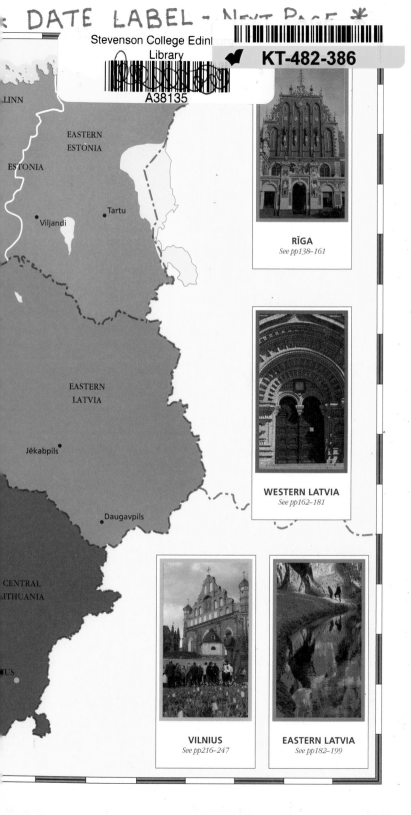

LINN

EASTERN
ESTONIA

ESTONIA

• Viljandi

• Tartu

RĪGA
See pp138–161

EASTERN
LATVIA

Jēkabpils •

• Daugavpils

WESTERN LATVIA
See pp162–181

CENTRAL
LITHUANIA

IUS

VILNIUS
See pp216–247

EASTERN LATVIA
See pp182–199

EYEWITNESS TRAVEL

ESTONIA, LATVIA AND LITHUANIA

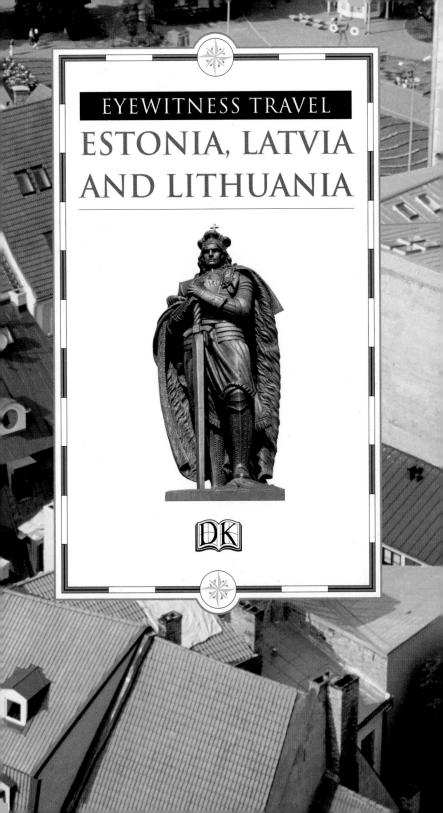

EYEWITNESS TRAVEL
ESTONIA, LATVIA
AND LITHUANIA

DK

DK

LONDON, NEW YORK,
MELBOURNE, MUNICH AND DELHI
www.dk.com

MANAGING EDITOR Aruna Ghose
DESIGN MANAGERS Sunita Gahir, Priyanka Thakur
PROJECT EDITOR Alka Thakur
PROJECT DESIGNER Rajnish Kashyap
EDITORS Jyoti Kumari, Ipshita Nandi
DESIGNERS Namrata Adhwaryu, Anchal Kaushal
SENIOR CARTOGRAPHIC MANAGER Uma Bhattacharya
CARTOGRAPHERS Mohammad Hassan, Jasneet Kaur
SENIOR PICTURE RESEARCHER Taiyaba Khatoon
PICTURE RESEARCHER Sumita Khatwani
ASSISTANT PICTURE RESEARCHER Shweta Andrews
SENIOR DTP DESIGNER Vinod Harish
DTP DESIGNER Azeem Siddiqui

CONTRIBUTORS
Howard Jarvis, John Oates, Tim Ochser, Neil Taylor

PHOTOGRAPHERS
Demetrio Carrasco, Nigel Hicks, Linda Whitman

ILLUSTRATORS
Chapel Design & Marketing Ltd, Chinglemba Chingtham,
Sanjeev Kumar, Surat Kumar Mantoo, Arun Pottirayil,
Suman Saha, Gautam Trivedi, Mark Warner

Reproduced in Singapore by Colourscan
Printed and bound by L. Rex Printing Company Limited, China

First published in Great Britain in 2009
by Dorling Kindersley Limited
80 Strand, London WC2R 0RL

Copyright © 2009 Dorling Kindersley Limited, London
A Penguin Company

A CIP CATALOGUE RECORD IS AVAILABLE FROM THE BRITISH LIBRARY.

ISBN 978-14053-3341-2

Front cover main image: Trakai Island Castle, Lithuania

We're trying to be cleaner and greener:

- we recycle waste and switch things off
- we use paper from responsibly managed forests whenever possible
- we ask our printers to actively reduce water and energy consumption
- we check out our suppliers' working conditions – they never use child labour

Find out more about our values and best practices at www.dk.com

---

**The information in this
DK Eyewitness Travel Guide is checked regularly.**

Every effort has been made to ensure that this book is as up-to-date as possible at the time of going to press. Some details, however, such as telephone numbers, opening hours, prices, gallery hanging arrangements and travel information are liable to change. The publishers cannot accept responsibility for any consequences arising from the use of this book, nor for any material on third party websites, and cannot guarantee that any website address in this book will be a suitable source of travel information. We value the views and suggestions of our readers very highly.
Please write to: Publisher, DK Eyewitness Travel Guides, Dorling Kindersley, 80 Strand, London, WC2R 0RL.

◁ A splendid overview of the colourful buildings of Riga, Latvia

CONTENTS

Door knocker, Tallinn

St Nicholas's Orthodox Cathedral in Karosta, near Liepāja, Latvia

Picturesque Island Castle at Trakai, Lithuania

Statue of King Gustav Adolphus of
Sweden, Tartu, Estonia

Amber jewellery, sold in souvenir
shops all over the Baltic region

The spectacular Vilnius Cathedral, Lithuania

HOW TO USE THIS GUIDE

This guide helps you get the most from your visit to the Baltic States. It provides detailed practical information and expert recommendations. *Introducing Estonia, Latvia and Lithuania* maps the three countries and sets them in their historical and cultural context, and describes events throughout the year. Each country has its own chapter, with its portrait, history and descriptions of important sights using visuals and maps. Information about hotels, restaurants, shops and markets, entertainment and sports is found in *Travellers' Needs*. The *Survival Guide* has tips on everything from making a telephone call to using local transportation.

ESTONIA, LATVIA AND LITHUANIA ON THE MAP

The orientation map shows the location of the Baltic States in relation to their neighbouring countries. In this book, each country is divided into three main sightseeing areas that are covered in a full chapter, such as *Estonia Region by Region* and so on. These areas are highlighted on other maps throughout the book.

A locator map shows where you are in relation to the other European countries.

ESTONIA, LATVIA AND LITHUANIA REGION BY REGION

Each country has been divided into three regions with a map at the start of the section. The key to the symbols is on the back flap.

Sights at a Glance lists the chapter's sights by category, such as Churches and Cathedrals, Towns, Resorts and Villages and Islands and National Parks.

1 Introduction
The landscape, history and character of each region is described here, explaining how they have changed over the centuries and what they have to offer to the visitor today.

2 Regional Map
This map shows the road network and gives an overview of the topography of the entire region. All the sights are numbered and there are also useful tips on getting around by car, bus and train.

3 Street-by-Street Map
This gives a bird's-eye view of interesting and important parts of each sightseeing area. The numbering of the sights ties in with the area map and the fuller description of the entries on the pages that follow.

A suggested route takes in some of the fascinating and attractive streets in the area.

Numbers refer to each sight's *position* on the area map and its place in the chapter.

Colour tabs refer to the regions. The same tab is used for pages relating to a particular region.

Stars indicate the sights that no visitor should miss.

4 Detailed Information
All the major cities, towns and tourist attractions are described individually. They are listed in order following the numbering on the area map at the start of the section.

The visitors' checklist gives all the practical information needed to plan your visit.

Story boxes provide information about historical or cultural topics relating to the sights.

Practical information provides everything you need to know to visit each sight. Map references pinpoint the sight's location on the road map on the inside back cover. For the three capital cities, map references relate to the *Street Finder* maps.

5 Major Sights
Historic buildings are dissected to reveal their interiors.

The list of star features recommends the details that no visitor should miss.

INTRODUCING ESTONIA, LATVIA AND LITHUANIA

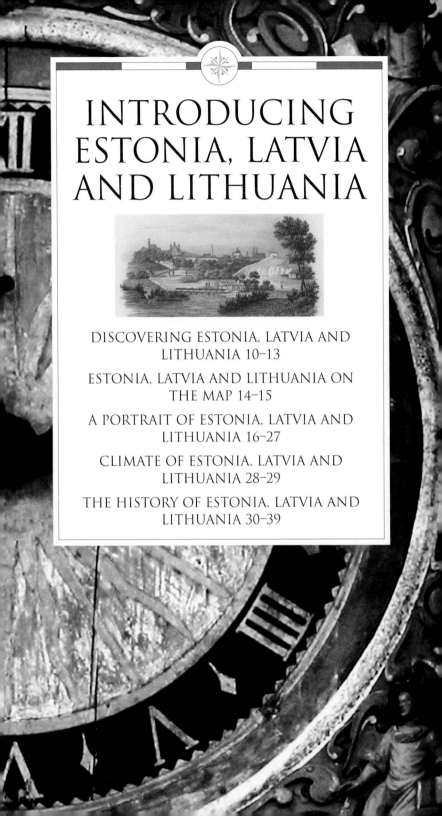

DISCOVERING ESTONIA, LATVIA AND LITHUANIA

The Baltic States all share a fairly similar landscape. Their western coastline is a sinuous and seemingly endless pristine beach stretching from Lithuania to Latvia and into Estonia, with beautiful resort towns such as Palanga, Jūrmala and Pärnu. Estonia's islands embody the diversity of all aspects of nature in the Baltics, while the southeastern part of the country has some of the hilliest and most picturesque terrain in the entire region. Western Latvia and Lithuania are rich in virgin forests and gently undulating landscapes that become wilder further east. The capital cities, while bound by many historical affinities, each have a distinctly different character, from the medieval splendour of Tallinn, to the decadent Art Nouveau of Rīga and the elegant Baroque of Vilnius.

Splendid outburst of autumn yellow at Kadriorg Park, Tallinn, Estonia

TALLINN

- **Medieval Old Town**
- **Excellent museums**
- **Lively art scene**
- **Exhilarating nightlife**

Tallinn's medieval Old Town is the heart of the city and an ideal starting point for visitors. **Town Hall Square** *(see pp58–9)* gloriously personifies Tallinn's medieval past and is an easy walk from the Old Town's other attractions. With spectacular views over the city, **Toompea** *(see pp68–9)* is the seat of the Estonian government. The city boasts some small but fascinating museums, especially the **Tallinn City Museum** *(see p63)*, with its concise overview of the city's history. The **Estonian Open-Air Museum** *(see p81)* offers a glimpse into traditional Estonian life. The magnificent surroundings of **Kadriorg Park** *(see pp74–7)* include many small specialist museums as well as the impressive **Kumu Art Museum** *(see p76)*. Beyond the park stands the popular **TV Tower** *(see p80)*.

Tallinn strikes a perfect balance between cultural refinement and youthful hedonism. An abundance of good restaurants, cafés and bars are concentrated in and around the Old Town.

WESTERN ESTONIA

- **Unspoiled islands**
- **Marvellous beach resorts**
- **Stunning nature parks**
- **Paldiski's Soviet relics**

Western Estonia is rich in natural beauty. The amazingly untouched islands here offer numerous scenic drives and splendid hiking routes. **Saaremaa Island** *(see pp92–5)* is the largest and its capital **Kuressaare** *(see p94)* is home to the Bishop's Castle. **Kihnu Island** *(see p101)* is one of the few remaining places where a traditional Estonian way of life still persists.

Pärnu *(see pp98–9)* is a gorgeous resort town with delightful architecture and an extremely attractive long stretch of beach. The resort town of **Haapsalu** *(see p88)* has not altered much since its 19th-century heyday as a fashionable spa resort.

Soomaa National Park *(see pp100–101)* and **Matsalu National Park** *(see p89)* are notable wildlife sanctuaries with exceptionally intricate ecosystems, and are surrounded by some historic sights.

The former Soviet naval base at **Paldiski** *(see p88)* has some spectacular coastal scenery full of relics of the country's Soviet past.

Windmill Tavern in Kuressaare, Saaremaa Island, Western Estonia

Eastern Estonia's sweeping coastline, with Narva-Jõesuu beachside resort hidden among pine trees

EASTERN ESTONIA

- Lahemaa National Park
- Picturesque towns
- Religious heritage
- Setu culture

Eastern Estonia has a wealth of diverse attractions. The stunning scenery of **Lahemaa National Park** *(see pp106–10)* includes little fishing villages and stately manor houses.

The coast passes through some intriguing industrial areas, such as the former Soviet town of **Sillamäe** *(see p111)*, before culminating in the historic Russian border city of **Narva** *(see p112)*. The resort of **Narva-Jõesuu** *(see p112)* boasts of one of the country's prettiest beaches.

The village of **Kuremäe** *(see p112)* is visited for its spectacular Russian Orthodox Pühtitsa Convent. **Lake Peipsi** *(see p123)* dominates Estonia's eastern border and its atmospheric shores are home to a community of Old Believers *(see p122)*.

Both historic and modern, the vibrant city of **Tartu** *(see pp114–17)* in the southeast lies at the very heart of Estonian culture. The beautiful landscape of this region abounds with little villages and towns, such as **Rõuge** *(see p120)* and **Viljandi** *(see p118)*, and is also generously strewn with countless historic sights.

In the far southeast corner of Estonia the unique Setu people *(see p120)* still hold on to their old way of life.

RĪGA

- Atmospheric Old Town
- Excellent dining
- Art Nouveau architecture
- Vibrant cultural scene

Rīga's colourful Old Town is full of historic sights, shops and museums as well as cafés, bars and restaurants. The superb **Dome Cathedral** *(see p142)* dominates Dome Square, while the imposing **St Peter's Church** *(see p149)* is one of Riga's most recognized landmarks. Of the many museums in the area, the **Museum of the Occupation of Latvia** *(see p148)* is one of

the best and should not be missed. The imposing **Freedom Monument** *(see p150)*, the revered symbol of Latvian nationhood, serves as a border between the Old Town and the city centre.

Art Nouveau architecture *(see pp152–3)* can be seen throughout the city centre, but is most impressive on Alberta Street. The elegant neighbourhood of **Mežaparks** *(see p156)* is close to Rīga Zoo and the venerable **Rīga's Cemeteries** *(see p157)*.

Across the Daugava river lies **The Left Bank** *(see p155)*, which is home to several intriguing sights, including **Victory Park** *(see p155)* and the **Railway Museum** *(see p155)*. Further afield is the **Latvian Ethnographic Open-Air Museum** *(see p159)*, among Rīga's best.

Cobblestoned street with historic buildings in Rīga, Latvia

Rundāle Palace set in verdant surroundings, Western Latvia

WESTERN LATVIA

- Beach resorts of Jūrmala
- Delightful towns
- The Livonian Coast
- Exquisite palaces

Some of the Baltic region's best sights can be found in Western Latvia. A string of pretty resort towns, **Jūrmala** *(see pp170–71)* has a pine forest-lined beach. Its tightly clustered summer houses, which include rare examples of wooden Art Nouveau, are architectural marvels.

Ventspils *(see pp176–7)*, a coastal city, has an immaculately renovated historic centre. **Liepāja** *(see pp180–81)* is arguably Latvia's most attractive city besides its capital and is famed for its vibrant music scene. The region's lush landscape is also filled with delightful small towns, such as **Tukums** *(see p171)*, wine-producing **Sabile** *(see p178)* and **Kuldīga** *(see p179)*.

The Livonian Coast, along the Gulf of Rīga and Baltic Sea, is a scenic drive and is lined with countless pretty old fishing villages before ending in **Cape Kolka** *(see p173)*. Kolka is part of the densely forested Slītere National Park, which is also home to the Livs *(see p172)*, the oldest of Latvia's indigenous peoples.

The Baroque-Rococo **Rundāle Palace** *(see pp168–9)* and the Neo-Classical palace,

Mežotne Palace *(see p166)*, are just some of the sights attesting to the distinguished history of Western Latvia.

EASTERN LATVIA

- Gauja National Park
- Unspoiled coastline
- Abundant lakes
- Historic Daugavpils

The country's most stunning landscape can be experienced in **Gauja National Park** *(see pp186–9)*. The park encompasses the Gauja Valley, a vast forested basin with steep sandstone banks and jaw-dropping cliffs. The sharply winding and deceptively placid-looking Gauja river is ideal for kayaking and canoeing, while the entire park is well served by a range of nature trails.

Girls in traditional outfits, near the castle at Cēsis, Eastern Latvia

Sigulda *(see p188)* is the perfect starting point for exploring the area, although the historic town of **Cēsis** *(see pp188–9)* on the eastern border of the park is another good entry point.

The coastline east of Rīga is not quite as popular as Jūrmala, but it is no less beautiful. The pleasant resort town of **Saulkrasti** *(see p192)* serves as the main focal point of a whole string of small coastal villages that line the amazingly unspoiled stretch of beach here.

In southeastern Latvia, the area known as **Latgale** *(see p198)* is famed for its abundance of lakes, all of which are used by locals for fishing or taking a refreshing dip.

The predominantly Russian-speaking city of **Daugavpils** *(see pp196–7)* is rich in architecture and places of historic interest.

VILNIUS

- Well-preserved Old Town
- Baroque architecture
- Impressive environs
- Cheery nightlife

The Lithuanian capital's UNESCO-protected Old Town holds the majority of the city's sights, such as the labyrinthine courtyards of **Vilnius University** *(see pp220–22)* and the Chapel of St Casimir inside **Vilnius Cathedral** *(see pp224–5)*. The spires and interiors of Catholic churches such as **St John's** *(see p222)*, **St Anne's** *(see p228)* and **St Theresa's** *(see p234)* and the mystical **Gates of Dawn** *(see p235)* have survived the ravages of the centuries.

The Baroque architecture that characterizes Vilnius sets it apart from any other city in Europe. The **Church of Sts Peter and Paul** *(see pp242–3)*, one of Vilnius's finest Baroque jewels, lies within easy walking distance of the Old Town.

The bohemian quarter of **Užupis** *(see p240)* and the views from **Verkiai Palace** *(see*

Vilnius Cathedral and Gedimino Bell Tower lit up at night, Vilnius

p245) make a good day-trip. On the city's fringes, the **Pushkin Museum** *(see p244)* and the **Paneriai Holocaust Memorial** *(see pp244–5)* draw the more serious visitors.

In addition to its lively nightlife, Vilnius is famed for its rich cultural life. It has two symphony orchestras and hosts several important music festivals.

CENTRAL LITHUANIA

- Trakai Island Castle
- Sprawling national parks
- Idyllic spa towns
- Museums of Kaunas

The ideal day-trip from Vilnius is **Trakai** *(see pp252–3)*, with its fairytale Island Castle set amid a lake that is dotted with countless islands. Exploring the castle, renting a rowing boat, going for a swim and sampling the village's distinctive Karaim dishes all make for memorable experiences.

The region is blessed with a verdant landscape and crystal-clear lakes. The amazingly untouched **Aukštaitija National Park** *(see pp266–7)*, with its network of lakes and rivers, attracts canoeists. The ancient forests of **Dzūkija National Park** *(see p256)* are interspersed with secluded villages with bubbling streams and thatched cottages.

One of Lithuania's major spa resorts, **Druskininkai** *(see p255)* is located in a bend in the Nemunas river, lined with

towering pines. It is famed for its mineral muds and healing waters. The quiet spa town of **Birštonas** *(see p257)* is popular for Birštonas Jazz, Lithuania's oldest jazz festival.

The heart of Central Lithuania is **Kaunas** *(see pp258–61)*, arguably the most intriguing of the Baltic region's second cities. The city's varied collection of museums offers insights into the Lithuanian character.

WESTERN LITHUANIA

- Unique spit and lagoon
- Serene Palanga resort
- Lively port city of Klaipėda
- Žemaitija National Park

Western Lithuania may be comparatively isolated, being well away from Vilnius, but it has, nonetheless, plenty of captivating places to see. The main highlight is the

unique coastal landscape, particularly the **Curonian Spit National Park** *(see pp284–5)*, a thin wedge of land covered in towering dunes and pine forest that stretches almost 100 km (60 miles) into the Baltic Sea. Its fishing villages and yachting harbours facing the sheltered Curonian Lagoon make the area extremely beautiful. The sublime little town of Nida, and a sandy beach that extends along the edge of the sea, provide the spit with an appealing coastal scenery. In contrast to this peaceful, UNESCO-protected landscape, the resort of **Palanga** *(see p282)* further north is packed in summer with holidaying families and fun-loving teenagers and youngsters. In or out of season, Palanga is worth visiting for attractions such as the Amber Museum.

The port city of **Klaipėda** *(see pp280–81)*, with timber-framed houses and a quaint Old Town, has retained its old Prussian atmosphere. The city's love of festivities is epitomized in the Sea Festival, which draws tourists in droves every year.

The region's secluded nature is most apparent in and around **Žemaitija National Park** *(see pp278–9)*. Isolated villages and wooden farmsteads carry a mystical blend of Catholic and pagan imagery, seen in the wayside crosses and shrines, or at the **Orvidas Garden** *(see p277)*.

One of the popular beaches around Palanga, Western Lithuania

Estonia, Latvia and Lithuania on the Map

With Estonia in the north, Latvia in the centre and Lithuania in the south, the Baltic States lie on the southeastern shore of the Baltic Sea. The region is bordered in the east by Russia and in the south by Poland, Belarus and the Russian enclave, Kaliningrad. The Baltic States' total land area is 173,000 sq km (66,778 sq miles). Latvia and Lithuania are of roughly equal size, while Estonia is about a third smaller and has a relatively flatter terrain in comparison to the other two countries. The three capital cities – Tallinn, Rīga and Vilnius – are home to almost a quarter of the region's 7 million people.

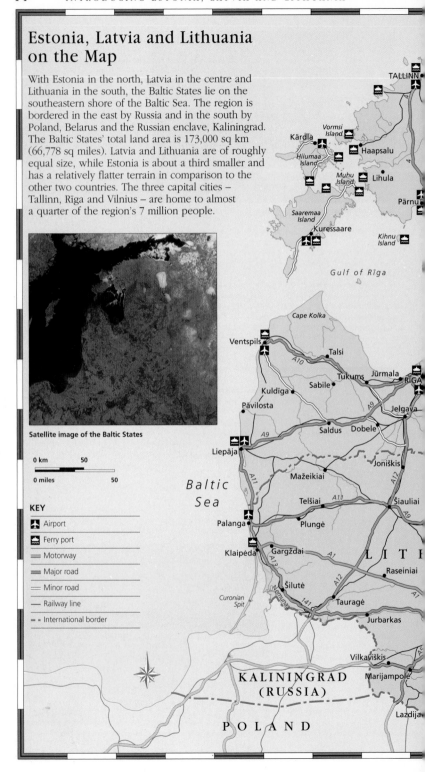

Satellite image of the Baltic States

0 km   50

0 miles   50

KEY

✈ Airport

⛴ Ferry port

━ Motorway

━ Major road

═ Minor road

— Railway line

– ∙ – International border

TALLINN

Vormsi Island

Kärdla

Hiiumaa Island

Haapsalu

Muhu Island

Lihula

Pärnu

Saaremaa Island

Kuressaare

Kihnu Island

Gulf of Rīga

Cape Kolka

Ventspils

Talsi

A10

Tukums

Jūrmala

RĪGA

Kuldīga

Sabile

Pāvilosta

Jelgava

A9

Saldus

Dobele

Liepāja

A9

Joniškis

Mažeikiai

A12

Baltic Sea

Telšiai

A11

Šiauliai

A11

A9

Palanga

Plungė

Klaipėda

Gargždai

A1

L I T H

A13

Raseiniai

Šilutė

A12

Curonian Spit

Nemunas

141

Tauragė

A1

Jurbarkas

Vilkaviškis

KALININGRAD
(RUSSIA)

Marijampolė

Lazdija

P O L A N D

Aerial view of Sillamäe, Estonia

Sillamäe
Narva
Jõhvi
Tapa
Rakvere
Paide
Lake Peipsi

E S T O N I A
Tartu
Viljandi
Lake Vōrtsjärv
Otepää
Võru
Valga
Valmiera
Alūksne
Cēsis
Smiltene
Sigulda
Gulbene
L A T V I A
Ērgli
Ogre
Daugava
A12
Ludza
Rēzekne
Jēkabpils
Preiļi
A13
Biržai
Krāslava
Rokiškis
Daugavpils
Panevēžys
Utena
U A N I A
Ukmergė
Molėtai
Jonava
Kaišiadorys
Kaunas
VILNIUS
A1
A3
A16
A15
Alytus
Varėna
Nemunas
Druskininkai

R U S S I A

B E L A R U S

EUROPE
NORWAY
FINLAND
SWEDEN
Tallinn
ESTONIA
DENMARK
Riga   LATVIA
RUSSIA
LITHUANIA
KALININGRAD   Vilnius
GERMANY
POLAND
BELARUS
CZECH REPUBLIC
UKRAINE
AUSTRIA
SLOVAKIA

Architectural Styles

Ever since the wooden fortifications of the Baltic tribes were replaced by stone castles in the 13th and 14th centuries, foreign influences have dominated the architecture of Estonia, Latvia and Lithuania. Today, the Baltic capitals are architectural treasure troves, with Tallinn particularly noted for its medieval buildings, Vilnius for its Italian Baroque and Rīga for its Art Nouveau. The Soviet era saw the building of inexpensive mass housing. Since independence private investment has funded ambitious new projects.

Detail of the extravagant Gothic brickwork of Perkūnas House, Kaunas

ROMANESQUE AND GOTHIC

Brought to Tallinn and Rīga by medieval German invaders, the Romanesque style, with its heavy vaulting, round arches and restrained ornamentation, lasted briefly in the region. The ornate Gothic ribbed vaults, pointed arches and decorative façades were more popular. Tallinn boasts the finest examples, while most of Rīga's were destroyed as part of the 19th-century rebuilding of the city.

Estonian History Museum *was built in Tallinn for the Great Guild, a powerful organization of German-speaking merchants. This early 15th-century building has a stern Gothic façade and vaulted halls.*

Church of St Anne, *Vilnius's most celebrated Gothic building, was constructed using 33 types of red brick. So impressed was Napoleon Bonaparte that he is said to have wanted to take it back to Paris.*

Kuressaare Castle, *on Saaremaa Island, is the only intact Gothic-style medieval castle in the Baltic States. It is built in local dolomite.*

RENAISSANCE AND BAROQUE

The 15th- and 16th-century revival of Classical learning, which favoured architectural features such as regularity, symmetry and a central axis, found little expression in Lithuania. In Latvia and Estonia, however, it led to the addition of new façades to existing buildings. The bold 17th- and 18th-century Baroque style, endorsed by the Catholic church, found favour in the religious climate of Vilnius.

Pažaislis Monastery, *in Kaunas, is one of Eastern Europe's most prominent Baroque monuments. Built in the 17th century by Italian architects, the monastery church has a twin-towered façade, behind which soars the 52-m (171-ft) dome. A wealth of marble enriches the interior.*

House of Blackheads, *in Tallinn, was used by the Brotherhood of Blackheads. It was formerly a 14th-century building, which was redesigned in a Renaissance style in 1597. The interiors were renovated in Neo-Classical style in 1908.*

NEO-CLASSICAL AND HISTORICIST

The Neo-Classical style arrived in the Baltic States as late as the 1780s. The style had a strong influence on Tartu, as well as some of the finest manor houses throughout Estonia. However, most examples today are found in Tallinn, often as façades on earlier buildings; some Latvian and Lithuanian palaces also exhibit the style. Around 1820, the Historicist movement became popular, drawing inspiration from various styles including Gothic, Renaissance and Neo-Baroque.

Tartu's Town Hall *is an elegant Neo-Classical edifice, eye-catchingly painted in lilac and orange. It was designed in the 18th century by J H B Walter for the Pistohlkors family.*

Kaunas's Town Hall, *locally known as the "White Swan", was renovated in 1870 in Neo-Classical style. It also bears Baroque traces, most obviously in its 53-m (174-ft) tall stepped tower.*

Latvian National Theatre, *in Rīga, was designed in a superb Neo-Baroque style. It was completed in 1902 by architect Augusts Reinbergs under the influence of Historicist aesthetics.*

ART NOUVEAU, MODERNIST AND CONTEMPORARY

The second half of the 19th century saw Art Nouveau gaining a hold in Rīga. After World War I there was a reaction against earlier flamboyant styles, with Modernists emphasizing function and Soviets favouring severe Functionalism. Since independence, new construction has taken place in the capitals, but it is not always in harmony with old architectural styles.

Alberta iela 13, *in Rīga, is a fine example of eclectic Art Nouveau, blending Classical and Symbolist imagery and Neo-Baroque stylistic features.*

Europa Tower, *in Vilnius, is one of a growing number of skyscrapers in the Baltic capitals, marking the return of the private sector.*

National Library, *in Tallinn, is one of the architectural triumphs of the late Soviet period. Raine Karp, the Estonian architect who designed it, used local dolomitic limestone.*

Landscape and Wildlife

The three Baltic countries are heavily forested with pine, spruce and birch and enjoy a predominantly flat terrain, although there are hilly areas such as the Vidzeme Upland in Latvia. The highest point in the region is Estonia's Suur Munamägi peak, which rises to about 318 m (1,043 ft) above sea level. The Baltic States are known for a dramatic coastline, innumerable lakes and rivers as well as extensive wetlands which, along with forests, provide habitats for a wide range of wildlife. The countries are also on major bird migration paths, making them popular with ornithologists all over the world. All three countries are still extensively covered with peat bogs, marshes and lakes.

Erratic boulders, *some of them very large, are common on the coastline of Estonia's Käsmu Peninsula (see p110). They were dragged there by glaciers during the last Ice Age.*

FOREST
Around 40 per cent of the total landscape in Estonia, Latvia and Lithuania is forested. Pine, spruce and birch are the main species, alongside other trees such as oak, ash, elm and maple. Trees were highly valued in the region's pre-Christian religions.

WETLANDS
The extensive wetlands of the region are ideal habitats for migrating birds, and for supporting plants such as cranberries and orchids. In Estonia, raised bogs in which thick layers of peat have built up are common. Many are protected by national parks.

FAUNA
The Baltic States are home to large mammals such as lynx, elk, deer, wolves and brown bears. With the region lying on major migration routes there are numerous nesting bird species including white stork, crane, barn swallow and grouse. The rivers and lakes teem with fish such as perch, trout and carp.

Bees *are highly valued in the region, as apiculture is an important industry and a part of the Baltic States' cultural heritage.*

White storks *are emblematic of the region and are often found nesting atop chimney pots or telegraph poles. Black storks are a relatively rare sight.*

Wolves *are found in the region's forests, especially in Lithuania. However, they are a rare sight, as hunting has resulted in the dwindling numbers of this predatory animal.*

FLORA

The Baltic States' forests and wetlands provide an environment in which a diverse range of plants can thrive. Many edible varieties of fungi and berries grow here. There is an orchid trail near Lake Engure, in Latvia, and yellow rattle and sea holly grow on Saaremaa and the Curonian Spit.

Arctic lichen *is a type of fungus found in Hiiumaa Island's Landscape Reserve. Like other lichen, it usually grows in two layers with a growth of algae in between.*

Mushrooms *are mostly wood decomposers or parasites. As the virgin forests are depleting, species of the former are becoming rarer.*

Orchids *grow mostly in the wetlands and woods. Those found here include rare North European species that are facing extinction.*

Berries, *such as cranberries, are eaten and also turned into wine.*

LAKES AND RIVERS

The region is dotted with lakes, of which Lake Peipsi in Estonia is the largest. There are a number of short rivers in the area. The low salinity of the Baltic Sea limits the number of plants and animal species it can support. Thus many of those present are freshwater species.

COASTLINE

Estonia has a sprawling coastline. It includes a stretch of the Baltic Klint, which is a long erosional escarpment stretching from Sweden to Russia. Another striking coastal feature is the Curonian Spit, a long sandy strip in Lithuania stretching to Kaliningrad.

The barn swallow, *the national bird of Estonia, often builds its nests in man-made structures.*

Ringed seals *are protected and can be found off the coast of Saaremaa and other Estonian islands.*

Brown bears *are omnivores and can be spotted in the forests of Estonia and Latvia, although they are usually sighted only with the help of a guide.*

Elk *is a game species that usually lives in forests and wetlands. It often appears on restaurant menus in the Baltic States.*

Religion

Although the Baltic lands were officially Christian by the end of the 14th century, pagan beliefs persisted and mingled with the new religion. Protestantism left its mark in the 16th century, but Lithuania soon returned to the Catholic fold. Today, it is the only country where the church plays a major public role. In Estonia and Latvia, the surge in religious participation after independence in 1991 proved short-lived. A significant number of ethnic Russians belong to the Russian Orthodox church, while other minority religious groups include Jews and Muslims.

Aerial view of the Orthodox Cathedral in Rīga, Latvia

Priest performing a Romuvan ritual, a popular modern religion

PAGANISM

Christianity came late to the Baltic region, with the Grand Duchy of Lithuania holding out until 1387, a year after Grand Duke Jogaila was baptized. The details of pagan beliefs are sparse, and scholars rely on surviving traditions and folk songs. Animism, the belief that plants and animals possess spirits, prevailed. Trees had great significance, with prayers offered at sacred groves.

Shamans communicated with the gods, but there was no organized priesthood. For Latvians and Lithuanians major deities included Dievs (the Sky God), Saule (the Sun), Pērkons or Perkūnas (Thunder), Velns (Trickster), Mēness (the Moon) and Laima (Fate). The Estonians and Livs *(see p172)* worshipped Taara (War), Uku (Thunder and Lightning), Vanetooni (the Dead), Maaema (Land), Ahti (Water) and Vanejumi (Fertility). Some scholars argue that these various

deities show aspects of one divine being. Pagan overtones are still present in a number of Christian celebrations.

The first period of independence of the 20th century saw attempts to revive old traditions. Some local organizations, such as Dievturība in Latvia, were nationalist in tone. After years of Soviet marginalization, Dievturība has now been revived, and in Lithuania, the pagan group Romuva has a fairly strong following.

ORTHODOX CHRISTIANITY

Orthodox missionaries arrived in the region as early as the 10th century but had little success, and Orthodox Christianity was largely eclipsed by Catholicism except among the Setu *(see p120)*. This changed only under Russian rule in the 19th century, with many magnificent Orthodox churches built at that time.

Today, almost all Orthodox worshippers in the region are ethnic Russians. Their churches are known for the abundance of icons – images of Christ, Mary and various saints – often displayed in rows on a screen called an iconostasis. The region also contains small communities of Old Believers *(see p122)*, descendants of worshippers who broke away from the Orthodox Church in protest against reforms introduced by Patriarch Nikon in 1652. Bringing Russian Orthodox rites in line with the Greek, his motives were both

Devotees lined up in Alexander Nevsky Church, Tallinn, Estonia

religious and political. The Old Believers sought to retain the purity of their faith, and the result was a schism (*raskol* in Russian) and their subsequent persecution. Many Old Believers fled from Russia, and today the main communities in the Baltic States are around Lake Peipsi (*see p123*) in Estonia and in the Latgale region of Latvia. Differences in rites include making the sign of the cross with two fingers (the Orthodox church now uses three) and changes to the wording of the Creed. Old Believers regard shaving a man's beard as sinful, and there are restrictions on smoking tobacco. Members often wear long traditional Russian shirts.

Catholic Church of the Holy Spirit, Vilnius, Lithuania

Old Believers' Church made of wood near Lake Peipsi

CATHOLICISM

Catholicism was brought to the region by force, with Pope Innocent III authorizing a crusade against the northern pagans in 1198. The areas which are now known as Estonia and Latvia fell first, with Lithuania hanging on until 1387.

The new religion was regarded as alien by the indigenous population, a feeling exacerbated by the use of Latin in services. Catholicism found its strongest roots in Eastern Latvia and Lithuania, both under the influence of Poland. These foundations were strengthened by the Counter-Reformation, the Catholic Church's response to the threat posed by Lutheranism. The newly established Jesuit order built schools and made efforts to use the native language, also emphasizing the importance of the Virgin Mary in an attempt to win back worshippers. Today Lithuania is the only country out of the three Baltic States where religion is central to national identity.

PROTESTANTISM

The Reformation was quickly felt in Estonia and Western Latvia, with the introduction of the revolutionary ideas of Lutheranism, a major branch of Protestant Christianity. The offshoot emphasized receiving God's grace through faith alone, rather than through good works. It first appeared in Estonian urban centres during the 1520s. Initially, the landowners resisted the change, but soon they recognized it as a useful way to resist the influence of the Pope. Peasants were expected to follow the faith of their landlords. The new beliefs were further bolstered by Swedish rule in the 17th century, when more pastors were trained and there was an increased use of indigenous languages for religious activities. The first Bible in Latvian was published in 1689 by the Lutheran theologian Ernst Glück (1654–1705).

There was a brief revival in religious activity after independence from the oppressive regime of the Soviet era, when many churches were converted to be used for other purposes. Although many Estonians and Latvians still follow Lutheranism, participation has declined in recent years and there are now marginally more Catholics than Lutherans in Latvia.

Virgin Mary's Lutheran Church, Otepää

Famous People

A history of cultural domination by other nations explains why only a handful of figures from the Baltic States are internationally known. It was only with the 19th-century national awakening movements that the notion of distinctive Baltic cultures gained popularity. After the brief confidence of the first independence, the restrictions of the Soviet era meant that most famous people from the region were either of Russian heritage or were living outside their native countries. In the years since independence in 1991, the arts have been hampered by reduced state funding and a population with little disposable income.

A portrait by Michael Sittow, a 15th-century Tallinn-born artist

VISUAL ARTS

Estonia's best-known painter was Eduard Wiiralt (1898–1954), while in the 20th century animators Elbert Tuganov (1920–2007) and Priit Pärn (b.1946) gained international praise. Within Latvia, painter Janis Rozentāls (1866–1916) remains most beloved, although Mark Rothko *(see p196)* is more famed abroad. Lithuania has produced several notable photographers, including Antanas Sutkus (b.1939).

Sergei Eisenstein *(1898–1948), one of the most influential film directors and theorists of all time, was born in Rīga. His groundbreaking use of editing is best seen in his early Marxist cinematic works, including* Strike! *(1924) and* Battleship Potemkin *(1925).*

Mikalojus Konstantinas Čiurlionis *(1875–1911), Lithuania's pre-eminent composer, was also an accomplished artist. His work draws extensively upon Symbolism and the influence of music can be found in his emphasis on mood, interest in harmony and development of themes across a series of paintings. The tempera on canvas shown above is entitled* The Offering *(1909).*

LITERATURE

Key to the 19th-century national awareness was the preservation of traditional stories and the creation of new myths by authors such as Latvian Andrejs Pumpurs (1841–1902), Estonian Friedrich Kreutzwald (1803–82) and Lithuanian Jonas Mačiulis (1862–1932). Modern literature is equally celebrated and famous authors include Estonian poets Jaan Kaplinski (b.1941) and Jaan Kross (1920–2007), and Lithuanian novelist Ričardas Gavelis (b.1950).

Anton Hansen Tammsaare *(1878–1940) is regarded as the greatest Estonian writer. His work,* Truth and Justice, *is a five-volume series of novels covering subjects that include rural Estonia and the Russian Revolution of 1905.*

Czesław Miłosz *(1911–2004) was born into a Polish aristocratic family and educated in Vilnius. Poet and intellectual, Miłosz won the Nobel Prize for Literature in 1980. He is perhaps best known for* The Captive Mind, *a prose critique of Communist ideology.*

MUSIC

Estonia has a strong tradition of classical composition. Veljo Tormis (b.1930) is influenced by Estonian folk music, while Erkki-Sven Tüür (b.1959) mixes avant-garde techniques with early music and progressive rock. The father of Latvian classical music is Jāzeps Vītols (1863–1948), and the country is also known for pop and rock performers such as the band Brainstorm. Lithuania is renowned for jazz musicians including the Ganelin Trio, while its finest classical composer was M K Čiurlionis.

Arvo Pärt (b.1935), an Estonian composer, experimented with Schoenberg's 12-tone technique and the use of chance early on in his career. He is internationally known for "sacred minimalism", drawing on medieval traditions and Orthodox Christianity. Pärt describes his music as tintinnabuli (like bells).

THEATRE AND DANCE

Professional theatre was once the domain of the ruling classes, but from the mid-19th century plays were written by authors such as Estonia's Eduard Vilde (1865–1933) and Latvia's Rūdolfs Blaumanis (1863–1908). Lithuania's lively theatre scene is dominated by director E Nekrošius (b.1952). Ballet thrived during the Soviet era, with the Rīga Ballet promoting Alexander Godunov (1949–95).

Mikhail Baryshnikov (b.1948), born in Rīga, is of Russian descent. Baryshnikov began his ballet studies in the Latvian city before progressing to Leningrad (now St Petersburg). He defected while on tour in Canada in 1974. He later became a citizen of the USA and founded a dance centre in New York.

Voldemar Panso (1920–77), the famous theatre director, rejected Soviet ideology in favour of complex characters and the ambiguity of Symbolism. He also founded the Estonian Youth Theatre (later the Tallinn City Theatre).

SPORT

The talent of Baltic athletes was, for many decades, obscured by their status as Soviet citizens. Estonia's most famous Olympian was heavyweight wrestler Kristjan Palusalu (1908–87), while Latvian long-distance walker Jānis Daliņš (1904–78) won the Olympic silver in 1932. Lithuania's top Olympic athlete is discus-thrower Virgilijus Alekna (b.1972). The region has also produced exceptional basketball players, including Lithuanian Arvydas Sabonis (b.1964), Latvian Uljana Semjonova (b.1952) and Estonian Tiit Sokk (b.1964).

Erki Nool (b.1970) won a gold medal in the decathlon at the 2000 Sydney Olympics, a controversial result since a judge had disallowed all three of his discus attempts before the competition referee overruled him. In 2007, he was elected to the Estonian Parliament.

Uljana Semjonova (b.1952), a basketball player of Russian-Latvian origin, won two Olympic gold medals in 1976 and 1980. She dominated the world basketball scene throughout the 1970s and 80s and never lost any official international match.

Folk Songs and Music

The traditional songs of Estonia, Latvia and Lithuania typically deal with everyday events, calendar rituals and rites of passage, though stories of epic heroism and grandeur also exist. These songs are generally sung by women. Efforts to compile the songs began in earnest in the late 19th century and this was an important facet of the region's growing national awareness. Later, between 1987 and 1990, the struggle for freedom from the Soviet Union came to be known as the Singing Revolution, partly due to the role played by huge open-air concerts.

Cover of the 1998 album *Beyond the River: Seasonal Songs of Latvia*

Traditional Lithuanian songs*, or* dainos, *deal with daily life. They are sung solo, in unison or polyphonically. One of the best-known forms is the duophonic* sutartinė *from the northeast.*

Monophonic Estonian songs*, or* runo, *are related to those from Finland, and their roots are much older than those of Latvia and Lithuania. The Setu people of Eastern Estonia have their own distinctive polyphonic singing traditions.*

BALTICA FESTIVAL

This annual international folklore festival was first held in Estonia in 1987 and is hosted cyclically by the Baltic States. The three Baltic flags were hoisted together for the first time during the second festival in 1988. Today, the festival brings together around 3,000 participants and includes concerts, parades and workshops.

Latvian folk songs*, or* dainas, *consist of one or two stanzas each with two non-rhyming couplets. This singing tradition is lyrical and usually draws inspiration from pagan mythology or daily life. Traditionally, these songs were accompanied by instruments such as bagpipes and psalteries, with accordions and fiddles added in the 17th century.*

Veljo Tormis *(b.1930) is a celebrated composer of choral music based on the folk songs of his native Estonia. Many of his more political pieces of the 1970s and 80s were censored by the Soviet government.*

Iļģi, *the famous Latvian folk music band, was formed in 1981. Like most folk musicians of the country, they revived forgotten traditions and developed into a band that used folklore as an impulse for creating music of their own.*

BALTIC FOLK SINGERS

The Soviet era saw government-approved performers refine folk songs with classical harmonies and accompaniment, but enthusiasts worked to preserve genuine traditions. Today, a number of festivals are held all over the region.

Veronika Povilioneine *(b.1946) has enjoyed success since the late 1960s, promoting folk singing as a mode of anti-Soviet protest. In recent years, she has also recorded pop and jazz albums.*

THE BALTIC PSALTERY

The most characteristic instrument used by the region's folk singers is the Baltic psaltery. It exists in numerous variations, and is known as *kokle* in Latvia, *kanklės* in Lithuania and *kannel* in Estonia. In the late 19th century, hybrids influenced by German and Austrian zithers were developed.

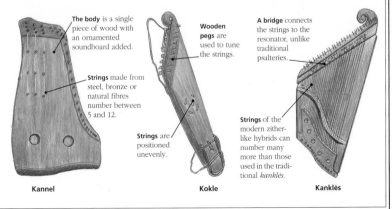

The body is a single piece of wood with an ornamented soundboard added.

Strings made from steel, bronze or natural fibres number between 5 and 12.

Wooden pegs are used to tune the strings.

Strings are positioned unevenly.

A bridge connects the strings to the resonator, unlike traditional psalteries.

Strings of the modern zither-like hybrids can number many more than those used in the traditional *kanklės*.

Kannel　　　　　**Kokle**　　　　　**Kanklės**

Baltic Amber

Amber has been valued for millennia, with amber jewellery found dating back to the early Neolithic period (around 7000 BC). Many medical authorities of the ancient world, including Hippocrates, believed that amber had healing properties. A trade network, now known as the Amber Route, arose at the height of the Roman Empire. In the medieval period, amber was used to make rosaries. Today, it still washes up on Latvian and Lithuanian shores, although 90 per cent of the world's amber is mined in the Curonian Spit of neighbouring Kaliningrad.

One of the many amber stalls found in tourist areas

IDENTIFYING AMBER

Sellers may pass off copal or plastic as genuine amber. Genuine amber floats in salt water and exudes a pine scent when touched with a red-hot needle, but only laboratory tests are conclusive.

Amber-catchers *in the Baltic Sea are shown in this lithograph from the 1850s. In the 13th century, local amber-gathering was forbidden by the Teutonic Knights. Their monopoly was lifted only in the 19th century, reviving amber-working traditions.*

Unpolished amber of different colours and shapes

Amber pieces *are regularly washed ashore in Pāvilosta (see p179), a small port town in Latvia. There are a handful of professional amber-catchers, and tourists can arrange to go out with them.*

FORMATION OF AMBER

Before it is washed up on the coasts of the Baltic States, especially after raging storms, amber takes millions of years to transform from pine resin into a sought-after substance. Often clear, it can also have pine needles or insects trapped in the resin before it solidified.

Tree Exuding Resin
Certain trees exude a sticky resin, which has a range of defensive functions. Its antiseptic qualities kill bacteria and fungi, while its stickiness inhibits physical attack from insects.

Insects Trapped in Amber
Any insects stuck in the resin are prevented from decaying, as the substance is antiseptic and lacking in water. Slowly, the volatile components evaporate, leaving behind copal.

Copal Formation
Copal, or hardened resin, becomes incorporated into the ground after the tree dies. The solidification process continues for millions of years, until the inert substance becomes amber.

USES OF AMBER

In addition to its decorative value, amber was once considered to have healing powers and even today some Lithuanians consider it to be a cure for goitre. The Aztecs and Maya are known to have burnt amber as incense.

Delicately crafted amber jewellery

Knife decorated with amber

Typical amber box

Exquisite brooch fashioned in amber

THE AMBER ROUTE

An EU-funded project has devised a modern-day Amber Route that links a series of cities along the Baltic Coast. Starting from Ventspils *(see pp176–7)*, the route takes in Palanga *(see p282)*, Liepāja *(see pp180–81)* and Klaipėda *(see pp280–81)*. While some of these towns have amber museums, Palanga also has an amber-processing workshop. Nida in Lithuania has a museum that exhibits amber. The route also takes in Karklė and Pāvilosta, with professional amber-catchers. Juodkrantė, once the site of major amber-mining activity, boasts a collection of prehistoric amber artifacts. Further south is Kaliningrad, a Russian outpost, which is the source of the vast majority of the world's amber.

KEY

━━ Amber Route

Amber Museum in Palanga
(see p282) *features a stunning collection of amber pieces with prehistoric insects trapped inside, as well as amber jewellery. There is also a display presenting the natural history of amber.*

An amber-polishing workshop, *held by experts, offers participants the opportunity to create their own jewellery. Some amber museums across the Baltic States conduct these worskshops.*

AMBER IN FOLKLORE

A popular Lithuanian folk tale recounts the love between the fisherman Kastytis and the goddess Juratė, who lived in an amber palace at the bottom of the sea. Angry that a mortal had dared to touch a goddess, the god Perkūnas sent lightning to destroy the palace and drown Kastytis. It is believed that pieces of the palace have been washing up on the shore ever since. The well-known story was first recorded in writing by Liudvikas Adomas Jucevičius in 1842, and the tale has even been adapted into a rock opera.

Jūratė kaj Kastytis **by Nijolė Ona Gaigalaitė**

The Climate of Estonia, Latvia and Lithuania

With the Baltic Sea as a moderating influence, the
Baltic region has a temperate climate without the
extremes that afflict neighbouring Russia. Winters are
gloomy, however, with short days and bitter winds.
The first snow usually falls in November, and inland
there can be constant snow cover from December
to April. The snowy season is shorter on the coast,
where temperatures are noticeably lower in summer
and higher in winter. At other times the weather
is unpredictable, with rain even in the middle of
summer when days are long and warm.

PÄRNU

	°C/F			
	21/70			
	13/55	9/48		
7/45		4/39		
0/32			-3/27	
				-9/16

6 hrs	10 hrs	3 hrs	1 hrs
36 mm	72 mm	60 mm	36 mm
month **Apr**	**Jul**	**Oct**	**Jan**

Average monthly maximum temperature

Average monthly minimum temperature

Average daily hours of sunshine

Average monthly rainfall

LIEPĀJA

	°C/F			
	20/68			
	14/57	11/52		
8/47		6/43		
2/36			-1/30	
				-5/23

6 hrs	9 hrs	3 hrs	1 hrs
37 mm	66 mm	77 mm	53 mm
month **Apr**	**Jul**	**Oct**	**Jan**

KLAIPĖDA

	°C/F			
	20/68			
	14/57	12/54		
9/48		6/43		
2/36			0/31	
				-5/23

6 hrs	9 hrs	3 hrs	1 hrs
36 mm	74 mm	80 mm	50 mm
month **Apr**	**Jul**	**Oct**	**Jan**

RĪGA

	°C/F			
	22/72			
	12/54	10/50		
10/50		4/39		
1/34			-2/28	
				-8/18

6 hrs	10 hrs	3 hrs	1 hrs
41 mm	85 mm	60 mm	34 mm
month **Apr**	**Jul**	**Oct**	**Jan**

KAUNAS

	°C/F			
	22/72			
	12/54	11/52		
11/52		4/39		
2/36			-3/27	
				-9/16

6 hrs	9 hrs	3 hrs	1 hrs
42 mm	80 mm	45 mm	39 mm
month **Apr**	**Jul**	**Oct**	**Jan**

WESTERN ESTONIA

Kuressaare

Pärnu

Ventspils

WESTERN LATVIA

RĪGA

Liepāja

Jelgava

Klaipėda

WESTERN LITHUANIA

Šiauliai

Panevėžys

Kaunas

TALLINN

° C/F			
8/46	21/70 12/54	9/48	
0/32		4/39	-2/28
			-8/18

☀	6 hrs	10 hrs	2 hrs	1 hrs
☂	36 mm	78 mm	73 mm	48 mm
month	Apr	Jul	Oct	Jan

TARTU

° C/F			
9/48	22/72 11/52	9/48	
0/32		3/37	-4/25
			-11/12

☀	8 hrs	10 hrs	3 hrs	1 hrs
☂	33 mm	71 mm	52 mm	29 mm
month	Apr	Jul	Oct	Jan

DAUGAVPILS

° C/F			
10/50	23/73 12/54	10/50	
1/34		3/37	-4/25
			-10/14

☀	6 hrs	8 hrs	3 hrs	1 hrs
☂	42 mm	79 mm	52 mm	37 mm
month	Apr	Jul	Oct	Jan

VILNIUS

° C/F			
11/52	22/72 12/54	10/50	
2/36		3/38	-4/25
			-9/16

☀	6 hrs	10 hrs	3 hrs	1 hrs
☂	46 mm	78 mm	53 mm	41 mm
month	Apr	Jul	Oct	Jan

TALLINN

EASTERN ESTONIA

Viljandi

Tartu

EASTERN LATVIA

Jēkabpils

Daugavpils

CENTRAL LITHUANIA

VILNIUS

0 km   50
0 miles   50

Estonia's winter landscape with snow-capped forest

THE HISTORY OF ESTONIA, LATVIA AND LITHUANIA

T*he history of the Baltic region begins only in 2000 BC with the arrival of the early Baltic tribes, the ancestors of today's Estonians, Latvians and Lithuanians. Despite a shared experience of conquests, foreign occupations and struggles for independence, the three countries have preserved their distinct cultural identities, emerging in 1991 as sovereign states.*

Archaeological evidence suggests that the Baltic region was inhabited as early as 10,000 BC, at the end of the Ice Age. The earliest occupied site, at Kernavė in Lithuania, dates as far back as 9000 BC. These Stone Age people used bows, arrows and spears for hunting and fishing. It was not until 3000 BC, however, that the ancestors of the current inhabitants began to arrive in the region. Surviving by hunting and fishing, the Finno-Ugrians – the future Finns and Estonians – were among the first to drift across Europe from Asia. They were pushed back by the Indo-European groups that arrived in 2000 BC. The Indo-Europeans, who introduced crop cultivation and animal rearing to the traditional modes of subsistence, mingled with the existing groups, eventually forming the races now known collectively as the Balts.

During the first centuries AD, distinctive regional tribes began to form. These were the Samogitians and Aukštaitijans in western and eastern Lithuania, the Curonians along

Coin dedicated to Kernavė, Lithuania

the coast, the Prussians beyond the Nemunas river, the Zemgalians in central Latvia and the Selonians and Latgalians further east. For several centuries, the Balts remained firmly rural, living off the land. Until the early 13th century, there were similar but unrelated settlements all along the coast from what is now Klaipėda as far as St Petersburg. There are very few records of life at that time as the local communities used wood rather than stone for all their fortifications and housing. Recent archaeological research has shown that there were extensive trading networks across the sea from this area to Sweden and Germany and inland towards Russia. The little written material from that time talks about the Balts as good boat-builders and dreaded pirates.

At a time when the rest of Europe had embraced Christianity, the Balts staunchly practised paganism. After haphazard attempts by small groups of Western European missionaries to convert the area to Christianity failed, the first Baltic crusade was sanctioned by Pope Innocent III in 1198.

TIMELINE

Pope Innocent III (1160–1216)

10,000 Earliest traces of human life in the Baltic region	**3000** Finno-Ugrians arrive in the region	**98** Roman writer Tacitus describes the "Aestii" people	**700** Vikings use Latvian rivers to trade with Persia and Turkey	**1198** The first Baltic crusade sanctioned by Pope Innocent III
10,000 BC	**5000 BC**	**AD 1**	**AD 600**	**AD 1190**
9000 Hunting-fishing groups flourish in Kernavė	**2000** Indo-European groups arrive	**100** Romans begin trading in amber along the Baltic coast		**1009** The name Lithuania appears in written form for the first time

Early Neolithic bone objects, Narva, Estonia

◁ **Detail from Jan Matejko's** *Battle of Grünwald* **(1878) showing Grand Duke Vytautas defeating the Teutonic Knights**

GERMANS IN ESTONIA AND LATVIA

After the papal declaration of the crusade, the Teutonic Knights, or the German warrior-monks who called themselves the Brotherhood of the Sword, began to venture along the Baltic coast. The phrase *"Drang nach Osten"* ("Thrust Eastwards"), which would become notorious in World War II, dates from this time. Religious and commercial zeal drove the crusaders to establish colonies along the Baltic coast. In 1201, a bishopric was set up in Rīga, which became the basis for the Baltic conquest. Expanding into Estonia from the south, the Knights created Livonia in 1207. Comprising Latvia and Estonia, Livonia was recognized as part of the Holy Roman Empire, with Rīga as the capital. Estonia's largest island,

Saaremaa, was subjugated in 1227. A fortress built in 1260 at its capital, Kuressaare, is the only one in the Baltic region to be preserved largely as the Teutonic Knights built it. Livonia flourished under the Knights, as they built cities throughout the region. After joining the Hanseatic League, a trading confederation of German port-cities and merchants' associations, Tallinn and Rīga began to thrive. The new social order, dominated by the Germans, excluded the local inhabitants not only from mercantile activities, but also agriculture, where they could only be hired as serfs.

POLISH DOMINATION IN LITHUANIA

Lithuania had a very different history from that of the area to its north. While Christianity was dominant in much of the Baltic region, Lithuania continued to be resolutely pagan until 1385, when Duke Jogaila married a Polish princess, embraced Christianity and assumed the crowns of Poland and Lithuania. Long before him, in 1251, Mindaugas had briefly adopted Christianity so that he could be crowned by the Pope. In 1410, Jogaila and his cousin Vytautas (r.1410–30), Grand Prince of Lithuania, decisively defeated the Teutonic Knights in the Battle of Žalgiris, or Grünwald. Under Vytautas, the Grand Duchy of Lithuania *(see pp212–13)* emerged as one of the largest states in Europe. Eventually, however, it came increasingly under the control of the Poles, with the relationship culminating in the creation of Polish-Lithuanian Commonwealth in 1569. With

A 19th-century lithograph showing the Battle of Grünwald (1410)

TIMELINE

Kuressaare Castle

1200	1250	1300	1350	1400	1450

1201 German crusaders set up a bishopric in Rīga

1237 The Brotherhood of the Sword becomes Livonian Order

1260 Building of Kuressaare Castle starts

1372 German replaces Latin as the official language in Rīga and Tallinn

1410 Lithuanians and Poles defeat the Teutonic Knights at the Battle of Žalgiris (Grünwald)

1230 Mindaugas unites the Grand Duchy of Lithuania

1207 Livonia becomes part of the Holy Roman Empire

1282 Rīga joins the Hanseatic League; Tallinn follows three years later

1385 Lithuania united with Poland under Jogaila

1430 The Grand Duchy reaches the Black Sea

Siege of Narva by the Russians in 1558 during the Livonian Wars

the Polish takeover, the right to own land was lost, privileges of the peasantry were curbed and serfdom was firmly established in Lithuania.

THE SWEDES AND THE RUSSIANS

Sweden and Russia fought two major wars to ensure control over the Baltic Sea and the surrounding land. In the Livonian Wars (1558–83), Poland and Lithuania were involved in resisting the armies of Russia's Ivan the Terrible (r.1533–84), in view of the destruction he had wrought in Livonia. The immediate aftermath of the war resulted in most of Estonia coming under Swedish rule, while Latvia endured a Polish occupation and Lithuania's full union with Poland was formalized. Southern and Eastern Latvia, commonly known as Courland and Latgale respectively, became duchies owing allegiance to Poland.

War soon broke out again, this time between the Poles and the Swedes, and in 1621, the Swedes seized Rīga and northern Latvia. The Duchy of Courland stayed in Polish hands, although the dukes almost became rulers in their own right. The most prominent of them, Duke Jakob Kettler (r.1642–82), brought the duchy to the pinnacle of its wealth and power. The Swedish occupation, regarded as the gentlest Livonia ever endured, was marked by a benign governance. The Germans, meanwhile, continued to hold sway in Livonia, socially and culturally. When an alternative to Latin was needed in the churches, German was the obvious choice. The universities at Rīga and Tartu taught exclusively in German. German merchants were granted special rights by the Swedish rulers, Charles XI (r.1660–97) and Charles XII (r.1697–1718), to ensure the continuity of commerce.

After the German barons' estates were expropriated by the Swedish crown, they turned to Russia for help. In 1700, Charles XII defeated Peter the Great of Russia at Narva, marking the beginning of the Great Northern War (1700–21). The loss at Narva inspired the Tsar to create a modern army and, in 1709, using a bitter winter to his advantage, he defeated the Swedes at the Battle of Poltava. In 1710, Tallinn and Rīga were occupied and soon Estonia and Latvia were brought under Russian control.

Battle of Poltava, a work by M Lomonosov (1711–65)

1520 Lutheranism established in Estonia, and a year later in Latvia	**1572** First reference to a synagogue in Vilnius	**1600–29** Polish-Swedish War	**1642–82** Courland flourishes under Duke Jakob Kettler	
1500	**1550**	**1600**	**1650**	**1700**
1536 First record of Jewish merchants in Riga		**1558–83** Livonian Wars between Sweden and Russia	**1700–21** Great Northern War between Sweden and Russia	

King Charles XII of Sweden (1682–1718)

Tsar Alexander I with a soldier holding the Imperial Standard

UNDER TSARIST RULE

Peter the Great treated his new conquests with respect, as the Swedes had done before him. He continued to give the local German community considerable autonomy, both with their trading rights in the towns and with their manor houses in the countryside. After his death in 1725, a unique century of peace followed. There were neither invasions nor local uprisings. The Jews *(see pp36–7)*, who had flourished under the Duchy of Lithuania, gradually spreading into Latvia and parts of Estonia, continued to thrive. By the 18th century, Vilnius had become the Jewish capital of Eastern Europe, referred to as Vilna. Under Catherine the Great (r.1762–96), the Russian Empire expanded to include Lithuania's Grand Duchy, which resulted from the third, and final, partition of Poland in 1795.

Tsar Alexander I (r.1801–25) was forced to forsake his dreams of reconstituting the Grand Duchy, when, in

An 1864 print in Lithuanian using the Latin alphabet

1812, Napoleon's Grand Army marched through Vilnius en route to Moscow, and was greeted by the people as liberators. In the same year Napoleon returned there, retreating ignominiously, not because the Russians had fought him successfully, but because they denied him supplies. In a pre-emptive move, the Russians burnt down the wooden suburbs of Rīga to give them a clear firing line for defending the town. Eventually, the French army was forced to retreat.

A CENTURY OF UNEASY PEACE

Under Alexander I, a series of agrarian laws were passed. Serfdom was abolished between 1816 and 1819, and peasants were allowed to buy and sell land. Civil unrest, however, came from the intelligentsia in the towns, dissatisfied by the religious domination of the Orthodox Church and the increasing use of the Russian language. Between 1830 and 1831, the movement was at its strongest in Lithuania and one of the countermeasures taken by the Russian authorities was to close Vilnius University in 1832, hoping that this would quell the unrest. In 1864, they resorted to banning the publication of books in Lithuanian using the Latin alphabet; books were now to be transcribed into Cyrillic. This encouraged publishers in Prussia to produce books in the Latin

TIMELINE

1721 Sweden surrenders Estonia and Latvia to Russia

Napoleon Bonaparte (1769–1821)

1812 Napoleon's failed attempt to conquer Russia

1725	1750	1775	1800

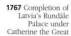

Catherine the Great (1729–96)

1767 Completion of Latvia's Rundāle Palace under Catherine the Great

1795 Lithuania absorbed into the Russian Empire

alphabet and to smuggle them across the border. By the 1860s, nationalist movements were equally active in Latvia and Estonia. In 1869, the first Estonian Song Festival was held, and in the following year, the writer Lydia Koidula produced her first play in Estonian, having previously only written in German. It is significant that both events took place in Tartu and not in Tallinn, where German and Russian influence was still too strong. The Latvian writer Krišjānis Valdemārs also caused a stir in Tartu by printing his name-card in Latvian. It was not until 1900, however, that Estonians, Latvians and Lithuanians could freely proclaim their nationalities in their capital cities.

Latvian writer Krišjānis Valdemārs (1825–91)

In the 19th century, as in the 18th, the Russians delegated local administration to the Germans. It was, therefore, the Germans, and not the Russians, who gained from the commercial potential of mass production, railways and steamships. Rīga and Tallinn expanded hugely as ports and manufacturing centres. The prospect of work drew many people from rural areas into the larger towns.

WAR RETURNS

Strikes and demonstrations took place in 1905 in many cities throughout Russia, to pressurize the Tsarist regime to grant civil rights and improve social conditions. Given the size of its industrial workforce at this time, Rīga was an active participant in this unrest. In the countryside, protests were directed against the German landed gentry and manor houses all over the region were attacked. These were social rather than nationalistic movements, partly as the Balts were now able to use their own languages openly and could also take part in local administration. National aspirations were, however, forcibly dampened at the outbreak of World War I (1914–18). The Russian Revolution of 1917, which resulted in the collapse of Tsarist Russia and which brought the Bolsheviks to power, played a significant role in changing the course of the region's history. The Civil War that followed soon after was seen as an opportunity for the Baltic States to take control of their destiny.

A turn-of-the-19th-century postcard impression of Rīga, one of Eastern Europe's most vibrant cities

1854 Crimean War breaks out; British Navy blockades Russian Baltic ports

1870 Tallinn–St Petersburg railway opens

1917 Russian Revolution and Civil War stimulate Baltic independence movements

| 1825 | 1850 | 1875 | 1900 |

1832 Russians close Vilnius University to curtail spread of nationalist ideas

Liepāja tram 1 at Liela iela, Latvia

1899 First Baltic electric tram line opens in Liepāja

1905 Urban and rural attacks on German and Russian business

1916 Election of first Latvian mayor of Rīga

Jewish History

Star worn by Jews during the Holocaust

The history of Jewish settlement in the Baltic region began in the 14th century, when King Gediminas invited merchants and craftsmen into the Grand Duchy of Lithuania. Estonia only ever had a small Jewish population, while Jews arrived in Latvia in the 15th century, but were only allowed to settle in Rīga much later. During World War II, almost all Jews who did not flee were killed. Although some returned, the Jewish communities today are dwindling, partly due to emigration to Israel.

Jewish Vilna's itinerant clothes-sellers photographed in 1915

The Gaon of Vilna (1720–97) *was Lithuania's most famous Jewish scho-lar, whose writing and research still guide many in the Jewish community today. In 1997, the celebration of the bicentenary of his birth brought Litvaks, former Lithuanian Jews, back to Vilnius from all over the world.*

JEWS IN THE BALTIC REGION

Banned from buying property and taking up professions until the late 19th century, the Jewish population lived largely as itinerant tradesmen and market stall-holders. After World War I, Jews were granted full rights as citizens. Until their persecution by the Nazis in 1941, when they were killed in large numbers, the Jews were active in the professions, business and politics.

Rīga's Great Choral Synagogue *was built in 1869 for the city's Jews, who thrived after the laws restrict-ing Jewish residence were lifted in 1840. The site of a Jewish massacre executed by the Nazis in 1941, the synagogue no longer exists.*

Children celebrating Purim *were photo-graphed in 1933 in Vilnius. Purim, a joyful festival in the Jewish calendar, is still celebrated by the Jewish commu-nity in the Baltic region today.*

Kenesa, a 20th-century synagogue in Trakai, *is where the Karaim (see p253) congregate. An ethnically Turkish community from the northern shores of the Black Sea, they first settled in Trakai in the 14th century.*

Makkabi Sports Association *was one of the Jewish organizations that thrived in independent Latvia between 1920 and 1940, when the government worked hard to eliminate anti-Semitism.*

The Paneriai Holocaust Memorial (see p244), *just outside Vilnius, commemorates the 70,000 Jews who were murdered here during the Nazi occupation (1941–44). In Latvia, 66,000 Jews were massacred, while Estonia, where 4,300 Jews lived prior to World War II, was declared "Jew free".*

Rīga's Museum of the Jews in Latvia *documents 500 years of Jewish history in the region, and includes this poster used by anti-Semitic groups.*

Tallinn's Beit Bella Synagogue *was opened on 16 May 2007. The city had been without a synagogue since the destruction of an earlier one during World War II. Today, a 3,000-strong Jewish community lives in Estonia, while in Latvia and Lithuania, Jews now number over 9,000 and 4,000 respectively.*

Estonia's Constituent Assembly in session, 1919

INDEPENDENCE DECLARED

As Western Europe welcomed peace in November 1918, the Baltic area was one enormous battlefield. Anti-Bolsheviks still hoped to overthrow the new Soviet regime, and the Germans wanted to make up for losses in the West with victories in the East. The Poles were keen to form another commonwealth with Lithuania. As a result, there was little interest in supporting the declarations of independence made by the three Baltic States early that year. Only a large British fleet, stationed off the Estonian coast, was happy to supply arms to Estonia and Latvia and, therefore, help them achieve independence.

By early 1920, Estonia and Latvia were able to fight off all their enemies and get them to agree to borders, which would hold until 1940. Lithuania was forced to give up Vilnius, after the Poles seized it later that year. Subsequently, Kaunas was made the

temporary capital. Lithuanians compensated themselves to some extent by seizing Memel (Klaipėda) in 1923 from French troops.

For the next 20 years, the three countries operated in a very similar manner. Weak, ever-changing governments in the 1920s gave way in the 1930s to strong statesmen who ran the state on Mussolini's corporatist model. Even though nobody in any Baltic government had had a senior position before independence, it was remarkable what they were able to achieve in such a short period of time. In Estonia and Latvia, the German estates were seized but the many successful urban businesses that had been established in the previous century were allowed to continue as before.

THE SOVIET OCCUPATION

On 17 June 1940, the Baltic countries fell to the Russians, as agreed in the Molotov-Ribbentrop Pact, a non-aggression treaty signed between Germany and the USSR. All traces of the previous 20 years of independence were removed. Senior members of the three governments were executed. Flags, national anthems and Bibles were banned. The Soviet Union did not want to be reminded of its failure to conquer the Baltic States at the end of World War I. In June 1941, a massive deportation to Siberia was organized of around 10,000 Estonians, 15,000 Latvians and 30,000 Lithuanians, most of whom died. A week later, Germany invaded the Baltic States, violating the Molotov-Ribbentrop Pact.

The USSR and Germany signing the Molotov-Ribbentrop Pact of 1939

TIMELINE

1918 The three Baltic States declare independence

1922 Russia becomes Soviet Union (USSR)

1920 Russia recognizes independence of the three Baltic States

1939 Molotov-Ribbentrop Pact signed between the USSR and Germany

1940 The three Baltic countries incorporated into the USSR

1941 German occupation of the Baltics begins

1945 Soviet reoccupation

1956 Baltic deportees allowed back from Siberia

1960 Foreign tourists begin to be allowed to visit the Baltic capitals

1925	1935	1945	1955	196

Soviet tanks in Riga, 1940

A chain of people joining hands to form the "Baltic Way" across the three Baltic States

Soviet forces, who called themselves "liberators", slowly reconquered most of the Baltic region during the autumn of 1944, as they drove the Germans westwards. In anticipation of their return, many locals fled to Sweden or Germany. Others who stayed joined the partisans based in the countryside. Known as Forest Brothers, they were a very effective guerrilla force until the mid-1950s, disrupting the Soviet administration throughout the region. All the links with the outside world were broken, including trading routes.

Aware that it had only minimal popular support, the Soviet government knew that the incorporation of the Baltic States could only be achieved and maintained by brute force. In each country, the Russian military occupied large parts to which access was strictly controlled and all the paperwork needed was only in Russian. The Russification policies followed by the Tsars were enforced once again in order to stamp out the national identities of Estonia, Latvia and Lithuania. They imposed such uniformity that it became challenging for an outsider to distinguish one Baltic State from the other. In 1989, a human chain, referred to as the "Baltic Way",

Soviet President Mikhail Gorbachev

was formed across the three Baltic States to draw the world's attention to their shared history of suffering.

INDEPENDENCE RETURNS

Perestroika (reform) and *glasnost* (openness), the two buzz words of Mikhail Gorbachev's regime (1985–91), had a dramatic effect in the Baltic region. Independence could be discussed openly and national flags reappeared. By 1990, independence for Estonia, Latvia and Lithuania could be predicted, but only in the long term. However, its sudden arrival on 21 August 1991, when an attempted coup in Moscow against Gorbachev failed, was unexpected. In 48 hours, when there was total uncertainty, the three Baltic countries took the opportunity of declaring independence. Russia under Boris Yeltsin did likewise, dissolving the USSR. Suddenly, what had been provincial backwaters became serious European countries, with their own airlines, currencies and embassies and, above all, recognition on a worldwide basis. In 2004, the three Baltic States joined the EU and NATO (North Atlantic Treaty Organization), and in 2007, acceded to the Schengen Agreement.

1994 Last Russian troops leave the Baltic region

1991 Independence restored to the three Baltic countries

2002 Eurovision Song Contest held in Tallinn; a year later in Riga

Eurovision Song Contest 2002

| 1975 | 1985 | 1995 | 2005 | 2015 |

1980 Moscow Olympics' sailing events held in Tallinn

1989 Two million people hold hands from Tallinn to Vilnius, known as the "Baltic Way"

2004 Baltic States join EU and NATO; accede to the Schengen Agreement three years later

Coin issued in 1999 to mark the tenth anniversary of the "Baltic Way"

ESTONIA

Estonia at a Glance

The smallest of the Baltic States, Estonia is divided into two geographical regions, Western Estonia and Eastern Estonia. Apart from the hilly region in the southeast, most of the country is low-lying and is punctuated with innumerable lakes and rivers. Estonia's deeply indented coastline and archipelago of many islands offer some dramatic scenery. The country's predominantly flat landscape is sparsely populated and made up of forests, wetlands and peatbogs that teem with wildlife.

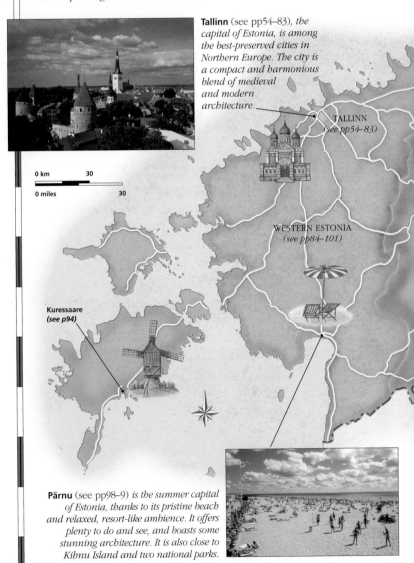

Tallinn (see pp54–83), *the capital of Estonia, is among the best-preserved cities in Northern Europe. The city is a compact and harmonious blend of medieval and modern architecture.*

TALLINN
(see pp54–83)

WESTERN ESTONIA
(see pp84–101)

Kuressaare
(see p94)

0 km   30

0 miles   30

Pärnu (see pp98–9) *is the summer capital of Estonia, thanks to its pristine beach and relaxed, resort-like ambience. It offers plenty to do and see, and boasts some stunning architecture. It is also close to Kihnu Island and two national parks.*

◁ **Street in Old Town Tallinn, with St Nicholas's Orthodox Church in the background**

Lahemaa National Park (see pp106–109), *the largest national park in Estonia, has diverse terrain criss-crossed by biking trails. It is dotted with villages such as Palmse, whose manor house contains the park's information centre.*

Narva (see p112) *has a fortified medieval castle that illustrates how this largely Russian-speaking city was at the frontline of regional power struggles for centuries.*

EASTERN ESTONIA
(see pp102–123)

Lake Peipsi (see p123) *is a huge body of water bordering Russia. A number of settlements with wooden houses mark the lakeshore. The Old Believers live in numerous little lakeshore villages towards the north, while the Setu live in the southern environs.*

Tartu (see pp114–15), *Estonia's second-largest city, is famed for its university and has an exciting cultural and nightlife scene. The city rivals Tallinn in charm and splendour, as well as historic significance.*

A PORTRAIT OF ESTONIA

*P*resenting *a heady mix of medieval heritage and technological advancement, Estonia has rebuilt itself in the post-Soviet era, adapting to the demands of the modern world while preserving a distinct cultural identity. With its rich historic architecture, natural landscapes and dynamic culture, the country makes a significant impression on the ever-growing number of visitors that it attracts.*

Estonia's tumultuous history has resulted from its geographical position as a crossroads between Eastern and Western Europe. With Russia dominating its eastern border, Scandinavia surrounding it to the north and west and the other two Baltic States to its south, Estonia was considered a prize strategic asset among the regional powers through the centuries.

Sign outside Olde Hansa restaurant

After regaining independence from the Soviet Union in 1991, Estonia was left severely dilapidated. During the long slog towards NATO and EU membership throughout the 1990s, Estonia was often held up by Eastern Europe as an example of how to rapidly modernize while preserving national heritage and improving overall living conditions. Estonia is sometimes referred to as e-Estonia due to its reputation for technological innovation. It has almost total Wi-Fi coverage and one of the highest rates of mobile phone usage in the world. Although the rural areas still lag behind the cities in raising living standards, Estonia has grown into a major travel destination. Its forests and marshlands, pristine islands and traditional villages are as alluring as its capital Tallinn, a pulsating city with a medieval Old Town.

Estonia's typical river scenery with yellow leaves and green mossy stones

◁ **A group of Estonian folk dancers performing in national costume**

Participants awaiting their turn at the All-Estonian Song Festival

significant icon for the nation, rousing affirmation of Estonian identity.

Religion does not play a particularly large part in Estonian life, although hundreds of years of foreign occupation led to many people converting to Christianity, including Lutheranism and Russian Orthodoxy. The most important aspects of Estonian culture are distinctly pagan in origin. The hugely popular midsummer festival Jaanipäev (John's Day), characterized by drinking, dancing and revelry, has a pagan origin.

SOCIETY AND CULTURE

In general, Estonians are more strongly influenced by Scandinavian culture than by that of their Baltic neighbours. Finns and Estonians also share close linguistic links through the Finno-Ugric language family. A sizeable Russian-speaking minority remained in Estonia after the Soviet withdrawal, leading to some diplomatic skirmishes with Russia over the years. Today, there are fewer instances of conflict between Russians and Estonians.

Estonians take great pride in their heritage. The country's medieval past is visible not only in some of its architecture, but also in festivals that have their roots in that era. Folk culture is central to national identity, as Estonians were predominantly reduced to serfdom, with no right to own land or property, until the country's first spell of independence in 1918. The All-Estonian Song Festival, which was first held in 1869 and has since taken place every five years, remains a

POLITICAL LIFE

The Communist Party of Estonia, which had previously shaped the political life of the people, gave way to a multi-party system in the post-independence years. The most prominent of these parties, the Estonian Centre Party, was joined by several political groups with diverse political ideologies. As a result, the Estonian government is made up of fragile cross-party coalitions.

Most politicians that hold senior political posts previously served in the Communist Party, leading to a sense of cynicism among many Estonians towards politics. However,

Parliamentary session in progress

Tallinn's new modern city centre, with the Radisson SAS Hotel *(left)* and SEB Uhispank bank buildings *(right)*

while corruption was certainly an issue in the 1990s, the situation has now improved, mainly due to the introduction of stringent EU laws and a far more stable economy.

ECONOMY

Successive governments have proven remarkably consistent in transforming the economy into a prosperous, competitive and flexible enterprise. Estonia has the largest GDP growth of the Baltic States and one of the lowest unemployment rates in the European Union. Its capital Tallinn abounds with ultra-sleek shops, restaurants, bars and nightclubs, reflecting the hedonistic nature of the youthful Estonian with a large disposable income.

While wages are still behind those of Western Europe, Estonia is quickly catching up. The country's main exports are machinery and electronic goods, along with wood and paper. The economy also depends heavily on a thriving IT sector, tourism and transporting Russia's oil through its ports.

TOURISM

Large parts of the Estonian countryside fell into total desolation after the break-up of the Soviet Union, which constructed entire communities around singular industrial and agricultural production. Tourism has been instrumental in transforming Estonia from a drab post-Soviet state into a thriving nation. The Estonian Tourist Board began marketing Estonia as a travel destination, while the private sector has been quick to adapt and respond to the business opportunities this has opened up. Tallinn was inevitably the first part of the country to benefit from the boom in tourism. In recent years, tourism has stimulated a social renaissance in parts of the country that had languished in poverty for many years. Estonian islands and villages, as well as towns throughout the mainland, have seen a steady increase in tourism-related investment.

Tourists enjoying Tallinn's roof-top panorama

ESTONIA THROUGH THE YEAR

Estonians celebrate a host of seasonal festivals through the year. These encompass everything from religion, folk culture and handicrafts to art, music, dance and theatre, making the festival calendar both colourful and remarkable. Much of the festive frenzy occurs in the summer, peaking with the Midsummer's Eve

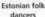

Estonian folk dancers

celebrations. Summer is also the time when a series of concerts are held throughout the country, and when the Folklore Baltica Festival *(see p132)*, which showcases the region's distinct traditional culture, takes place. In addition to the annual festivals, a number of commemorative days are observed throughout Estonia.

SPRING

As expected from a country so attuned to the seasons, spring is a joyful time marked by a lively range of long-established festivals.

MARCH

Estonian Film Days *(early Mar)*, Tallinn. The best in all Estonian film genres are given awards. Selected movies are shown with English subtitles.
Student Jazz Festival *(early Mar)*, Tallinn, Tartu and Viljandi. This long-running event features jazz concerts.

APRIL

Estonian Music Days *(mid-Apr)*. Contemporary Estonian classical music is showcased in Tallinn and other cities.
Jazzkaar *(late Apr)*. The biggest jazz festival held throughout Estonia includes local and international names.

Saxophonist playing at a concert during Jazzkaar

Horse-riders in medieval costumes, celebrating Tallinn Old Town Days

Tartu Student Days *(late Apr–early May)*. During this festival, Tartu's students hold bizarre concerts, shows and parties open to everybody.

MAY

Home Tourism and Handicraft Fair *(late May)*, Tallinn. Held at the Estonian Open-Air Museum, this annual craft fair displays the best traditional products and offers a series of cultural events.
Tallinn Old Town Days *(late May–early Jun)*. Tallinn's medieval past is celebrated with re-enactments of old traditions like jousting. The streets are filled with market stalls and people in costume.

SUMMER

After months of wintry gloom and darkness, Estonians make the best of their short but resplendent summers, with an abundance of festivals.

JUNE

Summer Music Festival *(early Jun–late Aug)*, Tartu. Classical, contemporary and jazz concerts are held in the town.
Midsummer's Eve *(24 Jun)*. This summer celebration is marked by a night of joyous drinking, eating and age-old rituals around a bonfire.
Pärnu Hanseatic Days *(late Jun)*. This two-day festival includes a procession, craft fair and knights' tournament.
Pühajärve Beach Party is a popular pop festival with live bands and DJs.

JULY

Haapsalu Early Music Festival *(early Jul)*. Set in the pretty surroundings of Haapsalu Castle, this is a celebration of early classical music.
Õllesummer Festival *(early Jul)*, Tallinn. This unique beer festival also features major concerts, from jazz to rock, as well as sideshows.

Audience watching performers on stage, Viljandi Folk Festival

Old Town Medieval Market *(early Jul)*, Tallinn. An exciting series of concerts, workshops, costumed performers and traditional market stalls.

Viljandi Folk Festival *(late Jul)*. Folk music ensembles from all over Estonia perform in the castle grounds.

AUGUST

Birgitta Festival *(mid-Aug)*, Tallinn. Operas, concerts and recitals are held in the ruins of Pirita Convent. Food is served on the summer terrace.

August Dance Festival *(late Aug)*, Tallinn. The best in contemporary dance, including guest performances by famous international troupes.

AUTUMN

The festival season winds down a bit in the autumn, though most cities have a few annual events on offer.

A brightly illuminated Christmas tree, Tallinn

SEPTEMBER

Autumnal Farming Days *(mid-Sep)*, Tallinn. Celebrates the harvest. Traditional farming methods are also shown.

Credo International Festival of Sacred Music *(early–late Sep)*, Tallinn. Orthodox sacred music concerts held in churches and concert halls.

Matsalu Nature Film Festival *(late Sep)*. An unusual festival screening the works of various nature-filmmakers.

OCTOBER

NYYD *(mid-Oct)*, Tallinn. The best in experimental compositions from Estonia and abroad are featured.

NOVEMBER

Black Nights Film Festival *(Nov–Dec)*, Tallinn. A comprehensive selection of independent and world cinema celebrating the best in film. Most films are screened with English subtitles.

WINTER

Despite the long and bitterly cold spells, winter also holds the promise of a wonderful snow-blanketed landscape and a season of festivity.

DECEMBER

Christmas Jazz Festival *(early Dec)*. A series of jazz concerts held in Tallinn and several other towns in the run-up to Christmas.

Old Town Christmas Market *(Dec–early Jan)*, Tallinn. Equally popular with tourists and locals, the market has a variety of goods on sale from the traditional to the novel.

JANUARY

Pärnu Contemporary Music Days *(mid–late Jan)*. An outstanding festival of classical music, which also features lectures, workshops and theatre performances.

Skiiers participating in the popular Tartu Ski Marathon

FEBRUARY

Baroque Music Festival *(early–mid-Feb)*, Tallinn. A festival favourite offering a series of Baroque music concerts in various venues around the Old Town.

Tartu Ski Marathon *(early Feb)*. This hugely popular ski-fest features events and competitions but the highlight is the 63-km (39-mile) ski marathon.

PUBLIC HOLIDAYS

New Year's Day (1 Jan)
Independence Day (24 Feb)
Good Friday (Mar/Apr)
May Day (1 May)
Võidupüha Victory Day (23 Jun)
St John's Day (24 Jun)
Restoration of Independence (20 Aug)
Christmas (24–26 Dec)

THE HISTORY OF ESTONIA

*H*istorical references to Estonia date from the early 13th century, when the Teutonic Knights arrived, introducing a new social order in which the Germans dominated for several centuries. A brief benevolent Swedish rule in the 17th century was followed by Russian and German oppression, which continued with a short-lived inter-war independence. Estonia became a republic only in 1991.

The German Knights, or the Brotherhood of the Sword, started a bitter struggle for the control of Estonia that lasted from 1208, when they established their hold over Otepää, until 1211. The Danes, too, were contending for the control of Estonia. In 1206, they tried in vain to subjugate Saaremaa, the country's largest and most prosperous island. Denmark's King Valdemar II (r.1202–41) occupied Tallinn in 1219, but his attempts to expand the Danish territory further were unsuccessful.

Fragment of a seal of Danish King Valdemar II

which the Germans owned manor estates and the local inhabitants were obliged to work as serfs, survived until the 19th century.

Tallinn was acquired again by the Germans in 1347, when large-scale protests against feudal exactions forced the Danes to relinquish their possessions in Estonia. During this time, many guilds and merchants' associations emerged, and towns such as Tallinn, Tartu, Viljandi and Pärnu thrived as members of the Hanseatic League. Tallinn, particularly, prospered as one of Northern Europe's largest towns.

GERMAN CONQUEST

In 1227, the Teutonic Knights conquered the whole of Estonia, also controlling Tallinn until 1238, when it was returned to the Danes. The Knights took over a stone castle built by the Danes and rebuilt it as the Toompea Castle the same year. The foundations for a new social order were laid, with the Germans serving as the nobility, as well as merchants and craftsmen. The Estonians were forcibly converted to Christianity and their land given away to the Knights and bishops. The feudal system, in

An impression of Tallinn's Toompea Castle in 1227

TIMELINE

1208 Germans capture Otepää in southern Estonia

1227 Germans conquer all of Estonia

1219 Danes seize Tallinn

1343 Peasants' uprising (St George's Night) against the Danes

1347 Danes sell Tallinn to the Germans

1372 German replaces Latin as the official written language

1422 Tallinn Town Hall Pharmacy opens on site where it still operates

Detail, Town Hall Pharmacy door

1574 First Lutheran service preached in Estonia at St Olav's Church in Tallinn

St Olav's Church, Old Town, Tallinn

1200   1300   1400   1500

Tartu University, Estonia's prestigious seat of learning

THE SWEDISH RULE

The 16th century saw Estonia as the major battleground between Russia and Sweden in the Livonian Wars *(see p33)*. By 1629, the whole country was in Swedish hands. The Swedes achieved much over the next 50 years, including the establishment of Tartu University, the introduction of schools all around the country, printing of books in Estonian and the construction of several buildings, especially in Narva and Tartu. Narva was built as the second Swedish capital. The social system created by the Germans was left undisturbed, however. Later Swedish kings interfered by seizing German-owned estates, incurring the wrath of the Germans who turned to Russia's Peter the Great for help.

STRUGGLE AGAINST THE RUSSIANS

Although the Swedish troops were initially able to resist the Russians, in 1709, the final battle between the Swedish King Charles XII and Peter the Great sealed Estonia's fate for the next 200 years, during which time there would be little threat to Tsarist rule. The Russians as well as the Baltic Germans actively kept Estonians out of any positions of responsibility, besides curbing the Estonian language. The discontent of the intelligentsia found expression in the rebellion led by the students of Tartu University in the 19th century.

In 1905, in common with many other places in Russia, Estonia witnessed unrest that spread to the towns. The factory-workers lent support to the nascent Bolshevik movement, while several German manors were burnt down in the countryside. During World War I (1914–18), the prospect of Estonian independence seemed bleak. However, the 1917 Revolution that ended the Tsarist regime in Russia and the chaos that followed in Moscow, encouraged Estonia to declare independence in February 1918, in Pärnu. The Treaty of Tartu, signed with Russia in February 1920, formally confirmed Estonian independence.

Estonian Army recruiting poster, 1918

Declaration of independence in February 1918, Pärnu

1632 Opening of Tartu University by Swedish Lutherans

1629 Estonia passes into Swedish hands

Diamond order of Peter the Great

1710 Treaty of Nystadt brings Estonia into the Tsarist Empire

1872 The first strike organized by the women of Narva

1864 First Estonian newspaper, *Postimees*, launched

1869 First Estonian Song Festival held in Tartu

1885 Russification of the Baltics begins

1918 Declaration of Estonian independence signed

1920 Treaty of Tartu confirms Estonia's independence

1905 Uprisings in Tallinn

1600   1700   1800   1900

President Konstantin Päts *(centre)* in 1939

FREEDOM AND WORLD WAR II

Although there were 20 coalition governments between 1919 and 1933, they all agreed to immediately distribute the Baltic-German landholdings among the local community. Education and state pension systems were introduced nationwide. People who had been active in the national movement before World War I took senior positions in government. The most prominent of these politicians was Konstantin Päts, who staged a coup in February 1934 and dissolved Parliament, although he began to restore democratic institutions in 1938. Day-to-day life for most Estonians was hardly affected by these developments. Industry, agriculture and international trade continued as before. Päts ruled until the Soviet invasion on 16 June 1940, which brought a sudden and brutal end to independent Estonia. The Russians executed several prominent Estonians, including Päts himself, and many others were deported to Siberia. The German invasion,

Soviet tanks thwarting the Germans' landing attempt in Estonia in September 1941

which came a year later, was seen by many in Estonia as a sort of liberation. Tallinn-born Alfred Rosenberg, who was appointed by Nazi Germany to run the Baltic States, treated the general population less harshly compared to most other countries subjected to Nazi occupation. In September 1944, the advancing Red Army returned to Estonia, forcing the Nazis to surrender and Estonia once again became part of the Soviet Union.

SOVIET ESTONIA

The ten years which followed the Soviet reoccupation were traumatic for Estonia. The deportation programme, restarted in 1944, saw its climax in March 1949 with the arrest of 20,000 Estonians. The Soviets wanted to curb any opposition to the establishment of collective farms. The deportations were also meant to sabotage the successful guerrilla campaign run by the Forest Brothers, a resistance group active until the early 1950s throughout Estonia. Stalin's death in 1953 led to a slightly less oppressive regime in Estonia, as it did throughout the USSR. From the 1960s, Estonia's link with the non-Soviet world began to grow. A ferry link between Tallinn and Helsinki was started twice a week. The 1980 Moscow Olympics turned out to be invaluable for Estonia, when it staged the yachting events, which brought thousands of foreign visitors to Tallinn. As a

TIMELINE

1921 Flights from Tallinn to Stockholm begin

1939 Molotov-Ribbentrop Pact puts Estonia under USSR

1934 Bloodless coup staged by Konstantin Päts

Estonia's Tallink ferry service linking Tallinn and Helsinki

1941 Nazi Germany occupies Estonia

1965 A ferry linking Tallinn and Helsinki begins sailing

1925	1935	1945	1955	1965

1924 Coup attempted by Estonian Communists

1937 The navy acquires its first British-built submarine

1944 Return of Soviet forces; Stalinist era begins

1940 Soviet occupation begins

1964 Finnish president visits Estonia

1953 Stalin dies; Soviet oppression slightly relaxed

Olympic torch inaugurating the yachting events held in 1980, Tallinn

INDEPENDENCE

The years 1992 and 1993 turned out to be a challenging time for Estonia. The immediate reintroduction of the kroon as the national currency wiped out savings accumulated in Soviet roubles and inflation was not immediately curtailed. Prime Minister Mart Laar, who served the first term from 1992 to 1994, coined the phrase "the little country that can" and it did, very quickly. Many suffered temporarily, as factories closed and collective farms were abandoned, but few suffered long-term as tourism, Finnish assembly plants and international call centres quickly absorbed any spare labour. Returning to power in 1999, Laar was able to steer the country out of the financial crisis that stemmed from the collapse of Russia's economy in 1998.

result, foreign newspapers, direct-dial international phone calls and a range of consumer goods not seen in Tallinn since 1940 were introduced. After the Games, all these quickly disappeared, but the memory of them did not; frustration with the USSR turned in the 1980s to total disillusionment as Finnish TV showed what a different style of life was being enjoyed just 50 km (31 miles) from Tallinn.

When Mikhail Gorbachev came to power in 1985 as General Secretary of the Communist Party of the Soviet Union, Estonians took advantage of his liberal policies to revitalize the cultural scene and to restructure factories and small businesses. Plans to reform the economy were made, the key element of which was the introduction of a stable currency. At the time of the collapse of the USSR in 1991, Estonians were better prepared, at least in theory, for a capitalist economy than were any of the other Soviet republics.

Estonian Prime Minister
Mart Laar

By late 2007, 16 years after independence, Estonia still had not experienced an economic slump and its entry into the EU in 2004 makes this even more unlikely. However, as about 10 per cent of the potential workforce now live abroad, unemployment remains an issue for the government. Relations with Russia will remain difficult while its governments still cannot accept the loss of their "near abroad". However, with trade turning westwards and NATO ensuring permanent security, this will matter less and less in the future.

1980 Olympics sailing and yachting events open in Tallinn

1992 Lennart Meri elected as president

President Lennart Meri (1929–2006)

2004 Estonia joins NATO and EU

| 1975 | 1985 | 1995 | 2005 | 2015 |

1991 Estonia declares independence

1994 Russian troops withdrawn; *Estonia* sinks, claiming 850 lives

2007 World's first national Internet election held

Pirita Yachting Centre, venue for Olympics yachting events in 1980

TALLINN

*I*n little over a decade, the Estonian capital has grown into a dynamic, chic and exciting city. An architectural wonder, Tallinn has some stunning examples of modern architecture that reflect the newly found confidence of its people. In addition to restoring the medieval architecture of its Old Town, the city has recently undergone a major construction boom.

An overview of Tallinn from Toompea Hill shows how the city has made the best of its extraordinary historic foundations. Tallinn first appeared on the Western European map in 1154. The city came to be known as Tallinn after the Danes conquered it in 1219 and built a stronghold on Toompea Hill. "Tallinn" is an abbreviation of the Estonian name Taani Linnus, meaning "Danish stronghold". However, Tallinn officially bore the Teutonic name of Reval until Estonia's first period of independence in 1918. With the arrival of German merchants in 1230, the city was divided into the Upper Town (Toompea) and the Lower Town.

In 1347, the Danish king sold Tallinn to Germany. The city flourished in the 14th and 15th centuries, when it was one of the leading members of the powerful Hanseatic League. The brilliantly restored Old Town, a UNESCO World Heritage Site since 1991, is a living monument to this golden period of Tallinn's history.

Tallinn was relatively stagnant during the Tsarist Russian period, which began in 1710 under the rule of Peter the Great. For most of the 19th century, it was little more than a summer resort for wealthy Russians. However, the introduction of the Tallinn–St Petersburg railway in 1870 restored the city's former glory as a major trading centre. During the Soviet occupation a vast influx of predominantly Russian-speaking workers swelled Tallinn's population.

Since independence in 1991, improving air and sea transport links with Western Europe have made Tallinn easily accessible. The city has forged close ties with neighbouring Finland and the Tallinn–Helsinki ferry line is among the busiest in the world.

Young ballerinas performing in a street in Tallinn during the summer festivities held in June

◁ Striking domes of Alexander Nevsky Cathedral soaring above the trees

Exploring Tallinn

The vast majority of sights in Tallinn are concentrated in and around Town Hall Square and Toompea, in medieval Old Town. Relatively easy to explore on foot, the winding cobbled streets are dotted with elegant back alleys, courtyards and spired churches, as well as fascinating museums that present the city's historic and cultural traditions. There are also many notable buildings around the fringes of the Old Town, all within easy walking distance. On the eastern section of the city wall, Viru Gate serves as one of the main access points into the Old Town.

Viru Gate, one of the best-known landmarks in Tallinn

SIGHTS AT A GLANCE

Churches and Monasteries
Alexander Nevsky Cathedral ⑲
Cathedral of St Mary
  the Virgin ⑳
Church of the Transfiguration
  of Our Lord ⑭
Dominican Monastery ⑩
Holy Spirit Church ❸
Niguliste Church pp64–5 ❻
St Olav's Church ⑮

Museums
Adamson-Eric Museum ㉔
Estonian Museum of Applied
  Art and Design ⑬
Great Guild Hall ❹
Museum of Estonian
  Photography ❺
Museum of Occupations ㉑
Museum of Theatre
  and Music ❼
Tallinn City Museum ⑪

**Historic Buildings and
Sites of Interest**
Fat Margaret Tower ⑰
House of Blackheads ⑫
Kiek-in-de-Kök ㉓
Knights' House ㉒
St Catherine's Passageway ❾
Three Sisters ⑯
Toompea Castle ⑱
Town Hall ❶
Town Hall Pharmacy ❷
Viru Gate ❽

0 metres		200
0 yards		200

SEE ALSO

KEY

▢	Street-by-Street map *pp58–9*
▢	Street-by-Street map *pp68–9*
ℹ	Tourist information
⊠	Post office
🚓	Police station
✝	Church

Pikk Hermann Tower, in the scenic Toompea area

GETTING AROUND

Walking is the best way to explore Tallinn's Old Town. However, motorized transport is required to see some major sights, such as Kadriorg Park east of the Old Town, as well as Pirita, the TV Tower and the Botanical Gardens, which are all situated to the northeast of Kadriorg Park. The city's public transport system is a network of buses, trolleybuses and trams. Nearly all buses and trolleybuses leave from Vabaduse Square or the Viru Keskus terminal, while most tram lines pass by the Old Town. Tallinn has transport links with all major towns and cities in Estonia.

View of the city's skyline from Toompea Hill

Street-by-Street: Around Town Hall Square

Medieval carving, Town Hall Square

In the heart of the Old Town, the magnificent Town Hall Square has, for centuries, served as a marketplace. Gently sloping, the cobblestoned square is surrounded by a ring of elegantly designed medieval buildings. The early 14th-century Town Hall is Northern Europe's only surviving late Gothic town hall. A meeting point for locals and visitors, the square captures the essence of the Old Town. In summer, it is filled with open-air cafés and restaurant tables.

Busy market in Town Hall Square, seen from the Town Hall tower

House of Blackheads

Tallinn City Museum
Housed in a medieval merchants' house, this museum presents Tallinn's history through a variety of fascinating exhibits and artifacts ⓫

★ Town Hall Pharmacy
Worth a visit just for the impressive interior, this long-running pharmacy also has a charming little museum displaying old curiosities ❷

KEY

— — — Suggested route

STAR SIGHTS

★ Town Hall Pharmacy

★ Town Hall

PÜHAVAIMU

KINGA

VOORIMEHE

DUNKRI

Holy Spirit Church
Regarded as one of Tallinn's most attractive churches, this splendidly preserved structure houses a treasure trove of medieval and Renaissance features ❸

For hotels and restaurants in this region see pp292–4 and pp322–5

Dominican Monastery
Among Tallinn's oldest buildings, the monastery complex also includes an atmospheric museum which has some beautiful stone carvings ⑩

Viru Street
One of the most famous in the Old Town, this busy street is packed with a variety of restaurants, bars, cafés and shops.

★ Town Hall
Taking pride of place in Town Hall Square, this imposing Gothic building with an octagonal tower has been the focus of civic life since the Middle Ages ①

Museum of Estonian Photography has an extensive collection housed in two buildings ⑤

MÜÜRIVAHE

VIRU

SAUNA

ENE

SUUR KARJA

KUNINGA

HARJU

VANA POSTI

NIGULISTE

RÜÜTLI

0 metres 100
0 yards 100

Niguliste Church
This remarkable Gothic church is now a Tallinn landmark boasting an excellent museum of religious art. The church holds organ recitals every weekend ⑥

Town Hall ❶
Tallinna raekoda

Raekoja plats 1. **Map** 1 C2. **Tel** 645 7900. 🚌 5, 40. 🚎 1, 2, 3, 4. ⏱ Jul–Aug: 10am–4pm Mon–Sat (by appointment), Sep–Jun: 9am–4pm Mon–Fri. 📷 📹 💻 www.tallinn.ee/raekoda

One of the most revered symbols of Tallinn, the Town Hall dates back to 1404. Its high-pitched roof is supported by two tall gables and a late-Renaissance spire crowns the slender octagonal tower. The narrow windows and crenellated parapet complete the building's impressive appearance. Facing Town Hall Square, a vaulted arcade runs along the north façade, where a small café puts out tables in the summer. Inside the building, it is possible to see the Citizens' Hall and the Council Hall, although most visitors head straight for the tower and the 115-step ascent to the top.

Town Hall Pharmacy ❷
Raeapteek

Raekoja plats 11. **Map** 1 C2. **Tel** 631 4860. 🚌 5, 40. 🚎 1, 2, 3, 4. ⏱ 9am–7pm Mon–Fri, 10am–5pm Sat. 📷

The Town Hall Pharmacy is famed for being one of the oldest-established pharmacies in Europe. The building's exterior dates back to the 17th century but there is evidence that a pharmacy existed on the site as long ago as 1422. In one corner of the shop's interior there is a modest museum with a small selection of historical exhibits including medical instruments and curative treatments. Ask to try the spiced wine, which was a popular purchase in medieval times. According to a local legend, marzipan was accidentally created here and named Martin's Bread.

Graceful Baroque tower of Holy Spirit Church

Holy Spirit Church ❸
Pühavaimu kirik

Pühavaimu 2. **Map** 1 C2. **Tel** 644 1487. 🚌 5, 40. 🚎 1, 2, 3, 4. ⏱ May–Sep: 9am–5pm Mon–Sat, Oct–Apr: 10am–3pm Mon–Sat. 📷 🔔 3pm (in English). www.eelk.ee/tallinna.puhavaimu

The 13th-century Holy Spirit Church is one of the most beautiful churches in Tallinn. The Gothic building served as the Town Hall chapel before being converted into a church. Its whitewashed exterior includes the oldest public clock in Tallinn, with carvings dating from 1684. The stepped gable is topped by a striking Baroque tower. The spire was nearly destroyed by fire in 2002, but was restored within a year. Inside, the church is a treasure trove of religious artifacts and architecture, from the magnificently intricate Baroque pews to the Renaissance-era pulpit. The sublime altar triptych, *The Descent of the Holy Ghost* (1483), by Lübeck artist Berndt Notke, is the main highlight. The church holds a special place in Estonian history, as the first Estonian-language sermons were delivered here in 1535 following the Reformation.

Great Guild Hall ❹
Suurgildi hoone

Pikk jalg 17. **Map** 1 C2. **Tel** 641 1630. 🚌 5, 40. 🚎 1, 2, 3, 4. ⏱ 11am–6pm Thu–Tue. 📷 🔔 www.eam.ee

One the most important buildings in medieval Tallinn, the Great Guild Hall was constructed in 1417. It was owned by a powerful union of wealthy merchants. The building holds a significant place in the town's history. It was mainly used as the gathering place for its members but at times it was also rented out for wedding parties and court sessions. It was the starting as well as the end point of most festive processions of Tallinn. The late-Gothic building has retained its original appearance through the centuries, although the windows were remodelled in the 1890s.

The Great Guild Hall's majestic interior provides a perfect setting for a branch of the **Estonian History Museum** *(see p78)*. The museum's collection of historical artifacts covers Estonian history from the Stone Age to the mid-19th century in fine detail. The exhibits, which include everything from jewellery to weaponry, are accompanied by explanatory texts in Estonian, Russian and English.

Interior of the Town Hall Pharmacy, with well-stocked shelves

Medieval Architecture

Tallinn's Old Town is one of the best-preserved examples of medieval architecture in Northern Europe. With its winding cobblestoned streets and rows of elegantly gabled façades, the Old Town retains the true character of a medieval town centre. The labyrinthine street structure developed in relation to the power seat of Toompea above and the harbour below, with the

Door knocker, Estonian History Museum

all-important Town Hall Square and marketplace at the heart of it. Although Tallinn flourished as a centre of trade in medieval times, it was relatively quiet in the 19th century, which is probably why the Old Town was spared from being demolished. Tallinn's medieval fortifications are also very well preserved, with some 2 km (1 mile) of the town wall and half of the original 46 towers still intact.

The gabled upper storey was used for storage, with a winch used to hoist up merchandise.

A model of a medieval merchant's house *can be seen at the Tallinn City Museum (see p63), a 14th-century building. The upper storey was used to store merchandise, and guests were entertained on the first floor.*

Medieval towers *are famous symbols of the city's history. Kiek-in-de-Kök (see p71) and Fat Margaret Tower (see p67) are now museums. Visitors can get a view of the area by climbing the adjoining Nunna, Sauna and Kuldjala towers.*

Saiakang alley, *which is just off Town Hall Square, is one of the narrow medieval streets and passageways that make the Old Town so fascinating.*

Lühike jalg, *also known as the "Short Leg", is a steep, atmospheric passageway that was built in the 13th century as a link between the stronghold of Toompea, or the Upper Town, and the rest of Tallinn. In the Middle Ages, a number of coppersmiths and locksmiths had their workshops on Lühike jalg.*

A dragonhead waterspout *can be seen just below the Town Hall's roof. The delightful waterspouts of the Town Hall are fine examples of the mischievous details that adorn many of Tallinn's medieval buildings.*

An 1898 photograph, Museum of Estonian Photography

Museum of Estonian Photography ❺
Fotomuuseum

Raekoja tänav 4/6. **Map** 1 C3. **Tel** 644 8767. 🚌 5, 40. 🚊 1, 2, 3, 4. ⭕ Mar–Oct: 10:30am–6pm Thu–Tue, Nov–Feb: 10:30am–5pm Thu–Tue. 🏷️ 🏛️ www.linnamuuseum.ee

Tucked away behind the Town Hall, the Museum of Estonian Photography consists of two separate buildings, one dating back to the 14th century and the other to the 18th century. They once served as the town prisons and were also used to hold court sessions. The buildings now house an extensive collection of Estonian photography covering the period from 1840 to 1940. The display, which includes rare daguerreotypes, ambrotypes and ferrotypes, showcases some of the finest works by well-known early Estonian photographers including H Tiidermann, B Lais and N Nyländer. Pride of place is given to the tiny Minox camera which was reputedly invented in Estonia in 1936. The gallery also hosts temporary exhibitions of contemporary works.

Niguliste Church ❻
Niguliste kirik

See pp64–5.

Museum of Theatre and Music ❼
Teatri-ja muusikamuuseum

Müürivahe 12. **Map** 1 C3. **Tel** 644 6407. 🚌 5, 40. 🚊 3, 4. ⭕ 10am–6pm Wed–Sun. 🏷️ 📷 call in advance. www.tmm.ee

Located in the stately-looking Assauwe Tower of the city wall, this museum focuses on a much-loved part of the country's cultural heritage, and also serves as an academic centre. Founded in 1924, the music museum was combined with a theatre museum in 1941. There is much for music and theatre aficionados to enjoy, from a fine selection of folk instruments to a collection of original theatre production programmes. The papers and instruments of the eminent Estonian composer, Peeter Süda (1883–1920), form a small part of the museum's collection. The staff are happy to play the instruments for a small fee. The museum owns the copyright to the work of composer Heino Eller (1887–1970) and since 1998, has been awarding the prestigious Heino Eller Music Prize to distinguished figures.

Viru Gate ❽

Viru tänav. **Map** 2 D3. 🚌 5, 40. 🚊 1, 2, 3, 4.

On the eastern section of the city wall, the Viru Gate serves as one of the main access points into the Old Town. A picturesque sight, its slightly skewed stone towers are one of Tallinn's best-known images. The pair of towers that make up the gate were built in the 14th century and were part of a larger gate-system. The surrounding stretch of city wall dates back to the 16th century. A moat and water mill, which once existed between the foregates and the main gate, were demolished in 1843. In the early 20th century, Viru Street was regarded as one of the city's most fashionable and is now a major tourist spot.

Stone towers of Viru Gate, one of the most renowned images of Tallinn

St Catherine's Passageway ⑨
Katariina käik

Katariina käik. **Map** 2 D2. 🚌 5, 40. 🚋 1, 2, 3, 4.

A fascinating medieval alleyway with uneven stone walls and overhead vaulting, St Catherine's Passageway joins Vene and Müürivahe Streets. A string of arts and crafts workshops line the passage, where it is possible to watch resident artisans working with jewellery, ceramics and glass or binding books. The passage runs along the surviving wall of St Catherine's Church, which was built in 1246. The church was Tallinn's largest in its day and several gravestones, some dating from the 14th century, still line this narrow passageway.

The cobblestoned St Catherine's Passageway

Dominican Monastery ⑩
Dominiiklaste klooster

Vene 16/18. **Map** 2 D2. **Tel** 644 4606. 🚌 5, 40. 🚋 1, 2, 3, 4. ◯ mid-May–23 Sep: 10am–6pm daily. Other times for pre-booked groups only. 🎫 📷 tour offered to the monastery's inner chambers through the cloister. 🏠 www.kloostri.ee

Founded by Dominican monks in 1246, this monastery was a renowned centre of learning. It thrived until the Reformation riots broke out in 1524. The Lutherans

A passageway in the medieval Dominican Monastery, Old Town

destroyed the monastery and forced the monks into exile. In 1531, a fire damaged most of the desecrated St Catherine's Church, which had formed its south wing.

After suffering neglect for four centuries, the ruined monastery was renovated in 1954. Today a serene cloister, its atmospheric passageways and its pretty inner garden draw visitors. The star attraction, however, is the fine **Dominican Monastery Museum**, with Estonia's largest collection of medieval and Renaissance stone carvings by local stonemasons. One of the prominent works, a decorative relief of an angel on a triangular slab, is attributed to Hans von Aken, the 16th-century German Mannerist painter.

🏛 **Dominican Monastery Museum**
◯ mid-May–mid-Sep: 10am–6pm daily. 🎫

Tallinn City Museum ⑪
Tallinna linnamuuseum

Vene 17. **Map** 1 C2. **Tel** 644 6553. 🚌 5, 40. 🚋 1, 2, 3, 4. ◯ Mar–Oct: 10:30am–6pm Wed–Mon, Nov–Feb: 10:30am–5pm Wed–Mon. 🎫 📷 www.linnamuuseum.ee

Located in a 14th-century merchant's house, the Tallinn City Museum was opened in 1937 to introduce locals to the city's rich cultural heritage. Today, the vast collection, set over three floors, offers a fascinating overview of Tallinn's history. Highlights include a cutaway model of a 16th-century merchant's house and a fine model recreating a 19th-century domestic interior. There is also a replica model of Old Thomas, the famous weathervane that sits atop the Town Hall steeple. The floors are interspersed with lifelike wax figures, dressed in period costumes. Also on view are a collection of silverware, porcelain and pewter and numerous tapestries.

The museum's display of 20th-century exhibits includes photographs of the vast crowds that congregated in the Old Town after Estonia regained its independence from the Soviet Union in 1991. One of the main draws is the intriguing exhibit entitled *The Town That Will Never Be Ready*. It was inspired by a local legend that claims Tallinn will disappear the moment someone proclaims it is finally completed as a city.

Model of Tallinn from the 1820s displayed in the Tallinn City Museum

Niguliste Church ⑥
Niguliste kirik

Dedicated to St Nicholas, Niguliste Church was originally built in the 13th century, although nearly all that remains today is from the 15th century. Most of Tallinn's medieval artworks were destroyed in the Reformation riots of 1524. However, according to legend, Niguliste Church escaped being ransacked due to the laudable efforts of the church warden, who sealed the door with melted lead. Today, Tallinn's most impressive collection of medieval religious artworks are housed here. The building has served as a museum ever since it was extensively rebuilt during Soviet times after being damaged by Soviet air raids in World War II. The church regularly holds organ and choral concerts.

Exterior of Niguliste Church, one of Tallinn's medieval treasures

★ Altarpiece Depicting St Nicholas
Painted in 1482 by Herman Rode of Lübeck, this superbly detailed altarpiece shows a variety of scenes from the life of St Nicholas, as well as the beheading of St George.

A collection of bells from churches all over Estonia is displayed inside the church.

The Silver Chamber is located on the extreme corner of the church.

Altar Triptych of St Mary and the Brotherhood of Blackheads
The main panel shows St George and St Maurice standing beside the Madonna, while St Francis and St Gertrude stand in the wings.

STAR FEATURES

★ Altarpiece Depicting St Nicholas

★ Bernt Notke's Dance Macabre

Stone Figure
This sculpture is one of the wonderfully evocative stone figures that are part of the original design of Niguliste Church.

Entrance

The spire, originally built in 1696, was finally restored in 1984.

Stone Carving

Carved in stone, the skull and crossbones can be seen at the entrance to the chapel near the church's main door. Stone carving, a vital element in Estonian architecture, was largely done in dolomite and sandstone.

★ Bernt Notke's Dance Macabre

The 15th-century frieze by Bernt Notke (1440–1509) is widely considered the pièce de résistance of the church. Only a fragment of the 30-m (98-ft) original remains.

Display, Silver Chamber

The small side chamber contains a fascinating display of ornate silverware that belonged to various guilds and organizations, such as the influential and wealthy Brotherhood of Blackheads.

DANCING WITH DEATH

Part of a 15th-century frieze by Bernt Notke, *Dancing with Death* is considered one of Estonia's most prized works of art, as it is the only known surviving example of its genre on canvas. Skeletal figures of death are shown as enticing a king and nobles to dance along with them. No one knows exactly how the painting came to Tallinn, but it is possible that Notke had reproduced a similar frieze he completed in 1461 in his native Lübeck in Germany.

Detail showing a king

Bernt Notke's frieze, *Dance Macabre,* which is kept inside the church, depicts the universality of death.

Renaissance-style House of Blackheads, with ornate front door

pieces of porcelain, dating from the 1930s to the 60s, by the legendary Estonian artist Adamson-Eric *(see p71).*

Since the museum opened in 1980 it has done a formidable job of promoting Estonian design at home and abroad. Be sure to pick up a copy of the map, which highlights some notable examples of public design around Tallinn.

House of Blackheads ⑫
Mustpeade maja

Pikk 26. **Map** 1 C2. *Tel 631 3199.*
5, 40. 1, 2, 3, 4. only for chamber music concerts (call for timings). **www**.mustpeademaja.ee

This 15th-century Renaissance building was the meeting place of the Brotherhood of Blackheads, an association of unmarried merchants and shipowners, who were then able to join the more powerful Great Guild upon marriage. The unusual name was derived from the North African St Maurice, the organization's patron saint, whose image can be seen on the ornate front door of the building.

Unlike their counterparts in Rīga *(see p148),* the Tallinn Blackheads were obliged to defend the city in times of strife and proved themselves especially formidable adversaries during the Livonian Wars (1558–82). However, in general, it seems that the wealthy young Blackheads lived somewhat leisurely and hedonistic lives. The association survived until the Soviet invasion in 1940, and today,

the House of Blackheads regularly hosts chamber music concerts in its elegant main hall, which is noted for its wood-panelled interior.

Estonian Museum of Applied Art and Design ⑬
Eesti tarbekunsti ja disainimuuseum

Lai 17. **Map** 1 C2. *Tel 627 4600.*
3. 1, 2. 11am–6pm Wed–Sun. **www**.etdm.ee

Housed in a converted 17th-century granary, the Estonian Museum of Applied Art and Design features the best in Estonian design from the early 20th century to the present day. The vast selection of exhibits, which include jewellery, ceramics, glass, furniture and textiles, is a splendid example of the pride that Estonia takes in applied arts.

Many of the exhibits meld Scandinavian-style refinement with subtle Baltic irony to excellent effect. Some of the fantastic examples of furniture are especially eye-catching and a delight for art collectors. There are also some fine

Church of the Transfiguration of Our Lord ⑭
Issandamuutmise kirik

Suur-Kloostri 14–1. **Map** 1 C2.
Tel 646 4003. 3. 1, 2.
10am–noon Sun.
www.teelistekirikud.ekn.ee

Located close to a stretch of the medieval city wall, the secluded Church of the Transfiguration of Our Lord has an impressive Baroque-style spire and a richly decorated interior. The church originally belonged to St Michael's Convent of the Cistercian Order but was closed down during the Reformation. Briefly serving as a church for the Swedish garrison, it was handed over to the Orthodox Church in 1716 during the rule of Peter the Great, who donated the extraordinary iconostasis by Russian architect Ivan Zarudny. The church also has a bell dating from 1575, the oldest in Tallinn.

Baroque spire of the Church of the Transfiguration of Our Lord

View of Tallinn and the Baltic Sea from St Olav's Church

St Olav's Church ⓯
Oleviste kirik

Lai 50. **Map** 1 C1. **Tel** 641 2241. 🚌 3. 🚋 1, 2. ⭕ Apr–Oct: 10am–6pm daily. 🅿️ 🚻 www.oleviste.ee

St Olav's 124-m (407-ft) spire is a major Tallinn landmark and the church holds a proud place in local history. The legend goes that Tallinners wanted to build the tallest spire in the world to attract merchant ships and a complete stranger promised to help them. As payment he wanted the city people to guess his name. When the church was nearing completion, the city fathers sent a spy to his home and found out his name. They called out "Olev" when he was fixing the cross and he lost his balance and fell. In fact, the name of the church was in homage to King Olav II of Norway. The 159-m (522-ft) spire made the church the tallest building in the world until a lightning-strike burned it down in 1625. Amazingly, the church was struck by lightning six times and burned down twice between then and 1820.

The original 16th-century structure of the church was renovated extensively in the 19th century. St Olav's interior is not especially

striking, although the vaulted ceiling is impressive and the church tower has a viewing platform with breathtaking vistas of the city. The exterior rear wall features an elaborately carved 15th-century tombstone of Johann Ballivi, a victim of the plague.

Three Sisters ⓰
Kolm õde

Pikk 71. **Map** 2 D1. 🚌 3. 🚋 1, 2.

Situated at the northern end of Pikk Street, the Three Sisters are three adjoining medieval merchants' houses that have been tastefully converted into a single luxury hotel *(see p294)*. The houses were built in 1362 and were functional commercial premises, complete with loading hatches and winches to hoist sacks of goods up and down. The houses' original owners, who were mostly guild elders, town councillors and burgomasters, also used their premises to entertain foreign guests whom they met on their business trips abroad. The elegant gabled houses are among the best-preserved buildings from the 14th century and form a valuable addition to the magnificent surroundings of Pikk Street. The Three Sisters Hotel proudly counts Queen Elizabeth II and the singer Sting among the many luminaries who have stayed there.

Detail of stone carving on rear of St Olav's Church

Fat Margaret Tower ⓱
Paks Margareeta

Pikk 70. **Map** 2 D1. **Tel** 641 1408. 🚌 3. 🚋 1, 2. ⭕ 10am–6pm Wed–Sun. 🅿️ 🚻 call in advance. 🚻 www.meremuuseum.ee

The 16th-century tower's evocative name derives from the fact that it was the largest part of the city's fortifications, with walls measuring 4 m (13 ft) thick. It was originally built to defend the harbour as well as to impress visitors arriving by sea. Later, the tower was transformed into a prison and was the scene of an outbreak of violence during the 1917 Revolution, when the prison guards were murdered by a mob of workers, soldiers and sailors.

Fat Margaret Tower now serves the more peaceful function of housing the **Estonian Maritime Museum** (Eesti meremuuseum), with a curious collection of nautical paraphernalia spread out over four storeys. The exhibits include an insight into shipbuilding and historical accounts of Estonia's harbours. There is also a scale model of the *Estonia*, the car and passenger ferry that sank between Tallinn and Stockholm in 1994. There are gorgeous views of the Old Town and Tallinn's harbour and bay from the top of the tower.

🏛 **Estonian Maritime Museum**
Pikk 70. **Tel** 641 1408. ⭕ 10am–6pm Wed–Sun. 🅿️

Metal ship replica on the entrance wall, Estonian Maritime Museum

Street-by-Street: Toompea

Set on Toompea Hill, some 50 m (164 ft) above sea
level, Toompea lies southwest of the Old Town. It
dates back to the 13th century, when the Danes erected
a stone castle on the site. The hill has changed hands
many times over the centuries, but still remains
enclosed in the impressive limestone fortifications built
during the Livonian War (1558–82). The eclectic complex of Toompea Castle now houses the Riigikogu,
Estonia's Parliament, in Castle Square. The centre of
the square is dominated by the imposing Alexander
Nevsky Cathedral. Toompea Hill offers a spectacular
vantage point of the Old Town and makes an ideal
starting point for a tour of Tallinn.

**Pikk Hermann Tower, one of
Tallinn's main landmarks**

**Pikk Hermann
Tower**

★ **Toompea Castle**
*This hilltop castle compound
comprises several architectural
styles, from medieval stone towers to
a vibrant pink Baroque façade* ⑱

★ **Alexander Nevsky Cathedral**
*Tallinn's most grandiose Russian
Orthodox cathedral was
named after the war hero
who victoriously led
Russian soldiers into battle
at Lake Peipsi in 1242* ⑲

**Kiek-in-
de-Kök
Museum
entrance**

STAR SIGHTS
★ Toompea Castle
★ Alexander Nevsky Cathedral
★ Kiek-in-de-Kök

★ **Kiek-in-de-Kök**
*The superbly preserved medieval
cannon tower now houses a large
museum on Tallinn's history* ㉓

Cathedral of St Mary the Virgin
Originally built as a wooden church by the Danes in 1240, St Mary's is the oldest church in mainland Estonia. Most of its austere Gothic exterior, however, dates from the 14th century ⑳

Patkuli Viewing Platform
One of Toompea's secluded hideaways, this picturesque spot has great panoramic views of the Old Town's red roofs as well as of the harbour.

KEY

– – – Suggested route

KOHTU

PLATS

Kohtuotsa viewing platform, swarming with postcard sellers and tour groups, looks out over the Old Town.

Pikk Jalg Gate Tower
With a striking red roof, the tower at the end of cobbled Pikk jalg dates from the 14th century.

0 metre 100
0 yards 100

Knights' House
The Neo-Renaissance building was built in 1848 to serve as the headquarters of the Knighthood, the then local aristocracy. The well-preserved interior is a blend of various styles ⑩

The Neo-Byzantine Alexander Nevsky Cathedral

Toompea Castle ⑱
Toompea loss

Lossi plats 1a. **Map** 1 B3. **Tel** 631 6357. 🚏 3, 4. 🕐 10am–4pm Mon–Fri. 📞 call in advance. ♿ 💽 www.riigikogu.ee

The elegant and unassuming pink Classical façade of Toompea Castle belies the history behind this vital seat of power. The castle is now home to Riigikogu (Estonia's Parliament), but for some 700 years it belonged to various occupying foreign powers. In the 9th century, a wooden fortress stood on the site, which was conquered by the Danes in 1219, who then constructed the stone fortifications around the hill, much of which still survives.

The architecturally diverse castle complex features the 50-m (164-ft) Pikk Hermann Tower, above which flies the Estonian flag. The unique-looking Riigikogu, which was built in 1922, is situated in the castle courtyard. Toompea as a whole enjoyed its own rights and privileges until 1878, when it was officially merged with the rest of the town below.

Alexander Nevsky Cathedral ⑲
Aleksander Nevski katedraal

Lossi plats 10. **Map** 1 B3. **Tel** 644 3484. 🚏 3, 4. 🕐 8am–7pm daily. ♿ 💽 www.teelistekirikud.ekn.ee

The imposing Alexander Nevsky Cathedral was built between 1894 and 1900, under orders from Tsar Alexander III. As intended, the Neo-Byzantine edifice dominates Castle Square with its towering onion domes and golden crosses.

Legend has it that the cathedral was built on the grave of the Estonian folk hero Kalev. It is named after the sainted Russian duke Alexander Nevsky (1219–63), who defeated the Livonian Knights on the banks of Lake Peipsi in 1242. Disliked by many Estonians as a symbol of the Russification policies carried out by Alexander III, it was due to be demolished in 1924, but the controversial plan was never carried out.

The extravagant altar is made up of a dazzling display of icons, while the sheer scale of the cathedral's interior is equally impressive.

Cathedral of St Mary the Virgin ⑳
Toomkirik

Toomkooli 6. **Map** 1 B2. **Tel** 644 4140. 🚏 3, 4. 🕐 9am–4pm Tue–Sat, 11:30am–4pm Sun. www.eelk.ee/tallinna.toom

Popularly known as Dome Church, St Mary's is believed to be the oldest church in Estonia. It was built in 1240 by the Danes and underwent extensive rebuilding over the years. The somewhat plain Gothic exterior dates from the 14th century, while the beautiful interior boasts an elaborate Baroque pulpit and a widely admired organ built in 1878. Other significant features include 107 aristocratic coats of arms and the fine Renaissance tomb of the French-born mercenary, Pontus de la Gardie, who captured Narva for the Swedes from the Russians in 1581, during the Great Northern War (1558–82). In 1684, the

Intricately designed Baroque pulpit, Cathedral of St Mary the Virgin

For hotels and restaurants in this region see pp292–4 and pp322–5

church was badly damaged in a fire that swept Toompea and had to be substantially reconstructed. Today, the church remains at the very heart of Estonian Lutheranism.

Museum of Occupations ㉑
Okupatsioonide muuseum

Toompea 8. **Map** 1 B3. **Tel** 668 0250. 🚊 *3, 4.* 🕒 *11am–6pm Tue–Sun.* 📷 📷 *call in advance.* ♿ 🚻 🏠 www.okupatsioon.ee

Opened in 2003, this comprehensive museum provides a look at life in Estonia under both the Nazi and Soviet occupations. The fascinating exhibits include examples of bureaucratic paperwork, gut-wrenching accounts of mass deportation and execution, as well as poster-art propaganda, which was an essential weapon for the occupying forces.

The open-space museum remembers the countless victims of the occupations, and its symbolic location at the foot of Toompea adds a certain poignancy. It was partly founded by Kistler-Ritso, an Estonian World War II refugee to the United States. He donated 2 million dollars to the museum, the largest private donation in Estonian history.

Knights' House ㉒
Rüütelkonna hoone

Kiriku plats 1. **Map** 1 B2. 🚊 *3, 4.*

Built in 1848, the Knights' House originally served as a meeting place for the knight-hood, an influential segment of the Toompea gentry. It was home to the Foreign Ministry during the first independent republic, which lasted from 1920 to 1940. During Soviet times, the building housed the Estonian National Library.

More recently, it temporarily accommodated the main collection of the Art Museum of Estonia before it moved to its new permanent home in the Kumu Art Museum (*see p76*). The building, which

Exterior of the 19th-century Knights' House, now a venue for concerts

also occasionally hosted concerts till recently, is currently closed to the public.

Kiek-in-de-Kök ㉓

Komandandi 2. **Map** 1 B3. **Tel** 644 6686. 🚊 *3, 4.* 🕒 *10:30am–6pm Tue–Sun.* 📷 📷 *call 644 6553 for a guided group tour of secret tunnels under the bastion.* 🏠 www.linnamuuseum.ee

One of the most powerful cannon towers in Northern Europe in the 16th century, Kiek-in-de-Kök was built in 1475 as Toompea's main bas-tion. The tower stands 38 m (125 ft) tall and its walls are 4 m (13 ft) thick. The curious Low German name means "to peek into the kitchen", suggesting that soldiers had a good vantage point over the enemy. Some, however, believe that they literally peeked into people's kitchens. The tower fell into disuse in the mid-18th century and

Painted porcelain plate, Adamson-Eric Museum

now houses a five-floor museum devoted to Tallinn's history. The highlights include medieval artillery and a plague doctor's protective uniform.

Adamson-Eric Museum ㉔

Lühike jalg 3. **Map** 1 C3. **Tel** 644 5838. 🚊 *3, 4.* 🕒 *11am–6pm Wed–Sun.* 📷 📷 *call in advance.* 📷 *allowed only with-out the flash.* 🏠 www.ekm.ee

Located in a medieval house on a narrow stairway con-necting the Old Town with Toompea, the Adamson-Eric Museum is a branch of the Art Museum of Estonia. Adamson-Eric (1902–68) is one of the key figures of 20th-century Estonian art. His idiosyn-cratic and diverse body of work spanned several decades and influenced countless artists after him.

The Tartu-born artist was primarily a painter, but also worked with ceramics, metal forms, jewellery and leather, among other media. Although he held several prominent positions in various Soviet art committees during the latter part of his life, he was thrown out of the Communist Party in 1949 and forced into fac-tory work for four years. After suffering a stroke in 1955 and losing the use of his right hand, he taught himself to paint using his left hand. The collection on display was donated to the Art Museum of Estonia by the artist's widow.

Bitter Death, a cannon replica displayed in Kiek-in-de-Kök

Exploring Beyond the Old Town

There is much more to Tallinn than its tourist-packed Old Town. A little way east is Kadriorg Park, with its splendid palace, the Kumu Art Museum and the nearby Song Festival Grounds. Further east is Maarjamäe Palace, which houses the Estonian History Museum. Just off lies the fascinating Pirita Convent. A short distance west of the Old Town is the Estonian Open-Air Museum with some of Estonia's oldest rural architecture. The well-connected suburb of Nõmme to the south is also worth exploring. Most places are within easy reach of public transport.

SIGHTS AT A GLANCE

Historic Buildings
Pirita Convent ⑩
Rotermanni Quarter and
  Salt Storage Warehouse ③
Russalka Memorial ⑥
Soviet War Memorial ⑨
TV Tower ⑪

Theatres, Concert Halls and Museums
Energy Centre ④
Estonian Concert Hall ②
Estonian Drama Theatre ①
Estonian Open-Air Museum ⑮
Maarjamäe Palace ⑧
Song Festival Grounds ⑦

Parks and Gardens
Kadriorg Park pp74–7 ⑤
Tallinn Botanical Gardens ⑫

Islands and Suburbs
Aegna Island ⑯
Lasnamäe ⑬
Nõmme ⑭

KEY
✈ Airport
🚉 Railway station
⚓ Ferry port
▬ Motorway
▬ Main road
— Minor road

Estonian Drama Theatre ①
Eesti draamateater

Pärnu mnt 5. *Tel 680 5555.* 🚌 5, 36, 40. 🚊 3, 4. ◯ *Sep–Jul: 11am–7pm daily (box office).* 🖼 ♿ ⌀ ▢ www.draamateater.ee

This popular theatre occupies one of the most striking buildings on the fringes of the Old Town. Built in 1910 as a German-language theatre, it was purchased by the Estonian Drama Theatre in 1939.

The elegant Art Nouveau exterior combines rustic-style features in a manner unique to the Baltic States. Under Soviet occupation, the theatre's name was changed to the Tallinn Drama Theatre, in an effort to remove nationalist affinities associated with it. However, in 1989 it reverted to its original name.

The theatre is the largest in Estonia with a 40-member company and an average of 500 performances per season. The productions are usually in Estonian, with rare exceptions during theatre festivals.

Grand entrance of the Estonian Drama Theatre

Estonian Concert Hall ②
Kontserdisall

Estonia pst 4. *Tel 683 1260.* 🚌 5, 36, 40. 🚊 3, 4. ◯ *11am–7pm daily (box office).* 🖼 ♿ ⌀ ▢ www.opera.ee

The imperious bulk of the Estonian Concert Hall dominates the view along the stretch of Estonia Avenue, skirting the eastern edge of

Imposing façade of the Estonian Concert Hall

the Old Town. The sprawling building houses the Estonian National Opera (ENO) in one wing and the Estonian Philharmonic Orchestra (Rahvusooper Estonia) in another, while the Winter Garden is regularly used to host state functions.

The Concert Hall was completed in 1913, through public donations, and was intended to serve as an impressive showcase for Estonian culture that would overshadow similar German and Russian institutions in Tallinn. In recent years, the ENO has gained an outstanding international reputation and its cutting-edge productions can be seen for a fraction of the price visitors would pay in most European capitals.

Rotermanni Quarter and Salt Storage Warehouse ❸
Eesti arhitektuurimuuseum

Ahtri 2. **Tel** 625 7000. 🚌 all buses to Viru Bus Terminal. 🚊 1, 2, 3, 4.
Museum of Estonian Architecture
⬭ mid-May–Sep: noon–8pm Wed–Fri & 11am–6pm Sat–Sun, Oct–mid-May: 11am–6pm Wed–Sun.
🎨 📷 ♿ ⊘ 🛍 www.arhitektuurimuuseum.ee

The Rotermanni Quarter is situated east of Mere Avenue on the fringes of Tallinn's port

area and within comfortable walking distance of the Old Town. The district is named after Charles Abraham Rotermann, a 19th-century industrialist, and was a major industrial hub before most of its factories and warehouses fell into disuse and disrepair during the Soviet era. The area has been earmarked for a massive redevelopment project and looks set to become a fashionable new business and residential area.

Charles Abraham Rotermann

The impressive limestone building of the Salt Storage Warehouse, located nearby, is home to the **Museum of Estonian Architecture**. It was once used as the city's salt warehouse. Today, it houses a range of architecture-related exhibits, spread out over its vast three-floor interior.

Energy Centre ❹
Tehnika-ja teaduskeskus

Põhja pst 29. **Tel** 715 2650. 🚌 3.
🚊 1, 2. ⬭ 10am–5pm Mon–Sat.
🎨 📷 ⊘ www.energiakeskus.ee

Situated in a former power station, the Energy Centre is an enormous museum that forms part of the Tallinn Science and Technology Centre. It has numerous interactive exhibits which are used to demonstrate the rudiments of science.

The centre is charmingly old-fashioned and relies on the joy of learning through entertainment, rather than the slick presentation and hi-tech gadgetry used by most modern-day institutes. There is an especially enjoyable array of hands-on exhibits downstairs. The centre also hosts various other more serious science-related exhibitions and seminars.

Salt Storage Warehouse, home to the Museum of Estonian Architecture

Kadriorg Park 5

Kadriorg Park is one of Tallinn's most interesting features outside the Old Town. It centres on the magnificent 18th-century Baroque palace built as a summer residence for Peter the Great and boasts a wealth of small museums, historic monuments and art galleries. The park stretches for 1.5 km (1 mile) from its southwest corner to the northeast. It is a popular and picturesque place for a leisurely stroll. The elegant and affluent residential streets near the south entrance are also well worth a look and include museums dedicated to Eduard Vilde and Anton Hansen Tammsaare, two of Estonia's most prominent 20th-century literary figures.

Statue of Friedrich Reinhold Kreutzwald
This grand statue honours the writer of Kalevipoeg, considered the founding work of Estonian literature.

Swan Lake
The Swan Lake is one of the park's focal points, although its elegant island pavilion is mostly enjoyed by swans.

0 metres   200

0 yards   200

Anton Hansen Tammsaare Museum
The museum offers an insight into how the writer Tammsaare (1878–1940) lived and also exhibits his literary works.

Eduard Vilde Memorial Museum
This attractive summer house serves as a living memorial to one of Estonia's most revered writers. Vilde lived and worked here until his death in 1933.

STAR SIGHTS

★ Kadriorg Palace

★ Kumu Art Museum

For hotels and restaurants in this region see pp292–4 and p322–5

★ **Kadriorg Palace**
*Peter the Great's Baroque palace now houses
the Estonian Art Museum's foreign collection.
However, the museum's main exhibits are
displayed at the Kumu Art Museum.*

**Russalka
Memorial**
*This imposing
monument
(see p78) com-
memorates the
sinking of the
Russalka near
Finland in 1893.*

**President's
Palace**

**Peter the Great
House Museum**
*The great Russian Tsar
once used this cottage as a
temporary residence.*

Mikkel Museum
*The small museum
is renowned for its
porcelain vases and
beautiful figurines.*

★ **Kumu Art
Museum**
*Arguably the most
architecturally imp-
ressive museum in
the Baltic States, the
magnificently designed
Kumu houses the main
exhibits of the Estonian
Art Museum.*

Exploring Kadriorg Park

With forested paths, statues and ponds, Kadriorg Park is a charming place to explore. The area has a number of beautiful houses and manicured gardens and is also associated with art because of the number of museums, such as the Kumu Art Museum and Mikkel Museum, located here. Nearly all the park's main sights are on, or close to, Weizenbergi. Kadriorg Park is not very large and it is quite easy to cover its entire length on foot. A short distance from the Old Town, the park's quiet neighbourhood is, nevertheless, a pleasant 30-minute stroll away. Regular buses and trams connect Kadriorg Park with the Old Town.

The attractive garden of Kadriorg Palace

🏛 Kadriorg Palace

Weizenbergi 37. **Tel** 606 6400.
⬜ May–Sep: 10am–5pm Tue–Sun,
Oct–Apr: 10am–5pm Wed–Sun. 🖼
🗺 ♿ 🖥 🚻 www.ekm.ee
This palace was built in 1718 under orders from the Russian Tsar Peter the Great, who intended it to serve as a summer residence for the royal family. It was later named in honour of his wife Catherine. Kadriorg Palace was designed in the Northern Baroque style by the famous Italian master architect Nicolo Michetti. The Russian emperor intended for the three-winged palace was supposed to look like an Italian villa. No expense was spared in creating a magnificently lavish palace in the Italian Baroque style of which he was so fond.

After undergoing extensive renovation, the palace now houses the Estonian Art Museum's foreign collection.

Portrait of Thomas Chaloner by Van Dyck

Johannes Mikkel (1907–2006), whose collections are exhibited in the Mikkel Museum, donated some 600 works of foreign art to the Estonian Art Museum in 1994. The museum boasts a fine selection of European painting. However, the museum's main attraction is the astonishingly ornate Great Hall, which ranks among the finest examples of Baroque exuberance in Northern Europe. The well-manicured ornamental garden with fountains behind the palace is also open to the public.

🏛 Mikkel Museum

Weizenbergi 28. **Tel** 601 5844.
⬜ 10am–5pm Wed–Sun. 🖼 🖥
www.ekm.ee
Located in the former kitchen of Kadriorg Palace, the Mikkel Museum comprises the private collection of Johannes Mikkel. He began collecting art during the inter-war period and over the years amassed a valuable collection. It is today considered one of the best private collections in Estonia.

The exhibits range from the 16th to 20th centuries and include an impressive selection of porcelain vases and figurines. There are some fine examples of classical European art, such as *Portrait of Thomas Chaloner*, attributed to the Flemish painter Anthony Van Dyck.

🏛 Kumu Art Museum

Weizenbergi 34. **Tel** 602 6000. ⬜
May–Sep: 11am–6pm Tue–Sun, Oct–Apr: 11am–6pm Wed–Sun. 🖼 🖥
♿ 🚻 🖥 🚻 www.ekm.ee
Opened in 2006, the Kumu Art Museum is the Estonian Art Museum's first purpose-built building; it was designed to provide a fitting home for the museum's main collection. The structure is built into a limestone bank on the edge of Kadriorg Park and is a work of art in itself.

The museum's enormous and beautifully designed interior is a labyrinth of artistic discovery with one exhibition hall leading to another. The exhibits in the rooms are arranged in chronological order. Among the many delights on show, Konrad Mägi's brilliantly coloured canvases stand out as a wonderful example of early 20th-century Estonian art. Eduard von Gebhardt's *Sermon on the Mount* is another painting to relish for both its epic excellence and

Row of busts on display in a room at the Kumu Art Museum

subtle irony. The fourth floor is devoted to a permanent exhibition entitled "Difficult Choices", exploring the complex relationship between art and the Soviet state, while the fifth floor is given over to the best in contemporary art. However, the most striking exhibition of all is the room filled with hundreds of busts eerily staring into space.

EDUARD VILDE (1865–1933)

Author of Estonian classics such as *The War in Mahtra* and *The Milkman from Mäeküla*, Eduard Vilde is one of the most revered figures in Estonian literature and is generally credited as being the country's first professional writer.

Vilde spent a great deal of time travelling abroad and he lived for some time in Berlin in the 1890s, where he was influenced by materialism and socialism. His writings were also guided by the naturalism of the French writer Emile Zola (1840–1902). In addition to being a writer,

Eduard Vilde, writer and diplomat

Vilde was also an outspoken critic of Tsarist rule and of the German landowners. With the founding of the first Estonian republic in 1919, Vilde served as a diplomat in Berlin for several years. He spent the last years of his life editing and revising an enormous volume of his collected works.

Catherine I's bedroom, Peter the Great House Museum

🏛 Peter the Great House Museum

Mäekalda 2. **Tel** 644 6686. ⬤ May–Aug: 11am–5pm Tue–Sun, Sep–Apr: 11am–1:30pm Tue–Sun. 🖼
www.linnamuuseum.ee

This museum is housed in the 17th-century cottage which the Russian emperor used as a summer residence while Kadriorg Palace was being built. The cottage was purchased along with the surrounding land in 1713 and was enlarged with an additional wing so that it contained a hall, a kitchen and four rooms.

After Peter the Great died in 1725, his successors opted to stay in the more lavish Kadriorg Palace and the cottage fell into disrepair until Alexander I ordered it to be restored after a visit to Tallinn in 1804. The house contains few remains of Peter the Great's time, but it still affords an intriguing glimpse into the life of the enigmatic ruler. The bedroom has a four-poster bed and a pair of slippers which supposedly belonged to the Tsar himself. There is an exhibition in the basement about his life and achievements.

🏛 A H Tammsaare Memorial Museum

Koidula 12a. **Tel** 601 3232. ⬤ 10am–5pm Wed–Mon. 🖼 🎦
www.linnamuuseum.ee

Anton Hansen Tammsaare (1878–1940) is Estonia's most important literary figure. His five-volume epic, *Truth and Justice*, takes a sweeping look at Estonian society from the 1870s to the 1930s.

The museum is situated in the attractive wooden house in Kadriorg where the novelist and his wife lived from 1932 until his death in 1940. The building was converted into a museum in 1978. On the first floor is the couple's five-room flat, while a separate wing serves as a museum dedicated

Exterior of the modest A H Tammsaare Memorial Museum

to Tammsaare's life and work. The collection of almost 6,000 artifacts includes several photographs, letters and manuscripts and even the writer's death mask.

🏛 Eduard Vilde Memorial Museum

Roheline aas 3. **Tel** 601 3181. ⬤ 11am–4pm daily. 🖼 🎦
www.linnamuuseum.ee

The Eduard Vilde Memorial Museum is housed in a Neo-Baroque summer house beside Kadriorg Park which was presented to the writer as a 60th birthday gift by the Estonian government.

Vilde was one of Estonia's most prolific writers, and his works amount to a staggering 33 volumes. The museum showcases the six-room flat where Vilde lived with his wife from 1927 to 1933. The authentic furnishings are accompanied by period art pieces and provide a fascinating look at literary life in Tallinn in the 1920s. It is said that Vilde could often be seen enjoying long talks with his neighbour, the famous writer A H Tammsaare, in the nearby park.

The museum has been in existence since 1946 and is an interesting monument. The balusters of the wooden staircase, dating from the turn of the 19th century to the 20th century, have survived.

Russalka Memorial ❻

Near the junction of Pirita tee & Narva mnt. 🚍 *1a, 34, 38.* ♿

This imposing memorial was erected in honour of the 177 soldiers who drowned when the Russian ship *Russalka*, or "Mermaid", sank en route to Finland in 1893. Designed by the renowned Estonian sculptor Amandus Adamson (1855–1929), the monument was erected in 1902. It features a bronze angel standing on tiptoe, holding aloft an Orthodox cross. The pedestal on which the angel stands is made of roughly hewn blocks of granite evoking stormy sea conditions. The monument is one of several locations around Tallinn which young couples visit to be photographed on their wedding day.

Angel with an Orthodox cross, standing atop Russalka Memorial

Song Festival Grounds ❼
Lauluväljak

Narva mnt 95. **Tel** *611 2102.* 🚍 *1, 1a, 34, 38 (to Lauluväljak); 19, 29, 35, 44, 60, 63 (to Lasnamägi).* ◯ *Wed–Mon.* ♿ www.lauluvaljak.ee

The centrepiece of the Song Festival Grounds is the **Song Festival Bowl**, the large shell-like amphitheatre, built in the 1960s. During the four-yearly all-Estonia Song Festival, the stage holds up to 15,000 choral singers, with room for many

Aerial view of the impressive shell-like Song Festival Bowl

more on an extra platform. It has been a strong symbol for Estonians ever since thousands of people gathered here during the 1988 Song Festival in a show of unity against Soviet occupation.

In summer, the venue hosts rock and classical concerts, as well as the Beer Festival. The 42-m (138-ft) high Light Tower beside the Song Festival Bowl offers good views of the Old Town. On weekday evenings, the tower is used as a climbing post.

Maarjamäe Palace ❽

Pirita tee 56. **Tel** *601 4535.* 🚍 *5, 34, 38.* 🅿 📷 *call in advance.* www.eam.ee

An elegant Neo-Gothic summer house, Maarjamäe Palace was built in 1874 by the Russian Count Orlov-Davydov. The building has since served as a consulate, a hotel and restaurant, and a base for trainee pilots as well as the Soviet army. However, today, it houses another branch of the **Estonian History Museum** (*see p60*).

The museum, inaugurated in 1987, picks up where its counterpart in the Old Town leaves off in the mid-19th century to cover the political and social upheavals of the 20th century. The exhibits include historically dressed

mannequins and re-creations of domestic interiors. The 1940s and 50s are represented by army uniforms, photographs and weapons. There is an original hut used by the Forest Brothers (*see p118*), the legendary partisans who fought against the Soviet occupation, and a replica of a desk used by a Communist Party secretary.

Visitors can go to the back of the palace to see some of the gigantic Soviet-era bronze monuments lying in an unceremonious heap.

🏛 **Estonian History Museum**
◯ *Mar–Oct: 11am–6pm Wed–Sun, Nov–Feb: 11am–5pm. Research: 9am–5pm Mon–Fri.*

Maarjamäe Palace, housing a branch of the Estonian History Museum

Peter the Great (1672–1725)

Russia had long coveted Estonia as a much-needed outlet to Western Europe, but it was Peter the Great who finally achieved this. When the Treaty of Nystad ended the Great Northern War between Russia and Sweden in 1721, Estonia finally fell under Russian control. The Russian Tsar visited Tallinn 11 times during his reign and left an impressive legacy behind. From the magnificent Kadriorg Palace *(see p76)*,

The Tsar's bust in Kadriorg Park

which was built as a royal summer residence, to the reconstruction of the ports in Tallinn and Paldiski, Peter the Great's formidable influence is still visible. The Tsar so loved Estonia that he once remarked, "If Tallinn and Rogewiek [Paldiski] had been mine in 1702, I would not have established my residence and the capital of European Russia on the low-lying river Neva but here."

Peter the Great *is represented as a great statesman in this portrait by Hippolyte Delaroche, painted in 1838. The Tsar's political intelligence and military prowess turned Russia into a major European power.*

The epic battle of Narva *took place in 1700 between Russia and Sweden during the Great Northern War. It ended in a severe loss for Peter the Great. By 1721, Russia had defeated the Swedes to become the dominant regional power.*

The cottage in Kadriorg Park (see p77) *was used by Peter the Great and his wife Catherine I as a summer residence while Kadriorg Palace was being built. The cottage is now a museum.*

Portrait of Catherine I, painted by Jean-Marc Nattier in 1717

CATHERINE I (1684–1727)

Originally named Marta Skavronskaya, Catherine I was a Lithuanian peasant's daughter and is thought to have been born in present-day Estonia. A beautiful girl, Marta joined the household of Prince Aleksandr Menschikov, who introduced her to Peter the Great in 1703. They became lovers soon after that. In 1705, she converted to Orthodoxy, whereupon she changed her name to Catherine. The couple lived a modest life in a two-room log cabin during the construction of St Petersburg and were secretly married in 1707. In 1709, Catherine gave birth to Elizabeth, who later ruled Russia from 1741 to 1762. In 1724, Catherine was officially declared co-ruler of the Russian empire with her husband. Kadriorg *(see pp74–7)*, or Catherine's Valley, was named in her honour.

Soviet War Memorial ❾
Maarjamäe

Pirita tee. 🚌 5, 34, 38. ♿

The Soviet War Memorial is
a typical example of Soviet
war monuments in both its
grand scale and rather kitsch-
aesthetic appearance. The
35-m (115-ft) obelisk at the
centre of the complex was
erected in 1960 to commemorate the Russian sailors who
died in 1918, during World
War I. The surrounding features were built in the 1970s,
in memory of the Soviet
soldiers killed in 1941 under
the Nazi onslaught. In a dilapidated state today, the site
includes an eerie concrete
amphitheatre and large concrete and iron figures.

A German cemetery filled
with stone crosses lies just
behind the memorial site,
serving as yet another reminder of the fierce struggle for
control over the region.

Pirita Convent ❿
Pirita klooster

Kloostri 9. **Tel** 605 5044. 🚌 1, 8, 34,
38. ⭘ Apr–May, Sep–Oct: 10am–
6pm daily; Jun–Aug: 10am–7pm
daily. ♿ **www**.piritaklooster.ee

Founded in 1407 by the
St Bridget Order, Pirita
Convent was finally consecrated in 1436. It served as
the largest convent in then
Livonia (present-day Estonia
and northern Latvia), until it
was badly damaged in a siege
by Ivan the Terrible in 1577.
Over the following decades,
the convent was reduced to
a skeletal structure, as locals
plundered it for building
materials. In the 17th century,
a cemetery was established
in the compound.

Despite centuries of neglect
and oblivion, the impressive
ruins retain some splendour.
The most striking feature is
the perfectly intact 35-m (115-
ft) high gable and the walls of
the main hall. The site is run
by Bridgettine nuns, who live
in a state-of-the-art award-
winning building close by.
The nuns offer lodgings in

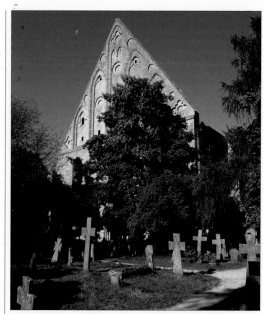

Pirita Convent screened by trees, with the cemetery in the foreground

their new home, continuing
a tradition that has existed
for hundreds of years.

TV Tower ⓫
Teletorn

Kloostrimetsa 58a. **Tel** 600 5511.
🚌 34, 38. ⭘ to the public. 🚻
www.teletorn.ee

Inaugurated in 1980, the TV
Tower, or Tallinn Tower, was
designed as an impressive
demonstration of superior
Soviet engineering. It was
the scene of a tense stand-off

TV Tower, a brilliant example of
Russian engineering

between Estonians and Soviet
troops in 1991, which was
resolved peacefully when
the Soviet troops withdrew.
An amazing spectacle, despite
its increasingly crumbling
condition, the tower stands
314 m (1,030 ft) tall.

Tallinn Botanical Gardens ⓬
Tallinna botaanikaaed

Kloostrimetsa tee 52, 10 km
(6 miles) NE of city centre. **Tel** 606
2666. 🚌 34a, 38. ⭘ May–Aug:
11am–6pm daily, Sep–Apr: 11am–
4pm daily. ♿ **www**.tba.ee

Located in a beautiful stretch
of woodland, the Tallinn
Botanical Gardens have an
exotic palm house as the
main attraction. Adjoining the
palm house are several greenhouses containing a superb
selection of rare orchids and
fascinating cacti. The outdoor
collections include a rose
garden, arboretum, limestone
rock garden and a permanent
display of "useful plants".

The grounds are set over
123 ha (304 acres) in a protected area of the Pirita River
Valley and have a designated
4-km (2-mile) nature trail

For hotels and restaurants in this region see pp292–4 and pp322–5

that goes through a lush range of habitats, from dry meadows to pine forests.

Lasnamäe ⑬

5 km (3 miles) NE of Tallinn.

A vast Soviet-era suburb founded on a limestone plateau in 1977, Lasnamäe houses almost a third of the city's population. The industrial part of the district is centred around Peterburi Street. Seemingly endless rows of housing blocks are lined up beside Laagna Street, which is a smaller road that passes through the so-called "Canyon", a road blasted through limestone.

The ambitious plans for the making of Lasnamäe were never finished and several aborted building projects that abruptly came to a halt when Estonia broke away from the Soviet Union, can still be seen. Although there is little of interest, the area as a whole is a strangely impressive sight and offers an intriguing glimpse of a side of the city that most visitors rarely see.

Nõmme ⑭

8 km (5 miles) S of Tallinn.
🚉 from Tallinn. 🚌 36.

The beautiful residential district of Nõmme was developed as a suburb after a railway station opened there in 1872. Soon afterwards wealthy Tallinners began building elegant summer villas with spacious gardens, and by 1926, the area had grown sufficiently to officially become a town. However, in 1940 the Soviets incorporated it into Tallinn.

Today, Nõmme is one of the most attractive areas of the city, with its own outdoor market, historic centre, cafés and restaurants, and some fine museums. The **Kristjan Raud Museum** is dedicated to the artist who illustrated the epic poem, *Kalevipoeg*, while the **Baron von Glehn Castle**, built by a Baltic-German landlord who largely founded

Baron von Glehn Castle in lush surroundings, Nõmme

the area, is an impressive sight. The castle is not open to the public. However, the surrounding park, with some particularly eye-catching statues, can be visited any time.

🏛 **Kristjan Raud Museum**
Raua 8. **Tel** 670 0023. ◯ 10am–5pm Thu–Sat. 📷 call in advance.

Estonian Open-Air Museum ⑮
Eesti vabaõhumuuseum

Vabaõhumuuseumi tee 12.
Tel 654 9100. 🚌 21, 21b. ◯ May–Sep: 10am–8pm daily, Oct–Apr: 10am–6pm daily. 📷 📷 call in advance. 🚻 📷 🖥 www.evm.ee

One of the few major sights outside the city centre, the Estonian Open-Air Museum is situated in the sprawling grounds of the former Rocco al Mare summer estate with a stunning backdrop of Kopli Bay. The museum is an enormous village made up of

historical rural buildings from all around the country. The exhibits range from the 18th to the 20th centuries and give a fascinating picture of how rural architecture developed in Estonia over the years. There are wooden windmills, thatched barns, a village inn and a 300-year-old wooden church alongside numerous farmsteads and outbuildings.

A variety of activities are offered, including nature trails as well as horse and carriage rides, while regular music and theatre productions are held here. Annual highlights include the Midsummer's Eve celebrations *(see p48)* and the Autumn Fair.

Aegna Island ⑯
Aegna saar

14 km (9 miles) NE of Tallinn.
🚢 from Pirita Harbour.

The tiny 3-sq km (1-sq mile) island of Aegna is situated in the northeastern part of Tallinn Bay. However, its pristine sandy beaches and unspoiled nature may be the target for future development.

What few traces can be found of human activity are nearly all military. There was a cannon battery here during Tsarist rule, and after being briefly used by the Estonian army during the country's first period of independence, Aegna became a closed Soviet military zone.

The island is now governed by Tallinn City Council and improved ferry links have led to a steady increase in visitors. It is a popular place to pitch a tent in summer.

Old wooden house by the sea, Estonian Open-Air Museum

WESTERN ESTONIA

*T*he region enjoys some of the country's most stunning natural landscapes and is also historically entwined with the Estonian national identity in countless ways. The erratic, time-worn coastline is punctuated with numerous places of cultural interest as well as some lively summer resorts, while the archipelago is remarkable for its unspoiled, timeless beauty.

Estonia's history has, to a large extent, been shaped by its west coast. Swedes settled in large numbers on the islands and around Haapsalu, as they were in the path of Nordic trading routes. Peter the Great seized Estonia and, in 1718, built a port and navy base at Paldiski because he wanted a "window into the West". In Soviet times, the coastline served as a heavily guarded border zone.

Western Estonia's main coastal town is Pärnu in the south, the country's "Summer Capital". Further north, Haapsalu was a stylish 19th-century resort and has remained every bit as attractive today. Soomaa National Park, which lies just inland, is an enchanting waterworld of bogs and rivers, while Matsalu National Park is one of the biggest nesting grounds for birds in Europe. On the northwest coast, Paldiski offers testimony to the Soviet occupation in the form of countless crumbling buildings that once served the enormous submarine base there, while the beautiful cliffs around the peninsula make it a wonderful place for hiking. The whole coastline is dotted with tiny, picturesque villages, while countless manor houses, medieval churches, iconic lighthouses and other places of interest are strewn throughout this region.

Of the Estonian islands, Saaremaa is both the largest and the most popular. The island of Vilsandi is the remotest of all of Estonia's national parks but, covered with interesting sights, it is one of the most rewarding to visit. The islands of Hiiumaa, Vormsi and Muhu are less developed, but their rugged beauty is a strong attraction for visitors seeking the serenity of a pristine and somewhat remote environment.

Traditionally attired dancers forming a circle at a celebration on Hiiumaa Island

◁ Awe-inspiring icefall and rock formation near Paldiski

Exploring Western Estonia

Western Estonia offers an irresistible blend of cultural heritage and wild natural beauty. Pärnu is a good base from which to explore the bogs and wetlands of Soomaa National Park to the east and the flourishing bird sanctuary of Matsalu National Park to the north. The popular spa resort of Haapsalu is within easy driving distance of Tallinn and visitors can explore the ruggedly beautiful coastal area around Paldiski on the way. The islands of Kihnu, Muhu, Saaremaa, Vormsi and Hiiumaa are well connected to the mainland by ferry and can be reached from Pärnu and Haapsalu.

Wooden trail through a bog in Soomaa National Park

Row of old buildings in cobblestoned Rüütli Street, Pärnu

SIGHTS AT A GLANCE

Towns and Cities
Haapsalu ❷
Lihula ❻
Paldiski ❶
Pärnu pp98–9 ❾

National Parks and Reserves
Matsalu National Park ❹
Soomaa National Park pp100–101 ❿

Islands
Hiiumaa Island ❺
Kihnu Island ⓫
Muhu Island ❼
Saaremaa Island pp92–5 ❽
Vormsi Island ❸

Sights of Interest
Tori Stud Farm ⓬

KEY

▬	Motorway
▬	Main road
▬	Secondary road
▬	Minor road
▬	Railway
▬	International border

Gulf of Rīg

For additional map symbols *see back flap*

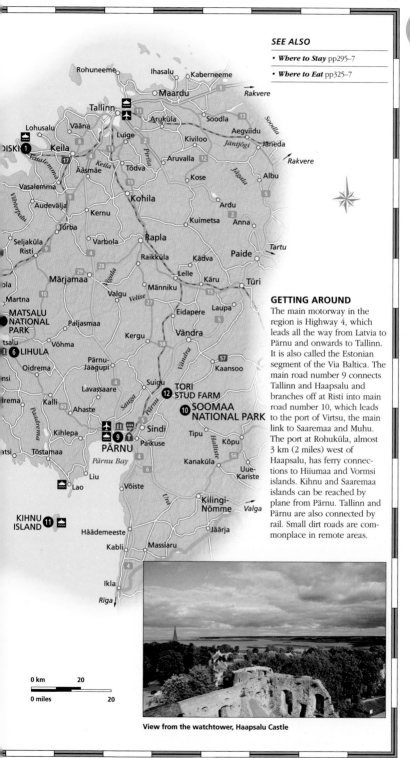

SEE ALSO

• *Where to Stay* pp295–7

• *Where to Eat* pp325–7

Rohuneeme Ihasalu Kaberneeme

Maardu

Tallinn

Lohusalu Vääna   Arukůla Soodla

DISKN Keila Luige Kiviloo Aegviidu

Vasalemma Tõdva

Ääsmäe Aruvalla Jäneda

Vasalemma Kose Albu

Audevälja Kernu Ardu

Türba Varbola Kuimetsa Anna

Seljaküla Rapla

Risti Raikküla Kädva Paide

Märjamaa Valgu Lelle Käru Türi

Martna Männiku

MATSALU Paljasmaa Eidapere Laupa

NATIONAL Kergu Vändra

PARK

Võhma Kaansoo

LIHULA Pärnu-

Oidrema Jäägupi

Lavassaare Suigu TORI

STUD FARM

Kalli Ahaste SOOMAA

NATIONAL PARK

Kihlepa Sindi Tipu Kõpu

PÄRNU Paikuse

Tõstamaa Kanaküla Uue-

Pärnu Bay Kariste

Liu Võiste

Lao Kilingi-

Nõmme Valga

KIHNU

ISLAND Häädemeeste

Kabli Massiaru

Ikla

Rīga

Rakvere

Soodla

Rakvere

Pirita

Keila

Jänijõgi

Jägala

Vääna

Tartu

Vigala

Velise

Vändra

Sauga

Pärnu

Halliste

Ura

GETTING AROUND

The main motorway in the
region is Highway 4, which
leads all the way from Latvia to
Pärnu and onwards to Tallinn.
It is also called the Estonian
segment of the Via Baltica. The
main road number 9 connects
Tallinn and Haapsalu and
branches off at Risti into main
road number 10, which leads
to the port of Virtsu, the main
link to Saaremaa and Muhu.
The port at Rohuküla, almost
3 km (2 miles) west of
Haapsalu, has ferry connections to Hiiumaa and Vormsi
islands. Kihnu and Saaremaa
islands can be reached by
plane from Pärnu. Tallinn and
Pärnu are also connected by
rail. Small dirt roads are commonplace in remote areas.

0 km 20

0 miles 20

View from the watchtower, Haapsalu Castle

Paldiski ❶

Road Map C1. 🚶 *4,000.* 🚆
🚌 *157, 241 from Tallinn.*
www.paldiski.ee

Deriving its name from the
Estonian pronunciation of
baltiyskiy, which means
"Baltic" in Russian, Paldiski
was established by Peter the
Great in 1718. Paldiski was
known to be of strategic importance for the Russian empire.
In 1962, when the Soviet Navy
nuclear submarine training
centre was set up here, the
area already had two nuclear
reactors and employed some
16,000 people. The Soviets
finally withdrew in 1994 and
the town quickly fell into
chronic disrepair. The Swedish
director Lukas Moodysson shot
his extraordinarily bleak film
Lilya-4-Ever (2002) in Paldiski,
though it was described as an
unnamed "former republic of
the Soviet Union".

Located 52 km (32 miles)
west of Tallinn, Paldiski is a
fascinating place to visit and
it attracts a steady stream of
tourists. The countless derelict
military buildings testify to
the prominent role Paldiski
once played in the Soviet
defence system. Today, however, the town is slowly, but
surely, being revitalized. The
port area is booming and
Paldiski's natural beauty
makes it an attractive site
for residential development.

Haapsalu's medieval castle, with an adjoining cathedral

Environs
Pakri, a stunning peninsula
3 km (2 miles) west of Paldiski,
boasts Estonia's tallest lighthouse. Also here are the ruins
of Peter the Great's ambitious
but unfinished fortress project.

The red-painted lighthouse at Pakri,
near Paldiski

Haapsalu ❷

Road Map C2. 🚶 *12,000.* 🚆 *from
Tallinn.* ⛴ *from Hiiumaa, Vormsi.*
ℹ️ *Posti 37, 473 3248.* 🎵 *Early
Music Festival (4–8 Jul), White Lady
Days (Aug).* **www**.haapsalu.ee

Situated on a small spit of
land jutting out into a narrow
bay, the popular resort town
of Haapsalu dates back to the
13th century. Its impressive
Bishop's Castle ruins still
serve as the main focal point
for the town despite the fact
that its formidable fortifications were largely dismantled
by Peter the Great in the 18th
century. The castle watchtower
houses the **Castle Museum**,
displaying medieval weaponry.
The adjoining **Dome Cathedral**
is the largest single-nave
church in the Baltic region.

Over the course of the 19th
century, Haapsalu became a
fashionable holiday resort,
famed for its curative mud
treatments and pretty beaches.
The town's landmark 216-m
(709-ft) long train platform is
an enduring monument to
the era when Russian royalty
and high society flocked to
the town every summer. The
platform was built in 1904 to
receive Tsar Nicholas II and
his entourage, and its ornate
wooden canopy was designed
to protect them from bad
weather. The station closed
in 1995 and the building now
houses the **Estonian Railway
Museum** with models of
engines used between the late
19th and early 20th centuries.

Paralepa Beach, just to
the west of the station, is
Haapsalu's most popular bathing spot. On the east coast,

ESTONIA'S SWEDISH COMMUNITY

Swedish settlers in Estonia were first mentioned in 1294 in
Haapsalu's town records. It is generally thought that Swedes
settled along the western coastal areas in the 13th and 14th
centuries to secure trade routes. From 1561 to 1700 Estonia
was directly under Swedish rule. By the early 20th century,
there were some 8,000 Swedish-speaking Estonians, most of
whom lived on Vormsi Island and in the Haapsalu region.

Swedish circular crosses in St
Olav's Church cemetery, Hullo

The Estonian-Swedes were a
recognized minority with
their own periodical and
distinct cultural identity.
However, the majority of
them fled to Sweden during
World War II. It is estimated
that some 2,000 Estonian-
Swedes remained behind,
but life in the Soviet Union
soon effaced their way of life
and they effectively dis-
appeared as a minority.

the promenade is another fine legacy of the town's imperial glory days. From Africa Beach the promenade winds its way past the spa hall at Kuursaal and leads to the **Museum of Coastal Swedes**, which traces the history of the Swedes.

🏛 **Museum of Coastal Swedes**
Sadama 31/32. **Tel** 473 7165.
⬜ May–mid-Sep: 10am–4pm
Tue–Sat, mid-Sep–Apr: 10am–6pm
Tue–Sat. 📷

Picturesque houses in one of the villages on Vormsi Island

Vormsi Island ❸

Road Map C1. 🏞 350. 🚌 from Haapsalu. ⛴ from Rohuküla, 10 km (6 miles) W of Haapsalu. **www**.vormsi.ee

Estonia's fourth-largest island, Vormsi is only 10 km (6 miles) by 20 km (12 miles) in size. The island is ruggedly beautiful and blissfully unspoiled despite being only 3 km (2 miles) from the mainland. The

---

TCHAIKOVSKY IN HAAPSALU

Tchaikovsky and his brothers Anatoly and Modest spent the summer of 1867 in Haapsalu. Living in a small house on Suur-Mere Street, the 27-year-old Tchaikovsky worked on *The Voyevoda*, his first opera and one of his major compositions. Tchaikovsky Bench on the promenade commemorates his stay and, at the press of a button, blares out a part of the Sixth Symphony, thought to be inspired by an Estonian folk song.

Tchaikovsky Bench on the promenade in Haapsalu

---

size of the island and its beautiful landscapes make it perfect for hiking and cycling. The island is well known for its lush pine forests and an abundance of juniper bushes, as well as spectacular stretches of rocky coastline.

Some people believe that Vormsi means "Snakes Island", as the name derives from the old Swedish word for snake. Others, however, claim that it was named after a pirate called Orm. Either way, Vormsi Island was home to some 2,000 Swedes prior to World War II, and their influence can be seen all over the island.

The island's main settlement is **Hullo**, 3 km (2 miles) west of the ferry port at Sviby. The 14th-century **St Olav's Church** is especially worth visiting for its Baroque pulpit and a cemetery with a striking collection of circular Swedish crosses looming out of handmade mounds of grass.

Matsalu National Park ❹

Matsalu rahvuspark

Road Map C2. 🏠 Matsalu Nature Centre, Penijõe Manor; 472 4236.
⬜ 8am–5pm Wed–Sun, 8am–3:45pm Fri. 🖥 **www**.matsalu.ee

Situated around the narrow Matsalu Bay, Matsalu National Park was founded in 1957 as a sanctuary for nesting and migratory birds. The area is a bird-watcher's paradise, with some 275 species found in its coastal wetlands. Six observation towers dotted along the coast offer the chance to see the fauna and birdlife up close. Viewing platforms overlook some of the islets and coastal meadows. Most of the observation towers are reached by car or bus, although Penijõe tower, on the bank of the Penijõe river, is a short walk from the Matsalu Nature Centre.

View of the Matsalu Bay islet, part of the idyllic Matsalu National Park

View of the pristine coastline of Hiiumaa Island

Hiiumaa Island ❺

Road Map C2. ✈ *Hiiesaare, 5 km (3 miles) E of Kärdla.* 🚌 *from Tallinn.* ⛴ *from Rohuküla, Triigi.* ℹ *Hiiu 1, Kärdla, 462 2232.* 🎭 *St John's Day (Jun).* **www**.hiiumaa.ee

Estonia's second-largest island, Hiiumaa is a paradise for nature-lovers due to its rugged and diverse landscape. Although it is only 22 km (14 miles) from the mainland, it is far less developed as a tourist destination than neighbouring Saaremaa *(see pp92–5)*. Over half the island is covered in forest that is home to an abundance of wildlife, such as elk, wild boar and lynx. The rest of the territory consists of meadows, peat bogs, heathland and endless miles of unspoiled coastline. Although there are plenty of interesting sights on the island, the majority of visitors come to Hiiumaa to enjoy its amazing natural beauty

and revitalizing atmosphere. The shallow waters off the northeast coast are very popular for canoeing and kayaking in the summer, and numerous hiking and cycling routes traverse the island. Public transport is limited and is best not relied on as the main means of getting around.

Kärdla

🏘 *4,000.* ℹ *Hiiu 1, 462 2232.* **www**.hiiumaa.ee **Hiiumaa Museum** Vabrikuväljak 8. ◯ *10am–5pm Mon–Fri, 11am–2pm Sat.* 🌐 This small town is of interest primarily as a base for exploring Hiiumaa. However, it is also a picturesque place, full of pretty wooden houses,

nearly all of which have well-tended gardens. A branch of the **Hiiumaa Museum** is housed in a one-storey wooden building, which was the home of a Swedish manager of a textiles factory in the 19th century. A seaside park lies just north of the museum and is filled with families and sunbathers throughout the summer.

The **Hill of Crosses** (Ristimägi), located 4 km (2 miles) west of Kärdla, is an impressive sight. The hill is packed with crosses made out of local wood. It is believed that the tradition of placing crosses at the site began with the deportation of Swedes in 1781 by the Russians. Today, most of the new crosses at the site are brought by tourists.

⚓ Suuremõisa Manor

Suuremõisa.
Although Estonians customarily refer to Suuremõisa (Big Manor) as a castle, it is actually a manor house. It was built in 1755 for Ebba Margaretha Stenbock, a relative of the powerful de la Gardie family, who owned much of Hiiumaa until the Russians acquired it in 1710. The widowed Stenbock lived in the manor with her children, after winning back the rights to her ancestral land.
In 1796, the manor was bought by a shipping magnate who was deported to Siberia in

Tahkuna • Lehtma

82

Malvaste
Reigi • ✈ Kärdla Paluküla

Kõrgessaare • Otste 81 80 • Hellamaa

Baltic Sea Lauka

Luidja • Heiste Nõmba

Kalana • HIIUMAA Heltermaa
Kaleste Kõpu Puski *Lake Tihu* Männamaa Suuremõisa

Mardihansu Bay 83

84 Käina
Taterma *Käina Bay* Kassari
Orjaku
Leisu Jausa *Sääre Tirp*
Valgu

83

KEY
═══ Major road
══ Minor road

Sõru Emmaste

0 km 10
0 miles 10

Key to Symbols *see back flap*

Sprawling Suuremõisa Manor, fronted by a verdant lawn

1803 for murdering one of his ships' captains in the house. There are 64 rooms in this grand manor that currently houses two schools. Although the interior is not open to the public, it is possible to take a stroll around the manor's vast grounds.

Kassari
90. from Kärdla. **Hiiumaa Museum** *10am–5pm Mon–Fri.*

A small island connected to Hiiumaa by a causeway, Kassari is known for its natural beauty. The 18th-century Kassari chapel-turned-church is the only functioning church with a reed roof in Estonia. Near the church is the village of Kassari itself, home to the **Hiiumaa Museum**, which gives an overview of Hiiumaa from the Stone Age through to the present. The island culminates in the stunning Sääre Tirp peninsula in the south, a 2-km (1-mile) spit that can be covered on foot or by car.

The Orjaku Nature Trail explores Käina Bay, a major bird sanctuary. The coastal water around Kassari is said to be the warmest in Estonia and the island has plenty of good beaches, especially in the south. With only four villages, Kassari retains its peace even in the height of summer.

Kõpu Lighthouse
Kõpu village, 35 km (22 miles) W of Kärdla. *May–mid-Sep: 10am–8pm daily.* **Tel** 469 3474.

Midway along the rocky Kõpu peninsula, this is the world's third-oldest working lighthouse. Built on the highest hill of Hiiumaa, it was commissioned by the Hanseatic League in 1500 and

completed in 1531. At the end of the 1980s, the crumbling edifice was reinforced with four thick sloping buttresses, giving it its highly distinctive appearance.

The equally distinct Ristna Lighthouse (1874) stands only 10 km (6 miles) further west, at the tip of the peninsula.

Kõpu Lighthouse, one of the world's oldest functioning lighthouses

Lihula ❻

Road Map C2. *1,600.* Tiigi 5, 477 8214. **www**.lihula.ee

The quiet town of Lihula leads to Matsalu National Park *(see p89)* and also serves as the last stopping-off point en

route to the islands of Muhu and Saaremaa. Lihula was the site of a major castle in the 13th century, which was almost destroyed during the Livonian Wars (1558–82). The impressive ruins stand atop a hill offering spectacular views of the region. Housed in an old manor house, the nearby **Lihula Museum** offers a comprehensive account of the town's history.

Lihula Museum
Linnuse tee 1. **Tel** 477 8880. *irregular hours; call for timings.*

Muhu Island ❼

Road Map C2. *from Tallinn, Pärnu. from Virtsu.* **www**.muhu.info

Most people generally pass through Muhu Island on their way to Saaremaa without spending much time here. However, Muhu is an extremely attractive island, whose small size makes it easy to explore. The village of Liiva, just 6 km (4 miles) from the ferry terminal, is home to the 13th-century St Catherine's Church, while the nearby coastal village of **Koguva** is a picturesque ensemble of stone farmhouses with thatched roofs.

Muhu Island has preserved its charming tradition of brightly painted farmhouse doors, some of which depict symbols that are said to keep evil spirits away.

The rugged natural beauty of the island also makes it a wonderful place for long walks, especially along the pristine coastline.

Stone farmhouses in the fishing village of Koguva, Muhu Island

Saaremaa Island ❽

Saaremaa is Estonia's largest island and the jewel of its archipelago. The capital, Kuressaare, is a strikingly picturesque town, whose relatively tranquil atmosphere makes it an ideal base from which to explore the island. The place has a lot to offer in terms of things to see and do, but its extraordinary natural beauty is the real attraction and the reason why so many people feel compelled to return here. The breathtaking landscape of Vilsandi National Park, the abundance of old churches and fascinating historical relics dotted throughout the island are just some of the main highlights *(see pp94–5)*.

Art Nouveau lion statues outside the information centre, Kuressaare

★ Vilsandi National Park
Known for its awe-inspiring landscapes, unspoilt islets and bird sanctuaries, this park was established in 1993 to preserve the ecology of Estonia's coast.

Kihelkonna Church, a splendid 13th-century place of worship, has an impressive steeple that was added in 1897.

Mihkli Farm Museum, an authentic 19th-century farmstead, offers a fascinating glimpse into rural life on the island in the past.

Sõrve Peninsula
The scenery along Sõrve Peninsula is some of the most spectacular on the island, culminating in the magnificently wild and windswept tip. The best way to explore the ravishing coastline is to take a bike or car trip.

STAR SIGHTS

★ Vilsandi National Park

★ Angla Windmills

★ Bishop's Castle

★ **Angla Windmills**
Standing along the main road from Kuressaare to Leisi, the five wooden windmills at Angla are an iconic symbol of Saaremaa Island and one of Estonia's most photographed sights.

VISITORS' CHECKLIST

Road Map C2. ✈ *Kuressaare.*
🚌 *from Tallinn, Tartu, Pärnu to Kuressaare.* ⛴ *from Virtsu to Kuivastu (Muhu Island), Hiiumaa Island to Triigi, Roomassaare to Ruhnu. Book ferry in advance.*
ℹ *Tallinna 2, Kuressaare, 453 3120.* ◯ *mid-May–mid-Sep: 9am–7pm daily, mid-Sep–mid-May: 9am–5pm daily.*
www.saaremaa.ee

Kaarma Church, which dates from the 13th century, has a striking 15th-century pulpit.

Poppy Fields
Due to its temperate climate and fertile soil, Saaremaa is rich in flora. Over 200 local species enjoy protection. Orchids and poppies grow wild in some parts.

★ **Bishop's Castle**
The formidable castle is the most important landmark in Kuressaare. It has Teutonic-order architecture with a powerful defence tower and a slender watchtower. The castle today houses an informative museum.

KEY

✈	Airport
⛴	Ferry port
ℹ	Visitor information
✝	Church
▬▬	Major road
═══	Minor road
- - -	Ferry route
▬ ▬	Park boundary

Exploring Saaremaa Island

The best way to explore Saaremaa Island is by car. The island's size makes it difficult to visit the major sights by bicycle, while public transport is extremely limited and erratic. Saaremaa has excellent, well-signposted roads on the whole, although bumpy dirt tracks are common in the more remote parts. The majority of visitors stay in Kuressaare but there is an abundance of excellent farmstead-style guest houses scattered throughout the island for a more authentic experience of rustic island life. All the major sights are within comfortable driving distance of the capital.

Buildings interspersed with greenery in the attractive town of Kuressaare

Kuressaare

🏯 16,000. ✈ 4 km (2 miles) SW of town centre. 🚌 Tallinna 2. 🎭 St John's Eve (23 Jun). **www**.kuressaare.ee

This small, but attractive and serene, town epitomizes the spirit of Saaremaa. Kuressaare's main thoroughfare, Lossi, which turns into Tallinna, is lined with a stunning stretch of beautiful buildings, including the green-domed St Nicholas's Church (Nikolai kirik) and the step-gabled Weigh House, which now serves as a pub known as Vaekoja. Most of all, though, the town makes a delightful place to stroll around, especially on a pleasant evening.

🏰 Bishop's Castle

Lossihoov 1, Kuressaare. **Tel** 455 6307. ⬤ May–Aug: 10am–7pm daily, Sep–Apr: 11am–7pm Wed–Sun. 📷 📹 call in advance. 🖥
www.kuressaare.ee

Dating back to the 14th century, the Bishop's Castle (Piiskopilinnus) in Kuressare is one of the best-preserved medieval castles in the Baltic States. Built out of local dolomite, it is a spectacular sight, as visitors approach it through the surrounding landscaped park. The castle houses the intriguing Saaremaa Regional Museum, whose labyrinthine interior is a joy to explore. The exhibits about Saaremaa are well arranged and offer a vivid account of the island's epic history.

Highlights of the castle include the Bishop's Living Quarters with a dingy, spartan little room where the resident bishop could retire for reflection, and a particularly eye-catching medieval lavatory.

Kaali Meteor Crater

Kaali. 🚌 from Kuressaare to Kõnnu, 15 km (9 miles) NE, then walk for 3 km (2 miles). 🛈 Kaali Visitors' Centre, 514 4889. 🍴 🏛
www.kaali.kylastuskeskus.ee

The meteor crater at Kaali is arguably one of the most extraordinary geological sights in Estonia. At a glance, it appears like a small lake, until visitors notice the perfectly rounded banks above the water and the shards of dolomite sticking out that were thrown up by the impact.

Scientists estimate that the meteor struck sometime between 4,000 and 7,500 years ago. With a diameter of 110 m (360 ft), it is the eighth-largest in the world. The crater exudes atmosphere, which inspires visitors to look upwards.

🏭 Angla Windmills

15 km (9 miles) N of Kaali. 🚌 from Kuressaare.

Lined up along the Upa–Leisi road, the five Angla Windmills (Angla tuulikud) are the last remaining group of windmills in Saaremaa. In the mid-19th century, there were 800 working windmills on the island.

Four of the Angla Windmills are constructed on the traditional Saaremaa model, while the largest is a wooden version of a Dutch windmill. Together, they form a mesmerizing sight amid the wide open landscape. Although the

Bishop's Living Quarters set in the lush grounds of the Bishop's Castle

Two of the five Angla Windmills, standing tall in an open landscape

windmills are not open to the public, there is a wonderful assortment of traditional play apparatus for children just behind them.

🔒 Karja Church
2 km (1 mile) NE of Angla Windmills, Karja village. ⬜ *mid-May–mid-Sep: 10am–6pm daily.* 🔆

The medieval Karja Church (Karja kirik) is the smallest church in Saaremaa, but also one of the most beautiful. It is well known for its elaborate stone carvings, which include a relief of the Crucifixion above the side door and some remarkable figures inside depicting saints. There is also a famous bas relief showing Mary and John at Cavalry, along with the two thieves whose souls depart their bodies in the form of children.

Stone carving outside Karja Church

🔒 Kaarma Church
15 km (9 miles) NW of Kuressaare, Kaarma village. **Tel** *459 5322.* ⬜ *Jun–Aug: 9am–5pm daily.* 🔆

Dating from the 13th century, Kaarma Church (Kaarma kirik) is one of the oldest churches in Western Estonia. A stone tablet over the front portal attests to repairs made to the church in 1407 and is considered to be the first written example of the Estonian language. The 15th-century pulpit with a polychrome figure of Joseph beneath it is especially impressive. The church may appear incongruously large, standing in the

middle of nowhere, but people once flocked here for Sunday services from the surrounding villages.

🏛 Mihkli Farm Museum
28 km (17 miles) NW of Kuressaare. Viki. **Tel** *454 6613.* ⬜ *mid-Apr–Sep: 10am–6pm daily.* 📷 www.muuseum.ee

In the sleepy village of Viki, the Mihkli Farm Museum (Mihkli talumuuseum) is a picturesque farmstead consisting of beautiful thatched cottages, a windmill, a brewery and even an old sauna. Most of the buildings date from the years between 1827 and 1856. The museum has one of the most authentic displays of rural architecture and traditional living styles. The farm was active until Soviet times, when collectivization broke it up. Today, visitors can learn traditional methods of making bread and butter.

🔒 Kihelkonna Church
3 km (2 miles) NW of Kihelkonna. **Tel** *454 6558.* ⬜ *Jun–Aug: 10am–5pm daily.* 🔆

On the west coast of the island along the border of Vilsandi National Park, this 13th-century church is a treasure trove of religious architecture and artifacts. The organ, built in 1805, is the oldest in the country, while the beautiful pulpit dates from 1604. The altar triptych, *The Last Supper*, is a superb example of Renaissance church art.

🦅 Vilsandi National Park
10 km (6 miles) W of Kihelkonna. ⛴ *from Papisaare.* **Tel** *454 6880.* 🛈 *Vilsandi National Park Visitors' Centre, Loona Manor.* ⬜ *9am–5pm Mon–Fri.* 📷 🖥 www.vilsandi.ee

This huge national park comprises Vilsandi Island along with some 150 islets and a narrow strip of coast culminating in the rugged Harilaid Peninsula. The park was established thanks to a lighthouse keeper named Artur Toom, who set up a bird sanctuary here in 1910. The 23,880-ha (59,010-acre) park in its present form was founded in 1993.

The most significant bird sanctuaries are located on the Vaika Islands, off the western tip of Vilsandi, from where the imposing 40-m (131-ft) Vilsandi Lighthouse can be seen. For some of the most striking scenery, head to the Harilaid Peninsula. From here, it is possible to take an invigorating hike up to the leaning lighthouse. The trail offers evocative scenery.

Display showing the interior of a rural household, Mihkli Farm Museum

Tallinn's medieval city wall covered with snow in winter ▷

Pärnu

Wooden door carving

Often referred to as Estonia's summer capital, Pärnu has historic buildings, pastel-coloured wooden houses and elegant late 19th-century villas set along leafy streets. The town centre is situated on an estuary between the Pärnu river and the Baltic Sea, with all the main sights located within walking distance. The Old Town is centred around the pedestrianized Rüütli Street, with the most popular beach a ten-minute walk away. With an ultra-modern concert hall and high-quality theatre, Pärnu also has an exciting cultural scene.

Town Hall
Uus 4/Nikolai 3.
The elegant Neo-Classical building that is now the Town Hall was erected in 1797 as a wealthy merchant's residence. In 1819, the structure was slightly altered to serve as the house for the town's governor and, in 1839, it took on its current function as Pärnu's Town Hall. What makes it worth visiting is the magnificent Art Nouveau extension built in 1911. Its brooding dark exterior is in total contrast to the bright yellow façade of the original structure and provides a fascinating juxtaposition of two radically different architectural styles.

Elizabeth's Church
Nikolai 22. **Tel** 443 1381. ◯ Jun–Aug: noon–6pm daily, Sep–May: 10am–4pm Mon–Fri.
www.eliisabet.ee
Another excellent example of local Baroque architecture, Elizabeth's Church (Eliisabeti kirik) has an elegant ochre exterior and maroon spire towering above the surrounding narrow side streets. It was founded specifically as a Lutheran church, in 1747, by the Russian Empress Elizabeth (1709–61). Today, it serves as the largest Protestant place of worship in Pärnu.

The wood-panelled interior is refined and understated, but all the more impressive for it. The church's spire was built by Johann Heinrich Wülbern, who also constructed Rīga's St Peter's Church. Elizabeth's Church is also renowned for its organ, one of the best in Estonia, built in 1929 by H Kolbe.

Green domes and yellow walls of St Catherine's Church

St Catherine's Church
Vee 16. **Tel** 444 3198. ◯ 9am–5pm daily.
Built in 1768 for the Pärnu garrison during the reign of Catherine the Great, St Catherine's Church (Ekateriina kirik) is arguably the finest example of a Baroque-style church in Estonia. With bottle-green domes and lemon-yellow walls, the church boasts an elegant exterior and an equally opulent interior. Intended as an architectural showpiece, St Catherine's had a significant influence on Orthodox churches throughout the Baltic States.

Pärnu Concert Hall
Aida 4. **Tel** 445 5800. ◯ 11am–8pm daily (box office).
www.concert.ee
Completed in 2002, the Pärnu Concert Hall is a source of great pride for local people. The curvaceous glass and steel building is a strong example of modern architecture in the country and compares favourably with similar structures in other European cities. Its seashell-like shape was intended to symbolize Pärnu's status as a coastal town. The multifunctional building mostly hosts theatre performances and concerts, although it also houses an art gallery, music school and music shop.

Tallinn Gate
Mere pst.
The only trace of the 17th-century ramparts that protected Pärnu at one time, Tallinn Gate still offers a significant glimpse of the once impressive fortifications. Until 1710, when Swedish rule came to an end, it was known as Gustav's Gate, named after King Gustav Adolphus of Sweden (1594–1632).

Today, the Tallinn Gate's only function is to provide an elegant portal between the Old Town and the area leading to the sea. The cobble-stoned passageway offers a relaxed walk.

Verdant setting of the Tallinn Gate, formerly known as Gustav's Gate

Detail featuring an Art Nouveau mask, Ammende Villa

Ammende Villa

Mere pst 7. **Tel** 447 3888.
noon–11pm daily (restaurant).
www.ammende.ee

Built in 1905 by a wealthy local merchant for the wedding party of his beloved daughter, Ammende Villa is one of the most impressive examples of Art Nouveau architecture in the country. Over the years, it has served as a casino, a health establishment and a library, before two Estonian businessmen renovated it and converted it into a luxury hotel (see p296). The villa is located a short walk from the sea and the Old Town.

Lydia Koidula Museum

J V Jannseni 37. **Tel** 443 3313.
10am–5pm Wed–Sun.
call in advance. www.pernau.ee

Situated a short walk across the Pärnu river, the Lydia Koidula Museum provides a moving testimony to Estonia's most revered female poet. The museum, which was established in 1945, is situated in the building where her father, Johann Valdemar Jannsen, ran a primary school from 1857 to 1863.

One of the main highlights of the museum is a reconstruction of the bedroom where Koidula died of cancer in 1886 in the Russian town of Kronstadt. Although very little of Lydia Koidula's work is available in English, the museum is worth visiting for an interesting insight into the history of Estonian literature at that time.

VISITORS' CHECKLIST

Road Map D2. 44,000.
Riia mnt 116. Pikk tänav. Rüütli 16, 447 3000.
Pärnu Film Festival (Jul), Oistrakh Festival (Jul).
www.parnu.ee

LYDIA KOIDULA (1843–86)

Lydia Emilia Florentine Jannsen is a highly influential figure in Estonian history. Although she was forced to write anonymously in her day under the pseudonym Koidula, meaning "of the dawn", her poetry was ecstatically received. Her *My Country is My Love* became the unofficial national anthem during Soviet times. Some critics believe that Koidula's finest writing was her passionate correspondence with the writer Friedrich Reinhold Kreutzwald, although his jealous wife eventually put an end to it. Koidula later married a Latvian doctor. She died of cancer in Kronstadt, in the Gulf of Finland, pining for her country to the last.

Lydia Koidula, Estonia's beloved writer and poet

PÄRNU

Ammende Villa ⑥
Elizabeth's Church ②
Pärnu Concert Hall ④
St Catherine's Church ③
Tallinn Gate ⑤
Town Hall ①

0 metres 200
0 yards 200

Key to Symbols see back flap

Soomaa National Park ⑩

Soomaa National Park, an enchanting self-enclosed world of bogs, rivers, swampland, meadows and virgin forest, was established in 1993. The 371-sq km (143-sq mile) park gets flooded in spring, which locals call the "fifth season". However, Soomaa's five bogs are its best natural feature. Approximately 6 m (20 ft) high in places, they can be accessed along a series of hiking trails set on wooden platforms. The park's stunning wildlife includes wolves, roe deer, brown bears, lynx, elk, wild boar and lesser spotted eagles.

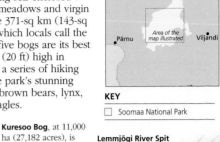

ESTONIA

Pärnu   *Area of the map illustrated*   Viljandi

KEY

☐ Soomaa National Park

Kuresoo Bog, at 11,000 ha (27,182 acres), is the largest bog. Birds come to nest here in spring.

Lemmjõgi River Spit Forest Trail is 5 km (3 mile) long.

★ Riisa Bog Trail
The 5-km (3-mile) long bog trail, close to the border of the park, culminates in a group of bog pools.

Navesti

Hälliste

Pärnu

Riisa

Raudna   Lemmjõgi

Tõramaa

Ingatsi Bog Trail
Half of the 4-km (2-mile) trail is a boardwalk that leads through swamp forest and bog pools.

Hälliste   Tõramaa

Meiekose Hiking Trail, a 5-km (3-mile) trail, is also suitable for cycling.

Karuskose Farm
Close to hiking trails and bog-land, this farm offers accommodation and fishing, canoeing and traditional canoe-building courses.

Viljandi

Kuuraniidu Study Trail has information boards describing the local flora.

STAR SIGHTS

★ Riisa Bog Trail

★ Tõramaa Wooded Meadow Trail

★ Tõramaa Wooded Meadow Trail
A 2-km (1-mile) walk leads to this pretty trail, which allows visitors to explore the park and its well-preserved meadow.

For hotels and restaurants in this region see pp295–7 and pp325–7

```
0 km           2
0 miles        2
```

**Hüpassaare Hiking
Trail** is 5 km
(3 miles) long, and
passes through forest
and bog pools before
culminating at the
Mart Saar House
Museum.

Flora
*The peat moss of the bogs
is ideal for heather, cranberries and Labrador
tea. The sundew plant
gets additional nutrition
by catching insects.*

Öördi Hiking Trail, a 7-km
(4-mile) forest trail, starts from
Iia village on the Kõpu-Jõesuu
road and leads to Lake Öördi.

KEY

ℹ️	Visitor information
🅰️	Campsite
🌿	Viewpoint
═══	Minor road
‒ ‒	Trail
▪▪	Park boundary

**Kihnu Jõnn's grave on Linaküla,
the main village on Kihnu Island**

Kihnu Island ⑪

Road Map C2. 🏘️ *600.* 🚶 *from
Pärnu.* ⛴️ *from Munalaid, 40 km (25
miles) SW of Pärnu.* **www**.kihnu.ee

The tiny island of Kihnu has
a significant place in Estonian
culture. It is the only part of
the country where women
still wear traditional dress
and the islanders continue
to live largely traditional life-
styles. Fishing remains a
major source of livelihood,
as do the much-admired
hand-made clothing and
mittens. There are four villages on the island, but as it
is only 7 km (4 miles) long
and 3.5 km (2 miles) wide,
it is easy to get around.
    In the main village of
Linaküla lies the grave of
the legendary Kihnu Jõnn
(1848–1913), the island's most
famous inhabitant. Born on
Kinhu, Jõnn was a larger-
than-life, hard-drinking sailor
who sailed around the globe.

Tori Stud Farm ⑫
Tori hobusekasvandus

Pärnu mnt 13, Tori. **Road Map** D2.
🚌 *from Pärnu.* **Tel** *522 6538.* 🕐
8am–5pm Mon–Fri. 📷 🎫 *call one
day in advance.* **www**.torihobune.ee

Situated in the beautiful
village of Tori, Tori Stud Farm
is a good stopping-off point
on the way to nearby Soomaa
National Park. Estonia's oldest
horse farm, it was established
in 1856 by the Livonian gentry with the aim of breeding
a strong local stock. After
several failed attempts at
improving the local breed,
a crossbred Norfolk-Roadster
horse was brought in, which
became the basis for the
new breed. The stud farm is
still used for breeding purposes today, although its
horses are far more likely
to be used for giving horse-
riding lessons than for
ploughing the fields.
    Tori Stud Farm is also a
worthwhile excursion in
itself. Visitors to the farm
can partake in a range of
activities, including a guided
tour of the farm which
introduces them to some of
the 90-odd horses. Those
interested in old-fashioned
transport can take a tour of
the farm and village in a
horse-driven carriage for a
small fee charged on an
hourly basis. It is possible to
go sleigh-riding in winter.
    The farm also boasts a
wonderful little museum situated in a thatched wooden
barn. Its collection features a
fascinating assortment of exhibits relating to the history of
horse-breeding as well as the
history of the local village.

Tori Stud Farm, breeder of some of Estonia's finest horses

EASTERN ESTONIA

T*he landscape of Eastern Estonia, punctuated with rolling hills, lush forests, limestone escarpments and pristine lakes, is more diverse than the country's western part. This truly fascinating region combines idyllic scenery with picturesque old manor houses and the unique cultural heritage of the Setu people and Old Believers, which have survived through the centuries.*

Despite being geographically stunning, some parts of Eastern Estonia are less frequented by tourists, especially the far northeast, southeast and around Lake Peipsi. The vast mass of Lake Peipsi dominates the central part of this region. The western shores of the lake are dotted with the sizeable settlements of Russian Old Believers who have been living here for countless generations.

Captured and conquered repeatedly by Russians since 1558, the historic fortress town of Narva still bears testimony to the enormous role Russia has played in shaping Estonia's history. During World War II, the value of oil-shale mining rose significantly, bringing Kohtla-Järve into sharp focus. Today, this heavily industrial town serves as a vast, sprawling, living monument to Soviet-era industry.

East of Tallinn, Lahemaa National Park is arguably the most beautiful of the country's nature reserves for the variety of its landscape and natural features. Further along, the Ontika coastline, with its huge limestone escarpments and cascading waterfalls, is breathtaking.

Social, cultural and political history abounds in the southeast as a whole. Viljandi hosted the country's very first Song Festival, while Estonia's national flag was sanctified in Otepää. Tartu, Estonia's second-largest city and its spiritual capital, is at the heart of the country's history and culture.

With attractions such as the grand Sangaste Manor and the captivating Suur Munamägi viewing tower at the country's highest point, the south and southeast are among Estonia's most scenic areas. In the far southeast, the ethnographically distinct Setu people continue to live traditionally.

Migrating flock of gulls flying across Lake Peipsi

◁ **Stretch of the Jägala river on its course through the lush landscape of Lahemaa National Park**

Exploring Eastern Estonia

Eastern Estonia has strikingly diverse
attractions. Lahemaa National Park boasts
some of the country's most beautiful
landscapes, with countless villages dotted
throughout the area. A stunning coastline
stretches to the medieval city of Narva and
the pristine beach at Narva-Jõesuu. To the
south is Lake Peipsi. The picturesque landscape
of the southeast provides a beautiful backdrop
to attractive towns such as Viljandi and Otepää,
as well as to countless places of historic
significance. Tartu makes an ideal base from
which to explore the region.

SIGHTS AT A GLANCE

Towns, Cities and Resorts
Kuremäe **7**
Narva **5**
Narva-Jõesuu **6**
Otepää **16**
Paide **11**
Põltsamaa **12**
Põlva **23**
Rakvere **8**
Rõuge **19**
Sillamäe **4**
Tartu pp114–17 **13**
Väike-Maarja **9**
Vastseliina **21**
Viljandi **15**
Võru **22**

**Buildings and
Sites of Interest**
Kohtla Underground
  Mining Museum **2**
Kiidjärve Watermill **24**
Mõniste Open-Air Museum **18**
Sangaste Manor **17**

**National Parks
and Reserves**
Endla Nature Reserve **10**
*Lahemaa National
  Park pp106–109* **1**

Areas of Natural Beauty
Lake Võrtsjärv **14**
Ontika Coast **3**
Suur Munamägi **20**
Taevaskoja Sandstone Cliffs **25**

Tour
Lake Peipsi p123 **26**

Medieval Ivangorod Castle, seen from Narva

Gulf of Finland

Mahu

ONTIKA **3**
COAST Kohtla- Toila
Kiviõli Järve **2** Jõhvi
Anguse Tarumaa
Tudu
Roela Peressaare
Tudulinna
Ilavere Mägi
5 m (509 ft)
rukse Kauske
Avinurme Lohusuu

KOHTLA
UNDERGROUND
MINING MUSEUM

Metsa
järve

SILLAMÄE
4

NARVA- **6**
JÕESUU

5
NARVA

Sirgala *Narva*
veehoidla

7 KUREMÄE
Kuningaküla
Jaama
Isaku
Vasknarva

Sadala Mustvee
küla Torma Raja
Kallavere
geva Omedu
Ranna
Kaarepere
mani Tabivere
Laeva
Kärevere
Rekusaare Reola

Kallavere

26 LAKE
PEIPSI

Kallaste
Alatskivi
Kolkja
Koosa Kasepää
Vara Varnja
Kevastu Meerapalu

13 TARTU

Võnnu
Ahja Rasina Naha

Kambja KIIDJÄRVE
Elva WATERMILL
Vastse- **24**
Kuuste
Maaritsa **25** TAEVASKOJA
Rõngu SANDSTONE CLIFFS **45**
Saverna PÕLVA **23** Mikitamäe
Vana- Viluste
autse Mägi Kojala
7 m (712 ft) OTEPÄÄ **16** Väimela Värska
Pühajärv **64** Vaartsi
Keeni Kärgula Lasva *Piusa*
17 SANGASTE Sõmerpalu **22** VÕRU Obinitsa
MANOR Antsla Meremäe
Laatre Haanja **2** **21** VASTSELIINA
ja **18** RÕUGE **19** **20**
MÕNISTE OPEN- SUUR MUNAMÄGI
AIR MUSEUM
Koikküla
Taheva Krabi

SEE ALSO

• *Where to Stay* pp297–9

• *Where to Eat* pp327–9

GETTING AROUND

Highway 1 leads east out of Tallinn and skirts Lahemaa National Park before following the coast to Narva. Highway 2 connects Tartu and Võru and Highway 3 links Tartu and Valga, skirting the northern part of Lake Peipsi along the way. The town of Rakvere also has a road leading to Tartu. A railway connects Tallinn with Rakvere, Narva, Tartu and Viljandi. Tartu also has a small airport. In the southeast an intricate network of signposted dirt roads connects most of the villages in the area.

Fishing village in Lahemaa National Park

0 km   20

0 miles   20

KEY

═══ Motorway

═══ Main road

─── Secondary road

═══ Minor road

─── Scenic route

─── Railway

▓▓▓ International border

△ Peak

Lahemaa National Park ❶

Extending across the north coast of Estonia, Lahemaa
National Park is a nature-lover's paradise. It is the
largest park in Estonia and also the first area to be
designated a national park in the erstwhile Soviet
Union. The diverse terrain covers four peninsulas jutting
out into the Gulf of Finland and stretches inland over an
area of 725 sq km (280 sq miles). The park teems with
wildlife and has several marked trails through its forests
and bogs and along its meandering coastline. Many
impressive manor houses and picturesque villages can
be found throughout the area *(see pp108–109)*.

KEY

☐ Lahemaa National Park

Viinistu
*Once a fishing village, Viinistu has
developed into a local cultural centre.
It is home to an impressive art gallery.*

★ Käsmu Peninsula
*The rugged coastline of Käsmu Peninsula, strewn
with giant boulders left behind by retreating glaciers
after the last Ice Age, has an ethereal beauty.*

Flora and Fauna
*With forest covering
more than 70 per cent of
Lahemaa, the area is rich
in flora and fauna. The
landscape has many
raised bogs, including
the 7,000-year-old
Laukasoo Reserve. The
thriving wildlife includes
a population of wolves,
bear and lynx.*

Pärispea

Viinistu

Suurpea

*Pärispea
Peninsula*

GULF OF
FINLAND

Hara
Bay

Kasispea

Eru Bay

Loksa

Vihasoo

*Lake
Lohja*

Kotka

Lobu

Ilum

Käs
Reni

Valgejõgi

Joaveski

0 km   2

0 miles   2

STAR SIGHTS

★ Käsmu Peninsula

★ Altja Village

★ Palmse Manor House

For hotels and restaurants in this region see pp297–9 and pp327–9

Võsu
A beautiful stretch of beach, tranquil atmosphere and stunning natural surroundings make this historic village a very popular holiday resort.

VISITORS' CHECKLIST

Road Map D1. 🚌 from Tallinn to Võsu, Altja, Käsmu, Viinistu. 🛈 National Park Visitors' Centre, Palmse, 329 5555. ⬭ May–Aug: 9am–7pm Mon–Fri, Sep: 9am–5pm Mon–Fri, Oct–Apr: 9am–5pm Mon–Fri. 🍴 ⬛ 🅿 🛖 🅰 available at Võsu (May–Sep). www.lahemaa.ee

The Oandu Forest Trail is a well-signposted, 5-km (3-mile) long route. Foraging wildlife can be seen along the mostly moss-covered path.

★ Altja Village
With its ornately thatched roofs and timber houses, the fishing village of Altja provides an authentic glimpse of a bygone era, when its survival depended on the sea.

Sagadi Manor
The grounds of Sagadi Manor, one of the most attractive in the region, are covered with sculptures, while its numerous outhouses include the Forestry Museum.

★ Palmse Manor House
The stately Baroque house has now been restored as a museum, while its converted outhouses and extensive grounds offer several other attractions.

KEY

🚌 Bus station

🛈 Visitor information

🅰 Campsite

═══ Minor road

– – Trail

– ▪ Park boundary

Exploring Lahemaa National Park

The sheer size of Lahemaa National Park makes getting around it by bike or car the best option. When driving to Lahemaa along the Tallinn-Narva Highway, turn off at the crossroads at Viitna and head north towards Palmse village, where there is a National Park Visitors' Centre. From Palmse, it is a relatively short drive to all the main villages, sites and areas of natural beauty. Käsmu and Võsu make convenient hiking and cycling bases with plenty of good accommodation, although most places are often booked up well in advance during summer.

Regal interior of the ornately decorated Palmse Manor House

🏛 Palmse Manor House
8 km (5 miles) N of Viitna. *Tel 324 0070.* ⬜ *May–Sep: 10am–7pm daily, Oct–Apr: 10am–3pm Mon–Fri.* 🅿 ✔ *call in advance.* ♿ 🍴 ⬜ www.muuseum.ee

The attractive village of Palmse is the ideal starting point for a tour of the enchanting Lahemaa National Park. It also has a well-run visitors' centre. The focus of the village is the splendid Palmse Manor House, an elegant Baroque building that originally served as a Cistercian convent. In 1677, it became the family home of the von Pahlens, a leading family of Baltic barons.

Today, the manor house serves as a museum, offering an interesting overview of the estate's history. The old distillery has been converted into a hotel with an excellent restaurant, while a lovely café now occupies the bathhouse.

The manor house organizes a wine tour, where visitors can enjoy a glass of sparkling wine or locally produced wine made from berries grown in the nearby Brest Pavilion. The manor grounds are beautifully landscaped. In summer, visitors can take a boat tour of the serene Swan Lake and soak up the surrounding tranquility.

🏖 Võsu
8 km (5 miles) N of Palmse. 🚌 *from Tallinn.* ⬜ *May–Sep: 10am–7pm daily, Oct–Apr: 10am–5pm Mon–Fri.* 🍴 ⬜ www.lahemaa.ee

A charming and quiet little coastal village, Võsu is a popular holiday resort. Its peaceful ambience and stunning natural beauty have made it a favourite summer getaway for families since the

Tourists enjoying themselves at the pine-fringed beach in Võsu

late 19th century. The resort is 2 km (1 mile) long and packed with elegant wooden houses from end to end.

The most distinctive building in the village is the old Fire Tower, which now houses an art gallery. Its beach, with Blue Flag status, is also one of the most attractive along the north coast. With its soft white sand and pine-fringed dunes, it offers gentle shade during the hot summer days. It is also a convenient base for further explorations of Oandu and Altja.

🏖 Käsmu
16 km (10 miles) N of Palmse.) 🍴
⬜ **Käsmu Maritime Museum**
⬜ *May–Sep: 10am–7pm daily, Oct–Apr: 10am–5pm Mon–Fri.*

Approximately 6 km (4 mile) long and 3 km (2 mile) wide, Käsmu village is situated on the smallest of the four peninsulas in Lahemaa National Park. It is often referred to as the prettiest village in the region due to its distinguished history and proudly kept homesteads.

Käsmu was a shipbuilding centre of repute in the 19th century, while the largely ice-free bay made it a regular place of anchor in winter. A maritime school was set up in the village in 1884 which now houses the **Käsmu Maritime Museum**. The museum's emphasis is on the 1920s and 30s through World War II and the Soviet era. It has an eclectic collection of artifacts honouring the village's seafaring past.

The village is also called the Captain's Village, because of the 62 captains that resided in Käsmu between World War I and World War II. Käsmu was decimated by the Soviets in the 1940s, with many families sent to Siberia and others fleeing across the sea.

Today, the village enjoys the reputation for being one of the best holiday resorts in the park. Käsmu also boasts a fascinating coastline strewn with giant boulders, a large and erratic scattering of which lie in a stone field near the village. This is the highlight of the famous Käsmu Boulder Walk *(see p110)*.

🎣 Altja

15 km (9 miles) E of Võsu. ☐ May–
Sep: 10am–7pm daily, Oct–Apr:
10am–5pm Mon–Fri. 🍴 **Oandu**
10 km (6 miles) S of Võsu.
🏕 free National Park campsite.
www.altja.ee

Situated to the east of Lahemaa
National Park, Altja is a lovely
fishing village that skirts the
rugged coastline of the park.
Its main landmark is a large
wooden swing that stands in
an open space, at the eastern
end of the village. Just
beyond, along the
beach, are the aban-
doned huts of fisher-
men. The timber
houses with
thatched roofs
make the village
seem like an open-
air museum. There
is a picturesque
wooden suspension
bridge in the same corner.

**Water barrel, Viinistu
Art Museum**

Beyond Altja, in nearby
Oandu, there are two fantastic
nature trails where visitors
can get a taste of Lahemaa
National Park's varied forest
landscape. The 2-km (1-mile)
long Oandu Beaver Trail
passes by several beaver
dams and countless skilfully
gnawed tree stumps. The
5-km (3-mile) long circular
Oandu Forest Nature Trail,
on the other hand, passes
through sweet-smelling and
lush pine forest. Visitors are
likely to spot tracks left by
foraging wild boar, elk and
brown bears.

Viinistu

9 km (6 miles) W of Käsmu. ☐ Jan–
Aug: 11am–6pm daily, Sep–May:
11am–6pm Wed–Sun. 🍴 💻
Viinistu Art Museum ☐ 11am–
6pm daily. 💳 **www**.lahemaa.ee

Lying on the eastern tip of the
Pärispea Peninsula, the village
of Viinistu is an intriguing
little place. It profited
from the smuggling
of vodka to Finland
during prohibition
in the 1920s, but
during the Soviet
era it was incor-
porated into the
nearby Loksa ind-
ustrial complex.
Today, it has been
reinvented due to
the efforts of Jaan Manitsky
(b.1943), a wealthy local
businessman who opened
a hotel and the **Viinistu Art
Museum** by the harbour.
Inaugurated in 2003, the
museum has an impressive
collection of 20th-century
Estonian art and uses two
converted water-towers for
temporary exhibitions.

The harbour has been
restored and it is possible to
travel northeast from Viinistu
to the barren Mohni Island.

**View of the beautiful Sagadi
Manor, Lahemaa National Park**

🏛 Sagadi Manor

8 km (5 miles) NE of Palmse. **Tel** 676
7888. ☐ May–Sep: 10am–6pm daily,
Oct–Apr by prior arrangement. 💳
📷 call in advance. 🚻 💻
www.sagadi.ee

Built in 1749, the Sagadi
Manor (Sagadi mõis) consists
of several buildings sym-
metrically laid out around a
sprawling courtyard in front,
with a manicured park and
pond to the rear. The attractive 18th-century Baroque
manor house is now home to
a museum which offers an
authentic glimpse of the lives
of the Baltic-German aristocratic family who lived in
the region in the mid-18th
century. The manor house
later served as a primary
school and part of a collective
farm until it finally opened
as a museum in 1987.

The Baroque gatehouse,
which used to be the main
entrance to the manor house,
is particularly grand. There
are also some truly fascinating
sculptures scattered around
the grounds.

Today, the outhouses on
one side of the courtyard are
occupied by the Forestry
Museum (Metsamuuseum),
which provides a detailed
overview of the diverse flora
and fauna of Estonia's forests.
Housed in the building
nearby is a hotel called Sagadi
Manor (see p298). A former
bailiff's residence now serves
as the Sagadi hostel. The
historic estate is also home to
a Nature School where ecolo-
gical research is carried out.

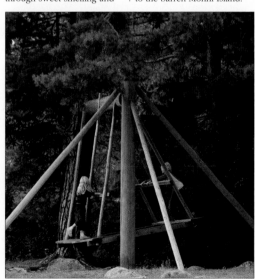

Landmark wooden swing at the quaint fishing village of Altja

Käsmu Boulder Walk

The smallest of the four peninsulas in Lahemaa, Käsmu boasts the most impressive chain of boulders. These form a formidable outcrop in the shallow waters, creating a dramatic coastline. Old Jüri, the tallest boulder at 5.5 m (18 ft), lies just off the northwest tip. Starting from Käsmu village, a path leads along the coast to the northwest tip of the peninsula before turning back towards the village through dense forest. There are clearly marked hiking trails and a cycling route.

Cosy wooden cottage snuggled in the heart of Käsmu village

Scenic Views ③
One of the most stunning routes in the park, this path follows the whole length of the coast.

Saartneem Island
GULF OF FINLAND
Eru Bay
Käsmu Bay
KÄSMU PENINSULA
LAKE KÄSMU
Võsu

Saartneem ②
A path leads from Käsmu village to the northwest tip of the peninsula, where a chain of erratic boulders stretches out to the island of Saartneem.

Cycle Route ④
The scenic bicycle route is about 14 km (9 miles) long and is marked with blue ribbons.

Käsmu Village ①
Käsmu village is one of the most popular resorts in Lahemaa. With plenty of B&B accommodation, it is an ideal base for exploring the Käsmu Peninsula as a whole, as well as the other regions of Lahemaa.

KEY

🚌	Bus station
ℹ️	Visitor information
🅰️	Campsite
– –	Walk route
▬▬	Bicycle route
══	Other road

TIPS FOR WALKERS

Starting point: Käsmu village.
Length: 11 km (7 miles).
Walking trails: An 11-km (7-mile) long path marked with red ribbons leads north of Käsmu village from Old Jüri. A shorter walk is the path west of Käsmu village which leads through the Stone Plantation.

Erratic Boulders ⑤
The Stone Plantation on the trail west of Käsmu village has a bizarre expanse of boulders. These attract a large number of visitors to the area.

0 km   1
0 miles   1

Kohtla Underground Mining Museum ❷

Kohtla kaevanduspark-muuseum

Road Map E1. **Tel** 332 4017. 🚌 from Kohtla-Järve. ⏰ 10am–5pm Mon–Fri, 11am–3pm Sat & Sun. 📷 book in advance. ⏳ summer only. **www**.kaevanduspark.ee

Undoubtedly one of the most fascinating museums in Estonia, Kohtla Underground Mining Museum is located in the sprawling industrial area of Kohtla-Nõmme. Set in a massive oil-shale mining complex, the museum operates guided tours where the history, technology and purpose of mining are explained before visitors are taken to explore the dark, damp labyrinth of the mines.

Visitors can see the infernal mining machines at work and can even attempt to drill or ride an underground bike. There is also the added option of sampling a miner's lunch under ground.

The outdoor tour continues on to the very impressive mountains of mined stone and it is possible to see one of the biggest diggers in the world. Wall and mountain climbing are some of the adventure sports offered here. Located nearby is the vast industrial town of **Kohtla-Järve**. A small town

Exhibit at the intriguing Kohtla Underground Mining Museum

before World War II, it saw speedy development during the Soviet era with the expansion of the oil-shale mines in the area.

Ontika Coast ❸

Road Map E1. 🚌 from Tallinn to Jõhvi, then bus or taxi to Toila, Ontika. **www**.ida-virumaa.ee

The coastal limestone cliffs of Ontika make it one of the most striking areas of natural beauty in Estonia. Sprawling over almost 20 km (12 miles) between Saka and Toila, the plateau is the highest point of the North-Estonian limestone escarpment. At Ontika, the cliff reaches a height of 57 m (184 ft) and offers a view across the Gulf of Finland. **Valaste**, which lies 5 km (3 miles) east, has Estonia's highest waterfall. The 26-m

(85-ft) stream of cascading water has carved its way through a bed of 470 to 570 million-year-old rocks to create an amazing sight.

Environs

The beautiful **Toila-Oru Park** is located 14 km (9 miles) east of Ontika Coast and is worth visiting. The park is spread out over an area of 105 ha (260 acres) along the coast.

Sillamäe ❹

Road Map E1. 🚶 17,000. 🚌 from Tallinn, Narva. **www**.sillamäe.ee

Situated midway between Kohtla-Järve and Narva, Sillamäe makes for a fascinating excursion. This Soviet-era town was the site of a uranium mine for the Soviet nuclear programme. However, it was so secret that it was not even marked on official maps.

The town is a living example of the more elegant side of late-Stalinist residential architecture. Many of the ornately decorated apartment blocks set along tree-lined boulevards and manicured parks are very attractive. The mine was closed in 1991 and a number of other industries have since moved in. Sillamäe is slowly but surely reinventing itself as an upcoming coastal and historic tourist destination of interest.

View of the limestone cliffs set against the azure Baltic Sea, Ontika Coast

For hotels and restaurants in this region see pp297–9 and pp327–9

Narva ❺

Road Map E1. 👥 *68,000.* 🚆 *from Tallinn.* 🚌 *from Tallinn, Tartu.* ℹ️ *Puškini 13, 356 0184.* 🎭 *Narva Days (5–10 Jun), Narva Historic Festival (Aug).* **www**.narva.ee

After centuries of being bitterly fought over, Narva now marks the EU border with Russia. Although most of the city's much-admired medieval centre was levelled by the Soviet air force towards the end of World War II, there is still plenty to see and do.

On the west coast of the Narva river stands the impressive Narva Castle, whose main tower, Tall Hermann, houses the predominantly war-themed **Narva Museum**. A splendid riverside park surrounds the castle.

With a population that is 96 per cent Russian-speaking, Narva has a different feel from Tallinn. The city is also close to a number of attractions in the area.

🏛 **Narva Museum**
Tel 359 9245. ⏰ *10am–6pm daily.* 🖥 **www**.narvamuuseum.ee

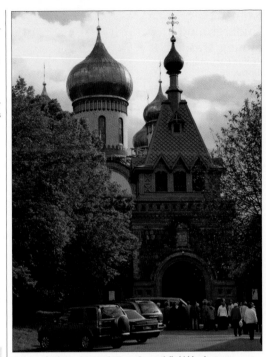

Exterior of Pühtitsa Convent in Kuremäe, partially hidden by trees

Narva Castle, home to the war-themed Narva Museum

Narva-Jõesuu ❻

Road Map E1. 🚌 *from Narva.* 🍴 💻 **www**.narva-joesuu.ee

The attractive summer resort of Narva-Jõesuu is famed for its pristine beach. Lined with pine trees and old wooden houses, the beach stretches for 7 km (4 miles) from Narva-Jõesuu to Meriküla. The area was a fashionable spa resort in the 19th century and was popular with St Petersburg's high society. Present-day Narva-Jõesuu enjoys a beach, a lively nightlife and a booming water-sports industry.

Kuremäe ❼

Road Map E1. 🚌 *from Tallinn, Narva.*

The small village of Kuremäe is celebrated for its Russian Orthodox **Pühtitsa Convent**, one of the most notable sights in Estonia. The convent was founded in 1891 and today some 170 nuns live there. There are six churches in the complex which is dominated by the striking Dormition Cathedral, built in 1910. The convent is surrounded by a thick granite wall and has a majestic entrance gate with seven large bells. The bright façade and pristine appearance of the

Statue of a bull on Vallimägi Hill, Rakvere

place gives it a cheerful air. The convent also has a hostel for guests and pilgrims.

⛪ **Pühtitsa Convent**
Tel 339 2124. ⏰ *8am–8pm daily.* 🖥 🚻 💻 **www**.orthodox.ee

Rakvere ❽

Road Map D1. 👥 *17,000.* 🚌 *from Tallinn, Narva.* ℹ️ *Laada 14, 324 2734.* **www**.rakvere.ee

The town of Rakvere, with restored historic buildings and a striking main square, has recently been transformed into an attractive tourist destination. Its most famous landmark, the 13th-century **Rakvere Castle** on Linnamägi Hill, is a medieval theme park now. The exhibits cover the castle's history from its early existence until it fell to ruins. A grand and slightly Picasso-esque statue of a bull, created by local artist Tauno Kangro (b.1966), stands on top of Vallimägi Hill and is a new symbol for the town. Rakvere's inhabitants are proud of the fact that the renowned composer Arvo Pärt *(see p23)* went to school and had begun his music studies here.

♣ Rakvere Castle
Rakvere linnus. *Tel* 322 5500. ◯ *May–Sep: 11am–7pm daily.* ▧ **www.**svm.ee

Väike-Maarja ❾

Road Map D1. ▒ *5,000.* ▨ *from Rakvere.* ❶ *Pikk 3, 326 1625.* **www.**v-maarja.ee

A typical parochial Estonian town, Väike-Maarja is steeped in history and has a number of quirky sights of interest. Housing the local tourism information centre, the **Väike-Maarja Museum** offers an eclectic and detailed overview of the town's history, including a fascinating tour of how the Forest Brothers *(see p118)* used to live. It is also possible to have a "Forest Brothers' picnic" in a reconstructed bunker. Other interesting sights include a Soviet missile base, the Vao Stronghold Tower Museum and the 14th-century town church.

❶ Väike-Maarja Museum
Pikk 3. *Tel* 326 1625. ◯ *May–Sep: 10am–5pm Tue–Sat, Oct–Apr: 10am–5pm Mon–Fri.*

Endla Nature Reserve ❿
Endla looduskaitseala

Road Map D1. ▨ *from Tartu.* ❶ *Reserve Headquarters, Tooma, 70 km (43 miles) NW of Tartu, 776 3375.* ☑ *call in advance.* **www.**endlakaitseala.ee

A scenic maze of peat bogs, rivers, swamp forests and lakes, the Endla Nature Reserve is considered to be one of the most important freshwater systems in the country. Although the reserve straddles three counties, its relatively small size makes it much easier to explore than the larger national parks. One of the six hiking trails, the stunning **Männikjärve Trail** stretches for 1 km (0.5 mile) over a long plank platform. To the east of the reserve, **Emumägi Hill** is the area's highest point. Its observation tower offers a superb view of the countryside.

The medieval octagonal tower amid castle ruins, Paide

Paide ⓫

Road Map D1. ▒ *11,000.* ▨ *from Tallinn.* ❶ *Pärnu 6, 385 0400.* **www.**paide.ee

Located in the centre of Estonia, Paide makes the ideal base from which to explore the heartland of the country. To emphasize its central location, the town has adopted a heart shape as its official logo. Paide's biggest tourist draw is the beautifully restored 13th-century octagonal castle tower and surrounding ruins. The tower houses a museum focusing on the town's early history, while the **Järvamaa Museum** offers a much broader look at the nature and history of the area. The Town Hall Square is the focal point of the well-kept town centre and offers a small variety of decent restaurants and cafés.

🏛 Järvamaa Museum
Lembitu 5. *Tel* 385 1867. ◯ *Apr–Oct: 11am–6pm Wed–Sun, Nov–Mar: 10am–5pm Wed–Sun.* ▧ **www.**jarva.ee/muuseum

Põltsamaa ⓬

Road Map D2. ▒ *5,000.* ▨ *from Tallinn, Tartu.* ❶ *Lossi 1, 775 1390.* **www.**poltsamaa.ee

The idyllic town of Põltsamaa is set amid the ruins of Põltsamaa Castle. Once the centre of power for Duke Magnus, the King of Livonia in the 16th century, the castle stronghold is an amazingly eclectic jigsaw of historical pieces. The exquisite Rococo palace was built in the 18th century on the site of an old convent, while the elegant Lutheran **St Nicholas's Church** dates from 1633 and was reconstructed in 1952. Located in an old storehouse in the castle yard, the **Põltsamaa Museum** boasts some fine exhibits.

❶ St Nicholas's Church
Lossi 3. *Tel* 776 9915. ◯ *Jun–Aug: 10am–3pm daily.* ❶ *11am Sun.* ▧

🏛 Põltsamaa Museum
Loss tänav 1. *Tel* 775 1390. ◯ *10am–6pm Mon–Sat.* ▧

Well-maintained building inside the castle grounds at Põltsamaa

Tartu ⑬

Best known for being home to the venerable Tartu University, the town is frequently referred to as the intellectual capital of Estonia. The university was founded in 1632 by King Gustav Adolphus of Sweden (1594–1632) and has played a major role in Estonian history ever since. With the second-largest population in the country, Tartu has a thriving cultural scene and exciting nightlife, and makes a convenient base from which to explore the southeast of the country.

Statue of King Gustav Adolphus

Town Hall Square, with the Kissing Students Fountain in the centre

🏛 Town Hall Square

Tartu's historic centre is set around Town Hall Square (Raekoja plats), with the Emajõgi river in the front and Toomemägi *(see pp116–17)* just behind it. The gently sloping cobblestoned square is distinctly Neo-Classical, with the pink Town Hall overlooking it from the top. The Great Fire of 1775 burned down most of the city and today the square's Neo-Classical look is in sync with the rest of the city centre. The famous **Kissing Students Fountain**, in front of the Town Hall, was erected in 1998.

🏛 Tartu University Main Building

Ülikooli 18. **Tel** 737 5384. ☐ 11am–5pm Mon–Fri. 📷 📹 ♿ **www**.ut.ee

Finished in 1809, Tartu University Main Building (Tartu ülikooli peahoone) is one of Estonia's finest Neo-Classical buildings. It contains the impressive Art Museum, from which the imposing Assembly Hall and the far more amusing Lock-Up can be seen. Unruly students were confined to the Lock-Up as punishment. Their scribbling and doodling on the walls makes for amusing reading.

⛪ St John's Church

Jaani 5. **Tel** 744 2229. ☐ May–Sep: 10am–6pm Tue–Sat, 10am–1pm Sun. 📷 ⛪ **www**.eelk.ee/tartu.jaani

Dating from 1330, St John's Church (Jaani kirik) was severely damaged by bombing during World War II. However, even after extensive renovations and having a new spire added in 1999, the church remains one of the best examples of brick Gothic architecture in Northern Europe. Hundreds of elaborate terracotta figures, dating from the Middle Ages, adorn the church interior. It is believed that there were originally more than 1,000 of them.

TARTU

Father and Son Statue ⑤
Tartu Art Museum ④
Town Hall Square ①
St John's Church ③
Tartu University Main Building ②

0 metres   150
0 yards   150

KEY

▨ Street-by-Street area: see pp116–17

Key to Symbols see back flap

Leaning building in which the Tartu Art Museum is housed

🏛 Tartu Art Museum

Raekoja plats 18. *Tel* 744 1080.
⏱ *11am–6pm Wed–Sun.* free on Fri. call in advance.
www.muuseum.ee

Housing one of the finest collections in the country, Tartu Art Museum (Tartu kunstimuuseum) features the works of prominent Estonian artists such as Elmar Kits (1913–72), Ülo Sooster (1924–70) and Marko Mäetamm (b.1965). A thorough and captivating overview of Estonian art, which spans the 19th century through to the present, is also provided. The museum's other impressive aspect is the building that houses it. Leaning conspicuously to one side, it belonged to the famous Russian Field Marshal Barclay de Tolly *(see p118)*, who successfully led the Russian army against Napoleon in 1812.

Father and Son Statue

Küüni (close to Poe St).

Originally planned for Tallinn, this delightful little statue by Ülo Õun (1940–88) was conceived in 1977. It was cast in bronze in 1987, purchased by the Tartu Town Government in 2001 and, finally, unveiled on Children's Day (1 June) in 2004. The father figure is modelled after the sculptor, and the child is modelled after his son Kristjan, when he was around one-and-a-half years old. Interestingly, both father and son are proportionately equal in this highly unusual and extremely touching monument.

🏛 KGB Cells Museum

Riia 15b. *Tel* 746 1717. ⏱ *11am– 4pm Tue–Sat.* www. linnamuuseum.tartu.ee

Situated in the basement of the regional headquarters of the KGB/NKVD, the KGB Cells Museum (KGB kongid) offers grim testimony to the nightmare of the Soviet occupation. Some of the former cells have been turned into exhibition spaces, while others have been restored to their original condition to provide a picture of what so many Estonians suffered under the Soviet regime. Much attention is paid to the mass deportations that took place between 1940 and 1949, including the official plans for carrying them out. There are gut-wrenching artifacts from the Gulags, the notorious correction camps where thousands of Estonians died.

A desk in the KGB Museum, with Stalin's portrait on the wall

🏛 Estonian National Museum

Kuperjanovi 9. *Tel* 742 1311.
⏱ *11am–6pm Wed–Sun.* free on Fri. call in advance. www.erm.ee

Estonia's most important ethnological centre, the Estonian National Museum (Eesti rahva muuseum) boasts over 1 million artifacts collected over the past 100 years. The museum focuses on Estonia and other Finno-Ugric cultures, and its collection covers every imaginable aspect of life. From chairs made of gnarled birch wood to warped wooden beer tankards, the displayed objects eloquently attest to a way of life that seems quaintly anachronistic in today's times.

In addition, there are vast photographic and documental archives, including a punk jacket (circa 1982–85), among the fascinating collection of costumes. The museum is dedicated to the great Estonian folklorist and linguist Jakob Hurt (1839–1907). The museum occasionally holds temporary exhibitions that encompass themes from furniture to photography.

KARL ERNST VON BAER (1792–1876)

A Baltic-German biologist, Karl Ernst von Baer was one of the founders of embryology. His pioneering work in this area was recognized by Darwin, although Baer himself was extremely critical of the evolutionary theory. Baer studied at Tartu University and later taught at Königsberg and the St Petersburg Academy of Sciences, before living out his last years in Tartu. A statue of him sitting pensively atop a large plinth has pride of place on Toomemägi. A rather endearing tradition takes place every year, on the eve of St Philip's Day (1 May), when Tartu University students wash Baer's bronze hair.

Statue of Karl Ernst von Baer on Toomemägi

Street-by-Street: Toomemägi

With its labyrinthine layout of narrow, winding streets and elegant historic buildings, Toomemägi (Cathedral Hill) is full of delightful surprises. In medieval times a fortress and cathedral stood on the hill but both were abandoned during the Livonian Wars (1558–82). Today, Toomemägi is home to a variety of prominent public buildings. Many of them belong to Tartu University, which was re-established here in 1802. There are several impressive monuments to some of the university's most esteemed graduates in the landscaped parks dotted around the hillside. The hill also commands some wonderful rooftop views of the city of Tartu spread out below.

Statue of two Wildes outside
The Wilde Irish Pub

Devil's Bridge
The bridge was built in 1913 to honour three centuries of rule by the Russian Romanov dynasty. The bridge was dedicated to Tsar Alexander I.

KEY

- - - Suggested route

| 0 metres | 100 |
| 0 yards | 100 |

★ University Observatory
When it was built in 1820, the observatory had the most powerful achromatic telescope in the world. It was separated from the university in 1946 and now serves as a science centre.

STAR SIGHTS

★ University Observatory

★ Angel Bridge

★ Statue of Karl Ernst von Baer

★ Angel Bridge
According to tradition, making a wish and holding one's breath while crossing this 19th-century yellow-and-black bridge will fulfil it.

Cathedral Ruins
The massive ruins bear testimony to the original grandeur of the cathedral. Damaged during the Livonian Wars, it was rebuilt as a library after the reopening of the university in 1802. Visitors can climb the renovated towers.

The sacrifical stone was the site of worship for pagan Estonians.

★ **Statue of Karl Ernst von Baer**
This impressive monument befits Tartu University's most eminent graduate and founder of modern embryology.

Tartu University
When the first students registered here in 1632, it was only the second university in the province of Swedish Livonia. Since its establishment, the university has played a crucial role in Estonia's history.

Town Hall
Dating back to 1786, the current Town Hall is the third of its kind to occupy this position at the heart of Tartu. The elegant early Classicist architecture was considered very fashionable in the 18th century.

Lake Võrtsjärv

Road Map D2. ⬚ *from Viljandi,
Otepää.* ⓘ *Centre for Limnology,
Vehendi, 529 8561.* ◷ *May–Sep:
10am–6pm Mon–Sat, 11am– 4pm
Sun; Oct–Apr: 10am–5pm daily.* ▨
call in advance. **www**.vortsjarv.ee

Straddling the three counties
of Viljandi, Tartu and Valga,
Lake Võrtsjärv is the second-
largest lake in Estonia after
Lake Peipsi *(see p123)*. The
northern part of the
lake has some beautiful sandy
beaches, while the southern
part is notably swampier.

Magnificent view of Otepää, set amid lush landscape

There are several attractions
scattered around the lake.
The mausoleum of Barclay
de Tolly (1757–1818), the
Russian general credited with
helping to defeat Napoleon,
is in **Jõgeveste**, south of
the lake. The bagpipe farm
in Riidaja, at the southwest
corner of the lake, is one
of the area's more unusual
sights. A popular summer
activity is to take a tour of
the lake aboard a *kaleship*,
a type of timber boat that
was used to get around Lake
Võrtsjärv in the olden days.

A section of the medieval castle
on Castle Hill, Viljandi

Viljandi ⓯

Road Map D2. ⬚ *20,000.* ⬚ *from
Tallinn.* ⬚ *from Tartu.* ⓘ *Vabaduse
6, 433 0442.* ☙ *Viljandi Folk Festival
(late Jul).* **www**.viljandi.ee

The pleasant town of Viljandi
is centred on the medieval
castle ruins sitting atop Castle
Hill, which affords spectacular
views of the nearby lake and

surrounding landscape. A
crucial staging post on the
Hanseatic trade route *(see
p32)*, Viljandi emerged as
one of Estonia's leading
strongholds in the 16th
century. By the end of the
19th century, the local area
had become one of the
wealthiest in Estonia.

A busy provincial centre
today, Viljandi is notable for
its well-preserved historic
buildings, with an abundance
of pretty timber cottages
and early 20th-century brick
houses. There are also several
manor houses.

In the small plaza, at the
junction of Lossi and Tartu,
is a statue that pays homage
to Carl Robert Jakobson
(1841–82). This zealous 19th-
century Estonian nationalist
helped get the National
Awakening underway by founding the Estonian-language
newspaper *Sakala* in Viljandi
in 1878. The statue is also the
main focal point for the town.

Otepää ⓰

Road Map E2. ⬚ *2,300.* ⬚ *from
Tartu, Võru, Tallinn.* ⓘ *Tartu mnt 1,
766 1200.* ☙ *Tartu Marathon (Feb).*
www.otepaa.ee

Situated amid the beautiful
rolling hills of southeast
Estonia, Otepää is equally
popular as a summer and
winter holiday retreat. The
town also holds a special
place in Estonian history.
In 1884 the national flag
was consecrated in the parish
church, which now houses
the **Flag Museum**. The totemic
Energy Column at Mäe Street
is an intriguing reminder of
how strongly pagan beliefs
prevail in Estonia.

Lake Pühajärv, 3 km
(2 miles) south of Otepää,
has some splendid beaches
and dining spots to enjoy
the magnificent scenery.

🏛 **Flag Museum**
Tel *765 5075.* ◷ *by appointment.*

THE FOREST BROTHERS

After the Soviet Union reoccupied Estonia in 1944,
thousands of men fled to the woods to take up arms. They
became known as the Forest
Brothers and fought a guerrilla-
style campaign against the
Soviet system, most prominently
in Viljandi and Tartu, with
strong support from locals.
However, the NKVD units
ruthlessly targeted the partisans'
families and by 1949 their
support network had largely
been broken. By 1953, only a
few of the Forest Brothers were
left. The last active member
died in 1980.

Illustration of an underground
bunker used by Forest Brothers

Skiing and Snowboarding

Skiing is a popular winter pastime in Estonia. When Estonia won three gold medals for skiing events at the 2006 Winter Olympics, the medallists were hailed as national heroes and "ski fever" gripped the country. Although Estonia has a flat terrain, there are numerous ski hills, such as the 318-m (1,043-ft) high Suur Munamägi, that offer snowboarding and downhill skiing. There are many ski resorts around Otepää. However, since Estonia is blanketed in snow throughout winter, the ski resorts are crowded until spring. The annual Tartu Ski Marathon *(see p49)* is held at Kuutsemäe Ski Resort and has seen as many as 10,000 participants Snowboarding is also fast gaining popularity in the region and Baltic snowboarders compete with the best in Europe in "trick park" acrobatics.

Snowboarding

The Tartu Ski Marathon *is one of the highlights of the winter sports calendar in Estonia. This 63-km (39-mile) WorldLoppet series event attracts competitors from all over the world. The festive proceedings also provide plenty of other skiing activities for non-professionals as well as children.*

Winter time in Otepää *draws hordes of ski-lovers, as this idyllic "Winter Capital" has several resorts, such as the one on Väike Munamägi (Small Egg Hill), 2 km (1 mile) from Otepää. Snowboarding, ice skating and snowtubing are popular in this attractive southern town.*

Kuutsemäe Ski Resort *is a seven-slope skiing facility located about 14 km (9 miles) outside Otepää. Its cross-country skiing tracks are well marked out.*

KRISTINA ŠMIGUN (B.1977)

A cross-country skier, Tartu-born Kristina Šmigun has achieved remarkable success in her field, which has made her a national hero among sports enthusiasts in Estonia. Her parents, Anatoli Šmigun and Rutt Rehemaa, were also successful skiers. Kristina has won six medals at the FIS Nordic World Championships, including a gold medal in 2003.

Her greatest success to date, however, was to become the first Estonian woman to win two gold medals at the 2006 Turin Winter Olympic Games. She won the 2 X 7.5 km (4.5 miles) double pursuit and the 10 km (6 miles) classical.

Kristina Šmigun at the Turin Winter Olympic Games

Andrus Veerpalu, *winner of two Olympic gold medals and one silver medal, is Estonia's most successful Olympic athlete. The cross-country skier has also won gold and silver in the World Championships.*

The English Gothic Revival-style exterior of Sangaste Manor

Sangaste Manor ⑰
Sangaste loss

Road Map D2. **Tel** 767 9300. 🚌 *from Tartu, Otepää.* ⭘ *10am–4pm daily.* 🎫 🅿 *call in advance.* ♿ 🍴 💻 www.sangasteloss.ee

One of the most attractive buildings of its kind in Estonia, Sangaste Manor was built in the English Gothic Revival style between 1879 and 1883. It was commissioned by Count Friedrich von Berg to prove to an English aristocrat, whose daughter he was wooing, that he was not the "savage from Russia" that the prejudiced nobleman deemed him to be. Sangaste's striking red-brick façade, crenellated gables and elegant towers lend it the appearance of a whimsical castle rather than a parochial manor house. The arched vestibule Dome Hall on the ground floor used to hold grand balls and still retains an air of grandeur, while the spacious dining room, which is criss-crossed with Tudor-style rafters, is particularly impressive. Sangaste is surrounded by a 75-ha (185-acre) forest park, making it a favourite place for wedding receptions.

Mõniste Open-Air Museum ⑱
Mõniste muuseum

Road Map E2. Kuutsi, Mõniste village. 🚌 *from Tartu.* **Tel** 789 0622. ⭘ *Apr–Sep: 10am–5pm daily, Oct–Mar: 10am–2pm Mon–Fri.* 🎫 🅿 www.hot.ee/monistem

Established in 1948, Mõniste Open-Air Museum is the oldest museum of its kind in the country. The museum is located in 19th- and early-20th century farm buildings, which are surrounded by the tranquil and beautiful forests of the Võru countryside. The museum offers plenty of activities for visitors. Special days are regularly held throughout the summer, which focus on the essential aspects of traditional rural life such as milking cows, working with wood and flax and baking bread. Apart from authentic farm work, visitors can also spin yarn, roll linen and make rope. One of the most interesting activities provided here is learning how Estonian farmers used local plants and trees to treat ailments.

St Mary's Church, set in lush rolling fields, Rõuge

Rõuge ⑲

Road Map E2. 🚌 *from Võru.* ℹ *Haanja mnt, 785 9245.* ⭘ *10am–6pm Mon–Fri.* www.rouge.ee

The small village of Rõuge perfectly embodies the languid charm of southeast Estonia and is considered by many Estonians to be the most beautiful village in the country. Situated on the shores of Lake Rõuge Suurjärv, the deepest in the country at 38 m (125 ft), and with the magnificent Valley of the Nightingales looming in the background, it is an exceptionally tranquil place. There are a series of nature trails through the valley which start from behind **St Mary's Church**. The church dates back to 1730 and was the site

---

THE SETU PEOPLE

A Setu woman wearing traditional clothes

Living in the southeast of Estonia, the Setu people form a distinct ethnographic group. Unlike the majority of Estonians, the Setu are Orthodox, having lived in a region that was Christianized by the Russian Orthodox Church. They also have their own unique language known as Võru-Setu, which differs considerably from standard Estonian. Traditional Setu folk music is among the most beautiful in Estonia, although its plaintive polyphonic form is strikingly Slavic-sounding. The Setu people are also famous for their traditional costumes and handicrafts. The best starting point to explore Setu culture is Obinitsa. Located at the centre of Setumaa, or "the Land of the Setu", the little village celebrates several Setu festivals.

of an Estonian stronghold until the 12th century. Adjacent to the church is an old wooden school dating from 1888, which has some beautiful wooden carvings and sculptures on its exterior. Opposite the church is a monument honouring those Estonians who lost their lives in the war of independence (1918–20).

Suur Munamägi ⓴

Road Map E2. ⛟ *from Võru.*
***Tel** 786 7514.* ⏱ *mid-Apr–Aug: 10am–8pm daily, Sep: 10am–5pm daily, Oct: 10am–5pm Sat & Sun, Nov–mid-Apr: noon–5pm Sat & Sun.* ♿ ▯ www.suurmunamagi.ee

Situated just south of the village of Haanja, Suur Munamägi (Great Egg Hill) is the highest point in the Baltic States. At a mere 318 m (1,043 ft) above sea level, it gives an idea of how flat the Baltic region is. However, the surrounding landscape of farmsteads, forests and hills is breathtaking enough to merit a trip to the top of the hill. On clear days, it is possible to see all the way to Russia and Latvia.

At the peak, there is an elegant observation tower which was built in 1939 and recently renovated to include the glass-fronted Suur Munamägi Tower Café *(see p329)* and a lift. Delightfully quirky wooden carvings, which peer down from the trees, can be seen while walking up the steep path to the top of the forested hill.

View from the observation tower, Suur Munamägi

F R KREUTZWALD (1803–82)

One of Estonia's best-loved writers, Friedrich Reinhold Kreutzwald is revered by Estonians as one of the most pivotal figures in the National Awakening of the 19th century. The enormous body of literature created by him in the Estonian language still instils a strong sense of identity and confidence among patriotic Estonians. Despite being impoverished, he studied medicine at Tartu University, where he developed a passionate interest in national folklore. He wrote many epics based on Estonian folklore, the most celebrated of which is *Kalevipoeg* (Son of Kalev). Published between 1857 and 1859, it was part fiction, part influenced by existing folk stories.

Kreutzwald Memorial Monument in Võru

Vastseliina ⓴

Road Map E2. ⛟ *from Võru.*
www.visitvoru.ee

The small town of Vastseliina is visited mainly for the 14th-century castle located 4 km (2 miles) east of it. The castle was originally a border stronghold built by the Germans as a defence against the Russians. It became the site of a miracle in 1353, when a cross was seen suspended in the middle of the castle's chapel altar. The incident was reported by the Bishop of Riga to Pope Innocent and the castle subsequently became a place of pilgrimage. In 1702, the castle was completely destroyed during the Northern War (1700–21), but the ruins are a vivid reminder of this once fiercely-contested area.

In Vana-Vastseliina, at the foot of the castle hill, **Piiri Tavern** – first mentioned in 1695 – still serves food.

Wooden houses lining Jüri Street in Võru

Võru ⓴

Road Map E2. 👥 *14,000.* ▯ ⓘ
Tartu 31, 782 1881. 🎭 *Võru Folklore Festival (19–22 Jul).* www.voru.ee

Situated in the centre of the southeast corner of Estonia, Võru is a good base for exploring the surrounding region. The town is best known for its impressive 18th-century wooden architecture.

Võru's main sight is the **Kreutzwald Memorial Museum**, the former house of writer F R Kreutzwald, who had a medical practice in the town. The sandy shores of Lake Tamula almost stretch up to the town centre, providing a perfect setting for walks.

Environs
Obinitsa, 30 km (19 miles) east of Võru, is the largest village of the Setu community.

🏛 **Kreutzwald Memorial Museum**
⏱ *11am–6pm Wed–Sun.* ♿

Sweeping view of Lake Põlva with the spire of St Mary's Church in the background

Põlva ❷❸

Road Map E2. 🏘 *6,500.* 🚌 *from Tartu.* ℹ *Kesk 42, 799 5001.* 🎭 *Town Days (penultimate weekend of May).* **www**.polva.ee

The town is set around the artificial Lake Põlva, whose sandy shores are crowded with sunbathers in summer. Legend has it that a girl was immured in a kneeling position in **St Mary's Church** to keep the devils away. This is reputedly how Põlva, meaning "knee" in Estonian, got its name.

The town was developed around St Mary's Church, which lay in ruins for a long period until it was rebuilt after the Northern War *(see p33)*. Nearby, the Cultural Centre, an award-winning building, houses an art gallery, concert hall and café, and offers panoramic views of the town from its terraced roof. Põlva is also famous for the Intsikurmu Song Festival Grounds. Set in a small forested area on the west side of the town, it regularly hosts concerts.

Kiidjärve Watermill ❷❹

Road Map E2. 🚌 *from Põlva.* ℹ *Kiidjärve village, 799 2122.* 🌐 **www**.polvamaa.ee

Built in 1914, the Kiidjärve Watermill is situated in the Kiidjärve-Taevaskoja Recreational Area, a 32-sq km (12 sq-mile) pocket of

stunning natural beauty that also includes sandcliffs. The watermill is the largest red-brick structure of its kind in the Baltic region. There are many hiking trails that start at Kiidjärve village. Horse-riding, cycling and canoeing are also popular ways to see the area. The famous Akste Anthills, some of which stand 2 m (7 ft) high, are among the area's most fascinating sights.

Taevaskoja Sandstone Cliffs ❷❺

Road Map E2. 🚌 *from Põlva.* 🚂 *from Tartu.* 🎯 *Taevaskoja Tourism & Holiday Centre, 799 2067.* **www**.taevaskoja.ee

Taevaskoja, meaning "Heaven's Hall", is famous for its sandstone cliffs and natural beauty. The Big and Small Taevaskoja cliffs are among the main attractions in the Põlva area. They run along the striking Ahja river, which is regarded

as one of Estonia's most beautiful. Close to the Small Taevaskoja is the Maiden's Cave, which was carved out by the spring water flowing out of the Devonian sandstone and is also a source of numerous legends and myths. Nearby is the Big Taevaskoja, a striking sandstone wall, widely regarded as a national symbol.

Sandstone cliffs at Taevaskoja, along the Ahja river

THE RUSSIAN OLD BELIEVERS

Opposing the sweeping reforms brought about by Patriarch Nikon (1605–81), the Old Believers split from the Russian Orthodox Church in the 17th century. Due to persecution, many moved to southeast Estonia, especially near Lake Peipsi where they have adhered to their traditional way of life ever since. Today, there are 11 congregations of Old Believers in Estonia, comprising about 15,000 members. They are known for their love of onions which they grow in abundance. It is a local belief that onions ward off various ills if eaten in large amounts.

Congregation of Old Believers

Lake Peipsi ㉖

Setu craftwork

The fifth-largest lake in Europe, Lake Peipsi stretches across a large part of the eastern border with Russia. It is a tranquil place steeped in history and tradition, with the immense lake dominating every aspect of life. The region is famous for being home to the Old Believers as well as the Setu people (see p120). The lakeshore has beautiful stretches of sandy beaches dotted with small fishing villages.

Fishing, a common activity on the coast of Lake Peipsi

Mustvee ①
A small museum dedicated to the Old Believers and three churches are the main sights here.

Raja ②
Famed for its Old Believers' Church, the 4.5-km (3-mile) long Raja is considered to be the longest village in Estonia.

Kolkja ③
The Museum of Old Believers is the highlight of Kolkja. The village also has a good restaurant that offers a taste of local cuisine.

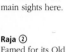

| 0 km | 15 |
| 0 miles | 15 |

TARTU
35 km (22 miles)

Lohusuu

Omedu

Ranna

Kallaste

Lake Peipsi

ESTONIA

RUSSIA

Varnja

Emajõgi

Meerapalu

Laaksaare

Mehikoorma

Räpina

Piirissaar ⑤
This island, on which fishermen and onion-growers live, can be reached by boat from Tartu and Värska.

Kasepää ④
Kasepää is part of a 7-km (4-mile) stretch of villages that adhere to the Old Believers' way of life.

TIPS FOR DRIVERS

Starting point: Mustvee.
Length: The road stretching from Mustvee to Varnja is 46 km (28 miles) and Meerapalu to Värska is 56 km (35 miles).
Driving conditions: It is not possible to drive the entire length. There are plenty of stay options just north of Kallaste.

Värska ⑥
Sandy beaches and wildlife make this village a pleasant getaway. The Setu Village Museum is a big draw.

KEY

🚢	Riverboat pier
ℹ	Visitor information
▬	Tour route
═	Other road
---	Ferry route
■·■	International border

LATVIA

Latvia at a Glance

Latvia is traditionally divided into four regions, roughly corresponding to the territories of the old Baltic tribes. Its long sandy coastline includes two of the country's largest ports, while the western region of Kurzeme is heavily forested in the north. To the south, the flat and fertile plains of Zemgale border Lithuania. In the north, Vidzeme has the most varied landscape, with a long coastline as well as forests, wetlands and hills. Bordering Russia and Belarus, the culturally distinct easternmost Latgale region remains largely rural and undeveloped.

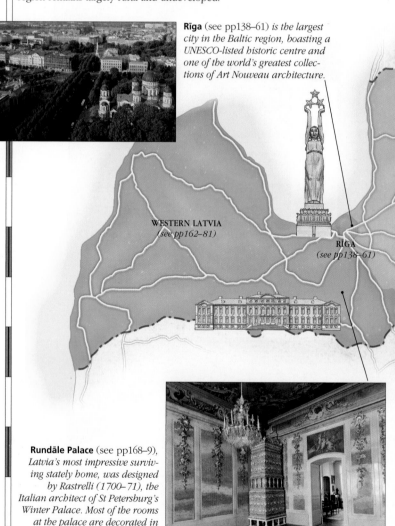

Rīga (see pp138–61) *is the largest city in the Baltic region, boasting a UNESCO-listed historic centre and one of the world's greatest collections of Art Nouveau architecture.*

WESTERN LATVIA
(see pp162–81)

RĪGA
(see pp138–61)

Rundāle Palace (see pp168–9), *Latvia's most impressive surviving stately home, was designed by Rastrelli (1700–71), the Italian architect of St Petersburg's Winter Palace. Most of the rooms at the palace are decorated in the fanciful Rococo style of the second half of the 18th century.*

◁ **View of the sandstone cliffs on the Salaca river, in Eastern Latvia**

Gauja Valley (see pp186–9) *is one of the most attractive parts of the country and a popular destination for both local and foreign tourists. In addition to providing a compelling mix of natural attractions and historic sites, it also offers some of Latvia's best opportunities for outdoor activities, from canoeing to bobsleighing.*

0 km 25

0 miles 25

EASTERN LATVIA
(see pp182–99)

Latgale lake area
(see p198) *is studded with almost 5,000 lakes. Although the Latgale upland rises no higher than 300 m (984 ft), the crystal-clear lakes enhance the beauty of this region, which is blessed with unspoiled countryside.*

Aglona (see p195), *the most important site of Catholic pilgrimage in the region, is famed for a 17th-century icon of the Virgin Mary which is only displayed on special occasions. The busiest day of the year is the feast of the Assumption, on 15 August, when thousands of visitors flock to the Baroque church.*

A PORTRAIT OF LATVIA

Lying between the other two Baltic States, Latvia is characterized by delightful forests and lakes, fascinating historical towns and dynamic cities, which are, by and large, under-explored. By contrast, the country's exciting capital, Rīga, draws hordes of Western Europeans round the year. The largest city in the Baltic region, Rīga revels in its cultural treasures and hedonistic nightlife.

Long before the arrival of the German crusaders in 1201, local Latvian tribes had established trading links with merchants as far afield as Byzantium, while Orthodox Christianity had made inroads from the East. Yet, it was the crusaders who were responsible for ushering in eight centuries of foreign domination. A short period of self-determination in the early 20th century ended with occupation first by Nazi Germany and then by Soviet Russia. The Soviet era brought rapid industrialization, while the restoration of independence in 1991 further hastened the pace of the country's modernization. Nonetheless, a distinctively Latvian culture developed and survived, assimilating foreign influences and substantial regional differences. A connection with nature, reflecting centuries of rural toil, has remained intact at the same time. While still trying to come to terms with the social, economic and political legacies of the 20th century, the country has entered the 21st century with confidence. The historic cores of Rīga and other major cities have been restored, while rural areas are being developed for ecotourism.

Statue on the House of Blackheads, Rīga

A splendid view of the countryside in Sigulda, Gauja National Park

◁ Latvian women in traditional dress at Turaida Castle, Gauja National Park

Traditional Latvian folk dancers performing at the Latvian Ethnographic Open-Air Museum, near Rīga

PEOPLE

The most obvious ethnic divide is between the country's Latvian and Russian communities, which respectively make up 58 and 29 per cent of the population of 2.3 million. Although Russians form the majority in Latvia's major cities, a small but significant proportion of them are not citizens, as they have not passed the mandatory language and citizenship tests. They cannot vote in national elections, nor are they allowed to work or travel freely in the EU.

Other minorities include Lithuanians, Poles, Belarussians and Ukranians. Although most of Latvia's Jews were executed or fled during World War II, some survivors returned, and small Jewish communities exist today.

SOCIETY AND CULTURE

Most Latvians are socially conservative, and although employment levels are equal for women and men, the latter are usually better paid. Women have played prominent public roles, not least in Latvian politics, yet the female domain is still often considered to be the home.

The strict social hierarchy, imposed by the Baltic Germans, ensured the survival and adaptation of many folk traditions. Echoes of Latvia's pagan past remain to this day, most obviously in the passionate celebration of Midsummer, and even city-dwellers profess a connection with nature. This is also reflected in the popularity of flowers as gifts, although it is important to give bunches with an odd number of stems, as even numbers are associated with funerals.

Latvians never took strongly to organized religion and today only around a third of the population identify themselves as Christians, mostly Evangelical Lutheran.

POLITICS AND ECONOMY

Since the restoration of independence, Latvia has seen the birth of dozens of political parties that have formed a succession of short-lived centre-right coalition governments. The end of

People attending the anniversary of the proclamation of the Republic of Latvia in Rīga

Communist rule has not meant the end of widespread corruption, with a small number of powerful oligarchs using political influence to promote vested financial interests. All this has bred a general sense of scepticism towards the political system.

The Soviet authorities took a primarily agricultural economy and transformed it

Ships docked in Liepāja harbour, a former Soviet naval base

to one based largely around heavy industry, with an associated influx of Russian workers into the cities. The collapse of the Soviet-planned economy meant a sudden loss of markets for Latvia's goods, and the country was plunged into further crisis when four newly privatized banks crashed in 1995. Since then, however, privatization, economic reform and low wages have fostered rapid growth. Most raw materials are imported, with the exception of timber, but industry has thrived on foreign investment. Exports include pharmaceuticals, timber, textiles, electrical and electronic goods, ships, dairy products, beef and grain. Latvia has capitalized on its status as an East–West trade hub, with oil transit from the former USSR to Western Europe particularly lucrative.

Although money has been flooding into Latvia, the living conditions of ordinary people has not improved much. A lack of opportunities has precipitated migration from rural areas, either to Latvian cities or to other EU countries.

TOURISM

One very evident change in recent years has been the rapid growth in tourism. While much of the country remains under-explored by foreign visitors, Rīga has established itself firmly on the tourist map. The city is

served by several airlines, including low-cost carriers, and the area around the Old Town is transforming to accommodate the growing number of visitors. The city is striving to recover its prized epithet of "Paris of the North", which it once shared with several other European cities.

However, the most fertile area for growth probably lies outside urban areas, where forests, rivers and lakes seem serenely untouched. Even though tourist infrastructure is still developing, tourism offers genuine opportunities for the revival of rural economies, with some farmsteads already embracing the possibilities of ecotourism.

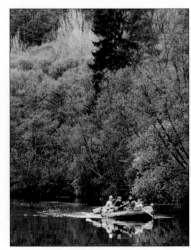

A group of rafters in the forested Kurzeme region

LATVIA THROUGH THE YEAR

With the pagan past never entirely erased by the German crusaders, the Latvian calendar is punctuated by celebrations which mark the rhythm of passing seasons. Many folk traditions are incorporated into Christian festivals, and they provide a chance to experience traditional activities. International cultural events are concentrated in Rīga, although other cities, particularly Liepāja, have their share, and many smaller towns celebrate folk festivals. The best time to visit is from May to mid-September. Rīga, however, gets plenty of tourists throughout the year due to its vibrant cultural life and it can look very attractive on a clear winter's day.

Violinist performing at a concert

SPRING

The rain and mud of early spring can dampen the spirits. However, by April the countryside comes alive with dance and music.

MARCH

Piano Stars *(early Mar)*, Liepāja. This festival was established in 1993 and attracts pianists from around the world.

APRIL

International Baltic Ballet Festival *(Apr–May)*. The festival, which features styles of dance ranging from classical to avant-garde, is held in Rīga as well as other towns.

MAY

Skaņu Mežs *(early–mid-May)*, Rīga. Performances by experimental and innovative musicians are held in a disused dockyard.

Art Days and Museum Nights is a lively festival, during which artists display their work in streets and squares throughout the country. Concerts and theatre performances are held, and many museums stay open into the night.

SUMMER

The summer months are the best time to visit, not only because the weather is at its most enjoyable, but because it is festival season.

JUNE

Artisans' Festival and Fair *(first weekend)*, Rīga. This event has been in existence since 1971, with music, theatre, dance and traditional craft demonstrations.

Rīga Opera Festival *(mid-Jun)*, Rīga. An international festival marking the end of the season for the Latvian National Opera, with an overview of the previous year.

Knights fighting in the Baltic Medieval Festival

Baltic Medieval Festival *(second weekend)*, Valmiera. Highlights include medieval music, food, craft workshops and battle re-enactments held at the foot of the town's Livonian Order castle hill.

Midsummer *(23–24 Jun)*. On Herb Day (Līgo), houses and barns are decorated with branches, flowers and leaves. In the evening, songs are sung around fires which remain lit until the dawn of St John's Day (Jāņi).

JULY

Sea Festival *(second weekend)*. Fishermen are honoured along with the God of the Sea in this festival.

Latvian Song and Dance Festival, Rīga. A major event in the calendar, this festival is held every five years and will next take place in 2013.

Folklore Baltica Festival, Rīga. The three Baltic capitals host the event in turns.

Performers at the Skaņu Mežs, a music festival in Rīga

Dancers in a street performance during Rīga City Festival

Baltic Beach Party *(late Jul)*, Liepāja. This festival confirms the city's claim to be the home of Latvian rock music.

AUGUST

Assumption of the Blessed Virgin Mary *(15 Aug)*, Aglona. Thousands of pilgrims visit Latvia's most important Catholic place of worship.
Rīga City Festival *(mid-Aug)*. First held in 2001 to celebrate the 800th anniversary of the city's founding, the festival consists of concerts.

AUTUMN

Autumnal colours can make this season a pleasant time to see the countryside, but temperatures fall rapidly from mid-September.

SEPTEMBER

Railway Festival *(first Sat)*, Gulbene–Alūksne Narrow-Gauge Line. Events are held at stops along the line, with a restored steam engine as the star attraction.

OCTOBER

New Music Festival Arēna *(Oct–Nov)*, Rīga. A month-long showcase for contemporary compositions.

NOVEMBER

Mārtiņdiena *(10 Nov)*. This marks the beginning of winter. Events take place at Rīga's Ethnographic Museum.
Lāčplēsis Day *(11 Nov)*. A number of events are held on this day in honour of Latvian freedom fighters.

WINTER

Short days and poor weather can make travelling in winter challenging, but on a clear day Latvia's snow-bound landscape can be beautiful.

DECEMBER

Christmas *(25–26 Dec)*. Yule logs are dragged from house to house, collecting the misfortune of the previous year before being ceremonially burnt.

Old Town Christmas Market *(Dec–early Jan)*, Rīga. Popular with tourists and local people, the market has a variety of goods on sale.

JANUARY

Latvian Blues Festival *(mid-Jan)*, Rīga. This festival has been running since 2000 and attracts international artists.
Silver Bells International Sacred Music Festival *(mid-Jan)*, Daugavpils. A competition with performances from a range of choirs, ensembles and soloists.

Exhibit at the International Ice Sculpture Festival, Jelgava

FEBRUARY

International Ice Sculpture Festival *(early Feb)*, Jelgava. One of the largest festivals of its kind in the world. After the event, the sculptures remain on display until they melt in the sun.

PUBLIC HOLIDAYS

New Year's Day (1 Jan)
Good Friday (March/April)
Easter Sunday and Monday (March/April)
Labour Day (1 May)
Restoration of the Independence of the Republic of Latvia (4 May)
Mother's Day (second Sunday in May)
Midsummer (23–24 June)
Proclamation of the Republic of Latvia (18 Nov)
Christmas (24–26 Dec)

Visitors enjoying the beautiful city of Rīga in autumn

THE HISTORY OF LATVIA

*L*atvia's history is traditionally considered to begin with the advent of the Teutonic Knights in 1201, which started German dominance of the area for three centuries. From the mid-16th to the early 18th century, Latvia was divided between Poland and Sweden. By 1795, all of Latvia had been absorbed into Russia. Final independence from foreign domination was only achieved in 1991.

Latvia's strategic geographical position, which prompted its more powerful neighbours to gain control over the region, largely decided the course of its history. By the late 12th century, Latvia's trade route up the Daugava river was increasingly visited by merchants from Western Europe. The Teutonic Knights, German warrior-monks, who first arrived in 1200, were looking for conquests as well as new converts in a pagan land. In 1201, they founded Rīga, which grew into an important centre for trade between the Baltic region and Western Europe.

Teutonic Knight in battle gear

THE GERMANS AND THE SWEDES

The power of the Germans quickly extended across all of Latvia. Castles were built in Cēsis (1209), Kuldīga (1242) and Valmiera (1283) to prevent any local resistance. Meanwhile, Rīga, Cēsis and Ventspils began to thrive as members of the Hanseatic League *(see p32)*. The beneficiaries of this growth were the Germans, who also owned large manors in the countryside. The Latvians, on the other hand, were dispossessed and forced to become serfs.

The early 16th century saw the townspeople lending zealous support to the Reformation movement, and soon after Protestantism was declared as the state religion. In 1561, during the Livonian Wars *(see p33)*, Poland conquered Latvia and Catholicism was firmly established. The separate Duchy of Courland, owing allegiance to Poland, was created in the south and west.

The clash between the Protestant Swedes and Catholic Poles in the late 16th century resulted in Swedish rule in

King Gustav Adolphus landing near the Baltic coast in 1630

TIMELINE

Stone coat of arms of the Hanseatic League

1201 Rīga founded by Albrecht of Bremen

1282 Rīga joins Hanseatic League

1561 Latvia occupied by Poland

1558 Livonian Wars begin

1200	1300	1400	1500

1211 Building of Rīga Cathedral begins

Rīga Cathedral

1372 German replaces Latin as official language

1520 First Lutheran service held

1536 Fir record o Jewish merchan in Rīga

northern Latvia for much of the 17th century. The Swedes were responsible for spreading education in the Latvian language throughout the country. Under Gustav Adolphus (r.1611–32), Sweden consolidated its hold over Livonia, which was then under Polish rule. Around the same period, the Duchy of Courland flourished under Jakob Kettler (r.1642–82), who built a powerful navy at Ventspils and also founded Latvia's only colony, the Caribbean island of Tobago.

Jakob Kettler, Duke of Courland

THE RUSSIAN EMPIRE

In 1710, during the Great Northern War *(see p33)*, the Swedes surrendered Rīga to Peter the Great of Russia. The Russians introduced 200 years of stability. Serfdom was abolished in 1819, which enabled farmhands to migrate to the towns as industrialization and the railways created a wide range of new employment. Power and money would, however, stay firmly in German and Russian hands. German merchants still enjoyed the privileges that they had secured from the Swedish rulers.

Towards the end of the 19th century, the Russians attempted to replace German with Russian as the national language. This infuriated the Latvian intelligentsia, who saw it as a sign of oppression. They began organizing political movements hostile to the Tsarist regime and continuing

German control of many businesses and farms. The 1905 uprisings in Russia found a sympathetic echo in Rīga and across the Latvian countryside, where over 100 manor houses were burnt down.

THE FIGHT FOR FREEDOM

When World War I broke out in 1914, Latvia became the main battleground between Germany and Russia, neither ever seizing its entire territory. Latvia's national aspirations took a blow as many Latvians were forced to join the Russian army. The Latvians, who were permitted to form their own army in 1915, put up a spirited fight against the Germans at the Battle of Christmas, which began on 23 December 1916. However, the Latvians were ultimately defeated and the Germans captured Rīga. The Allied victory in 1918 forced the German troops to withdraw. Within a few days, on 18 November, Latvian independence was declared.

A 19th-century oil painting of ships at a Latvian port

1621 Rīga seized by King Gustav Adolphus of Sweden		*King Gustav Adolphus of Sweden (1594–1632)*				**1905** Socialist revolution demands independence
1680 Rīga's first newspaper, in German, started	**1689** Bible translated into Latvian		**1822** First Latvian newspaper printed	**1873** First Latvian Song Festival held		**1917** Russian Revolution
600	**1700**		**1800**		**1900**	
1629 Sweden colonizes Latvia	**1710** Riga conquered by Peter the Great	**1817** Serfdom outlawed in Kurzeme	**1850s** National Awakening Movement formed	**1914** German occupation of Latvia begins	**1918** Formal declaration of Latvian independence	

THE FIRST INDEPENDENCE

Latvia's newly formed government was forced to flee to Liepāja in January 1919, returning to Rīga in July, when the city had been freed of Bolshevik troops. Throughout that year, many forces were ranged against Latvian independence and against each other, including the Germans, Poles and Russians. Latvia was only assured of its independence when it signed a peace treaty with Russia on 11 August 1920.

Despite the constantly changing governments that ruled until 1934, much was achieved during this period of independence. Trade was re-directed westwards and away from Russia, the Latvian language was used throughout the country and Rīga came to be regarded as the Baltic region's capital. The leading political figure throughout this period was Kārlis Ulmanis (1877–1942), who staged a coup in 1934 and abolished parliament. He proclaimed himself president, taking Mussolini as his role-model.

President Kārlis Ulmanis (1877–1942)

Progress came to a grinding halt with the Soviet invasion on 17 June 1940, making Latvia a part of the USSR. Anyone who had played a significant role in "bourgeois" Latvia was either executed or deported to Siberia. The German invasion followed a year later in June 1941, and most of Latvia was occupied within ten days. The Nazi regime was as brutal, but with different targets. Most of its victims were from the Jewish community, which had grown considerably after the laws which restricted Jewish residence were lifted in 1840.

THE RETURN OF THE RUSSIANS

The Soviets returned to Eastern Latvia and Rīga as "liberators" in autumn 1944, though the Germans held out until May 1945 in the country's west. This enabled nearly 100,000 Latvians to escape to Germany and Sweden, from where many continued on to Britain, Canada and Australia. In March 1949, the Russians carried out more deportations; this time their victims were mostly farmers unwilling to join the new collectives. As Latvians were forcibly removed from their own country, Russians were happy to take their place, and their numbers grew throughout the Soviet era. By 1990, half the population of the country was Russian-speaking and there was a serious threat that Latvian would disappear as the national language. The first public protest took place in 1987, when a crowd gathered around the Freedom Monument in Rīga, to commemorate the 1941 deportations to Siberia. New political groups began to emerge a year later. The most forceful

Soviet soldiers marching through Rīga in 1940

TIMELINE

1919 Bolshevik government in power in Riga for six months	**1934** Coup establishes Kārlis Ulmanis as President	**1939** Russia and Germany sign the Ribbentrop-Molotov Pact		**1956** Athlete Inese Jaunzeme becomes the first Latvian to win Olympic gold
		1940 First Soviet occupation		

	1925	1935	1945	1955

| **1920** Russia recognizes Latvia's independence | **1935** The Freedom Monument erected in Rīga
Freedom Monument, Rīga | **1945** Reoccupation by Soviet Union
1941 Occupation by Nazi Germany | | |

PLF supporters campaigning during the 1990 elections

Moscow's conservative Communists staged a coup against President Mikhail Gorbachev, but it collapsed within two days and Latvia suddenly found itself free.

Latvia was led during the first eight years of independence by Guntis Ulmanis (b.1939). Governments came and went as they had done in the 1920s, but they largely agreed on a slower policy of privatization than the Estonians were practising. The poor salaries being paid in the public sector continued the low-level corruption prevalent in the Soviet era and introduced it at higher levels too.

The beginning of the 21st century saw the effective integration of Latvia into Western Europe, particularly with its joining the EU (European Union) in 2004. Nonetheless, Latvia has still managed to maintain its trading links with Russia. The citizenship of half of Latvia's population, who speak Russian as their first language, is a problem likely to trouble its post-independence governments. However, sensitive handling of this issue can ensure the country's long-term security.

of them, the Popular Front of Latvia (PLF), demanded full independence and won the elections in 1990.

INDEPENDENCE AT LAST

The violence that broke out in January 1991 showed the determination of the Latvians for independence. Eight people were killed in clashes with Soviet forces in Rīga. In August,

JEWS IN LATVIA

In the early 19th century, Jews in the Russian Empire were barred from the academic world, government and the army officer corps. Anti-Semitism worsened under Tsar Alexander III (1881–94). Between the two World Wars, President Ulmanis firmly suppressed the activities of fringe groups that wanted to promote anti-Semitism. As part of its Latvian invasion in June 1941, Nazi Germany put its extermination policies into practice at once. The genocide was carried out in two phases that year. By 1945, only about 1,000 Jews, from a pre-war population of 95,000, had survived. Jewish institutions were

Pro-German Latvian militia standing guard over captured Jews in Liepāja in 1941

re-established in 1988, at the end of the Soviet era. A proper evaluation of Jewish history in all eras could only be carried out after independence in 1991.

President Vaira Viķe-Freiberga (b.1937)

1975	1985	1995	2005	2015

1991 Latvian independence re-established

1999 Vaira Viķe-Freiberga becomes Latvia's first woman president

2004 Latvia joins NATO and EU

2007 Valdis Zatlers sworn in as president

1970 Latvia's Jewish population grows to 50,000, most of whom live in Rīga

1990 PLF wins elections

1993 A democratic constitution adopted

2001 Riga celebrates its 800th anniversary

2006 Latvia hosts the 70th IIHF Ice Hockey Championships

RĪGA

With its long history as a mercantile centre, Rīga is the largest and most cosmopolitan city in the Baltic States. This is reflected in the buildings that line its streets and squares. The Old Town boasts an engaging array of medieval warehouses and Dutch Renaissance apartments. Remarkable Art Nouveau buildings, which secured the city UNESCO World Heritage Site status, can also be found.

When German crusader Bishop Albert von Buxhoevden chose Rīga as a strategic location for his fortress in 1201, the area was already inhabited by tribes who traded with Russian and Scandinavian merchants. The German settlement became the headquarters for the subjugation of the region and prospered as a member of the Hanseatic League of trading cities. Ruled by Sweden from 1621 to 1710, Rīga experienced a 19th-century heyday under the Russians. New suburbs were built for incoming workers, the harbour was expanded, a ring of boulevards was created in place of the old fortifications, and in the 20th century, industries such as automobile construction were developed.

The capital of an independent Latvia between the World Wars, Rīga suffered heavily during both conflicts and many of its oldest buildings were devastated. Several, including the striking House of Blackheads, have recently been rebuilt or restored. The "liberation" of Rīga by the Red Army in 1944 ushered in almost six decades of Communist rule, and there are still more ethnic Russians than Latvians in Rīga; relations between the two communities are cordial but rarely warm.

Since Latvia regained independence in 1991, Rīga has flourished, becoming a vibrant tourist destination with an impressive range of museums and a spirited nightlife. Change has been rapid and not always smooth, with the arrival of low-cost airlines in particular bringing its own challenges. Fashionable new bars and restaurants cater to growing crowds of visitors, and new glass and steel buildings have sprung up alongside the cobbled streets and church spires of the medieval Old Town. This is not a picture-perfect city stuck in time, but a lively metropolis intent on shedding the trappings of Soviet rule.

Outdoor café lining Cathedral Square (Doma laukums)

◁ Dutch Renaissance façade of the House of Blackheads, Rīga's Old Town

Exploring Rīga

For many centuries Rīga was largely contained within
the city walls on the right bank of the Daugava river.
Now known as the Old Town, this area contains most
of the city's sites of interest. The main route through
the tangle of picturesque streets and squares is Kaļķu
Street, leading from the Stone Bridge (Akmens tilts)
to Brīvības Street and the Freedom Monument. When
the city walls were removed in the mid-19th century,
the space was developed into a ring of boulevards
and parks. The main train and bus stations lie on the
southeastern edge of this ring. To the north is the late
19th- and early 20th-century extension of the city
known as the Centre (Centrs), which includes some of
the city's most impressive Art Nouveau architecture.

Café in Town Hall Square

KEY

- Street-by-Street map *pp146–7*
- ![] Tourist information
- ⊠ Post office
- 🚓 Police station
- ✝ Church
- P Parking

SEE ALSO

- *Where to Stay* pp300–302
- *Where to Eat* pp330–32

GETTING AROUND

The Old Town is compact and best seen on
foot: cars require an expensive permit and there
is no public transport. The main Art Nouveau
district is within walking distance of the Old
Town, while a network of trams, trolleybuses
and buses provides access to further-flung
attractions. Taxis are also abundant outside the
Old Town. The main tourist information office
can offer advice on guided tours.

0 metres   200

0 yards   200

SIGHTS AT A GLANCE

Churches and Cathedrals
Dome Cathedral ❶
Orthodox Cathedral ㉘
St Jacob's Cathedral ❼
St John's Church ㉓
St Peter's Church ⑳
St Saviour's Church ❹

Museums and Galleries
Arsenal Museum of Art ❾
Janis Rozentāls and Rūdolfs
　Blaumanis Memorial
　Museum ㉜
Krišjānis Barons Memorial
　Museum ㉗

Latvian National Museum of Art ㉙
Museum of Decorative Arts and
　Design ㉑
Museum of Jews in Latvia ㉚
Museum of the Barricades of 1991 ❷
Museum of the Occupation
　of Latvia ⑰
Museum of Rīga's History and
　Navigation ❸
Pauls Stradiņš Museum of
　the History of Medicine ㉛
Photography Museum ㉔
Porcelain Museum ㉒
Powder Tower/Latvian War
　Museum ⑫
Rīga Castle ❺

Buildings and Monuments
Bastejkalns ㉕
Cats' House ⑬
Freedom Monument ㉖
Great Guild ⑭
House of Blackheads ⑯
Latvian Riflemen Monument ⑱
Mentzendorff House ⑲
Parliament ❽
Small Guild ⑮
St Jacob's Barracks ⑪
Swedish Gate ❿
Three Brothers ❻

Panoramic view of Rīga's Old Town and the Daugava river

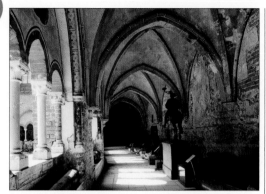
Impressive Cross-Vaulted Gallery of the Dome, Dome Cathedral

Dome Cathedral ❶
Doma baznīca

Doma laukums 1. **Map** 1 C3.
Tel 6721 3498. ☐ 10am–6pm
Mon–Thu, Sat–Sun; 10am–5pm Fri.
◑ for special events. ▨ ⬧ 8am
Mon–Sat; noon Sun. **www**.doms.lv

Founded as St Mary's by
Bishop Albert von
Buxhoevden in 1211, the
cathedral became one of the
city's three seats of power
alongside the town hall and
the castle. It gained its current
name from the German word
dom, meaning "cathedral", during the Reformation. The cathedral looks as if it has sunk, but
in fact the land around it has
been raised to keep out flood-
water from the Daugava river.

The largest place of worship
in the Baltic region, the
cathedral has been altered
over the years and its bulky
structure exhibits a variety of
styles. The altar alcove and
the east wing crossing are
Romanesque, with a cross-
vaulted ceiling and rows of
semi-circular windows.
Simpler Neo-Gothic additions
are characterized by pointed
arches, large windows and
lierne vaulting, while the
eastern pediment and the
steeple are in an 18th-century
Baroque style. The portal was
added in the 19th century,
followed by an Art Nouveau
vestibule in the 20th century.

Most of the interior decor
was destroyed during the
Reformation, and it is now
very plain except for the
tombs of merchants and the
19th-century stained glass. The

woodwork of the 17th-century
pulpit is ornate, however, as
is the organ case, which is
Mannerist with Baroque and
Rococo additions. The organ
itself was built in Germany
in 1884, and was then the
largest in the world. In the
summer it is possible to visit
the **Cross-Vaulted Gallery of
the Dome**, a Romanesque
cloister and courtyard.

Museum of the Barricades of 1991 ❷
1991 Gada barikāžu muzejs

Krāmu iela 3. **Map** 1 C4. **Tel** 6721
3525. ☐ 10am–6pm Mon–Fri,
11am–5pm Sat. ▨ donations.
www.barikades.lv

This museum recalls the
pivotal days of January 1991
when the people of Rīga took
to the streets, following the
threat of direct presidential
rule from Moscow and the

stationing of Soviet tanks
outside the Supreme Council
in Vilnius. Exhibits include
photographs of the demonstrations and a diorama of Dome
Square (Doma laukums) full
of people huddled around
bonfires. Most fascinating is
video footage shot around the
barricades, showing people
installing huge blocks of
concrete to defend strategic
points, including the Interior
Ministry and TV Tower. Scenes
shot at night are punctuated
by gunfire and shouting. A
final room is dedicated to the
people who were killed in
Bastejkalns *(see p150)*.

Museum of Rīga's History and Navigation ❸
Rīgas vēstures un
kuģniecības muzejs

Palasta iela 4. **Map** 1 C4. **Tel** 6721
1358. ☐ 10am–5pm Wed–Sun.
▨ ▨ **www**.rigamuz.lv

Founded in 1773, this
museum is the oldest in Rīga.
Housed in an impressive
building with tiled stoves
and stained-glass windows,
it is also one of the city's
most interesting and varied
museums. The exhibition on
navigation stresses the strong
maritime history of the city
up until World War I, and
includes several large model
ships and material on
Krišjānis Valdemārs *(see
p191)*. Other rooms cover
everything from prehistory
to independence, with
particular emphasis on the

Interior of the Museum of the Barricades of 1991

mid-19th to mid-20th centuries. Highlights from the Middle Ages include the *Madonna on a Crescent Moon*, a sculpture of the patroness of the Great Guild which was taken to Germany during World War II, and *Big Kristaps*, a large 16th-century statue of St Christopher.

Model ship at the Museum of Rīga's History and Navigation

St Saviour's Church ④

Anglikāņu baznīca

Anglikāņu iela 2a. **Map** 1 C3. *Tel* 6722 2259. 🕀 *11am first Sun of the month. Free lunchtime concerts are held at 1pm every Wed.* **www**.anglicanriga.lv

Funded by British merchants, this small Neo-Gothic church, built in 1857, is the only Anglican place of worship in the city. The English bricks were brought as ballast on trading ships, and the church was even built on a layer of British soil. During the Soviet era it was used by students as a disco and recording studio, but since the second independence in 1991 it has been reopened for worship with a congregation including English-speaking expatriates.

Rīga Castle ⑤

Rīgas pils

Pils laukums 3. **Map** 1 C3. **Museum of Foreign Art** *Tel* 6722 6467. 🕘 *11am–5pm Tue–Sun.* 🅿 📷 **www**.amm.lv **History Museum of Latvia** *Tel* 6722 1357. 🕘 *10am–5pm Wed–Sun.* 🅿 📷

The city's original Livonian Order castle was destroyed by Rīga's citizens during a war against the Order lasting from 1297 to 1330. After losing, the townspeople were forced to build a new castle on the present site just outside the city. Continuing quarrels led the Master of the Order to leave the capital, but Rīga Castle was destroyed by the citizens once more in 1484.

Again they were defeated and the next castle the townspeople were compelled to build forms the core of the current structure and was the headquarters of the Livonian Order until 1561.

As well as being the official residence of Latvia's president, the building now houses two museums.

Exhibits at the **Museum of Foreign Art** (Ārzemju mākslas muzejs) begin with copies of Egyptian and Greek statues, and continue with a collection of paintings. Most visitors will find the **History Museum of Latvia** (Latvijas vēstures muzejs) more absorbing. The exhibits take in religious sculpture, traditional regional costumes and consumer goods from the first period of independence. There are also rooms decorated in styles including Biedermeier and Art Nouveau.

Three Brothers ⑥

Trīs brāļi

17–21 Mazā pils iela. **Map** 1 C3. **Museum of Architecture** *Tel* 6722 0779. 🕘 *9am–6pm Mon, 9am–5pm Tue–Thu, 9am–4pm Fri.* 🅿 *donations.* **www**.archmuseum.lv

This row of buildings on Mazā pils Street covers three distinct architectural styles. Number 17, with a stepped gable and Gothic niches, dates from the 15th century and is Rīga's oldest stone residential building. The ears of wheat on the stones beside the door indicate

that it was owned by a baker. The wooden interior of the 17th-century building at number 19 now houses the small **Museum of Architecture**. The green building at number 21 was built in the 18th century.

Entrance of St Jacob's Cathedral, the seat of Rīga's Catholic archbishop

St Jacob's Cathedral ⑦

Sv Jēkaba katedrāle

Klostera iela 1. **Map** 1 C3. *Tel* 6732 6419. 🕘 *9am–7pm Mon–Fri, Sun.*

Sited outside the old city walls, St Jacob's was built in 1225 to serve the surrounding villages. The church was renowned for having its bell not in the Gothic steeple but hanging from a cupola, which is still visible on the southern side although the bell has gone. It was rung to signal that an execution was taking place in the city, although another story insists that it was heard when unfaithful women passed by the church. Today, it is the seat of Rīga's Catholic archbishop.

Changing of the guard outside Rīga Castle in the Old Town

Parliament ❽
Saeima

Jēkaba 11. **Map** 1 C3.
www.saeima.lv

This rather anonymous building, constructed from 1863 to 1867 with Florentine Renaissance features, and renovated several times since, was originally used for meetings of the local landed gentry. From 1919 to 1934, as today, it served as the seat of Latvia's parliament, while during World War II it was the headquarters of Friedrich Jeckeln – the SS officer who oversaw the killing of Latvia's Jews, Roma and other "undesirables". Later it was used by the Supreme Soviet of Latvia. In 2001, the Museum of the Barricades of 1991 was opened nearby to recall the days of January 1991 *(see p137)*.

Imposing façade of Latvia's Parliament

Arsenal Museum of Art ❾
Mākslas muzejs Arsenāls

Torņa 1. **Map** 1 C3. **Tel** 6735 7527.
⬚ *Apr–Sep: 11am–7pm Tue–Sun, Oct–Mar: 11am–5pm Tue–Sun.* 🖼
www.lnmm.lv

Until the completion of the highly anticipated Museum of Contemporary Art, designed by renowned architect Rem Koolhaas and scheduled to open in 2011, this is Rīga's premier venue for shows of cutting-edge art. There is no permanent collection, but the temporary exhibitions are generally of high quality. The emphasis is on art from the middle of the 20th century onwards, either produced in Latvia or by Latvians living abroad. The imposing one-storey building on Jēkaba Square was built between 1828 and 1832 in the style of Russian Classicism as a customs house. The name "Arsenal" comes from a previous building on the same spot, built by the Swedes. The downstairs exhibition space particularly benefits from airy rooms and high ceilings.

Swedish Gate ❿
Zviedru vārti

Between Torņa iela & Aldaru iela.
Map 1 C3.

The sole remnant of eight city gates, the Swedish Gate was built in 1698 during a period of Swedish rule in Rīga. It runs through the ground floor of the house at Torņa 11, and legend has it that the gate was created illegally by a wealthy merchant to give him more direct access to his warehouse. More likely, it was built for the use of the soldiers stationed at St Jacob's Barracks. Today the gate provides access between the popular strip of shops and bars on Torņa Street and the quieter, but pleasant, Aldaru Street. Newly-married couples include the gate on their tour of the city, as passing through it is said to bring good luck.

Swedish Gate, built through the ground floor of an old house

St Jacob's Barracks ⓫
Jēkaba kazarmas

Torņa iela. **Map** 2 D3.

Built in the 17th century to house Swedish soldiers, this yellow block is now home to shops and restaurants. The barracks also played a brief role in the nation's cultural development, as the site of an artists' commune opened in 1917, although the building retained its military purpose. Many of the members went on to join the influential Rīga Artists' Group of the 1920s and 30s. Opposite is the oldest remaining stretch of the city wall, dating from the 13th to 16th centuries but restored during the Soviet era.

Paintings and sculpture exhibited at the Arsenal Museum of Art

For hotels and restaurants in this region see pp300–302 and pp330–32

Powder Tower/ Latvian War Museum ⑫

Pulvertornis/Latvijas kara muzejs

Smilšu 20. **Map** 2 D3. **Tel** 6722 8147. ☐ May–Sep: 10am–6pm Wed–Sun, Oct–Apr: 10am–5pm Wed–Sun. 🖼 donations. 🖳 www.karamuzejs.lv

The cylindrical Powder Tower is all that remains from a total of 18 towers that were once part of the city's defences. Its 14th-century foundations are among the oldest in the city, but the rest of the structure dates from 1650, being rebuilt after it was destroyed by the Swedish army in 1621. The 2.5-m (8-ft) thick walls were intended to protect the gun-powder stored inside, after which the tower was named. Nine Russian cannonballs remain embedded in the walls as proof of the tower's strength.

The tower was bought by a German student fraternity at the end of the 19th century and in 1919 it housed a military museum reflecting on the then-recent fight for independence as well as on World War I. The annexe building was constructed from 1937 to 1940, but the Soviet occupation meant that it did not fulfil its function until several decades later. From 1957 the tower housed the Museum of the Revolution in the Soviet Republic of Latvia.

The current museum occupies both the tower and the annexe. While the oldest exhibit – part of a cannon discovered during the 1930s – dates from the 15th century, the museum largely concentrates on 20th-century warfare. World War I is covered with displays of weapons, uniforms and propaganda posters, as well as items made by the Latvian Riflemen *(see p148)*. Other rooms examine the role of Latvians in the Russian Revolution, the Latvian War of Independence, World War II and the Soviet occupation. Recent additions include an impressive collection of 360 models of military machinery.

Old issue of Lāčplēsis magazine at the Latvian War Museum

Cats' House ⑬

Kaķu māja

Meistaru iela 10. **Map** 2 D3.

This yellow Art Nouveau building on the corner of Meistaru and Amatu streets is a popular image of Rīga for its two feline statues. The story goes that before World War I a merchant who owned the building was refused entry to the Great Guild because he was Latvian and membership was reserved for Germans only. In retaliation, he put two statues of black cats – with arched backs and tails up – onto the roof, positioning them so that their backsides faced the guildhall. After a lengthy court battle the merchant eventually gained entry into the guild and turned the cats around.

Statue on the roof of Cats' House

Great Guild ⑭

Lielā Ģilde

Amatu 6. **Map** 2 D3. **Tel** 6721 3798.

Established in the 13th century, the Great Guild had a monopoly on trade in Rīga for centuries. The building that served as the guild's headquarters was built from 1853 to 1860. An old guild chamber displays symbols of Hanseatic cities and the bridal chamber was once used by guild members' children on their wedding nights. Today, the building holds concerts by the Philharmonic Orchestra.

Small Guild ⑮

Mazā Ģilde

Amatu iela 5. **Map** 2 D3. **Tel** 6722 3772. ☐ for concerts and conferences only. www.gilde.lv/maza

While the Great Guild counted the city's merchants as its members, the less powerful Small Guild existed to promote the interests of Rīga's German artisans. This guild may have been less prestigious than its neighbour, but with its turret and spire it is a more attractive building. The Italian mosaic floor in the entrance hall is particularly noteworthy. The current structure was started between 1864 and 1866, and then completed after an interval of 20 years. It was renovated in 2000.

Splendid exterior of the Small Guild

Street-by-Street: Around Town Hall Square

The Blackheads' patron

Until a local government reform in 1877, the Town Hall Square was Rīga's administrative centre. Built in 1334, the Town Hall was one of three focuses of power alongside Dome Cathedral and Rīga Castle, representing the interests of the city's residents. The square has functioned as a marketplace and a site where festivals were held and executions carried out. The impressive step-gabled House of Blackheads has been completely rebuilt, while the Town Hall is a modern building behind a Neo-Classical façade. Out of place at the square's edge is a Soviet-era building housing the Museum of the Occupation of Latvia.

Mentzendorff House, extensively restored in the 1980s

KEY

--- Suggested route

Town Hall

Town Hall Square
Many of the square's elaborate buildings, destroyed by the Russians after World War II, have benefited from a restoration project tied to the city's 800th anniversary in 2001.

GRĒCINIEKU IELA

Statue of Roland
A legendary medieval figure and one of Charlemagne's knights, Roland became a symbol of the independence of cities from the local nobility.

Museum of the Occupation of Latvia

STAR SIGHTS

★ House of Blackheads

★ Museum of the Occupation of Latvia

★ St Peter's Church

★ House of Blackheads
The exquisite Assembly Hall was restored to its former glory during the 1990s ⑯

★ **Museum of the Occupation of Latvia**
This incongruous slab of contrete houses a chilling and detailed testament to the suffering of Latvians during the Soviet and Nazi occupations in the 20th century ⑰

Konventa Sēta
The winding Convent Courtyard has been renovated and is now home to shops, galleries and the Porcelain Museum (see p149).

0 metres 100

0 yards 100

SKĀRŅU IELA

MĀRSTAĻU IELA

St John's Church

Photography Museum

Mentzendorff House

Jāņa Sēta
The courtyard of St John's Church is lined with tables and chairs in summer.

Dannenstern House was the largest dwelling in 17th-century Rīga.

★ **St Peter's Church**
This striking building has been destroyed and rebuilt several times over since its original 13th-century incarnation ⑳

House of Blackheads, set behind Schwab House

House of Blackheads ⑯
Melngalvju nams

Rātslaukums 7. **Map** 1 C4. **Tel** 6704 4300. 🛈 Schwab House. ◯ 11am–5pm Tue–Sun. 📷 🚫 🛗 🏛

Together with the adjoining Schwab House, the House of Blackheads is one of Riga's most impressive reconstruction projects. It was originally built in 1334 for the city's guilds, after the Livonian Order seized the existing guild buildings. Over time, the Blackheads, a guild of unmarried foreign merchants, became the sole occupants. Their name derives from their patron, St Maurice (who was often depicted as a Moor), and they were known for their riotous parties.

The ground floor of the building was occupied by shops, while the guildhall was on the first floor. The step-gabled Dutch Renaissance façade was added in the late 16th century, the astronomical clock in 1622, and the Hanseatic emblems and the four figures (Neptune, Mercury, Unity and Peace) in 1896. Schwab House was built to complement its neighbour in 1891.

The Blackheads disbanded when the Baltic Germans were asked by Hitler to return home at the beginning of World War II. Both buildings were devastated by bombing in 1941 and the Soviet authorities demolished the remnants seven years later; the current structures date from 1999. Rooms open to the public include the Grand Hall and a concert hall, which once welcomed composers including Richard Wagner and Franz Liszt. The city's main tourist information office can be found in Schwab House.

Museum of the Occupation of Latvia ⑰
Latvijas okupācijas muzejs

Strēlnieku laukums 1. **Map** 1 C4. **Tel** 6721 2715. ◯ May–Sep: 11am–6pm, Oct–Apr: 11am–5pm Tue–Sun daily. 📷 donations. 🚫 🏛 **www.** occupationmuseum.lv

This Soviet-era concrete structure was built to house a museum honouring the Latvian Riflemen, but since 1993 it has provided a sobering account of Latvians' suffering at the hands of Nazi Germany in World War II and later during the Soviet occupation. The collection includes photographs and eyewitness accounts of deportations and political represssion. The replica of a Gulag barracks room offers an insight into the hardship experienced by deportees.

Latvian Riflemen Monument ⑱
Strēlnieku piemineklis

Strēlnieku laukums. **Map** 1 C4. ♿

Depicting three brooding Latvian Riflemen, this controversial granite sculpture has stood in the square bearing its name since 1970. The Riflemen were a unit of the Russian army, formed to defend their homeland against Germany in 1915. Radicalized by the heavy losses they suffered during fierce fighting, they went on to support Lenin during the 1917 Revolution. Some of the Riflemen later returned to Latvia, while others became Lenin's most trusted troops. Some local people see the Riflemen as Latvian military heroes, while for others they recall the repressive Soviet period.

Mentzendorff House ⑲
Mencendorfa nams

Grēcinieku 18. **Map** 2 D4. **Tel** 6721 2951. ◯ 10am–5pm Wed–Sun. 📷 🚫 **www.**mencendorfanams.com

Constructed in 1695 as the premises for an apothecary, this tall building got its current name from a delicatessen based on the ground floor in the early 20th century.

Beautifully restored wall paintings in a room of Mentzendorff House

Extensively restored in the 1980s and 90s, the building is now a museum devoted to the life of Rīga's merchant class in the 17th and 18th centuries. Each room, including a saloon, kitchen and dancing hall, is decorated in period style. One highlight is the wall paintings, influenced by the work of French artist Antoine Watteau, depicting the wealthy relaxing.

St Peter's Church ⑳
Pēterbaznīca

Skārņu 19. **Map** 2 D4. **Tel** 6722 9426. ◯ 10am–5pm Tue–Sun. 🖼 tower only. ♿ except tower & exhibits. **www**.peterbaznica.lv

First mentioned in 1209, St Peter's Church was, unlike other churches, largely built by the Livs (see p172) and not by foreigners. None of the original wooden church remains, although parts of the walls date from the 13th century. The semi-circular apse and its five chapels were built in the 15th century, while the three Baroque dolomite entrance portals were added in the late 17th century. The church, which had become Lutheran in 1523, was damaged by fire in 1721, when Peter the Great is said to have headed the failed efforts to rescue it.

Lenin plate, Porcelain Museum

The church's steeple has been rebuilt several times over. The current one was built in 1973. Reaching a height of 123 m (403 ft), it provides excellent views across the city.

Museum of Decorative Arts and Design ㉑
Dekoratīvās mākslas un dizaina muzejs

Skārņu iela 10/20. **Map** 2 D4. **Tel** 6722 7833. ◯ 11am–5pm Tue, Thu–Sun; 11am–7pm Wed. 🖼 🎥 🔲 **www**.dlmm.lv

This museum is housed in the former St George's Church, Rīga's oldest surviving stone

Vera Viduka's 1977 textile at the Museum of Decorative Arts and Design

building. It was constructed as the chapel for Rīga's original Livonian Order castle in 1208, and became a separate church after the castle was destroyed in 1297. After the Reformation it was used as a warehouse, and traces of sacred and profane uses have been retained in the building.

The museum gives an overview of decorative arts from the 1890s to the present day. Temporary exhibitions are shown on the ground floor, while the first floor, covering the 1890s to the 1960s, is the most interesting part of the main collection. Highlights include painted ceramics from the Baltars studio and carpet designs by Jūlijs Madernieks.

Porcelain Museum ㉒
Rīgas porcelāna muzejs

Kalēju 9/11. **Map** 2 D4. **Tel** 6750 3769. ◯ 11am–6pm Tue–Sun. 🖼

Opened in 2001 in the Convent Courtyard, this museum reflects the history of porcelain manufacturing in Latvia, which dates back to the early 19th century. The 6,000 exhibits include a wide range of dinner services, as well as a huge red-and-gold vase made to celebrate the city's 700th anniversary in 1901. Of historic importance is a display of vases and statues portraying Soviet leaders.

St John's Church ㉓
Jāņa baznīca

Jāņa 7. **Map** 2 D4. **Tel** 6722 4028. ◯ 10am–5pm Tue–Sat. ✝ 8am Mon–Fri; 8am, 6pm Sat; 8am, 9am, 11am, 6:30pm Sun (in Latvian).

Built as the cloister chapel for a Dominican Order monastery in 1234, St John's was devastated by 15th-century fighting between the Livonian Order and the city. Only the main door and porch remain, with the rest rebuilt in Gothic style, including a web-vaulted red-brick nave with an apse, choir and tower. In 1582, the Polish king Stefan Bathory gave the church to the Lutherans, and it was further expanded in the Mannerist style. The interior includes a Baroque altar dating from 1769 and a painting, *Krustā sistais* (The Crucified, 1912), by Janis Rozentāls in the sacristy.

Impressive ceiling and nave of St John's Church

Boating on the city canal in Bastejkalns park

Photography Museum ㉔

Latvijas fotogrāfijas muzejs

Mārstaļu iela 8. **Map** 2 D4. **Tel** 6722 7231. ☐ 10am–5pm Tue, Fri–Sat; noon–7pm Wed–Thu. 🖼 **www.fotomuzejs.lv**

This museum traces the development of photography from 1839 to 1941 through displays of photographs and camera equipment. The images also serve to illustrate life in Latvia, depicting events such as the 1905 Revolution *(see p135)* and scenes of daily life during the first period of independence. In one room, an early 20th-century photographic studio has been re-created and in another there is a display dedicated to the Minox, or "spy" camera, invented by Rīga-born Walter Zapp (1905–2003). More unusual items include stereoscopic images and viewers and there is also a gallery that holds temporary exhibitions.

Large plate camera, exhibited at the Photography Museum

Bastejkalns ㉕

Basteja bulvāris. **Map** 2 D3.

Situated next to the Freedom Monument, this leafy park was set out in the mid-19th century on the mound of a 17th-century bastion. It is a pleasant place to relax, but it also contains a reminder that the path to Latvia's independence was not without bloodshed. On the night of 20 January 1991, OMON troops – also known as the Black Berets – tried to storm barricaded government buildings. Two filmmakers (Gvido Zvaigzne and Andris Slapiņš), two militiamen (Sergejs Kononenko and Vladimirs Gomanovics) and a schoolboy (Edijs Riekstiņš) were killed in the ensuing gunfire in Bastejkalns. Local people regularly renew the flowers on the memorial stones which bear their names, located close to a small bridge.

Freedom Monument ㉖

Brīvības piemineklis

Brīvības bulvāris. **Map** 2 D3. ♿

Built in 1935 on a site previously occupied by a statue of Peter the Great, the 42-m (138-ft) tall Freedom Monument is a potent symbol of Latvian independence. It was designed by the sculptor Kārlis Zāle, also responsible for the ensemble at the Brothers' Cemetery *(see p157)*. The granite base is decorated with reliefs and statues representing four virtues – work, spiritual life, family and

protection of the fatherland – as well as Latvian heroes including Lāčplēsis. It also bears the motto "*Tēvzemei un brīvībai*" (For Fatherland and Freedom). The slender granite column is topped by a female figure, commonly known as Milda, holding aloft three golden stars, which represent the three cultural regions of Latvia – Kurzeme, Vidzeme and Latgale. During the Soviet era the authorities banned people from laying flowers at the base of the monument and placed a statue of Lenin a short distance away.

Imposing Freedom Monument, designed by Kārlis Zāle

Krišjānis Barons Memorial Museum ㉗

Krišjāņa Barona memoriālais muzejs

Kr Barona iela 3. **Map** 2 E3. **Tel** 6728 4265. ☐ 11am–6pm Wed–Sun. 🖼 🎥 🖼 **www.baronamuzejs.lv**

Located in an apartment where the famous folklorist spent the last years of his life, this museum displays photographs and documents relating to Barons's life and work. The most important exhibit is the *Dainu skapis* (Cabinet of Latvian Folk Songs), a specially designed chest of drawers in which

KRIŠJĀNIS BARONS

In a nation where singing is one of the most important forms of cultural expression, Krišjānis Barons (1835–1923) is perceived as a hero. Influenced by Krišjānis Valdemārs *(see p191)* and part of the group of nationalist intellectuals known as the Young Latvians, Barons is known for systematizing Latvia's four-line folk songs *(dainas)*. He did not collect them in person, but by selecting certain songs as central and then enlisting to the differences between them, he was able to include 217,996 songs in the six-volume work he published between 1894 and 1915.

Photograph of Krišjānis Barons

Barons organized the texts of over 350,000 four-line folk songs sent by thousands of singers and informants. Each was written according to Barons's instructions on a slip of paper the same size as cigarette-paper boxes, which he used for storage before the cabinet was built. Contrary to popular belief, not all the slips were rewritten by Barons.

Orthodox Cathedral 🟤

Pareizticīgo katedrāle

Brīvības iela 23. **Map** 2 D3. **Tel** 6721 1297. 🔲 8am, 5pm Mon–Fri; 7am, 9:30am, 5pm Sat; 8am, 10am, 5pm Sun.

Situated on the edge of Esplanade Park (Esplanāde), this Neo-Byzantine Russian cathedral is officially called the Cathedral of Christ's Nativity (Kristus dzimšanas katedrāle). An attractive structure topped by five domes, it was built from 1876 to 1884 for the city's growing Russian community and was part of a deliberate process of Russification. It became a Lutheran church during the brief German occupation of Rīga in World War I, and once again an Orthodox church in 1921.

As with many places of worship, the Soviet authorities found alternative uses for the building during their occupation. In the 1960s they turned it into a lecture hall and planetarium. The interior decorations were nearly destroyed, and are still being replaced.

Latvian National Museum of Art 🟤

Latvijas Nacionālais mākslas musejs

Kr Valdermāra 10a. **Map** 2 D2. **Tel** 6732 5051. 🔲 Apr–Sep: 11am–7pm Mon, Wed, Sun; Oct–Mar: 11am–5pm Mon, Wed–Sun. 🌐 📷 **www**.vmm.lv

The interior of this early 20th-century Neo-Baroque building still has its original gilt and marble embellishments. While the collection was originally eclectic, in the 1920s and 30s the director Vilhelms Purvītis (1872–1945), himself one of the country's most famous artists, decided to focus on Latvian works. The first floor, therefore, traces the development of Latvian art from the mid-19th century to 1945, while the ground floor displays 18th- and 19th-century Balto-Germanic and Russian art. The latter collection also includes many icons from the 16th to 20th centuries.

There are, unsurprisingly, many paintings by Latvia's best-known artist Janis Rozentāls *(see p22)* and his works on display include *Leaving the Cemetery* (1895), and *Portrait of Malvīne Vīgnere-Grinberga* (1916). Other Latvian artists represented include Jēkabs Kazaks (1895–1920) and Romāns Suta (1896–1943), who were both members of the Rīga Artists' Group.

Museum of Jews in Latvia 🟤

Muzejs Ebreji Latvijā

Skolas iela 6. **Map** 2 D2. **Tel** 6728 3484. 🔲 noon–5pm Mon–Thu, Sun. 📷 donations.

Housed inside a Jewish cultural centre, this museum is based around the collections of Holocaust survivors Zalman Elelson and Marģers Vestermanis. It tells the story of the Jewish community in Latvia, which begins in the 16th century with the first records of Jews in the country and progresses to photographs of early 20th-century family life. Inevitably, though, the focus is on the horrific years of the Nazi occupation. The museum does not shy away from distressing images of the Holocaust, including footage of the massacre of Jews on Liepāja beach. A guidebook to Rīga's Jewish sites is available for those who want to see the places from which the once-vibrant community was erased.

View of the elaborate domed roof of the Orthodox Cathedral

Pauls Stradiņš Museum of the History of Medicine ③①

Paula Stradiņa medicīnas vēstures muzejs

Antonijas iela 1. **Map** 2 D2.
Tel 6722 2656. 🚌 2, 24. Trolleybus
1, 19. ⬜ 11am–5pm Tue–Wed, Fri–
Sat, 11am–7pm Thu. ⬛ last Fri of
the month. 🖼 🗹 www.mvm.lv

Opened in 1961, this museum is based around the collection of cancer specialist Dr Pauls Stradiņš. Its aim is to explore the history of medicine in relation to scientific development. Ancient uses of medicinal herbs, trepanning (the oldest known surgery, which involves making a hole in the patient's skull) and Soviet developments in space biology and medicine are covered. The oddest exhibit is a stuffed two-headed dog, which was the result of experimental grafting.

Janis Rozentāls and Rūdolfs Blaumanis Memorial Museum ③②

Jaņa Rozentāla un Rūdolfa Blaumaņa memoriālais muzejs

Alberta iela 12, flat 9. **Map** 2 D2.
Tel 6733 1641. ⬜ 11am–6pm
Wed–Sun. 🖼 🗹 www.rtmm.lv

A chance to see the interior of one of Rīga's Art Nouveau buildings, this museum is set in the apartment where Latvian artist Rozentāls *(see p22)* and his wife lived from 1904 to 1915. The elaborate painted staircase leading up to the fourth-floor museum is worth a look in itself. Some of Rozentāls's paintings are on display in the apartment and studio where he taught. The rooms are decorated in period style and include striking Art Nouveau motifs.

Writer Rūdolfs Blaumanis (1863–1908) rented a room next to the studio from 1906 to 1908, and it now contains copies of his manuscripts.

Art Nouveau Architecture

Owl motif, Elizabetes iela 10b

Rīga's collection of Art Nouveau buildings has been recognized by UNESCO as unparalleled anywhere in the world, with the majority concentrated in the Centre (Centrs). Many of the early examples – dating from the turn of the 20th century – are categorized as eclectic Art Nouveau, making use of asymmetry, symbolic ornamentation and details drawn from nature. Two other Art Nouveau styles found here are perpendicular, which placed emphasis on vertical composition, and National Romanticism, which incorporated folk motifs and the use of natural materials.

0 metres 100

0 yards 100

VIDUS IELA

RŪPNIECĪBAS IELA

VILANDES IELA

AUSEKĻA IELA

⑬ ⑫

ELIZABETES IELA

Elizabetes iela 13 ⑫
Less ornately decorated than others in the area, and judicious in its use of space, the façade of this building illustrates the principle of *amor vacui* (love of space).

Strēlnieku iela 4a ⑨
Symbols of victory adorn this eclectic Art Nouveau edifice, including maidens clutching wreaths and bald eagles. The building, designed by Mikhail Eisenstein, now houses a private school.

Strēlnieku iela 2 ⑪
An example of perpendicular Art Nouveau, the architectural design of this building is relatively restrained, with ornamental details integrated into the structure, including carvings of grain at the top.

Elizabetes iela 23 ⑩
This building has anthropomorphic carvings and a pediment with the words "*Labor vinvit omnia*" (Work conquers all), which commemorates architect Mārtiņš Nukša.

Alberta iela 13 ⑧
Numerous female figures on this building display a range of emotions.

Alberta iela 4 ④
Lions are uncommon in Art Nouveau, but in this eclectic building their wings indicate their traditional connection with the sun.

KEY LIST OF SITES

Alberta iela 2a ③
Alberta iela 4 ④
Alberta iela 8 ⑤
Alberta iela 11 ⑥
Alberta iela 12 ⑦
Alberta iela 13 ⑧
Elizabetes iela 10b ①
Elizabetes iela 13 ⑫
Elizabetes iela 23 ⑩
Elizabetes iela 33 ②
Strēlnieku iela 2 ⑪
Strēlnieku iela 4a ⑨
Vīlandes iela 2 ⑬

Elizabetes iela 33 ②
This early experiment with Art Nouveau by Mikhail Eisenstein, one of the foremost proponents of the eclectic style, draws upon Historicist architecture.

Alberta iela 11 ⑥
A fine example of National Romanticism, this building, constructed in natural stone, has bay windows resembling turrets.

ELSEWHERE IN THE CITY

Although the Centre includes some of Rīga's finest examples of Art Nouveau, there are many other buildings worth visiting elsewhere in the city. Examples in the Old Town include Kalēju iela 23, with its tree-shaped portal, and the city's oldest Art Nouveau building at Audēju iela 7. There are excellent examples of National Romanticism at Tērbatas iela 15/17 and A Čaka iela 26, and several impressive buildings on Brīvības iela and Hamburgas iela. *Art Nouveau in Rīga* (Silvija Grosa, published by Jumava) is available from tourist information offices and has good walks of the city.

Brightly coloured façade, Kalēju iela 23

Further Afield

Although primarily residential, Rīga's suburbs include numerous places of interest for visitors. The Moscow Suburb, southeast of the Old Town, has long been home to immigrant communities, including many Jews before World War II. In contrast, the exclusive Mežaparks to the north was built for wealthy Baltic Germans. Across the Daugava river is the Left Bank, where old wooden buildings and a variety of museums can be found.

SIGHTS AT A GLANCE

Aviation Museum ❺
Biķernieki Forest ❾
Botanical Gardens ❹
Central Market ❷
Dauderi ❻
Latvian Ethnographic
  Open-Air Museum ⓮
Left Bank ❸
Mežaparks ❼
Moscow Suburb ❶
Motor Museum ❿
Rīga's Cemeteries ❽
Rumbula Forest ⓬
Salaspils ⓫
Vecāķi ⓭

KEY

▨	Central Rīga
✈	Airport
⚓	Ferry port
▬	Motorway
▬	Major road
▬	Minor road

Moscow Suburb ❶

Maskavas forštate

🚌 18, 18a; trolleybus 15. 🚋 3, 7, 9.

The area to the east of the Central Market has long been known as the Moscow Suburb, for the road to Moscow ran through it and many of its inhabitants were impoverished Russians. They were joined by Jews – who had previously been banned from settling in the city – in the second half of the 19th century. When the German army arrived in 1941, they established a Jewish ghetto in the suburb, bounded by Kalna, Lauvas, Ebreju, Jersikas and Daugavpils streets.

Still home to many non-Latvians today, it is a quiet area with cobbled sidestreets and numerous wooden and religious buildings. The Museum of Jews in Latvia (see p151) has a booklet detailing a former Jewish site here, although there is little left to see. A memorial was, however, unveiled at the **Choral Synagogue Ruins** on 4 July 2007, exactly 66 years after German soldiers had filled the building with Jewish families and burned it to

the ground. The memorial includes the names of the 270 Latvians known to have rescued Jews during the war and the image of Žanis Lipke, who, with his wife Johanna, saved more than 50 lives.

Other religious buildings in the area include the small and atmospheric **Russian Orthodox Church of the Annunciation** (Tserkva blagoveshtenya) and the domed **Grebenshchikov Church** (Grebenščikova baznīca) where Old Believers (see p122) worship. The distinctive octagonal Lutheran **Jesus Church** (Jēzus baznīca), the largest wooden church in the city, is also worth visiting.

The **Academy of Sciences** (Latvijas zinātņu akadēmija) is a more controversial landmark. Rīga's first skyscraper, it was built between 1953 and 1957 in a pseudo-Baroque style which earned it the nickname "Stalin's Birthday Cake". The ornamentation includes both Latvian folk imagery and hammer-and-sickle motifs, and while parts of it are in need of repair it remains an impressive structure. The balcony on the 17th floor is open to the public.

🎵 **Choral Synagogue Ruins**
Corner of Gogoļa & Dzirnavu iela.

🏛 **Russian Orthodox Church of the Annunciation**
Gogoļa iela 9. **Tel** 6722 0566.

🏛 **Grebenshchikov Church**
Krasta iela 73. **Tel** 6714 4565.

🏛 **Jesus Church**
Elijas iela 18. **Tel** 6722 4123.
🕐 6pm Thu, 10am Sun.

🏛 **Academy of Sciences**
Akadēmijas laukums 1.
Tel 6722 5361. **Balcony** ◯ May–Sep: 9am–8pm daily. 🎫 📷 11am–3pm Mon–Fri.

Academy of Sciences, nicknamed "Stalin's Birthday Cake"

Well-maintained locomotives on show at the Railway Museum, Left Bank

Central Market ❷
Centrāltirgus

Centrāltirgus 1. ☐ 8am–5pm daily.
📷 www.centraltirgus.lv

Housed in five Zeppelin hangars, Rīga's Central Market is one of the most distinctive in Europe. The hangars, which the German Kaiser's army had abandoned in Kurzeme during World War I, were moved to their current site during the 1920s. The market building sells mostly fresh food, while the area around it is crammed with stalls selling other goods.

Left Bank ❸
Pārdaugava

🚌 8, 9. 🚊 1, 2, 4, 5, 8, 10.

Although most sites of interest lie on the right bank of the Daugava river, the Left Bank includes specialist museums and some of the country's best wooden architecture found in Āgenskalns district.

Just across the Stone Bridge (Akmens tilts) is the city's **Railway Museum** (Latvijas dzelzceļa muzejs), the highlight of which is the collection of rolling stock in the yard outside. Exhibits housed inside a renovated engine warehouse include photographs of Latvian stations, old tickets and posters, railway staff uniforms and signalling equipment.

Close by is **Victory Park** (Uzvaras parks), named after the Red Army's victory over the Nazis, which was depicted by the Soviet regime as a "liberation" of the city. The war memorial depicting soldiers being greeted by a welcoming figure of Victory is controversial and Latvian nationalists have twice tried to blow it up.

Also on this bank is the **Eduards Smiļģis Theatre Museum** (Eduarda Smiļģa teātra muzejs), which is set in the former home of engineer-turned-actor Smiļģis (1886–1966). The centrepiece is the small private theatre in which he rehearsed, and there are also exhibits relating to stage actors from the nation's first period of independence.

🏛 **Railway Museum**
2–4 Uzvaras bulvāris. **Tel** 6723 2849. ☐ 10am–5pm Tue–Sat.
📷 www.railwaymuseum.lv

🏛 **Eduards Smiļģis Theatre Museum**
Smiļģa iela 37/39. **Tel** 6761 1893.
☐ 11am–6pm Wed–Sun. 📷

Botanical Gardens ❹
Botāniskais dārzs

Kandavas iela 2. **Tel** 6745 0852.
🚊 5 to Konsula iela. ☐ May–Sep: 9am–7pm, Oct–Apr: 9am–4:30pm.
📷 🎧 in English, Russian or German by arrangement. ♿

Founded in 1922 as part of the University of Latvia, the Botanical Gardens have been in their current location since 1926. The site includes 5,400 species of plants, with approximately 400 of them native to Latvia; many of them are rare or endangered. In the centre of the garden is a complex of five greenhouses, including a palm house, a large collection of ferns, and a greenhouse devoted to cacti and other succulents. The gardens are particularly attractive from spring through to summer.

Greenhouse set amid the lush grounds of Rīga's Botanical Gardens

Aviation Museum ⑤
Aviācijas muzejs

Rīga Airport. *Tel* 2686 2707.
◻ Apr–Nov: 8am–7pm Tue–Sun,
Dec–Mar: 8am–5pm Tue–Sat. 🖼
🎫 🖥 🚻 www.aviamuseum.org

Located just beside Rīga's airport, this private open-air museum claims to have the largest collection of Soviet aircraft outside the Commonwealth of Independent States. The impressive array of aeroplanes and helicopters is the legacy of the Young Pilot's Club, an organization founded in 1956, which was granted used military aircraft for training purposes. After the break-up of the Soviet Union, funding dried up, but in 1998 the equipment was moved onto airport territory. In addition to the aircraft, both military and civilian, there is a small exhibition of uniforms and other equipment. Opening hours can be erratic so visitors should call ahead.

M16 airplane, on show at the Aviation Museum

Dauderi ⑥

Sarkandaugavas iela 30. *Tel* 6739 1780, 6739 2229. 🚌 5 or 9 to Aldaris. ◻ 11am–5pm Mon, Wed–Sun. 🖼 www.dauderi.lv

This late 19th-century Neo-Gothic mansion, 6 km (4 miles) from Rīga's city centre, was the summer residence of Latvian president Kārlis Ulmanis from 1937 to

Neo-Gothic façade of Dauderi mansion dating from the 19th century

1940, although he only ever stayed here for short periods of time. The Soviet army later occupied the building, and in turn the Germans placed anti-aircraft guns in the grounds. The mansion has also been used as a kindergarten and as tasting rooms for the Ministry of Food.

Now converted into a museum, the rooms are decorated and furnished in the style of the 1920s and 30s. There are displays dedicated to the life of Ulmanis, the nation's first period of independence and the cultural activities of Latvian exiles during World War II and the subsequent Soviet occupation. The collection is eclectic and includes photographs, medals, puppets and folk costumes. The mansion is surrounded by a park containing sculptures and artificial ruins.

Cherubs decorating the ceiling of Dauderi mansion

Mežaparks ⑦

🚆 11.

Previously called Kaiserwald (German for "Emperor's Forest") in reference to its use as a base by the invading Swedish king Gustav Adolphus in the 17th century, this part of northeast Rīga became Europe's first garden city in the early 20th century. Renamed Mežaparks, meaning "Forest Park", it was designed as a suburb for

wealthy Baltic Germans, most of whom later returned to Germany at the beginning of World War II. During the war a concentration camp was set up in the area by the Nazis, housing Jews brought from liquidated ghettos across Eastern Europe. The camp was closed when the Red Army invaded in 1944 and nothing remains of it today. During the Soviet period many of the suburb's buildings fell into disrepair. Since independence, however property prices in Mežaparks have risen, and the area is now predominantly Latvian with a significant number of foreign owners including several embassies. Some of the new residents are building homes which are grand, if not always tasteful, while others are restoring older buildings. The area is fascinating to walk around for its mix of contemporary, Modernist and Art Nouveau buildings, with Hamburgas Street a particular highlight of the area.

Another reason to visit the area is **Rīga Zoo** (Rīgas zooloģiskais dārzs), a well-maintained site which is popular with families. It is known for its bears and has an excellent tropical house, although the zoo's star attraction is a pair of rare Amur tigers. Rides in a horse-drawn carriage are available during the summer, and special events take place

For hotels and restaurants in this region see pp300–302 and pp330–32

throughout the year, including the weighing of the zoo's tortoises in June, and Wolves' Day in September.

Close to the zoo is the **Song Stadium** (Mežaparka estrāde), which was built to host the National Song Festival, held every five years. With the finale including more than 10,000 singers on stage at one time, the stadium is built on a very large scale.

🗗 Rīga Zoo
Meža prospekts 1. *Tel* 6751 8669.
◻ *May–Sep: 10am–6pm daily,*
Oct–Apr: 10am–4pm daily. 🖼 ☑

Rīga's Cemeteries ❽

Aizsaules iela. 🚌 4, 9. 🚋 11.
◻ daily.

Rīga's three most interesting cemeteries are located just south of Mežaparks along Aizsaules Street. The grandest is the **Brothers' Cemetery** (Brāļu kapi), built for Latvians who died defending their country during World War I and the War of Independence. The best-known sculptures are three patriotic works by Kārlis Zāle: *Two Brothers, The Wounded Horseman* and *Mother Latvia*. The memorial features the 19 coats of arms

of the Latvian administrative districts as well as soil from every *pagasts* (parish).

The **Rainis Cemetery** (Raiņa kapi) existed before the writer and atheist Janis Pliekšāns, known as Rainis, was buried there in 1929, but it was renamed in his honour. His memorial allegorically depicts a youthful Latvia awakening from its slumber. Rainis's wife Elza Rozenberga, who wrote under the name Aspazija, lies beside him, and many other Latvian artists and musicians have also been buried here.

The **Woodlands Cemetery** (Meža kapi) opened in 1913 and is the burial place for many political figures from Latvia's first period of independence. It was intended that the main alley would lead straight to the memorial to Latvia's first president Janis Čakste (1859–1927), but during the Soviet era smaller gravestones were put in the way. Janis Rozentāls *(see p22)* is also laid to rest at the site, while the most famous sculpture is the *Grieving Mother*, which marks the suspicious death of the nation's foreign minister in 1925.

Mother Latvia statue,
Brothers' Cemetery

Biķernieki Forest ❾
Biķernieku mežs

🚋 14 to Ķeguma. 🚌 24a.

This site was chosen by the Nazis for the execution and burial of around 40,000 Jews and other "undesirables" brought from Germany and several occupied European countries between 1941 and 1944. The memorial, unveiled in 2001, is the most moving of those in the Rīga area.

A path leads from Biķernieku Street under a white concrete arch, revealing a field of jagged stones huddled together into sections, each representing a city from which Jews were deported. The centrepiece is a concrete canopy under which a black stone stands, with an inscription reading "O earth, cover *not thou my blood, and let my cry have no place*" (Job 16:18). Further smaller memorials nearby mark mass graves. The site can be reached on foot from the Motor Museum *(see p158)* although the route is not signposted; the trolleybus stop is about 1 km (0.6 miles) from the memorial.

Evocative jagged stones of the Holocaust Memorial, Biķernieki Forest

Auto Union V16 racing car on display at the Motor Museum

Motor Museum ⑩
Rīgas motormuzejs

S Eizenšteina 6. **Tel** 6709 7170. 🚌 5, 21; minibus 207, 263. 🕙 10am–6pm daily. 🈂 📷 in English or Russian. 💻 **www**.motormuseum.lv

Row after row of gleaming cars, motorcycles and bicycles are housed in this modern hangar-like building. There are over 240 vehicles in total – both Latvian-made and foreign. The highlight is a series taken from the Kremlin's collection. The former Soviet president Leonid Brezhnev, in particular, was a motor enthusiast and one of the exhibits is a 1966 Rolls Royce Silver Shadow which he crashed in Moscow – a startled-looking waxwork sits behind the wheel. There is also a heavy armoured ZIS 115S limousine used by Stalin. Small panels give background information on the vehicles and tell the story of the automotive industry in Latvia. The museum shop sells model cars.

Salaspils ⑪

15 km (9 miles) SE of central Rīga. 🚉 Dārziņi.

Although its history stretches back to the 12th century, Salaspils is notorious as the location of a World War II German concentration camp. Its original inmates were prisoners of war, but they were joined by Jews brought from several occupied countries after Rīga's main ghetto was closed. The number of people who died in the camp is disputed as the Soviet regime subsequently exaggerated the figures as a propaganda tool, but it is thought that hundreds were either killed directly or died as a result of the camp's harsh conditions.

The entrance to the camp is marked by a long, sloping concrete block placed at an angle to the ground, intended to symbolize the boundary between life and death. The text on the block reads *"Behind this gate the earth groans"* – a line from a poem by Eižens Vēveris, who was a prisoner of the camp. Inside the block is a small exhibition which, like the rest of the site, has a rather neglected air. Beyond this, the shape of the camp has been indicated, and a metronome ticks inside a block of stone – its slow beat seemingly coming from deep inside the earth. Dominating the site is a series of huge sculptures erected in 1967, with titles such as *The Humiliated* and *The Unbroken.*

Sculpture at Salaspils

Rumbula Forest ⑫
Rumbulas mežs

11 km (7 miles) from central Rīga, along Maskavas iela. 🚉

At least 25,000 Jews were murdered in Rumbula Forest on 30 November and 8 December 1941. The victims, mostly women, children and the elderly from the Rīga ghetto, were shot and their bodies dumped in five mass graves. Just three people are known to have survived. The location of the killings came to light after the war, when two local people tried to sell jewellery found in the area.

Until the late 1980s, the memorials identified the dead as Soviet citizens, although members of the Jewish community illegally tended the site and were eventually allowed to add a modest stone bearing Hebrew text. The focal point of the memorial, constructed in 2002, is a large menorah (seven-branched candlestick), surrounded by broken stones, each of which is inscribed with the names of a murdered family.

Vecāķi ⑬

15 km (9 miles) NE of central Rīga. 🚉 🚌 24a.

This stretch of coast is a popular escape from the city during summer, although its beach is rarely crowded. At the eastern end there is an area reserved for naturists. It is worth walking west along the coast, towards the mouth of the Daugava river, for the remains of fortifications built to protect what was one of Europe's biggest ports. Many of the bunkers date from the time of the Napoleonic Wars, but were last used during World War I. The fortifications have not been well maintained, so exercise caution.

Vast sandy coastline of Vecāķi, northeast of central Rīga

For hotels and restaurants in this region see pp300–302 and pp330–32

Latvian Ethnographic Open-Air Museum ⑭
Latvijas etnogrāfiskais brīvdabas muzejs

Occupying 86 ha (213 acres) of woodland on the shores of Lake Jugla, this site includes over 118 homesteads, churches, windmills and other structures from across Latvia. Founded in 1924, the site is organized according to Latvia's administrative regions – Vidzeme, Kurzeme, Zemgale and Latgale – drawing attention to variations in building design and living arrangements in different parts of the country. With craftspeople working on-site during the summer, and many buildings containing every-day artifacts, the museum offers an insight into 19th-century rural life and takes at least two hours to explore.

VISITORS' CHECKLIST

Brīvības gatve 440.
Tel 6799 4510. 🚌 1, 19, 28.
🕐 May–Sep: 10am–5pm daily.
📷 ♿ 🚻 Sun. 🅿
www.muzejs.lv

Dutch Windmill
The windmill (1890) is from Latgale and has a movable "cap" including sails, a shaft and a gear wheel.

Vidzeme Spinning Wheel-Maker's Homestead

★ Kurzeme Peasants' Homestead
This wooden building with a reed-thatched roof is typical of 19th-century rural architecture in southwest Kurzeme.

Zemgale Peasants' Homestead includes a dwelling-house, a bath-house and a granary.

Handicrafts
Handicraft displays include traditional wicker-work.

Kurzeme Fishermen's Village

★ Usma Church
Most wooden churches were replaced by stone buildings in the 19th century, making this a rare example.

Entrance

STAR SIGHTS

- ★ Kurzeme Peasants' Homestead
- ★ Usma Church

Old Believers' House
Located in a Latgale village, the house exhibits a loom for weaving thread and a samo-var used to boil water for tea.

WESTERN LATVIA

*K*nown for its dense forests and fertile plains, lively cities and sleepy rural towns, Western Latvia enchants visitors with its contrasts. The Kurzeme region is quiet and sparsely populated, with the major exceptions of the busy ports of Ventspils and Liepāja. Running along the Lithuanian border, the largely agricultural Zemgale region is dotted with castles and manor houses recalling past glories.

Prior to the arrival of the German crusaders, the heavily forested western region now called Kurzeme was dominated by the Kurši tribe, while the Livs inhabited its northern coast. The fertile and well-drained terrain running along the Lielupe river in the south was home to the Zemgaļi; together with an eastern region formerly called Selonia, this area is now known as Zemgale. The Kurzeme tribes were defeated in 1267 and just over two decades later the same fate befell the Zemgaļi – the last of the Latvian tribes to surrender.

When the Livonian Order collapsed in the 16th century its last master, Gotthard Kettler, retained control of the entire region as a largely independent fiefdom of Poland. With Jelgava as its capital, the Duchy of Courland and Semigallia reached its zenith under Duke Jakob Kettler (r.1640–81). The Duchy was incorporated into the Russian Empire in 1795, and its fate was thereafter tied up with that of the rest of what is now Latvia.

Today, most of Kurzeme retains its rural character, although the cities of Liepāja and Ventspils are among the largest and most vibrant in the country. The few remaining speakers of the Liv language continue their fishing traditions on the northern coast. The area has several picturesque small towns, including Kuldiga and Talsi. The Zemgale countryside consists mainly of flat farmland, with exceptions such as forest parks in the hills around Tērvete. Jelgava's old town was devastated during World War II, although the duke's palace is still standing. The most popular tourist attraction, however, is Rundāle Palace with its Baroque exterior and restored Rococo interior.

Splendid yellow rape fields in full bloom, Kurzeme

◁ Entrance of the beautiful St Nicholas's Orthodox Cathedral in Karosta, Liepāja

Exploring Western Latvia

Kurzeme's long, unspoiled coastline has some tranquil villages as well as the cities of Ventspils and Liepāja. Ventspils is one of Latvia's busiest ports, while Liepāja has transformed from a derelict port to a vibrant cultural centre. Further inland, Kuldīga is among the country's most attractive small towns and makes a good base for exploration, while Pedvāle is popular for its outdoor sculptures. In Zemgale, Rundāle Palace, Bauska Castle and a Neo-Classical palace at Mežotne are highlights. Jelgava, a major transport hub, is a good base from which to explore the region.

SIGHTS AT A GLANCE

Towns and Cities
Bauska ④
Dobele ⑦
Dundaga ⑬
Jelgava ①
Ķemeri ⑨
Kuldīga ㉑
Liepāja pp180–81 ㉓
Sabile ⑱
Saldus ⑳
Talsi ⑰
Tukums ⑩
Ventspils pp176–7 ⑮

Sites and Buildings of Interest
Jaunpils Castle ⑧
Mežotne Palace ②
Pedvāle Open-Air Museum ⑲
Rundāle Palace pp168–9 ③
Skaistkalne Roman
  Catholic Church ⑤
VIRAC ⑯

Park and Reserve
Lake Pape Nature Reserve ㉔
Tērvete Nature Park ⑥

Area of Natural Beauty
Lake Engure ⑫

Beaches and Resorts
Jūrmala pp170–71 ⑪
Pāvilosta ㉒

Tour
The Livonian Coast p173 ⑭

SEE ALSO

• *Where to Stay* pp303–305

• *Where to Eat* pp333–5

THE LIVONIAN
COAST

Slītere Natio

P124

VIRAC ⑯ Miķeļtornis

Oviši

DUNDAGA

Ance

Virpe

Staldzene Ģibze

VENTSPILS ⑮ A10 Blāzma

Vārve

Stende

Ugāle

Lībciems

Ušava Spāre

Ziras P123 Lake Usmas

Venta

Zlēkas Abava Rend

P111

Ulava Ozoli P120

Ēdole P108

Rīezup

P119 KULDĪGA ㉑

Alsunga Krogsētas

Rīva Birži Vārme

P116

PĀVILOSTA ㉒ Snēpele P10

Saka P112

Tebra Aprīķi

Durbe Ķikuri

Ziemupe Aizpute Kazdanga

Cirava Kurzeme

Vērgale P115

Saraiķi Kalvene P107

P111 P112 Durbe A9 Venta P116

Grobiņa Tadaiķi Embūte Pamp

LIEPĀJA ㉓ Dubeņi P106

Lake Liepāja P106 Priekule Vaiņode

Pērkone P113 P114

Rude Gramzda

Klampjuciems Bārta Bārta

Jūrmalciems

Dunika

A11

LAKE PAPE ㉔ Lake
NATURE Pape Rucava
RESERVE

0 km   20

0 miles   20

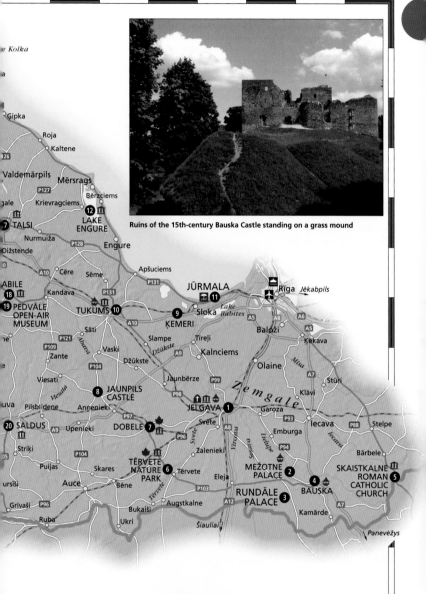

e Kolka

a

Gipka

Roja

Kaltene

P26

Valdemārpils   Mērsrags

P127

Bērzciems

gale   Krievragciems

Ⓜ

7 TALSI   **12** Ⓜ

LAKE

ENGURE

Nurmuiža

Dižstende   Engure

0   **A10**   Cēre   Sēme   Apšuciems

P128

Ruins of the 15th-century Bauska Castle standing on a grass mound

ABILE   Kandava   **P131**   JŪRMALA   🚉 Ⓜ Rīga   *Jēkabpils*

18 Ⓜ   **P131**   **11**   ✈

19 PEDVĀLE   TUKUMS **10**   Sloka   *Lake*   **A5**   **A8**   **A6**

OPEN-AIR   **9**   *Babītes*

MUSEUM   Sātī   ĶEMERI   Baloži   **A5**

ne   **P121**   Slampe   Tireļi   Ķekava

P109   Vaski   *Dzūkste*   Kalnciems

Zante   **P104**   Džūkste   Olaine   *Misa*

Viesati   Jaunbērze   **P99**   **A7**   Stūri

Viesatā   **P98**   *Z e m g a l e*   Klāvi

8 JAUNPILS   🏛 Ⓜ

uva   Pilsblidene   CASTLE   JELGAVA **1**   Garoza   Iecava   **P88** Stelpe

Anneņieki   Svēte   **P93**

20 SALDUS   **A9** Upenieki   DOBELE **7** 🍁   **A8**   Emburga   Bārbele

Ⓜ   **P96**   Zalenieki   *Svēte*   **P94**

Strīķi   **P104**   TĒRVETE   Ⓜ   *Svēte*   MEŽOTNE   SKAISTKALNE Ⓜ

Puijas   Skares   NATURE   Tērvete   PALACE **2**   **4** 🍁   ROMAN

ursīši   Auce   Bēne   PARK **6**   Eleja   BAUSKA   **5** CATHOLIC

Tērvete   RUNDĀLE **3**   CHURCH

Grīvaši   **P96**   Bukaiši   Augstkalne   **A12**   PALACE   Kamārde   **A7**

Ruba   Ukri   *Šiauliai*

Panevėžys

GETTING AROUND

To explore Western Latvia's remote towns and villages, it is generally best to travel by car. However, it is also possible to visit the region's many other attractions by using public transport. While buses are a good option for reaching Bauska and most of Kurzeme's sights, taking a train is preferable for trips to Jelgava and Tukums. However, as there are no direct rail links between Rīga and Rundāle, travellers must change at Bauska. The port towns of Ventspils and Liepāja have good ferry connections with Rīga as well as with other European cities. There are also airports at Liepāja and Ventspils.

Jelgava Palace, built on an island in the Lielupe river, Jelgava

Jelgava **❶**

Road Map C4. 🏘 *66,000.*
🚆 *from Rīga.* 🚌 *from Rīga.* 🛈
Pasta iela 37, 6302 2751. 🎭
International Ice Sculpture Festival
(Feb). **www**.jelgava.lv

Between 1578 and 1795,
Jelgava was the capital of the
Duchy of Courland. Much of
the town was damaged during
the two World Wars. The most
prominent remnant of the
duchy period is the **Jelgava
Palace** (Jelgavas pils), the winter residence of Ernst Johann
Biron *(see p169)*. Built in the
18th century by Francesco
B Rastrelli, the building today
houses the Latvian University
of Agriculture. None of the
original interiors remain
intact, but a small museum
houses archive photographs
of the palace's pre-war state.
Museum staff also provide
access to the burial vault
of the Dukes of Courland.

The old town offers a
handful of interesting sights.
The impressively restored
**Orthodox Cathedral of
St Simeon and St Anna** (Sv
Sīmaņa un Annas pareizticīgo
katedrāle) was designed by
Rastrelli for Biron's patron,
Anna Ivanovna. A Baroque
building houses the **History
and Art Museum** (Vēstures un
mākslas muzejs), which documents local history, while the
quirky little **Latvian Railway
Museum** (Latvijas dzelzceļu
muzejs) attracts rail enthusiasts.

Environs
The small **Nikolai Cemetery**,
4 km (2 miles) southeast of
Jelgava, contains the graves of
36 British soldiers and sailors

who died in 1917 in Latvia
as German prisoners of war
during World War I.

🏛 **Jelgava Palace**
Lielā iela 2. **Tel** *6300 5617.*
⏰ *May–Sep: 9am–4pm daily, Oct–*
Apr: 9am–4pm Mon–Fri. 🎟 🎫

🛕 **Orthodox Cathedral of
St Simeon and St Anna**
Raiņa iela 5. **Tel** *6302 0207.*

🏛 **History and Art Museum**
Akadēmijas iela 10. **Tel** *6303 5830.*
⏰ *10am–5pm Wed–Sat.* 🎟

🏛 **Latvian Railway Museum**
Stacijas iela 3. **Tel** *6309 6494.*
⏰ *10am–3pm Wed–Sat.* 🎟

Mežotne Palace **❷**

Road Map D4. **Tel** *6396 0711.*
⏰ *9am–5pm daily.* 🎟
www.mezotnespils.lv

This restored Neo-Classical
structure was built in 1802 for
Charlotte von Lieven, govern-
ess to the grandchildren of the
Russian Tsarina Catherine II.

Pastel-coloured exterior of the
Neo-Classical Mežotne Palace

The original design by Italian
architect Giacomo Quarenghi
was developed by local architect J G Berlitz. The Lieven
family lost the manor in 1920
during the agrarian reforms,
and it was partly destroyed
during World War II. Today,
the palace is used to host
functions and as a hotel *(see
p304)*, although it is also open
to visitors. The highlight is the
Dome Hall, with artificial
marble pillars and walls, and a
dome painted to give the
illusion of three-dimensional
decoration. The grounds are
in the style of an English park,
and in summer boats take
visitors across the Lielupe
river. On the other side of the
river is a castle mound, site of
one of the largest Semigallian
castles and scene of their final
battle against the German
crusaders (1290).

Rundāle Palace **❸**

See pp168–9.

Bauska **❹**

Road Map D4. 🏘 *11,000.* 🚌 *from*
Rīga. 🛈 *Rātslaukums 1, 6392 3797.*
🎭 *Early Music Festival (Jul).*
www.tourism.bauska.lv

A small country town, Bauska
is known mainly for its 15th-
century **Bauska Castle**
(Bauskas pils), which was
built at the confluence of the
Mēmele and Mūsa rivers to
help control the trade route
between Rīga and Lithuania.
Later, it became the property
of the Duchy of Courland and
Semigallia and a fortified

residence was added for the duke. In recent years, restoration work has reversed inauthentic Soviet alterations, including the renewal of the original sgraffito decoration on the towers. It is possible to climb one of the towers for a small fee.

Besides a number of fine wooden buildings, the town also boasts a 16th-century Lutheran church and the riverside **Bauskas Alus** brewery.

♣ **Bauska Castle**
Tel 6392 3793. ⬤ May–Oct: 9am–7pm daily. ✉ ▢

Bauskas Alus
Tel 6396 0013. ⬤ by appointment.
✉ www.bauskasalus.lv

Embellished altarpiece, Skaistkalne Roman Catholic Church

Skaistkalne Roman Catholic Church ❺
Skaistkalnes Romas katoļu baznīca

Road Map D4. Slimnīcas iela 2, Skaistkalne. **Tel** 6393 3154. ✉

Built for the Jesuits in 1692 and now maintained and administered by monks of the Paulian Order, Skaistkalne Church is Latvia's most popular place of pilgrimage after Aglona *(see p195)*. Raised on a mound, the white building has a red roof and a rounded apse. The Baroque interior features artificial marble palisades and an ornate altarpiece. Plump pastel-painted cherubs decorate the pulpit and organ, and

two sets of paintings represent the Stations of the Cross. Call ahead, as the church is often locked.

Tērvete Nature Park ❻
Tērvetes dabas parks

Road Map C4. 🚌 🚹 Pagasta ēka, 6376 3472. ✉ ♿ partial.
www.tervetesnov.lv

This popular nature park was developed in the forest around Tērvete, which was famous as the home of Sprīdītis, a Tom Thumb-like character in the beloved fairy-tale written by Anna Brigadere (1861–1933). Her summer house has been preserved as the **Anna Brigadere Museum**.

The theme of the fairytale is evident throughout the park, with its Dwarf Forest and Fairytale Forest dotted with carved wooden creatures. Summertime attractions include the park's own witch, while there are also quieter paths through the Old Pine Forest. Nearby are a Livonian Order castle mound with replica fort and the **Tērvete History Museum**, which displays a collection of farm utensils and textiles.

🏛 **Anna Brigadere Museum**
Sprīdīši. **Tel** 2653 2691. ⬤ May–Oct: 10am–5pm Wed–Sun. ✉

🏛 **Tērvete History Museum**
Jerumi. **Tel** 2989 6804. ⬤ May–Sep: 10am–5pm Tue–Sun. ✉

Dobele ❼

Road Map C4. 🏃 11,100. 🚏
🚌 🚹 Brīvības iela 15, 6370 7255.
www.zemgaletourism.lv

Situated on the banks of the Bērze river, Dobele is visited mainly for its ruined Livonian Order castle, built in 1335. Destroyed several times during the Polish-Swedish Wars (1600–29), the castle began to be restored only in 2002. The small **Dobele History Museum** recounts the town's history and mounts temporary exhibitions. On the edge of town, the **Dobele Horticultural Plant Breeding Experimental Station** houses a museum dedicated to noted horticulturalist Pēteris Upītis (1896–1976). One of the largest lilac collections in the world can also be found here. Classical music concerts are held in the gardens every spring while the flowers are in bloom.

Wooden figure, Tērvete Nature Park

Environs
A drive of 13 km (8 miles) down a gravel road west of town, the **Pokaiņi Forest** is an area of spiritual significance due to its numerous unusual rock formations.

🏛 **Dobele History Museum**
Brīvības 7. **Tel** 6372 1309. ⬤ noon–6pm Wed, 11am–4pm Thu–Sat. ✉

♣ **Dobele Horticultural Plant Breeding Experimental Station**
Graudu iela 1. **Tel** 6372 2294.
⬤ 9am–5pm Mon–Fri.

Ruins of the 14th-century Livonian Order castle in Dobele

Rundāle Palace ❸

Designed by Francesco Bartolomeo Rastrelli (1700–71), Rundāle is one of the finest palaces in the Baltic region. Work began in 1736 on a Baroque summer residence for Ernst Johann Biron, but was left unfinished when he was exiled. Following Biron's return, the interiors were renovated in the Rococo style. Biron's son removed most of the embellishments when he left in 1795, after Courland was annexed by Russia. The structure suffered damage during the 20th century, and the rooms have served as government offices, an elementary school and a granary. Restoration began in 1972 and is still in progress.

Detail, Rose Room
Rococo touches, such as fake marble, silver detailing and floral motifs, adorn the room.

Marble Hall was used as a school gym in the 20th century.

Duke's Reception Room

★ Duke's Bedroom
This room was the focal point of Biron's private apartments, which occupied the central block of the palace.

Rose Room

The Corner Room
The Russian Neo-Classical style reflects the taste of Count Zubov, who inhabited the palace after Courland was absorbed into the Russian Empire.

Grand Gallery was where the guests would dine before dancing in the White Hall. Wall paintings were uncovered during restoration.

STAR FEATURES

★ Duke's Bedroom

★ Gold Hall

★ White Hall

★ Gold Hall
The initials of the palace's owner, "EJ", can be seen amid the ornate gilt scrolls.

Formal French-style gardens, re-created from the original plans

VISITORS' CHECKLIST

Road Map D4. from Bauska.
Tel 6396 2197. May, Sept–
Oct: 10am–6pm daily; June–Aug:
10am–7pm daily; Nov–Apr
10am–5pm daily.
www.rundale.net **Park**
May–Oct: 10am–7pm daily,
Nov–Apr: 10am–5pm daily.

Old photos of Jelgava Palace are one of the many exhibits displayed in the palace complex.

Duchess's Boudoir
The duchess could rest and receive visitors during the day in the splendidly decorated boudoir, which has now been restored. The duchess and other family members lived in the western wing.

The exhibition of period clothes in Room 107 mostly features items belonging to the duke's family.

The courtyard has gateposts topped by the duke's emblem – a heraldic lion.

The Oval Porcelain Cabinet, made by Johann Michael Graff, was designed to exhibit exquisite artifacts.

★ **White Hall**
This ballroom boasts a parquet floor and lavish stucco work by German sculptor Johann Michael Graff. The restrained colour scheme gives the room its name.

ERNST JOHANN BIRON

The son of a minor landlord, Ernst Johann Biron was asked to leave the academy in Königsberg (present-day Kaliningrad) for bad behaviour. Failing to establish himself in the Russian court, he returned to Jelgava and became close to the widowed Duchess of Courland, Anna Ivanovna. In 1730, Anna became empress of Russia, and three years later Biron was appointed Duke of Courland. After his patron died in 1740, the unpopular Biron was sent into exile, returning only in 1763. A year later, Catherine II made him duke once more but he abdicated in 1769 in favour of his son Peter.

Duke of Courland, Ernst
Johann Biron (1690–1772)

Jaunpils Castle **8**
Jaunpils pils

Road Map C4. **Tel** 6310 7082. ☐
10am–6pm Mon–Fri. 🎟 📷 during
summer. 🖥 www.jaunpilspils.lv

Built by the Livonian Order in
1301, with its distinctive round
tower added in the 15th
century, Jaunpils Castle was
owned by the German von
der Recke family from 1561 to
1922. On 24 December 1905,
the castle was burnt down by
revolutionaries *(see p135)*,
and the current structure is
almost entirely the result of
subsequent reconstruction.
The small museum inside
includes replicas of weapons
and armour, as well as some
interesting photographs of the
castle before 1905. Across the
courtyard from the museum is
a pub, and the castle also has
four atmospheric hotel rooms
(see p303). Guided tours
also take in Jaunpils town's
Evangelical Lutheran Church
and the 200-year-old watermill.

One of a dozen bridges across the Vēršupīte river, Ķemeri Park

Ķemeri **9**

Road Map C3. 🚌 from Rīga.
🏠 Meža Māja, 6714 6819. 🛶 canoe
trips & wildlife tours arranged at
visitors' centre. www.kemeri.gov.lv

A popular resort in the early
20th century, Ķemeri is considered part of Jūrmala, although
it has not seen the same scale
of rejuvenation experienced
further east. The town's main

attraction, **Ķemeri Park**
encompasses an Orthodox
church, pavilions and bridges
across the Vēršupīte river.

Ķemeri is also the entry
point to **Ķemeri National Park**,
which has rivers, lakes, meadows, inland dunes, sulphur
springs and forests. A 3-km
(2-mile) wooden pathway
traverses the park's 6,000-ha
(14,830-acre) bog, which
attracts bird-watchers.

Jūrmala **⑪**

Literally meaning "seaside" in Latvian, Jūrmala is an
attractive stretch of beaches, pine forests and small
towns alongside the Gulf of Rīga. During the 19th
century, the area became famous for its medicinal
mud and sulphur-rich spring water. Jūrmala soon
grew into a popular resort and it became fashionable
to own a summerhouse here. The wooden houses
as well as older sanitaria still dot the area, standing
alongside modern guest houses and upmarket spas.

Jomas Street in Majori *is a
pedestrianized strip that forms
the heart of Jūrmala. It is lined
with a large number of outdoor
cafés, restaurants and hotels, as
well as a variety of shops.*

JŪRMALA

GULF OF RĪGA

Area of the map illustrated

To Jaunķemeri (4 km)

Lielupe
Dubulti
Bulduri
Majori

Sloka
Vaivari
Jaundubulti

To Ķemeri (6 km)

GULF RĪGA

**Marienbāde
Sanitarium** was
built in 1870.

Majori
Beach

Aspazija House
*is the last home
of one of Latvia's
most famous
poets, Elza
Rozenberga
(1865–1943),
nicknamed
"Aspazija".
The house is
now a branch
of the Jūrmala
Town Museum.*

Z MEIEROVICA PROSPEKTS

Lielupe

DUBULTI

DUBULTU PROSPEKTS

SLOKAS IELA

JŪRAS IEL

JOMAS

LIE

Hotel Majori, built in
1925 in Historicist style,
stands at the western
end of Jomas Street.

Tukums ⓾

Road Map C3. ⚄ *19,000.* ⚄ *from Riga.* ⚄ ⚄ *Pils iela 3, 6312 4451.* ⚄ *Tue, Thu, Sat.* ⚄ *Festival of Female Choirs and Men's Choruses (Jun).* **www**.tukums.lv/turisms

Meaning the "Land of the End" in Livonian, Tukums stands at the point where the Zemgale plains meet the Kurzeme uplands. Little remains of the town's history as an ancient Liv settlement, while the only remnant of the Livonian Order castle is the Castle Tower (Pils tornis). Restored in 1767 to serve as a granary and jail, it now houses the **Local History Museum**, which displays dioramas and temporary exhibitions.

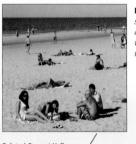

Monument to freedom fighters, Tukums

The oldest buildings in the old town date from the late 19th and early 20th centuries. The main highlight, **Tukums Art Museum**, houses Latvian art from the 1920s and 30s. It is considered to be Latvia's foremost gallery outside Rīga.

Environs

Durbes Pils, a manor house on the eastern edge of Tukums, is an 1820s Neo-Classical building with a 17th-century core. The restored rooms include displays on local history, but the foremost exhibition is the ethnological collection in the former servants' quarters.

About 5 km (3 miles) east of Tukums is the 15th-century Šlokenbeka Manor. It is home to the **Latvian Road Museum**. Many exhibits are of specialist interest but the collections of horse-drawn carriages and road building machines have a more general appeal.

Jaunmoku Pils (*see p303*), 5 km (3 miles) west of Tukums, is a distinctive red-brick manor house with step gables and chimneys. Many of the rooms of this former hunting lodge are decorated in an ornate style. A highlight is a large tiled stove bearing images of Rīga and Jūrmala. The forest museum upstairs includes oddities such as a collection of silver cigarette holders. It is possible to climb the tower for stunning views of the surrounding countryside.

🏛 **Local History Museum**
Brīvības laukums 19a. **Tel** 6312 4348. ⬜ *10am–5pm Tue–Sat, 10am–6pm Sun.* ⚄

🏛 **Tukums Art Museum**
Harmonijas 7. **Tel** 6318 2392. ⬜ *10am–5pm Tue–Sat, 11am–4pm Sun.* ⚄

♣ **Durbes pils**
Mazā parka 7. **Tel** 6312 2633. ⬜ *10am–5pm Tue–Sat, 11am–4pm Sun.* ⚄ ⚄ ⚄

🏛 **Latvian Road Museum**
Milzkalne. **Tel** 6318 2354. ⬜ *8am–noon & 1–5pm Mon–Fri, Sat & Sun by appointment.* ⚄ ⚄

Dzintari Beach, *a popular stretch of sand in summer, draws hordes of tourists. It is dotted with beer tents and volleyball nets during this time.*

0 km   1

0 miles   1

VISITORS' CHECKLIST

Road Map C3. ⚄ *from Rīga.* ⚄ *Jomas iela 42/2, Majori, 6776 4276.* **Aspazija House** Meierovica prosp 20, Dubulti. **Tel** *6776 9445.* **Hotel Majori** Jomas iela 29, Majori. **Tel** *6776 1380.* **Dzintari Concert Hall** Turaidas iela 1. **Tel** *6776 2086.* **Museum of Old Machinery** Turaidas iela 11, Dzintari. **Tel** *2926 3329.* **Pegasa Pils** Jūras iela 60, Dzintari. **Tel** *2923 6425.*

Dzintari Concert Hall hosts open-air summer concerts.

Bulduri Beach 🏖

Dzintari Beach 🏖

BULDURU PROSPEKTS

MEŽA PROSPEKTS

DZINTARI

ZINTARU PROSPEKTS

EDINBURGAS PROSPEKTS

BULDURI

BRĪVĪBAS PROSPEKTS

LIENES IELA

RĪGAS IELA

Pegasa Pils is an elegant Art Nouveau restaurant (*see p333*).

Key to Symbols *see back flap*

Museum of Old Machinery mostly displays antique bicycles and cars.

Coastal towns, *which make up Jūrmala, are situated among picturesque pine forests. Strict building regulations preserve the 19th-century wooden summerhouses and restrict construction in the area.*

Reed-filled part of Lake Engure, with boats moored along the shore

Lake Engure @
Engures ezers

Road Map C3. 🛥 for boating: *Abragciems Kempings, 4 km (2 miles) N of Engure, 6316 1668; for fishing permits: Ornithological Centre, Bērzciems, 6947 4420 (open by appointment only).* **www**.eedp.lv

Latvia's third-largest lake, Engure is a significant bird habitat. Around 160 species have been spotted in the wetlands, including cranes and grey herons. A road leads around the western edge of the lake between the towns Mērsrags and Engure, while the **Ornithological Centre** on the eastern side of the lake can be reached by turning inland just north of Bērzciems. One bird-watching tower is situated close to the centre, while another is directly opposite it across the lake. A 3.5-km (2-mile) orchid trail starts

close to the Ornithological Centre, running through dry pine forest and a chalky grass swamp in which 22 species of orchid can be found.

Many parts of the lake are choked with reeds as a result of pollution by chemical fertilizers, and a number of fish species have disappeared, although fishing permits can still be obtained at the centre.

Coat of arms at the castle, Dundaga

Environs
The small fishing port of **Roja**, 26 km (16 miles) northwest of Mērsrags, offers more accommodation options than most places on the coastal route from Rīga to Ventspils. Exhibits in the town's **Sea-Fishing Museum** (Rojas jūras zvejniecības muzejs) look at the naval schools of Krišjānis

Valdemārs *(see p191)*, sailing ships in the late 19th and early 20th centuries, fish canning and the local Banga fishermen's collective.

🏛 **Sea-Fishing Museum**
Selgas iela 33. **Tel** 6326 9594.
May–Oct: 10am–6pm Wed–Sat, 10am–4pm Sun; Nov–Apr: 10am–5pm Tue–Sat.

Dundaga ⑬

Road Map C3. 🚶 *4,000.*
ℹ *Pils iela 14, 6323 7858.*

First mentioned in historical sources in 1245, Dundaga has a restored 13th-century Livonian Order castle which today houses the tourist office. The seven coats of arms inscribed on the castle belong to its owners. The Lutheran church nearby has an altarpiece painted by Janis Rozentāls (1866–1916). The church's 19th-century wooden organ case is unusual, as it is the work of Latvian craftsmen who generally produced functional items while foreign masters made decorative pieces.

Dundaga features a large, bizarre sculpture of a crocodile at the corner of Talsu and Dinsberga streets, honouring local crocodile hunter Arvīds Blūmentāls (1925–2006). He emigrated to Australia during World War II and is said to be the inspiration for the film *Crocodile Dundee* (1986).

THE COAST-DWELLING LIVS
A Finnic people related to the Estonians, the Livs settled along the Gulf of Rīga around 5,000 years ago, long before the arrival of the Latvian tribes. They referred to themselves as *raandalist* (coast-dwellers) and *kalāmīed* (fishermen), and the sea has always been central to their way of life.

German crusaders devastated Livonian culture in the 13th century and the Livs were gradually assimilated into the other Baltic tribes. During the 19th and 20th centuries, children were educated in German and later Russian rather than in Livonian. Many of the remaining Livs were forced to leave the region when the Soviets declared the coast a military zone. Since 1991 there have been concerted efforts to preserve and strengthen Liv culture. Today, not more than 200 people are officially registered as Livs.

Monument to Livonian Culture in Mazirbe

Large concrete crocodile sculpture on a bed of stones in Dundaga

The Livonian Coast ⑭

A narrow strip of land running along the edge of the Gulf of Rīga and the Baltic Sea and dominated by sand dunes and pine forests, the Livonian Coast is separated from the rest of Kurzeme by the Zilie kalni (Blue Hills). It is home to one of Europe's smallest ethnic groups, the Livs. The coastal route also provides access to some of Latvia's most beautiful scenery. It is only a short walk between fishing villages and attractively secluded beaches.

TIPS FOR DRIVERS

Tour length: 60 km (37 miles).
Stopping-off points: There are small guest houses and campsites in several of the coastal villages. Booking ahead is advisable.
Road conditions: Conditions can be difficult once off the main roads, particularly in poor weather.

Cape Kolka ②
The point at which the Baltic Sea meets the Gulf of Rīga is a popular place for Latvian holidaymakers.

Vaide ③
The Museum of Horns is the main highlight of Vaide. It showcases the personal collection of a forest warden, formed over decades.

Pūrciems White Dune ①
A walkway leads across the dune, while signboards indicate a Neolithic settlement.

Košrags ④
The typical coastal village of Košrags is dotted with 18th-century wooden buildings, including a small B&B.

Mazirbe ⑤
Located in Mazirbe village, the Folk House of the Livs is a museum with a collection of old photographs depicting rope-making, leather-softening and other daily activities of the Livs.

Slītere Lighthouse ⑥
Indicating the start of the Slītere nature trail, the lighthouse can be climbed for a view of Slītere National Park's forests. Inside, there is a display focusing on the lighthouses along Latvia's coastline.

KEY

🏖	Beach
▬	Tour route
═	Other road

0 km 7
0 miles 7

Map labels: Cape Kolka ②, Uši, Vaide ③, 131, Melnsils, Pitrags 124, Slītere National Park, Gipka, Žocene ①, Mazirbe ⑤, Vidale, Pilsupe, Sīkrags, Slītere, Muņi, Jaunciems, Neveja 125, Kalķi

Picturesque view of the village of Sabile, known as the Switzerland of Latvia ▷

Ventspils ⑮

Founded in 1290, Ventspils has long been a trading centre and was a member of the Hanseatic League. In the 18th century, war and plague ravaged the city, but it later thrived as part of the Russian Empire.

A hub for Russian oil tankers till recently, Ventspils has gained an air of affluence since independence. In order to limit its reliance on Russia, the city has been spruced up to boost tourism. Enlivened by parks, flower beds and fountains, Ventspils has a bustling modern centre and a well-restored old town. The historic core is best explored on foot and a walk along Ostas Street gives a chance to see bovine sculptures left after the 2002 Cow Parade.

and touch screens. As a Livonian Order stronghold, it was a self-contained world complete with a dormitory, refectory, chapel and meeting hall. Later, the chapel was used as a Lutheran church, while the building served as a prison at various times from 1824 to 1959. It became the barracks for the German army during World War I and for Soviet border guards from 1962 to 1983. The rooms in which the exhibits are laid out bear fragments of wall paintings from the 15th to 17th centuries, and there are also displays of traditional costumes and jewellery.

The pleasant restaurant on the premises, Melnais Sivēns (see p335), is one of the best places to eat in the city. During summer, it is possible to try archery and, by arrangement, fire a small cannon in front of the castle.

⛪ Russian Orthodox Church of St Nicholas

Plosta iela 10. **Tel** 6362 1616.
The onion-domed Russian Orthodox Church of St Nicholas (Sv Nikolaja pareizticīgo baznīca) was consecrated in the early 20th century. Although the Neo-Byzantine exterior needs to be restored, the interior has an excellent collection of icons.

Exterior of the 13th-century Livonian Order castle, Ventspils Castle

🏛 Ventspils Castle

Jāṇa iela 17. **Tel** 6362 2031.
⬜ May–Oct: 9am–6pm daily, Nov–Apr: 10am–5pm Tue–Sun. 🅿 ✉
♿ 📷 🅗 www.ventspilsmuzejs.lv
On the bank of the Venta river, this Livonian Order castle is one of the finest in Latvia. Although it began life as a late 13th-century stone tower, its

current form largely dates from the 14th century. Devastated by the Swedish army in 1659, the castle has been restored many times since. Parts of the red-brick gallery in the inner courtyard were built as recently as the 1870s.

The museum inside the castle recounts its history through engaging displays

⛪ Lutheran Church of St Nicholas

Tirgus 2. **Tel** 6362 2750.
With a portico at the front and a tower with an observation platform, this attractive yellow-and-white church (Sv Nikolaja Luterāļu baznīca) stands on the old market square. Dating from 1835, it was built according to the wishes of Tsar Nicholas I.

🏛 Seaside Open-Air Museum

Riņķa 2. **Tel** 6362 4467. ◻ May–Oct: 10am–6pm daily, Nov–Apr: 11am–5pm Wed–Sun. 📷 ♿ ⌀ www.ventspilsmuzejs.lv **Narrow-Gauge Railway** May–Oct: Sat–Sun.
The Seaside Open-Air Museum (Piejūras brīvdabas muzejs) was opened in 1954 to preserve the heritage of Latvia's fishing villages, which began to disappear as the Soviet authorities regarded the shores as areas of military importance. Buildings were moved from their original location and reassembled here and the site now includes homesteads, smokehouses, curing cabins, net sheds and even a large windmill.

Traditional crafts are displayed around the site in summer. There are also large collections of fishing

---

boats and anchors, and a **Narrow-Gauge Railway**. Until the 1960s, the steam engine linked seaside villages, but now it takes a 1.4-km (0.8-mile) trip through Seaside Park.

Water slides and swimming pools at the Aqua Park

Aqua Park

Medņu iela 19. **Tel** 6366 5853. ◻ May–Sep: 10am–10pm daily. 📷 🅿
With three pools, several slides, Jacuzzis and saunas as well as a variety of water playgrounds, the Aqua Park (Akvaparks) is popular with families. Swimming gear can be rented on site.

🏖 Ventspils Beach

2 km (1 mile) S of town. ♿
The residents of Ventspils are proud of their beach, particularly the 1.2-km (0.7-mile) stretch that received an EU Blue Flag in 1999 for meeting international standards. This was a remarkable achievement, since the coast had been contaminated by industrial pollution during the Soviet era. Parts of the beach have been set aside for windsurfers, nudists and smokers, and there are playgrounds for children. At the northern end of the beach is a breakwater, with a promenade leading to a lighthouse at the end.

VIRAC (Ventspils International Radio Astronomy Centre) ⑯

Ventspils Starptautiskais Radioastronomijas Centrs

Road Map B3. **Tel** 2923 0818. ◻ 10am–5pm daily. 📷 📹 call in advance. ⌀ www.virac.venta.lv

Situated in a former Russian army town, the 1970s military installation is believed to have spied on communications between Europe and the USA for at least a decade. When they left in 1994, the Russians took the smallest dish, leaving the two heavier ones which are 16 m (52 ft) and 32 m (105 ft) in diameter. The bigger one is the largest radio telescope in Northern Europe and the world's eighth largest.

A combination of size and precision engineering makes the larger dish especially valuable to scientists. Guided tours of it begin with the ground-floor laboratory. Visitors can climb up to a viewing platform and then step into one of the suspended laboratory pods. The structure was built by a naval factory in the Ukraine, and the interiors are reminiscent of a ship.

The unmarked road to VIRAC, leading past eerily empty residential buildings, is just east of an electrical substation on the P124. Book in advance for a guided tour.

Radio telescope at VIRAC, the largest in Northern Europe

Talsi ⑰

Road Map C3. 🏛 12,500. 🚌 ℹ
19–21 Lielā, 6322 4165. 🎭 Mara's
Craft Market Fair (Aug). www.talsi.lv

The administrative centre of
northern Kurzeme and a
transport hub for the region,
Talsi is an attractive town
spread out around two lakes
and across nine hills. It was
originally a Liv settlement,
captured by the Kurši during
the 10th century, and then by
the Livonian Order in 1263. A
mound remains where the
Order's castle stood on
Watermill Hill (Dzirnavkalns).

Talsi's oldest surviving
building is the 18th-century
Lutheran church, atop Church
Hill (Baznīckalns). The most
noted pastor of the church
was Karl Amenda (1771–1836),
a close friend of composers
Beethoven and Mozart.
Nearby, the cobblestoned
Kalēju and Ūdens streets are
notable for water troughs.

The **Talsi Regional Museum**
(Talsu novada muzejs),
housed in a late 19th-century
Neo-Classical residence, features an interesting exhibition
on the Livs. The building's
original painted ceiling can
be seen in one of the rooms,
where several layers of white-
wash have been removed.

Environs
Laumas Nature Park, 20 km
(12 miles) north, has several
walking and cycle paths.
Guided tours are available,
including one focusing on
bees. It also has a campsite.

🏛 **Talsi Regional Museum**
K Milenbaha 19. **Tel** 6323 2213.
⏰ 10am–5pm Tue–Sun. 🎟 📷

Vīna Kalns, Sabile's renowned vineyard

Sabile ⑱

Road Map C3. 🏛 3,500. 🚌
ℹ Pilskalna iela 6, 6325 2344.
🎭 Wine Festival (Jul). www.sabile.lv

A small town on the banks of
the Abava river, Sabile was
first mentioned in 1253, by
which time it had long been
inhabited by the Kurši tribe.
Only a mound remains of the
tribe's castle, although the
stones were used to repair the
town's 17th-century Lutheran
church. Sabile's former
synagogue was
built in 1890
and restored in
2003 as the
**Centre of
Contemporary Art
and Cultural
Heritage**.

According to the
Guinness World
Records, Sabile's
wine hill, **Vīna Kalns**, is the
northernmost vineyard in the
world. The strong and sour
wine was popular in the
court of the Kurzeme Duchy

**Sculpture, Pedvāle
Open-Air Museum**

(1561–1795), but vini-
culture may have begun long
before. In the 1930s, the
vineyard was used to experiment with grape varieties, but
this ceased during the Soviet
period. Work began again in
1989, and there are now 650
vines of 15 varie-
ties. Wine-tasting is possible
at the annual wine festival.

Environs
Mara's Caves (Māras kambari),
named after an ancient
Latvian goddess, are located
12 km (7 miles) southwest of
Sabile. In the Middle Ages,
these sandstone caves were
the hiding place of bandits.

🏛 **Centre of Contemporary
Art and Cultural Heritage**
Strautu iela 4. **Tel** 6325 2249.
⏰ May–Oct: 10am–5pm daily. 🎟

Pedvāle Open-Air Museum ⑲
Pedvāles brīvdabas
mākslas muzejs

Road Map C4. Strauta 4. **Tel** 6325
2249. 🚌 ⏰ 10am–4pm daily. 🎟
📷 📧 www.pedvale.lv

The near-derelict buildings
and grounds of
Pedvāle Manor,
a short walk
uphill from
Sabile, were
bought by sculptor
Ojars Feldbergs in
1991. A year later,
they were opened
as the Pedvāle
Open-Air Museum,
one of Latvia's most interesting
museums. Scattered around
the 100-ha (247-acre) site are
over 150 works by Latvian and
international artists. Many of
the artworks are designed
specifically for the museum
during conferences and workshops. The on-site ticket office
provides a map to help
visitors in their exploration.
Some of Feldbergs's own
work can be found exhibited
in the attractively decaying
estate buildings at the far end
of the site, while other
buildings have been renovated
to accommodate visiting
artists. The former manor
house is now a guest house
open to the public.

Picturesque view of Talsi with a canopy of trees rising behind

Rows of crosses marking the graves of German soldiers, near Saldus

Saldus 20

Road Map C4. 🚉 ℹ️ *Avotu iela 12, 6388 1666.*

Set amid scenic countryside, close to Lake Ciecere, Saldus is best known for the **Janis Rozentāls Museum of History and Art** (Jaņa Rozentāla Saldus Vēstures un Mākslas Muzejs). Rozentāls (*see p152*), who was born near Saldus, reconstructed the building in 1900. The artist's home till 1901, it is now a museum that showcases his works. Temporary art exhibitions are housed in an adjacent building.

Statue of Janis Rozentāls, Saldus

Environs
Vācu Karavīru Kapi, 7 km (4 miles) south of town, is a war cemetery where German soldiers who died in Latvia were re-buried in a single place.

🏛 **Janis Rozentāls Museum of History and Art**
Striķu iela 22. **Tel** 6388 1603.
🕐 10am–4pm daily. 🈂️

Kuldīga 21

Road Map B3. 🏯 14,000. 🚉 ℹ️
Baznīcas iela 5, 6332 2259. 🎏 *Town Festival (mid-Jul).* **www**.kuldiga.lv

With a well-preserved old town and an attractive location alongside the Venta river, Kuldīga is one of Latvia's most alluring provincial towns. It was founded in 1242 by the Livonian Order, who chose the site to capitalize on the river and a land route linking Prussia with the lower Daugava Valley.

In the 16th century, Kuldīga's castle was one of the residences of Duke Gothard Kettler and the town traded with Rīga and Jelgava. The streets near the attractive old town hall square, running alongside the Alekšupīte river, feature 17th- and 18th-century timber buildings. Also here are a couple of attractive churches, St Catherine's (Sv Katrīnas baznīca) and the Holy Trinity (Sv Trīsvienības Katoļu baznīca). A short walk away is the Venta Waterfall (Ventas rumba), the widest in Europe. Close by is a 164-m (538-ft) brick bridge, one of Europe's longest. Overlooking the river is **Kuldīga District Museum** (Kuldīgas novada muzejs), best known for its collection of playing cards.

Environs
The **Riežupe Sand Caves** (Riežupes smilšu alas), 4 km (2 miles) north of Kuldīga, form the longest cave system in Latvia. A quarter of the 2-km (1-mile) site is open to visitors.

🏛 **Kuldīga District Museum**
Pils iela 5. **Tel** 6332 2364.
🕐 11am–5pm Tue–Sun. 🈂️

Pāvilosta 22

Road Map B4. ℹ️ *Dzintaru iela 2, 6349 8229.* 🎏 *Sea Festival (Jul).*

Founded in 1879, the small port town of Pāvilosta was named after Paul Lilienfeld, Governor of Kurzeme from 1868 to 1885. Tourist activities in Pāvilosta revolve around the sea, including yacht and canoe hire and trips out in a fishing boat. The surrounding area is also popular for windsurfing, and in 2006, the country's first world-class yacht marina, **Pāvilosta Marina**, was opened here.

The **Regional Studies Museum** (Pāvilostas novadpētniecības muzejs), located in the town's oldest building, exhibits everyday items from the region and Latvian-only displays about local history.

⛵ **Pāvilosta Marina**
Ostmalas iela 4. **Tel** 6349 8581.
www.pavilostamarina.lv

🏛 **Regional Studies Museum**
Dzintaru iela 1. **Tel** 6349 8276. 🕐
mid-May–mid-Sep: 11am–5pm Wed–Fri, noon–4pm Sat & Sun; mid-Sep–mid-May: 9am–5pm Mon–Fri. 🈂️

Ferries anchored at the harbour in the port town of Pāvilosta

Liepāja ㉓

Although Liepāja was officially declared a town in 1625, it expanded only in the early 19th century. The deepening of the ice-free port and the building of a railway link were followed, in 1890, by the foundation of a Tsarist naval port at Karosta. Today, Liepāja is Latvia's third-largest city with a vibrant cultural life. It is dotted with many interesting sights, most of which are located in its historic core. Many of the city's older buildings have been extensively restored.

Wooden sculpture, Liepāja Museum

Beautifully carved Baroque altar of St Anne's Basilica

🏛 Holy Trinity Church

Baznīcas 1. **Tel** 2943 8050. ⬜ 10am–6pm daily. 🅿 donations. **Organ recital** Jul: Sat (call for timings).
The modest exterior of the mid-18th-century Holy Trinity Church (Svētās Trīsvienības baznīca) belies one of the finest interiors in the Baltic region, adorned with gilt

Details on the exterior of Holy Trinity Church

detailing and woodcarvings. The centrepiece is an organ built in 1773 by H A Contius, a favourite of composer J S Bach. Expanded in 1885, it was the world's largest organ until 1912. Wooden steps lead up the clock tower for views.

House of Craftsmen

Kungu iela 26. **Tel** 6342 3286. ⬜ 9am–5pm Mon–Fri. 🅿 📷
With a wide variety of fine handicrafts on sale, the House of Craftsmen (Amatnieku namiņš) is a place where one can watch skilled artisans as they weave traditional textiles. The world's longest amber necklace, 123 m (404 ft) long and weighing 60 kg (132 lb), is also on display along with photographs documenting its creation.

🏛 St Anne's Basilica

Veidenbauma iela 1. **Tel** 6342 3384.
First documented in 1508, the current Neo-Gothic St Anne's Basilica (Sv Annas baznīca) dates only from the end of the 19th century. The plain interior is dominated by the huge Baroque altar, carved for Duke Jakob Kettler *(see p135)* in 1697 by Nicolas Sefrens. The altar painting depicts the Passion of Christ in three panels, with the Crucifixion at the bottom, the wrapping of his body in the centre and the Ascension at the top.

🏛 Occupation Museum

K Ukstiņa iela 7/9. **Tel** 6342 0274. ⬜ 10am–5pm Wed–Sun. 🅿
The interesting Occupation Museum (Okupāciju režīmos) offers an absorbing account

LIEPĀJA

Holy Trinity Church ①
House of Craftsmen ②
Liepāja Museum ⑥
Occupation Museum ④
St Anne's Basilica ③
St Joseph's Cathedral ⑤

Liepāja Airport
8 km (5 miles)
Railway Station 800 m (875 yards)
Bus Station 800 m (875 yards)
KAROSTA
K ZĀLES LAUK

Liepāja Museum ⑥
Liepāja Beach

Holy Trinity Church ①
Alexander Nevsky Church
Seaside Park
St Joseph's Cathedral ⑤
House of Craftsmen ②
St Anne's Basilica ③
Occupation Museum ④

0 metres   250
0 yards   250

Key to Symbols see back flap

of the city's treatment at the hands of Nazi Germany and the Soviet Union, with copious notes available in English. Exhibits include everyday objects left behind by repatriated Baltic Germans at the start of World War II, photographs of people deported en masse by the Soviets in June 1941 and an account of the killing of the city's Jews and other "undesirables".

The exhibits end with a display about the events leading up to independence. The offices of the Popular Front, which was based in the building, have been left intact. Rooms upstairs house an exhibition of antique photographic equipment.

🔒 St Joseph's Cathedral
Rakstvežu iela 16/18. **Tel** 6342 9775. Decorated inside with scenes from the Bible, the yellow St Joseph's Cathedral (Sv Jāzepa katedrāle) attained its current towering form in the 19th century. The congregation needed a larger church, but had no land on which to build, which is why they simply expanded the existing building upwards.

🏛 Liepāja Museum
Kūrmājas prospekts 16/18. **Tel** 6342 2327. ⏱ 10am–6pm Wed–Sun. 🌐 www.liepajasmuzejs.lv
Set amid a small sculpture garden, the Liepāja Museum (Liepājas muzejs) is housed in an ornate early 20th-century building with an impressive galleried hall. The displays trace local history, with exhibits including the heads of stone cherubs from St Anne's Basilica, a series of pewter drinking vessels topped by human figures and traditional southern Kurzeme costumes. Also here is a reconstruction of the workshop of the famous sculptor Mikelis Pankoks (1894–1983), who vanished in 1944 and was presumed dead. He had fled the country incognito, and ended his days in a Swiss mental hospital.

🚌 Liepāja Beach
Although the coast here was once an environmental disaster area, it has now been thoroughly cleaned up and proudly flies its EU Blue Flag.

The long, sandy Liepāja Beach (Liepājas pludmale) is separated from the Old Town by the wooded **Seaside Park** (Jūrmalas parks). The nearby streets are lined with elegant Art Nouveau buildings that used to be summer houses.

Façade of St Nicholas's Orthodox Cathedral, Karosta

Karosta
4 km (2 miles) N of town. 🚌 3, 4, 7. **www**.karosta.lv **St Nicholas's Orthodox Church** Katedrāles 7. **Military Prison** Invalīdu 4. 🌐 🎫
A military harbour built by the Russians during the late 19th century, Karosta was off-limits to civilians. In its heyday, it housed 40,000 personnel. Today, it has a ghost-town feel, with streets of huge unoccupied buildings.

One reason for visiting Karosta is to see the striking onion-domed **St Nicholas's Orthodox Cathedral** (Sv Nikolaja pareizticīgo catedrāle), used as a cinema and gym by the Soviets. The old **Military Prison** (Karostas cietums) is now the Kurzeme region's major tourist attraction, offering a chance to be locked up and yelled at by "guards" for a couple of hours or overnight.

Lake Pape Nature Reserve ㉔
Papes dabas parks

Road Map B4. **Tel** 2948 9775. 🛈 Dabas Māja, Pape village, 348 9485; Zvaniņš, Rucava village, 349 4766. ⏱ 10am–6pm daily. 🌐 🖥 **www**.pdf-pape.lv

Just 10 km (6 miles) from the Lithuanian border, the wetlands, pine forests, dunes, grasslands and coastline of the Lake Pape area make an excellent trip from Liepāja. Sponsored by the World Wide Fund for Nature, the reserve covers around 52,000 ha (128,495 acres), and is best known for its *savvaļas zirgi* (semi-wild horses) and *sumbru ganības* (European bison). Guided tours, taking around 90 minutes, are available from the ticket office at the entrance to the signposted grazing area.

The reserve is popular with bird-watchers, due to its location on a migration path. Some 271 species have been sighted here, 15 of which are on the European Red List of endangered species. The area is sparsely populated, although there are three villages within the reserve. One of them is the dune-enclosed settlement of Pape, home to **Vītolnieki**, a branch of the Latvian Ethnographic Open-Air Museum *(see p159)*.

🏛 Vītolnieki
Pape village. **Tel** 6340 0332. ⏱ 9am–5pm Tue–Wed, Fri–Sun.

Bird-watching tower at the Lake Pape Nature Reserve

EASTERN LATVIA

he eastern part of Latvia includes some of the country's most popular attractions, both natural and man-made, as well as rarely visited rural districts. Although far from mountainous, the terrain is not as flat as in the west and there are two extensive upland areas dotted with myriad lakes, some of which have well-developed tourist facilities, while others remain isolated and untouched.

When the German crusaders arrived, they found the Livs and Lettgallians inhabiting the region which now forms Vidzeme, while Latgallians and Selians lived further east in what is now Latgale. The Bishop of Rīga took control of the west and east of Vidzeme, while central Vidzeme and most of Latgale was claimed by the Livonian Order. After the collapse of the Livonian Order in 1561 the whole of the east fell under Lithuanian, and later Polish, rule.

The end of the Polish-Swedish Wars in 1629 saw Sweden ruling both Estonia and Vidzeme. The Russians conquered Vidzeme in 1721. Reliant economically on agriculture, forestry and wood processing, the region is sometimes claimed as the cradle of Latvian culture as it produced many of the country's best-known writers and musicians. Today Vidzeme is second only to Rīga as a travel destination, with the Gauja National Park combining natural beauty and historical attractions.

Latgale, on the other hand, was ruled by Poland until 1772. The Polish influence fostered a strong Catholic tradition, particularly evident in the pilgrimage centre of Aglona. Latgale was later absorbed directly into the Russian Empire, unlike other Latvian regions which were ruled as separate provinces. This isolation delayed the national awakening in Latgale, and today it is neglected as a predominantly Russian backwater. Despite this, its villages and lakes charm visitors and the regional capital Daugavpils is slowly shaking off its image as a grey Soviet throwback.

Old houses and tower in Cēsis, a town steeped in history

◁ **Bank of the Gauja river below Eagle Cliff, Gauja National Park**

Exploring Eastern Latvia

The most popular tourist attraction in Eastern Latvia is Gauja
National Park, which combines beautiful forests with attractions
such as the historic town of Cēsis and the restored Turaida
Castle. A significant part of the region is covered by the
North Vidzeme Biosphere Reserve, famous for its
coastal meadows, sandstone cliffs and extensive
wetlands. The route from Rīga to Daugavpils, the
capital of Latgale, runs along the Daugava Valley
and includes several worthwhile stops, while
the cathedral at Aglona is a major centre for
Catholic pilgrimage. For most visitors,
though, the main attraction in Latgale is its
patchwork of lakes, including Rāzna and
Lubāns, the two largest in the country.

SIGHTS AT A GLANCE

Sandstone cliffs on the banks of Salaca river, Vidzeme

KEY

▬▬ Motorway

▬▬ Main road

— Secondary road

═══ Minor road

━ Railway

▬▬ International border

Map labels: Unguriņ, MAZSALACA 5, Staicele, Lake Burtnieks, Ren, AINAŽI 3, Salaca, Vilzēni, P15, SALACGRĪVA 4, Drieliņi, A1, VALMIE, Vidzem, P13, P11, LIMBAŽI 6, Umurga, Jelgavkrasti, DUNTE 7, Vidriži, P14, Skulte, Inciems, GAUJA NATIO PARK, A3, SAULKRASTI 8, P9, A2, A1, Gauja, Sigulda, Vangaži, P8, Ķīšezers, P10, Ropaži, Mergupe, Mālpils, Ķeipe, Rīga, P4, A2, A4, A6, Ogre, IKŠĶILE 9, Daugava, LIELVĀRD 10, SKRĪVE, Taurkaene, Ērbe

GETTING AROUND

The highlights of Gauja National Park are easily reached by bus or train from Rīga, while even small towns in Vidzeme usually have at least one bus a day. Rīga and Daugavpils are well connected by buses and trains that run several times a day. The public transport network elsewhere in Latgale is not well developed and it is easier to use a private vehicle, particularly when exploring the lakes. A few buses ply between the towns but the service is unreliable and erratic.

Gauja National Park ❶

Latvia's first and most popular national park was established in 1973, stretching for about 100 km (62 miles) along the Gauja River Valley. But the area has been attracting tourists to its so-called "Alpine trails" since the 19th century. Almost half of the 92,000-ha (227,337-acre) park is forested, and it is home to about 900 plant, 149 bird and 48 mammal species. Around 4 per cent of the park forms a closed nature reserve, but the rest is accessible by road. Canoeing and boating are great ways to see the caves, cliffs and ravines carved out by the river since the glaciers receded 12,000 years ago. In addition to its natural attactions, the area also has some of Latvia's most fascinating historic sites (see pp188–9).

KEY

☐ Gauja National Park

0 km   5

0 miles   5

★ Turaida Museum Reserve
The extensively restored Turaida Castle houses historical exhibitions, while the grounds include outbuildings and a sculpture park.

New Castle in Sigulda
This fanciful manor house was built in 1867 near the main castle. It is one of the centrepieces of the town and houses the Pilsmuiža restaurant (see p336).

STAR SIGHT

- ★ Turaida Museum Reserve

- ★ Līgatne Education and Recreation Centre

- ★ Cēsis

Bobsleigh Run
Sigulda offers a rare chance to experience the thrill of a world-class bobsleigh run at a reasonable price. In summer, a slower inflatable vehicle is used.

★ **Līgatne Education and Recreation Centre**
Inside the park, footpaths and tracks for vehicles wind past spacious enclosures housing animals, including elk, brown bears and European bison.

VISITORS' CHECKLIST

Road Map D3. 🚉 *from Rīga.*
🚌 *from Rīga.* ℹ️ *Gauja National Park Visitors' Centre, Baznīcas iela 3, Sigulda, 6797 4006.* 🛶 *guided canoe trips organized by Campo in Rīga (2922 2339), Makars in Sigulda (2924 4948).* 🛅 www.*gnp.lv*

★ **Cēsis**
Once the seat of the German crusaders, Cēsis is a romantic town with a lakeside park.

CĒSIS

Raiskums

Cīruliši

Āraiši

Drabeši

Kārļi

Skaļupe · Zvārte Rock

Jasmala

Līgatne

Lēriķi

Augšlīgatne

Lake Āraiši
Archaeologists found remains of a fortress on the lake bed. This reconstruction offers a glimpse into Latgallian life in the 9th and 10th centuries.

Zvārte Rock, a 35-m (115-ft) high sandstone outcrop, boasts excellent views. It is locally believed to be a haunt of witches and demons.

KEY

🚉 Railway station

ℹ️ Visitor information

🚠 Cable car

🛅 Campsite

☆ Viewpoint

— Major road

— Minor road

— Other road

— Railway line

- - Park boundary

ROSE OF TURAIDA

According to a popular legend, in 1601 a young orphan girl was found in the aftermath of a battle between the Swedish and Polish armies. She was named Maija and raised in Turaida Castle. She fell in love with Viktor, a gardener from Sigulda Castle. One day a deserter from the Polish army lured her into the nearby Gūtmaņa Cave under false pretences, but she tricked him into killing her rather than surrendering her chastity. The so-called grave of the Turaida Rose in the Turaida Museum Reserve is considered a romantic spot for newlyweds.

Gravestone of the Turaida Rose, the beautiful Maija

Exploring Gauja National Park

The park follows the Gauja River Valley as it flows southwest from Valmiera. Road access to the park is good, with the A2 and A3 running alongside. The most convenient access points from Rīga are Sigulda, where the park information office is located, and Cēsis. In addition to hotels and guest houses along the major routes and close to the tourist sites, the park includes a network of 22 campsites. They are arranged along the Gauja, Amata and Brasla rivers, making canoeing an appealing way to see the area. The stretch between Sigulda and Cēsis is particularly attractive.

Sigulda

🚉 *from Rīga.* 🚌 *from Rīga.*
ℹ️ *Valdemāra iela 1a, 6 797 1335.*
www.sigulda.lv

A spacious town set in scenic woodland, Sigulda is a centre for outdoor activities and is also a good base for visiting Krimulda and Turaida. After the Brotherhood of the Sword subdued the Liv population in 1207, they gave the valley's right bank to the Bishop of Rīga and built their own castle on the left bank. The Brotherhood, renamed the Livonian Order, lost the town to the Poles in 1562, and it passed between the Poles and Swedes for 150 years, until it was taken by Russia in the Great Northern War (1700–21).

The castle ruins are tucked away behind the 19th-century New Castle (Jaunā pils), which now houses city council offices and a restaurant. Close by is a Lutheran church and the impressive viewpoint called Artists' Hill (Gleznotāju kalns). Paths run through the woodland to Satzele Castle Mound, once a Liv fortress, and Peter's Cave on the bank of the Vējupīte river.

Krimulda

🚎 *from Sigulda.* 🚟 *from Sigulda (10am–7:30pm Mon–Fri, 6:30pm Sat–Sun).* **www**.krimuldaspils.lv

The Bishop of Rīga had a castle built in Krimulda after taking control of the right bank of the Gauja Valley in 1207. Krimulda Castle (Krimuldas pils) was destroyed by the Swedish army in 1601, and little remains of the ruins. It is easier to spot the nearby 19th-century Neo-Classical manor house (Krimuldas muižas pils). It is now a

Cable car carrying visitors from Sigulda to Krimulda

rehabilitation centre for children, with a café and basic accommodation.

⛰ Turaida Museum Reserve

6 km (4 miles) N of Sigulda. 🚌 *from Sigulda.* **Tel** *6797 1402.* 🕐 *May–Oct: 10am–6pm (site & some buildings open until 8pm), Nov–Apr: 10am–5pm.* 🅿️ 📷 ℹ️ *second & fourth Sun.* 💻 **www**.turaida-muzejs.lv

The Turaida Museum Reserve mainly consists of a castle and a group of outbuildings. Turaida Castle was built by the Brotherhood of the Sword

in 1214. It was left in ruins after a fire in 1776 and has since been extensively restored. Plaques help visitors to understand the site, while exhibitions inside deal with the history of the castle and illustrate the restoration process. Near the museum entrance are the remains of the Turaida estate, including a working smithy and exhibitions on farming and woodcraft.

Close to the castle is the Turaida Church. Built in 1750, it is one of the oldest wooden churches in Latvia. Outside the church is a memorial to the Turaida Rose *(see p187)*. Tucked away behind the church is the Folk Song Park (Dainu kalns), where 25 sculptures celebrate the work of Krišjānis Barons *(see p151)*. Nature trails lead down slopes from the park.

Cēsis

35 km (22 miles) NE of Sigulda.
🚉 *from Rīga.* 🚌 *from Rīga.* ℹ️ *Pils laukums 1, 6412 1815.* **www**.cesis.lv
Museum of Art and History
Pils laukums 9. 🎟️ *includes access to the Old and New Castles.*

One of the oldest towns in Latvia, Cēsis has winding streets lined with attractive wooden and stone buildings. It was once an important trading centre, becoming a member of the Hanseatic League in 1383. The town served as the headquarters of the Brotherhood of the Sword, and later the Livonian Order, for much of the period between 1237 and 1561.

In 1577, Ivan the Terrible took Cēsis. Further damage was inflicted during the Great Northern War and the town

Row of wooden and stone houses in the old town, Cēsis

Picturesque view of the wooden dwellings of Āraiši Lake Fortress

also witnessed extremely fierce fighting during the War of Independence (1918–20).

The Cēsis castle complex is the town's major attraction. Visitors are given builders' helmets and lanterns for the tour of the 15th- to 16th-century towers of the 13th-century Old Castle. The pink New Castle, built in 1777, is home to the **Museum of Art and History** (Cēsu vēstures un mākslas muzejs). The highlight is the well-presented "Treasures of Cēsis" exhibition. Cēsis Exhibition House (Cēsu izstāžu nams), a renovated 18th-century coach house, stands on the square in front of the New Castle. To the north, the Castle Park is a popular place to relax in the summer, while the Old Town is to the southeast of the castle.

Other attractions include the 19th-century Cēsis Brewery, although the beer is now brewed outside the town.

♣ Āraiši Lake Fortress
10 km (6 miles) S of Cēsis. **Tel** 419 7288. ◻ May–Nov: 10am–6pm daily. 🖼 🈺

Tales of sunken castles are common in Latvian folklore, appearing to stem from the 9th- to 10th-century Latgallian practice of building settlements on islets. In 1965, archaeologists found one such settlement in Lake Āraiši, now

Sign, Ligatne Education and Recreation Centre

reconstructed as a tourist sight. A wooden platform holds 16 single-room dwellings with log walls and bark roofs. Each of them could accommodate three to eight people. A clay stove was used for heating and cooking, while a small structure to the right of each doorway was used for storage or to keep cattle.

Today, guides in costume re-create the atmosphere of the settlement, and a dugout boat can be hired. Back on shore is a ruined Livonian Order castle and several reconstructed Stone, Bronze and Iron Age dwellings.

♣ Ligatne Education and Recreation Centre
15 km (9 miles) NE of Sigulda. 🚌 from Cēsis. **Tel** 6415 3313. ◻ May–Oct: 9:30am–5pm Mon, 9:30am–6:30pm Tue–Sun. 🖼 www.gnp.lv

A wooded nature park, Ligatne Education and Recreation Park (Līgatnes mācību un atpūtas parks), is home to animals such as brown bears, lynx, beavers, elk and European bison. Large enclosures are connected by 5.5 km (3.4 miles) of walking trails and a 5-km (3-mile) route for vehicles. The site includes a 22-m (72-ft) viewing tower, horse-riding facilities, spots for campfires and several car parks. Dogs are not allowed on the trails.

THE LATVIAN FLAG

According to tradition, the Latvian national flag was born in Cēsis around 1280. The story goes that warriors from one of the Latvian tribes wrapped their dying chieftain in a white flag, which they had captured from their Estonian enemies. After a stirring speech, the chieftain died and the warriors removed the flag from his body to find that his blood had left two red stripes on it; the white stripe in the middle was where he had lain. The warriors took the new flag into battle and defeated their enemies. The present-day version of the flag was designed by artist

Latvian flag hoisted on the New Castle, Sigulda

Ansis Cīrulis in May 1917. The Museum of Art and History in Cēsis has an exhibition dedicated to the Latvian flag.

Forlorn remains of the Livonian Order castle in Valmiera

Valmiera ❷

Road Map D3. 🏠 30,000. 🚌 from Rīga. 🚆 from Cēsis. 🛈 Rīgas iela 10, 6420 7177. 🎭 Winter Music Festival (Jan), City Festivities (Jul), Craftsmen's Festival (Aug), St Simeon's Fair of the Middle Ages (Oct). **www**.valmiera.lv

Once a Hanseatic League member, Valmiera was founded in 1283 and has a distinguished history of trade due to its position on the Gauja river. Today, it is the second-largest city in Vidzeme after Rīga, although its old town was devastated during World War II. Most sights of interest are clustered together beside the river, just east of the city's main roundabout.

The 13th-century **St Simon's Church** (Sv Sīmaņa baznīca) has been destroyed several times and its current appearance dates from 1739. The altarpiece shows a depiction of the Temptation of Christ by Christiana Vogels-Vogelstein. Visitors can climb the church tower for a view of the city.

Just beyond the church lie the ruins of the Livonian Order castle and the **Museum of Local Studies** (Valmieras novadpētniecības muzejs). The museum covers local history and hosts exhibitions. Close by is the city's oldest wooden building, a former pharmacy built in 1735. The slope behind the museum forms a pleasant riverside park.

🏠 **St Simon's Church**
Bruņinieku iela 2. **Tel** 6420 0333.

🏛 **Museum of Local Studies**
Bruņinieku iela 3. **Tel** 6422 3620.
⏱ 10am–5pm Tue–Sat. 📷

Ainaži ❸

Road Map D2. 🏠 1,800. 🚌 from Cēsis.

Close to the Estonian border, Ainaži occupies a crucial place in Latvia's maritime history. For centuries, the coastline was sparsely inhabited, justifying the town's name, which is derived from the Livonian word *ainagi* meaning "solitary". However, by the 19th century, it had become an important fishing centre, and in 1864, was chosen by Krišjānis Valdemārs as the location for his naval school, which closed only in 1919 during the civil war. The original school building is now the **Naval College Museum** (Ainažu jūrskolas muzejs), which displays photographs, documents, model ships and a collection of anchors. Ainaži also boasts the **Fire-fighters' Museum** (Ainažu ugunsdzēsības muzejs). Exhibits in the main building include hand-operated water pumps, uniforms and insignia, while the garage displays fire trucks. The museum staff are former fire-fighters.

🏛 **Naval College Museum**
Valdemāra iela 47. **Tel** 6404 3349.
⏱ 10am–4pm daily. 📷

🏛 **Fire-fighters' Museum**
Valdemāra iela 69. **Tel** 6404 3280.
⏱ 10am–4pm Wed, Fri–Sat.

Striking snowcapped Liv Sacrificial Caves near Salacgrīva

Salacgrīva ❹

Road Map D3. 🏠 6,000. 🚌 from Rīga. 🛈 Rīgas iela 10a, 6404 1254. **www**.salacgriva.lv

Positioned at the mouth of the Salaca river, the fishing port of Salacgrīva officially became a town in 1928. There is evidence that German traders may have visited the Salaca before they reached the Daugava river. Salacgrīva is a good jumping-off point for exploring the area nearby.

Environs
On the banks of the Svētupe river, 10 km (6 miles) east of town, are the **Liv Sacrificial Caves** (Lībiešu upurala). Coins and artifacts dating from the 14th to 19th centuries have been found here, and there are runes carved into the walls. The **Randu Meadows** (Randu pļavas), about 8 km (5 miles) north of Salacgrīva, are rich in birdlife and rare plants.

Nautical objects displayed in the garden of Naval College Museum, Ainaži

Mazsalaca ⑤

Road Map D2. 🚍 *from Rīga.*
🛈 *Rīgas iela 1, 6425 1781.*
www.mazsalaca.lv

The sleepy town of Mazsalaca has little to detain visitors, except for the **Museum of Little Devils**, an unusual collection of woodcarvings on a Satanic theme by Valters Hirte. However, the town serves as an ideal base for exploring the attractions nearby, such as the spookily named Werewolf Pine and Devil's Caves, 2 km (1 mile) from Mazsalaca, where the spring water is said to have healing powers.

Skaņaiskalns (Sound Hill), a sandstone cliff southwest of Mazsalaca, is noted for the echoes it creates. It can be reached via a park filled with wooden sculptures, which can be viewed on the drive through, but are better seen on foot. The 2-km (1-mile) path begins at the Valtenburg manor house (now a secondary school) on Parka Street.

🏛 **Museum of Little Devils**
Rīgas iela 1. **Tel** *6425 1781.*
🕐 *11am–4pm Wed–Sun.*

Carved wooden soldiers in the park leading to Skaņaiskalns, Mazsalaca

Limbaži ⑥

Road Map D3. 🏠 *9,200.* 🚍 *from Rīga.* 🛈 *Burtnieku iela 5, 6407 0608.* **www**.limbazi.lv

Although one of Latvia's oldest towns, Limbaži has retained little of its prosperous past. The area, which was known during the 13th century as Metsepole (Indriķis in Latvian), was one of three Liv territories mentioned in the early 13th-century chronicle written by Henry of Livonia.

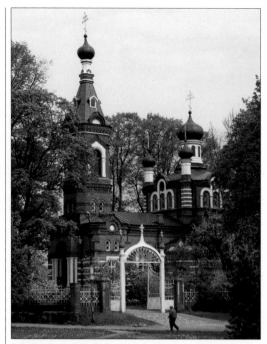

Orthodox Church, dating back to the early 20th century, in Limbaži

Limbaži's stone castle, built by the Brotherhood of the Sword in 1223, served as the Archbishop of Rīga's residence. A town grew up around the castle and formed part of the Hanseatic League. The castle, now in ruins, was destroyed in the 1602 Polish-Swedish War.

Offering tours of the castle ruins is the **Museum of Regional Studies** (Limbažu muzejs), with its fascinating display of artifacts that recount the region's history. Close by is the 1903 **Orthodox Church**, which still retains some of its original splendour. A statue of Kārlis Baumanis, composer of the national anthem, stands in Jūras Street.

🏛 **Museum of Regional Studies**
Burtnieku iela 7. **Tel** *6407 0632.*
🕐 *mid-May–mid-Oct: 10am–6pm Tue–Sat, mid-Oct–mid-May: 10am–5pm Tue–Sat.* 🎟 *for castle.* 📷

KRIŠJĀNIS VALDEMĀRS

One of the key figures of the Latvian National Awakening, Krišjānis Valdemārs (1825–91) was a writer, educationist, political thinker and ideologist. During his time the majority of Latvian works were written by Baltic Germans, which he sought to change. From 1862 until its suppression in 1865, Valdemārs edited a Latvian-language publication, *Pēterburgas Avīzes*, alongside Krišjānis Barons and poet Juris Alunāns, which criticized the Baltic German sense of cultural superiority. He encouraged Barons and Fricis Brīvzemnieks to start a Latvian folk songs collection *(see pp24–5)*, and was instrumental in establishing the Ainaži Naval College, where tuition was free and not dependent on social status.

Valdemārs's bust, Naval Museum

House set amid idyllic scenery reflected in one of the many clear-water lakes near Dunte

Dunte ❼

Road Map D3. 🚌 *from Valmiera.*

Otherwise unremarkable, Dunte is known for the **Münchausen Museum** dedicated to Karl Friedrich Hieronymus von Münchhausen (1720–97). An officer in the Russian cavalry, Baron Münchhausen married a local woman and visited Dunte on his honeymoon. He became unwittingly famous when a collection of fantastical stories featuring him was published anonymously in 1781, and his association with exaggeration continues to this day. Museum staff dress in period costumes, and one room is a fanciful reconstruction of his wife's boudoir. A screen shows a 1943 German film adaptation of his tales. Upstairs are waxworks of famous Latvians.

🏛 **Münchausen Museum**
Daugavas iela 58. **Tel** 6406 5633.
🕐 *Jun–Aug: 10am–5pm Mon–Thu, 10am–7pm Fri–Sun; Dec–Feb: 10am–5pm Wed–Sun.* 📷 🔲 🔳

Saulkrasti ❽

Road Map D3. 🏚 *5,550.*
🚆 *from Rīga.* 🚌 *from Rīga.*
ℹ️ *Ainažu iela 10, 6795 2641.*
🎷 *Town Festival (Jul), International Jazz Festival (Jul), Organ Music Festival (Sep).* **www**.saulkrasti.lv

A seaside resort since the 19th century, Saulkrasti is little more than a string of

homes and guest houses along the main road. Nonetheless, it remains a popular getaway for Rīga residents. The main activity is walking along the coastline, and a trail stretching for 4 km (2 miles) has several viewing points, including a platform on the White Dune (Baltā kāpa). The privately owned **Bicycle Museum** (Saulkrastu velosipēdu muzejs) is housed in a large shed in the owners' garden. The superb collection, a work of many years, features oddities such as a wooden bicycle made by an aeroplane engineer. There are also mock-ups of a workshop used for repairs and of a bicycle parts shop.

Cycle badges at Bicycle Museum, Saulkrasti

🏛 **Bicycle Museum**
Rīgas iela 44a. **Tel** 2962 1580. 🕐 *call ahead.* **www**.velomuseum.tk

Ikšķile ❾

Road Map D3. 🏚 *6,250.*
🚆 *from Rīga.* 🚌 *from Rīga.*

In the mid-12th century, the Augustinian monk Father Meinhard, the first Bishop of Ikšķile, accompanied German merchants along the Daugava river. He built **St Mary's Church** here, now the oldest surviving church ruins in Latvia. The local Livs resisted being converted to Christianity and Meinhard made little headway. The church was the first stone building in the Baltics, and its ruins have been covered with a metal roof to protect them from the elements. Following the construction of a hydroelectric dam on the river, the ruins stand on an island, although there is nothing much to see.

Ruins of St Mary's Church in Ikšķile, one of Latvia's earliest churches

For hotels and restaurants in this region see pp305–307 and pp335–7

Lielvārde ❿

Road Map D4. 7,350. from Rīga. Ausekļa prosp 7, Ogre, 19 km (11 miles) NW of town, 6507 1883. Regional Festival (Jul), Birthday of Andrejs Pumpurs (Sep).
www.lielvarde.lv

The town of Lielvārde is best known as the site of the climactic battle between the heroic Lāčplēsis and the Black Knight. The conflict ended when the two warriors disappeared into the Daugava river close to an early 13th-century castle, the ruins of which stand on a hillock. Tall wooden sculptures nearby illustrate Lāčplēsis's story, while a pair of large stones are said to be the bed and blanket of the hero, who reputedly returns to the bank each night to sleep.

Also close to the river is the **Andrejs Pumpurs Museum** (Andreja Pumpura muzejs), dedicated to the eminent writer. A small display is devoted to *Lielvārdes josta*. These belts, used in traditional weddings, are for sale at the museum.

At the western end of town is **Uldevena Castle** (Uldevena pils), a reconstruction of a wooden Liv fortification. It was built in 1997 to the design of a local artist and takes elements from other structures, thus representing an "ideal" rather than a replica of a single castle.

🏛 **Andrejs Pumpurs Museum**
E Kauliņa aleja 20. **Tel** 2505 3759.
10am–5pm daily.

♣ **Uldevena Castle**
Parka iela 3. **Tel** 2946 5792.
Apr–Nov: 10am–7pm daily.

Wooden sculpture of Lāčplēsis

ANDREJS PUMPURS AND LĀČPLĒSIS

Born in Birzgale, close to Lielvārde, Andrejs Pumpurs (1841–1902) was an unlikely literary figure. Working on the land before volunteering to fight in Serbia against the Ottoman Empire in 1876, he became a loyal officer in the Russian army but was also a staunch promoter of Latvian culture. Convinced of the need for a national epic, he chose the folk story of Lāčplēsis the Bear Slayer, whose mixed animal-human parentage is evident in his bear-like ears. Pumpurs also drew from Latvian folklore to create a strongly allegorical plot filled with demons and witches. Lāčplēsis defeats the Estonian giant Kalapuisis and convinces him of the need to work together against their foreign foes. Towards the end of the epic, Lāčplēsis unites the Latvian people and repels the invaders, but the wicked turncoat Kangars reveals the hero's secret – his strength is in his ears. The Black Knight, a Germanic giant, cuts off Lāčplēsis's ears, plunging Latvia into 700 long years of misery. The story goes that Lāčplēsis will rise again after he defeats his rival.

Mural of Lāčplēsis and Laimdota at the Andrejs Pumpurs Museum

in Latvian literature. The exhibition about the noted author, critic and Communist polemicist is displayed in his former home. The **Tree Park** (Dendroloģiskais parks) close to Skrīveri is a pleasant place to wander, its paths running through almost 400 species of trees from around the world. Each tree has been tagged with its Latvian and Latin names and, except for the occasional dog-walker, it is a surprisingly quiet site.

🏛 **Andrejs Upīts Memorial Museum**
Daugavas iela 58. **Tel** 2949 6725.
mid-May–Nov: 10am–5pm Mon–Fri.

Skrīveri ⓫

Road Map D4. from Rīga.
www.skriveri.lv

Although the town has a long history, Skrīveri was devastated during World War I. Its main attraction is the **Andrejs Upīts Memorial Museum** (Andreja Upīša memoriālmāja), which draws visitors interested

Koknese ⓬

Road Map D4. from Rīga. International Folk Music Festival (Jul).

Once the main settlement of the Selonian tribe, which was subjugated by the Livonian Order in 1208, Koknese also appears in the tale of Lāčplēsis as the home of Laimdota – the beautiful and virtuous young woman with whom the hero falls in love. Today, the picturesque ruins of the Livonian Order castle, built in 1209 but destroyed during the Great Northern War (1700–21), makes Koknese a popular stop for visitors. The site was even more attractive before a hydroelectric power station was built on the Daugava river in 1965.

Livonian Order castle with the Daugava river in the distance, Koknese

Neo-Byzantine St Nicholas's Orthodox Church in Jēkabpils

Jēkabpils ⑬

Road Map D4. 🏛 28,000.
🚆 *from Rīga.* 🚌 *from Rīga,
Daugavpils.* ℹ️ *Brīvības iela 140/142,
6523 3822.* **www**.jekabpils.lv

Founded as a settlement for
Old Believers *(see p122)*,
Jēkabpils received town rights
from Jakob Kettler, Duke of
Courland *(see p135)*, in 1670.

Located in the town centre,
the Neo-Byzantine **St
Nicholas's Orthodox Church**
(Sv Nikolaja pareizticīgo
baznīca) was built in 1910.
Close by, the large private
Mans's Gallery was one of the
first to open in post-Soviet
Latvia. East of the town centre,
the **Selian Farmstead** (Sēļu
sēta) is an open-air museum
with 19th-century buildings,
including a farmhouse, a
smithy and a windmill.

On the opposite side of
the Daugava river lies the
13th-century **Krustpils Castle**
(Krustpils pils). Destroyed
during the Livonian Wars
(1558–82), it was reconstructed in 1585 and modified in
1849. Though the castle is

largely dilapidated, several of
its rooms have been restored,
and one of them displays
Russian military memorabilia.

🔒 **St Nicholas's
Orthodox Church**
Brīvības iela 202. *Tel 6523 1486.*

🏛 **Mans's Gallery**
Brīvības iela 154. *Tel 6523 1953.* ⬜
9am–5pm Mon–Fri. **www**.manss.lv

🏛 **Selian Farmstead**
Filozofu iela 6. *Tel 6523 2501.*
⬜ *May–Oct: 9am–5pm Mon–Fri,
10am–4pm Sat–Sun.* 📷

⚜ **Krustpils Castle**
Rīgas iela 216b. *Tel 6523 3822.*
⬜ *May–Oct: 9am–5pm Mon–Fri,
10am–3pm Sat & Sun; Nov–Apr:
9am–5pm Mon–Fri, 10am–3pm Sat.*

Līvāni ⑭

Road Map E4. 🏛 11,000. 🚆
ℹ️ *Rīgas 77, 6530 7810.* 🎭 *Town
Festival (Jul), International Folk
Festival (Sep).* **www**.livani.lv

With a long history as an
industrial centre, Līvāni takes
pride in its 120-year-old glass
factory. The on-site **Glass
Museum** (Stikla muzejs) offers

glass-blowing demonstrations.
During the post-war era, the
Soviet regime built large bio-
chemical and construction facilities, many of which became
obsolete after independence.
Recent efforts to improve the
town's fortunes include the
establishment of the **Latgale
Art and Craft Centre**, which
hosts exhibitions, besides con-
ducting ceramics and weaving
workshops for visitors.

🏛 **Glass Museum**
Zaļa iela 23. *Tel 6530 7162.* 📷 📷

🏛 **Latgale Art and
Craft Centre**
Domes 1. *Tel 6538 1855.* ⬜ *May–
Oct: 9am–5pm Tue–Fri, Nov–Apr:
9am–5pm Tue–Fri.* 📷 ♿ 📷

Daugavpils ⑮

See pp196–7.

Krāslava ⑯

Road Map E4. 🏛 11,500.
🚆 *from Daugavpils.* ℹ️ *Brīvības
iela 13, 6562 2201.*

Attractively set alongside the
Daugava river, the town of
Krāslava is largely composed
of two-storey wooden buildings. Although there are few
specific sights to draw visitors,
it is a pleasant place to visit.

Standing on an artificial hill,
the 1750 Baroque Krāslava
Castle (Krāslavas pils) houses
the **Krāslava Museum**, dedicated to local arts and history.
The Catholic church (Katoļu
baznīca) stands on the town's
other hill. It is the finest of
the Baroque buildings in
Latgale. Its imposing fresco,
depicting St Ludovik leaving

Panoramic view of Krāslava town, with rows of pretty houses along the Daugava river

For hotels and restaurants in this region see pp305–307 and pp335–7

for the crusades, was painted by the Italian artist Philippo Kastaldi in the 18th century.

🏛 **Krāslava Museum**
Pils iela 8. **Tel** 6562 3586. 🖼

Attractive exterior of the majestic Aglona Basilica 🖼

Aglona ⑰

Road Map E4. 🚌 from Rīga.
ℹ Somersetas 34, 6532 2100. 🖼
Feast of the Assumption (15 Aug).

Catholic pilgrims from across the Baltic region and Russia flock to this otherwise unremarkable town to visit **Aglona Basilica** and attend the Feast of the Assumption. Lithuanian members of the Dominican Order were invited by a local landowner to build a monastery and school in 1697. The basilica, then a church, was built in the 18th century. Pope John Paul II declared it a basilica in 1980, marking the 200th anniversary of its completion, and visited it in 1993. The basilica is famous for its early 17th-century icon of the Virgin Mary, brought by the Dominicans and said to have healing powers. It is hidden behind a lesser icon, which slides down only during special services.

Preiļi ⑱

Road Map E4. 🚹 10,000. 🚌 from Rīga. ℹ Tirgus laukums 1, 6532 2041. **www**.preili.lv

From about 1475 until 1866, the market town of Preiļi was under the control of the Borgh family, who were

originally from Southern Italy. The most recent of the family's three manor houses still survives, though in poor condition. Located in the gatekeeper's house, the **History and Applied Arts Museum** (Preiļu vēstures un lietišķ mākslas muzejs) has exhibits including old photographs of the town and samples of the pottery for which Preiļi is renowned. More local ceramics can be found – and bought – at the **P Čerņavskis Pottery Workshop-Museum** (P Čerņavska keramikas darbnīca-muzejs). The late 19th-century **Roman Catholic Church** (Romas katoļu bazīca) contains an 18th-century crucifix, and two sculptures stand outside; one is dedicated to Mother Latvia and the other is a monument to the politically oppressed during the Soviet regime.

Jug, Latgale Culture and History Museum

🏛 **History and Applied Arts Museum**
Raiņa 28. **Tel** 6532 2731. 🕙 11am–6pm Tue–Fri, 10am–4pm Sat. 🖼

🏛 **P Čerņavskis Pottery Workshop-Museum**
Talsu iela 21. **Tel** 6532 2946.

🛉 **Roman Catholic Church**
Tirgus laukums 11. **Tel** 6532 2801.
🕙 by appointment.

Rēzekne ⑲

Road Map E4. 🚹 37,000. 🚌 from Rīga. 🚌 from Daugavpils. ℹ Hotel Latgale, Atbrīvošanas 98, 6460 5005.

Although most of its old buildings were destroyed during World War II, Rēzekne

is one of the cultural centres of the Latgale region and also serves as good base for visiting the area's lakes.

The best-known sight, *Latgales Māra*, a statue created by Leons Tomašickis, stands in the centre of a large roundabout on Atbrīvošanas Avenue. The religious iconography of the statue depicting the pagan goddess Māra holding aloft a Christian cross may be ambiguous but the politics are not: the plinth simply reads "*Vienoti Latvija*" ("United for Latvia"). Unveiled in 1939, it commemorates the 1917 meeting in Rēzekne which decided that Latgale would no longer remain a part of Russia's Vitebsk province. Removed by the Russian authorities in 1940, the statue was reinstated by the occupying German army. Destroyed in 1950, the statue was rebuilt by Tomašickis's son after Latvia gained its independence in 1991. The inauguration of the replica took place in 1992.

Just north of the statue is the **Latgale Culture and History Museum** (Latgales kultūrvēstures muzejs), which focuses on the ceramics of the region, including traditional branched candelabra. South of the statue, on a small mound with excellent views of a Catholic church, are the ruins of the city's castle.

🏛 **Latgale Culture and History Museum**
Atbrīvošanas aleja 102.
Tel 6462 2464. 🕙 10am–5pm Tue–Fri, 10am–4pm Sat. 🖼

Exhibits displayed inside the History and Applied Arts Museum, Preiļi

Daugavpils ⑮

The second-most populous city in Latvia, Daugavpils is often regarded as a "Russian city" as the majority of its residents are Russian. Its history can be traced to 1275 and a Livonian Order castle called Dinaburga. In the 16th century, a settlement grew on the banks of the Daugava river, and was occupied by Poles, Russians and Swedes at various times. When the town was developed into a Tsarist fortress in the early 19th century, civilians were relocated southeast to the land that today forms the city centre. An industrial hub for the erstwhile Soviet Union, Daugavpils has suffered from economic neglect since independence, though the city's image is improving.

Stately exterior of the Museum of Regional Studies and Arts

🏛 Museum of Regional Studies and Arts

Rīgas iela 8. **Tel** 6542 4155.
🕐 11am–6pm Tue–Sat. 🎫
📷 📷 www.dnmm.lv

Housed in an attractive Art Nouveau building, this museum dedicates its ground floor to local history from the second half of the 18th century until 1918. The highlight of the museum is a room dedicated to Mark Rothko, an artist who was almost unknown in Latvia during the Soviet era. Sadly, the cost of an original painting was well outside the museum's budget, so a series of high-quality reproductions were commissioned instead. There has, however, been discussion about original works being pledged to the museum by Rothko's children.

✡ Synagogue

Cietokšņa 42. **Tel** 6542 0092.
🕐 by appointment.

Prior to World War I, over half of the town's population was Jewish. There were at one time 48 synagogues, of which only one remains in use. It was renovated in 2006 with the help of Mark Rothko's children, who had visited it in 2003, the centenary of their father's birth.

⛪ Cathedral of Sts Boris and Glebe

Tautas iela 2. **Tel** 6545 3544.

This blue-and-white building, resplendent with its ten golden cupolas, is the largest Russian Orthodox cathedral in the country. Built in 1905, it is named after the two saints on whose feast day the Russian army entered Daugavpils in 1656. The Russian name for the town, Borisoglebsk, was also taken from the saints' names. The icons and frescoes inside were copied from those in Sophia Cathedral in Kiev.

⛪ St Mary's Church

Puškina 16a. 🕐 services only. 📷
A solid pink structure with diminutive blue domes, this Old Believers' *(see p122)*

Beautiful interior of the Cathedral of Sts Boris and Glebe

MARK ROTHKO (1903–70)

Mark Rothko was born Marcus Rothkowitz into a Jewish family in Daugavpils at a time when the Russian Empire was scarred by pogroms. His family emigrated to Portland, Oregon, in 1913. He received a scholarship to study at Yale University, but left after two years and trained in art in New

York. Rothko changed his name in 1940, and by 1950 he developed a unique style, in which soft-edged rectangular forms are aligned in front of coloured backgrounds. They are described as Abstract Expressionist, although Rothko insisted that he was interested not in pure form but in expressing basic human emotions. Following an aneurysm and the breakdown of his marriage, Rothko committed suicide in 1970.

Mark Rothko, Abstract Expressionist

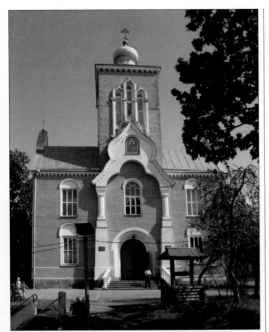

Rose-coloured façade of St Mary's Church

VISITORS' CHECKLIST

Road Map E4. 🏘 *110,000.*
🚉 *Rīgas iela.* 🚌 *Viestura iela
10.* ℹ️ *Saules iela 23a, 6542
2818.* 🎭 *City Festival (Jun)*

At one point, during the
Soviet regime, it was used
as a boxing gym.

🔔 Virgin Mary
Catholic Church
A Pumpura 11a. ◯ *evening mass.*
According to local legend the
daughters of a rich merchant
drowned in a lake on the spot
where the church now stands.

⛰ Daugavpils Fortress
Cietokšņa iela. 📷 📹
The construction of this
self-contained Russian fortress
began in 1810, but was inter-
rupted when Napoleon's
army attacked in July 1812.
It is surrounded by earth
walls. The moat encircling
it once contained tunnels
which connected it to the
Daugava river, but they have
since been blocked. The
fortress served as a German
concentration camp, and was
later occupied by the Soviet
Army until 1993. Today, on the
river's left bank is a prison,
while the right bank is largely
abandoned. Visitors enter at
Michael's Gate (Mihaila vārti).

church is rarely open to public.
Visitors may, however, be able
to look inside during services,
when candles are lit in front
of the dozens of icons that line
the walls. The solemn chant-
ing of the congregation adds
to the atmosphere.

🔔 Martin Luther Church
18 Novembra iela 66. **Tel** *2957
4349.* ◯ *Sun or by appointment.*
Built in red-brick Neo-Gothic
style, Martin Luther Church
dates from 1893, and has
benefited from complete
renovation in recent years.

DAUGAVPILS

Cathedral of Sts Boris
  and Glebe ③
Martin Luther Church ⑤
Museum of Regional Studies
  and Arts ①
St Mary's Church ④
Synagogue ②
Virgin Mary Catholic Church ⑥

0 metres   500

0 yards   500

Key to Symbols *see back flap*

Latgale Lakes ⑳

Latvia's relatively hilly southeastern corner, known as the Latgale Uplands (Latgales augstiene), is covered with a patchwork of more than 800 lakes. On a sunny day it is easy to see why this part is called the Land of Blue Lakes. Unfortunately, public transport is limited here, although if time permits the area can be explored by bus. The route also passes through Rēzekne, where the tourist office can provide advice on activities such as angling and bird-watching in the area, and a trip to Ludza en route is also possible.

Lake Lubāns, one of Latvia's favourite spots for bird-watchers

Lake Lubāns ⑧
One of the best places for bird-watching and fishing in the country, this is Latvia's largest lake by surface area.

Teirumnīki ⑦
A boardwalk circles the lake and runs through a swamp where cranberries grow.

Musical Instruments Workshop, Gaiglava ⑥
Visitors can watch artisans at work and learn to play traditional instruments.

Rēzekne ⑤
The cultural centre of Latgale, Rēzekne is known for its statue of pagan goddess Māra.

Mākoņkalns ③
Cloud Hill, at 248 m (814 ft), is a popular viewpoint, with ruins of a castle on the summit.

Lake Rāzna ④
The largest in Latvia by volume, Lake Rāzna offers a number of decent accommodation options.

KEY

ℹ️	Visitor information
▬	Tour route
═══	Other road

Lielais Liepukalns ②
At 289 m (948 ft), this hill is the highest point in the region and the third-highest in the country.

TIPS FOR DRIVERS

Starting point: *Lielais liepukalns.*
Length: *114 km (71 miles).*
Stopping-off points: *Rēzekne is an ideal stop. It is possible to stay at Ežezers, Rāzna and Lubāns.*
Driving conditions: *Avoid driving around the western edge of Lake Rāzna in bad weather.*

Map labels: Iča, P36, Ideņa, ⑧, Lake Lubāns, ⑥, Pudinava, ⑦, Žogotas, Nagli, Dricāni, Malta, Ivgolova, Kantinieki, Rēzekne, P36, Ludza, ⑤ RĒZEKNE, A12, Sakstagals, Janopole, Balbiši, A13, Viškeri, ④ Kaunata, Lake Rāzna, Zosna, Lipuški, ②, ③, 57, Andrupene, Andeņi, Lake Ežezers, ①, Dagda

0 km   10
0 miles   10

Lake Ežezers ①
Translated as "Hedgehog Lake", Lake Ežezers is considered one of the most beautiful lakes in Latgale. Its 36 islands can be explored by boat.

For hotels and restaurants in this region see pp305–307 and pp335–7

Ludza ㉑

Road Map E3. 🏘 *10,500.* 🚉 🚌 **i** *Baznicas 42, 6570 7203.* ⛴

Perhaps the oldest town in Latvia, Ludza traces its foundation back to about 1177. The central square is home to the tourist information office and the Orthodox Cathedral.

The **Handicrafts Centre** (Ludzas amatnieku centrs), close to the central square, has a potter's kiln and space for artisans. Visitors can participate in workshops by prior arrangement. Handicraft objects are on sale here as well. There is also a monthly food and crafts market.

The town's **Museum of Local Studies** (Ludzas novadpētniecības muzejs) occupies the former villa of Jakov Kulnev (1764–1812), a Russian war hero who lived in Ludza. The grounds contain late 19th- and early 20th-century wooden buildings from various parts of Latgale.

🏛 **Handicrafts Centre**
Tālavijas iela 27a. **Tel** *6570 7203.* **www**.ludzasamatnieki.lv

🏛 **Museum of Local Studies**
Kulneva iela 2. **Tel** *6572 3931.* ◷ *9am–5pm Mon–Fri, 10am–5pm Sat & Sun.* 🎟

Vecpiebalga ㉒

Road Map D3. 🚌 **i** *2656 5977.* **www**.vecpiebalga.lv

With a history dating back to the early 14th century, this small town is famed as the home of prominent cultural figures. Notable among them were the brothers, Reinis (1839–1920) and Matīss Kaudzīte (1848–1926), who wrote *Mērnieku laiki* (The Times of the Land Surveyors). Among the best-loved Latvian novels, it is based on the sale of a landlord's estates to peasant farmers. The authors' home is now the **Kaudzīte Brothers Memorial Museum**.

Environs
There are other interesting sites close to Vecpiebalga. The Kārlis Skalbe Museum is about 4 km (2 miles) from

Statue of Liena, heroine of *Mērnieku laiki,* **in Vecpiebalga**

the town. It occupies the summerhouse of revolutionary writer Kārlis Skalbe (1878–1945). Further along the road is the Janskola Museum, housed in the former home of composer Emīls Dārziņš (1875–1910). The displays include works by Latvian poet Janis Sudrabkalns (1894–1975).

🏛 **Kaudzīte Brothers Memorial Museum**
Kalna kaibēni. **Tel** *6447 3037.* ◷ *May–Oct: 10am–5pm daily.* 🎟

Alūksne ㉓

Road Map E3. 🏘 *9,500.* 🚉 *from Gulbene.* 🚌 *from Cēsis.* **i** *Pils 74, 6432 2804.* **www**.aluksne.lv

In 1342, the Brotherhood of the Sword built a castle on an island in Lake Alūksne, after destroying the existing fortress. The Swedish army demolished the castle in 1702 rather than let it fall into Russian hands.

Alūksne is best known for its association with Ernst Glück (1654–1705), a German Lutheran clergyman who was the first to translate the Bible into Latvian. His home has been turned into the **Ernst Glück Museum of the Bible**.

The Museum of Local Studies and Art is housed in a manor house built in 1861 for Baron Vietinghoff. In addition to displays on local history, arts and crafts, the museum can arrange excursions in the surrounding area.

🏛 **Ernst Glück Museum of the Bible**
Pils 25a. **Tel** *6432 3164.* ◷ *noon–5pm Wed–Sat, 1–5pm Sun.* 🎟

Gulbene–Alūksne Narrow-Gauge Railway ㉔

Road Map E3. 🎪 *Railway Festival (first Sat in Sep).* **www**.banitis.lv

This 33-km (21-mile) stretch of railway track constitutes the only functioning narrow-gauge passenger railway within Latvia. The 90-minute journey has stops en route, including Stāmeriena, which has a manor house, and Umernieki.

The **Ates Mill Museum** is the primary incentive for visiting Umernieki. Around the mill is an ethnographic museum, consisting of 13 buildings which have been brought from around Vidzeme.

🏛 **Ates Mill Museum**
Ate, Kalncempji village. **Tel** *2940 0393.* ◷ *9am–5pm Wed–Mon.* 🎟 ♿ 🎪 *Harvest Festival (Sep).*

Old Soviet steam engine locomotive at Gulbene railway station

LITHUANIA

Lithuania at a Glance

An unblemished natural landscape of rolling hills, Lithuania is blessed with thousands of lakes that create a complex network of streams and rivers. In this low-lying post-glacial countryside, almost all the land lies at less than 200 m (656 ft) above sea level. The eastern half of the country is known as the "highlands" and the western half the "lowlands". The main features of the Lithuanian coast are its fascinating sandy dunes and beaches. Despite Lithuania's tumultuous history, many of the country's fine historic buildings have survived.

Hill of Crosses (see p273)

WESTERN LITHUANIA (see pp268–85)

Palanga (see p282) is a popular beach resort that draws hundreds of visitors each summer. Once a quiet little fishing hamlet, today it is a vibrant place filled with innumerable bars and cafés.

Pažaislis Monastery (see p261)

Parnidis Dune towers over the fishing village of Nida, on the Curonian Spit (see pp284–5). Views from the summit take in both the Baltic Sea and the Curonian Lagoon and stretch southwards to Kaliningrad.

◁ Statue of Jesus Christ amid thousands of crosses left by visitors on the Hill of Crosses, Western Lithuania

Kernavė (see p254) *is a UNESCO World Heritage Site, set in the Neris River Valley. Once the capital of the Grand Duchy of Lithuania, it is now one of the largest archaeological sites in the Baltic region. The state museum, established here in 1989, was converted into a cultural reserve in 2004.*

CENTRAL LITHUANIA
(see pp248–67)

Vilnius Cathedral (see pp224–5), *a Neo-Classical structure, houses the lavish Baroque Chapel of St Casimir and a crypt that provides an insight into Lithuania's complex history.*

VILNIUS
(see pp216–47)

| 0 km | 25 |
| 0 miles | 25 |

Trakai Island Castle (see pp252–3), *in the picturesque village of Trakai, is a fairytale fortress that makes a beautiful day-trip from the capital during any season of the year. An optional trip by yacht or rowing boat rounds off the experience.*

A PORTRAIT OF LITHUANIA

The largest of the three Baltic States and one of the hidden jewels of Europe, Lithuania takes pride in its relatively secluded landscape of clean lakes, ancient forests and coastal dunes. The capital Vilnius, which has a UNESCO-protected Old Town, combines the romance of its breathtaking Baroque architecture with the modern trappings of 21st-century Europe.

Lithuania successfully repelled the Germanic invaders as early as 1410 at the Battle of Grünwald. In the subsequent centuries, however, the country experienced a tumultuous series of invasions. Most recently, the two World Wars and the massacre of one of Europe's largest Jewish communities were followed by the neglect of the Soviet era.

The Vytis, emblem of Lithuania

Since its independence in 1991, Lithuania has strived to restore its national identity. Its capital Vilnius possesses one of Europe's finest old towns, with several Baroque masterpieces. Across the country, areas of serene natural beauty have become protected reserves teeming with wildlife. Excellent roads wind through attractive villages and towns that are remarkably tranquil. A resurgence in the popularity of folk culture is colouring every corner of the country, with wooden crosses, altars and shrines being crafted and folk song and dance traditions being explored. An explosion of printed and electronic materials in Lithuanian, a language related to Sanskrit, has taken place since the Singing Revolution (1987–90). At the same time, Lithuania is forging a positive political and cultural role for itself in the expanded European Union.

A sweeping view of Parnidis Dune, or the Great Dune, in the Curonian Spit National Park

◁ Dancers in traditional dress at a concert, Vilnius University

Catholics worshipping the Virgin Mary in Vilnius

ETHNIC AND RELIGIOUS IDENTITY

Lithuania is the most ethnically homogeneous of the Baltic countries. By staying largely agrarian it managed to stem the incoming tide of large numbers of Russians and other nationalities whom the Soviet authorities wanted to man the new factories being built across the Baltic region. Of its population of 3.4 million, 84 per cent are Lithuanian, while only 5 per cent are Russian and 6 per cent Polish. Other minorities include Belarusians and Ukrainians, besides a small group of Tatars and Karaim. In Vilnius, the most ethnically diverse city, Russian and Polish can commonly be heard.

Despite its pagan past, Lithuania has a strong Catholic identity that sets it apart from Estonia and Latvia, where the Germans introduced Lutheranism. The efforts of the Soviet authorities to stamp out religious worship by converting churches into warehouses, cinemas, art galleries and museums, destroying their interiors and deporting large numbers of priests to Siberia, failed. As a result, only 10 per cent of the people do not identify with any religious group today. Religious groups other than Catholics include Russian Orthodox (5 per cent) and small communities of Old Believers and Lutherans.

POLITICS

Since regaining independence in 1991, Lithuania has vacillated between left- and right-wing governments, while struggling to find its feet on the international stage. Achieving the goals of NATO and EU membership in 2004 was of huge significance for the Baltic region, wrenching it away from Russia's influence. The impeachment of President Rolandas Paksas for violating the constitution, also in 2004, was the climax of a wave of public scepticism in politics.

A Lithuanian folk dance group dressed in national costume

Lithuanian President Valdas Adamkus outside Vilnius Cathedral

High-profile corruption cases revealing how politicians have lobbied on behalf of business interests in exchange for money have created the feeling that moral leadership in Lithuania is waning. Some politicians, however, including two-time president Valdas Adamkus, remain untainted by scandal.

ECONOMY

The Lithuanian economy is one of the fastest-growing in Europe. A dynamic private sector feeds strongly on niche industries including laser optics and biotechnology, as well as core industries such as construction and energy. Lithuanian laser and biotech companies are among the strongest in Europe. Lithuania's largest company by turnover is the Mažeikių Nafta oil refinery near Mažeikiai. The Soviet-era Ignalina Nuclear Power Plant is being decommissioned, but a new nuclear power plant is likely to be constructed to reduce reliance on Russian energy.

Agriculture was rapidly privatized after independence, and heavily subsidized after EU membership. Although this has made much of the land more productive, negative results include large swathes of abandoned land and widespread rural poverty. However, ways are being found to invest in sustainable industries such as tourism. Many small farms have been turned into attractive countryside farmsteads providing tourist activities and accommodation.

MODERN LIFE

Lithuanians take immense pride in their rich cultural life. The countless art galleries in the cities and towns reveal the importance of art and culture to Lithuania. The walls of most households are adorned with real paintings and graphics rather than framed reproductions. Cultural figures, such as M K Čiurlionis and adored novelist and painter Jurga Ivanauskaitė, have apportioned their skills to more than one medium. Symphonies, chamber concerts, classical ballets and operas are performed regularly throughout the country. On the stage, the dark, post-industrial version of *Hamlet*, by acclaimed theatre director Eimuntas Nekrošius, is one of the most popular theatrical pieces.

In sport, although Lithuania has produced achievers such as the discus-thrower Virgilijus Alekna and ice-dancer Margarita Drobiazko, basketball remains its national obsession. While the Kaunas-based Žalgiris team dominates the domestic scene, the Lithuanian Olympic basketball team has put Lithuania on the world map.

The 2006 Euroleague basketball match in progress

LITHUANIA THROUGH THE YEAR

Lithuanians celebrate a host of festivals where traditional events and folk culture blend with ancient pagan and Catholic rituals. Most of the year's events take place in summer, when after months of wintry gloom the country comes alive with music, dance, cinema, folk culture, handicraft and food festivals. Music is at

Lithuanian accordonist

the centre of most of the country's events, and it ranges from classical, jazz and blues to electronic and contemporary. Christmas is usually white but the thick snows fail to thwart the merrymaking, which culminates in New Year's Eve celebrations. A number of commemorative days are observed in addition to the traditional annual events.

Kaziuko Crafts Fair, held every year to mark St Casimir's Day

SPRING

Lithuanians welcome spring with joyful celebrations. The warmer weather wakes the country up to a new season of fairs and festivals.

MARCH

Kaziuko Crafts Fair *(4 Mar)*, Vilnius. A feast of traditional arts and crafts marking St Casimir's Day, with stalls selling all manner of curios.
Cinema Spring *(late Mar–early Apr)*, Vilnius. One of the largest international film festivals in the Baltic region, it showcases the best foreign-language films of the year, most with English subtitles.

APRIL

Jauna Muzika, Vilnius. A festival of new electronic music, often featuring radical international songwriters.
Kaunas Jazz *(late Apr)*. One of the best international jazz festivals in the country.

MAY

New Baltic Dance *(early May)*, Vilnius and Klaipėda. This eclectic event celebrates modern dance and theatre.
Poetry Spring, Vilnius. An international poetry festival and the most outstanding annual literary event in Lithuania.
Kaunas City Day *(20 May)*. A folk art fair with concerts, funfairs and fireworks.

Local folk dressed in traditional costume, Kaunas City Day festival

SUMMER

The sultry Lithuanian summer initiates great festivities. Classical music takes precedence in the warm evenings, along with jazz and blues.

JUNE

Cow-Swimming Festival, Aukštaitija National Park. A quirky custom where locals dress in folk costumes and watch as cows wearing wreaths are led into a lake to swim to the other side.
Medieval Festival, Trakai. Knights' fights with swords and battleaxes are the festival's highlight.
Joninės *(24 Jun)*. The summer solstice is celebrated all over Lithuania on St John's Day. It is also known as Rasos, meaning "of the dew", for dew's healing properties.
Pažaislis Music Festival *(Jun–Aug)*, Kaunas. Hosted at the Baroque Pažaislis Monastery, it stages music performances.

JULY

Christopher Summer Festival *(Jul–Aug)*, Vilnius. A hugely enjoyable musical fiesta with performances at different venues all over the city.
Statehood Day *(6 Jul)*. Pomp and ceremony are the hallmarks of this national holiday dedicated to the coronation of King Mindaugas.
Lake Lukstas Blues Nights features blues and jazz performers with the isolated Lake Lukstas as the backdrop.

Guards at the Presidential Palace in Vilnius, on Statehood Day

Sea Festival *(late Jul)*, Klaipėda. The freedom of the seas expressed in a carnival.

AUGUST

Christopher's Guitars, Vilnius. A festival featuring classical guitar and flamenco concerts as its highlight.

Mėnuo Juodaragis *(late Aug)*. Translated as "Black Horned Moon", this annual musical event of folk, metal and electronica is held in a different location every three years.

Capital Days *(late Aug–Sep)*, Vilnius. A multi-art event when Gedimino Avenue is flooded with craft and food stalls, while the squares of central Vilnius become rock and pop music venues.

AUTUMN

A short but beautiful season, autumn in Lithuania is a visual treat. However, there are fewer annual events.

SEPTEMBER

Sirenos Theatre Festival *(Sept–Oct)*, Vilnius. Works by international and local artists are showcased.

Mushroom Festival *(late Sep)*, Varėna. The only traditional festival dedicated to mushrooms in Europe.

Fire Sculptures Festival *(21–23 Sep)*. Straw figures are set alight at night in this festival that honours Grand Duke Gediminas and also celebrates the autumn equinox.

OCTOBER

International Festival of Modern Dance *(early Oct)*, Kaunas. A festival of freestyle contemporary dance, it attracts the best dancers from all over the world.

Vilnius Jazz *(mid-Oct)*. Jazz, blues and swing are performed by a host of talented contemporary Lithuanian musicians and singers at this festival.

WINTER

Lithuania looks stunning in winter. The country is often covered in a blanket of snow. However, the chill fails to curb the festive spirit.

NOVEMBER

Scanorama *(mid-Nov)*, Vilnius. Ten days of Scandinavian films take over the capital's multiplexes for this annual film festival.

DECEMBER

Christmas *(24–26 Dec)*. The festivities culminate in most homes with a 12-course meat-free meal on Christmas Eve. Christmas Day is celebrated with mass in church, and concerts.

New Year's Eve *(31 Dec)*. Celebrations and parties take place throughout the country, and at the stroke of midnight fireworks light up the sky.

JANUARY

Epiphany *(6 Jan)*, Vilnius. Shortly after New Year, a colourful procession of the Three Kings graces the streets of the Old Town.

FEBRUARY

Užgavėnės *(mid-Feb)*. People throughout Lithuania don masks of witches, devils, goats and other creatures and feast on heartwarmingly rich food in this farewell to winter.

PUBLIC HOLIDAYS

New Year's Day (1 Jan)
Independence Day (16 Feb)
Restoration of Independence (11 Mar)
Easter (Mar/April)
Labour Day (1 May)
Midsummer's Day (23 Jun)
Joninės (24 Jun)
Statehood Day (6 Jul)
Assumption Day (15 Aug)
All Saints' Day (1 Nov)
Christmas (24–26 Dec)
Boxing Day (26 Dec)

Musicians jamming at the Vilnius Jazz festival

THE HISTORY OF LITHUANIA

urope's last pagan stronghold, Lithuania rose as a powerful state by the late 14th century, surviving until the 16th century. It was thereafter subjugated first by the Poles and then the Russians. The long periods of occupation endured by the country stirred a reawakening of national identity in its people. An independent republic, briefly created during the inter-war era, was finally established in 1991.

At the start of the 13th century, Lithuanian tribes, such as the Samogitians in the west and Aukštaitiai in the east, began to unite in the face of regular incursions by the Germanic crusaders. The brutal attacks grew with increasing intensity before the resolutely pagan Samogitians vanquished the Knights of the Sword at the Battle of the Sun in 1236.

13th-century seal of the Germanic crusaders

Lithuania *(see pp212–13)*, led by a dynasty established by Gediminas (r.1316–41). The crusaders occupied the Grand Duchy for 100 years, until they were finally and decisively defeated at the Battle of Grünwald (Žalgiris) in 1410 by the powerful allied armies of Lithuania and Poland.

THE LITHUANIAN GRAND DUCHY

Duke Mindaugas (r.1235–63), who was rapidly adding territory to his base in Aukštaitija, united the tribes in 1240, crowning himself king in 1253. His acceptance of Christianity to appease the crusaders enraged the Samogitians, who murdered him, took over his land and reverted to paganism. By the beginning of the 14th century, large numbers of crusaders returned from the Middle East and joined the fight against the pagan Grand Duchy of

POLISH-LITHUANIAN COMMONWEALTH

Grand Duke Jogaila (r.1362–1434) married Jadwiga of Poland in 1386 and accepted Christianity, which led to mass baptisms throughout Lithuania in the ensuing years. The marriage

Impression of the Union of Lublin by 19th-century artist Jan Matejko

TIMELINE

King Mindaugas (c.1203–63)

1236 Samogitian victory at the Battle of the Sun

1253 Duke Mindaugas crowned

1386 Lithuania and Poland unite

1392 Grand Duchy of Lithuania reaches the Black Sea

1200	1300	1400	1!

1240 Duke Mindaugas unites Lithuania

1316 Accession of Gediminas

1382 Crusaders seize Samogitia

1410 Battle of Grünwald (Žalgiris) destroys the Teutonic Knights formed a Polish-Lithuanian alliance that endured for centuries. This proved particularly effective as a bulwark against enemies in the West and in the East. Under Grand Duke Vytautas (r.1401–30), Lithuania was able to extend its reach between the Baltic and the Black seas. Throughout the first half of the 16th century, however, a militant Russia compelled a stronger union between Lithuania and Poland, cemented at the Union of Lublin in 1569. The Commonwealth that resulted lasted for over 200 years.

Portrait of Grand Duke Vytautas on a tile

DECLINE OF THE COMMONWEALTH

When King Sigismund Augustus (r.1548–72) died without an heir, the combined position of Grand Duke of Lithuania and King of Poland became an elected one, chosen by the all-powerful nobility. Warsaw, midway between the old capitals of Vilnius and Kraków, became the base. Stefan Bathory (1533–86) was one of the most successful of these elected heads of state. Apart from founding Vilnius University, he also introduced sweeping military and judicial reforms. During the Livonian Wars *(see p33)*, he successfully led a decisive campaign against the Russians, regaining control over Livonia in 1582.

Under the Commonwealth, Poland established its hegemony, with the Poles dominating the Lithuanian nobility. The bourgeoisie, on the other hand, were deprived of all political rights as well as the right to own land, while the peasants were forced to become serfs, subject to severe punishment if they attempted to flee.

The 17th century was a disastrous period for Lithuania, with misrule in Warsaw, plague and fires in Vilnius and a calamitous invasion by the Russians in 1655. Governed by a string of ineffective rulers and noblemen who were either deliberately divisive or simply uninterested in state affairs, the steadily weakening Commonwealth became, throughout the 18th century, little more than a puppet state to Tsarist Russia. In a series of partitions in 1772, 1793 and 1795, the vast lands of the Commonwealth were divided between Russia, Prussia and Austria, despite brave armed resistance by Lithuanian patriots. One such failed uprising was led by Jokūbas Jasinskis (1761–94). By 1795, with the final partition of the Commonwealth, Poland and Lithuania had ceased to exist.

Russians paying tribute to Stefan Bathory, a painting by Jan Matejko

---

The Grand Duchy of Lithuania

The royal seal of Vytautas

Founded in the 13th century by King Mindaugas and strengthened further by Grand Duke Gediminas in the 14th century, the Grand Duchy of Lithuania reached its greatest territorial extent under Vytautas the Great. Originally a defensive military union, the Duchy quickly started expanding eastwards and southwards, eventually stretching across much of present-day Belarus and Ukraine. The Duchy was dominated in Vilnius by a military class that later became a privileged nobility. Vilnius flourished as the capital of culture and architecture.

KEY

Grand Duchy under Vytautas

THE BATTLE OF GRÜNWALD

Nothing quite symbolizes the Grand Duchy at the height of its achievements like Jan Matejko's masterpiece painted in 1878. Vytautas the Great is shown at the centre, victorious in the Battle of Grünwald (Žalgiris) against the Teutonic Knights in 1410. The Knights were decisively defeated by the combined armies of the Grand Duchy and Poland, led by Vytautas and King Jogaila, respectively.

Grand Duke Gediminas (1275–1341) *extended the Duchy's borders, moved the capital to Vilnius and built a powerful chain of defensive fortresses.*

Albert II Radvila (1595–1656), *who was descended from a long line of influential nobles, effectively ruled the Grand Duchy as Grand Chancellor of Lithuania within the Polish-Lithuanian Commonwealth.*

Grand Duke Vytautas (1350–1430), *shown here in a 17th-century portrait, is today revered as a national hero. Under his reign, the Grand Duchy grew to its greatest geographical extent covering swathes of land, between the Baltic and Black seas.*

Tile, 16th century   Coin, 16th century

SURVIVING THE CENTURIES

Artifacts found during excavations of the remains of the Royal Palace in Vilnius include decorative tiles, coins and exquisitely crafted jewellery. While the tiles and coins date from the 16th century, some of the jewellery dates back to the 14th century. The collection is likely to go on display once the newly reconstructed palace is completed.

Vilnius University, *which the Jesuits had founded as an academy in 1568, was upgraded to a university 11 years later by Stefan Bathory (1533–86), the Grand Duke of Lithuania and King of Poland.*

Grand Duke Vytautas

The icon of the Virgin Mary *at the Gates of Dawn in Vilnius is a fine example of religious painting from the period. It was originally painted on oak panels in the 1620s.*

The first book printed in the Lithuanian language *was* Catechism *(1547) by Martynas Mažvydas. Appearing in the Duchy at a time when Polish was the preferred language of the aristocracy, the book had a great appeal for the pagan rural masses.*

The Christianization of Lithuania *took place in 1387, following the union of Lithuania and Poland. However, unlike the dramatic mass conversion depicted in this 19th-century painting by Jan Matejko, many parts of Lithuania remained pagan into the 16th century.*

Napoleon's Grand Army crossing the Nemunas river in 1812

TSARIST RUSSIAN RULE

Over 120 years of occupation followed the break-up of the Commonwealth, with most of the land once governed by the Grand Duchy of Lithuania now absorbed into the Russian Empire. Resistance constantly simmered under the surface, however, and hopes of independence were revived when Napoleon marched through Kaunas and Vilnius in June 1812. These hopes were crushed six months later when the demoralized, half-frozen remnants of the French Grand Army retreated from Moscow through Vilnius.

When a rebellion led mainly by the rural nobility failed in 1831, repressive measures were launched such as the closure of Vilnius University and the enforced use of Russian in Lithuanian schools. Even harsher oppression followed another rebellion in 1863, with over 100 of the resistance leaders hunted down and hanged, while others were deported with their families to Siberia. The Russification of the whole country followed, which involved a

President Antanas
Smetona (r.1926–40)

conscious eradication of all traces of traditional Lithuania. Catholic churches were converted to Orthodox ones and Lithuanian-language books in the Latin alphabet were banned. However, language and identity were kept alive by smuggling books in from East Prussia as well as the printing and circulation of the first Lithuanian-language newspapers, *Aušra* (Dawn) and *Varpas* (Bell).

NATIONHOOD REGAINED, AND LOST

As the chaos of World War I and the 1917 Revolution weakened Russia, an elected council in Vilnius declared Lithuanian independence on 16 February 1918. International recognition was slow in coming. In October 1920, Józef Piłsudski (1867–1935), the nationalist head of state of Poland, which had also regained its independence in 1918, sent an army to occupy Vilnius. The Lithuanian government was, therefore, forced to re-establish itself in Kaunas. Vilnius was indisputably Lithuania's historical capital, but by now, almost half of the city's population was Jewish, and the other half consisted of Polish-speakers. Kaunas was declared Lithuania's temporary capital and remained so until 1939. An element of pride was restored when Lithuania snatched control of Memel from a caretaker French garrison in early 1923 and renamed it Klaipėda.

TIMELINE

1812 Napoleon's advance and disastrous retreat

1832 Russians close down Vilnius University

Dr Jonas Basanavičius, one of the signatories of the Lithuanian Independence Act

1918 Lithuania declares independence

1815	1855	1895

1831 Rebellion against Tsarist rule

1863 Lithuanian rebels persecuted by Russia

1866 Ban on Lithuanian-language books in the Latin alphabet; 40 years of book-smuggling from East Prussia begins

Adolf Hitler entering Klaipėda in 1939

THE REPUBLIC OF LITHUANIA

In 1988, encouraged by the greater openness of Soviet premier Mikhail Gorbachev's reforms, a group of intellectuals founded the Sąjūdis movement to rally popular support for demonstrations that had begun the previous year. The response was immediate. Peaceful protests increased and, on 11 March 1990, Lithuania declared its independence, the first of any of the Soviet republics to do so. In January 1991, Soviet tanks and troops stormed the Vilnius TV Tower, killing 14 unarmed civilians and injuring 700.

In August 1991, the failure of the hardliners' putsch in Moscow finally gave Lithuania freedom. The first presidential elections brought Algirdas Brazauskas to power. Several years of economic hardship followed, marked by rising unemployment. Lithuania's EU and NATO membership in 2004 has brought the country far greater security and prosperity.

Independent Lithuania was led, between 1926 and 1940, by the authoritarian Antanas Smetona. For Lithuanians, this was a time of growing prosperity as agricultural exports boomed. However, these were uneasy times, as the resurgent powers of Germany and Russia loomed on either side. Klaipėda was retaken by the Nazis in 1939 and the Red Army occupied the rest of Lithuania following an ultimatum from Moscow in 1940. The Red Army carried out mass deportations and horrific massacres. The reign of terror continued under the Nazis, who, in June 1941, launched Operation Barbarossa, the code name for Germany's invasion of the Soviet Union. An estimated 200,000 people, most of them Jews, were taken outside virtually every town and city to be executed. In 1944, as part of its Baltic Offensive, the Red Army pushed back through Lithuania. Over the next ten years, between 120,000 and 300,000 people were deported to the Siberian Gulags. A brave, but futile, partisan war was fought from the Lithuanian forests until the early 1950s.

A Lithuanian independence rally in 1989, Kaunas

1939 Molotov-Ribbentrop Pact places Lithuania under Soviet control

1941 Nazi Operation Barbarossa launched

1988 Sąjūdis movement founded

1990 Declaration of independence

2004 Lithuania joins NATO; becomes member of EU

| 1935 | 1975 | 2015 |

1944 Soviets reoccupy Lithuania

1955 Partisan war against Soviet occupation dies away

Vilnius's TV Tower

2008 Lifting of visa requirements for Canada

1991 Bloody assault on Vilnius's TV Tower

President tona seizes er

VILNIUS

Whether viewed from one of the hills that overlook the Old Town or from one of the many pavement cafés with tall spires rising all around, Vilnius is unmistakably a city of great beauty. The Old Town, on the UNESCO World Heritage list since 1994, blends Gothic and Neo-Classical styles with a breathtaking late flourish of Baroque. Vilnius is in itself an architectural monument.

The character of Vilnius, the Lithuanian capital, has been retained partly because of its isolated location. Yet, the ebb and flow of history has given it a more multicultural feel than the country's other cities.

The earliest written reference to Vilnius exists in a letter from Grand Duke Gediminas in 1323, inviting citizens from towns in Germany to settle here, pledging freedom from taxes and granting other rights. Pagan Vilnius sustained many attacks during the Northern Crusades, yet by the 14th century it had become the capital of an empire that stretched from the Baltic Sea to the Black Sea. Vilnius was reduced to being a provincial city in the Polish-Lithuanian Commonwealth, but following a period of devastating wars, invasions and fires between the early 17th and mid-18th centuries, efforts to rebuild the city resulted in the rich offshoot of the Baroque style that is typical of Vilnius today.

Vilnius regained its status as the capital of Lithuania in 1918, but only for a year. Occupied by Poland, with Lithuania's government forced to relocate to Kaunas, it declined in economic importance until the Soviets invaded it in 1939. World War II devastated Vilnius and annihilated most of its Jewish population. However, under the ensuing Soviet occupation the city expanded.

A recent spate of development has transformed the city from a sleepy backwater to a lively, modern European capital that provides a wonderful setting for shopping, dining and nightlife. However, with Vilnius University, Town Hall Square and several carefully restored churches, Vilnius has retained its charm.

Colourful mural by Antanas Kmieliauskas decorating the ceiling of Vilnius University's bookshop, Littera

◁ Bernardine Church rising between the Church of St Anne and the statue of Adam Mickiewicz

Exploring Vilnius

Although its Old Town is one of the largest in Europe, Vilnius is a surprisingly compact city that can easily be explored on foot. Two of the best places to begin a tour of the Old Town and its Baroque treasures are Vilnius Cathedral in the north and the Gates of Dawn in the south. Gedimino Avenue, the main shopping street where the KGB Museum is located, stretches west from Cathedral Square, while the Church of St Anne lies immediately to the east of the Old Town. Vilnius is also a good base for exploring much of Central Lithuania.

Outdoor cafés along cobblestoned Pilies Street, Old Town

SIGHTS AT A GLANCE

SEE ALSO

• *Where to Stay* pp308–10

• *Where to Eat* pp338–40

KEY

▣	Street-by-Street map *pp220–21*
▣	Street-by-Street map *pp230–31*
🚉	Railway station
🚌	Bus station
ℹ	Tourist information
⊠	Post office
✚	Hospital
⛪	Church

N e r i s

ARSENALO GATVĖ

T VRUBLEVSKIO GATVĖ

TILTO GATVĖ

...NO PROSPEKTAS

...DMINIŲ GATVĖ

ŠVENTARAGIO GATVĖ

B RADVILAITĖS GATVĖ

V i l n i a

L STUOKOS GUCEVIČIAUS GATVĖ

UNIVERSITETO GATVĖ

S SKAPO GATVĖ

BERNARDINŲ GATVĖ

PILIES GATVĖ

...TVĖ

ŠV JONO GATVĖ

LATAKO GATVĖ

SVARCO GATVĖ

MAIRONIO GATVĖ

STIKLIŲ GATVĖ

...GATVĖ

SAVIČIAUS GATVĖ

BOKŠTO GATVĖ

DIDŽIOJI GATVĖ

ŠVATO JONIŠKISTOS

...NIŲ GATVĖ

RŪDNINKŲ GATVĖ

ŠV KAZIMIERO GATVĖ

ARKLIŲ GATVĖ

SUBAČIAUS GATVĖ

MAIRONIO GATVĖ

AUŠROS VARTŲ GATVĖ

SUBAČIAUS GATVĖ

BAZILIJONŲ GATVĖ

M DAUKŠOS GATVĖ

0 metres	200
0 yards	200

🚌 **Bus Station**
660 m (720 yards)

🚉 **Railway Station**
550 m (600 yards)

GETTING AROUND

Walking is the best way to explore the Old Town.
Cycling is another popular way of getting around
the area. Bicycles can be rented from the tourist
office in the Old Town. Outlying sites, such as the
TV Tower and Pushkin Museum, can be reached by
bus or trolleybus, but others, for example Verkiai
Palace, are more easily reached by car or taxi.

Street-by-Street: Pilies Street and Vilnius University

Narrow lanes, hidden courtyards and some of the Old Town's finest architecture make Pilies Street and nearby Vilnius University a delight to stroll around and explore. The 550-year-old university is one of the oldest in Eastern Europe. Traffic is restricted, and in summer restaurants and cafés spill out onto the cobbled streets. Souvenir stalls and shops on Pilies sell amber and interesting gifts, while the surrounding buildings are testimony to the city's long and eventful history.

KEY

– – – Suggested route

Applied Arts Museum lies inside the C Arsenal.

Upper Castle
The best visual introduction to Vilnius is from the viewing platform on the castle's last surviving tower. The Lithuanian flag was raised here in 1919 and in 1988 **⓫**

Royal Palace
Also known as the Lower Castle, it was the main residence of the Grand Dukes and was the political and cultural heart of Lithuania **❿**

Vilnius Cathedral
The austere Neo-Classical exterior of Lithuania's main basilica belies its hidden jewels, which include the Baroque Chapel of St Casimir and the winding passages of the crypt **❽**

Presidential Palace
A 14th-century nobleman's residence, this building has hosted many historical figures. It became the Presidency in 1997 **❸**

STAR SIGHTS

★ Pilies Street

★ Vilnius University

UNIVE

★ **Pilies Street**
With a view of the Upper Castle ever present, Pilies is one of the city's oldest streets. It was once Vilnius's commercial centre but today the street is popular with visitors hunting for amberware and other local products.

Church of St Anne
The flamboyant Gothic red-brick church fell victim to Napoleon's soldiers, who used it as a barracks on their way to Moscow in 1812. Fortunately, the beautiful façade has survived the turbulent centuries ⑰

| 0 metres | 100 |
| 0 yards | 100 |

Littera Bookshop
This charmingly decorated bookshop at the eastern edge of the university's Sarbievijaus Courtyard also sells university souvenirs.

St John's Church has a sweeping Baroque façade.

★ **Vilnius University**
Lithuania's largest university, occupies a large part of the Old Town. It is 550 years old and has over 13 courtyards and multiple buildings ❶

BERNARDINŲ GATVĖ

PILIES GATVĖ

ŠV. MYKOLO GATVĖ

Vilnius University ❶
Vilniaus universitetas

Universiteto 3. **Map** 2 D3. *Tel 268 7001.* ◯ *10am–5:30pm Mon–Sat.* ▓ *for prior booking call 268 7298.* ▓ **www**.vu.lt

The oldest university in Eastern Europe was founded as a Jesuit College in 1568, before becoming a school of higher education in 1579. The current campus, constructed between the 16th and 18th centuries, is a combination of different architectural styles.

The most impressive of its 13 courtyards, the Great Courtyard has open galleries dating from the 17th century, which were later lined with dedications to professors. Accessed via a passage from the western side of the Great Courtyard, the Observatory Courtyard by contrast is a serene enclosed garden from which the observatory and its zodiac symbols can be seen.

North of the Great Courtyard is the Sarbievijaus Courtyard, the oldest part of the university. At its far end, a bookshop, **Littera**, can be found. Frescoes caricaturing professors and students that decorate the interior of the bookshop were painted in 1978 by Antanas Kmieliauskas (b.1932).

Façade of St John's Church and adjoining belfry

St John's Church ❷
Šv Jono bažnyčia

Universiteto 3/Šv Jono 12. **Map** 2 D3. *Tel 611 795.* ◯ *10am–5pm Mon–Sat.* ✝ *6pm Mon–Sat, 11am Sun.*

At the southern edge of the university campus, the impressive façade and separate bell tower of the Church of St John the Baptist and St John the Evangelist dominate the Great Courtyard. The original Gothic church, built here in 1426, was reconstructed in 1749 in flamboyant Baroque by Jan Krzysztof Glaubitz (*see p233*). The ten magnificent altars in faux marble with Corinthian columns illuminate the otherwise austere interior. Initially, there were 22 columns, most of which were removed during further rebuilding in the 19th century. At 68 m (223 ft), the bell tower, which was given two extra tiers by Glaubitz, is the tallest structure in the Old Town.

Presidential Palace ❸
Lietuvos respublikos prezidentūra

Daukanto aikštė 3. **Map** 2 D3. *Tel 266 4154.* ◯ *9am–5pm Sat (call in advance).* ▓ *for group tour call 266 4011.* **www**.president.lt

Formerly a residence for high-ranking bishops, this ornate building has existed since Lithuania's conversion to Christianity at the end of the 14th century. The palace was rebuilt in the late 1820s in the Neo-Classical style by Vasily Stasov (1769–1848), an architect from St Petersburg. It has hosted a number of important personalities, including Napoleon Bonaparte and Tsar Alexander I. The former used the palace during his doomed advance on Moscow.

The palace was later used for a variety of ceremonial purposes before becoming the Presidential Palace in 1997. When the president is in Vilnius, a flag flies showing his coat of arms.

Colourful interior of Littera, with its collection of books for leisure and study material, Vilnius University

For hotels and restaurants in this region see pp308–10 and pp338–40

Elegantly displayed paintings in one of the exhibition rooms, Vilnius Picture Gallery

Vilnius Picture Gallery ❹

Vilniaus paveikslų galerija

Didžioji 4. **Map** 2 D4. **Tel** *212 0841.* ☐ *noon–6pm Tue–Sat, noon–5pm Sun.* 🖼 🗚 🗗 🗖 **www**.ldm.lt

The imposing, enclosed Neo-Classical courtyard of this gallery offers a reflection of 19th-century Vilnius, when these premises were used by Vilnius University and the Medical Academy. Inside, the paintings on display show how the main art movements of the 19th and early 20th centuries influenced the development of Lithuanian art. *Lithuanian Girl with Verbos* by Kanutas Ruseckas (1800–60) is an icon of the Romantic aesthetic in Lithuanian art. Similarly, the later movements of Realism and Impressionism are reflec-ted, respectively, in intimate portraits, such as Alfredas Romeris's *Study of a Girl's Hands*, and open landscapes, such as Juozas Balzukevičius's *Across a Ryefield.*

Church of St Paraskeva ❺

Šv Paraskevos cerkvė

Didžioji 2. **Map** 2 D4. **Tel** *215 3747.*

Also known as Pyatnitskaya Church, this attractive little Orthodox church stands on a site that has been used for ritual and prayer for many centuries. In the mid-14th century, Grand Duke Algirdas built a church here for his Orthodox wife, before which it had been a pagan sanctuary.

Here, at the beginning of the 18th century, Peter the Great baptized a nine-year-old African slave by the name of Hannibal, later Major-General Abram Petrovich Hannibal (1696–1781), great grandfather of the Russian poet Alexander Pushkin. The current building, designed by Nikolai Chagin, dates from 1865. Closed during the Soviet period, it has been returned to the Russian Orthodox faith.

The small Russian Orthodox Church of St Paraskeva

House of Signatories ❻

Signatarų namai

Pilies 26. **Map** 2 D3. **Tel** *231 4442.* ☐ *May–Sep: 10am–5pm daily, Oct–Apr: 10am–5pm Tue–Sat.* 🗚 🗖

The House of Signatories, with an extravagant façade, has played a crucial role in Lithuania's modern history. It

was here that, on 16 February 1918, the newly created Council of Lithuania signed the deed that restored Lithuania's independence. The Štralis Coffee House on the ground floor, created during renovation in the 1890s, was a popular meeting place for leading figures in the Lithuanian national revival.

The second-floor room, where the independence act was signed, has been re-created. Unfortunately, the displays on this historic event are a little sparse.

Šlapelis House Museum ❼

Šlapelių namas-muziejus

Pilies 40. **Map** 2 D4. **Tel** *261 0771.* ☐ *11am–4pm Wed–Sun (call in advance).* 🗚

Presenting a journey back in time to Vilnius during the troubled first half of the 20th century, this modest, yet evo-cative, museum is dedicated to Marija and Jurgis Šlapelis. Although a native Polish-speaker, Marija secretly ran a Lithuanian-language book-shop on nearby Domininkonų Street while the city was under Russian, Polish, Nazi and Soviet occupations between 1906 and 1949.

On display are furnishings, newspapers, books, music sheets and postcards from this time. In addition, photo-graphs showing a number of family reunions following the end of Soviet occupation can be found beneath 17th-century beams in what used to be the kitchen.

Vilnius Cathedral **⓼**
Vilniaus arkikatedra bazilika

Having taken various guises since it was first built as a Christian church on the site of a pagan temple in 1251, Vilnius Cathedral today largely dates from the late 18th century. The young architect, Laurynas Stuoka-Gucevičius, brought the fashionable French Classicist style to Baroque Vilnius, his idea for the cathedral exterior and interior being a visual re-creation of a Greek temple. Vilnius Cathedral was closed by the Soviets in 1950 and initially mooted for use as a garage for truck repairs. In 1956, however, it opened as a picture gallery. It was eventually returned to the Catholic Church in 1989 and reconsecrated a year before independence was declared.

Valavičius Chapel
Members of the Valavičius family were governors and bishops of Vilnius. Their lavish chapel was created in the early 17th century.

Stucco Sculpture
The sculpture depicting a bird sacrifice can be seen on the tympanum of the façade.

The entrance
is via a huge Classical portico.

Wall Painting of the Crucifixion
The oldest surviving fresco in Lithuania, dating from the 14th century, can be found in the crypt. It was discovered in 1925.

STAR FEATURES

★ St Casimir's Chapel

★ Crypt

Statue of Luke, the Evangelist
Of the statues of the Four Evangelists on the southern façade, Luke appears with a bull, which is a symbol of service and sacrifice.

High Altar
The marvellously intricate tabernacle door on the High Altar, which was created in the 1620s, is fashioned from gold and silver. Two biblical scenes, the Last Supper and Christ Washing the Disciples' Feet, are beautifully depicted on the panel.

★ St Casimir's Chapel
Italian masters created this superb chapel, one of the major Baroque jewels of Vilnius, from 1623 to 1636. Its main highlights are the marble columns, magnificent stucco figures and colourful frescoes.

★ Crypt
A sombre mausoleum holds the remains of two Grand Dukes and two wives of Sigismund Augustus (r.1548–72), the last descendant of Gediminas (r.1316–41).

ST CASIMIR (1458–84)

Casimir was the second son of a Grand Duke, whose siblings became kings and queens of European states through lineage and marriage. Pious Casimir shunned the luxuries of court life and would often go to the cathedral to pray. When he died of tuberculosis aged 25, it was rumoured that his coffin could cure disease. A fresco in St Casimir's Chapel shows how a sick orphan, who prayed beneath the coffin, was miraculously cured.

Richly decorated altar of St Casimir's Chapel

Vilnius Cathedral Belfry, Cathedral Square

Cathedral Square ❾
Katedros aikštė

Map 2 D3. 🚋 10, 11, 33.

The paving stones around the square show the outline of the wall around the Lower Castle, a defence that made Vilnius a 14th-century bastion against the crusades.

At the square's western end is the **Vilnius Cathedral Belfry**. It was originally part of the fortifications. There was also a western gate where Vilnius Cathedral stands today. The square's eastern end is dominated by a statue of Grand Duke Gediminas. Unveiled in 1996, it conveys the city founder's predilection for diplomacy over force. In the square's centre is a tile marked *stebuklas* (miracle), reputed to be the point where the Baltic Way *(see p39)*, the human chain linking Vilnius, Rīga and Tallinn in 1989, started from. Locals believe that turning around on it three times makes a wish come true.

Lower Castle ❿
Žemutinės pilis

Katedros 3a. **Map** 2 D3. *Tel 261 4063.* 🚋 10, 11, 33. 🕐 call in advance. 🌐 www.lvr.lt

The buildings, including Vilnius Cathedral, the Arsenal and Royal Palace, the residence of the Grand Dukes that stood at the foot of Castle

Hill and survived the sieges of the 14th century, are known as Lower Castle. In the 1520s, the Royal Palace was renovated in Renaissance style by Italian architects invited by Sigismund the Old (r.1506–48) and his wife. The palace became the hub of a vibrant cultural life.Excavations carried out here between 1987 and 2001 unearthed decorative tiles, tapestries, jewellery and armour from this period and earlier. These objects are thought to have lain buried since the palace was destroyed by Tsarist authorities in 1802 as they did not want a symbol of Lithuanian power dominating the city.

Upper Castle ⓫
Aukštutinės pilis

Arsenalo 5. **Map** 2 D3. *Tel 261 7453.* 🚋 10, 11, 33. 🕐 10am–5pm Tue–Sun. 🌐

The western tower, the only remaining part of the Upper Castle complex, which once included defensive structures, is today the symbol of independent Lithuania. The viewing platform at the top provides a

panorama of the spires and rooftops of the Old Town to the south, as well as a glimpse of the new skyscrapers rising to the west. A funicular offers a ride to the Upper Castle.

The original stone buildings of the Upper Castle were built in 1419, with recent restoration work taking place in the 1950s. According to legend, while on a hunting trip, Grand Duke Gediminas dreamed of an iron wolf howling from the hills in the park. This, his pagan priest said, was a sign that a powerful fortress should be built there. Wooden upper and lower castles and another on the adjacent hill were the result.

Lithuanian National Museum ⓬
Lietuvos nacionalinis muziejus

Arsenalo 1. **Map** 2 D3. *Tel 262 9426.* 🚋 10, 33. 🕐 May–Sep: 10am–5pm Tue–Sat, 10am–3pm Sun; Oct–Apr: 10am–5pm Wed–Sun. 🌐 🌐

An early 19th-century building, known as the New Arsenal, houses the Lithuanian National Museum. In front of it stands a statue of King Mindaugas, which was unveiled together with the nearby bridge in July 2003.

Western tower, the Upper Castle's lone surviving structure

Lithuanian traditional costumes on display, Lithuanian National Museum

The museum presents a glimpse of everyday life in Lithuania before World War II. Ordinary lives are evocatively documented in the exhibits that include plates and spoons, decorative boxes and perfume bottles, and even an old stone with a hollow used for pagan rituals.

The museum's main highlight is the first-floor room, which gives a pictorial history of the Lithuanian Grand Duchy from the Battle of the Sun to the 18th-century partitions (see p211).

The museum as a whole gives a concise tour of Lithuanian history from the 13th century to the present. Fascinating exhibits showcased in the museum include an executioner's sword tellingly broken into two pieces, a wonderfully ostentatious 18th-century sleigh and a handprint in iron of Peter the Great. There is also a display of folk costumes and a superb life-size re-creation of a typical Lithuanian peasant family farmstead.

Applied Arts Museum ⑬
Taikomosios dailės muziejus

Arsenalo gatvė 3a. **Map** 2 E3.
Tel 262 8080. ◻ 11am–6pm Tue–Sat, 11am–4pm Sun. 🖼

The 16th-century Old Arsenal houses the Applied Arts Museum, which hosts major state-sponsored exhibitions on topics mainly relating to the history of Lithuania, the Grand Duchy and sacred art.

One of the permanent exhibitions in the museum displays Lithuanian folk art from the 17th to the 19th centuries, illustrating the heavy impact that Christian themes had on traditional mediums such as sculpture. The collection includes wayside wooden crosses, shrines, saints and *rūpintojėlis* (Lithuanian folk-art representations of a weary Christ holding his head in his right hand). Particularly illuminating is the work of Vincas Svirskis

(1835–1916), a prolific craftsman who carved hundreds of shrines for rural farmsteads and villages in the Kėdainiai and Kaunas regions (see pp258–61).

Hill of Three Crosses ⑭
Trijų kryžių kalnas

Kalnų parkas. **Map** 2 E3.

A recognizable landmark and symbol of Vilnius, the three crosses on the hill adjacent to the Upper Castle are replicas of a monument destroyed by the Soviet authorities in the 1950s. Three wooden crosses were first placed here in the 16th century to commemorate, according to legend, Franciscan friars tortured and murdered by a pagan rabble. The incident took place during the rule of Grand Duke Algirdas, when Lithuania was stubbornly resisting Roman Catholic conversions. Seven of the friars were hacked to death, while the others were tied to crosses and cast into the Vilnia river.

The view of the Old Town from the crosses is unrivalled. A footbridge and a path along the Vilnia leads to steps up the hillside. An easier alternative route is via a side road leading up through the park from where T Kosciuškos Street crosses the Vilnia.

Hill of the Three Crosses, a distinguished symbol of Vilnius

Elegant façade of the Russian Orthodox Holy Mother of God Church

Holy Mother of God Church ⑮

Skaisčiausios dievo motinos cerkvė

Maironio 14. **Map** 2 E4. *Tel* 215 3747. 🚌 10, 11, 33. 🕙 9am & 5pm Sat, 9am Sun.

The current structure of this Russian Orthodox church, designed by Russian architect Nikolai Chagin, dates from the 19th century. One of the icons, *The Mother of God*, was brought by Tsar Alexander II, who also gave funds for the reconstruction work. For over 60 years before its renovation the church had been used as dissection rooms for the Medical Academy and as a military barracks. Just like the Church of St Paraskeva (*see p223*), it stands where pagan Grand Duke Algirdas built a place of worship for his wife, in the 14th century.

Bernardine Church ⑯

Bernardinų bažnyčia

Maironio 8. **Map** 2 E3. *Tel* 260 9292. 🚌 10, 11, 33. 🕙 9am (in English), 10:30am, 5pm Sun.

In 1469, the austere Franciscan Observant friars, known in Lithuania as the Bernardines after their founder St Bernardino of Siena, arrived in Vilnius. The Bernardine Church, which they built in around 1525, still retains the late Gothic crystal vaulting above the aisles. In the 1770s,

a series of Baroque wooden altars and confessionals were added to the interior. However, of these only the main altar, carved by Italian craftsman Daniele Giotto, remains today. The intriguing façade combines Gothic windows and Baroque scrolls.

Both church and friary were closed after the 1863 uprising (*see p214*), becoming barracks for Russian troops, but were eventually given back to the friars. The church's original 16th-century frescoes are being restored and include depictions of the sobriety and solemnity observed by friars, as well as St Christopher, and scenes from the Passion of Christ.

Just outside the church grounds is a statue of Adam Mickiewicz, created in 1984. In August 1987, the statue was the meeting point for the first public rally under Soviet occupation that called for Lithuania's national rights.

Church of St Anne ⑰

Šv Onos bažnyčia

Maironio 8/1. **Map** 2 E3. *Tel* 625 48011. 🚌 10, 11, 33. 🕙 5:30pm.

According to local folklore, this church charmed Napoleon into exclaiming how he wished he could take

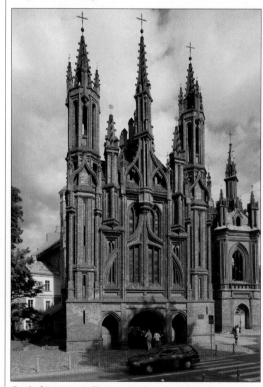

Church of St Anne, a Gothic gem said to have dazzled Napoleon

ADAM MICKIEWICZ (1798–1855)

"Oh Lithuania, my country, thou art like good health; I never knew till now how precious, till I lost thee." So begins *Pan Tadeusz*, the lyrical masterpiece of the great Polish Romantic poet Adam Mickiewicz. He was born into a family of Polish nobles near Nowogrodek, in present-day Belarus, three years after the partition of the Polish-Lithuanian Commonwealth. His nomadic life was dominated by a strong yearning for an idyllic lost homeland. His epic poems are full of ancient forests, groves and open landscapes. *Gražyna* (1822), written in his youth, is about the female chief of a pagan Lithuanian tribe who outwits the cross-and-sword-wielding Teutonic Knights. The Byronesque *Konrad Wallenrod* (1828) describes these battles with even greater mastery.

Statue of Adam Mickiewicz, outside the Bernardine Church

it back to Paris on the palm of his hand. St Anne's is a Gothic beauty; its ornate façade of flowing ogee arches and slender windows are a unique monument to the style in a city of Baroque. The finials and the spires are covered evenly with decorative crockets – bricks made to resemble flowers or curled leaves and so favoured by Gothic architects. One set of historians found 33 different shapes of brick used in the façade. Inside, the three Baroque altars were designed by Jan Krzysztof Glaubitz (*see p233*). The free-standing bell tower was built much later, in the 1870s.

Church of St Michael ⑱
Šv Mykolo bažnyčia

Šv Mykolo 9. **Map** 2 E3. **Tel** 261 6409. ◯ *11am–6pm Wed–Sun, 10am–1pm Mon.*

The Renaissance-style Church of St Michael was built during the early 17th century, as a convent for Bernardine nuns and a mausoleum for the Sapiega family. Its interior features several of the nobles' funerary monuments. These include one to Leonas Sapiega, whose initials mark some of the crests, motifs and rosettes

that decorate the ceiling. Between 1972 and 2005, the church housed the Museum of Architecture, the exhibits of which were later transferred to the Lithuanian National Museum (*see p226*).

Mickiewicz Museum ⑲
Adomo Mickevičiaus memoralinis butas-muziejus

Bernardinų 11. **Map** 2 E3. **Tel** 279 1879. ◯ *10am–5pm Tue–Fri, 10am–2pm Sat–Sun.*

The legendary poet Adam Mickiewicz, who romanticized his Polish-Lithuanian homeland, stayed at this apartment, which belonged to a university professor, for a brief period in 1822. Set inside a lovely enclosed courtyard, the museum attempts to re-create the atmosphere of the era in which the poet lived.

Period furniture, which Mickiewicz himself is said to have used while writing his first folk-inspired ballads, includes a table and chair from Kaunas and a chair from Paris. Portraits of the poet are set alongside

volumes of his works in various languages. The place also houses the first editions of a number of his great works. The museum often hosts literary meetings and poetry evenings.

Orthodox Church of St Nicholas ⑳
Šv Mikalojaus cerkvė

Didžioji 12. **Map** 2 D4. **Tel** 261 8559. ◯ *11am–4pm Wed–Sun.* ✝ *5pm Tue–Sat, 9am Sun.*

The serene, candlelit interior of the Orthodox Church of St Nicholas contrasts sharply with the bustle on Didžioji, the Old Town's main street. Originally a Gothic church dating from 1514, it passed into the hands of the Uniates, or Greek Catholics, in 1609 before getting a Baroque overhaul, including the bell tower. The church was returned to the Russian Orthodox Church in 1827. The overtly Russian Byzantine façade of the church, together with most of the interior, is an example of the change that took place in the city's religious landscape following the doomed January 1863 uprising.

The domed chapel on the left is dedicated to Count Mikhail Muravyov (1796–1866), the governor-general who dealt harshly with the uprising's participants.

Façade, Orthodox Church of St Nicholas

Street-by-Street: Town Hall Square to the Gates of Dawn

Lithuania's distinctive Baroque architecture, known as Vilnius Baroque, can be admired in the outstanding monuments clustered around the Gates of Dawn and the Church of St Casimir. The enchanting collection of towers and sculptures was created during the 17th and 18th centuries by Italian and Polish architects and their Polish-Lithuanian noble patrons. The buildings are elegantly designed with symmetrical façades, reflecting an unmistakable Italian influence. Nonetheless, the mystical atmosphere, so unique to Vilnius, distinguishes the area from any other European city.

★ Church of St Casimir
This church was the city's museum of atheism from 1963 to 1991. The crown symbolizes St Casimir's royal lineage ㉔

Town Hall
With a bold Classical portico, the Town Hall was designed by the renowned Lithuanian architect, Laurynas Stuoka-Gucevičius ㉒

DIDŽIOJI GATVĖ

VOKIEČIŲ GATVĖ

RŪDNINKŲ GATVĖ

KEY

– – – Suggested route

Contemporary Art Centre
is a Soviet-era venue for groundbreaking modern art ㉓

Vokiečių Street
One of the city's oldest, Vokiečių Street resembles a park during the summer months, with its outdoor cafés and a pleasant central tree-lined walkway.

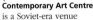

STAR SIGHTS

★ Church of St Casimir

★ Church of St Theresa

★ Gates of Dawn

Šv Kazimiero Street
A narrow cobblestone street named after St Casimir snakes around the back of the church towards Užupis with its jumble of roofs.

Church of the Holy Spirit

★ **Church of St Theresa**
Scenes from the life of St Theresa, revered for her mystical writings, adorn the vaulted nave of the church. The frescoes were painted in the late 18th century following a fire ㉗

0 metres 100
0 yards 100

SUBAČIAUS GATVĖ

AUŠROS VARTŲ GATVĖ

M AUKŠOS GATVĖ

BAZILIJONŲ GATVĖ

Basilian Gate

Basilian Monastery
The now dilapidated monastery complex was used as a prison to hold anti-Russian activists, including the poet Adam Mickiewicz, in the 1820s.

★ **Gates of Dawn**
A site of pilgrimage, this gateway to the Old Town protects a silver-covered painting of the Virgin Mary, said to have miraculous powers ㉘

Panoramic view of Town Hall Square, with flagpoles and church spires

Čiurlionis House ㉑
Čiurlionio namai

Savičiaus 11. **Map** 2 D4. **Tel** 262 2451. ◯ 10am–4pm Mon–Fri. Entrance from side door.

The former house of Mikalojus Konstantinas Čiurlionis *(see p261)* was turned into a museum in 1995, to mark the 120th anniversary of the birth of Lithuania's beloved artist and composer. Čiurlionis lived here in relative poverty with his wife Sofija, from October 1907 until June 1908, when they left Vilnius in search of success in St Petersburg.

Quite modest in scale, this museum does not attempt to rival the more extensive one dedicated to Čiurlionis in Kaunas *(see p260)*. Instead, the museum mainly serves as an educational resource and a venue to hear his chamber music concerts. Reproductions of the artist's paintings adorn the walls, as do photographs of him. Even today, Čiurlionis's grand piano stands here.

Town Hall Square ㉒
Rotušės aikštė

Didžioji 31. **Map** 2 D4. ◈ Kaziuko Crafts Fair (Mar). **www**.vilnius.lt **Town Hall Tel** 261 8007. ⓘ Didžioji 31, 262 6470. ◯ 8am–6pm Mon–Fri.

Fully repaved in 2006, Town Hall Square was for centuries a market place and the centre of public life. It still bustles with activity, mainly during the annual Kaziuko Crafts Fair *(see p208)*, when craft stalls line the square. The square's main building, the **Town Hall**, was earlier the site of a court,

and prisoners were marched from its cells to the square to be beheaded. The hall was constructed at the end of the 18th century and designed by the Classical architect, Laurynas Stuoka-Gucevičius *(see p224)*. Today, the hall hosts about 200 cultural and social events around the year.

"Extreme Crafts", art exhibits at the Contemporary Art Centre

Contemporary Art Centre ㉓
Šiuolaikinio meno centras

Vokiečių 2. **Map** 2 D4. **Tel** 212 1945. ◯ noon–7:30pm Tue–Sun. ◈ ▣ ⬛ **www**.cac.lt

The main gallery space for modern art exhibitions in Vilnius, the Contemporary Art Centre features works by both Lithuanian and international artists. The star attraction is the Fluxus Room, with a permanent exhibition dedicated to Fluxus, the radical art movement that emerged in New York in the 1960s. The room pays special tribute to the movement's creator, Kaunas-born George Maciunas (1931–78). Memorabilia evoking the populist spirit of Fluxus festivals and photographs of Maciunas fill the room.

Church of St Casimir ㉔
Šv Kazimiero bažnyčia

Didžioji 34. **Map** 2 D4. **Tel** 212 1715. ✚ 10:30am & 5:30pm Mon–Fri, noon Sun.

The city's first Baroque church, St Casimir was destroyed by fire three times after being built by the Jesuits between 1604 and 1635, prompting heavy reconstruction in the 1750s. Much of the interior was destroyed in 1812, when Napoleon's army used the church as a granary. It became a Russian Orthodox church during the 19th century and onion domes were added to it.

During World War I, it served as a Lutheran church for the German army and was then returned to the Jesuits and restored in the 1920s. The dome was rebuilt in 1942 and the crown was added. The Soviets used the church as a museum of atheism from 1963. It was reconsecrated in 1991.

Altarpiece at Church of St Casimir, depicting the saint's resurrection

Baroque Vilnius

The sensual waves, rich colours and theatrical stucco figures of Baroque architecture reached Lithuania during the first half of the 17th century, replacing Gothic and Renaissance. Italian masters, invited by Lithuania's rulers, built Baroque gems such as St Casimir's Chapel *(see p225)* and the Church of St Theresa. In the mid-17th century came a second resurgence of the style,

Angel with golden wings, Dominican Church

when architects living in Vilnius began to develop a distinct branch of Baroque. Led by Jan Krzysztof Glaubitz, they began to transform the Old Town's panorama by designing opulent façades, matched by voluptuous interiors and multiple altars. By the end of the 18th century Baroque had been replaced by the far more restrained values of Neo-Classicism.

St Casimir's Chapel, *in Vilnius Cathedral, is an early Baroque gem, beautified intricately with marble from Galicia and the Carpathians, lavish stucco and 17th-century frescoes.*

St John's Church (see p222), *one of Glaubitz's first works in Vilnius, boasts an overwhelming four-tier façade made up of clusters of columns. Inside there are ten interconnected altars.*

The Basilian Gate (see p234) *of the Basilian monastery was built by Glaubitz in 1761. The 18-m (59-ft) structure carries a depiction of the Holy Trinity, to which the church in the complex is dedicated.*

Church of St Theresa (see p234) *boasts radiant frescoes, glittering altars and an image of the Madonna, believed to be miraculous.*

JAN KRZYSZTOF GLAUBITZ (1700–67)

The most influential of Vilnius's late Baroque architects, Jan Krzysztof Glaubitz developed a distinct school of Lithuanian Baroque known as Vilnius Baroque. Born in Silesia, Glaubitz was a Lutheran of German origin who moved to Vilnius at the age of 37 and designed structures for all faiths in this multi-religious city. Among his most celebrated works are the magnificent façades of the Basilian Gate, St John's Church, Church of St Catherine *(see p237)*, the Church of the Holy Spirit *(see p234)* and the now destroyed Great Synagogue *(see p239)*.

Exterior of Church of St Catherine, Old Town

Ornate Baroque entranceway of the Basilian Gate

Basilian Gate ㉕
Bazilijonų vartai

Aušros vartų 7b. **Map** 2 D5.

The awe-inspiring Basilian Gate was designed in 1761 in flamboyant late Baroque style by J K Glaubitz *(see p233)*. An all-seeing eye peers out from the central niche. The white bas-relief at the top portrays the Holy Trinity, a hint of what lies beyond the gate. The **Church of the Holy Trinity**, placed in the hands of the Uniates in 1598, stands at the centre of an enclosed court-yard. This was once a seclu-ded monastery, but in 1823 the Tsarist authorities turned it into a prison for anti-Russian revolutionaries and kept Adam Mickiewicz *(see p229)*

there the same year. The Uniates who live here now, are sometimes willing to show visitors round.

> 🔒 **Church of the Holy Trinity**
> **Tel** 212 2578. 🕀 5:30pm Mon–Sat, 10am Sun.

Church of the Holy Spirit ㉖
Šv Dvasios cerkvė

Aušros vartų 10. **Map** 2 D5. **Tel** 212 7765. 🚫 🕀 6:45am, 8am, 10am, 5pm Mon–Sat; 5pm Sun.

This Baroque church is the religious centre of the city's Russian Orthodox faithful. Though completed in 1634, it remains rem-arkably intact, the only alterations to the exterior being a raised façade and a new dome added in the late 19th century. The painting over the doorway depicts Sts Anthony, Ivan and Eustachius, whose remains lie within, miraculously preserved. In the 14th century, the three were Christians in the court of pagan Grand Duke Algirdas. When the pagan priests demanded that they renounce their faith, they refused and were hanged from an oak tree. They were canonized in 1547 and the nearby Church of the Holy Trinity was built in place of the oak.

Church of St Theresa ㉗
Šv Teresės bažnyčia

Aušros vartų 14. **Map** 2 D5. **Tel** 212 3513. 🕀 9am, 6:30pm daily.

Another early feature of the Baroque landscape, built from 1630 to 1655, is the Church of St Theresa, which stands in front of the Gates of Dawn. Materials like black marble in the portal and sandstone from Sweden, used to beautify its façade, were also used in the St Casimir's Chapel inside Vilnius Cathedral *(see pp224–5)* around the same time. This has led some researchers to believe that Italian craftsmen who designed the chapel also contributed to the Church of St Theresa. The main attraction of the church is its interior, with its frescoes and altars dating back to the second half of the 18th century. The painting on the high altar is *The Exaltation of St Theresa* by Szymon Czechowicz (1689–1775). St Theresa of Ávila in Spain inspired the formation in 1593 of the Discalced (Barefoot) Carmelites, a Roman Catholic order whose emphasis was on discipline and prayer. A convent was located next door, but today it is a hotel, the Domus Maria *(see p308)*.

Painting, Church of St Theresa

Stunning frescoes on the ceiling of the Church of St Theresa

Image of the Virgin Mary, seen through the window of the Gates of Dawn

Renaissance furniture and French Baroque with 20th-century American modern art. Other rooms have over 150 maps, including some of Lithuania dating from 1507. The book section has around 7,000 volumes of unique publications. The collection includes a number of books by famous illustrators.

Varnelis, renowned for creating optical illusions based on geometric patterns in his paintings, rarely meets visitors now.

Gates of Dawn 28
Aušros vartai

Aušros vartų 12. **Map** 2 D5. *Tel* 212 3513. 🚩 7:30am, 9am, 10am, 5:30pm, 6:30pm Mon–Sat; 9am, 9:30am, 11am, 6:30pm Sun.

The Classical chapel of Gates of Dawn follows the centuries-old custom of having a chapel or a religious image in every gateway to safeguard the city from outside enemies and protect departing travellers. The focus of this chapel is *The Madonna of Mercy*, an image reputed to have miracle-working powers. It was painted on oak in the 1620s and encased in silver 150 years later. The miracles attributed to it were faithfully recorded by nuns at the neighbouring Carmelite convent. Hundreds of hearts of different sizes stand out on plates of silver around the painting.

The Classical chapel that houses the image dates from 1829, when it was rebuilt from an earlier Baroque version. A flight of steps leads up to the chapel from a door in the street. A site of pilgrimage, it was one of the first stops for Pope John Paul II when he visited Lithuania in 1993.

This is the only gateway from the early 16th-century city walls to have survived. It becomes more evident when viewed from the outside where round holes that were used for cannons are still visible.

Kazys Varnelis Museum 29
Kazio Varnelio namai-muziejus

Didžioji 26. **Map** 2 D4. *Tel* 279 1644. 🕙 10am–4pm Tue–Sat (by appointment only). 🖼️ 📷

An extraordinary collection of modern art, maps, graphics, paintings, sculptures, vintage furniture, books and ceramics, as well as art from around the world, fill the home of the famous Lithuanian-American artist Kazys Varnelis (b.1917). Some of the rooms look truly avant-garde, mixing Italian

Artillery Bastion 30
Bastėja

Bokšto 20/18. **Map** 2 E4. *Tel* 261 2149. 🕙 May–Sep: 10am–5pm Tue–Sat, 10am–3pm Sun; Oct–Apr: 10am–5pm Wed–Sun. 🖼️

Constructed as part of the city defences in the first half of the 17th century, the bastion had fallen into ruin by the end of the 18th century. It was used as an orphanage and the city's pre-eminent rubbish heap, and was finally cleaned up by the Germans during World War I to store ammunition. Its cool interior made it an ideal space for storing vegetables during the early Soviet period.

In 1987 it was opened as a museum. Although there is not a great deal to see, the museum holds a certain fascination for history enthusiasts. Outside, there are pleasant views of the Old Town and the hilly Užupis district.

Red-brick Artillery Bastion, dating from the 17th century

Church of
St Nicholas ③
Šv Mikalojaus bažnyčia

Šv Mikalojaus 4. **Map** 2 D4. **Tel** 262
3069. ☩ 7:30am, 6pm Mon–Fri;
9am Sat; 9am, 10am, 2pm Sun.

One of the oldest churches
in Lithuania, the Church of
St Nicholas was built when
the country was still pagan.
Most of its simple Gothic
façade and interior dates from
the 16th century. The interior
is defined by the decorative
brick veins of the vaulting.
Some colourful paintings
discovered here include a
striking image of the sun.

The church has patriotic
connotations for Lithuanians,
as from 1901 to 1939, when
Vilnius was occupied by
Russia and then Poland, it
was one of the few churches
allowed to hold Lithuanian-
language services.

In the churchyard, the
statue of St Christopher
carrying the Infant Christ,
created in 1959, also helped
to keep the spirits of the
people alive. The sculptor,
Antanas Kmieliauskas
(b.1932), was expelled from
the Association of Artists
because of it. He later
frescoed Littera bookshop in
Vilnius University (see p222).

Surviving fragment of a fresco on
the ceiling of the Franciscan Church

Franciscan
Church ③
Pranciškonų bažnyčia

Trakų 9/1. **Map** 1 C4. **Tel** 261 4242.
☩ 5:30pm Mon–Sat, 10am Sun.

The cracked and cavernous,
yet highly evocative,
Franciscan Church is also
known as the Church of Our
Lady of the Assumption. It
stands on a spot where, in the
14th century, Franciscan friars
established a base on the road
to Trakai (see pp252–3). The
Conventual Franciscans chose
to settle in the poorest of

urban areas, reaching out to
the destitute, often outside
the safety of the city walls.
The Gothic main doorway
dates from this earlier period,
but the rest of the structure
was built in the 1770s. After
the 1863 uprising (see p214),
the church and friary were
closed and used as a granary
and an archive. The altars and
the now unidentifiable frescoes above the nave were
virtually destroyed, as was a
tall Gothic bell tower that
stood on Pranciškonų Street.

Dominican
Church ③
Šv Dvasios bažnyčia

Dominikonų 8. **Map** 2 D4. **Tel** 262
9595. ☩ 7am, 7:30am, 3pm, 6pm
Mon–Sat; 8am, 9am, 10:30am, noon,
1:30pm, 6pm Sun.

Also known as the Church
of the Holy Spirit, the current
building of the Dominican
Church dates from the years
of repair that followed the
destructive war of 1655–61
during the Russian occu-
pation. However, a church
has stood on this spot since
the 14th century.

The unassuming doorway,
which can be easily missed,
belies the sumptuous interior.

Lavishly decorated interior of the Dominican Church, featuring Rococo altars

Figures in stucco stand out on 15 lavishly decorated Rococo altars. The altars, which are embellished with colourful paintings, also feature gilded frames and faux marble Corinthian columns – all hallmarks of the late Baroque style. The fresco-lined vestibule, which forms a passage into the nave from the street, gives the church a cavern-like quality, emphasized by the dark, candlelit interior.

During Napoleon's chaotic retreat in 1812, the friary next to the church was converted into a hospital and the crypt was used as a morgue. Today, the crypt is still full of stacks of mummified corpses from this time, preserved by the dry air. The crypt is, however, off-limits to visitors.

Movie cameras on display at the Theatre, Music and Film Museum

Façade of the Church of St Catherine, with strawberry-and-cream towers

Church of St Catherine ㉞
Šv Kotrynos bažnyčia

Vilniaus gatvė 30. **Map** 2 D3.

Originally a small wooden structure, the Church of St Catherine formed part of a Benedictine monastery in the early 17th century. The church was rebuilt in stone in 1703, almost 50 years after the Russians burned it down. The structure, as it appears today, was built and considerably expanded between 1741 and 1773. Its sophisticated design, highlighted by the delightful strawberry-and-cream twin towers, is attributed to Lithuania's much-celebrated Baroque architect Jan Krzysztof Glaubitz *(see p233)*.

The church suffered some damage during World War II and was recently reopened after lengthy renovation. It is now regularly used as a popular venue for classical music concerts and performances. In the garden facing the church, there is a bust monument of the well-known Polish composer Stanislaw Moniuszko (1819–72), who wrote his first operas while working as an organist in Vilnius. The area to the east of the church is where a large convent for Benedictine nuns stood from 1622 until the Soviet period. The church's interior is highly decorated but not fully repaired, giving it an air of authenticity.

Theatre, Music and Film Museum ㉟
Lietuvos teatro, muzikos, kino muziejus

Vilniaus 41. **Map** 1 C4. **Tel** 261 5848. ☐ noon–6pm Tue–Fri, 11am–4pm Sat, noon–5pm Sun. ✉ http://teatras. mch.mii.lt

Housed inside a 17th-century mansion once owned by the powerful Radvila family, who ruled Lithuania in the 16th century, this absorbing museum was founded by the Ministry of Culture. The museum's expansive collection is a tribute to the Lithuanians' love of theatre and classical music. The exhibits include theatre memorabilia ranging from old costumes and puppets to stage-set pieces, mostly from the 19th and early 20th centuries. The superb collection of folk instruments features a number of *kanklės* (decorated Lithuanian stringed instruments related to the zither).

The space given to cinema is limited and not as informative, although there are some displays on cinematography.

Radvila Palace ㊱
Radvilų rūmai

Vilniaus 22. **Map** 1 C3. **Tel** 262 0981. ☐ noon–6pm Tue–Sat, noon–5pm Sun. ✉ www.ldm.lt

The early 17th-century palace, once grand in size, was reduced to just one wing by the end of the Northern War (1700–21). Now an art gallery, it hosts a permanent display, including 165 portraits of members of the Radvila family. Temporary exhibitions feature little-known, but often surprisingly impressive, paintings by Lithuanian artists from the 19th and early 20th centuries.

Phonograph, Theatre, Music and Film Museum

Holocaust Museum in the Green House, annexe of the State Jewish Museum

State Jewish Museum ③⑦
Valstybinis Vilniaus gaono žydų Muziejus

Pylimo 4. **Map** 1 C3. **Tel** 212 7912. ⬭ 9am–1pm Mon–Fri. ▨ ▦ excursions of the museum & Vilnius Old Town offered. **www**.jmuseum.lt

The hub of the city's now tiny Jewish community, this small museum displays copies of ghetto diaries and handwritten notes on the backs of cigarette packets about life in the ghetto, plus items that remained from the museum that existed before World War II. Several objects that miraculously survived from the Great Synagogue include a bas-relief of the Ten Commandments.

The museum building also hosts a Union of Former Ghetto and Concentration Camp Prisoners, a Union of Jewish War Veterans, a youth club and a newspaper in Yiddish, English, Lithuanian and Russian called *Jerusalem of Lithuania*.

Holocaust Museum ③⑧
Holokausto ekspozicija

Pamėnkalnio 12. **Map** 1 C3. **Tel** 262 0730. ⬭ 9am–5pm Mon–Thu, 9am–4pm Fri, 10am–4pm Sun. ▨ ▦ **www**.jmuseum.lt

Located in the Green House, this annexe of the State Jewish Museum reveals some of the horror that befell the Jews of Lithuania during World War II. A display on Jewish life before the terror unfolded is followed by maps and photographs showing how and where the Holocaust was executed. Descriptions of how harsh life was in the ghettoes are followed by eyewitness accounts of the mass killings in the forests of Paneriai *(see p244)*.

Frank Zappa Statue ③⑨

Kalinausko 1. **Map** 1 C3.

The world's first statue of the prolific Californian rock legend Frank Zappa was created in Vilnius shortly after his death from cancer in 1993. A group of local artists wanted to test the limits of newly independent Lithuania's proclamations of democracy and freedom and were pleasantly surprised when their idea for the statue was approved. The bust was created by the then 70-year-old Konstantinas Bogdanas, known for his statues of Lenin and other notable Communists.

Bust of Frank Zappa

KGB Museum ④⓪
Genocido aukų muziejus

Aukų 2a. **Map** 1 C2. **Tel** 249 7427. ⬭ 10am–5pm Tue–Sat, 10am–3pm Sun. ▨ ▦ ▯ **www**.genocid.lt

Also known as the Museum of Genocide Victims, the KGB Museum was opened in 1992, on the ground floor of the former KGB building. In this effectively designed display area, personal stories are used to reveal the regime of terror under Stalin until 1940 and then until 1991 under the former Soviet Union.

The exhibits chronicle the Soviet occupation of Lithuania, the cattle-car deportations to Siberia and the futile efforts of the Forest Brothers *(see p118)* who fought the Soviets. Below ground, the cells were in use right up until the late 1980s and are even more overwhelming. They include tiny cells used in winter with no glass in the window and a floor filled with water, and an execution chamber displaying, under glass, the recently dug-up remains of victims. In 1997, the museum was taken over by the Genocide and Resistance Research Centre of Lithuania, a state institution dedicated to investigating atrocities that occured in the country during the the Nazi and Soviet occupations.

Exhibits in the corridor outside the former execution chamber, KGB Museum

Jewish Vilnius

Until it was eliminated during the Holocaust, Jewish Vilna, or Vilnius, was home to a large, influential Jewish community. About 250,000 Jews lived in Lithuania at the turn of the 19th century, compared to just 4,000 today, and 40 per cent of Vilnius's population was Jewish. By the early 19th century, Vilnius had emerged as a major centre of Jewish learning and bustled with life. The

Domed ceiling, Choral Synagogue

religious customs of the Litvaks, as Lithuanian Jews are known in Yiddish, were marked by a rigid analysis of the Talmud, the Jewish laws and traditions. As a result, other Jewish communities in Eastern Europe saw the Vilna Jews as being old-fashioned and staunch intellectuals. Decimated by World War II and ravaged further by the Soviets, Jewish Vilna is a ghostly reminder of a vanished world.

Jewish Vilna before World War II *had its cobbled lanes crowded with artisans' workshops and cafés. A maze of courtyards and passages that lay around Vokiečių and Žydų streets, concealed synagogues and prayer houses.*

The Great Synagogue, *built in 1572, was restored with an Italian Renaissance interior by Glaubitz. The Soviets destroyed the remains of the Jewish quarter after World War II, broadening Vokiečių Street and bulldozing this awe-inspiring building.*

Elijah Ben Solomon (see p36), *known as Vilna Gaon, or "genius", was a leading Talmud scholar who wrote extensive commentaries on ancient Hebrew books. He advocated an empirical study of religious scriptures over mysticism.*

Vilnius Choral Synagogue *is the only one in the country to survive World War II. Located on Pylimo Street 39, the synagogue started functioning in 1903. Although it was smaller in scale and simpler in design than Vilnius's other synagogues, the Choral Synagogue has an enchanting interior.*

A map of Vilna Ghetto *is shown on the wall at Rūdininkų 18. This is where the Jews of Vilnius were imprisoned during World War II, and the ghetto's only gate once stood.*

Further Afield

As most of Vilnius's main sites are concentrated in the Old Town, visitors often ignore the suburbs. It can be rewarding, however, to escape the bustling city centre and to discover Vilnius as a living city as well as a picturesque time capsule. A trip to the TV Tower affords excellent views on a clear day, while Vingis Park and Verkiai Palace are ideal for walking and a breath of fresh air. Paneriai and Antakalnis Cemetery, meanwhile, recount Lithuania's often tragic history.

SIGHTS AT A GLANCE

Antakalnis Cemetery ❸
Calvary Church of the
  Holy Cross ⓫
Church of Sts Peter and Paul ❷
Green Bridge ❹
Paneriai Holocaust Memorial ❿
Parliament ❺
Pushkin Museum ❽
Rasos Cemetery ❾
TV Tower ❼
Trinapolis Church ⓬
Užupis ❶
Verkiai Palace ⓭
Vingis Park and Žvėrynas ❻

KEY

▨	City centre
✈	Airport
🚉	Railway station
🚌	Bus station
▬	Motorway
▬	Main road
▭	Minor road

Užupis ❶

🚃 *11.* **www**.uzupis.com

Tucked inside a bend in the Vilnia river, Užupis translates as "Behind the River". This picturesque part of central Vilnius has narrow streets filled with cafés, art galleries and mysterious hidden courtyards. The artists who live here declared independence in 1997, with their own flag, president and independence day (1 April). Their constitution, which features articles such as "Everyone has the right to understand nothing", is nailed to a wall on Paupio Street. The statue of an angel, the symbol of Užupis, stands on nearby Užupio Street. The bizarre **Alternative Art Centre**, where the door is always open, stands by the river between Užupio and Malūnų. A stroll further east leads to the serene Bernardinų Cemetery.

The terrace of the Tores café *(see p339)* on Krivių has one of the town's best views. Another viewpoint can be found on an unmarked footpath behind the school on Krivių Street. The footpath then plunges down the Vilnia Valley into Kalnų Park.

Church of Sts Peter and Paul ❷

See pp242–3.

Antakalnis Cemetery ❸
Antakalnio kapinės

Karių kapų 11. **Tel** 234 0587.

The largest public cemetery in Vilnius brings together much of the city's modern history. Statues and memorial stones cover the verdant landscape, the crosses and tombs inscribed in Lithuanian, Russian and Polish. The main path leads past a wave of identical stone crosses dedicated to Polish soldiers who died during World War I. At the heart of the cemetery is a sweeping semicircular memorial cut into the hillside for the 14 civilians who were

Imaginatively painted façade of the Alternative Art Centre, Užupis

Graves of civilians killed by Russian tanks in 1991, Antakalnis Cemetery

killed while defending the TV Tower and the Parliament in 1991. A path to the right of the cemetery entrance leads to Soviet-era war memorials.

Green Bridge ❹
Žaliasis tiltas

The first bridge crossing the river at this point was built in the 16th century, but the current one dates from 1952, the year before Stalin's death. At its four corners stand Socialist Realist statues and reasons abound for not pulling them down. One is that they are a reminder of the ugliness of Soviet monoculture; another is that locals have come to regard them as genuine works of art. Whatever the reason, the statues of confident workers, peasants and soldiers, once built to instill optimism among the masses in a brave new Communist future, are here to stay, however odd they may seem amid Vilnius's skyscrapers.

Soviet-era statues that adorn Green Bridge

Parliament ❺
Lietuvos respublikos seimas

Gedimino 53. **Tel** 239 6060. 🚌 24.
📱 www.lrs.lt

The far end of Gedimino Avenue is marked by the Seimas, Lithuania's

Parliament. Built in 1982, the building is typical of the late Soviet era. The similarly monumental National Library, constructed 20 years earlier, stands beside it on the other side of Independence Square.

It was in the Seimas, on 11 March 1990, that the act declaring independence from the Soviet Union was signed. During the subsequent siege, in 1991, concrete barricades and Catholic shrines were put up around the building to protect it against Soviet tanks. These were finally removed in 1993, and the remnants emblazoned with graffiti demanding freedom and democracy can still be seen on the western side of the Seimas.

Vingis Park and Žvėrynas ❻

🚌 11. 🚻 🛒 🚹

The leafy Žvėrynas district was created from the Radvila family's forest-covered hunting grounds, which were sold off from 1893 as plots of land for development. The streets are lined with old wooden villas and contemporary mansions. The silver-domed Orthodox Church of the Apparition of the Holy Mother of God (1903) looms over the Neris river. The tiny Kenesa (1922), where the Karaim (see

p253) used to congregate, stands on Liubarto Street. Vingis Park, reached via a suspension footbridge on the western side of Žvėrynas, is filled with towering pine trees and footpaths. At the centre of the park is an open-air auditorium used for concerts and, every five years, the climax to the World Lithuanian Song Festival. To the east, where the pleasant M K Čiurlionio Street meets the park, a cemetery for German soldiers killed during the two World Wars has been restored.

TV Tower ❼
Vilniaus televizijos bokštas

Sausio 13–Osios 10. **Tel** 252 5333.
🚌 49. 🕙 10am–9pm daily. 🎫 🎥
🚻 🛒 www.lrtc.net

The grand 326-m (1,070-ft) TV Tower is set against a striking backdrop of tall pines. On the ground floor, there is a small display paying tribute to those who were shot or crushed beneath Soviet tanks while trying to defend the tower on 13 January 1991. Granite markers outside show where they fell.

The tower's observation deck houses a state-run café, Paukščių Takas, at a height of 165 m (541 ft). The rotating deck makes a full circle in about 50 minutes and offers spectacular views of the area. On a clear day, visibility is 70 km (43 miles) in every direction, with views stretching into Belarus, about 40 km (25 miles) away.

Elegant TV Tower, soaring high above its surroundings

Church of Sts Peter and Paul ❷
Šv Petro ir Povilo bažnyčia

With its breathtaking interior of over 2,000 white stucco figures featuring angels and demons, biblical scenes and some gruesome historical images, the Church of Sts Peter and Paul is essentially a glorified Baroque mausoleum to its wealthy patron Michal Kazimierz Pac (1624–82). He was a Lithuanian military leader and the provincial governor of Vilnius. Pac's portrait hangs by the altar, his crest is positioned over the door and his body lies under the front steps. Built over the remains of two earlier wooden churches, the second of which was badly damaged during a brutal war with Moscow from 1655 to 1661, the church was intended to stand as a lasting monument to peace.

Twin-towered façade of the Church of Sts Peter and Paul

The interior is a fine ensemble of exquisite stucco and richly decorated chapels.

Boat-Shaped Chandelier
A late addition to the interior and a reference to St Peter's profession as a fisherman, the glass-bead chandelier was made by Latvian craftsmen in 1905.

Altar
The original high altar was replaced by The Parting of St Peter and St Paul *(1801), created by the Polish historical painter, Pranciškus Smuglevičius (1745–1807).*

STAR FEATURES

★ Chapel of the Holy Queens

★ Vaulted Nave and Cupola

★ Chapel of St Ursula

★ Chapel of the Holy Queens
The chapel to the north of the nave is rich in stucco. The female figure perched over the arch giving a coin to a beggar denotes compassion.

★ Vaulted Nave and Cupola

The exuberance of the decoration attains a dizzying scale as the nave reaches the cupola, the rectangular reliefs, flowers and cartouches, giving way to a spiral of animated angels and the face of God at the apex.

The inscription above the balcony reads *"Regina pacis funda nos in pace"* ("Queen of Peace protect us in peace"), probably a play on the patron's name.

VISITORS' CHECKLIST

Antakalnio gatvė 1.
Tel 234 0229. 7am, 7:30am, 6pm Mon–Fri; 8:30am, 1pm Sat; 7:30am, 10am, 11:30am, 5pm, 6pm Sun. Services in Lithuanian & Polish only.

Smiling Madonna in the Chapel of St Casimir in Vilnius Cathedral

THE ITALIAN CONNECTION

The first flowering of Lithuanian Baroque in the early 17th century took place when Lithuania's rulers invited Italian architects and sculptors to redesign the city. Matteo Castello (1560–1632) designed St Casimir's Chapel *(see p225)*. His nephew, Constante Tencalla (1590–1646), completed it, then created the façade of the Church of St Theresa *(see p234)*. Half a century later, artists Perti, Galli and Palloni arrived in Vilnius to adorn the Church of Sts Peter and Paul.

★ Chapel of St Ursula

Ursula was an English princess seized by the Huns with ten virgin companions and shot with arrows. Images of their fate are balanced by four sculptures of female saints including Mary Magdalene.

Ornate Stucco Portico

The rippling central shield above the doorway, flanked by figures of young boys, displays a fleur-de-lis, a symbol from Pac's coat of arms. The glorious stucco work adorning the entire church is attributed to the Italian masters Pietro Perti and Giovanni Maria Galli.

Delightful wooden building of the Pushkin Museum

Pushkin Museum ⑧

Puškino memorialinis
muziejus

Subačiaus 124. **Tel** 260 0080.
🚌 10,13. ⏱ 10am–5pm Wed–Sun.
📷 ♿

This museum is located in a
bright yellow wooden house,
which stands out on a pleasant grassy hill. It was not
the great Russian poet, but
his son Grigorij (1835–1905)
who lived here with his wife
Varvara (1855–1935). Founded
in 1940 and opened in 1948,
the museum is now home to
many volumes of Alexander
Pushkin's works and the
ground floor is furnished in
the late 19th-century style.

At the back of the house,
behind a statue of Pushkin,
are acres of tranquil grounds
and a small onion-domed
family mausoleum. Steps lead
down to a lake, and the paths
that reach out into the surrounding countryside are a
delight to explore.

Rasos Cemetery ⑨

Rasų kapinės

Rasų gatvė. 🚌 31.

Revered national figures
and ordinary Vilnius folk lie
side by side in this cemetery
founded in 1769. Some of
the distinguished tombstones
include those of Jonas

Basanavičius (1851–1927),
founder of the first Lithuanian-
language newspaper *Aušra*
(Dawn), composer and
painter M K Čiurlionis *(see
p261)* and Marija and Jurgis
Šlapelis *(see p223)*. A more
controversial monument is
the tomb of the man res-
ponsible for Poland's annexa-
tion of Vilnius in 1920, Józef
Pilsudski (1867–1935). His
body lies among those of the
kings and queens of Kraków,
but by his wishes his heart
was cut out and placed
here under a granite slab.
The cemetery is spiritually
significant for the Lithuanians.
In 1956, a crowd gathered
here to protest the suppression
of the Hungarian uprising
against Soviet occupation.

Paneriai Holocaust Memorial ⑩

Panerių memorialinis
muziejus

Agrastų 17, 8 km (5 miles) SW
of Vilnius. **Tel** 260 2001. 🚆 from
Vilnius. ⏱ Mar–Dec: 11am–6pm
Mon, Wed, Fri, Sun.

Centuries of Jewish culture
and tradition in Vilnius ended
at this major Holocaust site.
About 70,000 Jewish men,
women and children were

Imposing tombstones of Marija and Jurgis Šlapelis at the Rasos Cemetery

slaughtered in the forests of Paneriai between July 1941 and August 1944. Around 29,000 Poles, Russians and people of other nationalities were killed, as were many of Roma and about 500 Catholic priests. The executions were carried out by Nazi units with the help of a squad of Lithuanians. The sites, including a large pit where, in 1944, the retreating Nazis attempted to destroy the last of the bodies with acid, are now an open-air memorial. The first memorial was raised here in 1948. The tiny visitor centre is closed in winter, but the rest of the site is accessible.

Fresco in a Station of the Cross, Calvary Church of the Holy Cross

Calvary Church of the Holy Cross ⓫

Kalvarijos bažnyčia

Kalvarijų 225, 5 km (3 miles) N of Vilnius Old Town. **Tel** 269 7779. 🚌 26, 35, 36, 50.

This twin-spire Baroque church towering over the green Neris Valley was built by the Dominicans in the 1750s. The prime feature of its interior is a series of frescoes on the ceiling depicting the life of Christ. The main highlights are the nearby Stations of the Cross. Some 35 chapels, set amid trees along a 7-km (4-mile) hillside route, many in the Baroque style, were a popular attraction for 19th-century pilgrims. In 1962, they were destroyed by the Soviets. Several of the chapels have so far been re-created.

Twin-towered façade of the 18th-century Trinapolis Church

Trinapolis Church ⓬

Šv Trejybės bažnyčia

Verkių 70. 🚌 26, 35, 36, 50.

The original wooden church lasted only six years before it burnt down in 1710. The solid Baroque structure that replaced it in 1722 was designed by Pietro Puttini, a Veronese architect. Following the 1831 uprising, the church was closed by the Russians and the interior destroyed. In 1849, it was converted into an Orthodox church and the Metropolitan, the city's highest-ranking Russian Orthodox personage, used the neighbouring monastery as his summer residence. In 1917, the church was returned to the Catholics and the Archbishop set up residence here. The church was closed during the Soviet era and is still not open to the public.

Verkiai Palace ⓭

Verkių rūmai

Žaliųjų ežerių 49. **Tel** 272 9834. 🚌 35, 36, 76. ⭘ by appointment. 📷 ♿ 🍴

This once-immense Classical mansion was designed by Laurynas Stuoka-Gucevičius (1753–98) and Marcin Knackfus (1740–1821). The two distinguished architects were commissioned in 1781 to create a summer retreat for the Bishop of Vilnius. They built the palace on a site that, some 400 years previously, had been granted by Grand Duke Jogaila *(see pp210–11)* on his conversion to Christianity, to the new diocese of Vilnius.

The Classical gem was unfortunately short-lived. It was ravaged so much by the French army in 1812 that the subsequent owners had the central part pulled down. Only two wings of the palace survive and some decoration is still visible on the ceilings and the woodwork.

Verkiai Palace is also visited for its magnificent location. Standing on a hilltop above the Neris river, it offers a stunning view of the surrounding forests. A centuries-old legend tells how a sacred fire here was once tended by a pagan priest and beautiful virgins. The Verkiai restaurant *(see p339)* is located behind one of the palace wings. A winding path leads from the mansion gates down to **Vandens Malūnas**, a former watermill, which is now also a restaurant *(see p338)*.

Vandens Malūnas, a former watermill near Verkiai Palace

CENTRAL LITHUANIA

Rolling hills, swathes of untouched ancient forest and thousands of clear lakes characterize Central Lithuania. Much of the land is protected, allowing birds, animals and plants to thrive. While Vilnius and Kaunas are the region's most vibrant cities, the less-visited towns and villages of the region, with their beautiful churches and farmsteads, also attract a number of visitors.

Lithuania's heartland is symbolized by the mysterious mounds and fort-hills of Kernavė where Mindaugas, the first king of Lithuania, is said to have united the Baltic tribes in an effort to hold back the crusading armies of the Teutonic Knights. Similarly, Trakai, with its fairytale Island Castle that once stood as the kernel of one of Europe's biggest empires, stirs romantic nationalism in Lithuanians. Kaunas, which served as the capital of independent Lithuania between the two World Wars, is often seen as the original seat of its nationhood, rather than Vilnius, the present-day capital.

Three of the country's four ethnographic regions, each with its own dialect and traditions, are located in this area. Much of Dzūkija, in the south, is thickly forested. In summer and autumn, villagers selling mushrooms or berries line the roads, particularly along the route from Vilnius to the spa town of Druskininkai. Some parts of Dzūkija, which stretches from Alytus in the west to Vilnius in the east, have large Polish-speaking communities.

Aukštaitija, which literally means "the highlands", consists of relatively high ground that is dotted with lakes. Although some forest has survived the centuries, much of Aukštaitija was used for agriculture during the 20th century. With the exception of the Russian-speaking town of Visaginas, Aukštaitija is almost exclusively Lithuanian-speaking and is the country's archaic hinterland. Centred around Marijampolė, Suvalkija, or Sūduva, is the smallest ethnographic region, with its dress and customs once influenced by Prussia as well as Poland.

Permanent display entitled "Space of Unknown Growth" at the open-air art museum, Europe Park

◁ Picturesque view of the fairytale Island Castle at Trakai

Exploring Central Lithuania

The well-kept roads winding through the region offer great opportunities for exploring the forests around the spa town of Druskininkai in the south as well as the lakes and villages of Aukštaitija National Park in the northeast. The best way to experience this pristine landscape is to venture off the main roads, onto the scenic minor routes connecting Trakai–Birštonas, Varėna–Marcinkonys–Merkinė and Molėtai–Ignalina. However, Central Lithuania is more than just lakes and forests. The towns are scenic and there is a good choice of old-fashioned farmsteads to visit.

Flowerbeds in the pedestrianized centre of Panevėžys

SIGHTS AT A GLANCE

GETTING AROUND

The A1 motorway between Vilnius and Kaunas and onwards to the coast, and the A2 motorway from Vilnius to Panevėžys are the region's major arteries. Good bases for exploring are Kaunas, Druskininkai, Anykščiai and Palūšė, each of which is reachable by bus. Buses traverse Aukštaitija and Dzūkija national parks, but the best way to enjoy the surroundings is to reach the pretty villages of Zervynos and Salos II on foot. Trains go to Kaunas and Ignalina from the capital, but road transport should be taken to all other areas. There are airports at Vilnius and Kaunas.

KEY

═══	Motorway
═══	Main road
───	Secondary road
───	Minor road
───	Scenic route
───	Railway
───	International border

0 km   20

0 miles   20

etkai Čedasai

Nemunėlis

ys **16** ROKIŠKIS

Aleksandrevėlė

emunėlis Kriaunos 122

Lake Sartai 117 *Daugavpils*

Kamajai 120 Zarasai A6

Dusetos 178 Degučiai

Svėdasai **19** VISAGINAS

Vyžuonos Dūkštas

onys Utena **20** AUKŠTAITIJA NATIONAL PARK *Lake Dysnai*

17 ANYKŠČIAI A14 Kuktiškės 102

A6 Ignalina 112 Didžiasalis

Alanta Labanoras 111 *Lake Kretunas*

Molėtai 114 Kaltanenai Mielagėnai

18 MOLĖTAI LAKELANDS 111 110 Adutiškis

115 Inturkė 173 Svencionys

Šešuoliai Arnionys Sariai

Širvintos Visalaukė 102

Magūnai

2 EUROPE PARK Nemenčinė

3 KERNAVĖ *Vilnia* Lavoriškės

Suderve *Verte* 103

TRAKAI ISLAND CASTLE Vilnius Rukainiai

Trakai Juodšiliai A3 *Minsk*

es A4 A15

220 Šalčininkėlia

Valkininkai 126 Šalčininkai

Salčia *Lida*

105 ARĖNA Eišiškės

Rudnia

Fishing at Lake Srovinaitis, Aukštaitija National Park

Trakai Island Castle ❶

An impressive stronghold for any invader to overcome, the Island Castle in Trakai was built as a seat of power during the reign of Vytautas the Great and completed just before the Grand Duchy's crushing victory over the Teutonic Knights at the Battle of Grünwald (see p212). As Vilnius grew in importance, Trakai lost its significance and was destroyed by the Cossacks during the 1655 Russian invasion. In the late 19th century, the elegiac island ruins captured the imaginations of poets and painters during the national revival. Oddly, it was the Soviet authorities who, in the 1950s, sanctioned the reconstruction of this monument to Lithuania's glorious past. It was completed in 1987.

Dry moat, separating the main castle from the outer courtyard

The circular defence towers have 4-m (13-ft) thick bases.

★ Lakeside Walk
One way to appreciate Trakai's idyllic lake-filled landscape and the scale of the castle's construction, is to take the pretty walk that follows the shore of the island.

A wooden footbridge links the shore to the Island Castle.

Yachts
Between May and October yachts from the nearby Žalgiris Yacht Club are moored next to the Island Castle. They can be hired by the hour, but charges vary.

STAR SIGHTS

★ Lakeside Walk

★ History Museum

Lake Galvė

Serving as a moat around the castle, the lake has 21 tiny islands. Rowing and paddle boats can be hired along the quayside for a spectacular view of the castle.

VISITORS' CHECKLIST

Road Map D5. 🚌 *from Vilnius.*
🚆 *from Vilnius.* ℹ️ Vytauto
gatvė 69. **Tel** *(528) 51 934.*
Žalgiris Yacht Club Žemaitės
gatvė 3. **Tel** *(528) 52 824.*
History Museum Tel *(528)
53 946.* 🕐 *May–Sep: 10am–
7pm Tue–Sun, Oct–Apr: 10am–
5pm Tue–Sun.* 🌐 **www.
trakaimuziejus.lt**

The Ducal Palace's keep, which is 30 m (100 ft) high, served as the residence of the Grand Duke.

★ **History Museum**
The museum showcases a wide array of weaponry as well as items found during excavations, including 16th-century tankards, tiles and coins.

THE KARAIM OF TRAKAI

The Karaim, a community of Turkic settlers practising a particular kind of Judaism, lend a distinctly exotic flavour to Trakai. Their ancestors were taken prisoners by Vytautas the Great on a military venture to the Crimea in 1397, and subsequently served as royal guards. The Karaim have maintained their customs and traditions. Their characteristic wooden houses, each typically with gable ends and three windows facing the street, the Karaim synagogue or Kenesa and the Karaim Museum are all on Karaimų Street. The Karaim cemetery is by Lake Totoriskiai.

Graves in the Karaim Cemetery, partially hidden by long grass

Europe Park ❷
Europos parkas

Road Map D5. **Tel** (370) 237 7077.
🚌 *from Vilnius.* ⬤ *9am–noon daily.* 🅿️ 📷 🖥️ 🏠 **www.europosparkas.lt**

The 55-ha (136-acre) park contains contemporary sculptures. The aim of its founder, Gintaras Karosas (b.1968), was to give an artistic response to the French National Geographic Institute's statement in 1989 that a point about 17 km (11 miles) north is Europe's precise geographical centre.

Around 100 works of art are set in a landscape of forests, hills and lakes. The American artist Dennis Oppenheim (b.1938) created two monumental pieces – *Chair/Pool* and *Drinking Structure with Exposed Kidney Pool. Double Negative Pyramid*, by Sol Le Wit (1928–2007), is a reflection in concrete of ripples on a lake. Karosas's own work, *LNK Infotree*, is a maze of 3,000 old TV sets.

Kernavė ❸

Road Map D5. 🏠 *500.* 🚌 *from Vilnius.* 🏠 *Kernius 4, (382) 47 315.* 🎭 *Days of Live Archaeology (Jul).* **www.kernave.org**

The small, sleepy village of Kernavė overlooks the idyllic Neris Valley, where steep-sided fort-hills hint at the passing of a long-lost

Wooden steps crossing fort-hills, Kernavė's archaeological reserve

civilization. Archaeological finds show that the site was inhabited as far back as 9000 BC. In the 13th century, Kernavė was the first capital of the united Lithuanian tribes and a busy trading centre. The Northern Crusaders ransacked the prosperous pagan town in 1365. In 1390, another attack was launched by a mighty army consisting of knights, soldiers and mercenaries from Germany, France, Italy and England. Henry IV (1367–1413), the future king of England, also participated in the assault, from which the town never recovered.

Today, Kernavė is Lithuania's foremost archaeological reserve. In 2004, it was declared a UNESCO World Heritage Site. The protected area comprises five large mounds, which contained medieval ramparts and fortifications. Wooden steps lead to the summits of the hills, where there are breathtakingly beautiful views of the surrounding terrain.

Environs
The scenic road from Vilnius to Kernavė passes several villages. **Sudervė**, 20 km (12 miles) south of Kernavė, has an unusual white circular church designed by Lithuania's legendary early 19th-century Neo-Classicist, Laurynas Stuoka-Gucevičius.

Varėna ❹

Road Map D6. 🏠 *11,000.* 🚌 *from Vilnius.* 🚌 *from Vilnius.* 🏠 *Basanavičiaus 9, (310) 31 330.* 🎭 *Mushroom Festival (Sep).* **www.varena.lt**

Surrounded on all sides by thick forest, Varėna is situated on the eastern edge of Dzūkija National Park *(see p256)*. The town is regarded as the mushroom capital of Lithuania. Although a rich variety of mushrooms grows all over the country, here they proliferate like a carpet on the forest floor. One day a year, usually the last Saturday in September, the sleepy town springs to life, to celebrate the Mushroom Festival *(see p209)*.

Environs
The road from Varėna to Marcinkonys, 22 km (14 miles) southwest, winds pleasantly through Dzūkija National Park. Immediately

Farmstead with wooden barns, on the edge of the forest in Zervynos, near Varėna

Russian Orthodox Church with striking purple domes, Druskininkai

on the left inside the park, a road leads to **Zervynos**, a village with unpaved streets and the scenic Ūla river bubbling underneath the foliage and wooden bridges.

Druskininkai ❺

Road Map D6. 🏘 *17,000.* 🚌 *from Vilnius.* ℹ️ *Gardino 3, (313) 52 984.* **www**.druskininkai.lt

Lithuania's foremost spa resort, Druskininkai is a haven of peace and tranquility. Main roads bypass the town, tucked inside a bend on the thickly forested Nemunas river, and noise restrictions allow peace to prevail. After thriving on 200 years of popularity, Druskininkai suffered an economic shock in the 1990s, when it found itself deprived of Polish, Belarusian and Russian tourists, who once stayed in its sanitaria.

In recent years, wellness tourism has been revived considerably. The sanitaria offer water and mineral mud treatments, massages, beauty programmes and fitness trails through the forest. Bike rides and long walks are possible along the Sun Path, which leads through the picturesque Ratnyčia Valley.

The boulevard-lined town centre preserves wooden villas from the 19th and early 20th centuries, mainly found on Laisvės Square. The delightful **Russian Orthodox Church** also stands in the same square. On Vilniaus Street,

some futuristic-style buildings still survive, including the now-closed Soviet-era physiotherapy treatment centre with decorative waves of solid concrete hanging in mid-air.

The serene town inspired painter and composer M K Čiurlionis *(see p261)*, who lived here from 1890 to 1911. The **Čiurlionis Memorial Museum**, located in his family's wooden house, displays period furniture, his notebooks and copies of his artwork. Another museum in the town, the **Jacques Lipchitz Museum**, is dedicated to the Cubist sculptor who was born here in 1891.

🏛 Čiurlionis Memorial Museum
M K Čiurlionio 35. **Tel** *(370) 313 51131.* ⏲ *11am–5pm Tue–Sun.* 🔒 *last Tue of the month.* 📷 🎥

🏛 Jacques Lipchitz Museum
Šv Jokūbo 17. **Tel** *(313) 56 077.* ⏲ *June–Aug: 11am–5pm daily.* 📷

Grūtas Park ❻
Grūto parkas

Road Map D6. **Tel** *(370) 3135 5511.* ⏲ *Jun–Aug: 9am–8pm daily, Dec–Feb: 9am–5pm daily.* 📷 🎥 ♿ 🖥 **www**.grutoparkas.lt

Around 90 statues and busts of figures once glorified by the Soviet regime stand in alcoves on a forest trail in Grūtas village. Most of them once graced squares and gardens, before being torn down by crowds of cheering Lithuanians in 1991. The park's owner, Viliumas Malinauskas, was awarded the IgNoble Peace Prize in 2001, the year the park opened.

Each of the ideological relics is explained in English in information stands. A massive metal statue of Lenin that once stood in front of the KGB building in Vilnius lost a thumb while being wrenched by a crane from its pedestal. Another Lenin statue, showing him as a well-dressed gentleman, poses with the Lithuanian Communist Party's First Secretary Vincas Mickevičius-Kapsukas. Both statues were decapitated in 1991, but their heads have since been joined back. There is an image of Stalin, which once stood outside Vilnius train station until it was dismantled in 1960. *Rusų Karys* (Russian Soldier) is a statue made by Nazi prisoners of war from metal taken from the wrecks of German planes shot down by the Soviets. There are also statues and busts of Red Army liberators, poets and other heroes.

Busts of Marx, Engels, Lenin and Stalin in Grūtas Park

View of the Nemunas river and surrounding area from the fort-hill at Merkinė, near Dzūkija National Park

Dzūkija National Park **❼**

Dzūkijos nacionalinis parkas

Road Map D6. 🚉 *from Vilnius to Zervynos, Marcinkonys.* 🚌 *from Vilnius to Merkinė.* ℹ️ *Vilniaus 2, Merkinė, (310) 57 245.* **Headquarters** *Miškininkų 61, Marcinkonys, (310) 44 466.* 📧 *English-speaking guides arranged in Merkinė, Marcinkonys.*

The densely forested Dzūkija National Park, established on Lithuanian independence in 1991, covers 550 sq km (212 sq miles) of countryside. Besides an enormous area of ancient pine forest in the sandy Dainava plain, the park also covers sweeping bends in the broad Nemunas Valley. More than 200 species of flora and fauna are protected in the park, including many rare species of stork.

White stork, Dzūkija National Park

The few villages that are located in the park offer a glimpse of Eastern European life that has remained the same for a century or more. The ethnographic reserve of **Zervynos** is on the park's eastern edge.

The ancient settlement of **Merkinė** lies at the confluence of the Nemunas and Merkys rivers. A fort-hill, the site of a 14th-century castle, offers extensive vistas of the park.

Another fort-hill overlooking the Nemunas river is in the scenic hamlet of **Liškiava**, at the southwestern edge of the park. The 14th-century castle that stood here defended the Grand Duchy against the mighty Teutonic Knights. Another striking landmark is the domed 18th-century Holy Trinity Church, with a rich interior featuring seven late Baroque altars. A series of frescoes depicting images from the history of Christianity were covered in plaster in 1823 and were only recently restored.

In **Marcinkonys**, a village 8 km (5 miles) southwest of Zervynos, a track leads southwards to **Čepkeliai Reserve**. This area protects the country's most extensive marsh, which stretches into Belarus, and the migratory birds that stop here. Paths and raised wooden walkways reach observation platforms offering great views.

Alytus **❽**

Road Map D6. 🏙️ *70,000.* 🚉 *from Kaunas.* 🚌 *from Vilnius, Kaunas.* ℹ️ *Rotušės aikštė 14a, (315) 52 010.* **www**.alytus.lt

Lithuania's sixth-largest city began as a hilltop fortress where the tiny Alytupis river trickles into the Nemunas.

The hill still offers views of both the city and the Dzūkija forests to the south.

In the centre, the **Museum of Local Lore** has a collection of 65,000 antiques. The bridge across the Nemunas has a bas-relief depicting a battle that occured here between Lithuanians and Bolsheviks in 1919. It claimed the life of Antanas Juozapavičius, the first Lithuanian officer to die in the independence struggle. His tomb lies by the **Guardian Angels' Church**.

Much of the city centre was destroyed in 1941. Soon after, all the city's 60,000 Jews were killed in Vidzgiris Forest, a site marked in 1993 by a monument of a broken Star of David. Gravestones in the city cemetery remember the Jews.

Mass of crosses in the churchyard of Guardian Angels' Church, Alytus

Environs

From Alytus, the Nemunas river sweeps towards Kaunas *(see pp258–61)* around several huge, forest-covered bends. One of these bends can be viewed from an evocative forthill at the far end of the quiet village of **Punia**, located 15 km (9 miles) north of Alytus.

🏛 **Museum of Local Lore**
Savanorių 6. *Tel* (315) 51 990.
⏱ *9am–6pm Tue–Sat.* 📷

Church of the Blessed Virgin Mary in Kalvarija

Kalvarija ❾

Road Map C6. 🏠 *6,000.*
🚌 *from Kaunas.* ℹ️ *Bažnyčios 4,*
(345) 60 759.

Another Lithuanian town deeply haunted by the Holocaust, Kalvarija emerged in the 17th century as a trading town on the Warsaw–St Petersburg road. Jews made up a significant part of the population, some of them wealthy merchants who exported grain to Germany, but the majority poor workers who manned several factories making brushes and medicinal alcohol. Wooden synagogues were built and, in 1803, a stone synagogue complex was constructed including a rabbi's house and *beit midrash* (a place of study and prayer).

In 1941, the Nazis and the Soviet army exterminated the entire Jewish population in town. Lithuanian and Jewish Communists were tortured,

then shot on the banks of Lake Orija. The synagogue has been partially restored as a national monument.

The **Church of the Blessed Virgin Mary**, with its statues of angels and kings on the pediments above the portico and gate, was built in 1840.

Marijampolė ❿

Road Map C6. 🏠 *49,000.*
🚆 *from Kaunas.* 🚌 *from Kaunas.*
ℹ️ *Kudirkos 41, (343) 51 109.*
www.marijampole.lt

This town takes its name from an 18th-century monastery built for the Marian Fathers, a religious order founded in 1673. The Church of St Michael became a part of the complex in 1824, but the monastery's activities were restricted after the 1831 uprising. The church was revived by Bishop Jurgis Matulaitis (1871–1927), whose remains are marked by a tombstone and sarcophagus. During the Soviet occupation in 1944, over 6,000 residents were deported to Siberia. Anti-Soviet partisans mounted a struggle, a story told at the **Tauras District Partisans and Deportation Museum**. A cemetery on Varpio Street and a chapel on Tylioji Street remember the victims of the Soviet regime.

🏛 **Tauras District Partisans and Deportation Museum**
Vytauto 29. *Tel* (370) 3435 0754.
⏱ *9am–5pm Tue–Sat.* 📷

Vytautas's statue, Birštonas

Birštonas ⓫

Road Map D6. 🏠 *3,000.* 🚌 *from Vilnius, Kaunas.* ℹ️ *Jaunimo gatvė 3, (319) 65 740.* 🎷 *Birštonas Festival (Jun), Birštonas Jazz (Mar, alternate years).* **www**.birstonas.lt

The secluded spa town of Birštonas is quite different from the bustling wellness centre of Druskininkai *(see p255)*. Though open to paying guests as well as patients, Birštonas's clinical sanitaria have remained trapped in a bygone era. Nonetheless, the well-ordered landscape planning and a pleasant pedestrian boulevard alongside the Nemunas river makes it a delightful town to explore. On the town's eastern edge stands Vytautas Castle Hill, the site of a hunting lodge of Grand Duke Vytautas. A large carved stone statue of Vytautas on horseback stands near the fort-hill.

Birštonas is dotted with wooden houses, which date from the mid-19th century, when the reputation of the town's mineral waters and muds began to grow. A tiny yellow building in the town centre contains a tap with free access to the rich well of water below. The town attracts a lot of visitors during Birštonas Jazz, Lithuania's oldest jazz festival. Held once every two years, the three-day marathon features a range of styles. Birštono Seklytėlė *(see p341)*, a valley-top restaurant, has a grand view of the pine-covered Nemunas.

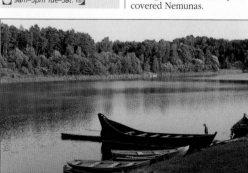

The Nemunas river seen from the promenade at Birštonas

Kaunas

Lithuania's second-largest city, Kaunas stands at the confluence of the Nemunas and Neris, the country's biggest rivers. A series of disasters hindered the city's development, including invasions by the Russians (1655), Swedes (1701) and Napoleon's Grand Army (1812). Rapid growth in the 19th century culminated in Kaunas becoming the temporary capital of newly independent Lithuania in 1919. Later, the city suffered under Nazi and Soviet occupations. Today, Kaunas is a modern city with a boulevard and a host of museums. The main historic sights are located in its well-preserved Old Town.

View of the bridge over the Nemunas river leading to the Old Town

Old Town Hall
Rotušės aikštė.
Known locally as the "White Swan" and resembling a church with its single-tiered tower, the Old Town Hall has been a marriage registry office since the 1970s. It continues to be the photogenic backdrop for newlyweds. Built in the mid-16th century, it housed merchants, magistrates and the mayor, as well as a subterranean prison. It has been used as an ammunition store, clubhouse, fire station and theatre. Town Hall Square, where it stands, was once a busy marketplace and the focal point of the Old Town.

Church of the Holy Trinity
Rotušės aikštė 22. **Tel** (37) 323 734. 10am Sun.
Built for a Bernardine convent in the late 1620s, this church has remained in good condition. Its blend of Renaissance and Gothic styles and pastel colours brighten up the northwestern corner of Town Hall Square. A redesign of the interior was completed just before the outbreak of World War II.

Church of St George
Papilio 9. **Tel** (37) 224 659. 6pm Mon–Fri, 10:30am Sun.
Constructed for Bernardine friars in the 15th century, this Gothic church was destroyed twice by fire before its interior was restored in the Baroque style. The church was further damaged by the Russians in the 17th century and in 1812 by Napoleon's soldiers, who used it as a warehouse. It was finally returned to the Franciscans in 1993.

Kaunas Castle
Pilies 17. **Tel** (37) 323 436. admission with guided tour only.
The ruins of Kaunas Castle are a reminder of the strategic importance of its location, between the two rivers, Neris and Nemunas. Little is known about what stood here before the first stone structure was erected in the 13th century. Crusaders damaged the castle in 1362. Soon after reconstruction, the Teutonic Knights were dealt their decisive blow at the Battle of Grünwald (*see p212*) and the castle consequently fell into ruins. The structure was used as a prison in the 18th century, but was restored in the 1920s.

Pharmacy Museum
Rotušės 28. **Tel** (37) 201 569. 10am–6pm Tue–Sat.
A powder for epilepsy made from the heads of corpses, a tincture of "Venus hair" to improve one's allure and a 19th-century herbal remedy

Elegant Old Town Hall, locally called the "White Swan"

0 metres　　500
0 yards　　500

for male vitality called Erektosan are among the exhibits at this unique museum. Chilling medicinal apparatus and the occasional waxwork, such as a shaman curing a baby, add to the atmosphere. The museum also runs a homoeopathic pharmacy.

🔒 Cathedral of Sts Peter and Paul
Vilniaus 1. *Tel* (37) 324 093. 🕂
7am, 8am, 9am, 6pm daily.
Several reconstructions have culminated in the Gothic and Renaissance exterior of this 15th-century cathedral. The broadly late Baroque interior, however, is largely unchanged since 1800. A tombstone on the exterior of the south wall is that of Maironis (1862–1932), a priest-poet whose verse romanticized Lithuanian legends and landmarks. Inside, the sculptures surrounding the high altar are overpowering. The oldest of the cathedral's

Painting, Cathedral of Sts Peter and Paul

paintings, the 17th-century *Suffering Mother of God*, reputedly has miraculous powers.

🏛 Perkūnas House
Aleksoto 6. *Tel* (37) 302 994.
⬜ 10am–4pm Mon–Fri, 11am–1pm Sun. 📷
The ogee arches and pinnacles of this red-brick Gothic building, resemble Church of St Anne *(see p228)*,Vilnius. It was named after Perkūnas, the pagan god of thunder, when renovation in the 19th century revealed that it may once have been the site of a pagan temple. Dating from the early 1500s, it was originally a meeting house for merchants in the Hanseatic League. Bought by the Jesuits, the house was converted into a chapel before becoming, in the 19th century, a theatre and then a school. Later, during the Soviet period, it was used as a warehouse. It is now back with the Jesuits.

VISITORS CHECKLIST
Road Map D5. 🏠 356,000.
✈ 10 km (6 miles) N of town.
🚉 🚌 ℹ Laisvės alėja 36, (37) 323 436. 🎷 International Jazz Festival (Apr). **www**.kaunas.lt

🔒 Vytautas Church
Aleksoto 3. *Tel* (37) 203 854. 🕂
6pm Tue–Thu, 10am & 6pm Sat–Sun.
Standing on the bank of the Nemunas river, this church was built on the orders of Vytautas the Great after the Holy Roman Emperor decided in 1413, much to the ire of the Teutonic Knights, that the land on the river's right bank belonged to the Grand Duchy of Lithuania. Already an army storehouse, the church was converted to serve a Russian Orthodox congregation. A full reconstruction took place after Lithuania's first independence in 1918, post World War I. In 1930, a medallion was placed in the church wall to commemorate the 500th anniversary of Vytautas's death.

Red-brick Gothic structure of Vytautas Church

🏛 Folk Music Museum
Zamenhofo 12. *Tel* (37) 206 820.
⬜ Oct–Mar: 9am–5pm Tue–Sat, Apr–Sep: 10am–6pm Tue–Sat. 📷 📷
This museum boasts a collection of 7,000 wind, brass and stringed instruments, including pipes and whistles. Only 500 of them are on display due to the museum's small size. The staff can give demonstrations of many of these. Stranger pieces, such as the table bass, a pine table with four strings and a pig's bladder, are also displayed.

KAUNAS

Key to Symbols see back flap

Exploring Modern Kaunas

Stretching eastwards from the Old Town is the city's modernized New Town. The process of its expansion began in the 19th century, and today it is as the hub of commercial and cultural life in the city. The museums and other sites are found around the heart of modern Kaunas in Laisvės (Freedom) Avenue. This broad, leafy, pedestrianized boulevard is lined with shops, pavement cafés, restaurants and bars, and is the place local people come to stroll and mingle.

View along Laisvės Avenue towards Church of St Michael

Laisvės Avenue

At the eastern end of this boulevard are the blue-silver onion domes of the Church of St Michael. Originally Russian Orthodox when it was built in the early 1890s, it was later converted to serve the Lithuanian army. A monument by the park outside the Music Theatre at Laisvės 4 marks the spot where Romas Kalanta, a Lithuanian student, set fire to himself on 14 May 1972 in protest against Soviet rule. His suicide sparked student protests, which were ruthlessly suppressed.

🏛 Mykolas Žilinskas Art Gallery

Nepriklausomybės 12. **Tel** *(37) 322 788.* ☐ *11am–5pm Tue–Sun.* 🏷 🔲 🔲
An exile who had fled from Kaunas to West Berlin in advance of the Soviets in 1940, Mykolas Žilinskas (1904–92) later built a valuable art collection, which he donated to Kaunas in the 1970s. Besides canvases and porcelain from the 16th to the 20th centuries, including *The Crucifixion* by Rubens and some early Soviet avant-garde art, there are also pre-war paintings and sculptures by Baltic artists.

🅰 Church of the Resurrection

Žemaičių 31. **Tel** *(37) 229 222.* ✚ *6pm Mon–Fri; 9:30am, 11am, 12:30pm Sun.*
With a 70-m (230-ft) steeple, this church was built to mark Lithuanian independence in 1918. After World War II, the Soviets turned it into a radio factory. With independence regained, the factory was evicted. After reconstruction the church was consecrated on Christmas Day 2004.

🏛 M K Čiurlionis Art Museum

V Putvinskio 55. **Tel** *(37) 221 587.* ☐ *11am–5pm Tue–Sun.* 🏷 🔲
Housing virtually all the paintings that Čiurlionis ever produced, this museum also gives an insight into the development of art in Lithuania. With 335,000 exhibits, it is Lithuania's biggest art gallery, but there is room for only a fraction of these. Artifacts from other cultures include some oddly juxtaposed pieces from Ancient Egypt.

🏛 Vytautas the Great War Museum

Donelaičio 64. **Tel** *(37) 320 939.* ☐ *10am–5pm Wed–Sun.* 🏷 🔲
Lithuania's national war museum exhibits weapons that the country has used to defend itself. However, the main focus of the museum is the re-creation of the story of the doomed transatlantic flight of the *Lituanica* in July 1933. The pilots Steponas Darius and Stasys Girėnas died in the crash, but the distance covered, 6,411 km (3,984 miles), was the second-longest flight ever recorded. The plane's wreckage and the suits of the pilots are on display.

🏛 Devil's Museum

V Putvinskio 64. **Tel** *(37) 221 587.* ☐ *10am–5pm Tue–Sun.* 🏷 🔲 🔲 🔲
This museum's fine collection of representations of devils, demons and witches from Lithuania and around the world, was brought together by avid collector Antanas Žmuidzinavičius (1876–1966). A sculpture of the horned figures of Hitler and Stalin fighting over Lithuania in a pit of bones is grim, but most of the devils are shown as playful, musical and frequently drunk.

🏛 Ninth Fort

Žemaičių 73. **Tel** *(37) 377 715.* ☐ *Apr–Oct: 10am–6pm Wed–Mon, Nov–Mar: 10am–6pm Wed–Sun.* 🔲
The ninth in a series of fortifications constructed by Tsarist Russia to protect its western borders, was built in the early 20th century, only to become a prison in 1924. During World War II, it was used for incarceration and extermination by the Nazis. The fort also housed Soviet political prisoners. Part of a fort after the war, it opened as a "museum to the victims of Fascism" in 1958. The dungeon and defence walls have displays on the Nazi and Soviet occupations.

Artillery on show at the Vytautas the Great War Museum

♣ Raudondvaris

5 km (3 miles) W of Kaunas.
🚌 *from Kaunas.*

Built by the crusaders in the 14th century, Raudondvaris (Red Manor) became a part of Lithuania after the Battle of Grünwald (1410). The legend says that it was presented as a gift, in 1549, by Sigismund August to Barbora Radvilaitė a year before their marriage. After her death in 1551, the castle fell into ruin and was rebuilt as a manor house in the 17th century by the Tyszkiewicz family. Its library and collection of paintings were lost during World War I. A chapel close by contains the Tyszkiewicz tombs that survived the 20th century.

A red manor with manicured lawns at Raudondvaris

🏛 Pažaislis Monastery

7 km (4 miles) E of town. 🕐 *10am–5pm Mon–Sat.*

One of Eastern Europe's great Baroque monuments, Pažaislis Monastery and its central, cupola-domed Church of the Visitation of the Blessed Virgin Mary were constructed by Italian architects in the 17th century. There is finely detailed stucco work inside the church and in the corridors of the monastery, much of it framing intricate frescoes painted by the Italian artist, Michelangelo Palloni.

🏛 Rumšiškės Open-Air Museum

15 km (9 miles) E of town.
Tel *(346) 47 392.* 🕐 *10am–6pm Tue–Sat.* 🔒 *1 Nov–Easter Mon.* 📷
📷 ♿

At Rumšiškės Open-Air Museum, traditional thatched farmsteads and other elements of village life have been carefully reassembled.

Colourful buildings and statue in the square of the Old Town, Kėdainiai

The rolling countryside overlooking Lake Kaunas creates a perfect backdrop.

🏛 Zapyškis Church

15 km (9 miles) W of town.

One of Lithuania's loveliest buildings, the triangular red-brick Gothic Zapyškis Church is set in a field by the Nemunas river. Built in the 16th century, it has remained miraculously intact despite invasions and occupations.

Kėdainiai ⑬

Road Map D5. 📷 *32,000.* 🚂 *from Kaunas, Vilnius.* 🚌 *from Kaunas, Vilnius.* 🛈 *Didžioji 1, (347) 60 363.* 📷 *Cucumber Festival (Jul), Ice Cream Festival (Aug).* **www**.visitkedainiai.lt

With a history as a trading town on the route between Kaunas and Rīga, Kėdainiai was first mentioned in written sources in 1372. Its colourful Old Town has a series of elaborately gabled merchants' houses in the main square. Close by, the Renaissance-style Town Hall dates from 1654 and holds Kėdainiai's administrative offices. In another square, two synagogues dating from 1837 stand side by side. They were once used by the town's thriving Jewish community. Another synagogue, now the **Multicultural Centre**, holds a museum on Kėdainiai's cultural history.

Environs

Paberžė, 30 km (19 miles) north of Kėdainiai, with its delightful wooden church, was the residence of Father Stanislovas (1918–2005), a revered Tolstoyan hermit and Capuchin friar.

🏛 Multicultural Centre

Senoji rinka 12. **Tel** *(347) 51 778.* 🕐 *10am–5pm Tue–Sat.* 📷

M K ČIURLIONIS (1875–1911)

A tortured soul and artistic genius, Mikalojus Konstantinas Čiurlionis is Lithuania's most famous painter and composer. He started out as a prodigious composer of atmospheric symphonic and organ works, but at the age of 27 he began to study drawing. The next nine years were filled with feverish creativity. Before his early death from pneumonia, he had created around 300 works of music, painting and poetry. Many of his mystical paintings mirrored his musical compositions and some were named as pieces of music, such as *Spring Sonata* and *Funeral Symphony*. Despite their melancholy, Čiurlionis's painted and musical works can be surprisingly uplifting.

Painting by Čiurlionis, displayed at the M K Čiurlionis Art Museum

View of the wooden steps across the mounds at Kernavė's archaeological reserve ▷

Interior of the Neo-Baroque Cathedral of Christ the King, Panevėžys

Panevėžys ⑭

Road Map D5. 🏠 *114,000.*
🚉 *from Klaipėda.* 🚌 *from Vilnius.*
ℹ️ *Laisvės aikštė 11, (45) 508 081.*
www.panevezys.lt

One of Lithuania's largest cities with a modern commercial centre, Panevėžys is a crucial transport hub in the region.

South of its centre lies the **Cathedral of Christ the King**, a Neo-Baroque structure built in 1904. A sweeping painting above the altar depicts a victorious medieval Lithuanian army. A few streets north, the **Civic Art Gallery** often holds eccentric exhibitions of local modern art. East of the centre is **Glasremis**, a working gallery creating glass items.

Environs
In **Pakruojis**, 50 km (31 miles) northwest of Panevėžys, the country's largest 18th-century manor lies in a 6-ha (15-acre) park, with a five-arch stone bridge and 40 other structures.

🏛 **Civic Art Gallery**
Respublikos 3. **Tel** (45) 584 802.
⭘ *11am–6pm Wed–Sun.* 🈂️

🏛 **Glasremis**
J Biliuno 12. **Tel** (45) 430 403.
⭘ *10am–5pm Mon–Fri.* ⬛

Biržai ⑮

Road Map D4. 🏠 *17,000.* 🚉 *from Panevėžys.* ℹ️ *J Janonio 2, (450) 33 496.* **www**.birzai.lt

The small town of Biržai is best known for its traditional breweries. The local brew can be sampled in the cellar of the **Sėla Museum**, housed in the 17th-century Biržai Castle. Visitors can enjoy live folk music performed here, but should book ahead.

In 1701, Peter the Great of Russia and King Augustus II of Poland signed the pact against Sweden in this castle on the eve of the Great Northern War *(see p33)*.

In the grounds are the ruins of an older castle, whose defences in the mid-1500s involved damming two rivers to create Lithuania's oldest man-made lake, Širvėna. A 525-m (572-yard) wooden bridge leads across the lake to Astravas Manor Park, with its sprawling 19th-century manor house, watermill and old dam.

🏛 **Sėla Museum**
J Radvilos 3. **Tel** (450) 31 883.
⭘ *10am–5:30pm Wed–Sat, 9am–4:30pm Sun.* 🈂️ ⬛

Rokiškis ⑯

Road Map D4. 🏠 *18,000.* 🚉 *from Panevėžys.* 🚌 *from Panevėžys, Vilnius.* ℹ️ *Tyzenhauzo 5, (458) 52 261.* 🐎 *Lake Sartai Horse Race (first Sat in Feb).* **www**.rokiskis.lt

Set amid glorious countryside, Rokiškis is blessed with fort-hills, forests and picnic sites. However, it is best known for its cheese company, Rokiškio Sūris. Having started as a small local dairy, it sells cheeses all over the Baltic region.

Rokiškis Manor House, the town's main sight, was built in 1801 by the Tyzenhaus family. The Polish architects who redesigned it in 1905 created an English-style interior, but its exterior has Baroque elements. It houses the **Rokiškis Museum**, which offers tours of the lavish Great Hall and a separate building that exhibits fine wooden folk sculptures by Lionginas Šepka (1907–85).

Environs
Kriaunos, 15 km (9 miles) southeast of Rokiškis, has a local **Historical Museum** filled with an eclectic collection of flax tools, linen fabrics, tubs and troughs. Hidden upstairs, the "loft of witches" is a coven of 400 witches, mermaids, fairies and goblins.

The island in Lake Dviragis in the village of **Salos**, 20 km (12 miles) southwest of Rokiškis, was a sanctuary for its inhabitants in the early 15th century. Now connected

Wooden bridge across the castle moat into the older castle, Biržai

Façade of Rokiškis Manor House, embellished with Baroque elements

by a bridge to the rest of the village, the island forms a calm backdrop to a Classical 19th-century manor and a Neo-Gothic wooden church.

🏛 **Rokiškis Museum**
Tyzenhauzo 5. **Tel** (458) 52 261.
◷ 10am–6pm Tue–Sun. 🖼 🎦

🏛 **Historical Museum**
Kriaunų village. **Tel** (458) 41 718.
◷ 10am–5pm Tue–Sat. 🖼 🎦

Anykščiai ⑰

Road Map D5. 🏠 13,000. 🚆 from Panevėžys. 🚌 from Panevėžys, Kaunas. 🚹 Gegužės 1, (381) 59 177. **Lithuanian Narrow-Gauge Railway** ◷ Aug–May: 11am Sat, Jun–Jul: 11am Sat–Sun. **www**.ngr.lt

Nestled in a landscape of rolling pastures, Anykščiai creates a picturesque setting for the 160-km (100-mile) **Lithuanian Narrow-Gauge Railway**. Only 68 km (42 miles) of Europe's longest functional narrow-gauge railway is in regular use today. Its locomotives pull carriages across open countryside along the Šventoji river to the scenic shores of Lake Rubikiai with its 16 islands. Tickets are sold at the tourist information centre. The old station boasts the **Anykščiai Northern Railway Museum**, providing further insights into train travel.

Environs

In **Niūronys**, 6 km (4 miles) north of Anykščiai, the **Horse Museum** hosts exhibitions on various horse-related products. Rides on real horses, around the paddock or in a horse-

drawn carriage, can be had for a small fee. There is also a mini-playground for children.

🏛 **Anykščiai Northern Railway Museum**
Vilties 2. **Tel** (381) 59 177.
◷ May–Oct: 10am–5pm daily, Nov–Apr: by appointment. 🖼 🎦
🖥 **www**.siaurukas.eu

🏛 **Horse Museum**
Niūronių village. **Tel** (381) 51 722.
◷ May–Aug: 9am–6pm daily, Sep–Apr: 8am–5pm daily. 🖼 🎦
www.arkliomuziejus.lt

Molėtai Lakelands ⑱

Road Map D5. 🏠 29,000. 🚆 from Vilnius, Daugavpils. 🚌 from Vilnius, Daugavpils. 🚹 Inturkė 4, (383) 51 187. 🎵 Visagino Country Music Festival (mid-Aug).

The lakes that extend east from the town of Molėtai are some of the Baltic region's cleanest, making it perfect for camping and swimming.

Lake Želva's Ethnocosmology Centre, Molėtai Lakelands

Forest-lined lakes with inlets, such as Baltieji and Juodieji Lakajai, and, further south, Asveja, are protected as part of the 55,000-ha (136,000-acre) Labanoras Regional Park. Molėtai is one of the oldest settlements in the country, although it has preserved very few historical monuments. The Molėtai Astronomical Observatory offers sweeping views of area. Inside, the **Ethnocosmology Centre** displays an intriguing exhibition on the links between cosmology and the pagan rituals of the ancient Lithuanians.

Exterior of the Ignalina Nuclear Power Plant, near Visaginas

Visaginas ⑲

Road Map E5. 🏠 29,000. 🚆 from Vilnius, Daugavpils. 🚌 from Vilnius, Daugavpils. 🚹 Taikos gatvė 11, (386) 52 597. 🎵 Visagino Country Music Festival (mid-Aug).

With only 15 per cent of its population ethnically Lithuanian, Visaginas has a unique atmosphere in a country that is 85 per cent Lithuanian. It was created in 1974 to house nuclear scientists who built and then worked at the nearby **Ignalina Nuclear Power Plant**, the Baltic region's only nuclear power station.

Hidden in forests down a single road, Visaginas has no discernable centre. High-rise housing blocks cover the town from east to west. To cool the reactors at the Ignalina plant, water is pumped in from Drūkšiai, Lithuania's biggest lake.

Aukštaitija National Park ⑳

The oldest and most beloved of Lithuania's national parks, Aukštaitija National Park was established in 1974 to protect local biodiversity. About 60 per cent of the country's plant species can be found here, in addition to its ancient pine forests, fort-hills, burial mounds and old thatched cottages in villages such as Salos II. Palušė makes an ideal base for exploring the 400-sq km (154-sq mile) park. However, the park's central point, Ladakalnis Hill, is its highest, from which five lakes are visible. Rowing boats can be hired from Palušė, enabling visitors to make a circular trip or drift at a leisurely pace along the water trail.

KEY

☐ Aukštaitija National Park

0 km 2

0 miles 2

Taurapilis, one of several ancient fortifications found in the park, is situated above Lake Tauragnas, affording extensive views in all directions.

Tauragnai

Šeimatis

Mokas Stones

Lake Tauragnas

Lake Utenas

Šėla

Stripeikiai

Ginučiai Watermill

Lake Rakasas

Kireikiai

Ladakalnis Hill
175 m/574 ft

Salo

★ Beekeeping Museum
Sculptures of characters from Lithuanian folklore stand together on a grassy hillside with wooden hives, in the village of Stripeikiai.

★ Ladakalnis Hill
The best panoramic view of the park can be experienced from the hill above Lake Linkmenas. The area is noted for its mesmerizing greenery and clear lakes.

★ Salos II Cultural Reserve
The ethnographic village is arranged like a live, open-air museum, with several well-preserved timber houses.

STAR SIGHTS

★ Beekeeping Museum

★ Ladakalnis Hill

★ Salos II Cultural Reserve

BEEKEEPING

Unusually shaped beehives at the Beekeeping Museum

Lithuanians have a long and enduring history of apiculture. Forest beekeeping, in which bees lived in tree hollows and their keepers mounted elaborate climbing apparatus to collect the honey, was widely practised in the Middle Ages. Beeswax and honey were vital to the economy in the Middle Ages. In the 15th century, a law was passed to prosecute people who harmed them, or the trees.

VISITORS' CHECKLIST

Road Map D5. 🚆 from Ignalina. 🚌 from Ignalina. 🛈 Park Headquarters and Visitors' Centre, Palušė, (386) 47 478. 🚶 on foot or by bus, offered at the Park Headquarters. Rowing boats and canoes can be hired during summer. 🖥 www.anp.lt

Trainiškis
In the village of Trainiškis stands a mighty tree, which is believed to be 800 years old and is said to have once been a site of pagan sacrifices.

Valčių Pervežimas Boat Way
Visitors can rent a boat for a circular trip around the park from lake to lake, going via Valčių Pervežimas, the water trail that links Lake Baluošas and Lake Dringis.

Vaišniūnai

ainiškis

Valčių ervežimas

Lake Dringis

Gaveikėnai

IGNALINA

Lake Lūšiai

Palušė

KEY

🚉	Railway station
🚌	Bus station
🚤	Boating
🛈	Visitor information
🏛	Museum
🏤	Historic building
⛺	Campsite
⛰	Viewpoint
══	Main road
──	Other road
—	Railway
– –	Trail
---	Water trail
▬ ▬	Park boundary
▲	Peak

Gaveikėnai Watermill
One of several original watermills in the park, Gaveikėnai Watermill was built around 1800. Today, it houses a café.

WESTERN LITHUANIA

*I*solated for centuries, the little towns and villages of Žemaitija, the local name for the low-lying land of Western Lithuania, have a mystical atmosphere. Rustic wooden farmsteads and settlements are nestled between knolls and marshes. Klaipėda and Šiauliai are charming cities with distinct surroundings characterized by tiny, hidden lanes with a surfeit of cafés and museums.

Žemaitija is the ancient heartland of Samogitia, a medieval pagan duchy that managed to repel the innumerable incursions of its hostile, mostly Christian neighbours. With stubborn determination the Samogitians fought off the crusaders for more than 250 years, before finally being absorbed into the Grand Duchy of Lithuania in 1422. It was the last corner of Europe to be converted to Christianity and age-old rituals dedicated to pagan deities continued in more isolated parts until the 20th century.

Klaipėda, the country's only seaport city, is an ideal base for embarking on day-trips into Western Lithuania. Although the port area was secretively closed off during the Soviet era, it has since reopened to cruise ship and ferry passengers. Originally known as Memel, Klaipėda was part of Prussia and Germany for over 500 years. Some of the surviving Germanic-style half-timbered houses, once used by merchants, characterize the streets of the Old Town today.

A short ferry ride from Klaipėda lies the Curonian Spit, with its towering dunes and scenic villages like Nida. Inland, quaint little towns, such as Šilutė and Kretinga, are easily reachable and a delight to stroll around. The quiet village of Rusnė and the surrounding Nemunas Delta region attract many rare birds which breed in their lush marshes. Žemaitija National Park, close to Lake Plateliai, conceals a former Soviet missile base. Cycle paths stretch all along the Lithuanian coast from Nida up to the Latvian border and pass the coastal resorts of Palanga and Šventoji, both offering beaches, spas and all-night bars and clubs.

Pretty wooden houses along a street in Nida, a village in the Curonian Spit National Park

◁ The Nemunas river flowing amid verdant scenery, near Šilutė

Exploring Western Lithuania

The northwest corner of Lithuania offers the twin attractions of Žemaitija National Park, with its Soviet-era missile base, and the memorable Orvidas Garden. The UNESCO-protected Curonian Spit, a long and narrow strip of land between the Baltic Sea and the Curonian Lagoon, is worth visiting for its towering dunes, charming fishing villages, cycle paths and beaches. Western Lithuania also gives an insight into the country's unique Catholic and pagan mysticism, which is keenly felt in small towns such as Tytuvėnai and Šiluva.

SIGHTS AT A GLANCE

Towns and Resorts

Saldus

163

MAŽEIKIAI **11**

Skuodas · Tirkšliai · Vie

170

Kaukolikai · 164

Seda

Lenkimai · 169

ŽEMAITIJA
NATIONAL PARK

Liepāja · 218

Eigirdž

Šventoji · Darbėnai · ORVIDAS **13** · PLATELIAI **15** · 🏛 🏠 **12**

GARDEN · TELŠIAI **10**

A13

Tūbausiai · A11 · PLUNGĖ **14** · Rain

PALANGA **18** 🚗 🏛 · Kartena · Žlibinai · Žarė

KRETINGA **17** 🏛 · Stalgėnai · 164

166

Giruliai · Rietavas · Var

A13 · Vežalčiai · La · Lūks

Gargždai · 197 · Jūra

KLAIPĖDA · A1

SMILTYNĖ **19** 🏛 🏠 **16** · Mickai · Veiviržėnai · Kvedarna

Priekulė · 193

CURONIAN SPIT NATIONAL PARK · Švėkšna · Š

Ašva · Pajūris

Curonian · Saugos · Tenenys · 165 · Pagrar

Lagoon · Žemaičių · Vainutas

20 · Minija · Naumiestis

Ventė · 🏛 **21** ŠILUTĖ · 199 · Tau

22 · Rusnė · Juknaičiai

NEMUNAS · Usėnai · Lauksargiai

DELTA · 141 · A12

Zelenogradsk

PANEMUNĖ **8**

Kaliningrad

| 0 km | 20 |
| 0 miles | 20 |

Beach on the eastern shore of Lake Plateliai, Žemaitija National Park

GETTING AROUND

The A1 motorway between Kaunas and Klaipėda is the fastest east–west route across the region. Buses serve the region well, and good bases from which to explore it are Palanga, Kaunas, Šiauliai and Klaipėda. Trains offer a less flexible means of transport, and even the Kaunas–Klaipėda line makes a detour via Šiauliai. The regional airport, at Palanga, provides international connections, most notably with the transit hub of Copenhagen.

KEY

▬	Motorway
▬	Main road
▬	Secondary road
▬	Minor road
▬	Railway
▬	International border

Rīga

Žagarė
Naujoji
kmenė
Skaistgiris
Kriukai
Žeimelis
Dameliai
209
Joniškis
156
211
Venta
155
Kinkiai
A12
152
Pašvitinys
Linkuva
Meškuičiai
Pamūšis
Mūša **151**
škiai
HILL OF CROSSES ②
Pakroujis
Kuršėnai
150
Žeimiai
Rozalimas
🏠🏛️🏛️
ŠIAULIAI ①
Derveliai
Uopyna **159**
Aukštelkė
Lake Bekyins
A9
212
Radviliškis
Panevėžys
215
Bubiai
A12
🏛️ **A9**
Užventis
Laikšės
Sidariai
③ **ŠEDUVA**
144
Kiaunoriai
Siaulėnai
Karkėnai
Kražiai
Kelmė
④ **TYTUVĖNAI**
Grinkiškis
⑤ **ŠILUVA**
Katauskiai
Vosiliškis
225
Nemakščiai
148
na **196**
Ilgižiai
Skaudvilė
⑥ **RASEINIAI**
Ariogala
Bebirza
A1
ašaltuonys
Eržvilkas
Šimkaičiai
Juodaičiai
198
146
Stakiai
Eičiai
RAUDONĖ
Veliuona
147
141
⑦
Kaunas
JURBARKAS ⑨
Nemunas
Gelgaudiškis
137
Slavikai
Lukšiai
Šakiai
140
Griškabudis
Nova
Kudirkos
Naumiestis
Marijampolė

SEE ALSO

• **Where to Stay** pp313–15

• **Where to Eat** pp343–5

Painting of Madonna and Child, Tytuvėnai

Šiauliai ●

Lithuania's fourth-biggest city, Šiauliai first appeared in historical sources in 1236, the date of the Battle of the Sun *(see p210)*. An major industrial centre since the 18th century, it saw its population rise from 6,200 in 1866 to 23,600 at the outbreak of World War I. The war destroyed more than 60 per cent of the city. Today, Šiauliai is enjoying a wave of development. New shopping centres are being built, pedestrianized streets laid and monuments renovated. The city's most attractive part, with traditional houses and museums is the Old Town.

Old bicycle outside the Bicycle Museum, a part of Aušra Museum

🏛 Aušra Museum

Vytauto 89. *Tel (41) 524 390.*
⏲ 9am–5pm Tue–Fri, 11am–4pm
Sat. 🈺 🎫 *opening times vary at each location and can be checked at Šiauliai tourist information centre.*
The Aušra Museum, founded in 1923, is the oldest museum in the city. It was named in honour of the first Lithuanian newspaper. The museum is a treasure trove of art and culture with a vast collection of historical, achitectural and archaeological artifacts, spread over 11 locations. The history of the daily life of the townspeople of Šiauliai is the focus of Aušra Avenue Palace, the museum's main building. A special section is dedicated to the repressions of the Soviet post-war period.

The **Bicycle Museum** (Vilniaus 139) reveals the story of cycling in Lithuania with almost 100 bicycles on display, including a child's tricycle from 1905. Replicas of a number of historic bikes are also exhibited.

One of Lithuania's very few Art Nouveau buildings from the early 20th century, the **Chaim Frenkel Villa** (Vilniaus 74), depicts Jewish daily life in centuries past. The bulk of the city's collection of art is housed at the **Venclauskų House** (Vytauto 89), which, together with the privately run **Laiptai Gallery** (Žemaitės 83), exhibits the work of local artists such as Marcė Katiliūtė (1912–37). Her prodigious talent, creating mostly intense and haunting portraits, ended when she took her own life at the age of 25.

🏠 Cathedral of Sts Peter and Paul

Aušros aleja 3. *Tel (41) 528 077.*
⏲ 7:30am, 5pm, 6pm Mon–Sat; 8am, 9:30am, 11am, 12:30pm Sun.
A church has stood on this spot since 1445 and the precise location of the earlier

ŠIAULIAI

Aušra Museum ①
Cathedral of Sts Peter
and Paul ②
Sundial Square ③

0 metres   500
0 yards   500

Key to Symbols *see back flap*

Prominent tower of the Cathedral of Sts Peter and Paul

wooden place of worship is marked by a metal cross. The old church was burnt down and in 1625, the existing one was built in stone to give it more permanence. Seen from afar, the cathedral's gleaming white 70-m (230-ft) tower makes the building look more modern than it actually is.

The cathedral is built in Renaissance style with some features typical of medieval architecture. Its thick walls are accompanied by details that appear to have been defensive but in fact were not. On the southern side of the cathedral is Lithuania's oldest sundial. Sts Peter and Paul Church was elevated to cathedral status in 1997.

⊓ Sundial Square
Ežero gatvė.
A sundial was erected in the square in 1986 to mark the 750th anniversary of the Battle of the Sun. The slender sundial, surmounted by a sculpture of a golden archer, towers over Lake Talšos.

Sundial Square is laid out like an amphitheatre and brings together three significant symbols for the city – the archer Šaulys, after whom, according to legend, the city was named; the sun, images of which can be found all over Šiauliai; and time, represented on the square by the numbers of the clock, 12, 3, and 6, which when brought together form the date of the battle.

VISITORS' CHECKLIST

Road Map C4. 🏙 130,000.
🚊 Višinkio gatvė 44, S of Draugystės prospektas. 🚌 Tilžės gatvė 109. 🛈 Vilniaus gatvė 213, (41) 523 110. 🎭 Saulės Žiedas Folk Festival (Jul), Šiauliai City Days (Sep). **www**.siauliai.lt

🏛 Cat Museum
Žuvininkų 18. **Tel** (41) 523 883.
◯ 11am–5pm Wed–Sun. 🖼
With almost 10,000 exhibits not just from Lithuania but across the world, from Austria to Zambia, this museum is a haven for cat-lovers. Established in May 1990, the museum has exhibits of cats in every conceivable pose cramming the display area. They have been crafted from porcelain, amber, marble, crystal, glass and other materials. There are cats in stained-glass windows, cats in artistic photographs, cats on postage stamps, in books and on cards. Interesting odes to cats have been collected in over 4,000 poems written in various languages. There are lamps with cats as ornamentation as well as furniture and a set of banisters with delightful feline designs.

Colourful wooden cats, Cat Museum

Hill of Crosses ❷
Kryžių kalnas

Road Map C4. 🚌 from Šiauliai.

One of Lithuania's most awe-inspiring sights, this saddle-shaped knoll in a field filled with thousands of crosses, crucifixes and rosaries is an insight into the significance of Catholicism to Lithuania.

Crosses started appearing on the hill after the ruthless suppression of the 1831 uprising against Tsarist Russian rule. By the end of the 19th century, 150 large crosses stood here, 200 by 1914, and many more by the time the Soviets came to occupy Lithuania in 1940. Seen by the fanatically atheist regime as being an unnecessary religious symbol, the Hill of Crosses was hacked down in 1961, but the crosses reappeared soon after. Bulldozed in 1973 and again in 1975 with sewage poured on top, the crosses kept appearing. Finally, the hill was left in peace and by the time Pope John Paul II visited it, in 1993, it had crosses and religious sculptures from all over the country and around the world.

Collection of crosses of all shapes and sizes at the Hill of Crosses

Šeduva ❸

Road Map C5. 🏚 *3,000.* 🚌 *from Šiauliai, Panevėžys.* 🚆 *from Šiauliai, Panevėžys.*

The little town of Šeduva is a composite of wooden houses preserved as a historic monument. One of its main sights is the twin-tower Church of the Holy Cross. Built in 1649, the church elegantly blends Renaissance and Baroque elements.

Šeduva's most delightful spot is the mid-19th-century estate of Prussian Baron Otto von Ropp, located 2 km (1 mile) east of town. Aside from the original red-brick buildings, which have given the estate the local name **Raudondvaris** (Red Manor), there is a school and a hotel, and the lakeside grounds are a pleasure to stroll through.

Environs
The grounds of **Burbiškis Manor**, 12 km (7 miles) east of Šeduva, are decorated with sculptures of lions, fauns and historical figures created in 1912 by sculptor Kazimieras Ulianskas. A dazzling display of tulips adorns the manor grounds in spring, when the Tulip Festival is celebrated.

🏛 **Burbiškis Manor**
Burbiškis village. **Tel** *(422) 51 747.*
⬜ *Apr–Oct: 9am–5pm Tue–Sun.* 🎟
🎏 *Burbiškis Tulip Festival (mid-May).*

Crucifix above the altar, Friary of the Blessed Virgin Mary, Tytuvėnai

Tytuvėnai ❹

Road Map C5. 🏚 *3,000.* 🚌 *from Šiauliai.* 🚆 *from Šiauliai.* **www**.trp.lt

Once the site of a 13th-century hilltop fortress, Tytuvėnai became the secluded setting for a magnificent monastery and the church of the **Friary of the Blessed Virgin Mary** in the 1630s. The buildings were created for the Franciscans and set amid rolling hills and tranquil lakes. The courtyard of the monastery is decorated with faded frescoes, while a beautiful painting on the wooden sacristy door depicts the Resurrection.

The highlight of the church's colourful interior is an elaborate altar encircled by four Baroque figures of Franciscan saints. In the grounds, the Chapel of the Holy Stairs was modelled on the Scala Sancta (Holy Stairs) in Rome. Each of the steps, which pilgrims mounted on their knees, contains a sacred relic brought here from Jerusalem in the 1730s.

Šiluva ❺

Road Map C5. 🏚 *800.* 🚌 *from Šiauliai.* 🎏 *Šilinės Pilgrimage (Sep).*

Šiluva is one of Lithuania's great pilgrimage places. Legend has it that 400 years ago, the town was the site of a miraculous apparition of a weeping Virgin Mary holding the Infant Jesus in her arms. In the late 16th century, as Šiluva became Calvinist, its last priest buried a bundle of Catholic documents and a miracle-working painting of the Virgin Mary in an iron box in the grounds of the ruined church.

In 1610, the Virgin Mary appeared standing on a rock before children tending their herds. The box was later discovered by the rock and, as fame about the apparition grew, a wooden chapel was built close by. It was replaced in 1785 by the Church of the Nativity of the Blessed Virgin Mary. The painting of Mary, now embellished by a golden frame, was hung on the altar. The painting is concealed,

Bright evening view of the lakeside buildings at Raudondvaris, near Šeduva

Façade of the Neo-Gothic castle at the Raudonė estate, seen from across its lush grounds

except on feast days, by a 1920 painting of the Annunciation. On his visit in 1993, Pope John Paul II prayed at the church.

The obelisk-style structure of the Church of the Apparition of the Blessed Virgin Mary, which was completed in 1924, can be seen from afar.

Raseiniai's attractive main square, featuring the *Independence Statue*

Raseiniai ⑥

Road Map C5. 🏘 *12,000.* 🚌 *from Kaunas.*

An important Samogitian town, Raseiniai played a crucial role in the region's history. In 1941, the town witnessed a fierce four-day battle between hundreds of German and Soviet tanks. By the end of World War II, 90 per cent of Raseiniai had been destroyed. Miraculously, the hilltop Church of the

Ascension, built in 1729, survived the war, as did the *Independence Statue* in the town's main square. Created by Vincas Grybas (1890–1941) in 1934, the statue shows a man in a flowing cloak and bast shoes together with a bear he has tamed. The bear is a symbol of Samogitia, the independent duchy that fought the Teutonic Order in the 13th century, but it was later ceded to the Grand Duchy of Lithuania.

Raudonė ⑦

Road Map C5. **Tel** *(447) 45 323.* 🕐 *mid-Nov–mid-Apr: 10am–4pm weekly.* 🚻

Originally a 16th-century family estate owned by Prussian timber merchants, the castle at Raudonė was acquired in 1810 by Platon Zubov, once a favourite consort of Catherine the Great. Catherine had played an important role in obtaining much of the Polish-Lithuanian Commonwealth during the partitions *(see p211)*. After her death, the count lived in seclusion at Rundāle Palace *(see pp168–9)* in Courland.

The count's daughter gave the family castle in Raudonė its current Neo-Gothic appearance and its tall and slender fairytale tower. Destroyed by the retreating Germans at the end of World War II, the tower was rebuilt in 1968 and today offers a panoramic view of the Nemunas Valley.

Environs
Veliuona, a village 10 km (6 miles) east of Raudonė, is known for its secluded fort-hill where Gediminas *(see p212)* was reputedly slain.

Panemunė ⑧

Road Map C5. 🚌 *from Kaunas.*

Situated on the banks of the Nemunas river, Panemunė boasts a castle with two tall circular towers and red-tiled rooftops. Most of the building was erected by a family of Hungarian nobles during the reign of Stefan Bathory, the Transylvanian prince who ruled the Polish-Lithuanian Commonwealth between 1575 and 1586. Two centuries later, the castle was bought by the Polish-Lithuanian Gelgaudas family. The Tsarist authorities seized it after Antanas Gelgaudas led the 1831 uprising *(see p214)*. Today, the castle belongs to the Vilnius Academy of Art.

One of the castle's tall circular towers in Panemunė

Jurbarkas

Road Map C5. 13,500. *from Kaunas.* Dariaus ir girėno 94, (447) 70 201. www.jurbarkas.lt

The ancient **Karšuva Forest**, about 3 km (2 miles) west of the tiny industrial town of Jurbarkas, is the site of one of the earliest fortresses built by the crusaders on the Nemunas river in 1259. The pagan Lithuanians erected their own castle above the Imsrė river, a tributary of the Nemunas, and both sides fought bitter battles for the next 150 years. Although nothing remains of the castles, the forest can be explored. One of Lithuania's largest and most secluded forests, the 427-sq km (165-sq mile) stretch has enchanting trails leading through its towering pines.

Environs
In **Gelgaudiškis**, 10 km (6 miles) east of Jurbarkas, lie the ruins of the 19th-century manor of the Gelgaudas family, the Polish-Lithuanian ancestors of actor Sir John Gielgud. The manor boasted a lavish interior with paintings, silver, crystal, bronze and porcelain works until it was ransacked during World War II. Today, the manor hosts village festivals and music evenings in its grounds.

Mount Rambynas, 60 km (37 miles) west of Jurbarkas, is a 46-m (50-yard) escarpment, and a mystical location for Lithuanians. A pagan altar that once stood here was used for rituals up until the 19th century. Today, the hill offers views over Kaliningrad.

Embellished interior of the Cathedral of St Anthony of Padua, Telšiai

Telšiai ⑩

Road Map C4. 30,000. *from Vilnius, Šiauliai, Klaipėda.* *from Vilnius, Šiauliai, Klaipėda.* Turgaus 21, (444) 53 010. www.telsiai.lt

According to legend, Telšiai was founded by a knight named Džiugas on a hill above Lake Mastis. In 1765, the Franciscans built a church here, which became the **Cathedral of St Anthony of Padua**, after Telšiai was made a diocese in 1926. An unbroken second-floor gallery has its own altar and paintings framed by Corinthian columns. These include an altar painting of St Anthony and Infant Jesus, embellished with faux gold and held aloft by angels garbed in pink and green.

Environs
One of the worst massacres by the Soviets took place in the forests near **Rainiai**, 4 km (2 miles) southeast of Telšiai.

The terrible event took place on the nights of 24 and 25 June 1941, shortly after Nazi Germany invaded the then Soviet Union. Today, a granite cross marks the spot and the **Rainiai Chapel of Suffering**, consecrated in 1991, stands nearby. Just 30 km (19 miles) southeast of Telšiai, **Šatrija Hill** offers splendid views of the Žemaitija landscape. **Lake Lūkstas**, 40 km (25 miles) south of Telšiai, has beaches that liven up in July during the Blues Night festival.

Mažeikiai ⑪

Road Map C4. 45,000. *from Šiauliai.* *from Šiauliai.* Ventos 8a, (443) 95 351. www.mazeikiai.lt

A minor village in the mid-19th century, Mažeikiai rapidly grew into Lithuania's eighth-largest city by the end of the 20th century. The Vilnius–Liepāja railway, which reached Mažeikiai in 1869, was responsible for its growth.

The **Mažeikiai Museum** has displays on the town's development and regional folklore, and paintings by Alfonsas Dargis (1909–96), a Lithuanian artist who joined the New York Modernist movement.

Environs
The 4,000-ha (9,884-acre) **Kamanos State Reserve**, 20 km (12 miles) east of Mažeikiai, protects one of the region's most valuable clayfields. Richly diverse in flora and fauna, the reserve has a lower area of marshland and a higher area of lakes and tiny islands.

In **Viekšniai**, a small town 15 km (9 miles) southeast of Mažeikiai, the **Pharmacy Museum** is considered miraculous. It survived two fires that devastated the town but spared the pharmacy building.

🏛 **Mažeikiai Museum**
Burbos 9. **Tel** (443) 25 759.
⬜ 9am–6pm Wed–Mon.

🌿 **Kamanos State Reserve**
Tel (425) 59 285.

🏛 **Pharmacy Museum**
Tilto 3. **Tel** (443) 37 420. ⬜ 9am–4pm Tue–Sat.

Rainiai Chapel of Suffering commemorating the massacre in 1941

Boats on the eastern shore of Lake Plateliai, bordering Plateliai village

Plateliai ⑫

Road Map B4. 🏘 1,000. 🚌 from Plungė. ℹ️ Didžioji 8, (448) 49 231. 🎭 Shrove Tuesday Carnival (Feb/Mar).

The administrative centre of Žemaitija National Park (see pp278–9), Plateliai is a sleepy lakeside village. It has the wooden Church of Sts Peter and Paul (1744) and a park that was the grounds of a manor. The Witch's Ash, Lithuania's biggest ash tree which stands in the park, has many legends attached to it. One involves a baker who threw a loaf of bread at a witch sitting on its branches. The loaf is still visible – the knobbly bit where the branches divide.

Across the road on Didžioji Street, elaborate Shrovetide masks are displayed in the manor barn. These masks are worn during the Shrove Tuesday Carnival. The most popular destination is **Castle Island**, which takes its name from a fortress that stood on the nearest island of Pilies.

Orvidas Garden ⑬
Orvido sodyba

Road Map B4. **Tel** (613) 28 624. ⏰ June: 10am–7pm Tue–Sun, July–May: 10am–7pm Wed–Sun. 📷

The creative work of local mystic and genius Vilius Orvidas (1952–92), the Orvidas Garden is one of Eastern Europe's most bizarre sights. Eclectic and enormous, it is a complex network of crosses and tombstones, boulders and tree-trunks, sculptures of odd creatures, carvings and rock paintings of pagan and religious imagery, painted missile shells and a disused Soviet tank. Hidden gardens appear out of nowhere and there is no set path, adding to the maze-like feel. The dark caverns conceal further oddities, and a pond-side hut hidden among trees is reputedly the home of pixies and gnomes.

Plungė ⑭

Road Map C5. 🏘 23,000. 🚌 from Šiauliai, Klaipėda. 🚉 from Šiauliai, Klaipėda. ℹ️ Parko 1, (448) 52 492. **www**.plunge.lt

The town of Plungė is the main gateway to Žemaitija National Park (see pp278–9). One of Lithuania's most opulent manors, the well-preserved **Plungė Manor** was built by Mykolas Oginskis, a descendant of a family of Lithuanian nobles. It includes 16 sculptures of Samogitian figures and a park featuring the Thunder Oak tree, now a natural monument. The manor also houses the **Samogitian Art Museum**, which displays works by Western Lithuanian artists.

Environs
About 2,236 Jews of Plungė died in the Holocaust. Much of the killing took place in **Kaušėnai**, a village 4 km (2 miles) west of town. Here, a series of moving wooden sculptures have been carved by Jacob Bunka (b.1922), chairman of Plungė's 13-member Jewish community.

Gandinga Hill, 5 km (3 miles) southwest of Plungė, offers a panoramic view of the Žemaitija forests. A fortress, Gandinga, once stood here, built as a defence against the Teutonic Knights. Pagan burial grounds dating from the 9th century have been discovered nearby.

Another remakable outdoor museum is the **Museum of Unique Rocks** in Mosėdis, 40 km (25 miles) northwest of Plungė. Exhibits range from a display of fossils and sands inside a restored watermill to a park full of mossy boulders and crude stone sculptures. The museum was founded in 1979 by Dr Vaclovas Intas.

🏛 **Samogitian Art Museum**
Parko 1. **Tel** (448) 52 492.
⏰ 10am–5pm Tue–Sat. 📷 📷

🏛 **Museum of Unique Rocks**
Salantų 2. **Tel** (440) 76 291. ⏰ 8am–6pm Mon–Fri, 10am–6pm Sat–Sun. ⏰ Nov–Apr: Sat & Sun. 📷 📷

Plungė Manor seen across a lake, with a sculpture in the foreground

Žemaitija National Park 🅫

Shrouded in folklore and legend, the Žemaitija region was the last stretch of Europe to accept Christianity. Pagan gods were worshipped here till the 19th century, and carvings and crosses in the villages still blend Catholic and pagan imagery. Established in 1991, the Žemaitija National Park spreads across 220 sq km (85 sq miles), with its headquarters and information centre in the town of Plateliai. There are several hiking trails that meander around Lake Plateliai through isolated stretches of forest. Campsites and rural farmsteads cater to tourists.

Wild lupin with purple flowers

KEY

ℹ	Visitor information
ⓐ	Campsites
🔆	Viewpoint
══	Minor road
– –	Hiking trail
▪ ▪	Park boundary

★ **Mikytai Hill and Devil's Footprint Stone**
The forest-covered "sacred hill" of Mikytai is believed by local people to be haunted. On the hill's northern slope, the Devil's Footprint Stone was once used for pagan sacrifices.

Plateliai serves as the park's main service and information centre.

Church of St Stanislav in Beržoras
This church (1746) is made of spruce logs. Its Chapels of the Cross were destroyed by the Soviets but restored in 2001.

Godeliai has a rare collection of obscure paintings and crucifixes in its Museum of Folk Art.

Mill-Gallery
A stone watermill, converted into a folk art gallery, stands in the riverside village of Babrungėnai, once famed for its beaver hunters.

STAR SIGHTS

★ Mikytai Hill and Devil's Footprint Stone

★ Žemaičių Kalvarija

★ Plokštinė Former Soviet Missile Base

Map labels: Barsty, Mikytai, Pūčk, Visvaini, Vi, Lake Pla, Plateliai, Beržoras, Lake Beržoras, Lake Ilgis, Grigaičiai, Godeliai, Salantai, Babrungėnai, Plu, 169

★ **Žemaičių Kalvarija**
Churches and white Chapels of the Cross give this town a spiritual atmosphere. The Church Festival, held in July each year, is its main attraction.

0 km   2

0 miles   2

VISITORS' CHECKLIST

Road Map C4. 🚌 *from Plungė to Žemaičių Kalvarija.* ℹ️ *Didžioji 8, Plateliai, (448) 49 231.* 🅰️ **www**.zemaitijosnp.lt **Mill-Gallery** ⏱ *9am–6pm daily.* **Plokštinė Former Soviet Missile Base** 🎫 *bookings at the park's information centre.*

Žemaičių Kalvarija

egrėnai

Skurvydai

Platakiai

164

lokštinė

Mound of Šarnelė
Excavations on this hill, in Šarnelė village, have revealed that it was a small fortified town in the third century BC.

★ **Plokštinė Former Soviet Missile Base**
Between 1962 and 1978, this secret Soviet rocket site, with its now rusty and overgrown silos, aimed missiles at cities in Western Europe.

Yacht moored along the shore of Lake Plateliai

FOLK LEGENDS OF LAKE PLATELIAI

Lake Plateliai had tremendous significance to the pagans of the historical regions of Samogitia and Žemaitija. Drownings occasionally occur here and according to one of the many legends associated with it, a great white horse lives in the water and takes the life of at least one swimmer every year. The water level has risen in recent times and archaeologists diving in the lake have excavated standing stones with pagan symbols under the surface. To this day, Plateliai, on the lake's western shore, celebrates many colourful traditional Samogitian festivals.

Klaipėda ⑯

First mentioned in 1252 when the Christian Livonian Order built a fortress named Memelburg at the mouth of the Danė river, Klaipėda for many centuries was an important Prussian port city called Memel. Today, as Lithuania's only sea port, Klaipėda is thriving despite serious damage during World War II and its status as a military-industrial centre during the Soviet years. For those who enjoy walking, central Klaipėda and its Old Town, with narrow, criss-crossing streets, is a delightful place to explore. Half-timbered buildings and cobbled lanes conceal gift shops, galleries and café-bars.

Visitors and local people relaxing in cafés in Klaipėda

🏛 Ännchen of Tharau
Teatro aikštė.

The heart of Klaipėda's Old Town is **Theatre Square**. A statue called *Ännchen of Tharau*, which stands in front of the theatre, is the focal point of the fountain dedicated to Simon Dach (1605–59), one of the city's distinguished personalities. Born in Klaipėda, then known as Memel, Dach became a leading Prussian poet from the late 1630s until his death. He is well known throughout Germany for his songs, hymns and dialect poems such as *Ännchen of Tharau*, written in 1637.

The original statue was created in 1912, but it mysteriously vanished on the eve of World War II. Adolf Hitler made a speech from the theatre balcony behind its original location, on 23 March 1939. In 1989, a replica of

Statue of *Ännchen of Tharau* in Theatre Square

the original *Ännchen of Tharau* statue, made by local artists, was placed in the middle of the fountain.

🏛 Castle Museum
Pilies 4. **Tel** (46) 313 323.
◯ 10am–5pm Tue–Sat. 🖼

Not much remains of the 17th-century castle that houses the Castle Museum. The castle was built on the foundations of the 1252 fortress when Memel was part of the Duchy of Prussia. In 2002, an exhibition opened inside one of the ramparts, illustrating the development of the fortress and the city. The exhibits on display include authentic furniture and re-created models. The highlight is a Renaissance-era gold ring encrusted with diamonds. Today, this castle has become one of the most recognized symbols associated with modern Klaipėda.

🏛 Lithuania Minor History Museum
Didžioji vandens 6. **Tel** (46) 410 524.
◯ 10am–5:30pm Tue–Sat. 🖼

Lithuania Minor is what the local people call East Prussia, which today is the territory of Kaliningrad as well as Klaipėda. The Lithuania Minor History Museum, inside one of the Old Town's loveliest buildings, paints an illuminating picture of the region's history. Coins, clothes, maps, postcards, old photographs and models give a glimpse of the lives and the differences between the local German- and Lithuanian-speaking communities before World War II. Situated opposite the museum is the town's old post office.

🏛 Blacksmiths' Museum
Šaltkalvių 2a. **Tel** (46) 410 526.
◯ 10am–5:30pm Tue–Sat. 🖼 🖼

Black metal crosses, fences and cemetery gates collected in a garden beside an old working smithy are among the exhibits of this museum. Some of the crosses were rescued from destruction when the Sculpture Park replaced the city's main cemetery in the 1970s. Lithuania's cross-crafting tradition, in metal and in wood, was recognized by UNESCO in 2001.

Old wooden clock inside the exceptional Clock museum

🏛 Clock Museum
Liepų 12. **Tel** (46) 410 413.
◯ noon–5:30pm Tue–Sat, noon–4:30pm Sun. 🖼 🖼

A fascinating insight into the development of man's attempts to measure time, from sundials to atomic clocks, is the focus of this unique museum. The Clock Museum was opened in 1984 inside a villa built in 1820 by John Simpson, an English merchant. Reconstructions of ancient calendars, sun, fire, water and sand clocks, and timepieces showing the changes in the faces and mechanisms of clocks from Renaissance times form the bulk of the exhibits.

The pleasant courtyard, featuring a large sundial, is a popular venue for music, dance and poetry evenings. The house next door was built by another English merchant and industrialist, Mae Lean. In 1905, it was reconstructed in the Art Nouveau style. The Neo-Gothic post office close by is another striking building in the neighbourhood.

🏛 Picture Gallery and Sculpture Park

Liepu 33. **Tel** (46) 410 412.
⬜ noon–6pm Tue–Sat, noon–5pm Sun. 📷
The city's main state-run art gallery is named after Pranas Domšaitis (1880–1965), a Lithuanian artist who was born near Königsberg and settled in South Africa in 1949. Heavily influenced by the Norwegian Symbolist painter Edvard Munch (1863–1944), Domšaitis won recognition for his art in inter-war Germany and later in South Africa. The gallery exhibits 20th-century Lithuanian art as well as a permanent exhibition of works by Domšaitis.

Dedicated to the author of the first Lithuanian book, Martynas Mažvydas (1510–63), the Sculpture Park is situated behind the gallery. Until the 1970s it was the site reserved for the city's cemetery. It covers almost 10 ha (25 acres) and is scattered mainly with

VISITORS' CHECKLIST

Road Map B5. 🏙 187,000.
🚉 Priestočio gatvė 1.
🚌 Priestočio gatvė. ⚓ Old Castle Port, Žvejų 8, (46) 314 257; New Port, Nemuno 7, (46) 345 780. Jun–Aug: 6:30pm–2:15am daily, Sep–May: at least hourly 6:30pm–2am.
ℹ Turgaus 7, (46) 412 186.
🎭 Klaipėda Jazz Festival (mid-Jul), Sea Festival (late Jul).
www.klaipeda.lt

abstract and intriguing sculptures by various artists. New works are added to the park each year.

Unique creations laid out in the Sculpture Park

KLAIPĖDA

Ännchen of Tharau ①
Blacksmiths' Museum ④
Castle Museum ②
Clock Museum ⑤
Lithuania Minor History Museum ③
Picture Gallery and Sculpture Park ⑥

0 metres 200
0 yards 200

Key to Symbols see back flap

Kretinga

Road Map B5. 🏘 *21,000.* 🚉 *from Klaipėda.* 🚌 *from Klaipėda.* ℹ *Vilniaus 20, (445) 55 459.*

This pretty town is based around a 17th-century Franciscan monastery, a manor house, now the **Kretinga Museum**, and gardens that stretch alongside a stream and open up into a park. The Franciscans played a major role in developing the town, particularly in independent inter-war Lithuania when they opened a college specializing in agriculture and beekeeping. They also arranged a Lourdes-style grotto in the park with an image of the Virgin Mary.

One of the highlights of the Kretinga Museum is the Winter Garden, originally built when Count Josef Tyszkiewicz reconstructed the manor in 1875. Destroyed during World War II, these gardens were re-created in 1987 and today house around 600 plants. Other museum exhibits include furniture and paintings rescued from the Tyszkiewicz mansions in Kretinga and Palanga, iron crosses that are a blend of Catholic and pagan imagery and Curonian clothing and jewellery. The Church of the Annunciation has a towering steeple and an ornate interior with 17th-century paintings.

🏛 **Kretinga Museum**
Vilniaus 20. **Tel** *(445) 77 323.*
🕙 *Sep–May: 10am–6pm Wed–Sun.*
www.kretingosmuziejus.lt

View of the sandy beach with locals and visitors, Palanga

Palanga ⑱

Road Map B5. 🏘 *17,500.* ✈ *5 km (3 miles) N of town.* 🚉 *from Klaipėda.* 🚌 *from Klaipėda.* ℹ *Kretingos 1, (460) 48 811.* 🎪 *Summer Feast (Jun).* www.palanga.lt

The coastal town of Palanga, first mentioned in a 13th-century land partition pact between the Teutonic Order and the Livonians, became a permanent part of Lithuania in 1435. Today, it is a popular sandy resort, with its dune-and-pine-bordered beach stretching 18 km (11 miles). It also has boulevards crammed with restaurants, clubs and bars, giving it a carnival-like atmosphere. The pier, first built in 1882, is a popular spot to watch the sunset.

A Neo-Renaissance palace was built in the 1890s by the Tyszkiewicz family, with grounds created by the French landscape architect Edouard André (1840–1911). Since 1963, the palace has housed the **Amber Museum**, which exhibits 4,500 pieces, including some unusual ones such as amber with trapped prehistoric insects and plants. At the far end of the palace's grounds is **Birutės Hill**, said to be where the future wife of Grand Duke Kęstutis tended a pagan sacred fire before he wed her. Close by is one of Lithuania's best-known sculptures, *Eglė, Queen of the Grassy Snakes* (1960), inspired by a fairytale.

Environs
The quiet fishing village of **Šventoji**, 15 km (9 miles) north of Palanga, is blessed with windswept dunes. It was a thriving port in the 16th and 17th centuries. An attraction here is *Fisherman's Daughters* (1982), a statue of three girls dancing on the dunes.

🏛 **Amber Museum**
Vytauto 17. **Tel** *(460) 51 319.*
🕙 *Jun–Aug: 10am–8pm Tue–Sat, 10pm–7pm Sun; Sept–May: 11am–5pm Tue–Sat, 11am–4pm Sun.* 🎫 🖼 www.pgm.lt

Smiltynė ⑲

Road Map B5. 🏘 *100.* 🚢 *from Klaipėda.*

Officially part of Klaipėda city (*see pp280–81*), Smiltynė is the northernmost settlement on the Curonian Spit, directly facing Klaipėda's busy port. In earlier times, the spit was the main land route used by dispatch riders, postmen and the military, between the Prussian cities of Königsberg and Memel, modern Kaliningrad and Klaipėda respectively. However, the final ferry trip was disrupted by storms or trapped ice. In 1525, an inn was established in Sandkrug (Sand Inn), as Smiltynė became known.

A string of elegant villas line the water's edge. The town's star attraction, however, is the **Sea Museum**. It is located in Kopgalis Fortress, a sea bastion built by Prussia in 1865. The

Tropical conservatory in Kretinga Museum's Winter Garden, Kretinga

Dolphins performing with trainers before an enthralled audience at the Sea Museum in Smiltynė

main highlights are the regular dolphin and sea lion shows. Permits must be purchased for photography.

🏛 **Sea Museum**
Smiltynės 3. *Tel* (46) 492 250.
⬜ 19 Apr–Sep: 10:30am–6pm Tue–Sun, Oct–18 Apr: 10:30am–5pm Sat & Sun. 🏛 🎥 📷 🔲
www.muziejus.lt

Curonian Spit National Park ⑳

See pp284–5.

Šilutė ㉑

Road Map B5. 👥 21,500. 🚌 from Klaipėda. 🚌 from Klaipėda.
ℹ Lietuvininkų gatvė 10/2, (441) 77 795. www.silute.lt

Originally the site of an inn for travellers riding between Klaipėda and Kaliningrad, Šilutė became a part of the German Empire in 1871. It was seized by Lithuania in 1923, but annexed by Nazi Germany 15 years later.

German influence is still visible in the low, red-tiled roofs of the public buildings. On tree-lined Lietuvininkų Street, the tiny **Šilutė Museum** displays 18th-century furniture and folk-themed exhibits. The Evangelical Lutheran Church, built in 1926, is decorated with startlingly colourful murals of biblical scenes.

Environs
Just 3 km (2 miles) northeast of Šilutė, **Macikai** was used as a German prisoner-of-war camp from 1939, then a Soviet

camp for German troops after 1944, and was an official unit of the Gulag from 1948 to 1955. Today, it comprises the **Macikai Concentration Camp Museum** and a grave site.

🏛 **Šilutė Museum**
Lietuvininkų 36. *Tel* (441) 62 207.
⬜ mid-May–Oct: 10am–6pm Tue–Sat, Oct–mid-May: 9am–5pm Tue–Sat. 🏛 🎥

🏛 **Macikai Concentration Camp Museum**
Macikai. *Tel* (441) 62 209. ⬜ 10am–4pm Tue–Fri, 10am–3pm Sat. 🎥

Nemunas Delta ㉒

Road Map B5. 👥 1,700. 🚌 from Šilutė.

The low-lying delta of the Nemunas, Lithuania's largest river as it streams into the Curonian Lagoon, has great potential for outdoor activities. The wetlands, protected as a regional park, are a popular spot for angling and bird-watching. Every spring, when

the snow and ice melt, 20 per cent of delta gets flooded, attracting 200 species of birds to breed, while hundreds of other species migrate through the area every year. A bird ringing station at **Ventė** is one of the oldest in Europe, dating from 1929.

The floods annually threaten to cut off **Rusnė**, located 11 km (7 miles) southeast of Ventė. A Lutheran church, built from 1809 to 1827, is a sign of Rusnė's East Prussian background. It was changed into a sports hall in the Soviet period, but reverted to receiving congregations in 1994. An ethnographic farmstead gives a snapshot of past life in the delta region.

Almost 8 km (5 miles) northwest from Rusnė is the village of **Minija**, situated where the Minija river meets the Nemunas Delta. The river functions as the main street in the area. Protected as architectural monuments, 19th-century wooden houses stand on both riverbanks.

Sunset view of Nemunas Delta countryside, near Šilutė

Curonian Spit National Park ⑳

A narrow 98-km (61-mile) strip of land on the Baltic Coast, the Curonian Spit (Kuršių nerija) was formed 5,000 years ago. Its landscape consists largely of pine forests, dunes and sandy beaches. The park's forests are also rich in wildlife such as roe deer, elk, foxes and wild boars. The dunes that tower over the village of Nida fall like cliffs into the Curonian Lagoon and villages have been buried beneath the shifting sands. The Curonian Spit National Park was created in 1991 to preserve the dunes, lagoons and surrounding area. The national park, which covers most of the spit, has been a UNESCO World Heritage Site since 2000.

KEY

☐ Curonian Spit National Park

★ **Nida**
The highly characteristic red-and-blue fishermen's cottages in Nida have remained unchanged for centuries. Some ancient weather-beaten fishing boats lie in the gardens outside the cottages.

Baltic Beach
The entire length of the spit on the side of the Baltic Sea is one long sandy beach. Areas adjacent to the villages are popular in summer, but other parts are little visited. Parking throughout the spit is allowed only at designated parking areas.

★ **Parnidis Dune**
Looming 52 m (171 ft) above Nida, Parnidis (Great) Dune offers stunning views and is one of the highest points on the spit. A sundial erected here in 1995 collapsed during a storm in 1999.

Vecekrug Dune, the highest wooded dune (67.2 m/220.5 ft), is bypassed by taking the cycling track.

★ Hill of Witches

Comically demonic wooden statues, such as this ghoulish figure, lurk alongside a path through the pine forest behind Juodkrantė. The statues were set up by a group of local sculptors in the 1980s.

Juodkrantė

VISITORS' CHECKLIST

Road Map B5. 🚌 Naglių 18e, Nida, (469) 52 859. ⛴ Naglių 14, Nida, (469) 51 101. Several operators offer cruises in vessels, including a replica kurėnas. Local trips, as well as excursions across the lagoon or along the shoreline to the Dead Dunes, are available. 🛈 Taikos 4, Nida, (469) 52 345. Bike rentals can be arranged at the centre.
www.visitneringa.com

Dead Dunes

These once-shifting dunes are now held in place with vegetation and offer a sanctuary to birds, animals and plants. Paths stretch from Avikalnio Dune in the north to Agilo Dune in the south.

Forest Trails

It is possible to walk or cycle the entire length of the spit. The path, marked by the dotted red line on the map, takes visitors past isolated stretches of sandy beach.

valka

KEY

⛴	Ferry port
🚌	Coach station
🛈	Visitor information
🏛	Museum
🏖	Beach
═	Main road
- -	Trail
····	Ferry route

0 km 2

0 miles 2

STAR SIGHTS

★ Nida

★ Parnidis Dune

★ Hill of Witches

SHIFTING DUNES

In the 17th century, when the forests on the Curonian Spit were cut down to fuel industry and constant military campaigns, the mountainous dunes were released. In the Baltic winds, the sand started to shift up to 20 m (66 ft) a year in places, burying entire villages. It was only in the 19th century, when a vast number of trees were planted to reforest the area, that the moving dunes were stopped.

Parnidis Dune seen from the harbour at Nida

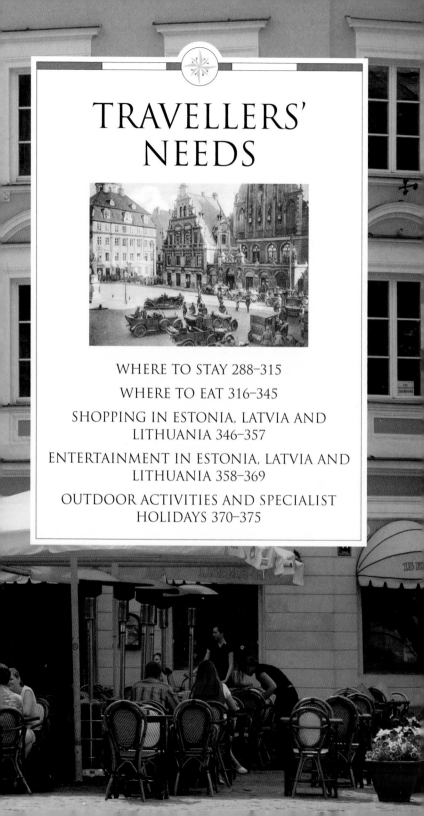

TRAVELLERS' NEEDS

WHERE TO STAY

In recent years, Estonia, Latvia and Lithuania have witnessed a growth in all forms of accommodation, from luxury hotels and city-centre hostels to rural guest houses. Although there is an abundance of good-quality mid-range and budget stay options in the three capital cities of Tallinn, Rīga and Vilnius, it is advisable to book well in advance during late spring, summer and early autumn. Hotels in the Baltic States share a classification code with Scandinavian countries, which has helped to improve

Logo, Monika Centrum, Rīga

standards throughout the industry. Before making a reservation it is advisable to cross-check the establishment, as some smaller hotels, particularly those converted from Soviet-era buildings, may not live up to expectations. The elaborate network of accommodation extends to smaller towns and the countryside, where it is very easy to find a place to stay for the night. Bookings are easy as even the smallest of guest houses have their own websites, apart from being advertised through several other sources.

BOOKING

For more out-of-the-way locations, there are specialist tour operators and websites listing choices. Reservations can be made by telephone, fax and through the Internet. Local tourist information offices also help book rooms.

PRICES & PAYMENT

All major hotels accept principal credit cards for payment. Cheques and traveller's cheques, however, are rarely used in the Baltic States. It is advisable to confirm acceptable modes of payment prior to arriving, especially for rural areas. Visitors need to make sure what they are getting for their money on the hotel's website. Many hotels include breakfast and use of amenities such as a fitness centre, while other facilities, such as

Three Sisters hotel *(see p294)*, a renovated house in Tallinn

saunas, can cost extra. Prices vary considerably from hotel to hotel, although there are often significant discount offers available during off-season months. It is also worth looking for special discounts or packages.

TIPPING

Generally, it is not customary to tip taxi drivers, bar staff and bellboys in the Baltic States. As a rule of thumb, tip those who provide you with good service.

LUXURY HOTELS

Tallinn, Rīga and Vilnius have a large range of luxury hotels. Often these are housed in historic buildings that have been converted to provide state-of-the-art facilities while retaining their original features. There are also several superb chain hotels that attract heads of state and other VIPs.

Swimming pools remain a rarity in the Baltic States, although fitness centres, spas and saunas are common, as is high-quality cuisine, Wi-Fi access, and in some cases, facilities for disabled guests.

Luxurious Diķļu Pils hotel *(see p307)*, a restored 19th-century manor house in the Valmiera region, Latvia

◁ **Open-air café in Cathedral Square (Doma laukums), Rīga, Latvia**

CHAIN HOTELS

Chains, such as the Radisson SAS and Reval Hotel Group, were among the first to get a foothold in the Baltic States and still occupy a leading position in the increasingly competitive market with a range of fine upmarket and mid-range hotels. The Reval Hotel Group currently boasts the largest hotel in the region with the recently expanded Reval Hotel Latvija *(see p302)*. The Domina Hotel Group has a couple of hotels in Tallinn and one in Rīga, while the Best Western chain has set up hotels in Estonia, Latvia and Lithuania. The more upmarket Europa chain has hotels in Rīga, Vilnius, Druskininkai and Klaipēda.

Façade of Rīga's Reval Hotel Latvija *(see p302)*, a major Latvian flagship

MID-RANGE HOTELS

Until quite recently, there were few affordable, good-quality hotels in Estonia, Latvia and Lithuania. Today, mid-range accommodation has greatly improved and there is now plenty of choice in all three Baltic States.

Most of the larger towns and cities provide a variety of mid-range hotels, although only a handful are located in the Old Town areas of Tallinn, Rīga and Vilnius. Most of the hotels can be found either in the city centre or in slightly more peripheral locations. The quality of the mid-range hotels can vary considerably so it is always

Shakespeare Boutique Hotel *(see p310)* in Vilnius

sensible to make enquiries about the services provided before booking a room.

HOSTELS

Hostels were another sorely missing accommodation category in the Baltic States until very recently, but that has definitely changed over the past few years. There has been a massive growth in budget accommodation in all the three countries, including several centrally located hostels that are too well-appointed to be called true hostels. By far the cheapest places to stay, hostels are well suited for budget travellers.

Most hostels are of a very decent standard and have beds in communal dormitories for reasonable rates, as well as a small selection of private rooms, offered for considerably less than the average hotel rate. The majority of hostels also offer an excellent range of amenities, including Internet, kitchen facilities and assorted tours and excursions, some of which can be quite fascinating and unusual in theme.

The International Youth Hostel Association (IYHA) has comfortable hostels in the three Baltic countries. The **Estonian Youth Hostel Association** is a part of the IYHA, while in Latvia these youth hostels are known as **Hostelling Latvia**. The **Lithuanian Youth Hostelling**

Lilija Plus
REAL ESTATE AGENCY

Logo of Lilija Plus Real Estate Agency

Association does not have an office. However, its website *(see p291)* provides contact details for hostels in different areas.

APARTMENTS & PRIVATE HOMES

Apartment rental is an excellent accommodation option that is comparatively under-used in the Baltic States. Several agencies in the capital cities offer this service – **Erel Apartments & Residences** and **Apartment.ee** in Tallinn, **Lilija Plus Real Estate Agency** and **Patricia LTD** in Rīga and **Eldorado Apartments** and **Eugenijus Apartments** in Vilnius. Also available in some other major cities, apartments can range from opulent to simple and cosy, but in general all are of a very high standard. Most agency-managed apartments are in central locations. Rates are usually very competitive and the apartments often provide better facilities than those offered at a hotel in the same price range.

Rooms in private homes are limited in the capital cities but are widespread in the countryside and can usually be found through the local tourist information office. As lodging categories can occasionally be blurred in the Baltic States, this option can sometimes be more fittingly described as guest houses or family B&Bs.

Ric and Diga's B&B in Rīga, bookable through Baltic Country Holidays

GUEST HOUSES

Guest houses have become a real Baltic speciality in recent years. Often, they can be the best form of lodging in rural areas, offering cosy, clean accommodation at very reasonable rates. Most guest houses tend to be built close to a family home so a personal touch is always assured. Aesthetically, they are loosely modelled on rustic-style timber buildings and have become an integral part of the Baltic countryside. They invariably offer a range of activities for guests, such as swimming, sports and saunas, and the owners can sometimes arrange guided tours of local sights. Meals are usually optional, but a hearty, home-made breakfast or dinner costs less than similar fare in a local restaurant.

The choice of guest houses is enormous throughout the Baltic States and their availability extends to the most remote areas of each country. Bookings can be made through the rural tourism association – **Estonian Rural Tourism** in Estonia, **Baltic Country Holidays** in Latvia and **Countryside Tourism** in Lithuania.

Rural tourism has become such a popular sector in the Baltic States that many guest houses are booked out all through the summer. It is advisable to make a reservation well in advance.

CAMPSITES

Camping is an extremely popular summer pastime in Estonia, Latvia and Lithuania. As a result, there are a number of campsites scattered throughout each of the Baltic countries. These are usually very cheap and offer basic amenities such as communal showers and an on-site pub-style restaurant. However, not all camps are equipped with washing facilities and toilet blocks. Many commercial campsites also offer basic accommodation in the form of small, simple wooden huts that can house up to four people. National parks have official camping spots, which are free of charge, and many guest houses allow people to pitch tent in their grounds for a minimal fee.

In general, there is a very relaxed attitude towards camping in the Baltic States and people often camp alongside beaches and lakes and in forests in improvised campsites. For camping on private property, however, it is important to get permission from the owner beforehand.

A full list of campsites can be found on national tourism websites and rural tourism specialist websites. In Estonia, **RMK** is an efficient organization that arranges camping.

HIDDEN EXTRAS

Most decent hotels in cities throughout the three Baltic States operate in a transparent manner and will not add any hidden extras to the bill. However, it is worth checking for extra expenses such as the minibar and telephone calls, as these can be exorbitantly priced in some cases. In smaller hotels, it is a good idea to find out if breakfast is included in the room rate.

Rural guest houses tend to be peculiarly reticent about the cost of extra services. Therefore, it is advisable to check out the exact prices of

Caravans lined at Nidos Kempingas, a well-equipped campsite at Nida

Promenāde *(see p304)*, a former grain warehouse in Liepāja, Latvia

meals, drinks, saunas, guided tours, or any such additional services well in advance, to avoid any awkwardness at the time of settling the bills.

CHILDREN

Children are amply catered for in nearly all hotels and guest houses in all three countries. A number of hotels have rooms designed for families travelling with children. If not, then most hotels gladly provide extra beds for children. Many rural guest houses offer special play areas and activities for children and most decent hotels can provide cots for very young children, while babysitting services are becoming increasingly common. Some larger hotels offer special family rates that include a number of family-oriented excursions. For more information see page 381.

SMOKING

In keeping with the recent ban on smoking in public places in Estonia, Latvia and Lithuania, all hotels prohibit smoking in their public areas. Smoking is not allowed in lobbies and restaurants, although some larger hotels provide special smoking zones. These zones can be recognized by a green smoking-allowed symbol.

Most hotels still offer guests a choice between smoking and non-smoking rooms.

DISABLED TRAVELLERS

Until recently, access and facilities for disabled travellers was limited to high-end establishments and large chain hotels. However, most major new hotels in the three capital cities have incorporated facilities for disabled guests into their design and the situation has greatly improved. In many upscale hotels, guest rooms are appointed with facilities for disabled people. It is important to remember, however, that very few rural guest houses have facilities for disabled visitors.

Disability signage

Modern lobby of the upscale Radisson SAS *(see p294)* in Tallinn

DIRECTORY

HOSTELS

Estonian Youth Hostel Association
Narva mnt 16–25, Tallinn.
Tel 646 1455.
www.balticbookings.com/eyha

Hostelling Latvia
Siguldas prospekts 17–2, Rīga. *Tel* 2921 8560.
www.hostellinglatvia.com

Lithuanian Youth Hostelling Association
www.lithuanianhostels.org

APARTMENTS & PRIVATE HOMES

Apartment.ee
Aasa 2, Tallinn. *Tel* 504 5444.
www.apartment.ee

Eldorado Apartments
Vilnius. *Tel* 6991 7391.
www.apartamentai.lt

Erel Apartments & Residences
Tartu mnt 14, Tallinn.
Tel 610 8780. www.erel.ee

Eugenijus Apartments
Vilniaus 25–1, Vilnius.
Tel 6994 2456.
www.bedandbreakfast.w3.lt

Lilija Plus Real Estate Agency
Rīdzenes iela 25, Rīga. *Tel* 6721 6040. www.lilarealty.lv

Patricia LTD
Elizabetes iela 22, Rīga. *Tel* 6728 4868. www.patriciahotel.com

GUEST HOUSES

Baltic Country Holidays
Kuģu iela 11, Rīga. *Tel* 6761 7600. www.traveller.lv

Country Tourism of Lithuania
Donelaičio gatvė 2–201, Kaunas. *Tel* (37) 400 354.
www.countryside.lt

Estonian Rural Tourism
Vilmsi tänav 53b, Tallinn.
Tel 600 9999.
www.maaturism.ee

CAMPSITES

RMK
Viljandi mnt 18b, Tallinn.
Tel 676 7500. www.rmk.ee

Choosing a Hotel in Estonia

These hotels have been selected for their good value, facilities and location. They are listed by region, starting with Tallinn, followed by the rest of Estonia. Under each town or area, hotels are listed alphabetically within each price category. For Tallinn map references, see pages 82–3; for road map references see inside back cover.

PRICE CATEGORIES
The following price ranges are for a standard double room for one night during the high season. Breakfast is included, unless otherwise specified.
Ⓚ Under 600 EEK
ⓀⓀ 600–900 EEK
ⓀⓀⓀ 900–1,200 EEK
ⓀⓀⓀⓀ 1200–1,500 EEK
ⓀⓀⓀⓀⓀ Over 1,500 EEK

TALLINN

Pääsu   🗐 🅿   Ⓚ
Sõpruse pst 182, 13424 **Tel** *656 1448* **Fax** *654 2013* **Rooms** *24*

Located in Mustamäe, a 15-minute drive from the centre, Pääsu has a range of sparsely furnished rooms with TV, refrigerator and shared showers. There is also a sauna and café-bar as well as free parking. Buses leave regularly for the city centre. **www.paasu.ee**

City Guesthouse   🅿 🖨   ⓀⓀ
Pärnu mnt 10, 10148 **Tel** *628 2236* **Fax** *628 2237* **Rooms** *32*   **Map** *2 D3*

Its convenient Old Town location and impressive Art Deco façade make the City Guesthouse a preferred option for budget travellers. The rooms are on the bare side but come with TVs, and there is also a cheaper dormitory for up to five people. There is limited Wi-Fi access and an inexpensive airport transfer. **www.cityguesthouse.ee**

Dorell   🅿   ⓀⓀ
Karu 39, 10120 **Tel** *666 4333* **Fax** *666 4334* **Rooms** *30*   **Map** *2 F2*

This cheap and cheerful hotel has standard rooms that are clean and comfortable, all with a pleasant café-bar and sauna. It is within walking distance of the centre or a short bus ride away. A fully equipped apartment with kitchen is also available. **www.dorell.ee**

Dzingel   🅿 🍴 🏊 🖨   ⓀⓀ
Männiku tee 89, 11213 **Tel** *610 5201* **Fax** *610 5245* **Rooms** *240*

Although the recently renovated Dzingel looks a bit grim on the outside, it is another good budget option, with comfortable rooms, a restaurant, sauna and conference facilities. Located in the picturesque suburb of Nõmme, a bus ride away from the centre, it offers a good alternative view of Tallinn. **www.dzingel.ee**

Hotel G9   🅿 🖨   ⓀⓀ
Gonsiori 9, 10117 **Tel** *626 7100* **Fax** *626 7100* **Rooms** *23*   **Map** *2 E3*

Located on the third floor of an office building, Hotel G9 offers decent, strikingly decorated rooms at good rates. Services are limited and there is no catering on-site. However, it is only a five-minute walk from the Old Town and is close to several restaurants, theatres, bars, casinos, cinemas and the general post office. **www.hotelg9.ee**

Lilleküla   🅿 🍴 🖨   ⓀⓀ
Luha 18b, 10131 **Tel** *627 1120* **Fax** *648 1333* **Rooms** *33*   **Map** *1 B3*

A good option for the more budget-conscious, this newly built hotel offers decent rooms at good rates, all of which come with Wi-Fi access. The hotel also has a pleasant little restaurant and is located about a 15-minute walk from the centre. **www.lillekulahotel.ee**

OldHouse Guesthouse   🅿 🖨   ⓀⓀ
Uus 22, 10111 **Tel** *641 1464* **Fax** *641 1664* **Rooms** *6*   **Map** *2 D2*

Well situated in the Old Town, this excellent-value guest house has unusually nice rooms for this price range. There is a lovely dining room with a fireplace and the kitchen is open to guests for self-catering. The owners also rent apartments. Free parking is available. **www.oldhouse.ee**

Romeo Family Hotel   🅿 🖨   ⓀⓀ
Suur-Karja 18, 10146 **Tel** *644 4255* **Rooms** *15*   **Map** *1 C3*

This Old Town family-run hotel is excellent value, offering a range of comfortable rooms at decent rates. The owners also rent out a range of Old Town apartments, which make a great alternative to hotels. Limited parking available. **www.romeofamily.ee**

City Hotel Portus   🅿 🍴 ♿ 🖨   ⓀⓀⓀ
Uus-Sadama 23, 10120 **Tel** *680 6600* **Fax** *680 6601* **Rooms** *107*   **Map** *2 E1*

Situated next to the D-Terminal of Tallinn's passenger port, Portus is unusually good value for money. It is within walking distance of the Old Town and shopping and entertainment centres, and offers pleasantly quirky, but comfortable, rooms with free Wi-Fi access. **www.portus.ee**

Key to Symbols *see back cover flap*

Go Hotel Shnelli

P ⑪ & ⚡︎ Ⓚ Ⓚ Ⓚ

Toompuiestee 37, 10133 **Tel** *631 0100* **Fax** *631 0101* **Rooms** *124* **Map** *1 B2*

Next to the railway station and a short walk away from the Old Town, the seven-storey Go Hotel Shnelli is not particularly attractive on the outside but it offers decent rooms at reasonable rates. Good Old Town views from the upper floors and a charming restaurant are definite advantages. **www.gohotels.ee**

Pirita Cloister Guesthouse

⊟ P & ⚡︎ Ⓚ Ⓚ Ⓚ

Merivälja 18, 11911 **Tel** *605 5000* **Fax** *605 5006* **Rooms** *20*

Just 7 km (4 miles) from the city centre, this award-winning modern guest house lies adjacent to Pirita Convent and close to the beach. The lovely rooms all come with a shower and Internet connection. Lunch and dinner have to be arranged in advance. Discounts are available from September to May. **www.piritaklooster.ee**

Reval Inn Tallinn

⑪ & ⚡︎ Ⓚ Ⓚ Ⓚ

Sadama 1, 10111 **Tel** *667 8700* **Fax** *667 8800* **Rooms** *163* **Map** *2 E1*

Neighbouring the passenger port, the comfortably-appointed Reval Inn Tallinn is hugely popular with ferry passengers. It has the usual high standards of the Reval chain, including perks such as free entrance to the Bonnie and Clyde nightclub *(see p361)* and an excellent buffet breakfast. **www.revalinn.com**

Skåne

P ⑪ ⚡︎ Ⓚ Ⓚ Ⓚ

Kopli 2c, 10412 **Tel** *667 8300* **Fax** *667 8301* **Rooms** *38* **Map** *1 B1*

Close to the train station and a short walk away from the Old Town, this attractive and reasonably priced hotel has light, airy and well-furnished rooms with Wi-Fi access. It offers a good buffet breakfast, but for larger groups lunch and dinner have to be arranged in advance. The parking is secure. **www.hotelskane.eu**

Susi

P ⑪ ⊟ & ⚡︎ Ⓚ Ⓚ Ⓚ

Peterburi tee 48, 11415 **Tel** *630 3200* **Fax** *630 3400* **Rooms** *101*

Although located a little way out of the city centre, Susi is well connected via a tram route. The hotel is an attractive option, thanks to its excellent amenities and large choice of rooms. It includes a restaurant, lobby bar, billiards table, beauty salon and sauna. Displays of local artwork add a touch of class. **www.susi.ee**

Tatari 53

P ⚡︎ Ⓚ Ⓚ Ⓚ

Tatari 53, 10134 **Tel** *640 5150* **Fax** *640 5151* **Rooms** *36* **Map** *2 D4*

A pleasant and comfortable hotel in the city centre, Tatari 53 is within easy walking distance of the Old Town. It offers clean, nicely furnished rooms with Wi-Fi access at good rates. Allergy-free rooms are also available. Pets are allowed for a small additional charge. **www.tatari53.ee**

Oru Hotel

P ⑪ & ⚡︎ Ⓚ Ⓚ Ⓚ Ⓚ

Narva mnt 120B, 10127 **Tel** *603 3300* **Fax** *601 2600* **Rooms** *51* **Map** *2 E2*

Conveniently close to the Song Festival Grounds, Oru Hotel may look a little dull on the outside but it has pleasantly furnished and inviting rooms, all of which come with free Wi-Fi access. There is also a sauna and a decent restaurant. **www.oruhotel.ee**

Reval Hotel Central

P ⑪ & ⚡︎ Ⓚ Ⓚ Ⓚ Ⓚ

Narva mnt 7c, 10120 **Tel** *633 9800* **Fax** *633 9900* **Rooms** *245* **Map** *2 E2*

Located close to Tallinn's town centre, Reval Hotel Central has a good choice of airy, well-appointed rooms, including large family rooms. There is a sauna, beauty salon and excellent restaurant and bar, as well as a play area for children. Children under 16 can stay for free. **www.revalhotels.com**

Reval Park Hotel & Casino

P ⑪ & ⚡︎ Ⓚ Ⓚ Ⓚ Ⓚ

Kreutzwaldi 23, 10147 **Tel** *630 5305* **Fax** *630 5315* **Rooms** *121* **Map** *2 F3*

About a ten-minute walk away from the Old Town and overlooking a beautiful park, this hotel has an enormous casino on the ground floor. The rooms are spacious and extremely comfortable, while the suites come with Jacuzzis. Excellent dining options include Tallinn's only all-day buffet. **www.revalhotels.com**

Uniquestay

P ⑪ ⊟ & ⚡︎ Ⓚ Ⓚ Ⓚ Ⓚ

Toompuiestee 23, 10137 **Tel** *660 0700* **Fax** *661 6176* **Rooms** *77* **Map** *1 B3*

The elegant limestone building of the Uniquestay hotel was built as a residence for a German baron. Its interior is warm but stylish, and the so-called Zen rooms and apartments come with NASA-designed gravity-free chairs. All rooms have flat-screen computers and digital safes. **www.uniquestay.com**

Uniquestay Mihkli

P ⑪ & ⚡︎ Ⓚ Ⓚ Ⓚ Ⓚ

Endla 23, 10122 **Tel** *666 4800* **Fax** *666 4888* **Rooms** *84* **Map** *1 A4*

Excellent value for money with great public transport links, this hotel is situated in a beautiful part of the city centre, just a short walk away from the Old Town. Sauna, gym and a free massage are included in the room rate. There is secure parking and the excellent La Bohème restaurant. **www.uniquestay.com**

Baltic Hotel Vana Wiru

P ⑪ ⊟ & ⚡︎ Ⓚ Ⓚ Ⓚ Ⓚ Ⓚ

Viru 11, 10140 **Tel** *669 1500* **Fax** *669 1501* **Rooms** *82* **Map** *2 D3*

This trendy hotel is ideally situated in the heart of the Old Town. The beautifully furnished, pastel-coloured rooms all come with free Internet access, while the deluxe rooms have a sauna or Jacuzzi. There is also a Turkish bath and Finnish sauna, a great restaurant and a lively pub. **www.vanawiru.ee**

Domina Inn City

P ¶¶ 🖥 �) 🏢 🏢 ⓌⓌⓌⓌⓌⓌ

Vana-Posti 11/13, 10146 **Tel** *681 3900* **Fax** *681 3901* **Rooms** *68* **Map** *1 C3*

Set in a fine 18th-century building in a great Old Town location, Domina Inn City is a top-class hotel. Elegant rooms all come with free Internet connection. Services and extras include babysitting, laundry, airport transfer and complimentary newspaper. Excellent business conference facilities are available. **www.dominahotels.com**

Kalev Spa Hotel

P ¶¶ 🏊 🏃 🖥 🍽 ⓌⓌⓌⓌⓌ

Aia 18, 10111 **Tel** *649 3300* **Fax** *649 3301* **Rooms** *100* **Map** *2 D2*

The centrally located Kalev Spa Hotel specializes in spa treatments and also boasts an enormous waterpark with three water slides and a large swimming pool. The rooms are stylishly decorated. Use of the waterpark, fitness centre and sauna facilities are included in the room rate. **www.kalevspa.ee**

Metropol

P ¶¶ 🖥 🍽 ⓌⓌⓌⓌⓌ

Roseni 13, 10111 **Tel** *667 4500* **Fax** *667 4600* **Rooms** *149*

Situated in the bustling port area close to the Old Town, Metropol has rather tasteful and refined rooms, all of which come with free Wi-Fi connection. There is a smart à la carte restaurant, casino, sauna and beauty salon. Free parking facilities are also available for guests. **www.metropol.ee**

Radisson SAS

P ¶¶ 🏃 🖥 🖥 🍽 ⓌⓌⓌⓌⓌ

Rävala pst 3, 10143 **Tel** *682 3000* **Fax** *682 3001* **Rooms** *280* **Map** *2 D4*

This sleek and immaculately run hotel is located in the centre of Tallinn's business and commercial district. Great views of the city, free Internet access and free morning sauna, a healthcare centre and superb dining are just some of the additional features. **www.tallinn.radissonsas.com**

Reval Hotel Olümpia

P ¶¶ 🏊 🏃 🖥 🍽 ⓌⓌⓌⓌⓌ

Liivalaia 33, 10118 **Tel** *631 5333* **Fax** *631 5325* **Rooms** *390* **Map** *2 D5*

The successful Reval chain began with this 26-storey hotel. It has numerous extra services such as trouser presses, safes, hairdryers and slippers in its cosy rooms, along with free Internet access and spectacular views. There are fantastic restaurants, pubs and a nightclub on the premises. **www.revalhotels.com**

Scandic Palace

¶¶ 🏃 🖥 🖥 🍽 ⓌⓌⓌⓌⓌ

Vabaduse väljak 3, 10141 **Tel** *640 7300* **Fax** *640 7288* **Rooms** *86* **Map** *1 C3*

Scandic Palace combines Scandinavian refinement and belle époque luxury to delightful effect. The 1930s building has great views of the Old Town, while the skylight in the seventh-floor sauna is a lovely touch. There is a chic café in the lobby and an excellent Mediterranean-style restaurant. **www.scandic-hotels.com**

Schlössle

P ¶¶ 🏃 🖥 🖥 🍽 ⓌⓌⓌⓌⓌ

Pühavaimu 13/15, 10123 **Tel** *699 7700* **Fax** *699 7777* **Rooms** *24* **Map** *1 C2*

This award-winning hotel fully deserves each of its five stars. The lavishly furnished rooms perfectly complement the splendid medieval-style interior, while the romantic restaurant is top-class. Facilities include 24-hour room service, babysitting, limousine hire and a private sauna and massage service. **www.schlossle-hotels.com**

Sokos Hotel Viru

P ¶¶ 🏃 🖥 🖥 🍽 ⓌⓌⓌⓌⓌ

Viru väljak 4, 10111 **Tel** *680 9300* **Fax** *680 9236* **Rooms** *516* **Map** *1 C2*

Located in the centre of Tallinn, Sokos is perfectly suited to everyone from families to business travellers. A wide range of excellent rooms comes with an equally impressive range of amenities. The huge complex includes a conference centre, two restaurants, a nightclub and shopping centre. **www.viru.ee**

St. Petersbourg

P ¶¶ 🖥 🖥 🍽 ⓌⓌⓌⓌⓌ

Rataskaevu 7, 10123 **Tel** *628 6500* **Fax** *628 6565* **Rooms** *27* **Map** *1 C2*

St. Petersbourg is a small but very classy hotel in a charming Old Town location. The rooms are furnished in eclectic Art Deco style with en-suite bathrooms. The hotel restaurant specializes in Russian cuisine in keeping with the hotel's historical connection with visiting Russian aristocrats. **www.schlossle-hotels.com**

Tallink City

P ¶¶ 🖥 🍽 ⓌⓌⓌⓌⓌ

Laikmaa 5, 10145 **Tel** *630 0800* **Fax** *630 0810* **Rooms** *332* **Map** *2 E3*

This sophisticated business-class hotel in the city centre has a range of spacious, well-appointed guest rooms, as well as two state-of-the-art conference rooms and superb tenth-floor meeting suites. There is an excellent restaurant buffet and the sauna is free for guests in the morning. **http://hotels.tallink.com**

Three Sisters

P ¶¶ 🖥 🖥 🍽 ⓌⓌⓌⓌⓌ

Pikk 71/Tolli 2, 10133 **Tel** *630 6300* **Fax** *630 6301* **Rooms** *23* **Map** *1 C2*

Tallinn's premier luxury boutique hotel is in three magnificently converted medieval houses. The beautifully fitted rooms come with flat-screen TVs and Internet connection, while the labyrinthine interior includes spiral staircases, a library with fireplace, a restaurant *(see p325)* and a supremely cosy wine cellar. **www.threesistershotel.com**

Ülemiste

P ¶¶ 🖥 🖥 🍽 ⓌⓌⓌⓌⓌ

Lennujaama tee 2, 11101 **Tel** *603 2627* **Fax** *603 2601* **Rooms** *130*

An ultra-modern hotel next to the airport, Ülemiste is a great option for overnight and short-stay guests. There is a good range of rooms, as well as a fitness centre, two saunas and a decent restaurant. The summer terrace has great views of a lake. There is easy access to the city centre by car and bus. **www.ylemistehotel.ee**

Key to Price Guide *see p292* **Key to Symbols** *see back cover flap*

WESTERN ESTONIA

HAAPSALU Päeva Villa

Lai 7, 90503 **Tel** 473 3672 **Fax** 473 3772 **Rooms** 18

Road Map C2

Päeva Villa is a charming little guest house with bright and inviting rooms decorated in different themes. The restaurant serves delicious Slavic cuisine as well as Estonian dishes. Facilities include a sauna. Pets are welcome for a small extra charge. **www.paevavilla.ee**

HAAPSALU Baltic Hotel Promenaadi

Sadama 22, 90507 **Tel** 473 7254 **Fax** 473 7250 **Rooms** 35

Road Map C2

This delightful hotel consists of a modern extension and a converted 19th-century villa. The lovely rooms, most of which have balconies, face out on to the sea. Rowing boat and bike rental services are available. There is free Internet acess in the lobby and partial Wi-Fi connection in some rooms. **www.promenaadi.ee**

HAAPSALU Fra Mare Spa Hotel

Ranna tee 2, 90403 **Tel** 472 4600 **Fax** 472 4601 **Rooms** 112

Road Map C2

Situated on the seafront, this modern hotel offers a huge range of spa and beauty treatments. The rooms are bright and airy and the whole place is suffused with a healthy atmosphere. There is an excellent pool complex, gym and even a children's playground. **www.framare.ee**

HIIUMAA ISLAND Liilia Hotel

Hiiu mnt 22, Käina, 92101 **Tel** 463 6146 **Fax** 463 6546 **Rooms** 13

Road Map C2

Located in an area of stunning natural beauty, Liilia Hotel is housed in a charming building which vaguely resembles a Spanish villa. The rooms are fairly nice but simple, while the hotel restaurant and pub are delightful. Various boat trips and boat rental options are available. **www.liiliahotell.ee**

HIIUMAA ISLAND Padu Hotel

Heltermaa mnt 22, Kärdla, 92414 **Tel** 463 3037 **Fax** 463 3023 **Rooms** 18

Road Map C2

Padu Hotel is a pleasant place to stay and is a convenient base from which to explore Hiiumaa. The rooms are somewhat sparsely decorated, but the apartments are much more comfortable and cost just a little more. All rooms have balconies. The restaurant serves local wild boar. **www.paduhotell.ee**

KIHNU ISLAND Tolli Tourism Farm

Sääre village, 88001 **Tel** 446 9908 **Rooms** 7

Road Map C2

This authentic farmstead provides a great way to experience the rugged beauty of Kihnu, with accommodation that includes beds in a converted barn. Guests can take trips out to sea with the island's famed fishermen and there are plenty of sporting activities on offer. Village musicians can be hired on request. **www.kihnutalu.ee**

LIHULA Luige Villa

Tallinna mnt 23, 90303 **Tel** 477 8872 **Rooms** 18

Road Map C2

The elegant-looking Luige Villa was built in 1912 and is a good place from which to explore the nearby Matsalu National Park. Decent double rooms are available along with cheaper accommodation in a separate building that has an attractive old electric sauna. **www.luigevilla.ee**

MATSALU NATIONAL PARK Altmõisa Guesthouse

Tuulu village, 90402 **Tel** 472 4680 **Fax** 472 4681 **Rooms** 12

Road Map C2

Situated on the northern shore of Matsalu Bay, this endearing guest house makes a great resting place after a long day's bird-watching or hiking trip. There are lovely views out to sea and of myriad kinds of birds. The restaurant is also very good, with a health-conscious, but delicious, menu. **www.altmoisa.ee**

MUHU ISLAND Pädaste Manor

Pädaste Manor, 94702 **Tel** 454 8800 **Fax** 454 8811 **Rooms** 13

Road Map C2

The hotel in Pädaste Manor has a heliport and has become famous after much high-profile media coverage. Its combination of refined luxury and rustic charm is certainly irresistible. Beautiful rooms, sumptuous food and a range of spa treatments make a perfect package. Ferry pick-up service is also available. **www.padaste.ee**

PALDISKI Laulasmaa Resort

Puhkekodu 4, 76702 **Tel** 687 0800 **Fax** 687 0801 **Rooms** 150

Road Map C1

Situated on a beautiful sandy bay just 30 minutes from Tallinn, this is an excellent resort with a superb wellness institute and spa facilities. More than half the rooms have balconies, and there are special allergy-free rooms as well. The resort's surroundings are fantastic for walking and cycling. **www.laulasmaa.ee**

PÄRNU Lepanina

Kabli village, 86002 **Tel** 446 5024 **Rooms** 34

Road Map D2

Lepanina is a pleasant seafront hotel some 52 km (32 miles) from Pärnu and 12 km (7 miles) from the Latvian border. Family rooms can sleep two children and all rooms have a balcony and view of the sea. Facilities include a sauna complex, swimming pool, restaurant, lobby bar, tennis courts and a mini golf course. **www.lepanina.ee**

PÄRNU Scandic Rannahotell
　　　　　　　　　　　　　　　　　　　　　　　　P ⅠⅠ & ≋　　ⓀⓀⓀⓀ

Ranna pst 5, 80010 **Tel** *443 2950* **Fax** *443 2918* **Rooms** *62*　　　　　　**Road Map** *D2*

Scandic Rannahotell is an elegant seafront hotel, equipped with modern facilities. It has an excellent à la carte restaurant and a rooftop terrace for warmer weather. Some rooms have sea views and balconies. Sauna, massage and beauty therapies are available. Free parking for guests. **www.scandic-hotels.com**

PÄRNU Strand Spa & Conference Hotel
　　　　　　　　　　　　　　　　　　　P ⅠⅠ ≋ & ≋　　ⓀⓀⓀⓀ

Tammsaare pst 35, 80010 **Tel** *447 5370* **Fax** *447 5371* **Rooms** *187*　　　　**Road Map** *D2*

The largest hotel in Pärnu, Strand Spa & Conference Hotel is close to the sea and city centre. Its spa and large swimming pool are free for guests, as is the popular Spa nightclub. Massage and beauty treatments are also available. The hotel specializes in organizing large conferences. **www.strand.ee**

PÄRNU Tervise Paradiis
　　　　　　　　　　　　　　　　P ⅠⅠ ≋ ⛲ 目 & ≋　　ⓀⓀⓀⓀ

Side 14, 80010 **Tel** *445 1606* **Fax** *445 1601* **Rooms** *122*　　　　　　**Road Map** *D2*

Warm and stylish rooms and a recreational atmosphere make Tervise Paradiis a good family option. The hotel boasts the largest waterpark in Estonia, as well as a huge swimming pool, bowling alley and a well-equipped fitness centre. It also has a good restaurant. **www.terviseparadiis.ee**

PÄRNU Ammende Villa
　　　　　　　　　　　　　　　　　　　　　P ⅠⅠ ≋　　ⓀⓀⓀⓀⓀ

Mere pst 7, 80010 **Tel** *447 3888* **Fax** *447 3887* **Rooms** *24*　　　　　　**Road Map** *D2*

A glorious Art Nouveau house, Ammende Villa has been converted into a luxury hotel. The rooms are beautifully furnished in authentic period style, while the service is second to none. The hotel is close to the beach and a short walk from the Old Town. Car rental is available. **www.ammende.ee**

SAAREMAA ISLAND Välja Tourism Farm
　　　　　　　　　　　　　　　　　　　　　≋ P　　Ⓚ

Hiievälja village, Angla Windmills, 94202 **Tel** *452 9050* **Rooms** *7*　　　**Road Map** *C2*

Situated on the less explored side of Saaremaa, Välja Tourism Farm is an excellent base for exploring this beautiful region. Comfortable rooms are on offer in quaint, farmstead-style surroundings. Camping is also available. Leisi, the nearest town, is almost 7 km (4 miles) away. **www.valja.maaturism.ee**

SAAREMAA ISLAND Kaali Visitors' Centre
　　　　　　　　　　　　　　　　　　　P ≋　　ⓀⓀ

Kaali village, Kaali Meteorite Crater, 94102 **Tel** *459 1184* **Rooms** *10*　　　**Road Map** *C2*

The Kaali Visitors' Centre offers comfortable guest house-style accommodation in a great location. The hotel can arrange excursions to Kuressaare and other major sights in Saaremaa, as well as boat trips to nearby islands, horse-riding and cycling. Transport available on request. **www.kaali.kylastuskeskus.ee**

SAAREMAA ISLAND Kase Holiday Village
　　　　　　　　　　　　　　　　　　　≋ P　　ⓀⓀ

Paiküla village, Mihkli Farm Museum, 93501 **Tel** *509 4279* **Rooms** *6*　　　**Road Map** *C2*

This converted farmstead really captures the spirit of the Saaremaa coutryside. Self-catering is available in each of the six houses and decent meals can be arranged on request. The owners can organize excursions around the island. Other activities on offer are fishing, hunting, tennis and cycling. **www.kase.ee**

SAAREMAA ISLAND Loona Manor
　　　　　　　　　　　　　　　　　　　≋ P ⅠⅠ　　ⓀⓀ

Loona, Kihelkonna, 93401 **Tel** *454 6510* **Rooms** *10*　　　　　　**Road Map** *B2*

Situated at the gateway to Vilsandi National Park, Loona Manor is a perfectly adequate hotel with cosy and well-furnished attic rooms as well as grounds for camping. Guided tours around the park are available, including a memorable trip to Vilsandi Island on a huge truck, especially popular with bird-watchers. **www.loona.ee**

SAAREMAA ISLAND Nasva Yacht Club Hotel
　　　　　　　　　　　　　　　　　　P ⅠⅠ & ≋　　ⓀⓀ

Nasva village, 93822 **Tel** *454 4044* **Fax** *454 4028* **Rooms** *21*　　　　　**Road Map** *C2*

Located in a fishing village 10 km (6 miles) from Kuressaare, this hotel resembles a ship on the outside and has a maritime theme on the inside. The rooms are bright and cheerful and all have balconies. The restaurant is reasonable but there are better places to eat in Kuressaare. **www.saaremaa.ee/nasvahotel**

SAAREMAA ISLAND Vanalinna Võõrastemaja
　　　　　　　　　　　　　　　　　　　　P ⅠⅠ　　ⓀⓀ

Kauba 8, Kuressaare, 93812 **Tel** *455 3383* **Rooms** *14*　　　　　　**Road Map** *C2*

A home-like hotel that is good value for money. The rooms are unexceptional but comfortable, while the two attic rooms have a more romantic and rustic feel. The hotel restaurant offers excellent food at reasonable prices. **www.vanalinna.ee**

SAAREMAA ISLAND Pilguse Manor
　　　　　　　　　　　　　　　　　　　≋ P　　ⓀⓀⓀ

Jõgela village, 93301 **Tel** *524 0033* **Fax** *454 5441* **Rooms** *15*　　　　**Road Map** *C2*

This relaxing family-run hotel is surrounded by stunning scenery. The comfortable rooms tastefully incorporate rustic elements. The hotel has free Wi-Fi access for guests. If weather permits, a prepacked country picnic on Katri Cliff is a great option. The area is perfect for hiking and cycling. **www.pilguse.ee**

SAAREMAA ISLAND Oti Manor
　　　　　　　　　　　　　　　　　　　　　　P　　ⓀⓀⓀⓀ

Oti, 94501 **Tel** *511 7773* **Rooms** *5*　　　　　　　　　**Road Map** *C2*

Oti Manor has been beautifully transformed into a charming hotel consisting of five suites, each of which is furnished on a different theme. The hotel is 8 km (5 miles) from the town of Orissaare and 50 km (31 miles) from Kuressaare. A stunning beach is within fairly easy reach. **www.otimanor.ee**

Key to Price Guide *see p292* **Key to Symbols** *see back cover flap*

SAAREMAA ISLAND Saaremaa Spa Hotel Rüütli   P ⫼ ♨ ⛷ ⚐ ⚡   ⓚⓚⓚⓚ

Pargi 12, Kuressaare, 93813 **Tel** *454 8100* **Fax** *454 8199* **Rooms** *93*   **Road Map** *C2*

Located next to the town park and the marina, this large spa hotel is a good option for families. Children's facilities include a play area and a designated pool in the water centre. There is also a squash court, sauna complex and plenty of health and beauty therapies, including water aerobics. **www.sanatoorium.ee**

SAAREMAA ISLAND Georg Ots Spa Hotel   P ⫼ ♨ ⛷ ▤ ⚐ ⚡   ⓚⓚⓚⓚⓚ

Tori 2, Kuressaare, 93815 **Tel** *455 0000* **Fax** *455 0001* **Rooms** *91*   **Road Map** *C2*

The interior of this award-winning hotel is minimalist, though warm and intimate. The swimming pool is a master-piece of design. An excellent range of spa and beauty treatments and top-notch dining are also on offer. The hotel is also close to all the main sights in Kuressaare. **www.gospa.ee**

SAAREMAA ISLAND Grand Rose Spa Hotel   P ⫼ ♨ ⛷ ⚐ ⚡   ⓚⓚⓚⓚⓚ

Tallinna 15, Kuressaare, 93811 **Tel** *666 7000* **Rooms** *65*   **Road Map** *C2*

This classy hotel offers extravagantly comfortable accommodation. Allergy-free rooms, as well as those with facilities for disabled guests are included. The spa and sauna centre is beautifully designed and offers guests free access between 7am and 10pm. **www.grandrose.ee**

SOOMAA NATIONAL PARK Soomaa Hostel   ⊟ P   ⓚ

Jõesuu village, 86802 **Tel** *447 4894* **Rooms** *10*   **Road Map** *D2*

Conveniently located in Jõesuu village, the main gateway to Soomaa National Park, this cheap but well-run hostel is a good budget option. Private rooms and dormitories are available. The hostel has a sauna, laundry facilities, barbecue area, free Wi-Fi access and bike rental. **www.hostel.soomaa.com**

VORMSI ISLAND Elle-Malle Guesthouse   ⊟ P ⚡   ⓚ

Hullo village, 91301 **Tel** *473 2072* **Rooms** *12*   **Road Map** *C1*

This is a charming and restful guest house that feels far from the bustle of the modern world. The main guest house has several rustic-looking but cosy rooms, while a narrow windmill on stilts has been converted into a romantic double room. Excellent local food is offered at great prices. **www.vormsi.ee**

VORMSI ISLAND Rumpo Mäe Farm   ⊟ P   ⓚ

Rumpo village, 91301 **Tel** *472 9932* **Rooms** *14*   **Road Map** *C1*

This charmingly converted farmstead makes an excellent place to stay. It is close to the sea and is well situated for hiking and cycling. The rooms are simple but pleasant. Self-catering facilities are available. Guests can also pitch a tent in the grounds. **www.hot.ee/streng**

EASTERN ESTONIA

KUREMÄE Wironia   P ⫼ ⚡   ⓚⓚ

Rakvere 7, 41531 **Tel** *336 4200* **Fax** *336 1210* **Rooms** *21*   **Road Map** *E1*

This simple, but pleasant, hotel is 20 km (12 miles) away from the spectacular Pühtitsa convent and close to several other areas of interest. The average-priced rooms are bright and cheery and there is a nice pub and restaurant with outdoor seating in summer. A good base for exploring the region. **www.wironia.ee**

LAHEMAA NATIONAL PARK Kolga Guesthouse   ⊟ P ⫼   ⓚⓚ

Kolga village, 74602 **Tel** *607 7477* **Fax** *607 7270* **Rooms** *20*   **Road Map** *D1*

This pleasant little hotel is housed in the stables of the impressive Kolga manor house and offers cosy, clean rooms that are perfect for a brief stay. The medieval-style cellar pub is a congenial place for an evening meal. The hotel surroundings are spectacular. **www.kolgahotell.ee**

LAHEMAA NATIONAL PARK Merekalda Guesthouse   ⊟ P   ⓚⓚ

Neeme tee 2, Käsmu, 45601 **Tel** *323 8451* **Rooms** *6*   **Road Map** *D1*

This relaxing guest house has five snug apartments and two double rooms. Rates do not include breakfast, although light breakfasts can be ordered, and the closest restaurant is in nearby Võsu. The stunning surroundings are a dream for hikers and cyclists. No pets are allowed. **www.merekalda.ee**

LAHEMAA NATIONAL PARK Park Hotel Palmse   ⊟ P ⫼   ⓚⓚ

Vihula district, Palmse, 45202 **Tel** *322 3626* **Fax** *323 4167* **Rooms** *27*   **Road Map** *D1*

Park Hotel has sparsely furnished, but bright and cheerful rooms housed in the converted distillery of Palmse Manor. The beautiful surroundings and central location in Lahemaa National Park make it an attractive option. There is a great beer cellar and rustic-style sauna for guests. **www.phpalmse.ee**

LAHEMAA NATIONAL PARK Rannaliiv Guesthouse   ⊟ P ♨   ⓚⓚ

Aia 4, Vosu, 45501 **Tel** *323 8456* **Fax** *323 8456* **Rooms** *13*   **Road Map** *D1*

Situated near a beautiful beach, Rannaliiv Guesthouse is a comfortable place to pass a few days. It has homely rooms with balconies and a pleasant garden for guests to sit in during summer. There is also a sauna and swimming pool, and hall with a fireplace for groups. **www.rannaliiv.ee**

LAHEMAA NATIONAL PARK Sagadi Manor
🅿 🍽 ⚡   ⓧⓧⓧ

Sagadi village, Sagadi, 45402 **Tel** *676 7888* **Fax** *676 7880* **Rooms** *28*   **Road Map** *D2*

The hotel is located on the grounds of the beautiful Sagadi Manor estate. The charming en-suite rooms are housed in the loft of converted stables. A hostel across the courtyard offers sparse but comfortable accommodation at more modest rates. Bicycle rental options are available. **www.sagadi.ee**

NARVA King
🅿 🍽   ⓧⓧ

Lavretsovi 9, 20307 **Tel** *357 2404* **Fax** *357 2404* **Rooms** *24*   **Road Map** *E1*

King is a charming, rustic-style hotel in the centre of town. The tastefully furnished rooms are comfortable and lavish and each comes with free Wi-Fi access. The restaurant, set over two floors, is excellent. Excursions are also available. **www.hotelking.ee**

NARVA Narva Hotel
🅿 🍽 ♿ ⚡   ⓧⓧⓧ

Puškini 6, 20308 **Tel** *359 9600* **Fax** *359 9603* **Rooms** *48*   **Road Map** *E1*

Excellently located, this establishment is close to all of Narva's most famous historic monuments. While the hotel's exterior is rather modest, the rooms are very clean and comfortable and some come with Internet connection. **www.narvahotell.ee**

NARVA-JÕESUU Narva-Jõesuu Spa Hotel
🅿 🍽 ≈ ♿ ⚡   ⓧⓧⓧ

Aia 3, 29002 **Tel** *359 9529* **Fax** *359 9525* **Rooms** *67*   **Road Map** *E1*

Offering a wide range of therapy treatments, this delightful spa hotel is a relaxing getaway. There is an excellent swimming pool and sauna, while the beautiful beach is only a short walk away. The hotel's reception staff can arrange excursions to nearby Narva and the Ontika Coast, among other leisure activities. **www.narvajoesuu.ee**

ONTIKA COAST Toila Spa Hotel
🅿 🍽 ≈ 🧍 ♿ ⚡   ⓧⓧⓧⓧ

Ranna 12, 41702 **Tel** *334 2900* **Fax** *334 2901* **Rooms** *161*   **Road Map** *E1*

A modern nine-storey spa hotel surrounded by sea and forest, this highly professional establishment specializes in health and wellness treatments. There is a huge range of quality accommodation, including apartments and a nearby camping site. The bathing pools are nicely designed in mock-Roman style. **www.toilasanatoorium.ee**

OTEPÄÄ Pühajärve Spa Hotel
🅿 🍽 ≈ 🧍 ♿ ⚡   ⓧⓧⓧ

Pühajärve, 67406 **Tel** *766 5500* **Fax** *766 5501* **Rooms** *97*   **Road Map** *E2*

This spa hotel is beautifully located and offers an excellent range of wellness and beauty treatments. There is also a sizeable swimming pool, bowling alley, gym and billiards room. Best of all, though, are the stunning natural surroundings. Pets are welcome. **www.pyhajarve.com**

PÕLTSAMAA Heleni Maja Guesthouse
🍽 🅿   ⓧ

Pajusi 12, 48106 **Tel** *776 2720* **Fax** *776 2721* **Rooms** *15*   **Road Map** *D2*

Situated in the tranquil environs of Põltsamaa, this is a pleasant, if rather functional, guest house. The rooms are clean and comfortable and the restaurant is similarly low-key. A pool table and sauna are available for evening relaxation. **www.helenimaja.ee**

PÕLVA Hotel Pesa
🅿 🍽 ≈ ⚡   ⓧⓧ

Uus 5, 63308 **Tel** *799 8530* **Fax** *799 8531* **Rooms** *24*   **Road Map** *E2*

Hotel Pesa is a congenial place with unexceptional, but comfortable, rooms and a good restaurant. Wi-Fi access is limited to the lobby and selected rooms. The hotel boasts a swimming pool, fitness centre and sauna. Among the many activities on offer is an excellent culture and nature tour. **www.kagureis.ee**

RAKVERE Wesenbergh
🅿 🍽 ⚡   ⓧⓧⓧ

Tallinn 25, 44311 **Tel** *322 3480* **Fax** *322 3524* **Rooms** *45*   **Road Map** *D1*

Named after an old local castle, this elegant little hotel also has a separate villa. Some rooms are provided with a private sauna. There is a gym and aerobics hall. In addition to a restaurant, café and a grill-house, Wesenbergh also has a 24-hour lobby bar. **www.wesenbergh.ee**

RÕUGE Rõuge Suurjärv Guesthouse
🅿 ♿   ⓧ

Metsa 5, 66201 **Tel** *785 9273* **Rooms** *17*   **Road Map** *E2*

This home-like guest house is a great base from which to explore the beautiful region. The rooms are simple but comfortable and a rustic-style breakfast is served. Lunch and dinner can be arranged on request. A real country sauna is also available. The area is fantastic for hiking. **www.hot.ee/maremajutus**

SANGASTE MANOR Sangaste Castle Hostel
🛏 🅿 🍽   ⓧ

Lossiküla village, 67001 **Tel** *767 9300* **Fax** *767 9303* **Rooms** *18*   **Road Map** *D2*

One of the most striking manor houses in Estonia, Sangaste Castle has charming high-ceilinged rooms which resonate with history. The restaurant is similarly authentic-looking, although its menu is fairly basic. The hotel is expected to undergo a thorough renovation in the near future. **www.sangasteloss.ee**

SETUMAA Piusa Ürgoru Holiday Home
🛏 🅿   ⓧ

Väiko-Härma village, 65302 **Tel** *528 9134* **Rooms** *16*   **Road Map** *E2*

This pleasant village-like ensemble consists of a main house, a converted granary and several simple log cabins at a lower price. The beautiful surrounding countryside and local places of interest make it a good choice. There is also a campsite and trout fishing is possible throughout the summer. **www.puhkemaja.ee**

Key to Price Guide *see p292* **Key to Symbols** *see back cover flap*

SILLAMÄE Hotel Krunk P ⑪ ⊗⊗

Kesk 23, 40231 **Tel** *392 9030* **Fax** *392 9035* **Rooms** *21* **Road Map** *E1*

Situated right in the middle of town, Hotel Krunk is a good example of Stalinist Neo-Baroque architecture and is an intriguing place to stay. The hotel was constructed during the Soviet era and was then a guest house. The spacious rooms all have Internet connection. The hotel also has a good restaurant and a sauna. **www.krunk.ee**

SUUR MUNAMÄGI Haanjamehe Farm P ⑪ ⚤ ⊗⊗

Vakari, 65101 **Tel** *786 6000* **Fax** *786 6001* **Rooms** *14* **Road Map** *E2*

This delightfully converted farmstead gives a real taste of rural life. The rooms are lovely and there is a staggering range of activities on offer, from excursions to local sights, to canoeing and amusing obstacle courses. The wonderful wooden restaurant is a great place to unwind. **www.kubija.ee/haanjamehetalu**

TAEVASKOJA Taevaskoja Holiday Centre Hostel ▤ P ⊗⊗

Taevaskoja, 63202 **Tel** *799 2067* **Rooms** *30* **Road Map** *E2*

This hostel is not exactly luxurious, but it is cheap and cheerful. Guests can make use of the self-catering facilities. There is also a volleyball court, sauna and rock-climbing wall. It is a good base from which to go for trekking and canoeing. **www.taevaskoja.ee**

TARTU Hansa Hotel P ⭐ ⇄ ⊗⊗⊗

Aleksandri 46, 43401 **Tel** *737 1800* **Fax** *737 1801* **Rooms** *22* **Road Map** *D1*

Strategically located close to the Tartu river, Hansa Hotel resembles an old merchant's house or a row of stores. This comfortable and modern hotel retains its period charm. The rooms are lovely, with a neat decor and facilities such as TV and telephone. Special rooms for disabled guests are available. **www.hansahotel.com**

TARTU Tartu Hotel P ⑪ ⭐ ⇄ ⊗⊗⊗

Soola 3, 51013 **Tel** *731 4300* **Fax** *731 4301* **Rooms** *62* **Road Map** *E2*

A reasonable budget option for a night or two, Tartu Hotel is located on the periphery of the city centre and offers rooms at a good price. The whole hotel has Wi-Fi access. The sauna can take groups of up to 15 people at one time. **www.tartuhotell.ee**

TARTU Draakon P ⑪ ▤ ⭐ ⇄ ⊗⊗⊗⊗

Raekoja plats 4, 51003 **Tel** *744 2045* **Fax** *742 3000* **Rooms** *41* **Road Map** *E2*

Located right on Town Hall Square, Draakon is a plush hotel mainly catering to businessmen and high-end tourists. The suites come with their own saunas. All rooms have Internet connection. There is an elegant Baroque-style restaurant and an atmospheric medieval-style beer cellar restaurant. **www.draakon.ee/eng**

TARTU Pallas P ⑪ ⭐ ⇄ ⊗⊗⊗⊗

Riia mnt 4, 51004 **Tel** *730 1200* **Fax** *730 1201* **Rooms** *61* **Road Map** *E2*

This slightly unusual but charming hotel sits atop a sleek new commercial building in the centre of town and offers great views. The wonderfully decorated rooms are all inspired by famous Estonian artists. The restaurant is decent and serves a range of set menus. **www.pallas.ee**

TARTU Barclay P ⑪ ▤ ⭐ ⇄ ⊗⊗⊗⊗⊗

Ülikooli 8, 51003 **Tel** *744 7100* **Fax** *744 7110* **Rooms** *49* **Road Map** *E2*

An elegant 1912 Art Nouveau building, the Barclay hotel served as the headquarters of the Red Army during Soviet times. The rooms are extremely comfortable, if unimaginatively furnished. The hotel has an excellent location in the centre of town. **www.barclay.ee**

VILJANDI Hotel Centrum P ⑪ ⭐ ⇄ ⊗⊗

Tallinna 24, 71008 **Tel** *435 1100* **Fax** *435 1130* **Rooms** *27* **Road Map** *D2*

Hotel Centrum is located on the third floor of the Centrum shopping centre. The rooms are comfortable, though sparsely decorated. A sauna, massage parlour and beauty salon are open to guests. The excellent restaurant *(see p329)* is a bonus. **www.centrum.ee**

VILJANDI Grand Hotel Viljandi P ⑪ ⯏ ⭐ ⇄ ⊗⊗⊗⊗

Tartu 11/Lossi 29, 71004 **Tel** *435 5800* **Fax** *435 5805* **Rooms** *49* **Road Map** *D2*

Housed in a 1938 Art Deco building, the Grand Hotel is decidedly opulent for its small-town setting. It has an impressive gym, a sauna divided into a Turkish bath and Finnish sauna and a very good restaurant. Check with the helpful staff about local excursions and cultural events. **www.ghv.ee**

VÕRU Tamula Hotel P ⇄ ⊗⊗

Vee 4, 65609 **Tel** *783 0430* **Fax** *783 0431* **Rooms** *24* **Road Map** *E2*

Located on the sandy shores of Lake Tamula, Tamula Hotel is a bright and pleasant establishment. The suites have a private sauna. The hotel also has tennis courts, while bike rental is available for exploring the nearby town of Võru. There is a pub and nightclub beside the hotel. **www.tamula.ee**

VÕRU Kubija Hotel P ⑪ ⯏ ⚤ ⭐ ⇄ ⊗⊗⊗

Männiku 43a, 65603 **Tel** *786 6000* **Fax** *786 6001* **Rooms** *57* **Road Map** *E2*

Kubija is a bright, welcoming and uniquely furnished hotel that takes special care of its guests. It even includes a sleep centre offering expert advice and diagnoses on sleeping problems. A good range of wellness treatments as well as plenty of fascinating local excursions can be found here. **www.kubija.ee**

Choosing a Hotel in Latvia

These hotels have been selected for their good value, facilities and location. They are listed by region, starting with Rīga, followed by the rest of Latvia. Under each town or area, hotels are listed alphabetically within each price category. For Rīga map references, see pages 160–61; for road map references see inside back cover.

PRICE CATEGORIES
The following price ranges are for a standard double room for one night during the high season. Breakfast is included, unless otherwise specified.

Ⓛ Under 30 Ls
ⓁⓁ 30–50 Ls
ⓁⓁⓁ 50–80 Ls
ⓁⓁⓁⓁ 80–110 Ls
ⓁⓁⓁⓁⓁ Over 110 Ls

RĪGA

Homestay
🖼 🅿 ⌦   Ⓛ
Stokholmas iela 1, LV-1014 **Tel** *6755 3016* **Rooms** *4*

Located in the upmarket Mežaparks district, a 20-minute tram ride from the Old Town, Homestay is well worth the journey. The owners, a Latvian and a New Zealander, are very attentive towards their guests. The rooms are cosy and the breakfast is excellent. **www.homestay.lv**

B&B Rīga
⌦ 🅿   ⓁⓁ
Ģertrūdes iela 43, LV-1011 **Tel** *2652 6400* **Fax** *6729 7594* **Rooms** *18*   **Map** *2 E2*

This family-run B&B is located in a quiet courtyard a short walk from the Old Town. The apartment-style rooms come in a range of sizes, although the smallest do not include cooking facilities. The largest are very good value for big groups. Breakfast is served at a café across the road. **www.bb-riga.lv**

KB
⌦   ⓁⓁ
Krišjānis Barona iela 37, LV-1011 **Tel** *6731 2323* **Fax** *6731 6953* **Rooms** *12*   **Map** *2 E3*

Named after Krišjānis Barons, a collector of Latvian folk songs, this B&B is owned by his great-grandson. The renovated Art Nouveau building is bright and spacious, while the bedrooms are basic but good value. The studio in the attic has a kitchenette. **www.kbhotel.lv**

Laine
🅿 🍴   ⓁⓁ
Skolas iela 11, LV-1010 **Tel** *6728 8816* **Fax** *6728 7658* **Rooms** *38*   **Map** *2 E2*

Housed in an Art Nouveau building, tucked away in a quiet street, this hotel is a great budget find. The bright and welcoming rooms show a Scandinavian influence and have paintings on the walls. Safes, Wi-Fi access, hairdryers and minibars are provided. The cheapest rooms have shared facilities. **www.laine.lv**

Radi un Draugi
🍴   ⓁⓁ
Mārstaļu iela 1/3, LV-1050 **Tel** *6782 0200* **Fax** *6782 0202* **Rooms** *76*   **Map** *2 D4*

An excellent budget choice in the centre of the Old Town, this popular hotel should be booked well in advance. Owned by British-Latvians, it is a no-frills place with basic but comfortable and clean rooms. The name means "friends and family", something which the helpful staff take to heart. **www.draugi.lv**

Viktorija
🅿 🍴   ⓁⓁ
Čaka iela 55, LV-1011 **Tel** *6701 4111* **Fax** *6731 0629* **Rooms** *64*   **Map** *2 E3*

A popular choice for travellers on a budget, Viktorija is located in a restored Art Nouveau building within walking distance of the Old Town. Rooms are on the small side, but are clean and represent good value for money. Most have en-suite bathrooms, but cheaper rooms with shared facilities are also available. **www.hotel-viktorija.lv**

Albert
🍴 🗐 ♿ ⌦   ⓁⓁⓁ
Dzirnavu iela 33, LV-1010 **Tel** *6733 1717* **Fax** *6733 1718* **Rooms** *246*   **Map** *2 E4*

The Albert in question is Einstein, and this theme is subtly present throughout this popular hotel in the main Art Nouveau district. The stylish rooms each contain a quote from the famous scientist, and there are atom motifs in the carpets. Bedrooms are simple but comfortable, decorated in calming colours. **www.alberthotel.lv**

Baltvilla
🅿 🍴 🗐 ♿ ⌦   ⓁⓁⓁ
Senču prospekts 45, LV-2146, LV-2164 **Tel** *6784 0640* **Fax** *6799 0888* **Rooms** *39*

Just 30 minutes from the centre of Rīga, this hotel on the edge of Lake Baltezers opened in 2007. It specializes in providing both medical and spa treatments for its guests, with good facilities for those with disabilities or allergies. The rooms are comfortable and stylish. **www.baltvilla.lv**

Ekes Konventa
ⓁⓁⓁ
Skārņu 22, LV-1050 **Tel** *6735 8393* **Fax** *6735 8395* **Rooms** *11*   **Map** *2 D4*

Right in the centre of the Old Town, this building has an interesting history. It was a guest house for travellers in the 15th century and later housed the widows of guild members. The downside is that rooms are small and noise tends to carry, which may cause problems for light sleepers. **www.ekeskonvents.lv**

Key to Symbols *see back cover flap*

Elizabetes Nams

Elizabetes iela 27, LV-1010 **Tel** *6750 9292* **Fax** *6750 9291* **Rooms** *20*　　　　**Map** *2 D2*

Housed in a restored 18th-century wooden building, this quiet and stylish hotel offers a range of accommodation options. The decor in the rooms ranges from warm to muted tones. One of the rooms has a washing machine and tumble dryer, while some have bathtubs. There is a pleasant restaurant in the cellar. **www.elizabetesnams.lv**

Europa City

Brīvības iela 199c, LV-1039 **Tel** *6716 6000* **Fax** *6716 6001* **Rooms** *143*　　　　**Map** *2 F1*

This oddly curvy building is a short tram ride from the Old Town, but its location means that its rooms are reasonably priced. The decor is groovy 1960s retro, with a range of different colour schemes in the bedrooms. The terrace is a pleasant place for cocktails in summer. **www.europacity.lv**

Hanza

Elijas iela 7, LV-1050 **Tel** *6779 6040* **Fax** *6779 6044* **Rooms** *80*　　　　**Map** *2 E5*

A newly renovated residential building in the Moscow District, a short walk beyond the Central Market, Hanza is a good choice if being absolutely central is not essential. Rooms are comfortable, with formal beige decor, heated bathroom floors and Wi-Fi. Streetside rooms have a view of Jesus Church. **www.hanzahotel.lv**

Islande

Ķīpsalas iela 20, LV-1048 **Tel** *6760 8000* **Fax** *6760 8001* **Rooms** *205*　　　　**Map** *1 A3*

A 20-minute walk from the Old Town, this large and modern hotel is located on the left bank of the Daugava river. The rooms are simple and reflect Scandinavian influence, and many have excellent views. The ninth-floor Arctic Lights restaurant looks out over the city. Spa treatments are also on offer. **www.islandehotel.lv**

Kolonna

Tirgoņu iela 9, LV-1050 **Tel** *6735 8254* **Fax** *6735 8255* **Rooms** *41*　　　　**Map** *1 C4*

A central and affordable option. The rooms of Kolonna are clean and spacious, but often oddly shaped because they have been fitted into a historic building, evidence of which can be seen in exposed sections of wall. The hotel also provides Wi-Fi access. **www.hotelkolonna.com**

Konventa Sēta

Kalēju iela 9/11, LV-1050 **Tel** *6708 7501* **Fax** *6708 7515* **Rooms** *141*　　　　**Map** *2 D4*

Named after the convent court in which it is set, this hotel benefits from a very convenient location in the Old Town. Although many of the rooms in the complex of medieval buildings are quite plain, some have features such as old wooden joists. Apartments with kitchenettes are also available. **www.konventa.lv**

Vecrīga

Gleznotāju iela 12/14, LV-1050 **Tel** *6721 6524* **Fax** *6721 4561* **Rooms** *16*

A friendly hotel located in a quiet part of the Old Town, this 18th-century town house retains plenty of old-world charm alongside facilities such as minibars and satellite TV. There is also outdoor dining in summer. The reception area proudly displays photographs of a visit by the Dalai Lama in 2000. **www.vecriga.lv**

Ainavas

Peldu iela 23, LV-1050 **Tel** *6781 4316* **Fax** *6781 4317* **Rooms** *22*　　　　**Map** *1 C4*

The name of this cosy boutique hotel means "landscape" and each room reflects a different aspect of Latvian scenery. The building dates from the 15th century and sections of bare wall add character to some rooms. The staff excel at little touches such as offering a glass of champagne to guests on arrival. **www.ainavas.lv**

Boutique Hotel Viesturs

Mucenieku iela 5, LV-1050 **Tel** *6735 6060* **Fax** *6735 6061* **Rooms** *13*

Each room in this boutique hotel is decorated differently, and is of uniformly high quality, although the bathrooms are on the small side. Exposed stone walls in the communal areas enhance the appeal of the medieval building, while the hotel's only suite has its own sauna, Jacuzzi and rooftop terrace. **www.hotelviesturs.lv**

Centra

Audēju iela 1, LV-1050 **Tel** *6722 6441* **Fax** *6750 3281* **Rooms** *27*　　　　**Map** *2 D4*

Minimalism is the keyword in this friendly and stylish hotel. Rooms on the upper floors are quiet despite the central location, and all are equipped with a plasma TV, minibar and safe. There is also free Wi-Fi access throughout the hotel. Airport transfers may be arranged by the hotel. **www.centra.lv**

Domina Inn

Pulkveža brieža 11, LV-1010 **Tel** *6763 1800* **Fax** *6763 1801* **Rooms** *110*　　　　**Map** *1 C1*

Situated in the city's main Art Nouveau district, this elegant hotel is itself architecturally impressive. Rooms vary somewhat in size, but are all modern and come with a safe, minibar and broadband Internet access. Allergy-free bedrooms are also available. Use of the sauna and Jacuzzi costs extra. **www.dominahotels.com**

Europa Royale

Krišjānis Barona 12, LV-1050 **Tel** *6707 9444* **Fax** *6707 9449* **Rooms** *60*　　　　**Map** *2 E3*

This 19th-century residence became a hotel in 2006, and has retained its original features. Everything about it is plush – parquet floors, high ceilings, huge doors, stained-glass windows and wooden staircases. The Presidential Suite has a private door to the restaurant. There is also a casino, sauna and gym. **www.europaroyale.com**

Garden Palace

Grēcinieku iela 28, LV-1050 **Tel** *6722 4650* **Fax** *6735 9749* **Rooms** *66*　　　　　　　**Map** *1 C4*

With an abundance of old-fashioned elegance, this is a well-priced option for visitors looking for a little luxury. The decor is a tasteful combination of cream and gold, set off by crystal chandeliers and vases of flowers. The suites are well appointed, while rooms at the top have terraces. **www.hotelgardenpalace.lv**

Gutenbergs

Doma laukums 1, LV-1050 **Tel** *6781 4090* **Fax** *6750 3326* **Rooms** *38*　　　　　　　**Map** *1 C3*

This cosy hotel is just around the corner from the Dome Cathedral. Rooms in the new wing have the most character, with wooden beams and interesting trinkets. In summer, there is dining on the rooftop terrace, with live Latvian music on weekend evenings and during Sunday brunch. **www.gutenbergs.lv**

Maritim Park

Slokas iela 1, LV-1048 **Tel** *6706 9000* **Fax** *6706 9001* **Rooms** *239*　　　　　　　**Map** *1 A5*

Located on the opposite side of the Daugava river, this large but quiet hotel is popular with business travellers and has a good link by tram to the Old Town. Rooms are modern and clean, coming in a range of sizes. The Bellevue restaurant *(see p332)* on the tenth floor, one of Rīga's most expensive, has superb views. **www.maritim.lv**

Metropole

Aspazijas bulvāris 36/38, LV-1050 **Tel** *6722 5411* **Fax** *6721 6140* **Rooms** *86*　　　　　　　**Map** *2 D4*

Open since 1871, this is the elder statesman of Rīga's hotel scene. It is conveniently located on the edge of the Old Town, although street-facing rooms can be noisy. The spacious, Scandinavian-style rooms come equipped with Wi-Fi, minibar and trouser press. Facilities include a gym, sauna and business centre. **www.metropole.lv**

Radisson SAS Daugava

Kuģu iela 24, LV-1048 **Tel** *6706 1111* **Fax** *6706 1100* **Rooms** *361*　　　　　　　**Map** *1 B4*

This classy hotel, on the left bank of the Daugava river, has spacious rooms and excellent facilities, including a swimming pool – something very unusual in Rīga. A shuttle bus runs regularly to the House of Blackheads. The hotel also offers its guests free transfers to the airport. **www.riga.radissonsas.com**

Rīga

Aspazijas bulvāris 22, LV-1050 **Tel** *6704 4222* **Fax** *6704 4223* **Rooms** *236*　　　　　　　**Map** *2 D4*

With a prime spot on the edge of the Old Town, this local landmark has been open since 1956. A little of the Soviet era lingers despite renovation. However, it has all the facilities of a large hotel such as Wi-Fi access, a business centre and sauna. The lobby includes a currency exchange, bar and jewellery store. **www.hotelriga.lv**

Bergs

Elizabetes iela 83/85, LV-1050 **Tel** *6777 0900* **Fax** *6777 0940* **Rooms** *38*　　　　　　　**Map** *2 D2*

A very stylish addition to the fashionable Berga Bazārs shopping precinct, this boutique hotel has won numerous awards in publications such as the *Tatler* and *Condé Nast Traveller*. Rooms are large and comfortable, and the service is professional; the only downside is that the place can be noisy at weekends. **www.hotelbergs.lv**

Grand Palace

Pils 12, LV-1050 **Tel** *6704 4000* **Fax** *6704 40014* **Rooms** *56*　　　　　　　**Map** *1 C3*

A classy option popular with celebrities, this hotel has two acclaimed restaurants, a sauna, gym and a cosy lobby bar with antler chandeliers. Bedrooms are elegantly decorated in blue, white and gold and equipped with Wi-Fi, a minibar, safe and pay TV. Bathrooms have tubs and heated floors. **www.schlossle-hotels.com**

Hotel de Rome

Kalķu iela 28, LV-1050 **Tel** *6708 7600* **Fax** *6708 7606* **Rooms** *88*　　　　　　　**Map** *2 D3*

This landmark building on a major thoroughfare close to the Freedom Monument boasts a spacious lobby and the highly regarded Otto Schwartz restaurant on the top floor. All the usual five-star facilities are included, although, as usual in Rīga, there is no swimming pool. Rooms are comfortable, if anonymous. **www.derome.lv**

Monika Centrum

Elizabetes iela 21, LV-1010 **Tel** *6703 1900* **Fax** *6703 1901* **Rooms** *80*　　　　　　　**Map** *2 D2*

An attractive Neo-Gothic building, reminiscent of a castle and located in the main Art Nouveau district, this hotel offers spacious and cosy rooms within easy reach of the Old Town. Suites come with four-poster beds, and facilities include free Wi-Fi, sauna and fitness centre. Breakfast is a hearty buffet. **www.centrumhotels.com**

Reval Hotel Latvija

Elizabetes iela 55, LV-1010 **Tel** *6777 2222* **Fax** *6777 2332* **Rooms** *586*　　　　　　　**Map** *2 D2*

Once an Intourist hotel where foreign guests were accommodated and spied upon, the building has been extensively renovated and is now counted among Rīga's leading hotels. The funky Skyline Bar *(see p365)* on the 26th floor is a big tourist draw, with fantastic views and a good cocktail list. **www.revalhotels.com**

Reval Hotel Rīdzene

Reimersa iela 1, LV-1050 **Tel** *6732 4433* **Fax** *6732 2600* **Rooms** *95*　　　　　　　**Map** *2 D3*

Formerly the exclusive domain of the Communist elite, this 1980s hotel is considered one of the best in town. The sauna and fitness centre on the top floor have glass walls with excellent views of the nearby park, while the glass pyramid covering the restaurant is a local landmark. **www.revalhotels.com**

Key to Price Guide *see p300* **Key to Symbols** *see back cover flap*

WESTERN LATVIA

BAUSKA Rožmalas
Ceraukstes pagasts, 7 km (4 miles) S of town, LV-3908 **Tel** *6779 1178* **Fax** *6779 1177* **Rooms** *15* **Road Map** *D4*

Rožmalas is a refreshingly modern roadside hotel and restaurant on the Via Baltica, in the direction of Vilnius. Standard rooms are comfortable, while the most expensive include whirlpool baths and a split-level layout. Guests can try their hand at baking bread in the 19th-century windmill, converted into a bakery. **www.rozmalas.lv**

BAUSKA Day & Night
Slimnicas iela 7, LV-3901 **Tel** *6399 1000* **Fax** *6399 1001* **Rooms** *78*   **Road Map** *D4*

This modern hotel, the first in a chain scheduled to open in several Latvian cities, brought a much-needed quality accommodation option to Bauska. Double and family rooms are well appointed with economical singles available. Services include a souvenir kiosk, banking facility and tourist information desk. **www.hoteldayandnight.lv**

DUNDAGA Pūpoli
Gipka iela, LV-3270 **Rooms** *4*   **Road Map** *C3*

This wooden guest house is ecologically run. Meals can be provided by arrangement, while there is also a kitchen for guests to use. Other facilities include a sauna and plunge pool. Berry- and mushroom-picking trips can be arranged in season. **www.hasselberga.se/pupoli/**

ENGURE Villa Elizabete
Jūras iela 88, LV-3113 **Tel** *6316 1421* **Fax** *6316 1421* **Rooms** *7*   **Road Map** *C3*

Small, clean double bedrooms as well as a larger deluxe room in the attic are offered at this wooden guest house. There is plenty to keep visitors busy, including basketball, table tennis, bicycle hire and a small gym. For children, there is a playground at the back, including a sandbox, swing and slide. **www.villaelizabete.lv**

JAUNMOKU PILS Jaunmoku Pils
Tume, LV-3139 **Tel** *6310 7126* **Fax** *6310 7125* **Rooms** *6*

The former hunting residence of George Armistead, Rīga's mayor from 1901 to 1912, this red-brick manor house has appealing rooms with slightly old-fashioned furnishings. The public areas are decorated with hunting trophies, while antique stoves add to the charm. It's a popular place for weddings in the summer. **www.jaunmokupils.lv**

JAUNPILS Jaunpils Pils
Tukuma rajons, LV-3145 **Tel** *6310 7082* **Rooms** *4*   **Road Map** *C4*

In addition to several basic rooms, this castle offers four atmospheric and individualistic places to stay. The Baron's Room is the most impressive, with a four-poster bed, Jacuzzi, under-floor heating and fireplace. The other three have a selection of these features. Tiled floors and exposed walls add further character. **www.jaunpilspils.lv**

JELGAVA Zemgale
Rīgas iela 11, LV-3002 **Tel** *6300 7707* **Fax** *6300 7710* **Rooms** *34*   **Road Map** *C4*

Just across the Lielupe river from the city's main tourist sights, this hotel is part of a recreation complex offering tennis, ten-pin bowling and ice-skating. Rooms are on the small side, but clean and modern, and staff are friendly and helpful. There are two cafés in the complex. **www.zemgale.info**

JŪRMALA Amber Sea
Dzintaru prospekts 68, Dzintari, LV-2015 **Tel** *6775 1297* **Fax** *6714 6601* **Rooms** *31*   **Road Map** *C3*

Tastefully decorated, predominantly in chocolate, red and cream, this is a very stylish option away from the busy resort of Majori. Rooms are spacious and the suites very large, some with access to a terrace. The restaurant is also classy. Prices rise considerably during the peak summer period. **www.amberhotel.lv**

JŪRMALA Baltic Beach
Jūras iela 23/25, Majori, LV-2015 **Tel** *6777 1400* **Fax** *6776 4044* **Rooms** *165*   **Road Map** *C3*

Although its wedge-shaped exterior is quite uninspiring, the Baltic Beach is one of Jūrmala's top hotels. Rooms come in a range of different sizes and degrees of luxury. The spa centre offers a long list of massages and treatments, as well as medical consultations. Staff have a reputation for being rather dour. **www.balticbeach.lv**

JŪRMALA Jūrmala Spa
Jomas iela 47/49, LV-2015 **Tel** *6778 4415* **Fax** *6778 4411* **Rooms** *190*   **Road Map** *C3*

This renovated Soviet-era block is a welcome addition to the hotel scene in Jūrmala. The style is retro-chic, with extensive use of natural materials, including stone in the bathrooms. The spa facilities are excellent and medical consultations are available. The bar on the 11th floor offers panoramic views. **www.hoteljurmala.lv**

KANDAVA Kandava
Sabiles iela 3, 14 km (9 miles) E of Sabile, LV-3120 **Tel** *2640 6733* **Fax** *6318 1643* **Rooms** *10*   **Road Map** *C3*

This centrally located hotel offers clean, comfortable and very basic rooms with red sheets and curtains. Most rooms have TVs, although, without satellite or cable, the viewing options are limited. The restaurant downstairs is fashionable, with retro furnishings and glowing oval lights in the floor and the bar. **www.hotelkandava.lv**

KOLKA Zītari
`P` `11` `≈`   Ⓛ

Rūtas, LV-3264 **Tel** *6332 0451* **Rooms** *15*   **Road Map** *C3*

Very convenient for visiting Cape Kolka, which is just a short walk away, this hotel is better than what might be expected from its outward appearance. Rooms are clean and light in tone, with pine furniture and sloping ceilings. The café has a standard Latvian menu, with plenty of fish options.

KULDĪGA Jāņa Nams
`P` `11` `≈`   Ⓛ

Liepājas iela 36, LV-3301 **Tel** *6332 3456* **Fax** *6332 3785* **Rooms** *8*   **Road Map** *B3*

Rooms in this central and friendly family-run hotel are on the small side, but are clean and decorated in cheerful colours. Some of the rooms are given additional character by their exposed wooden beams. The on-site restaurant is popular with locals, and there is also a sauna to help guests unwind. **www.jananams.lv**

KULDĪGA Metropole
`P` `11` `▤` `&` `≈`   ⒼⒼⒼ

Baznīcas iela 11, LV-3301 **Tel** *6335 0588* **Fax** *6335 0599* **Rooms** *14*   **Road Map** *B3*

Built as a hotel in 1919 and subsequently used for other purposes, the Metropole was gutted by fire in 1997. The interior has been fully renovated, with stylishly minimal decor and sloping ceilings lending the rooms character. The classy restaurant has an extensive wine list and a terrace for summer dining. **www.hotel-metropole.lv**

LIEPĀJA Poriņš
`P` `11` `&`   Ⓛ

Palmu iela 5, LV-3401 **Tel** *2915 0596* **Fax** *6342 8602* **Rooms** *20*   **Road Map** *B4*

This boutique hotel is stylish without being intimidating. Rooms have Scandinavian furnishings, wicker-finished wardrobes and stencilled walls. A glass lift provides wheelchair access, and parking is off the street. Its restaurant has circular lights recessed into the ceiling, and one of the walls is made from a stack of logs. **www.porins.lv**

LIEPĀJA Libava
`P` `11` `&` `≈`   ⓁⓁ

Vecā ostmala 29, LV-3401 **Tel** *6342 5318* **Fax** *6342 5319* **Rooms** *7*   **Road Map** *B4*

From the spacious lobby to the immaculate bedrooms, this canal-side hotel provides an affordable slice of luxury. Guests can take advantage of a discount in the basement spa, relax on cream leather sofas in the conservatory, or try the restaurant's adventurous menu. There is a working pier alongside the hotel. **www.libava.lv**

LIEPĀJA Promenāde
`P` `11` `▤` `&` `≈`   ⒼⒼⒼ

Vecā ostmala 40, LV-3401 **Tel** *6348 8288* **Fax** *6348 8588* **Rooms** *42*   **Road Map** *B4*

Retaining elements of the late 19th-century grain warehouse in which it is housed, this canal-side hotel is both cosy and modern. The lobby doubles as an art gallery, and the restaurant has a terrace for summertime dining. There is also a business centre and mooring space for yachts. **www.promenadehotel.lv**

MEŽOTNE Mežotnes Pils
`P` `11`   ⒼⒼⒼ

Mežotnes pagasts, LV-3918 **Tel** *6396 0711* **Fax** *6396 0725* **Rooms** *16*   **Road Map** *D4*

Built from 1797 to 1802, but partly destroyed in World War II, this exquisitely restored manor house has a Neo-Classical interior. Rooms range from singles to family apartments, with tasteful wooden furniture and wallpaper reminiscent of the 19th century. The grounds are also impressive. **www.mezotnespils.lv**

NĪCA Nīcava
`P` `11` `≈`   ⒼⒼⒼ

Nīcas pagasts, LV-3473 **Tel** *6348 6379* **Rooms** *6*   **Road Map** *B4*

Convenient for exploring Lake Pape Nature Reserve, this hotel offers rooms in an old post house. The decor is a little dated but rooms are clean and large; some are huge. The restaurant and less formal café share a menu which includes some hearty traditional Latvian dishes. **www.nicava.lv**

PĀVILOSTA Vēju Paradīze
`P` `11` `≈`   Ⓛ

Smilšu 14, LV-3466 **Tel** *2644 6644* **Rooms** *17*   **Road Map** *B4*

Rooms in this comfortable motel have wooden floors and exposed beams. Most bedrooms are doubles with en-suite facilities, but some can accommodate up to four people and have shared bathrooms. Facilities include a sauna and café, with a terrace for dining in summer. **www.vejuparadize.lv**

PEDVĀLE Firkspedvāle
`P` `11` `≈`   Ⓛ

Sabiles novads, LV-3295 **Tel** *6325 2249* **Rooms** *5*   **Road Map** *C4*

This manor house was part of the estate that forms the Pedvāle Open-Air Museum. The rooms have plenty of character, with wooden beams and photographs on the walls, although they would not suit visitors seeking luxury. Food is served in the pub nearby. There is also a sauna.

ROJA Rojas Pērle
`P` `11` `&` `≈`   Ⓛ

Selgas iela 4a, LV-3264 **Tel** *6326 9562* **Fax** *6326 9561* **Rooms** *10*   **Road Map** *C3*

With a sauna, café and restaurant, this hotel also holds discos at the weekends. Bedrooms, painted in soothing pastel shades, are equipped with pine furniture. Better rooms come with bathtubs instead of showers, and have balconies. Access for disabled people has been considered and there is a lift in the building. **www.rojasperle.lv**

ROJA Dzintarkrasts
`P` `11` `≋` `†` `&` `≈`   ⓁⓁ

Žocene, LV-3279 **Tel** *2860 0600* **Fax** *2937 0274* **Rooms** *19*   **Road Map** *C3*

Guests at this family-friendly complex can choose to stay in either a hotel room or cottage, and there is space for tents and caravans. Accommodation in the modern wooden buildings is comfortable and clean. Facilities include a good restaurant, sauna and swimming pool, and numerous activities are available. **www.dzintarkrasts.lv**

Key to Price Guide *see p300* **Key to Symbols** *see back cover flap*

RUNDĀLE Baltā Māja
🖼 P 🍴　　　　　　　　　　　　　　　Ⓛ

Pilsrundāle, LV-3921 **Tel** *2912 4374* **Rooms** *8*　　　　　　　**Road Map** *D4*

When restoring the run-down servants' quarters of Rundāle Palace, the owners left plenty of the original features such as paved floors and tiled stoves. Most rooms have shared bathrooms, although one has en-suite facilities. High-quality home-cooked Latvian dishes are served in the cosy restaurant. **www.kalpumaja.lv**

TALSI Saule
P 🚹 🍴　　　　　　　　　　　　　　Ⓛ

Saules iela 19, LV-3201 **Tel** *6323 2232* **Rooms** *6*　　　　**Road Map** *C3*

This pleasant guest house is run along environment-friendly lines. Rooms have wooden floors and pine furniture, while the Black Room features antique furniture made from dark wood, including an ornate 120-year-old bed. There are views of Lake Talsi from the terrace. Organic breakfast is served. **www.saulehotel.lv**

TĒRVETE Laima
🖼 P 🍴 🍴　　　　　　　　　　　　Ⓛ

Tērvete Nature Park, LV-3728 **Tel** *2949 5041* **Rooms** *6*　　　**Road Map** *C4*

With an excellent location within the nature park, this guest house offers basic bedrooms with en-suite facilities. All rooms have a TV and DVD player. Facilities include a sauna and pool table; bicycles are also available to hire. The ground-floor café boasts a bizarre mix of carpeted walls, mirrors, tiles and rocks. **www.laima.viss.lv**

TUKUMS Tuko
P 🍴 🚹 ♿ 🍴　　　　　　　　　　　Ⓛ

Stadiona iela 3, LV-3101 **Tel** *6312 2299* **Fax** *6310 7464* **Rooms** *47*　**Road Map** *C3*

Part of an outwardly uninspiring, but modern, recreation centre, this hotel offers simple, affordable and clean rooms. The centre also includes an ice-skating arena, sauna, café, gym and even a hairdressing salon. The bedrooms are located away from the other facilities and, thus, tend to remain quiet at night. **www.tuko.lv**

VENTSPILS Olimpiskā Centra
P 🍴 🏊 🚹 ♿ 🍴　　　　　　　　　Ⓛ

Lielais prospekts 33, LV-3601 **Tel** *6362 8032* **Fax** *6362 9032* **Rooms** *68*　**Road Map** *B3*

Part of the city's Olympic Centre, incorporating tennis courts, swimming pool, skate park and many other facilities, this hotel offers very good value for money. The rooms are devoid of character, with vertical blinds contributing to an office-like feel, but they are clean and comfortable. **www.ocventspils.lv**

VENTSPILS Raibie Logi
P ♿ 🍴　　　　　　　　　　　　　　Ⓛ

Lielais prospekts 61, LV-3601 **Tel** *2914 2327* **Rooms** *8*　　　**Road Map** *B3*

Aptly named Raibie Logi, translated as "vivid windows", this early 20th-century wooden building is decorated in jolly colours both inside and out. It offers clean rooms with pine furniture and laminated floors, with little touches such as sweets left on pillows. Light meals may be served in addition to breakfast. **www.raibielogi.lv**

VENTSPILS Vilnis
P 🍴 🍴　　　　　　　　　　　　　　ⓁⓁ

Talsu iela 5, LV-3602 **Tel** *6366 8800* **Fax** *6366 5054* **Rooms** *52*　**Road Map** *B3*

A decent three-star option for those wishing to stay outside the city centre, Vilnis is on the right bank of the Venta river. The hotel is geared towards business travellers. There is a classy restaurant with a grand piano, small aquarium and long wine list. **www.dzintarjura.lv**

EASTERN LATVIA

AGLONA Aglonas Cakuli
🖼 P 🚹 🍴　　　　　　　　　　　　ⓁⓁ

Ezera iela 4, LV-5304 **Tel** *2927 5701* **Fax** *6532 1465* **Rooms** *7*　**Road Map** *E4*

This friendly, family-run guest house with a rustic feel is located on a quiet residential road beside Lake Ciriss. Rooms are small, with somewhat cramped bathrooms. Breakfasts are hearty and the owners are keen to help their guests. Fishing equipment is available for hire, and there is ice fishing in winter. **www.aglonascakuli.lv**

DAUGAVPILS Leo
P 🍴 🍴　　　　　　　　　　　　　　Ⓛ

Krāslavas iela 58, LV-5403 **Tel** *6542 6565* **Fax** *6542 5325* **Rooms** *5*　**Road Map** *E4*

A regular winner of local tourist board awards, Leo is a small and centrally located hotel housed in a well-restored building. Organized in a motel style, the five rooms are arranged around the small car park. The clean, comfortable and reasonably sized rooms have en-suite bathrooms. The staff are friendly and helpful.

DAUGAVPILS Sventes Muiža
P 🍴 🍴　　　　　　　　　　　　　　ⓁⓁ

Alejas 7, Svente, LV-5473 **Tel** *6542 7822* **Fax** *6549 7322* **Rooms** *12*　**Road Map** *E4*

Sventes Muiža is an impressively restored manor house, complete with wooden floors and old tiled stoves. Each room is named after a month of the year and decorated accordingly. Facilities include two saunas, a gym and a separate smoking room. There is also a museum of military vehicles. **www.sventehotel.lv**

DAUGAVPILS Villa Ksenija
P 🍴 ♿ 🍴　　　　　　　　　　　　ⓁⓁ

Varšavas iela 17, LV-5404 **Tel** *6543 4317* **Rooms** *6*　　　**Road Map** *E4*

Standard bedrooms in this restored mansion, which dates from 1876, are tastefully decorated, although not as elegant as the common areas. The white bedding is, however, notably crisp. The executive suite has its own sauna and Jacuzzi. Hotel services include laundry, ticket booking and a concierge. **www.villaks.lv**

GAUJA NATIONAL PARK Province
Niniera iela 6, Cēsis, LV-4101 **Tel** *6412 0849* **Rooms** *5*

Road Map D3

This small guest house is close to Maija Park, a short walk from the centre of town. The rooms are simple but cosy and clean. The restaurant, located in a conservatory and with a terrace for summer, is popular with locals. There is also a playground for children. Breakfast is not included.

GAUJA NATIONAL PARK Sigulda
Pils 6, Sigulda, LV-2150 **Tel** *6797 2263* **Fax** *6797 1443* **Rooms** *44*

Road Map D3

One of the few establishments in town to enjoy a central location, this hotel offers unexceptional rooms at a reasonable price. The common areas are more interesting, particularly the small indoor bridges which link the 100-year-old hotel to its more modern annexe. There is paid Wi-Fi access. **www.hotelsigulda.lv**

GAUJA NATIONAL PARK Kārļa Muiža
Drabešu pagasts, Cēsis, LV-4138 **Tel** *6419 3330* **Fax** *6419 3310* **Rooms** *8*

Road Map D3

Housed in a converted 19th-century estate building, this place offers accommodation in apartments of different sizes, each with a kitchen. Breakfast is available on request. The hotel has 30 ha (74 acres) of land, and bicycles, quad bikes and boating equipment can be hired. Transfers and babysitters can be provided. **www.karlamuiza.lv**

GAUJA NATIONAL PARK Kolonna Hotel Cēsis
Vienības laukums 1, Cēsis, LV-4101 **Tel** *6412 0122* **Fax** *6412 0121* **Rooms** *40*

Road Map D3

Excellently located in the centre of town, the rooms are neutrally decorated, and some have pleasant views of the park in front. Studio rooms are worth the additional cost. The formal restaurant is only open in summer, while the café in the basement operates year-round. **www.hotelkolonna.com**

GAUJA NATIONAL PARK Lāču Miga
Gaujas iela 22, Līgatne, LV-4110 **Tel** *6415 3481* **Rooms** *13*

Road Map D3

This hotel takes its name, "Bear's Den", rather seriously, with teddy bears of all sizes placed throughout the wooden building. It is well above par for rural Latvia, with superior rooms equipped with sofas and large bathtubs. The restaurant Lāču Miga *(see p336)* is worth visiting in its own right. **www.lacumiga.lv**

GAUJA NATIONAL PARK Spa Hotel Ezeri
Sigulda pagasts, Sigulda, LV-2150 **Tel** *797 3009* **Fax** *6797 3880* **Rooms** *29*

Road Map D3

A modern hotel influenced by Scandinavian design, featuring a lot of wood. The spa centre includes indoor and outdoor pools, saunas and aroma baths and offers a range of massages. The restaurant, with a pleasant terrace for summer dining, serves Modern European cuisine. The gardens are attractive when in bloom. **www.hotelezeri.lv**

IKŠĶILE Meidrops
Rīgas iela 18, LV-5052 **Tel** *6503 6547* **Tel** *6503 0612* **Rooms** *16*

Road Map D3

A well-appointed riverside hotel and recreation centre on the route between Rīga and Daugavpils, with facilities including a swimming pool, sauna, Jacuzzi and children's playground. The restaurant is housed in a log cabin. There are views from the hotel of the ruins of Ikšķile Church, the oldest in Latvia. **www.meidrops.lv**

JĒKABPILS Hercogs Jēkabs
Brīvības iela 182/184, LV-5201 **Tel** *6523 3433* **Fax** *6523 3432* **Rooms** *6*

Road Map D4

This 19th-century red-brick building beside the Daugava river has an excellent location in the centre of town. Rooms are spacious and decorated in soothing pastel shades; some have sloping ceilings and wooden pillars. Many of the rooms offer stunning views of the river. The restaurant downstairs is cosy. **www.jnami.lv**

KOKNESE Baltā Gliemežnīca
Kokneses pagasts, LV-5113 **Tel** *2923 8990* **Rooms** *14*

Road Map D4

Bedrooms here are clean, bright and airy. The views of the surrounding area are excellent, and the hotel can arrange hire of boats, bicycles and other equipment. There are also volleyball and badminton nets. The restaurant menu has some surprises, such as venison *carpaccio* and dishes containing crocodile. **www.gliemeznica.lv**

KRĀSLAVA Priedaine
Klusā iela 2, LV-5601 **Tel** *2643 0798* **Rooms** *5*

Road Map E4

This small and popular guest house is located on the bank of the Daugava river, just across from the centre of town. Fishing can be arranged here, as can raft trips along the Daugavas Loki, a series of bends in the Daugava river. The area around it is a nature reserve with horses and bicycles available for hire.

LIELVĀRDE Lielvārdes Osta
Krasta iela 2, LV-5070 **Tel** *6505 3041* **Fax** *6505 4041* **Rooms** *9*

Road Map D4

With mooring for boats on the Daugava river, this friendly hotel boasts Lielvārdes Osta *(see p337)*, one of the best restaurants in town. Rooms are small but cosy and all come with a different theme. Pop Art, for example, is decorated with zigzag patterns. Some rooms do not have space for a wardrobe. **www.lielvardesosta.lv**

LIMBAŽI Birīņu Pils
Birīņi, LV-4014 **Tel** *6402 4034* **Fax** *6402 4035* **Rooms** *27*

Road Map D3

Built in 1860 in Neo-Gothic style, this manor house has been immaculately restored. The bedrooms in the main building are usually available only for events such as weddings; other guests stay in the gardener's house, which is also luxurious. Boats, bicycles and horses are available for hire. **www.birinupils.lv**

Key to Price Guide *see p300* **Key to Symbols** *see back cover flap*

LUDZA Cirmas Ezerkrasts

P 🏃 🌊 Ⓛ

Zvirgzdenes pagasts, LV-4600 **Tel** *2833 2523* **Fax** *6462 2756* **Rooms** *18* **Road Map** *E3*

The centrepiece of this recreation complex is a row of attractive log cabins overlooking Lake Cirmas, each with a living room, including fireplace, TV, Wi-Fi and sofa-bed, kitchen and three bedrooms. There is also a guest house with three double rooms, a kitchen and shared bathroom. **www.cirmasezerkrasts.lv**

LUDZA Dzerkaļi

P 🏃 ♿ 🌊 ⒷⓁ

Cirmas pagasts, LV-5701 **Tel** *2632 4735* **Rooms** *9* **Road Map** *E3*

This complex on the shore of Lake Cirmas includes nine log cabins which are self-catering, but food can also be ordered. There are plans to add a guest house. The cabins are comfortable and good value, although the furniture is slightly dated. Facilities include jet-ski rental, Russian sauna and Japanese-style hot tub. **www.dzerkali.lv**

PREIĻI Pie Pliča

P �🍽 🏃 📋 ♿ 🌊 Ⓛ

Raiņa bulvāris 9, LV-5301 **Tel** *2912 1689* **Fax** *6530 7075* **Rooms** *10* **Road Map** *E4*

Housed in the town's first hospital, an attractive wooden building with a veranda, Pie Pliča is the most highly regarded hotel in Preiļi. Many bedrooms are located under the eaves, and are simple but pleasant. Antique jugs and agricultural implements are displayed in the communal areas. There is also a sauna.

RĀZNA Rāzna

P �🍽 ♨ 🏃 ♿ 🌊 Ⓛ

28 km (17 miles) S of Rēzekne, LV-4622 **Tel** *2999 4444* **Fax** *6466 7288* **Rooms** *30* **Road Map** *E4*

Located on the banks of Lake Rāzna, this hotel complex is one of Latvia's largest recreation centres and includes spacious hotel rooms as well as six well-appointed villas. Activities available include boat and bicycle rental, fishing and horse-riding. The sauna has a glass wall for viewing the lake. **www.razna.lv**

RĒZEKNE Latgale

P ⍐🍽 🌊 Ⓛ

Atbrīvošanas alēja 98, LV-4601 **Tel** *6462 2180* **Rooms** *80* **Road Map** *E4*

This Soviet-era block has been extensively renovated in recent years, offering a range of decent rooms at good prices. The local tourist information office is located within the building, as is one of the best restaurants in town, also called Latgale *(see p337)*. There is also a bar with pool tables in the basement. **www.latgalehotel.lv**

RĒZEKNE Kolonna Hotel Rēzekne

P ⍐🍽 🌊 ⒷⓁ

Brīvības iela 2, LV-4600 **Tel** *6460 7820* **Fax** *6460 7825* **Rooms** *41* **Road Map** *E4*

Reopened after extensive renovation in 2005, this hotel has retained its original impressive 1940s façade but has been significantly modified inside. Rooms are clean and businesslike in appearance, with international TV and Wi-Fi access. There is also a beauty salon. **www.hotelkolonna.com**

SALACGRĪVA Rakari

P ⍐🍽 ♨ 🏃 ♿ 🌊 ⒷⓁ

Svētciems, LV-4033 **Tel** *6407 1122* **Fax** *2721 7254* **Rooms** *40* **Road Map** *D3*

Signposted by a giant yellow chair in a roadside field, this fully-featured recreation complex includes a hotel and restaurant in a huge barn-like building, 16 cottages (each for four people) and space for camping. Equipment can be hired for windsurfing and kitesurfing boards. Cross-country skiing in winter. **www.rakaricamp.lv**

SAULKRASTI Marve

P ⍐🍽 🏃 ♿ 🌊 ⒷⓁ

Rīgas iela 28, LV-2160 **Tel** *6795 1960* **Fax** *6795 1950* **Rooms** *22* **Road Map** *D3*

A short walk from the beach, this brightly coloured hotel offers two-room suites with balconies as standard. Pine furniture predominates, and all rooms come with TVs. Deluxe rooms include bathtubs and terraces. The hotel also has a Jacuzzi and sauna. Bicycles are available for hire. The restaurant specializes in Italian dishes. **www.marve.lv**

SAULKRASTI Medzābaki

P ⍐🍽 🏃 📋 ♿

Medzābaki-2, Carnikavas pagasts, LV-2163 **Tel** *6714 7070* **Fax** *6714 6061* **Rooms** *40* **Road Map** *D3*

With a wonderful location on the edge of Lake Lilaste, this complex includes a large thatch-roofed hotel, 14 self-contained holiday cottages and leisure facilities perfect for children. Unspoilt beaches on the Baltic Coast are just a ten-minute walk across the sand dunes. **www.medzabaki.lv**

STĀMERIENA Vonadziņi

P ⍐🍽 ♨ 🏃 ♿ 🌊 Ⓛ

Skolas iela 1, LV-4406 **Tel** *6447 1151* **Rooms** *17* **Road Map** *E3*

This recreation centre alongside Lake Ludza incorporates two thatch-roofed wooden guest houses and a bath-house with a sauna, pool and two bedrooms. The pleasant bedrooms come in a range of sizes, some with fantastic lake views. A wide range of activities are on offer, including boating and horse-riding. **www.vonadzini.lv**

VALMIERA Dikļu Pils

P ⍐🍽 🏃 ♿ 🌊 ⒷⓁ

Dikļi, LV-4223 **Tel** *6420 7480* **Fax** *6420 7485* **Rooms** *30* **Road Map** *D3*

Every room in this beautifully restored late 19th-century manor house is luxurious. There are many options for relaxation, with a sauna, steam room, whirlpool bath, swimming pool and billiards room with pool and snooker tables. There are plans to develop the 20 ha (50 acres) of parkland for sports and recreation. **www.diklupils.lv**

VALMIERA Wolmar

P ⍐🍽 📋 ♿ 🌊 ⒷⓁ

Tērbatas iela 16a, LV-4200 **Tel** *6420 7301* **Fax** *6420 7305* **Rooms** *30* **Road Map** *D3*

Taking the former name of the city, this large hotel with spacious rooms is a short walk from the main tourist sights. Unusually for a provincial Latvian hotel, the reception desk sells essentials such as toothpaste. The stylishly retro café is decorated with illuminated maps of Latvia. **www.hotelwolmar.lv**

Choosing a Hotel in Lithuania

These hotels have been selected for their good value, facilities and location. They are listed by region, starting with Vilnius, followed by the rest of Lithuania. Under each town or area, hotels are listed alphabetically within each price category. For Vilnius map references, see pages 246–7; for road map references see inside back cover.

PRICE DETAILS
The following price ranges are for a standard double room for one night during the high season. Breakfast is included, unless otherwise specified.
ⓛ Under 150 Lt
ⓛⓛ 150–300 Lt
ⓛⓛⓛ 300–450 Lt
ⓛⓛⓛⓛ 450–600 Lt
ⓛⓛⓛⓛⓛ Over 600 Lt

VILNIUS

Litinterp
P   ⓛ
Bernardinų 7/2, 01124 **Tel** *212 3850* **Fax** *212 3559* **Rooms** *16*   **Map** *2 E3*

Boasting a prime spot close to the Church of St Anne, this two-star hotel offers perhaps the cheapest and smallest rooms in the Old Town. However, it is a peaceful spot to spend a night. The rooms are well equipped, with refrigerator, tea- and coffee-making facilities and phone. Some rooms have en-suite bathrooms. **www.litinterp.com**

Paupio Namai
P   ⓛ
Paupio 31a, 01134 **Tel** *264 3113* **Fax** *264 3112* **Rooms** *25*   **Map** *2 F4*

A range of budget accommodation, from shared dormitories to basic, clean apartments with en-suite bathrooms, characterizes Paupio Namai. One of Vilnius's few genuine hostels, this huge grey house on the edge of the Užupis district, a few steps from the Old Town, has a communal kitchen and laundry room. **www.paupio.lt**

Victoria
P   ⓛ
Saltoniškių 56, 08105 **Tel** *272 4013* **Fax** *272 4320* **Rooms** *42*   **Map** *1 A1*

One of the most comfortable budget options in town, Victoria is located in the leafy district of Žverynas. It is a pleasant 30-minute walk away from the Old Town, but the Scandinavian management ensures that guests have a decent breakfast before they leave and the benefits of a cosy bar on their return. **www.victoria.lt**

Amicus
P ⑪ ⚡   ⓛⓛ
Kaminkelio 15, 02182 **Tel** *237 5880* **Fax** *283 3980* **Rooms** *20*

A modern-looking mansion located midway between the airport and city centre, this is a pleasant economy-class hotel, with helpful English-speaking staff. Facilities include a bar-restaurant and a sauna that can be hired by the hour. Guests should opt for a taxi rather than a bus to get to town. **www.amicushotel.lt**

Centrum Uniquestay
P ⚡   ⓛⓛ
Vytenio 9/25, 03113 **Tel** *268 3300* **Fax** *213 2760* **Rooms** *100*   **Map** *1 B5*

Tucked away in a fairly quiet street, this well-located hotel is just a 20-minute walk away from the Old Town. The elegant rooms are all equipped with flat-screen computers with free Internet access, as well as satellite TV, telephone, minibar, and complimentary tea- and coffee-making facilities. **www.uniquestay.com**

Domus Maria
P ♿ ⚡   ⓛⓛ
Aušros vartų 12, 01129 **Tel** *264 4880* **Fax** *264 4878* **Rooms** *39*   **Map** *2 D5*

One of the loveliest budget options in Vilnius, this former nunnery, tucked unobtrusively in a quiet courtyard, is close to the Gates of Dawn, with some rooms overlooking this landmark. Every room has a TV, Internet connection and en-suite bathroom. Some rooms have bathrooms adapted for disabled guests. **www.domusmaria.lt**

Ecotel Vilnius
P ♿ ⚡   ⓛⓛ
Slucko 8, 09312 **Tel** *210 2700* **Fax** *210 2707* **Rooms** *168*   **Map** *2 D2*

Situated on a quiet street across the river from the Old Town, Ecotel is a pleasant and unfussy two-star hotel. All rooms come with en-suite bathroom and TV. There are special rooms for guests with disabilities or allergies. With magnificent views of Vilnius, it is popular with both leisure and business travellers. **www.ecotel.lt**

Europa City Vilnius
P ⑪ 🌲 ▤ ♿ ⚡   ⓛⓛ
Jasinskio 14, 01112 **Tel** *251 4477* **Fax** *251 4476* **Rooms** *128*   **Map** *1 B2*

A tranquil place amid some of the capital's noisiest roads, modern-looking Europa City Vilnius is a perfect business-class hotel. It features comfortable rooms and spacious, well-appointed meeting rooms. The Old Town is about a 15-minute walk away, best accessed down Gedimino Avenue. **www.europacity.lt**

Apia
P ⚡   ⓛⓛⓛ
Šv Ignoto 12, 01120 **Tel** *212 3426* **Fax** *212 3618* **Rooms** *12*   **Map** *2 D3*

This tiny hotel is essentially an intimate guest house with an unbeatable location amid the spires of the Old Town. The rooms lack safes and minibars, but free access to the Internet and free parking facilities are available. Rooms at the front face an often-crowded street, but those at the back face a quiet courtyard. **www.apia.lt**

Key to Symbols *see back cover flap*

Barbacan Palace

P 11 🗐 🕭 �─── ⓛⓛⓛ

Bokšto 19, 01126 **Tel** *266 0840* **Fax** *266 0841* **Rooms** *33*   **Map** *2 E4*

This hotel is tucked away in one of the Old Town's darker, less visited lanes. Its best rooms boast a fine view across Užupis. Facilities include air-conditioned rooms and free Internet connection. It also has the odd distinction of having a bowling alley in the basement. **www.barbacan.lt**

Dvaras

P 11 🗐 �─── ⓛⓛⓛ

Tilto 3, 01101 **Tel** *210 7370* **Fax** *261 8783* **Rooms** *8*   **Map** *2 D3*

A classy guest house close to Vilnius Cathedral, Dvaras means, "manor house". However, the interiors resemble a richly designed country cottage, with creaky floors, thick carpets and elegant furnishings. Excellent meals are served in a cosy but little-visited cellar restaurant. **www.dvaras.lt**

Grybas House

P �─── ⓛⓛⓛ

Aušros vartų 3a, 01129 **Tel** *261 9695* **Fax** *212 2416* **Rooms** *10*   **Map** *2 D5*

This family-run guest house offers unpretentious, spacious rooms spruced up with personal touches. Heated bathroom floors and Wi-Fi Internet access are among its perks. Importantly for the Old Town, there is also secure parking in the courtyard. Prices are very reasonable for the location. **www.grybashouse.com**

Novotel Vilnius

11 ♨ 木 🗐 🕭 �─── ⓛⓛⓛ

Gedimino 16, 01103 **Tel** *266 6200* **Fax** *266 6201* **Rooms** *159*   **Map** *1 B2*

Despite its massive size, this relatively new addition to Gedimino Avenue maintains an intimate feel in its rooms, with tea- and coffee-making facilities and spacious bathrooms. The gorgeous views from the upper floors are an added attraction. The French-style restaurant, Garden Brasserie, serves well-prepared meals. **www.novotel.com**

Reval Hotel Lietuva

P 11 ♨ 木 🗐 🕭 �─── ⓛⓛⓛ

Konstitucijos, 09308 **Tel** *272 0200* **Fax** *272 6210* **Rooms** *291*   **Map** *1 C1*

One of Vilnius's lofty landmarks, the concrete-block Lietuva has been transformed by the pan-Baltic Reval Hotels chain into a radiant Scandinavian masterpiece. Friendly staff, Wi-Fi access, a lively lobby, a stunning view from the top-floor bar and the superb Riverside restaurant *(see p340)* add to the experience. **www.revalhotels.com**

Rinno

P �─── ⓛⓛⓛ

Vingrių 25, 01141 **Tel** *262 2828* **Fax** *262 5929* **Rooms** *17*   **Map** *1 C4*

A luxurious three-star hotel on the edge of the Old Town, Rinno is enthusiastically rated by many guests and has a high number of return visits. The rooms are cosy and spotless, the bathrooms huge and the service professional. Free Wi-Fi, secure parking and an optional bodyguard service are also available. **www.rinno.lt**

Scandic Hotel Neringa

P 11 ♨ 🗐 🕭 �─── ⓛⓛⓛ

Gedimino 23, 01103 **Tel** *268 1910* **Fax** *261 4160* **Rooms** *60*   **Map** *1 B2*

A fantastic combination of space, light and practicality is evident at the Scandic Hotel Neringa. The Nordic region's leading hotel chain renovated the age-old Hotel Neringa in 2001, preserving much of its original design. There is a mini-pool and sauna, besides a 1960s-themed retro disco called Neringa Café-Bar. **www.scandic-hotels.com**

Senatoriai

P 11 ⓛⓛⓛ

Tilto 2a, 01101 **Tel** *212 6491* **Fax** *212 6372* **Rooms** *11*   **Map** *2 D3*

An unassuming guest house, Senatoriai retains its simplicity, despite its location close to Vilnius Cathedral. Heavy wooden furnishing and flooring give it an ornate, old-fashioned feel. Standard services, including Wi-Fi access, laundry services and airport transfer, are available. **www.senatoriai.lt**

Atrium

11 ♨ 🗐 �─── ⓛⓛⓛⓛ

Pilies 10, 01123 **Tel** *210 7777* **Fax** *210 7770* **Rooms** *28*   **Map** *2 D3*

Sumptuously spacious suites and apartments, together with a location close to Vilnius Cathedral, are the main selling points of Atrium. The standard rooms are small but reasonably priced for the place. The ground floor has an excellent Argentinian-themed restaurant, El Gaucho Sano *(see p340)*. **www.atrium.lt**

Centrum Hotels Artis

P 11 ♨ 🗐 �─── ⓛⓛⓛⓛ

Liejyklos 11/23, 01120 **Tel** *266 0366* **Fax** *266 0377* **Rooms** *120*   **Map** *2 D3*

Located in the very centre of the Old Town, Centrum Hotels Artis places a heavy accent on fine furnishings and oil paintings. It is a lovely place, with impressively sized rooms, Wi-Fi and conference facilities. All the main attractions as well as the shopping and business streets are within walking distance. **www.centrumhotels.com**

Conti

P 11 ♨ 🗐 �─── ⓛⓛⓛⓛ

Raugyklos 7/2, 01140 **Tel** *251 4111* **Fax** *251 4100* **Rooms** *88*   **Map** *2 C5*

Located on the edge of the Old Town, Conti offers spa breaks and special packages for newly-weds. For regular guests, there is little missing in the comfortable rooms, particularly the luxury room. The garret rooms are an excellent low-cost option for those travelling alone. **www.contihotel.lt**

Crowne Plaza Vilnius

P 11 ♨ 木 🗐 🕭 �─── ⓛⓛⓛⓛ

Čiurlionio 84, 03100 **Tel** *274 3400* **Fax** *274 3411* **Rooms** *108*   **Map** *1 A3*

A towering five-star hotel where the upper floors offer sweeping views of the cityscape. The in-house amenities are extensive, but Wi-Fi is only available on some floors. There is also a restautant on the 16th floor. The pine-covered Vingis Park is close by and the Old Town is a 20-minute walk away. **www.cpvilnius.com**

Europa Royale Vilnius
Aušros vartų 6, 01129 **Tel** 266 0770 **Fax** 261 2000 **Rooms** 39   **Map** 2 D5

With a fantastic location close to the Gates of Dawn, Europa Royale Vilnius is a tastefully designed four-star hotel with innovatory facilities such as in-room spas, beauty treatments and babysitting services. The Druskininkai restaurant (see p341) serves delightful cuisine. **www.europaroyale.com**

Grotthuss
Ligoninės 7, 01134 **Tel** 266 0322 **Fax** 266 0323 **Rooms** 20   **Map** 1 C4

Luxury furniture, goose-feather beds and en-suite bathrooms with Spanish tiles and heated floors add a touch of glamour to the usual facilities such as Wi-Fi access, minibar, TV and safe. A location on one of Old Town's tranquil cobblestoned streets and a superb restaurant are further attractions. **www.grotthusshotel.com**

Holiday Inn Vilnius
Šeimyniškių 1, 09312 **Tel** 210 3000 **Fax** 210 3001 **Rooms** 134   **Map** 2 E1

Efficient and professionally run, Holiday Inn Vilnius stands on a busy city intersection, although the rooms have blackout curtains and soundproof windows. Guests can select from a variety of pillows from the pillow menu. Prices are high, in relation to the hotel's location. **www.holidayinnvilnius.lt**

Hotel Klaipėda
Styokos-Gucevičiaus 3, 01120 **Tel** 210 7461 **Fax** 210 7460 **Rooms** 77   **Map** 2 D3

A gleaming structure overlooking Cathedral Square, Hotel Klaipėda has rooms with tea- and coffee-making facilities, Wi-Fi Internet access and TVs, as well as heated bathroom floors. Sofi L, the hotel's restaurant, prides itself on its fresh seafood flown in from Italy. **www.citypark.lt**

Mabre Residence
Maironio 13, 01124 **Tel** 212 2087 **Fax** 212 2240 **Rooms** 41   **Map** 2 E4

One of the Old Town's most enchanting hotels, Mabre Residence is set in a former monastery. Fully enclosed in a peaceful courtyard, it is surrounded by church spires. The hotel's beauty centre offers facials, manicures and massages. Its restaurant, Steakhouse Hazienda, serves good steak, wine and beer. **www.mabre.lt**

Narutis
Pilies 24, 01123 **Tel** 212 2894 **Fax** 262 2882 **Rooms** 50   **Map** 2 D3

Each plush room here is individually decorated in luscious colours. Unique frescoes, wall paintings, original 16th-century beamed ceilings and Gothic vaults add to its charm. French designer Anne Toulous selected soft, noise-absorbing carpets for the rooms and corridors. Two suites even have a hammam and Jacuzzi. **www.narutis.com**

Ramada Vilnius
Subačiaus 2, 01127 **Tel** 255 3355 **Fax** 255 3311 **Rooms** 55   **Map** 2 E4

One of the Old Town's newest hotels, Ramada Vilnius is part of the Wyndham Hotel Group. The well-appointed rooms have DVD players and satellite TV, as well as free high-speed Internet access and a minibar. Some of the rooms facing the street may be noisy. **www.ramadavilnius.lt**

Shakespeare Boutique Hotel
Bernardinų 8/8, 01124 **Tel** 266 5885 **Fax** 266 5886 **Rooms** 31   **Map** 2 E3

The Shakespeare Boutique Hotel, with its Sonnets restaurant (see p340), is a favourite among regular visitors to Vilnius. A tasteful emphasis on art and literature and polite service sets it apart. Each room is stocked with a selection of books. There are rooms named after James Joyce, Oscar Wilde and Leo Tolstoy. **www.shakespeare.lt**

Best Western Naujasis Vilnius
Konstitucijos 14, 09308 **Tel** 273 9595 **Fax** 273 9500 **Rooms** 114   **Map** 1 C1

Set amid the skyscrapers of the capital's new business district, Best Western Naujasis Vilnius is clean and efficient. It has a decent restaurant, a small fitness centre, sauna and pool and all the in-room facilities expected of a four-star hotel. Visitors should note that rooms facing the front tend to be noisy well into the night. **www.hotelnv.lt**

Le Meridien Villon Resort
19 km (12 miles) N of Vilnius, Highway A2, 03005 **Tel** 273 9700 **Fax** 273 9730 **Rooms** 189

Set amid rolling countryside, Le Meridien Villion Resort is a sprawling resort hotel. All rooms as well as the hotel's Le Paysage restaurant (see p343) overlook lakes and forests. A golf course and Lithuania's biggest conference centre contribute to the feeling of space. **www.lemeridien.lt**

Radisson SAS Astorija
Didžioji 35/2, 01128 **Tel** 212 0110 **Fax** 212 1762 **Rooms** 120   **Map** 2 D4

One of Vilnius's best hotels, the Radisson SAS Astorija provides a broad range of professionally delivered services and amenities. The Brasserie Astorija (see p340) serves modern international cuisine, while Astorija Bar offers panoramic views of the Old Town. **www.vilnius.radissonsas.com**

Relais & Châteaux Stikliai
Gaono 7, 01131 **Tel** 264 9595 **Fax** 212 3870 **Rooms** 44   **Map** 2 D4

An opulent five-star hotel on one of the Old Town's most charming narrow streets, this place exudes elegance. The rooms boast beautiful upholstery in rich fabrics and luxurious en-suite bathrooms. This is where royalty and stars come to stay, particularly in the breathtaking King Mindaugas Suite. **www.stikliaihotel.lt**

Key to Price Guide see p308 **Key to Symbols** see back cover flap

CENTRAL LITHUANIA

ALYTUS Dzūkija
Pulko 14/1, 62133 **Tel** *(315) 51 345* **Rooms** *32* | **Road Map** *D6*

Despite being renovated in 2003, all rooms in Dzūkija reflect the ambience of a typical cottage in rural Lithuania, with creaky furniture and canvases of rural scenes. However, this is the biggest hotel in Alytus, situated in the town centre. All rooms have satellite TV and separate bathrooms. **www.hoteldzukija.lt**

ALYTUS Senas Namas
Užuolankos 24, 62111 **Tel** *(315) 53 489* **Fax** *(315) 51 643* **Rooms** *25* | **Road Map** *D6*

Opened in 1997, the three-star Senas Namas is one of the more comfortable and professionally run hotels in town. Located in a quiet neighbourhood close to the town centre, it is also among the region's best. All rooms have an en-suite bathroom, Internet access and a refrigerator that doubles as a minibar. **www.senasnamas.lt**

ANYKŠČIAI Mindaugo Karūna
Liudiškių 18, 29130 **Tel** *(381) 58 520* **Fax** *(381) 58 640* **Rooms** *27* | **Road Map** *D5*

This three-star hotel at the Mindaugo Karūna leisure and sports centre is clean and contemporary. Nestled on the eastern edge of Anykščiai at the base of a hill named "Light of Good Fortune", and close to a thick oak forest, the hotel reflects tranquillity. Only the suites and deluxe rooms have Internet access. **www.mindaugokaruna.lt**

AUKŠTAITIJA NATIONAL PARK Šakarva
Šakarva, 30204 **Tel** *(386) 6871 7290* **Rooms** *10* | **Road Map** *E5*

A set of comfortable wooden cottages amid the beautiful scenery of Lake Ilgis, Šakarva, within the national park, is best visited in summer. The highlight, however, is the bath house on wheels, which is a mobile hot tub that can be delivered to the national park's campsite. Guide services are available on request. **www.sakarva.lt**

AUKŠTAITIJA NATIONAL PARK Žuvedra
Mokyklos 11, Ignalina, 30119 **Tel** *(386) 52 314* **Rooms** *10* | **Road Map** *E5*

Situated just outside Aukštaitija National Park, Žuvedra is a pretty lakeside hotel in the town of Ignalina. All rooms come with self-regulated heating, and guests can also visit the saunas and baths at the relaxation centre. The deluxe rooms, which face the outdoor terrace and the lake, are the best. **www.zuvedra.com**

AUKŠTAITIJA NATIONAL PARK Miškiniškės
Kazitiškio sen, 30252 **Rooms** *15* | **Road Map** *E5*

A gorgeous and expansive farmstead deep in the Lithuanian countryside, Miškiniškės provides a combination of comfort and isolation. Its delightful cabins and family cottages built of logs are well-equipped. The on-site restaurant prepares all kinds of meals, including delicious game dishes. **www.miskiniskes.lt**

BIRŠTONAS Audenis Guest House
Lelijų 3, 59207 **Tel** *(319) 61 300* **Fax** *(319) 61 301* **Rooms** *9* | **Road Map** *D6*

This placid hotel resembles a modern residence. Well located close to the spa resort of Birštonas, Audenis Guest House has a selection of sparsely decorated, but comfortable rooms, with TV, telephone, minibar and Internet access. Fans and ironing facilities are available on request. **www.audenis.lt**

BIRŠTONAS Sofijos Rezidencija
Jaunimo 6, 59206 **Tel** *(319) 45 200* **Fax** *(319) 45 201* **Rooms** *14* | **Road Map** *D6*

While the exceptional decoration in every room may seem extravagant to some, the four-poster beds, silk and satin quilts, and Renaissance-style paintings may make others feel like royalty. Its multicuisine restaurant serves good food in a unique ambience. **www.sofijosrezidencija.lt**

BIRŠTONAS Sonata
Algirdo 34, 59204 **Tel** *(319) 65 825* **Rooms** *22* | **Road Map** *D6*

This restful hotel is tucked away in the quietest corner of town, on the banks of the Nemunas river. The rooms, decorated in subtle pastel shades, reflect the surrounding calm. A wide variety of optional facilities such as horse-riding, tennis and canoeing are available, but most guests prefer to just relax in this peaceful environment.

DRUSKININKAI Dalija
Vasario 16-osios 1, 66118 **Tel** *(313) 51 814* **Rooms** *11* | **Road Map** *D6*

The best budget option in the spa resort town of Druskininkai, Dalija is a 19th-century wooden building. Its basic rooms and wood-panelled walls have an old-fashioned, rustic charm. All rooms come with a shower room and toilet, as well as facilities such as kettle, fridge and a TV showing the local channels.

DRUSKININKAI Regina
T Kosčiuškos 3, 66116 **Tel** *(313) 59 060* **Fax** *(313) 59 061* **Rooms** *40* | **Road Map** *D6*

Located in the town centre, Regina has a spa centre, aqua park and pleasure grounds, and is among Druskininkai's more comfortable hotels. The rooms are modestly sized but immaculately furnished. The Regina restaurant *(see p341)* offers a choice of excellent European dishes and has floor-to-ceiling windows. **www.regina.lt**

DRUSKININKAI Spa Vilnius

`P` `11` `≈` `六` `⚡`   ①①

K Dineikos 1, 66165 **Tel** *(313) 53 811* **Fax** *(313) 59 019* **Rooms** *187*   **Road Map** *D6*

Popularly regarded as Druskininkai's premier wellness centre, Spa Vilnius offers a wide range of massages, water and mud baths as well as exercise facilities. The eight-storey, four-star hotel is a refreshing and sparklingly clean retreat. It is a favourite with families because of its in-house nanny and kids' games room. **www.spa-vilnius.lt**

DRUSKININKAI Europa Royale Druskininkai

`P` `11` `≈` `六` `目` `&` `⚡`   ①①①

Vilniaus 7, 66119 **Tel** *(313) 42 221* **Fax** *(313) 42 223* **Rooms** *101*   **Road Map** *D6*

Housed in a renovated 19th-century building, this hotel is part of the four-star Europa chain. It is directly connected to one of the resort's best spas, so that curative muds, mineral waters and beauty treatments are just a few steps away. There is a good restaurant, a café and a summer courtyard. **www.europaroyale.com**

KAUNAS Kaunas Archdiocese Guesthouse

`P` `11` `⚡`   ①

Rotušės 21, 44279 **Tel** *(37) 322 597* **Fax** *(37) 320 090* **Rooms** *21*   **Road Map** *D5*

Although the rooms at this guest house are simple and sparsely furnished, they are clean and boast spectacular views of the surrounding Old Town. Internet access is available and there are many good restaurants nearby. It is, therefore, a good choice for the budget-conscious. **www.kaunas.lcn.lt**

KAUNAS Apple Economy Hotel

`P` `⚡`   ①①

M Valančiaus 19, 44275 **Tel** *(37) 321 404* **Rooms** *14*   **Road Map** *D5*

A convenient Old Town location, cosy atmosphere and reasonable rates make the Apple Economy Hotel a very pleasant budget option for a short stay in Kaunas. Breakfast is not included in the room rate but can be ordered for a small charge. The hotel also has a small souvenir museum. **www.applehotel.lt**

KAUNAS Nemunas Tour

`目` `P` `六` `⚡`   ①①

Gėlių 50, Ringaudai, 44324 **Tel** *(37) 563 766* **Fax** *(37) 563 863* **Rooms** *6*   **Road Map** *D5*

A short drive from Kaunas and the Via Baltica motorway, Nemunas Tour is a comfortable and well-run guest house. It offers a huge range of activities from organized sightseeing to sports and is a good way to experience the best of the countryside and city. Hearty home-made meals can be ordered. **www.nemunastour.com**

KAUNAS Daugirdas

`P` `11` `≈` `目` `&` `⚡`   ①①①

T Daugirdo 4, 44279 **Tel** *(37) 301 561* **Fax** *(37) 301 562* **Rooms** *48*   **Road Map** *D5*

Located a stone's throw from most of Kaunas's sights, Daugirdas is a four-star hotel housed in a tastefully restored building. The comfortable, well-furnished rooms are well equipped, with Internet access, minibar and even air conditioning. Its Gothic-style basement, decorated with frescoes, has three restaurants. **www.daugirdas.lt**

KAUNAS Sfinksas

`P` `11` `⚡`   ①①①

Aukštaičių kudirkos 55/19a, 03000 **Tel** *(37) 301 982* **Fax** *(37) 301 983* **Rooms** *12*   **Road Map** *D5*

Although Sfinksas is a short drive away from the city centre, it is a pleasant, though slightly quirky, place to stay. Each room is uniquely decorated, while the overall eccentric design is a good example of Baltic idiosyncrasy. The restaurant is excellent and the staff are exceptionally helpful. **www.sfinksas.lt**

KAUNAS Best Western Santakos

`P` `11` `≈` `目` `⚡`   ①①①①

J Gruodžio 21, 44293 **Tel** *(37) 302 702* **Fax** *(37) 330 2700* **Rooms** *92*   **Road Map** *D5*

Set in an elegant historic red-brick building in the heart of the Old Town, this four-star hotel offers quality. The wonderful interiors and cosy rooms are matched by excellent service and a range of facilities. The restaurant is among the best in Kaunas and serves artfully garnished dishes in a Persian-themed ambience. **www.santaka.lt**

KAUNAS Reval Hotel Neris

`P` `11` `⚡`   ①①①①

K Donelaičio 27, 44240 **Tel** *(37) 306 100* **Fax** *(37) 306 200* **Rooms** *208*   **Road Map** *D5*

Opened in 2008, this is sprawling, contemporarily designed hotel has the city's biggest conference centre, with eight halls that can together seat up to 1,000 people. The hotel's Diverso restaurant serves fresh Mediterranean cuisine while the Ginger bar offers fine service. **www.revalhotels.com**

KĖDAINIAI Grėjaus Namas

`P` `11` `目` `&`   ①①

Didžioji 36, 57257 **Tel** *(34) 751 500* **Fax** *(34) 767 154* **Rooms** *18*   **Road Map** *D5*

Perhaps the best place to stay in the sleepy town of Kėdainiai, this boutique hotel is well appointed and elegantly furnished. It is housed in an 18th-century building constructed by Scots. The business and deluxe rooms are air conditioned and there is also a special room for disabled guests. **www.grejausnamas.lt**

MARIJAMPOLĖ Sudavija

`P` `⚡`   ①①

Sodo 1a, 68295 **Tel** *(343) 52 995* **Fax** *(343) 52 926* **Rooms** *10*   **Road Map** *C6*

Excellently located in an attractive part of the town centre, Sudavija is popular among businesspeople and tourists. The well-appointed rooms, with satellite TV channels and telephones, reflect a cosy, homey ambience. The on-site restaurant serves good food and the service is efficient. **www.sudavija.com**

MOLĖTAI LAKELAND Apple Island

`目` `P` `⚡`   ①①

Lake Grabuostas, Žalvariai village, 33284 **Tel** *(383) 50 073* **Rooms** *10*   **Road Map** *D5*

Ideal for families or groups, this well-equipped and well-run campsite offers a range of two- and four-bed wooden huts. Pitches for camper vans and tents are also available. There is a huge choice of sports and leisure activities on offer. A great place for wholesome, rugged countryside fun. **www.appleisland.lt**

Key to Price Guide *see p308* **Key to Symbols** *see back cover flap*

MOLĖTAI LAKELAND Belvilis
`P` `†1` `≋` `⇌`　　　　`Ⓛ Ⓛ`

Molėtų raj Kirneilė village, 33166 **Tel** *(383) 51 098* **Fax** *(383) 51 099* **Rooms** *20*　　　**Road Map** *D5*

A luxurious lakeside complex of beautifully designed rooms and cottages, Belvilis is an ideal place for a relaxing or a romantic getaway. It has a fine restaurant, spa and beauty treatments as well as a complex of swimming pools and baths. Given its quality and idyllic surroundings, it is excellent value for money. **www.belvilis.lt**

PANEVĖŽYS Romantic
`P` `†1` `≋` `⇌`　　　　`Ⓛ Ⓛ Ⓛ`

Kranto 24, 35173 **Tel** *(45) 584 860* **Fax** *(45) 581 162* **Rooms** *39*　　　**Road Map** *D5*

An hour's drive from Vilnius and only a short one from the Via Baltica motorway, Romantic is undoubtedly among the few decent hotels in Panevėžys. Housed in a thoroughly refurbished historic building in the town centre, the hotel has a lovely swimming pool, gym and spa centre, along with a quality restaurant. **www.romantic.lt**

TRAKAI Akmeninė Rezidencija
`P` `†1` `⇌`　　　　`Ⓛ Ⓛ`

Bražuolės village, 21100 **Tel** *(698) 30 544* **Fax** *(528) 25 186* **Rooms** *10*　　　**Road Map** *D5*

This rustic-style hotel, a complex of five hotel rooms and five villas, is a divine getaway with great views of Trakai Castle. It offers cosy accommodation with lakeside Russian baths and top-quality dining. Waters ports are available in summer, while in winter the lake turns into a giant ice-skating rink. **www.akmenineuzeiga.lt**

TRAKAI Trasalis
`P` `†1` `≋` `⇌`　　　　`Ⓛ Ⓛ`

Gedimino 26, 21118 **Tel** *(528) 51 588* **Fax** *(528) 51 589* **Rooms** *103*　　　**Road Map** *D5*

A comfortable new hotel and entertainment centre, Trasalis has well-furnished rooms with Internet connection and all the usual modern facilities. It boasts a mini aquapark, spa centre, bowling and two pleasant restaurants. The hotel also offers an array of sightseeing excursions and sports activities. **www.trasalis.lt**

VARĖNA Vila Ula
`⇌` `P`　　　　`Ⓛ Ⓛ`

Burokaraistėlės village, 65383 **Tel** *(620) 32 862* **Fax** *(374) 57 579* **Rooms** *15*　　　**Road Map** *D6*

Conveniently situated for exploring Dzūkija National Park, Vila Ula nestles by a lake, surrounded by forests. It is one of the many countryside retreats that are springing up across Lithuania. Both two-bed and four-bed rooms are available, as well as a fabulous sauna. **www.vilaula.lt**

VISAGINAS Gabriella
`P` `†1`　　　　`Ⓛ Ⓛ`

Jaunystės 21, 31230 **Tel** *(386) 70 171* **Fax** *(386) 70 151* **Rooms** *17*　　　**Road Map** *E5*

Although not the most charming of hotels, Gabriella is clean and comfortable and has enough facilities to make a stay in Visaginas pleasant. All rooms come with Internet connection and satellite TV. The restaurant is surprisingly cosy, while the spa centre is small but relaxing. **www.gabriella.lt**

WESTERN LITHUANIA

CURONIAN SPIT NATIONAL PARK Santauta
`⇌` `⇌`　　　　`Ⓛ`

Kalno 36, Juodkrantė, 93102 **Tel** *(469) 53 167* **Fax** *(469) 53 349* **Rooms** *46*　　　**Road Map** *B5*

One of the best and cheapest budget options on the Curonian Spit, Santauta has fairly rudimentary rooms, but that does not affect the jovial family-holiday atmosphere. The building itself has the aura of a wooden, Eastern European mountain chalet.

CURONIAN SPIT NATIONAL PARK Ąžuolynas
`P` `†1` `≋` `大` `⇌`　　　　`Ⓛ Ⓛ`

L Rėzos 54, Juodkrantė, 93101 **Tel** *(469) 53 310* **Fax** *(469) 53 316* **Rooms** *79*　　　**Road Map** *B5*

Perhaps the closest to a resort hotel on the Curonian Spit, Ąžuolynas, directly facing the lagoon, has a swimming pool and waterslide for families to enjoy. It also has a Turkish bath, besides a tennis court and fitness centre. A heath path over the dunes leads to the Baltic Sea. **www.hotelazuolynas.lt**

CURONIAN SPIT NATIONAL PARK Inkaro Kaimas
`⇌` `目`　　　　`Ⓛ Ⓛ`

Naglių 26–1, Nida, 93123 **Tel** *(469) 52 123* **Rooms** *3*　　　**Road Map** *B5*

Reflecting the gaudy reds and blues of a traditional Nida fisherman's home, the wooden apartments of Inkaro Kaimas are delightfully positioned on the edge of the Curonian Spit. The rooms are tastefully decorated and come with satellite TV and a kitchenette. Only a few rooms have air conditioning. **www.inkarokaimas.lt**

CURONIAN SPIT NATIONAL PARK Kuršių Kiemas
`P` `≋` `大` `&` `⇌`　　　　`Ⓛ Ⓛ`

Miško 11, Juodkrantė, 05872 **Tel** *(469) 53 004* **Fax** *(469) 53 114* **Rooms** *20*　　　**Road Map** *B5*

This charming and elegant building, tucked away from the rest of Juodkrantė down a pine-shrouded road, has been a hotel for over 100 years. Originally called the Hotel Bachmann, it was a retreat for well-off Prussians. Today, the well-equipped rooms are comfortable, some with balconies and kitchenettes. **www.neringatravel.lt**

CURONIAN SPIT NATIONAL PARK Linėja
`P` `†1` `⇌`　　　　`Ⓛ Ⓛ`

Taikos 18, Nida, 93121 **Tel** *(469) 52 390* **Fax** *(469) 52 718* **Rooms** *36*　　　**Road Map** *B5*

Named after the twin flower, a plant typical of the Curonian Spit region, the three-star Linėja sits on a slope above the town of Nida. Guests can choose between catering or non-catering accommodation. The rooms are cosy and suitable for families. Bowling, billiards and cycling are among the resort's activities. **www.linejahotel.lt**

CURONIAN SPIT NATIONAL PARK Litorina

Nidas–Smiltynės 19, Nida, 05872 **Tel** *(469) 52 528* **Fax** *(469) 51 102* **Rooms** *19*   **Road Map** *B5*

Unusual for the Curonian Spit, Litorina is located on the Baltic Coast rather than with the other settlements by the lagoon. It is a classy resort hotel with tennis, sauna and gym facilities and evening entertainment. The serene and secretive location makes it popular with the Lithuanian elite. **www.litorina-dubingiai.lt**

CURONIAN SPIT NATIONAL PARK Nerija

Pamario 13, Nida, 93124 **Tel** *(469) 52 777* **Fax** *(469) 52 777* **Rooms** *57*   **Road Map** *B5*

A three-star hotel, Scandinavian-style Nerija exudes space and openness, with high-ceilinged rooms, large beds, generous windows and balconies overlooking the pine forest. Tennis, volleyball and basketball courts are nearby, while the ground-floor restaurant provides a romantic setting for dinner. **www.neringahotels.lt**

CURONIAN SPIT NATIONAL PARK Nidos Kempingas

Taikos 45a, Nida, 93121 **Tel** *(469) 52 045* **Rooms** *10*   **Road Map** *B5*

Lithuania's best-organized and most popular campsite, Nidos Kempingas also has a selection of rooms and a spacious split-level apartment – the latter with kitchenette, modern bathroom with heated floor and a security system. The range of daytime activities for families and children is hard to beat. **www.kempingas.lt**

CURONIAN SPIT NATIONAL PARK Villa Banga

Pamario 2, Nida, 93124 **Tel** *(469) 51 139* **Fax** *(469) 52 762* **Rooms** *6*   **Road Map** *B5*

Exuding peace and tranquillity, Villa Banga is a gorgeous thatch-roofed building right in the centre of Nida, close to the Curonian Lagoon. Its rooms are replete with wooden furniture and come with kitchenettes. Breakfast is optional and may cost extra. Bikes and skis can be hired, depending on the time of year. **www.nidosbanga.lt**

CURONIAN SPIT NATIONAL PARK Nidus

G D Kuverto 15, Nida, 93123 **Tel** *(469) 52 001* **Fax** *(469) 50 016* **Rooms** *27*   **Road Map** *B5*

Situated midway between the beach destinations and the town of Nida, Nidus is a 15-minute walk from the beaches and the town centre. Guests rooms, which are clean and painted in warm colours, all have a balcony. Bike rental, a pleasant restaurant and a smart conference room are among the facilities on offer. **www.nidus.lt**

KLAIPĖDA Reval Inn Klaipėda

Minijos 119, 93231 **Tel** *(46) 380 803* **Fax** *(46) 482 030* **Rooms** *84*   **Road Map** *B5*

For drivers using the nearby port or business travellers on a budget, the modern high-rise Reval Inn Klaipėda offers comfort, safety and efficiency in equal measure. All rooms have colour-coded lighting to create an ambience to match the mood of the guests. Some rooms are also equipped for disabled visitors. **www.revalinn.com**

KLAIPĖDA Klaipėda

Naujoji Sodo 1, 92118 **Tel** *(46) 404 372* **Fax** *(46) 404 373* **Rooms** *307*   **Road Map** *B5*

Commonly referred to as the K-Centre, this hotel consists of two skyscrapers, both of which are city landmarks. One of them, constructed in the Soviet-era style, is archaic yet comfortable. The second is very modern, with stunning views, sunken baths and split-level suites. **www.klaipedahotel.lt**

KLAIPĖDA Preliudija Guest House

Kepėjų 7, 91247 **Tel** *(46) 310 077* **Rooms** *6*   **Road Map** *B5*

Located in the middle of the criss-cross lanes of the Old Town, this lovely guest house is a bargain. The building dates back to the 1850s and is a protected architectural monument. The rooms, however, appear stylishly modern, and come with free Internet access. Dry-cleaning and laundry services are available. **www.preliudija.com**

KLAIPĖDA Europa Royale Klaipėda

Žvejų 21, 91247 **Tel** *(46) 404 444* **Fax** *(46) 404 445* **Rooms** *50*   **Road Map** *B5*

Overlooking the Old Town, with its romantic sights and a multitude of noisy nightlife options, Europa Royale Klaipėda could not have a better location. However, even for guests who need solitude, this four-star hotel, with its unrivalled services and soundproof windows, is an ideal choice. **www.europaroyale.com**

KLAIPĖDA Navalis

Manto 23, 92234 **Tel** *(46) 404 200* **Fax** *(46) 404 202* **Rooms** *28*   **Road Map** *B5*

Housed in a refurbished 1863 building, this four-star hotel has retained most of its architectural features. The symbolic bow of a boat in the reception area and the general ambience reflects the hotel's naval theme. The decor is formal, but restful, in soft, warm colours with mahogany and beech furniture. **www.navalis.lt**

KLAIPĖDA Vecekrug

Jūros 23, 92125 **Tel** *(46) 301 002* **Fax** *(46) 312 262* **Rooms** *23*   **Road Map** *B5*

Named after the highest point on the Curonian Spit, Vecekrug is distinguished by its combination of friendly staff and modern structure. The rooms have soundproof windows, Internet connection, minibar and bathrooms with heated floors. A wall of windows overlooks the coast while other rooms face a quiet street. **www.vecekrug.lt**

KLAIPĖDA Radisson SAS Klaipėda

Šaulių 28, 92231 **Tel** *(46) 490 800* **Fax** *(46) 490 815* **Rooms** *74*   **Road Map** *B5*

With rooms decorated in 19th-century New England maritime style, Radisson SAS Klaipėda sets high standards. Free Wi-Fi access, a top-notch restaurant and cocktail bar, as well as steam bath and fitness studio with superb equipment, complete the picture. **www.klaipeda.radissonsas.com**

Key to Price Guide *see p308* **Key to Symbols** *see back cover flap*

NEMUNAS DELTA Ventainė

P **🍴** 🔵🔵

Ventės ragas, Kintųdoyen, 99361 **Tel** *(411) 68 525* **Fax** *(411) 47 422* **Rooms** *27*   **Road Map** *B5*

A snug hotel, campsite and leisure centre on the shores of the Curonian Spit, Ventainė is close to the bird-ringing station at Ventė and a short drive from the Nemunas Delta. Boats, jet-skis, tennis courts and multiple saunas can all be rented. The small on-site restaurant sometimes closes early. **www.ventaine.lt**

PALANGA Kungis Inn

P 🌿 🔵

Užkanavės 32, 00169 **Tel** *(460) 56 310* **Rooms** *8*   **Road Map** *B5*

Tucked away in the heart of a pine forest near Palanga International Airport and a short walk from the beach, Kungis Inn is an excellent budget option. The accommodation, though fairly basic, boasts thick carpets, bathrooms with heated floors and charcoal barbeque grills on the balcony. **www.kungis.lt**

PALANGA Alanga

P **🍴** 🏊 📋 🌿 🔵🔵

S Nėries 14, 00134 **Tel** *(460) 49 215* **Fax** *(460) 49 316* **Rooms** *47*   **Road Map** *B5*

The imaginative colours of the rooms and apartments, together with comfortable furniture, make Alanga a joy to stay in. A swimming pool, along with Finnish and Turkish saunas, makes it even more inviting. The staff are polite and professional. **www.alanga.lt**

PALANGA Smelio Takas

P **🍴** 📋 🔵🔵🔵

Naglio 17, 00136 **Tel** *(460) 20 025* **Fax** *(460) 20 026* **Rooms** *8*   **Road Map** *B5*

With gently swaying pines in the background and windows overlooking the sea and golden dunes, Smelio Takas appears more like a fairytale house. It is virtually on the beach, making the seaview from some of the rooms unbeatable, especially at sunset. There is also an on-site mini-spa. **www.smeliotakas.lt**

PALANGA Mama Rosa Villa

P **🍴** 🏊 🌲 📋 🌿 🔵🔵🔵🔵

Jūratės 28a, 00133 **Tel** *(460) 48 581* **Fax** *(460) 48 580* **Rooms** *8*   **Road Map** *B5*

Sumptuously decorated in classic English style, the rooms at Mama Rosa Villa have lovely wrought-iron beds and sleek, shiny bathrooms. With its tastefully designed interiors, this place could indeed be an English country cottage. The service is courteous and the exclusive restaurant and sauna complex a delight. **www.mamarosa.lt**

PALANGA Vanagupė

P **🍴** 🏊 🌲 📋 ♿ 🌿 🔵🔵🔵🔵

Vanagupės 31, 00169 **Tel** *(460) 41 199* **Fax** *(460) 31 199* **Rooms** *98*   **Road Map** *B5*

This plush five-star beach hotel has an unbeatable range of luxury services, a classy restaurant and a sprawling spa centre. It is perfect for couples on a romantic weekend. Its L'Ambra Rossa restaurant serves classic European cuisine. **www.vanagupe.com**

PLUNGĖ Beržas

P **🍴** 🔵

Minijos 2/Telšių 2 **Tel** *(448) 56 840* **Fax** *(448) 56 840* **Rooms** *10*   **Road Map** *C5*

Although the rooms of Beržas have a faded, rustic charm, the hotel offers some of the most comfortable beds to be found between Klaipėda and Šiauliai. Breakfast is available for an extra charge. The hotel tries hard to make guests feel welcome in this sleepy town. **www.berzas.goo.lt**

ŠEDUVA Prie Ežero

📋 **P** **🍴** 🔵🔵

Raudondvaris village, Radviliškio raj, 82213 **Tel** *(422) 44 430* **Fax** *(422) 44 436* **Rooms** *15*   **Road Map** *C5*

On the Panevėžys road, a few kilometres away from Šeduva, this three-star lakeside hotel is also one of the more pleasant accommodation options in these parts. Most rooms have satellite TV. For those on a budget, a boarding school across the lake rents out rooms in summer. **www.hotelprieezero.lt**

ŠIAULIAI Saulininkas

P **🍴** 🏊 🔵

St Lukauskio 5a, 76236 **Tel** *(41) 436 555* **Fax** *(41) 421 848* **Rooms** *13*   **Road Map** *C4*

An affable hotel with reasonably priced rooms, Saulininkas is set in a quiet neighbourhood a few blocks from the Church of Sts Peter and Paul. The sauna and pool can be booked ahead for evening parties and the gym is used by locals. The restaurant also delivers food to rooms. **www.saulininkas.com**

ŠIAULIAI Grafaitės Svetainė

P **🍴** 🏊 ♿ 🔵🔵

Aušros 1, Ginkūnai, 81493 **Tel** *(41) 589 120* **Fax** *(41) 502 152* **Rooms** *21*   **Road Map** *C4*

There are two streets in Šiauliai named Aušros. This one is out of the city centre in the direction of the Hill of Crosses, making it convenient for pilgrims or for those who wish to visit this Catholic landmark. Harmoniously furnished, the little guest house has well-equipped rooms. **www.hotelgrafaite.com**

ŠIAULIAI Šaulys

P **🍴** 🏊 🔵🔵

Vasario 16–Osios 40, 76351 **Tel** *(41) 520 812* **Fax** *(41) 520 911* **Rooms** *41*   **Road Map** *C4*

Safe and secure, with bright and comfortable rooms, Šaulys is not exactly upmarket, yet it offers the classiest rooms in Šiauliai. The on-site restaurant has a reasonable wine list, the pool and sauna are refreshing and the staff can help arrange ticket reservations and do laundry, all for a small extra charge. **www.saulys.lt**

ŽEMAITIJA NATIONAL PARK Linelis

P **🍴** 🔵🔵

Paplatelės, 90483 **Tel** *687 3 5058* **Fax** *4484 9422* **Rooms** *33*   **Road Map** *C4*

By far the most pleasant accommodation in Žemaitija National Park, Linelis is situated on the northeastern shore of Lake Platelai and has its own beach. Activities on offer include pedalos, sailing and even diving excursions. A small on-site spa is another highlight. **www.linelis.lt**

WHERE TO EAT

Restaurant culture in Estonia, Latvia and Lithuania has changed dramatically in recent years. Although traditional food is still very popular, there has been a huge increase in all kinds of new restaurants specializing in everything from an eclectic international cuisine to quality pizza. The considerable rise in the diversity and standards of restaurants is comparable across the three Baltic States, although the variety of eating places is much higher in the capital cities. A few other large cities

Sign for a café in the Old Town, Vilnius

and popular resort towns also have a fairly impressive choice of dining options. Good food is an integral part of Baltic culture and the abundance of traditional-style restaurants in each country attests to the pride many people take in their national cuisine. Traditional Baltic food may not be particularly subtle, but it is tasty and makes for a hearty meal. It is often best enjoyed in the countryside where portions are generous and ingredients tend to be deliciously fresh.

TYPES OF RESTAURANTS

Restaurants and cafés in the Baltic States are locally referred to as *restoran* and *kohvik* in Estonia, *restorāns* and *kafejnīca* in Latvia, and *restoranas* and *kavinė* in Lithuania. Both types of establishments vary widely in the type of food they offer.

Restaurants can either be very luxurious and modern establishments or basic food-and-beer places that do not differ significantly from pubs. Similarly, cafés can be pleasant and stylish. Most of them offer a decent but cheap meal of hearty proportions. Sometimes they act as a meeting place for local drinkers. All cafés have a good selection of alcohol on sale. Most modern bars often have a small but good-quality menu which is available until late.

A café in Town Hall Square in the Old Town, Tallinn, Estonia

Locally-run pubs are known as *kõrts* in Estonia, *krogs* in Latvia and *baras* in Lithuania. Although rare in Tallinn, Riga and Vilnius, pubs are common in small towns and in the countryside. Sometimes, they are rustically furnished places that offer an excellent standard of traditional food and local beer. Fast food has not really taken off in the Baltic States and can only be found in central locations in the capitals.

Bakery sign in Trakai, Lithuania

DINING HOURS

The rise in restaurant culture has seen a proliferation of restaurants which keep similar opening hours throughout the Baltic States. They open between 10 and 11am and close between 11pm and midnight. In small towns, restaurants are more likely to open later

and close earlier, and in tourist resorts some restaurants are open only during summer months. Big breakfasts are rare in the Baltic States. Until quite recently, the only breakfast food available were pastries or pancakes. These days, however, restaurants offer a range of breakfasts, including variations on the English fry-up. Lunch is still the main meal of the day for many people. Nonetheless, eating out has become such a recreational habit that restaurants often fill up in the evenings, although people tend to eat early, normally between 6 and 9pm.

Café culture is big in the Baltic States. Most cafés open any time from 8 to 10am and close around 9 or 10pm, although in small towns they often close earlier. In more remote places, many cafés

Modern interior of Vincent's restaurant *(see p332)* in Riga

Atmospheric street restaurant in the Old Town, Vilnius, Lithuania

remain closed on Sundays. Pubs and cafés always have an array of snacks available.

MENUS

English-language menus are commonplace in the capital cities and tourist resorts. In small towns and the countryside, however, such menus are much scarcer. Most people in the Baltic States speak some English, so it may be possible to ask for help in deciphering the menu. After German, Russian is the most common language in Latvia and Estonia. Consequently, menus often come with German or Russian translations.

VEGETARIANS

Meat is integral to Baltic cuisine, although there is an increasing choice of vegetarian (*vegetaarlane* in Estonian, *veģetārietis* in Latvian and *vegetaras* in Lithuanian) dishes on offer in most decent restaurants. However, these vegetarian menu options are limited to the capital cities.

RESERVATIONS

Reservations are usually made by phone, although in some cases they can be made via the Internet. It is unnecessary to make lunchtime bookings, but it is sensible to reserve a table for dinner, particularly on a Friday or Saturday evening, in a good restaurant in one of the capital cities.

Menu, Tallinn's Admiral restaurant (see p322)

PRICES & PAYMENT

Restaurant prices have gone up considerably in the Baltic States, but are still comparatively lower than in other European countries. The cost of alcohol is also notably lower than in other European countries. Prices are highest in the capitals, particularly in tourist spots. Tax is always included in the price. Cover charges are quite rare, and usually only apply to restaurants or bars which include special live music sets. Cafés are the most affordable eating option, but many only accept cash. However, credit and debit card payment is becoming common throughout the Baltic States.

TIPPING

Tipping is a relatively new concept to the Baltic States. Service charges are usually included in the bill. However, some leading restaurants add a service charge to the total, which should be clearly indicated. Tipping is only expected in larger establishments with table service. The general rule is to leave 10 per cent or less of the total bill. Tipping in cafés and bars is rare.

CHILDREN

Although children are welcome in restaurants, only a few popular chains offer provisions such as half-portions. In centrally located establishments in bigger towns and cities, however, menus for children are becoming more common. It is usually possible to arrange for something off the menu to meet the children's needs.

DISABLED VISITORS

Few restaurants, besides the new ones, offer easy access for disabled people in the Baltic States. The situation, however, is improving. Tallinn is slightly ahead of Vilnius and Rīga in this regard. Hotel restaurants remain a good option for disabled visitors as they have more facilities.

SMOKING

Smoking in enclosed public spaces is usually banned in the Baltic States. The only option for smokers is to sit at an outdoor table in the summer, although some restaurants even prohibit outdoor smoking. However, a few places do permit smoking. These are identifiable by a green smoking-allowed symbol on the entrance door.

Log-cabin restaurant at the LIDO Atpūtas Centrs (see p330) in Rīga

The Flavours of Estonia, Latvia and Lithuania

Traditional Baltic cooking is hearty and filling, designed to satisfy after hard physical labour and during long, gloomy winters. In the past, staple dishes were mostly soups and porridges made with grains such as barley, although coastal communities also ate fresh and preserved fish. Meat was usually reserved for festivals. Today it is central to most dishes, typically accompanied by boiled potatoes and rye bread. Popular seasonings include garlic, onions, caraway seeds and dill. Baltic cuisines have been influenced by those of neighbouring countries, particularly Russia and Germany in Estonia and Latvia, and Poland in Lithuania.

Bunch of fresh dill

Basket of wild mushrooms gathered in the woods of Latvia

MEAT, POULTRY & GAME

Pork is on almost every Baltic menu, whether breaded and fried like a schnitzel or in the form of bacon and sausages. Roast pork has long been a festive treat. Pork fat is also eaten, often accompanied by rye bread, and several dishes, such as Lithuanian *liežuvis* (cow's tongue), stem from a time when no part of the animal could be wasted. Chicken and beef are also widely available, while game, such as wild boar, hare and venison, may be found both in rural and in upmarket urban restaurants.

FISH & SEAFOOD

Fishing has a venerable history in the Baltic States, with the long coastlines of Estonia and Latvia and an extensive network of rivers and lakes throughout the region. Many traditional recipes fell out of use during the Soviet era when most fish was exported. The Baltic sprat, in particular, was canned and eaten throughout the Soviet Union. Today, fish is usually prepared by frying or baking, but is also smoked and salted. The prevalence of this in Estonia is said to show a link with Scandinavian traditions.

Trout   Plaice   Sprats   Herrings   Salmon fillet   Bream

Some of the many varieties of fish caught in the clear Baltic waters

BALTIC DISHES AND SPECIALITIES

The long list of Baltic soups and porridges includes Latvian *putra* (porridge with pork fat, often with meat or smoked fish added). Popular sausages include Lithuanian *vedarai*, made from pig's intestines stuffed with potato. Estonia is noted for *verevoorst* (blood sausage) and *verleib* (blood bread). Latvia's signature dish is *pelēkie zirņi* (grey peas with bacon). Lithuania's *kugelis* (grated potato pudding often incorporating bacon, onion and eggs) is served with sour cream. A favourite Lithuanian snack is *kepta duona*, also known as *grauzdini* (fried rye bread with garlic) in Latvia and served with cheese. Throughout the region, you can sample Russian-style *pelmeni* (dumplings).

Red caviar on rye bread

Pīrāgi *(Latvia) and pirukas (Estonia) are small leavened pasties, usually filled with bacon or cabbage.*

Stalls in the bustling market square in Vilnius, Lithuania

Popular freshwater fish include pike, eel and elvers. Caviar is also available, including the relatively affordable red variety.

FRUIT & VEGETABLES

The Baltic climate limits the cultivation of fruit and vegetables, and they are not strongly represented in traditional recipes. By far the most common vegetable is the potato, introduced in the 18th century and now served at almost every meal. Other accompaniments include simple salads, often just cucumber and tomato. Mushrooms are popular and, every autumn, people roam the forests to gather mushrooms either to eat or to sell *(see p373)*. Cepe is preferred, although varieties such as chanterelle and

rozites caperata, meaning "gypsy mushrooms", are also picked.

Local apples, plums and pears appear in fruit pies and tarts, but the true fruit bounty of the region is its berries and currants. Picking

Freshly picked redcurrants at an Estonian farm

berries is a popular summer pastime *(see p373)*. They are eaten raw, made into tarts, puddings or compotes, or preserved for the winter.

DAIRY PRODUCE

Dairy products feature strongly in Baltic cuisine. Local butter is held in high regard, while Estonian *kefir* (fermented cow's milk) and Latvian *rūgušpiens* (curdled milk) are also very popular. Caraway cheese is eaten by Latvians, especially in midsummer. The most ubiquitous dairy product is sour cream. A base for many Baltic sauces, it is also poured directly on to a wide range of dishes.

ON THE MENU

Kartupeļu pankūkas (Latvia) Potato pancakes.

Kibinai (Lithuania) Mutton and onion pies, a speciality of the Karaim community.

Preskučiai šližikai (Lithuania) Biscuits served with poppy seed milk, on Christmas Eve.

Rossolye (Estonia) Herring, meat, beetroot and apple salad, in a whipped cream and mustard dressing.

Seljanka (Estonia) and *Soļanka* (Latvia) A soup made with meat, pickled vegetables or fish, which has Russian origins.

Zrazai (Lithuania) Thin beef rolled with onion, bread and often mushrooms, then baked.

Šaltibarščiai *(Lithuania) is a chilled soup made of beetroot, cucumber, chopped egg,* kefir *and dill.*

Cepelinai, *or "zeppelins", are meat-stuffed potato dumplings in a sour cream, onion and bacon sauce.*

Pannkoogid, *huge, fluffy pancakes served with a berry compote, show the influence of Russian cuisine.*

What to Drink

Beer is popular in the Baltic States and several of the region's breweries date back to the 19th century. Vodka is not as popular as it was during the Soviet era, although it is still widely drunk and both local and Russian brands are available. The region also has some unusual spirits and liqueurs made with herbs. Although wine-drinking does not have a distinguished history, imported wine is available in restaurants and many affordable local sparkling wines are available. The most prominent traditional soft drink, *kali* in Estonia, *kvass* in Latvia or *gira* in Lithuania, has been claimed as a historical forerunner of strong beer. Customarily made from rye bread and very mildly alcoholic, it is a refreshing alternative to aerated drinks such as cola.

Viru Valge vodka

Rīga Black Balsam, Latvia

Bobelinė, Lithuania

WINES

Although the Baltic States are not a major wine producing region, both Latvia and Lithuania produce sparkling wines, such as Rīga Šampanietis and Alita Šampanas respectively. In Estonia, mulled red wine, known as *hõõgvein* or *glögg*, is popular in winter. Served warm, it has a spicy taste due to the cinnamon and cloves used to flavour it. Fruit wines, such as Põltsamaa Kuldne, which is made from apples, are also common.

Latvia has the distinction of being in the *Guinness Book of World Records* for the northernmost open-air vineyard in the world. Sabile vineyard, Vīna kalns (*see p178*), has a long history of viniculture, but production stopped during the Soviet occupation. It has been restarted but is very limited and often the only chance to try the wine is by attending the annual wine festival in summer.

SPIRITS & LIQUEURS

The best-known Estonian liqueur is the sweet-tasting Vana Tallinn, which has ingredients such as citrus oils, cinnamon, vanilla and rum. It can be drunk neat but is worth trying in coffee or over ice cream. It is also used to make cocktails or mixed with white wine or champagne. Vodka is also popular in Estonia, and Viru Valge is the most common local brand. In addition to the original version, it is available in flavoured varieties such as vanilla, lemon and watermelon.

For visitors to Latvia, Rīga Black Balsam is an unmissable drink and makes a popular souvenir, although perhaps as much for its ceramic bottle as for the liquid inside. Developed in 1752 as a medicinal tonic, it is composed of a top-secret list of ingredients and is an acquired taste. Occasionally drunk neat, it is often mixed with cola, hot blackcurrant juice or vodka. Specialist shops, and some bars, also sell Latvian liqueurs such as the caraway-flavoured Allažu Ķimelis.

Lithuania has a range of herbal liqueurs, including Trejos Devynerios. Concocted by a pharmacist in the late 19th century, Trejos Devynerios was listed as a legal patent medicine between the two World Wars. Vodka-drinkers may want to try Starka, which is distilled from rye grain, while other traditional drinks are honey-based mead and *bobelinė*, a liqueur made with cranberry juice. In rural areas throughout the region, local people brew their own, very potent vodka. Visitors should be wary of this, as it is usually of low quality and there have been cases where batches have been contaminated with methanol. In Lithuania, a legitimate drink takes the name of this illegal vodka, Samanė, but is not as strong.

Vana Tallinn liqueur

BEER

After independence in 1991, the region's state breweries were privatized and many of them were subsequently bought by large international corporations. Baltic Beverages Holdings, jointly owned by Carlsberg and Scottish & Newcastle, owns several of the region's biggest brands, such as Saku in Estonia, Aldaris in Latvia and Utenos and Švyturys in Lithuania. The Finnish company

Rīgas sparkling wine, Latvia

Põltsamaa Kuldne fruit wine, Estonia

Glögg mulled wine, Estonia

Olvi has bought Cēsis, which is Latvia's oldest brewery, A Le Coq in Estonia and Ragutis in Lithuania. Also in Lithuania, Kalnapilis is owned by the Danish Brewery Group. These major brands predominate in both bars and shops, although some of the more popular international beers are also available in the three countries. The two main categories are light (*helein* in Estonian, *gaišais* in Latvian and *šviesus* in Lithuanian) and dark (*tume* in Estonian, *tumšais* in Latvian and *tamsus* in Lithuanian). However, the major breweries have diversified their ranges and produce everything from very light US-style ice beers to rich and dark porters such as Ragutis, a chocolate porter. Lager-drinkers will certainly find a light beer to suit their palate, although visitors often find the dark beers appealing.

The arguably more interesting products of small and medium-sized breweries do make it into some bars, particularly in the area where they are produced and in the capital cities, and larger supermarkets also often have a decent range. Estonia's islands produce stronger drinks than most of the mainland breweries, and Saaremaa *õlu* is particularly well received. Interesting breweries in Latvia include Užavas, which produces unpasteurized beers that cannot be stored for long and are not exported. Other brands worth looking out for are Piebalgas, Tērvetes and Bauskas. The LIDO chain of restaurants brew

Saku Brewery, producer of some of the most popular beer in Estonia

their own brand of beer, with a microbrewery on the premises of the huge LIDO Recreation Centre, just outside Rīga. In Lithuania, the Biržai region is known for its long-standing brewing traditions and is home to several breweries, including the popular Rinkuškiai, which has both light and dark beer.

SOFT DRINKS

The most popular soft drink in the Baltic States is a drink traditionally made from fermented rye bread and sometimes flavoured with fruit or herbs, alternatively called *kali*, *kvass* and *gira*. Strictly speaking, it is not a soft drink and is beer-like, although it has a very low alcohol content, usually about 1 per cent. It vanished from the market at the time of the collapse of the Soviet Union because of concerns about the conditions of its production and storage, since it used to be dispensed from large outdoor tanks. Once reintroduced, it proved a threat to the market dominance of Coca-Cola, which responded by buying the drink manufacturers in the three countries, who now produce Linnuse Kali, Pilskalna Kvass and Bajorų Gira.

Today, this mass-produced drink is usually made from malt extract and flavourings. Another common lunchtime drink across the region is *kefir*, a very mildly alcoholic fermented milk, which is one of the key ingredients of *šaltibarščiai* (*see p319*).

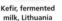

Kefir, fermented milk, Lithuania

Kvass, malted drink, Latvia

A very popular soft drink in Estonia is Tartu Limonaad, while Latvia has the very rustic *bērzu sula*, made from birch sap. It is fermented in a barrel with barley seeds sprinkled on top and sometimes rye bread crusts are added. Traditional flavourings for the juice include peppermint and sprigs of blackcurrant, while more modern additions include lemon or orange zest, raisins and cinnamon. Something else to look out for in Latvia is *veselība*, which is a soft drink sold in vessels akin to beer bottles and advertised as being fortified with an abundance of vitamins.

Saku Originaal, Estonia

Aldaris Zelta, Latvia

Kalnapilis Grand, Lithuania

Švyturys Gintarinis, Lithuania

Choosing a Restaurant in Estonia

Chosen for their impressive food, location and value
for money, these restaurants cover a wide price range.
They are listed by area, starting with Tallinn. Restaurants
within the same price category appear in alphabetical
order. For Tallinn map references, see pages 82–3; for
road map references see the inside back cover.

PRICE DETAILS
Based on the price per person of a
three-course meal with half a bottle
of wine, including cover charge,
service and tax.
Ⓚ Under 100 EEK
ⓀⓀ 100–200 EEK
ⓀⓀⓀ 200–300 EEK
ⓀⓀⓀⓀ 300–400 EEK
ⓀⓀⓀⓀⓀ Over 400 EEK

TALLINN

African Kitchen   ⓀⓀ
Uus 34, 10111 **Tel** *644 2555*   **Map** *2 D2*

The restaurant's vibrant and lively interior is matched by the excellent food, which is the most authentic African
cuisine in the Baltic States. African Kitchen is a hip, fun place to eat, with an impressively diverse menu of fresh-
tasting, spicy and exotic fare.

Amarillo   ⓀⓀ
Viru väljak 4, 10111 **Tel** *680 9280*   **Map** *1 C2*

Amarillo serves good Tex-Mex food in a relaxed environment. The menu covers everything from burritos and
fajitas to burgers and pizzas, and food can be made especially spicy on request. Lactose and gluten-free dishes
are highlighted on the menu. A popular place that mostly attracts families and large groups.

Americana   ⓀⓀ
Müürivahe 2, 10146 **Tel** *644 8837*   **Map** *2 D3*

A small restaurant, Americana specializes in thick-crust, American-style pizzas, which come with a huge variety of
toppings. The restaurant itself is small but popular, probably due to the sheer dimensions of the pizzas. Pizza and
wine can also be delivered anywhere in Tallinn.

Turg   ⓀⓀ
Mündi 3, 10146 **Tel** *641 2456*   **Map** *1 C2*

Turg means "market" in Estonian, which provides the theme for this popular cellar restaurant. The stalls, carts and
crowds give it a bustling market feel by day, but by night it is a more subdued, candlelit place. The menu offers a
number of meat dishes.

Admiral   ⓀⓀⓀ
Lootsi 15, 10151 **Tel** *662 3777*   **Map** *2 F1*

This restaurant offers a unique dining experience aboard an old steamer docked in the Tallinn passenger port. The
elegant but cosy interior boasts great views of the harbour and city through portholes, while the Balkan cuisine is
of high quality. The ship can also be chartered for cruises.

Ami-Ja   ⓀⓀⓀ
Narva mnt 36, 13628 **Tel** *646 6096*   **Map** *2 E2*

Popular with locals, Ami-Ja boasts an impressive range of quality Japanese food served up by kimono-clad
Estonian waitresses. The interior has a pleasant ambience and the service is excellent. Private rooms are available
for larger groups or special parties. Sushi can be ordered to take away.

Artemis   ⓀⓀⓀ
Pikk 35, 10133 **Tel** *644 1114*   **Map** *1 C2*

Artemis is an authentic, Greek-owned and run restaurant with all the frills. The plastic grapevines only add charm
to the homeliness of the place. The menu includes staple favourites such as moussaka and dolmades, among
others. It is one of the few places that serve ouzo, a Greek aniseed-flavoured liqueur.

Balthasar   ⓀⓀⓀ
Raekoja plats 11, 10146 **Tel** *627 6400*   **Map** *1 C2*

With superb views and a supremely elegant interior, Balthasar's speciality is an outstanding garlic-themed menu.
The restaurant is named after Balthasar Russow, who wrote *Chronicle of Livonia* on the premises. Even some
desserts contain garlic, but garlic-free dishes are also available.

Beer House   ⓀⓀⓀ
Dunkri 5, 10123 **Tel** *644 2222*   **Map** *1 C2*

A restaurant-cum-microbrewery, Beer House really does resemble an old German-style beer house. The menu
includes six kinds of sausage, along with some good meaty main courses. This place also serves the only unpasteurized beer in the country. There is live music and a sauna for up to 20 people.

Key to Symbols *see back cover flap*

Cathedral
Lossiplats 2/Toomkooli 1, 10130 **Tel** *627 6400*   **Map** *1 B3*

Cathedral takes its name from the nearby Alexander Nevsky Cathedral and is every bit as majestic. Specializing in French and Russian cuisine, the restaurant is a popular place, so book well in advance. Several alcove booths provide a more intimate setting.

Controvento
Vene 12/Katariina käik, 10123 **Tel** *644 0470*   **Map** *2 D2*

Hidden away in the beautiful Katariina Passage, Controvento is a hugely popular Italian restaurant because of its outstanding food and thoroughly charming atmosphere. The restaurant has excellent pizza and pasta along with a good choice of meat and fish dishes. Book ahead at weekends.

Dominic
Vene 10, 10123 **Tel** *641 0400*   **Map** *2 D2*

Combining a café with an Italian-inspired menu, a restaurant with a French menu and a cosy little wine cellar, Dominic is a stylish establishment with exceptionally good food. The historic and tastefully converted building dates back to the 14th century.

Elevant
Vene 5, 10123 **Tel** *631 3132*   **Map** *2 D2*

Elevant offers outstanding and imaginative fusion-style Indian fare that includes Ayurveda dishes and cross-over European elements such as moose soup and wild boar kebab. The extensive menu has plenty for vegetarians as well as more traditional Indian food. The interior is wonderfully relaxing.

Golden Dragon
Pikk 37, 10133 **Tel** *631 3506*   **Map** *1 C2*

Unarguably the best Chinese restaurant in Tallinn, Golden Dragon is housed in a cosy cellar with an extensive whitewashed vaulted ceiling. The vast menu is a dream for vegetarians, and the portions are gratifyingly large. Some Thai dishes are on offer as well. Usually fills up at weekends.

Grillhouse Daube
Rüütli 11, 10130 **Tel** *645 5531*   **Map** *1 C3*

Spread over two floors, Grillhouse Daube is an extremely pleasant place with welcoming staff. The quality menu offers a good selection of tender steaks as well as satisfying pasta and fish dishes. There are also some good-value and delicious set meals for groups of four or more.

Jasmine
Tatari 1, 10116 **Tel** *660 1842*   **Map** *2 D4*

Jasmine is a pleasant if rather unexceptional Chinese restaurant whose decor is almost cosily kitsch, with plenty of dangling lanterns and the obligatory fish tank. The menu, however, is reasonably priced and has a good choice of dishes. Also does takeaway.

Klafira
Vene 4, 10123 **Tel** *667 5144*   **Map** *2 D2*

The somewhat exorbitant prices of this Russian-themed restaurant are offset by its exuberant atmosphere and huge portions. The menu includes a few more exotic dishes than most Russian restaurants, although for large groups the set menus are a good option. Excellent live music acts at weekends.

Kuldse Notsu Kõrts
Dunkri 8, 10123 **Tel** *628 6567*   **Map** *1 C2*

Specializing in Estonian cuisine, Kuldse Notsu Kõrts is a charming cellar restaurant with an interior humorously described as "nouveau-rustic" by the owners. The menu abounds with meat, particularly pork, but there are some vegetarian options such as the Farm Girl's Stew.

Mõõkkala
Kuninga 4, 10122 **Tel** *641 8288*   **Map** *1 B5*

This aquatically themed cellar restaurant is a treat to look at and dine in. Offering, undoubtedly, the best seafood in Tallinn, Mõõkkala has a vast menu of superb dishes, from tiger shrimp kebab with red roe mousse to the signature swordfish with fried oyster.

Must Lammas
Sauna 2, 10140 **Tel** *644 2031*   **Map** *1 C3*

Must Lammas, meaning "black sheep", is a refreshingly modern Georgian restaurant, rather than the usual folksy one. The ultra-stylish interior does not, however, detract from the superb Caucasian cuisine. Try the spicy lamb soup for starters, with a classic Georgian wine such as Saperavi.

Olde Hansa
Vana turg 1, 10140 **Tel** *627 9020*   **Map** *1 C3*

A tourist attraction in its own right, Olde Hansa is an immensely enjoyable experience. Huge traditional dishes are served by waiting staff in medieval costumes in a candlelit atmosphere, while an ensemble plays live traditional music. The menu is reputed to be based on carefully researched recipes.

Oliver

Viru väljak 3, 10140 **Tel** *630 7898*

Map 2 D3

Oliver does a roaring trade simply by being on one of the most popular tourist routes in Tallinn. It is a pleasant-looking, if unremarkable, cellar restaurant which offers a good selection of grilled dishes, from Cajun ribs to steak tartare, along with a couple of vegetarian dishes.

Park Avenue

Kreutzwaldi 23, 10147 **Tel** *630 5345*

Map 2 F3

Part of the Reval Park Hotel & Casino *(see p293)*, Park Avenue is as sleek as its New York namesake. It offers a buffet of set hot, cold and sweet selections or a combination of all three from lunchtime until 5am. There is also an à la carte menu. The summer terrace has great views.

Pegasus

Harju 1, 10146 **Tel** *631 4040*

Map 1 C3

Pegasus is an ultra-hip restaurant for good reason. Its suberb menu is one of the most innovative in the area and changes regularly. Set in a three-storey building facing Niguliste Church, it also enjoys a prime location. The extensive menu features imaginative fusion cuisine. The ground-floor bar is a great weekend hangout.

Vanaema Juures

Rataskaevu 10/12, 10123 **Tel** *626 9080*

Map 1 C2

Meaning "grandma's place", Vanaema Juures definitely lives up to its name. It is an exceptionally cosy and homely cellar restaurant decorated with 1920s and 30s period furniture. The excellent Estonian-style cuisine is stylishly served and reasonably priced. Try the roast elk, a local speciality.

Bocca

Olevimägi 9, 10123 **Tel** *641 2610*

Map 1 C2

Sleek and minimalist, Bocca is a favourite with Tallinn's in-crowd. The suitably stylish menu includes some excellent pastas and fillets, along with delicacies such as vineyard snails with Fontina and Gorgonzola sauce and baked rabbit in red wine and balsamic sauce. The lighting is wonderfully atmospheric.

Gloria

Müürivahe 2 **Tel** *644 6950*

Map 3 C3

Opened in 1937, Gloria has very stylish 1930s European interiors decked out with Art Nouveau originals and artifacts from the owner Dimitri Demjanov's private collection. The food is served by very attentive waiters and waitresses. Gloria also serves fantastic wine from its own cellar and Cuban cigars.

Karl Friedrich

Raekoja plats 5, 10146 **Tel** *627 2414*

Map 1 C2

Overlooking Town Hall Square, Karl Friedrich offers fantastic European cuisine in luxurious but refined surroundings. Its claim to fame is the culinary use of capsicums. The à la carte menu is served in four tastefully furnished rooms on the second floor, while there is a more casual lounge on the first floor and a cosy cellar pub as well.

Maikrahv

Raekoja plats 8, 10146 **Tel** *631 4227*

Map 1 C2

One of the more reasonably priced and refined medieval-style restaurants in Tallinn, Maikrahv is set in an atmospheric arched hall under Town Hall Square. The menu offers a good selection of tasty international dishes. There is a great summer terrace and a hall to accommodate large groups.

Seasons

Rävala pst 3, 10143 **Tel** *669 0000*

Map 2 D4

Situated on the first floor of the Radisson SAS hotel *(see p294)*, this top-class restaurant is set in comfortable, if slightly charmless, surroundings. It is worth visiting if only to have an after-dinner drink at the Lounge 24 bar on the 24th floor. Seasons also does a superb breakfast buffet.

Troika

Raekoja plats 15, 10146 **Tel** *627 6245*

Map 1 C2

One of Tallinn's best Russian restaurants, Troika occupies a great spot on Town Hall Square. The beautiful vaulted interior creates an atmospheric fusion of medieval Tallinn and Slavic exuberance. The somewhat pricey menu offers the usual Russian classics with some exotic additons, such as bear stroganoff.

Egoist

Vene 33, 10123 **Tel** *646 4052*

Map 2 D2

Unashamedly opulent, Egoist specializes in old-fashioned haute cuisine in an aristocratic salon-style interior. Choose from favourites such as lobster carpaccio or pan-fried foie gras, or try something from the new menu of Estonian dishes. The *kama* (yoghurt made from four grains and sour cherries) is exquisite.

House

Rataskaevu 16, 10123 **Tel** *641 1900*

Map 1 C2

Housed in a magnificently renovated and modernized 14th-century building, which is reputed to be haunted, House is in reality a vibrant place full of culinary delights. The food ranges from sushi to European chic, depending on which part of the restaurant you visit.

Key to Price Guide *see p322* **Key to Symbols** *see back cover flap*

La Bonaparte

Pikk 45, 10133 **Tel** *646 4444*

Map *1 C2*

This highly esteemed French restaurant is set in a beautifully restored medieval merchant's house and has catered for French presidents. With dishes such as duck fillet with raspberry syrup and pike-perch with champagne and almonds, it is truly first-rate. The cellar offers more secluded dining.

Three Sisters Restaurant

Pikk 71/Tolli 2, 10133 **Tel** *630 6300*

Map *1 C2*

One of the most luxurious restaurants in Tallinn, Three Sisters simply oozes luxury. The food is excellent and can be enjoyed on the terrace or in the charming courtyard in summer. The private Angels Room has an 18th-century ceiling fresco, while the wine cellar stores over 300 wines.

WESTERN ESTONIA

HAAPSALU Central

Karja 21, 90502 **Tel** *473 5595*

Road Map *C2*

Housed in a big 19th-century wooden building, this restaurant has a great view of the local castle and serves traditional Estonian food. Colourful murals enrich the overall historic ambience. The cosy beer cellar is charmingly furnished and makes a good place for a family dinner, so a quiet evening cannot be guaranteed.

HAAPSALU Blu Holm

Sadama 9/11, 90502 **Tel** *472 4406*

Road Map *C2*

Among the highlights of the elegant and spacious Blu Holm are its outstanding service and sleek interior. The excellent fish dishes are subtly enhanced by the wonderful view of the sea. Folk music and dance performances are a regular feature of the restaurant.

HAAPSALU Fra Mare Restaurant

Ranna tee 2, 90403 **Tel** *472 4606*

Road Map *C2*

With its excellent facilities and seaviews, Fra Mare Restaurant is an attractive dining option. The menu is a collection of international dishes including some Estonian fare. The Panoramic Hall offers exceptional views of the town, and the outdoor Terrace Café is a pleasant option in summer.

HAAPSALU Haapsalu Kuursaal

Promenaadi 1, 90502 **Tel** *473 5587*

Road Map *C2*

Housed in a beautiful late-19th-century wooden building, Haapsalu Kuursaal is one of the best and most popular restaurants in Haapsalu. The excellent food is largely thanks to the efforts of the young and eager-to-please chefs from a local vocational college. The place offers great views and atmosphere.

HIIUMAA ISLAND Liilia Hotel Restaurant

Hiiu mnt 22, Käia, 92101 **Tel** *463 6146*

Road Map *C2*

This restaurant, a part of the Liilia Hotel *(see p295)* and situated adjacent to Pullu Pub, has a friendly atmosphere. The fare includes plenty of local meat and fish dishes that have been specially created to suit a variety of tastes. Beefsteak with juniper berries and fried bass with blue cheese, and a few vegetarian options are included.

HIIUMAA ISLAND Vetsi Tall

Kassari, 92111 **Tel** *462 2550*

Road Map *C2*

Vetsi Tall is located in the tastefully renovated stable of Kassari manor and resembles an old-style inn. There is an enticing range of traditional Estonian meals, including smoked fish, as well as many more European-style dishes. The atmospheric Gentry Room has a lovely fireplace.

KIHNU ISLAND Kurase Keskus Café

Sääre village, 88005 **Tel** *446 9938*

Road Map *C2*

The only eatery in Kihnu Island, this humble café serves a surprisingly decent fare. It offers a number of local specialities, including the island's famed fish dishes. Also somewhat unusually, the restaurant stays open until 1am between June and August.

MATSALU NATIONAL PARK Amanda Puhvet

Üdruma village, 90701 **Tel** *472 9044*

Road Map *C2*

Amanda Puhvet is a lovely little out-of-the-way place located en route to Saaremaa and Matsalu National Park. A large wooden bird-watching tower right outside makes it hard to miss. The filling fare includes hearty soups, decent main courses and special dishes for children.

MATSALU NATIONAL PARK Roosta Holiday Village Restaurant

Tuksi, 91202 **Tel** *479 7230*

Road Map *C2*

Part of a lovely ensemble of vacation cottages in the northwest of the country, this restaurant has a good mixture of Estonian and international dishes. There is a sizeable breakfast buffet each morning for guests and a restful summer terrace with delightful views.

MUHU ISLAND Muhu Restaurant

Liiva village, 94701 **Tel** *5333 4005*   **Road Map** *C2*

Situated in the heart of the island, Muhu Restaurant is a charming, friendly place. The walls are lined with traditional blankets along with other local paraphernalia. The eclectic menu is prepared with local produce and includes ostrich meat which comes from a nearby farm.

MUHU ISLAND Seahouse – Pädaste Manor Restaurant

Pädaste manor, 94702 **Tel** *454 8800*   **Road Map** *C2*

This restaurant is part of the top-quality Pädaste Manor hotel *(see p295)*, a converted manor house by the sea. The menu is surprisingly innovative, with some outstanding fish dishes. The chef prefers to use local produce and many herbs and vegetables are grown in the manor's grounds.

PALDISKI Valge Laev

Rae 32 **Tel** *674 2035*   **Road Map** *C1*

Valge Laev has been Paldiski's only restaurant for some time. The maritime-themed interior is rather charming, although the food is standard Estonian pub fare. However, it is very filling and suits the somewhat surreal surroundings of the town.

PALDISKI Laulasmaa Resort Restaurant

Puhkekodu 4, 76702 **Tel** *687 0870*   **Road Map** *C1*

This restaurant has a pleasant ambience, with herbs used to adorn the tables. The menu is not extensive but the food is good quality and includes some wonderful dishes, such as the gnocchi with Parmesan and blue cheese. A health food buffet is also available.

PÄRNU Lahke Magjar

Kuninga 18, 80011 **Tel** *444 0104*   **Road Map** *D2*

Lahke Magjar is a small, intimate and delightfully rustic-looking Hungarian restaurant that manages to avoid the trappings of kitschiness. The superb food is similiarly impressive, with generous portions at reasonable prices. There is also a good range of Hungarian wines on offer.

PÄRNU Pärnu Kuursaal

Mere pst 22, 80010 **Tel** *442 0368*   **Road Map** *D2*

This lively and popular place is set in an attractive late 19th-century seafront building. The tavern's menu has something for most tastes. The main courses are stodgy but satisfying and include meat dishes and local favourites such as herring and sour cream, grilled sausage and perch in beer pastry.

PÄRNU Postipoiss

Vee 12, 80011 **Tel** *446 4864*   **Road Map** *D2*

A Russian restaurant that offers an authentic taste of Russia, with everything from *blini* (pancakes) and *pelmeni* (dumplings) to *solianka* (Russian beef soup) on the menu. There is also a pretty decent home-made beer to wash it all down. Despite the quaint rustic interior, weekend nights are usually very lively.

PÄRNU Must Pärl

Supluse 22, 80042 **Tel** *442 6902*   **Road Map** *D2*

This marine-themed restaurant has wave-like walls and a shell-shaped stage for weekend dance performances. The food is fairly standard although the reasonable prices and pleasant atmosphere make Must Pärl a worthwhile place to visit. It has a good outdoor terrace.

PÄRNU Seegi Maja

Hospidali 1, 80011 **Tel** *443 0550*   **Road Map** *D2*

In spite of its unreliable doorways and rafters, this beautifully restored Old Town house is one of the most charming and atmospheric restaurants in Pärnu. Good, medieval-themed food is served in generous portions on earthenware dishes. The place also offers fantastic home-made beer.

PÄRNU Brasserie Strand

Tammsaare pst 35, 80010 **Tel** *447 5370*   **Road Map** *D2*

This sleek, modern restaurant has some extremely good dishes on offer, although the menu is not exactly huge. Try rounding off one of the excellent main courses with the intriguing roasted Camembert and cloudberry jam for dessert. The hotel complex also includes a popular nightclub.

PÄRNU Ammende Villa

Mere pst 7, 80010 **Tel** *447 3888*   **Road Map** *D2*

Ammnede Villa offers luxury dining that perfectly suits the opulent Art Nouveau surroundings. Exquisite French and Mediterranean food is served up in three halls with immaculate attention to detail. The sea breeze-swept summer terrace looks out over pleasant residential surroundings.

SAAREMAA ISLAND Kaali Tavern

Kaali Meteorite Crater, 94102 **Tel** *515 4205*   **Road Map** *C2*

Located very close to the Kaali meteor impact site, Kaali Tavern is a perfect resting place after a long day's sight-seeing. The tavern is housed in a creamery, and embellished with locally-made limestone and metalwork decorative elements. The place offers decent food in very pleasant surroundings.

Key to Price Guide *see p322* **Key to Symbols** *see back cover flap*

SAAREMAA ISLAND Suur Töll Tavern

Lilbi, 93826 **Tel** *454 5404* — **Road Map** *C2*

The tavern's decor is inspired by the folklore about the friendly giant of Saaremaa, Suur Töll, and his wife Piret. Suur Töll Tavern is part of a charming holiday village just 3 km (2 miles) from Kuressaare. The place serves a variety of hearty Estonian fare and has a special menu for children.

SAAREMAA ISLAND Vaekoda Pub

Tallinna mnt 3, 93811 **Tel** *453 3020* — **Road Map** *C2*

Housed in a 17th-century building known as the Weigh House, in the centre of the Old Town, Vaekoda Pub is a popular place with locals and tourists. The food is much above average for a pub while the amiable atmosphere makes for a lively and fun evening.

SAAREMAA ISLAND Grand Rose Spa Hotel

Tallinna 15, 93811 **Tel** *666 7000* — **Road Map** *C2*

This cosy cellar restaurant is one of the best places in town. Its arched brick ceiling and partitioned rooms provide an intimate setting, while the medieval-style feel to the place creates an interesting atmosphere. The excellent menu includes a few local Saaremaa specialities.

SAAREMAA ISLAND Hotel Saaremaa Restaurant

Mändjala, 93822 **Tel** *454 4100* — **Road Map** *C2*

With its idyllic location overlooking Mändjala beach and excellent cuisine, this restaurant is an attractive option. The food ranges from gourmet-style Estonian cuisine to health food-style minimalism. The chef can also prepare a special evening picnic package for the beach.

SAAREMAA ISLAND Georg Ots Spa Restaurant

Tori 2, 93815 **Tel** *455 0000* — **Road Map** *C2*

This restaurant offers wonderfully inventive cuisine that strikes a perfect balance between health and sumptuousness. There is also a range of rich pasta dishes for those unconcerned with counting calories. The open-air terrace has a great view of the bay during the summer season.

VORMSI ISLAND Hullo Tavern

Hullo, 91301 **Tel** *5191 5244* — **Road Map** *C2*

Located in a Swedish-style wooden house that is so characteristic of Vormsi Island, Hullo Tavern is a friendly family-run place that serves authentic Estonian home-cooked food. Large groups should book in advance. There is also a very cosy bar which stays open until midnight at weekends.

EASTERN ESTONIA

KUREMÄE Wironia Pub

Rakvere 7, 41531 **Tel** *336 4204* — **Road Map** *E1*

This cheery place is ideal for a meal after a long day of sightseeing. The food is fairly typical of Estonian pub fare and includes meat, fish and salad. There are some good main courses such as schnitzel, meat-and-spuds, pancakes and other hearty local favourites. There is a nice little pub with cosy wooden benches and pool tables next door.

LAAHEMAA NATIONAL PARK Kaminasaal

Rakvere tee 13, 45501 **Tel** *5648 2286* — **Road Map** *D1*

Situated in one of the most beautiful parts of Lahemaa, this is a lovely little restaurant. The rustic interior is the main attraction, although the food strikes a perfectly decent balance between local and European tastes. There are outdoor tables in summer and an open fire in winter.

LAHEMAA NATIONAL PARK Viitna Kõrts

Viitna, 45202 **Tel** *520 9156* — **Road Map** *D1*

Located along the Tallinn-Narva motorway, and by a main entry road to the centre of Lahemaa, this old-style tavern is a popular resting place for travellers. The food consists mainly of variations on potato, meat and fish dishes, but it is well made, filling and tastes great in the atmospheric surroundings.

LAHEMAA NATIONAL PARK Kolga Manor Restaurant

Kolga village, 74803 **Tel** *607 7250* — **Road Map** *D1*

Located in one of Lahemaa's most splendid manor houses, the tastefully renovated restaurant is an attractive and atmospheric place to dine. The house wine is imported from the French birthplace of Pontus de la Gardie (1520–85), who was once the Swedish governor of Livonia.

LAHEMAA NATIONAL PARK Sagadi Manor Restaurant

Sagadi village, Sagadi, 45402 **Tel** *676 7888* — **Road Map** *D2*

With its splendid interior and beautiful surroundings, the Sagadi Manor Restaurant is an immensely enjoyable experience. The menu includes specialities made with local game and fowl, as well as the famous Sagadi carrot cake. The first-floor terrace has magnificent views in summer.

NARVA 100% China
Tallinn mnt 6b, 20304 **Tel** *357 5099*   **Road Map** *E1*

One of the best restaurants in Narva, this pleasant little place boasts the only Chinese chef in the region, ensuring that the food is more or less authentic. The extensive menu includes many vegetarian options, something of a rarity in strictly non-vegetarian Estonia.

NARVA Café Geneva
Võidu 2, Narva, 21006 **Tel** *356 1135*   **Road Map** *E1*

A nightclub, bar and café that offers reasonably priced food of decent quality. It is useful to remember, however, that a side dish of rice, fries or vegetables is not included in the price for the main dishes and has to be ordered separately. Desserts and cocktails are probably the highlights here.

NARVA German Pub
Puškini 10, 20308 **Tel** *359 1548*   **Road Map** *E1*

A popular place with locals, German Pub offers hearty Estonian-style food in a relaxed environment. The rustic-looking cellar has a somewhat incongruous gallery of boxing photographs on proud display. This is also one of the few places that serves frogs' legs as a snack.

NARVA Salvadore
Puškini 28, 20306 **Tel** *688 1100*   **Road Map** *E1*

The centrally located Salvadore is a safe bet for a good meal that is a decent blend of Estonian and European dishes. The home-made pasta and risotto are worth trying. There is also a children's menu featuring the Matroskin Cat Sandwich, named after a famous Russian cartoon. The sandwich consists of rye bread, ham and butter.

ONTIKA COAST Mio Mare
Ranna 12, Toila, 41702 **Tel** *334 2916*   **Road Map** *E1*

Part of the Toila Spa Hotel *(see p298)*, Mio Mare is a low-key restaurant that has a fantastic menu. The main courses mostly feature exquisitely prepared meat and fish dishes, including local wild boar, but the vegetarian options are limited. At weekends, the restaurant remains open till late.

OTEPÄÄ Karupesa Hotel Restaurant
Tehvandi 1a, 67406 **Tel** *766 1500*   **Road Map** *E2*

A pleasant little place with romantic lighting and cosy tables. The food is mostly meat-based, though there is also a set vegetarian menu. The restaurant has a bar with billiard tables, as well as a tennis court outside which is turned into an ice-skating rink during winter.

PAIDE Bonatal
Pärnu 54, 72712 **Tel** *384 6010*   **Road Map** *D2*

Given the paucity of dining options in a parochial town like Paide, Bonatal is a decent place for a good meal. Situated in the town centre, it is a cheery little eatery that serves up a menu of typical small-town fare, largely including generous portions of meat, fish and salad.

PÕLTSAMAA Rivaal
Veski 1, 48106 **Tel** *776 2620*   **Road Map** *D2*

A lovely little riverside restaurant in the middle of town, Rivaal has a good range of Estonian-style dishes on offer. Large groups can be catered for. The nearby castle has a famous wine-tasting cellar and there is also a charming rose island a short walk away.

PÕLVA Pesa Hotel Restaurant
Uus 5, 63308 **Tel** *799 8530*   **Road Map** *E2*

About as good a place to eat as you will find in a provincial Estonian town. Unusually, the menu includes some decent vegetarian choices as well as generic Estonian and European dishes. The Sun Terrace is a pleasant place to eat, while the cosy pub stays open until late.

PÕLVA Põlva Restaurant
Kesk 10, 63308 **Tel** *799 9037*   **Road Map** *E2*

This establishment in the centre of town consists of a bistro, restaurant and bar. The interior is curiously charmless and the food is typical of a small town, though the menu is extensive enough for even the most fastidious visitor to find something to suit his or her liking.

RAKVERE Katariina Kelder
Pikk 3, 44307 **Tel** *322 3943*   **Road Map** *D1*

This restro-bar is located on the oldest street in Rakvere and is one of the best places in town for a satisfying meal. The food is more imaginative than local pub fare, and usually consists of a piece of meat with a small serving of salad. The nearby castle ruins provide a good way of walking off dinner.

SETUMAA Hirve Café
Silla 2, Värska, 64001 **Tel** *797 6105*   **Road Map** *E2*

Located in a holiday centre, Hirve Café mostly attracts visitors to the Setu Farm Museum. The menu is typical rural Estonian food with plenty of soup, potatoes and roasts. A range of sandwiches and other snacks makes it a good place for a quick bite.

SILLAMÄE Krunk

Kesk 23, 40231 **Tel** *392 9030*

Road Map *E1*

This Soviet-era hotel restaurant *(see p299)* has a strangely elegant and refined air about it. The food is the best in town, dressing up the usual meat and fish dishes with at least a veneer of style. Popular international dishes are served with fries. Live music at weekends adds to the ambience.

SUUR MUNAMÄGI Suur Munamägi Tower Café

Haanja Village, 65101 **Tel** *787 8847*

Road Map *E2*

It is definitely worth visiting this recently renovated glass-fronted café for a refreshing cold drink or cup of coffee simply because it is the highest point in the Baltic States and offers a truly breathtaking view. The place mainly serves basic refreshments. Remains open till 8pm during the summer.

SUUR MUNAMÄGI Café Suur Muna

Haanja village, 65101 **Tel** *786 6000*

Road Map *E2*

Café Suur Muna is a pleasant rural café with a small but decent menu. Its idyllic surroundings can be admired from the lovely wooden terrace. Taking inspiration from the name of the area, Suur Munamägi (Big Egg Hill), the menu of this café features several egg dishes.

TARTU La Dolce Vita

Kompanii 10, 51007 **Tel** *740 7545*

Road Map *E2*

This likeable little restaurant has an enormous selection of salads, pizzas and main courses. The pizzas are baked in the only wooden oven in Tartu, while the delightful interior is reminiscent of a genuine trattoria. The outdoor terrace looks out over a lovely park.

TARTU Tsink Plekk Pang

Küütri 6, 51007 **Tel** *730 3415*

Road Map *E2*

This excellent Old Town restaurant-cum-bar is spread out over four floors and has a relaxed and enjoyable atmosphere. The Asian-themed menu includes a choice of Chinese food, sushi and a few Indian dishes. A great place to come for a drink too.

TARTU Wilde

Vallikraavi 4, 30103 **Tel** *730 9764*

Road Map *E2*

A typical Irish-style pub, although much brighter than usual, Wilde has big windows and light coloured walls. The huge menu at this cheerful eatery includes Irish-themed dishes such as beef and Guinness pie as well as burgers and curries.

TARTU Atlantis

Narva mnt 2, 51009 **Tel** *738 5485*

Road Map *E2*

Atlantis occupies a glass-fronted building overlooking the Emajõgi river and forms part of a complex that includes a popular nightclub. The restaurant itself is bright, comfortable and elegantly furnished. The eclectic menu features some excellent fish dishes. The panoramic view of Tartu is another bonus.

TARTU Rasputin

Ülikooli 10, 51003 **Tel** *730 5996*

Road Map *E2*

With dishes such as Leningrad Casserole, Novgorod Fish Pot and Moscow Borsch, Rasputin offers a taste of authentic Russian cuisine in an intimate, tavern-style environment. All the staple Russian classics are there as well. The enclosed courtyard is a great spot to eat in during the summer.

VILJANDI Suur Vend Pub

Turu 4, 71003 **Tel** *433 3644*

Road Map *D2*

A friendly and welcoming pub with an eclectic and suprisingly good menu that offers everything from breaded broccoli to wok-fried pork and chicken. There is regular live music and even a cosy sauna which can be booked by the hour, on the premises.

VILJANDI Hotel Centrum Restaurant

Tallinna 24, 71008 **Tel** *435 1100*

Road Map *D2*

The restaurant at Hotel Centrum *(see p299)* offers great views of Viljandi's main street from its fourth-floor vantage point. It is a modern and comfortable place to eat in, with a menu that is arguably the best in town. It also has a better-than-average wine list for the provinces.

VÕRU Ränduri Pub

Jüri 36, 65603 **Tel** *786 8050*

Road Map *E2*

Ränduri Pub is situated on a main road running through the centre of town. With its traditional-looking wood and brick interior, it is a comfortable spot and has a decent range of Estonian pub-style food, including meat and fish dishes and salads at good prices. Plenty of parking space is available.

VÕRU Õlle 17

Jüri 17, 65609 **Tel** *782 8461*

Road Map *E2*

Õlle 17 is the only Irish-style pub in Võru. The friendly, relaxing environment includes a lounge area and a comfortable separate room for smokers. There is a range of fresh-tasting, well-made pub food, including meat and salads, along with an unusually large selection of beers, including Guinness.

Choosing a Restaurant in Latvia

These restaurants have been selected for their food, good value and location. They are listed by region, starting with Rīga, followed by the rest of Latvia. Under each town or area, hotels are listed alphabetically within each price category. For Rīga map references, see pages 160–61; for road map references see the back cover.

PRICE DETAILS
Based on the price per person of a three-course meal with half a bottle of wine, including cover charge, service and tax.
Ⓛ Under 10 Ls
ⓁⓁ 10–15 Ls
ⓁⓁⓁ 15–20 Ls
ⓁⓁⓁⓁ 20–25 Ls
ⓁⓁⓁⓁⓁ Over 25 Ls

RĪGA

Alus Sēta
ⓁⓁ
Tirgoņu iela 6, LV-1050 **Tel** *6722 2431*　　　　　**Map** 1 C4

The most central branch of the popular LIDO chain of self-service Latvian restaurants, Alus Sēta serves authentic local cuisine in a farmhouse setting. Popular dishes include shashlik and grey peas, teamed with the restaurant's own brand of beer or tasty Užavas ale.

Citi Laiki
ⓁⓁ
Brīvības iela 41, LV-1010 **Tel** *6724 0590*　　　　　**Map** 2 F1

Housed in a wooden building dating from 1824, Citi Laiki offers Latvian dishes in a rustic environment complete with local antiques. Unlike many of the capital's Latvian restaurants, it is not owned by the LIDO group and has table service instead of a buffet. Traditional folk music performances are among the weekend highlights.

Dzirnavas
ⓁⓁ
Dzirnavu iela 74/76, LV-1050 **Tel** *6728 4228*　　　　　**Map** 2 E4

Popular for offering Latvian cuisine at reasonable rates, Dzirnavas is one of several LIDO restaurants in the capital. The buffet spread is lavish, with plenty of salad options as well as favourites such as shashlik. The decor has a medieval feel, with exposed brickwork and torches hanging from the walls.

LIDO Atpūtas Centrs
ⓁⓁ
Krasta iela 76, LV-1019 **Tel** *6750 4420*　　　　　**Map** 2 D5

Part of the LIDO chain of recreation centres, this massive log cabin with an amusement park, ice-skating rink and live folk music performances is a tourist attraction in its own right. The buffet boasts over 500 items, including many traditional Latvian dishes. There is also a sit-down restaurant and a large beer hall.

Osīris
ⓁⓁ
Krišjānis Barona iela 31, LV-1011 **Tel** *6724 3002*　　　　　**Map** 2 E3

A sophisticated and atmospheric café with an excellent international spread, Osīris has a predominantly artistic clientele and hosts regular art exhibitions. The fireplace and foreign newspapers help to make it a cosy hangout, and the classical music playing in the background adds to the ambience. Reservations are recommended for dinner.

Soraksans
ⓁⓁ
Miesnieku iela 12, LV-1050 **Tel** *6722 9068*　　　　　**Map** 1 C3

An authentic Korean restaurant with an extensive menu, Soraksans offers the popular *kimbab* (rice wrapped in seaweed along with meat, eggs and vegetables, dressed with sesame oil). In traditional Korean style, food is served all at once, rather than in courses. It is also possible to cook your own dish on a hotplate at the table.

Staburags
ⓁⓁ
Čaka 55 iela, LV-1011 **Tel** *6729 9787*　　　　　**Map** 2 E3

Exposed brickwork and oak features create a mock-farmhouse setting for this vast branch of the LIDO chain. Its authentic Latvian meals, featuring pork shashlik and grey peas, are affordably priced yet hearty. Evenings at Staburags are often livened up with folk music performances.

Vērmanītis
ⓁⓁ
Elizabetes iela 65, LV-1050 **Tel** *6722 1318*　　　　　**Map** 2 D2

Located on the edge of Vērmanes Garden, this branch of the ubiquitous LIDO chain of restaurants is decorated like a farmhouse with staff dressed in traditional Latvian costumes. Self-service Latvian staples, such as meat, potatoes, rice and salads, are available at reasonable prices. Pizzas and other fast food are available in the cellar.

Alpen Rose
ⓁⓁⓁ
Jauniela iela 16, LV-1050 **Tel** *6722 0402*　　　　　**Map** 1 C4

A cheerfully painted exterior sets this charming Swiss restaurant apart. The menu includes home-made bread, meat-filled apples, raclette and fondue served by waitresses dressed in traditional Swiss costumes. The wine list also has Swiss selections. The top-floor terrace is open for dining in summer.

Key to Symbols *see back cover flap*

Alus Ordenis

Raiņa bulvāris 15, LV-1050 **Tel** *6781 4190*

Map *2 D3*

This beer cellar beneath the Black Cat bar serves rural Latvian dishes, with some unique treats such as *cuku pupas* (broad beans in butter sauce), bulls' testicles and boiled pigs' trotters. A wide range of locally brewed beer is also available. The food is authentic but more expensive than at similar Latvian restaurants.

Aragats

Miera iela 15, LV-1001 **Tel** *6737 3445*

Map *2 F1*

Specializing in authentic Armenian dishes, this Caucasian restaurant has a homely ambience with very friendly staff. Favourites include shashlik and *hashlama* (mutton and vegetable soup), as well as a range of wines from the region. Sweet coffee completes this traditional meal.

Baan Thai

Bruņinieku iela 59, LV-1011 **Tel** *6727 8602*

Map *2 E3*

This small Thai bistro is one of the few Latvian restaurants that serve spicy dishes. A typical meal, prepared by a Thai cook, consists of a soup, a curry dish or spicy salad and a dip with fish and vegetables. The options, though limited, are of good quality. Prices are high by local standards, but the business lunch on weekdays is reasonable.

Bon Vivant

Mārstaļu iela 8, LV-1050 **Tel** *6722 6585*

Map *2 D4*

The decor of this Belgian restaurant resembles a 1930s brasserie. Bon Vivant is a cosy place to tuck into steamed mussels and fries or sausages sold by the half-metre. The food here is accompanied by a decent selection of beers, each served in its own special glass.

Dada

Kalēju iela 30, LV-1050 **Tel** *6710 4433*

Map *2 D4*

Taking its name from an avant-garde artistic movement, Dada displays a playful irreverence in its decor, mismatched cutlery and staff uniform. Most people come here for its Mongolian Barbecue section, where visitors can pick from a selection of meat, seafood, vegetables, noodles and sauces which the chef will stir-fry.

Da Sergio

Tērbatas iela 65, LV-1001 **Tel** *6731 2777*

Map *2 E3*

The chefs at Da Sergio, considered one of the best Italian restaurants in the city, make their pizzas in a wood-fired oven. There is also an extensive menu of authentic pasta and seafood dishes. The Mediterranean atmosphere here is maintained by a strictly Italian music policy, with a wine list to match.

El Primero

Smilšu iela 6 (entrance on Aldaru iela), LV-1050 **Tel** *6732 3664*

Map *1 C3*

Oak furnishing and bullfight posters set the ambience for this Spanish restaurant, which serves a wide range of traditional meat and seafood dishes, along with a few vegetarian options. A good-value business lunch menu is available on weekdays. The atmosphere is further enhanced during weekends with live flamenco performances.

Gastronome

Brīvības iela 31, LV-1000 **Tel** *6777 2391*

Map *2 F1*

Despite the rapid development of restaurants in Rīga over the past years, seafood options are scarce, making this combined shop and restaurant a welcome addition. Situated in the Reval Hotel Latvija *(see p302)*, Gastronome's open kitchen serves delectable grilled fish and oyster dishes, as well as freshly baked pastries and pies.

Hongkonga

Valdemāra iela 61, LV-1050 **Tel** *6781 2292*

Map *1 A3*

Among the better Chinese restaurants, Hongkonga serves authentic spicy food instead of the bland options commonly available in Rīga. It is very atmospheric, with delightful decor and Chinese music creating a soothing background. A very popular place, it is especially busy during weekends.

Kamāla

Jauniela iela 14, LV-1050 **Tel** *6721 1332*

Map *1 C4*

Conveniently situated in the Old Town, Kamāla is one of the few vegetarian restaurants in Rīga. The menu combines Indian dishes with eclectic international fare. The relaxed Indian ambience is set with carved wooden furniture, appropriate music and the heady aroma of burning incense.

Kiploku Krogs

Mazā pils 23/25, LV-1050 **Tel** *6721 1451*

Map *1 C3*

Taking its name seriously, Kiploku Krogs, which means "garlic bar", has garlic in almost every dish, including the ice cream. In fact, the menu labels the few dishes that do not contain the pungent ingredient. The results are less gimmicky than might be expected, with some very exciting choices.

Lidojošā Varde

Elizabetes 31a, LV-1010 **Tel** *6732 1184*

Map *2 D2*

One of Rīga's oldest expatriate hangouts, Lidojošā Varde, which means "flying frog", is so named because of the frog decorations in all its three cellar rooms. It is especially popular with staff from the nearby embassies. The straightforward menu comprises burgers, ribs, salads and pasta.

Lotoss

Skārņu iela 9, LV-1050 **Tel** *6721 5075*   **Map** *2 D4*

The menu of this restaurant is truly international, with a variety of choices ranging from samosas to filet mignon as well as a decent range of meat-free dishes. Considering this breadth of choice, the standard is high, but the real reason to visit it is the view on to one of the city's prettiest streets.

Macaroni Noodle Bar

Barona iela 17, LV-1011 **Tel** *6721 7981*   **Map** *2 E3*

Justifying its name, the Macaroni Noodle Bar serves pasta and noodle dishes from Europe and Asia. Sushi is also available here, taken from the menu of sister restaurant Kabuki next door. The provenance of each dish on the menu is indicated with a national flag.

Melnie Mūki

Jāņa sēta 1, LV-1050 **Tel** *6721 5006*

Housed in a former cloister, with a chef who worked for a former Latvian president, Melnie Mūki (Black Monks) is renowned for its eclectic menu, available at surprisingly reasonable prices. The service is attentive and the atmosphere is relatively formal. It is wise to reserve in advance, as it is popular among local diners.

Rozengrāls

Rozena 1, LV-1050 **Tel** *6722 0356*   **Map** *1 C4*

Among the few restaurants in the city that still prepare food from old recipes, Rozengrāls attracts attention for the late 13th-century cellar it inhabits. Today, traditionally dressed staff serve strictly medieval fare. Venison soup, perch stuffed with prunes and carp prepared in a spicy cognac sauce are some of the house specialities.

Sue's Indian Raja

Vecpilsētas 3, LV-1050 **Tel** *6721 2614*   **Map** *2 D2*

While many of Latvia's Asian restaurants cater to local tastes by toning down their dishes, Sue's Indian Raja serves authentic cuisine from around the subcontinent. As a result, it is arguably more popular with expatriates than locals, and consistently wins plaudits from critics and visitors. Tandoori chicken is the chef's speciality.

Arbat

R vāgnera 3, LV-1050 **Tel** *6721 4057*   **Map** *2 F1*

The Russian cuisine here is well priced considering the elegant surroundings in which it is served. The menu includes *pelmeņi* (dumplings), caviar, elk steaks and "Tsar-style" soup, made of sturgeon, pike perch and vodka. Arbat's international wine list and non-alcoholic *kvass* (made from fermented rye bread) are also worth sampling.

Palete

Gleznotāju iela 12/14, LV-1050 **Tel** *6721 6037*

A favourite with both foreign visitors and local people, this cosy restaurant in the Vecrīga hotel *(see p301)* serves an eclectic international menu ranging from Cajun to Italian. There is something to suit most tastes, but seafood is a speciality. Paintings and an open fireplace in winter add to its old-world charm.

Bellevue

Skolas iela 1, LV-1048 **Tel** *6706 9000*   **Map** *2 E2*

An upmarket option on the left bank of the Daugava river, Bellevue sits on the 11th floor of the Maritim Park hotel *(see p302)* and offers a plush ambience and impressive views of the riverfront and Old Town. Specializing in fish and seafood dishes, the chef serves gourmet cuisine to a well-heeled clientele.

Benjamiņs

Barona iela 12, V-1000 **Tel** *6707 9444*   **Map** *2 E3*

Housed in an opulent 19th-century building, this elegant restaurant, in the Europa Royale hotel *(see p301)*, retains many of its original features, such as stained-glass windows and parquet floors. The menu offers international dishes, complemented by an extensive wine list which includes some sought-after vintages.

Bergs

Elizabetes iela 83/85, LV-1050 **Tel** *6777 0957*   **Map** *2 D2*

Located in the Bergs boutique hotel *(see p302)*, this restaurant is among Rīga's classiest dining venues. Overseen by one of the city's most esteemed chefs, Kaspars Jansons, the food here is good and the service attentive. Its eclectic menu highlights modern European and fusion cuisine, served in an intimate setting.

Skonto Zivju Restorāns

Vāgnera iela 4, LV-1050 **Tel** *6721 0087*

This cosy upmarket restaurant, specializing in seafood, has been a favourite with Rīga's wealthier diners for over a decade. The menu has some exciting options, such as a starter of swordfish and salmon carpaccio with daikon, quail eggs and wasabi sauce.

Vincent's

Elizabetes iela 19, LV-1000 **Tel** *6733 2634*   **Map** *2 D2*

With celebrity chef Mārtiņš Rītiņš at the helm, Vincent's has been a staple of Rīga's restaurant scene since it opened in 1994 and continues to attract most of the foreign dignitaries and celebrities who pass through the city. Adventurous international dishes are offered alongside a menu of classy versions of traditional Latvian fare.

Key to Price Guide *see p330* **Key to Symbols** *see back cover flap*

WESTERN LATVIA

BAUSKA Rožmalas
*Ceraukstes pagasts, 7 km (4 miles) S of town, LV-3908 **Tel** 6779 1178*   **Road Map** *D4*

Part of the Rožmalas hotel *(see p303)*, this restaurant is a cut above most provincial Latvian establishments. The spacious and well-lit interior is contemporary in style. The menu includes tempting dishes such as suckling pig roulades with hemp and pea purée served in a cream sauce, and fried cod with root vegetables.

DUNDAGA Jūras Sapņi
*Vīdāles iela 2, LV-3270 **Tel** 2917 7245*   **Road Map** *C3*

There are few dining options in Dundaga, and Jūras Sapņi is one of the best. The decor has a seaside theme, with palm trees, a large mural and a grotto in one corner. The food covers the standard Latvian fare of pork, chicken and potatoes. There is also a separate children's menu.

ENGURE Cope
*Rideļu dzirnavas, LV-3113 **Tel** 2912 0190*   **Road Map** *C3*

This wooden guest house next to Rideļļi Watermill includes a pleasant café, making it a convenient stop for visitors en route to Lake Engure. The flour which is still produced at the mill is used in several dishes on the menu, including the delicious pancakes. Boats can be hired here for a cruise along the lake.

JAUNMOKU PILS Huberts
*Tume, LV-3139 **Tel** 2870 9742*

Housed in Jaunmoku Pils *(see p303)*, Huberts is decorated with hunting trophies. The kitchen specializes in wildfowl and the menu has signature dishes such as "Potato Pancakes to the Taste of the Major-domo's Wife". The flat curd cakes served here are popular with children.

JELGAVA Stolovaja Nr. 5
*Driskas iela 4, LV-3001 **Tel** 2962 1580*   **Road Map** *C4*

Tucked away in a shopping centre, this restaurant serves authentic Russian cuisine in an atmospheric setting. The menu is in Russian and Latvian only, but the staff should be able to help. The live music is an acquired taste, with popular Russian tunes played on guitar and keyboard.

JŪRMALA Al Tohme
*Pilsoņu iela 2, LV-2015 **Tel** 6775 5755*   **Road Map** *C3*

A seaside Lebanese restaurant, Al Tohme offers breathtaking views of the Gulf of Rīga from its terrace, especially at sunset. The menu includes kebabs and pizza as well as various mezze, such as hummus and spicy sausage, all served on mosaic tables. Arabic music, belly-dancing and hookah aromas add to the atmosphere.

JŪRMALA Pegasa Pils
*Jūras iela 60, Majori, LV-2015 **Tel** 2923 6425*   **Road Map** *C3*

Housed in a restored wooden Art Nouveau building with a distinctive corner tower, this restaurant close to the Dzintari concert hall is one of the best choices in Majori. Food is typical Latvian fare with many fish dishes, as well as pasta options. Violinists liven up weekend evenings.

JŪRMALA Aquarius
*33 Bulduru prospekts, Bulduri, LV-2010 **Tel** 6775 1071*   **Road Map** *C3*

A surprisingly stylish dining option, slightly off the tourist trail in Bulduri, Aquarius derives its name from the fish tank behind the bar. The menu is an assortment of adventurous Asian and European dishes. The excellent food is complemented by music and chic decor. The extended wine list also has half-bottle options.

JŪRMALA Villa Joma
*Jomas iela 90, LV-2015 **Tel** 6777 1999*   **Road Map** *C3*

This pastel-coloured restaurant is bright and airy and considered among the best eateries in Jūrmala. The menu is helpfully displayed outside the restaurant and includes international favourites such as tuna carpaccio and breast of Barbary duck. In addition to the wine list, cocktails are also served at the bar.

KOLKA Zītari
*Rūtas, LV-3275 **Tel** 6322 0451*   **Road Map** *C3*

One of the better options on the Livonian Coast, this café in the Zītari hotel *(see p304)* has a relatively modest menu with limited choices. The simple Latvian fare served here includes a range of fish dishes, reflecting Kolka's proximity to the sea.

KULDĪGA Stenders
*Liepājas iela 3, LV-3301 **Tel** 6332 2703*   **Road Map** *B3*

Housed on the first floor of a former granary, Stenders offers an array of standard Latvian dishes and is very popular locally for its signature pancakes. The cosy open-air terrace makes an excellent spot for scenic views of the city, particularly appealing on a summer's day. Local DJs entertain on Friday and Saturday nights.

KULDĪGA Metropole   🅰🈁🈲🅿   ⓁⓁⓁ

Baznīcas iela 11, LV-3301 **Tel** *6335 0588*   **Road Map** *B3*

Housed in the Metropole hotel *(see p304)*, this restaurant is the most upmarket dining option in town. The menu comprises regular Latvian and international dishes. However, the vegetarian fare is limited to a selection of salads. The hotel's wine list is extensive, and the basement has a bar.

LIEPĀJA Ilze   🎵🈲   Ⓛ

Graudu iela 23, LV-3401 **Tel** *6342 3814*   **Road Map** *B4*

This brick-lined cellar restaurant with arched vaulting and romantic lighting is very popular with locals. It serves standard Latvian cuisine along with some exotic fare such as chicken wasabi or calamari at reasonable prices. Live music performances every evening.

LIEPĀJA Libava   🈲🅿   ⓁⓁ

Vecā ostmala 29, LV-3401 **Tel** *6342 9714*   **Road Map** *B4*

Emphasizing local cuisine, the restaurant specializes in fish and seafood. The menu includes signature dishes such as "Mrs Štrondfogt's Festive Chicken" (chicken marinated in fermented milk, grilled and served with shrimp sauce and vegetable pie). With white walls and red leather chairs, it is a pleasant place to dine.

LIEPĀJA Pastnieka Māja   🅰🈁🈲   ⓁⓁ

Fr Brīvzemnieka 53, LV-3401 **Tel** *6340 7521*   **Road Map** *B4*

This brick and timber building is located in a quiet street close to the centre of town. The structure may be old, but the restaurant's decor is resolutely modern. The menu largely sticks to the Latvian standards and the drinks list includes several local beers. There is also a large terrace.

MEŽOTNE Mežotnes Pils   🅰🎵🈲   ⓁⓁ

Mežotnes pagasts, LV-3918 **Tel** *6396 0711*   **Road Map** *D4*

This pleasant dining room in the Mežotnes Pils hotel *(see p304)* offers spectacular views of the palace grounds. The food is less grand than the surroundings might suggest. The modest menu comprises simple Latvian cuisine, including *escalope* (thin slivers of meat or fish), available at reasonable rates. It is best to book in advance.

NĪCA Nīcava   🈲   ⓁⓁⓁ

Nīcas pagasts, LV-3473 **Tel** *6348 6379*   **Road Map** *B4*

The restaurant is divided into a main dining room, with the entry from the Nīcava hotel *(see p304)* and a conservatory, with its entrance around the side of the building. The Latvian menu is the same in each and includes "Cuisine of the Mistress", a selection of traditional dishes such as pork knuckle roasted and served with horseradish.

PĀVILOSTA Pub Āķagals   🚹🅰🎵🈁🈲   ⓁⓁ

Dzintaru iela 3, LV-3466 **Tel** *6349 8212*   **Road Map** *B4*

The ornate wooden decor of this pub extends even to its quirky bar made from logs. Taking advantage of its proximity to the sea, the restaurant specializes in smoked and fresh fish dishes and also serves Latvian cuisine. There is an in-house sauna and a cosy fireplace for cold winter days.

PEDVĀLE Dāre   🈁🈲   ⓁⓁ

Pedvāles Brīvdabas Mākslas Muzejas, LV-3294 **Tel** *6325 2273*   **Road Map** *C4*

Only a short drive from Sabile and located close to the entrance to the Pedvāle Open-Air Museum, this café serves up a decent selection of Latvian favourites in a relaxed atmosphere. Art is sometimes exhibited inside the café. The pleasant outdoor terrace is a favourite dining venue in summer.

ROJA Rojas Pērle   🚹🅰🈁🈲Ⓥ   Ⓛ

Selgas iela 4a, LV-3264 **Tel** *6326 9562*   **Road Map** *C3*

The Rojas Pērle hotel *(see p304)* has a café and a restaurant catering for small and large appetites. The restaurant menu is surprisingly adventurous, with dim sum and paella, as well as Latvian staples such as pork cutlets with potatoes. The café has an outdoor terrace. The building also houses a disco which operates during weekends.

ROJA Dzintarkrasts   🚹🅰🈲Ⓥ🅿   ⓁⓁ

Žocene, LV-3264 **Tel** *2860 0600*   **Road Map** *C3*

Tastefully furnished with dark-wood tables and wicker chairs, this sophisticated restaurant is part of the Dzintarkrasts holiday complex *(see p304)*. The menu includes traditional Kurzeme dishes, such as sorrel soup with fried bacon and slices of boiled egg, and dark bread soup with dried apples and whipped cream.

RUNDĀLE Baltā Māja   🈲   Ⓛ

Rundāle, LV-3921 **Tel** *2912 4374*   **Road Map** *D4*

The Baltā Maja *(see p305)* is about 200 years old. In addition to bed and breakfast offered to guests, there is an excellent café serving authentic home-cooked Latvian food in an endearing farmhouse-style dining room. The black bread and berry dessert served here is unmissable. Book ahead.

RUNDĀLE Rundāles Pils   🎵🈲🅿Ⓥ   ⓁⓁ

Rundāle, LV-3921 **Tel** *6396 2195*   **Road Map** *D4*

Conveniently located for visiting Rundāle Palace, this restaurant occupies the Duke of Courland's former kitchens. The Latvian food here is fantastic but the vegetarian menu is comparatively sparse. The restaurant is open all year, but off-season (October–May) visitors must give prior notice if they wish to dine.

Key to Price Guide *see p330* **Key to Symbols** *see back cover flap*

SABILE Pie Vīna Kalna 🔲 ⓒⓛ

Rīgas iela 11, LV-3294 **Tel** *2921 6407*   **Road Map** *C3*

This café is a good option for those passing through Sabile or visiting the vineyard. The Latvian menu features chicken, fish and pork. A TV set, continually tuned in to a channel playing Russian pop hits, is the only available entertainment in the café.

TALSI Martinelli 🎵 🔲 🍴 ⓒⓒ

Lielā iela 7, LV-3201 **Tel** *6329 1340*   **Road Map** *C3*

A fireplace and wooden beams impart a cosy farmhouse-feel to this popular restaurant. Traditional Latvian pork, chicken and fish dishes are served, along with age-old family recipes such as peeled barley penny buns with soup. The owners have a wine shop next door with an interesting stock.

TUKUMS Alus Pagrabs 🎵 🔳 🔲 ⓛ

Pils iela 9, LV-3101 **Tel** *6312 5747*   **Road Map** *C3*

Alus Pagrabs has a pub-like atmosphere with a large TV in one corner. Grilled meat and fried fish are the menu highlights, but the selection is wider than that at most provincial restaurants. There is a bowling alley which opens daily, and the place turns into a disco on weekend evenings.

VENTSPILS Buginš 🚻 🔳 🔲 🍴 ⓒⓒ

Lielā iela 1/3, LV-3601 **Tel** *6368 0151*   **Road Map** *B3*

With wooden beams and old photographs adorning the wall, this lively place attempts to emulate the setting of a cosy rural log cabin. However, the TV in the main room somewhat disturbs the effect. The food, mostly standard Latvian, is decent. The service, however, is not particularly quick.

VENTSPILS Splīns 🎵 🔲 Ⓥ 🍴 ⓒⓒ

Kuldīgas iela 17, LV-3601 **Tel** *6362 2589*   **Road Map** *B3*

Popular with well-heeled locals, Splīns serves international cuisine cooked to a high standard. The austere dining room is fortunately enlivened by video monitors screening classical works of art. Some evenings feature live music performances, generally blues or classical. It doubles as a nightclub after hours.

VENTSPILS Melnais Sivēns 🔳 🔲 ⓒⓒⓒ

Jāņa iela 17, LV-3602 **Tel** *6362 2396*   **Road Map** *B3*

The most atmospheric dining option in Ventspils, Melnais Sivēns is housed in the basement of the city's Livonian Order castle. It serves interesting medieval cuisine, such as black pudding with apple and cranberry marmalade, and spice-marinated pork with sorrel sauce, in a candlelit ambience.

EASTERN LATVIA

AGLONA Upenīte 🔲 🚻 🔳 🔲 ⓛ

Tartakas iela 7, LV-5304 **Tel** *2631 2465*   **Road Map** *E4*

A member of the European Network of Regional Culinary Heritage, the Upenīte guest house offers one of the more interesting dining venues in Aglona. The dining room is styled after a medieval tavern and specializes in curd pancakes made according to a traditional Latgallian recipe.

DAUGAVPILS Gubernators 🔲 ⓛ

Lāčplēša 10, LV-5403 **Tel** *6542 2455*   **Road Map** *E4*

This lively cellar pub has plenty of choice on the menu, which is available both in French and English. The Russian influence on the city is clear, as *pelmeni* (dumplings) are served as well as the usual Latvian dishes of pork, potato and black peas. Russian Baltika beer is on offer alongside other options.

DAUGAVPILS Villa Ksenija 🔲 🍴 ⓒⓒ

Varšavas 17, LV-5404 **Tel** *6543 4317*   **Road Map** *E4*

Styled as a mansion house, this restaurant has an elegant dining room with a sideboard bearing a wide choice of brandy and single-malt scotch. The food is international in its scope, with particular emphasis on fish dishes. There is a prominent fireplace with framed collections of mounted butterflies on the walls.

DAUGAVPILS Eiropa ♿ 🔲 ⓒⓒⓒⓒ

Viestura iela 8, LV-5403 **Tel** *6545 4540*   **Road Map** *E4*

Concealed by a curtain at the back of a bowling alley, this upmarket restaurant comes as a surprise. Dining is formal, with meticulously folded napkins and piped classical music. The menu includes European dishes, such as stewed rabbit in white mushroom sauce and roasted squid fillet. Sushi is also served here.

GAUJA NATIONAL PARK Sarunas 🔲 ⓛ

Rīgas iela 4, Cēsis, LV-4101 **Tel** *6410 7173*   **Road Map** *D3*

This centrally located restaurant specializes in pizzas. However, there is also a separate menu of Russian-style meals that taste more Latvian than Russian. The red seating, lights embedded in the floor and visible air conditioning, make the place resemble a trendy bar. Friday and Saturday nights are enlivened by DJs.

GAUJA NATIONAL PARK Kolonna Hotel Cēsis

Vienības laukums 1, Cēsis, LV-4101 **Tel** *6412 0122* **Road Map** *D3*

A varied menu of Latvian cuisine is served in the rather formal dining room of Kolonna Hotel Cēsis *(see p306)*. Lamb, beef and pork grills, as well as fresh fish and seafood, are among its staples. However, it is only open during summer. The more casual and cheaper Café Popular in the basement is open year-round.

GAUJA NATIONAL PARK Lāču Miga

Gaujas iela 22, Līgatne, LV-4110 **Tel** *6415 3481* **Road Map** *D3*

Located in the hotel of the same name *(see p306)*, this restaurant is bear-themed and is signposted by orange paw prints. Wooden furniture and white leather chairs give the place a modern look, while the menu offers high-quality international dishes. Nice touches include freshly squeezed fruit juices and after-dinner chocolates on every plate.

GAUJA NATIONAL PARK Aparjods

Ventas iela 1a, Sigulda, LV-2150 **Tel** *6797 2230* **Road Map** *D3*

Themed on a farmhouse, Aparjods has a warm interior decorated with sepia photographs and cane and wood furnishings. Alongside traditional Latvian cuisine, more adventurous European dishes, such as snails, are also available. It is a popular dining venue despite being outside the town centre.

GAUJA NATIONAL PARK Kunga Rija

Krimuldas pagasts, Turaida, LV-2147 **Tel** *6797 1473* **Road Map** *D3*

Food is served in a relaxed atmosphere on the mezzanine and ground floors of this restaurant which resembles a large log cabin. The menu is quite adventurous for provincial Latvia, featuring dishes such as fried salmon trout in a herb crust with plums and a rosé wine sauce.

GAUJA NATIONAL PARK Pilsmuiža

Pils iela 16, Sigulda, LV-2150 **Tel** *6797 1425* **Road Map** *D3*

Housed in the New Castle built in 1867, this restaurant serves straightforward Latvian cuisine, such as steaks, shashlik and fish, in an appealing wood-panelled room. The Art Deco fireplace is a particularly imposing feature. There are also outdoor seating options in small pavilions during the summer.

GAUJA NATIONAL PARK Spa Hotel Ezeri

Siguldas pagasts, Sigulda, LV-2150 **Tel** *6797 3009* **Road Map** *D3*

The modern dining room in the Spa Hotel Ezeri *(see p306)* has a Scandinavian-influenced decor. The short yet interesting menu comprises modern European cuisine. It is an excellent place to dine, even for those not staying at the hotel or using the spa facilities. Closed on Monday and Tuesday.

GULBENE Kalna Lacītēs

Rankas pagasts, LV–4416 **Tel** *2922 5352* **Road Map** *E3*

A cut above most Latvian roadside eateries, this modern log cabin with a thatched roof is a pleasant restaurant. The Latvian menu offers local dishes with children's options and non-alcoholic cocktails. The staff are friendly and helpful. There is a watermill, Lacītēs Ūdensdzirnavas, close by.

IKŠĶILE Meidrops

Rīgas iela 18, LV-50522 **Tel** *6503 0466* **Road Map** *D3*

Located in a prime spot on the banks of the Daugava river, the restaurant in the Meidrops hotel *(see p306)* is a modern log cabin with thatched roof. Great attention has been paid to detail with decorative metalwork by a local artisan. Meals such as smoked duck salad with mushrooms and spinach are served on handmade dishes.

JĒKABPILS Uguntiņa

Pasta 23b, LV-5201 **Tel** *6523 1907* **Road Map** *D4*

A favourite among locals, this bustling self-service restaurant offers a wide selection of Latvian dishes such as pork, potatoes and black beans, as well as a few more unexpected items such as sushi. The menu is only in Latvian, but the staff are usually very helpful with deciphering it.

JĒKABPILS Hercogs Jēkabs

Brīvības iela 182, LV-5201 **Tel** *6523 3433* **Road Map** *D4*

This restaurant, set by the Daugava river, is a cosy spot for both lunch and dinner, with a menu that includes Latvian staples such as pork chops. It is more of a pub than a restaurant, with simple wooden chairs and tables as well as a few comfortable leather sofas.

KOKNESE Vino Rosso

Koknesis pagasts, LV-5113 **Tel** *2921 2909* **Road Map** *D4*

Located on the bank of the Daugava river, this restored warehouse is part of the Bilstiņi manor complex in Koknese. The restaurant serves Mediterranean cuisine, including antipasti, with a menu that changes weekly. The wine list has choices complementing specific dishes.

KRĀSLAVA Mārīte

Tirgus 2, LV-5601 **Tel** *6562 4039* **Road Map** *E4*

In the absence of any genuine restaurants in town, this centrally located café is popular with locals. The name Mārīte means "ladybird", and this is reflected in the predominantly scarlet decor. The menu is straightforward, covering the usual Latvian basics of chicken, pork and fish. There is live music on Friday evenings.

Key to Price Guide *see p330* **Key to Symbols** *see back cover flap*

LAKE RĀZNA Rāzna

Astiči, Kaunatas pagasts, LV-4622 **Tel** *2999 4444* — **Road Map** *E4*

Situated in a well-equipped lakeside complex, Rāzna offers authentic Latvian cuisine to travellers exploring the lakes of the Latgale region. The bright dining room, with white tablecloths and light wood furniture, has pleasant views of the waterfront. Call ahead as the café often hosts events.

LIELVĀRDE Lielvārdes Osta

Krasta iela 2, LV-5070 **Tel** *6505 3041* — **Road Map** *D4*

Part of the Lielvārdes Osta boutique hotel *(see p306)* on the Daugava river, this restaurant is undoubtedly one of the best in the region. The well-presented international fare is served in a cosy dining room with a roaring fire in winter. The bar has been made from the bow of a boat.

LIMBAŽI Bīriņu Pils

Bīriņi iela, LV-4014 **Tel** *6402 4033* — **Road Map** *D3*

Housed in the brick-lined cellar of Bīriņi manor house, Bīriņu Pils *(see p306)* is a pleasant hotel restaurant. However, it is slightly out of the way for those not staying at the hotel. The menu is limited and mostly covers simple Latvian meat dishes. Children's options are also available.

PREIĻI Pie Pliča

Raiņa bulvāris 9, LV-5301 **Tel** *2912 1689* — **Road Map** *E4*

Part of the hotel Pie Pliča *(see p307)*, this restaurant is furnished with wooden chairs, tables and panelling, and decorative features such as old jug displays, giving the place its desired rustic appeal. Its authentic Latvian cuisine is widely regarded as the best in town.

RĒZEKNE Little Italy

Atbrīvošanas aleja 100, LV-4600 **Tel** *6462 5771* — **Road Map** *E4*

Centrally located Little Italy is a favourite with locals. This first-floor restaurant has pleasant views and a menu that features a wide selection of Italian favourites. There are 30 types of pizza, in addition to pasta and other dishes. Desserts include an unusual folded pizza filled with fruit.

RĒZEKNE Latgale

Atbrīvošanas aleja 98, LV-4600 **Tel** *6462 2180* — **Road Map** *E4*

This restaurant, on the ground floor of the Latgale hotel *(see p307)*, is an appealing dining venue. The relatively formal setting with plush furnishing is brightened up with large windows. The restaurant's menu has a wide range of Latvian dishes, though vegetarian options are limited.

SALACGRĪVA Rakari

Svētciems, just off Via Baltica (Rīga–Tallinn), LV-4033 **Tel** *6407 1122* — **Road Map** *D3*

Part of a well-equipped recreation complex *(see p307)* that includes a hotel, guest houses and camping grounds, Rakari serves Latvian favourites in a large brick and timber building. Visible from the main road just south of Svētciems, its landmark is a giant yellow chair in a field.

SALACGRĪVA Zvejnieku Sēta

Rīgas iela 1, LV-4033 **Tel** *2962 4153* — **Road Map** *D3*

The fishing boat and nets displayed outside are a clue to the specialities of this restaurant. However, in addition to fish and other seafood, it serves salads and soups. Conveniently located in the centre of town, Zvejnieku Sēta is a pleasant place to sample hearty local fare.

STĀMERIENA Vonadziņi

Skolas iela 1, LV-4406 **Tel** *6447 1151* — **Road Map** *E3*

Attractively situated by Lake Ludza, the restaurant in the Vonadziņi hotel *(see p307)* makes an excellent refreshment stop for those touring the area. The restaurant is part of a complex of log buildings with thatched roofs, and there are plenty of recreation possibilities as well as a menu of international dishes.

VALMIERA Dikļu Pils

Dikļu pagasts, LV-4223 **Tel** *6420 7480* — **Road Map** *D3*

The impeccably restored Dikļu Pils *(see p307)* houses this restaurant, with a formal, though not stifling, ambience. The food here consists of an interesting array of Latvian and international dishes emphasizing seasonal and local ingredients, such as fish from nearby Lake Burtnieku. There is a decent selection of meals for vegetarians.

VALMIERA Rossini

Bruņinieku 3, LV-4201 **Tel** *6422 6622* — **Road Map** *D3*

Well-placed below the Museum of Local Studies, Rossini is a classy Italian restaurant with vaulted ceilings and an unusual bar partly made from wine-bottle corks. The menu specializes in popular Italian cuisine such as pizza and pasta, and also includes a reasonable choice of vegetarian dishes.

VECPIEBALGA Jumurdas Muiža

Jumurda, 19 km (12 miles) S of Vecpiebalga, LV-4844 **Tel** *6487 1791* — **Road Map** *D3*

This restaurant is part of a lakeside hotel complex developed from manor buildings. The modern European cuisine blends rural culinary traditions with urban sophistication. The summer terrace offers brilliant lakeside views and has a retractable roof that is useful in case of bad weather.

Choosing a Restaurant in Lithuania

These restaurants have been selected for their food, good value and location. They are listed by region, starting with Vilnius, followed by the rest of Lithuania. Restaurants are listed alphabetically within each price category. For Vilnius map references, see pages 246–7; for road map references see the back cover.

PRICE DETAILS
Based on the price per person of a three-course meal with half a bottle of wine, including cover charge, service and tax.
Ⓛ Under 55 Lt
ⓁⓁ 55–65 Lt
ⓁⓁⓁ 65–75 Lt
ⓁⓁⓁⓁ 75–85 Lt
ⓁⓁⓁⓁⓁ Over 85 Lt

VILNIUS

Briusly
🔲 V   Ⓛ

Šv Ignoto 14 **Tel** *614 95676*   **Map** 2 D3

Named after Kung Fu culture's most famous fighter, Briusly serves simple and tasty Pan-Asian meals at surprisingly affordable prices. This informal restaurant's modestly sized premises can get crowded with trendy young locals in the evening. It is one of the few places in Vilnius that serves hot curry.

Čili Kaimas
🚹🎵🔲🔲 V   Ⓛ

Vokiečių 8 **Tel** *231 2536*   **Map** 2 D4

Offering Lithuanian food in a vast barn-style venue complete with farming implements and a tree growing through the middle, Čili Kaimas is loud, kitsch and hugely popular. Two menu options are provided, one offering better food at higher prices. The vodka snacks followed by pigs' trotters and stuffed intestines must be sampled.

Forto Dvaras
🚹🔲 V   Ⓛ

Pilies 16 **Tel** *261 1070*   **Map** 2 D3

This restaurant employs a team of local culinary experts to regularly check the ingredients and kitchen implements for authenticity. Diners can choose between the village atmosphere upstairs and the cavernous cellar theme restaurant with a menu demonstrating that there is more to Lithuanian food than *cepelinai* (stuffed dumplings).

Gras'as
🎵🔲🔲   Ⓛ

Vokiečių 2 **Tel** *212 2031*   **Map** 2 D4

As its name suggests, Gras'as uses grass as the main feature of its interior design, especially on the walls. Despite their simplicity, dishes commonly take a while to prepare, but the merry evening atmosphere and the bizarre decor keep visitors occupied during the wait. Meals here are good value for money.

Mambo Pizza
🔲🔲 V   Ⓛ

Upės 6 **Tel** *656 82408*   **Map** 1 C2

Situated near the Reval Hotel Lietuva *(see p309)*, Mambo Pizza serves possibly the tastiest pizzas in Vilnius. In summer, tables are laid around the exterior windows amid the lush green expanse along the Neris river. Evenings attract a youthful crowd and the place sometimes turns into a lively nightclub.

Pas Rudolfą II
🔲   Ⓛ

Gedimino 46/2 **Tel** *249 6668*   **Map** 1 B2

Named after the 16th-century King of Bohemia, Pas Rudolfą II is a Czech restaurant serving cheap and quick meat and potato meals along with some of the world's best beers. Its decor sets the ambience of a medieval tavern with iron gloves that punch through walls to hold up lamps, assorted weapons and shelves full of helmets.

Transylvania
🔲 V   Ⓛ

Totorių 22/3 **Tel** *262 2301*   **Map** 2 D3

The casual pub-style Transylvania serves an unusual spread of inexpensive but authentic Carpathian dishes, with decor to match and rock music playing in the background. The menu is surprisingly long, with a fair smattering of vegetarian as well as meat dishes, such as Dacian roast and pepper steak served with flaming absinthe.

Užupio Klasika
🔲 V   Ⓛ

Užupio 28 **Tel** *215 3677*   **Map** 2 E4

A tiny, romantic café fashioned out of a living room, Užupio Klasika is a pleasant spot for a long, intimate rendezvous, partly because dishes often take a painfully long time to arrive. Meals are carefully created by a single chef, so more than a handful of guests can slow things down. The food is, however, well worth the wait.

Vandens Malūnas
🚹🎵🔲🔲 V

Verkių 100 **Tel** *271 1666*

The delightful setting of this restored 19th-century watermill is a lush valley just below Verkiai Palace. The indoor seating by the fireplace in winter is as lovely as sitting by the rushing water in spring and summer. The food is simple Lithuanian cuisine, but it undoubtedly complements the location.

Key to Symbols *see back cover flap*

Avilys
Gedimino 5 **Tel** *212 1900*   **Map** *1 B2*

Avilys is a microbrewery and the interior decor of vats, metal ducts and tubes adds to the feeling of it being like a factory. The atmosphere is warm and jovial, the fare tasty. The honey beer that is brewed in-house is delicious, and honey-flavoured dishes such as the honey steak are a perfect accompaniment.

Barcelona
Linkmenų 5/66 **Tel** *275 6873*

Not far from the capital's new business district, Barcelona is the only Spanish restaurant in Vilnius. Highlights include paella, which takes precisely 20 minutes to prepare and is served steaming in a pan, as well as tapas and sangria. The decor is slightly stark, but the lively weekend evenings warm things up.

Belmontas
Belmonto 17 **Tel** *6861 6656*

Nestled in the Vilnius Valley, just a 10-minute taxi ride from the Old Town, Belmontas is an enjoyable year-round choice consisting of three restaurants. Vila Gloria offers fireside dining with good wines, Joanos Carinovos Smuklė is a far less ceremonious barn-style eatery and Belmono Kriokliai has a summertime barbecue.

Cozy
Dominikonų 10 **Tel** *261 1137*   **Map** *2 D4*

Located in the heart of the Old Town, Cozy is one of the city's hippest café-restaurants with a DJ-bar. The contemporary jazz music complements the subtly lit interiors decorated with Buddhas and framed black-and-white photographs. It serves decent European cuisine and set lunches. The lounge-style DJ-bar is an ideal spot to unwind.

Didžioji Kinija
Konstitucijos 12 **Tel** *263 6363*   **Map** *1 C1*

Of the many Chinese restaurants scattered around the city, Didžioji Kinija is probably the best. It serves generous helpings of delicious food in almost overflowing plates. The main dishes are placed in the centre of the table. For the sake of variety, order two or three different dishes. The restaurant's candle-lit ambience is romantic.

Dubliner
Domininkonų 6 **Tel** *243 0807*   **Map** *2 D4*

Most Irish-style pubs in the Baltic States make do with serving Guinness and hanging a few pictures of Oscar Wilde on their walls. Fortunately Dubliner is not limited to this cliché. Fabulous Irish boxty is served here alongside chicken tikka and scrumptious pies. Attentive service and a relaxed, casual atmosphere complete the picture.

IdaBasar
Subačiaus 3 **Tel** *262 8484*   **Map** *2 E4*

This restaurant presents a choice between a reasonably priced atrium café and a more classy, less-frequented gourmet restaurant in the cellar. The food served in the café, such as the *tarte flambée* or onion tart, is cheap, filling and tasty, especially when teamed with Lithuanian beer. The European fare served downstairs is more refined.

Saint Germain
Literatų 9 **Tel** *262 1210*   **Map** *2 D3*

Modestly sized but hugely popular with expatriates, Saint Germain blends an excellent choice of wines, impressive food and a Provence-style atmosphere. Salmon and *dorado* (mahi mahi) are cooked to perfection and cheeses are given ample prominence. The outdoor seating beneath the spires of the Old Town is especially popular.

Sorena
Islandijos 4 **Tel** *262 7560*   **Map** *1 C3*

Superbly spicy Azerbaijani cuisine is the speciality at Sorena, which also serves the best hummus and falafel in Lithuania. *Tebriz*, which is a tender roll of beef served on a sword-like skewer with a pot of hot, home-made *adjika* sauce, is another of the menu's Eastern delights. Georgian wine is served with food as a thirst-quencher.

Tores
Užupio 40 **Tel** *262 9309*   **Map** *2 E4*

The outdoor terrace at Tores, with its sweeping view of the Old Town spires, the Upper Castle and surrounding parks, makes it worth the price. It is a lovely spot for a pre-dinner drink-with-a-view. The fish dishes and desserts are reasonable, but the menu and service never quite live up to the scenic wonders.

Verkiai
Žaliųjų ežerų 49 **Tel** *210 2333*

Tucked away behind one of the two surviving wings of Verkiai Palace, just north of the Vilnius city limits, is the wonderful Verkiai restaurant. It looks especially enchanting in summer, when the flowers surrounding the outdoor pavilion are in full bloom. The decor is subtle and the food enjoyable without being ostentatious.

Miyako
Konstitucijos 7a **Tel** *248 7060*   **Map** *1 C1*

Housed on the top floor of the elegant and thoroughly post-modern Europa shopping centre, Miyako has a restaurant with a sushi bar with subtle Japanese ambience. The restaurant's sashimi is delectable and cuts of fish are superb. Another highlight is the soup with crispy asparagus.

Riverside 🏃♿🏠✈Ⓥ♟ ①①①
Konstitucijos 20 **Tel** *272 6272* **Map** *1 C1*

Black lacquered furniture with drapes and a decor in warm earthy hues makes this restaurant housed in the Reval Hotel Lietuva *(see p309)* cosy. The big open kitchen is still an attraction and the food is always a delight. Seafood is the focus of the extensive menu. For wine, guests can peruse vintages at the restaurant's central wine station.

Sonnets 🎵🏠✈Ⓥ♟ ①①①
Bernardinų 8/8 **Tel** *266 5885* **Map** *2 E3*

Exuding elegance, Sonnets is housed in the Shakespeare Boutique Hotel *(see p310)*. Seating ranges from snug sofas by the bar and fine-dining tables in the library to the less formal balcony. The menu reads like Dante's *Inferno*. "Aleksandr", a mix of chestnuts, Gorgonzola and baked fig, is the restaurant's signature dessert.

Sue's Indian Raja 🎵🏠✈Ⓥ ①①①
Odminių 3 **Tel** *266 1887* **Map** *2 D3*

An old Vilnius favourite, Sue's Indian Raja is among the most reliable restaurants in town that serve authentic Indian cuisine. Ably managed by a retired Indian Air Force officer, the delicious korma and wonderfully spicy *jalfrezi* blend with less familiar enchantments for the palate. Occasional live Indian music recitals add to the atmosphere.

Da Antonio ♿🏠✈Ⓥ♟ ①①①①
Vilniaus 23 **Tel** *262 0109* **Map** *1 C2*

Opened as Vilnius's first quality Italian restaurant in 1997, Da Antonio combines an intimate elegance with traditional cooking. Pizzas are prepared in a wood-fired oven, pasta is created on the premises and the wines are an imaginative selection from Italy. Reproductions of Italian art add the final touch to the ambience.

El Gaucho Sano ♿✈ ①①①①
Pilies 10 **Tel** *210 7773* **Map** *2 D3*

Although not quite as authentically Argentinian as it advertises itself to be, El Gaucho Sano, in the Atrium hotel *(see p309)*, prepares some of the best steaks in Vilnius. Thick cuts of meat, served on wooden carving boards with a choice of sauce dips, makes it a carnivore's favourite. South American red wine served here suits the cuisine.

Garden Brasserie 🏃♿✈Ⓥ♟ ①①①①
Raugyklos 4a **Tel** *233 5648* **Map** *2 C5*

Novotel Vilnius's *(see p309)* restaurant knows how to serve a crème brûlée. The French-trained chefs never add too much spice in their creations, preferring instead to allow the ingredients to retain their natural flavour. Another highlight is the Sunday buffet, a family-friendly tradition. Closed from June to August.

La Mama 🎵✈♟ ①①①①
Didžioji 28 **Tel** *260 9009* **Map** *2 D4*

Housed inside an upmarket mini-entertainment centre in the Old Town, La Mama lays special emphasis on steaks and roasts. The menu ranges from a choice of beef, duck and ostrich to delicious grilled salmon and tuna steak. Seating by the windows offers a pleasant view of Town Hall Square.

Medininkai 🏠✈Ⓥ♟ ①①①①
Aušros vartų 8 **Tel** *266 0771* **Map** *2 D5*

The restaurant at the Europa Royale Vilnius *(see p310)* has an atmospheric courtyard for dining in summer and an evocative cellar for chillier weather. The chef likes to call her dishes Lithuanian fusion, but in reality Medininkai serves international cuisine with a certain panache. Service may sometimes seem tardy.

Brasserie Astorija 🏃♿✈Ⓥ♟ ①①①①①
Didžioji 35/2 **Tel** *212 0110* **Map** *2 D4*

One of the classiest restaurants in Vilnius and with the most cordial service, Brasserie Astorija is at the Radisson SAS Astorija *(see p310)*. The chef emphasizes the use of fresh, healthy ingredients in his cooking. Every course is a delight, especially the seafood, and the wine list is exceptional. The glass vestibule is great for people-watching.

La Provence ✈Ⓥ♟ ①①①①①
Vokiečių 22 **Tel** *262 0257* **Map** *2 D4*

This classy restaurant, with quality of service and prices to match, reputedly offers the most exquisite gourmet fare in town. Visited mostly by diplomats and entrepreneurs, La Provence stand out on account of its reliability at blending superb Mediterranean and French cuisine with unmatched presentation makes.

Stikliai 🎵🏠✈Ⓥ♟ ①①①①①
Gaono 7 **Tel** *264 9580* **Map** *2 D4*

Housed in Relais & Châteaux Stikliai *(see p310)*, this restaurant offers a choice of two different venues. The exquisite restaurant, with a French accent, serves jacket potatoes and great goulash besides desserts such as chocolate ice cream in gold leaf. The less pretentious beer hall in the cellar serves European and Lithuanian cuisine.

Tokyo ✈ ①①①①①
Vienuolio 4 **Tel** *7005 5599* **Map** *1 C2*

Located within the Grand Casino World complex, Tokyo ranks among the best Japanese restaurants in the Baltic States. Optionally served with excellent sake, the sushi, sashimi and tempura are first-rate, and the *hamachi* and tuna cuts superb. The bustling casino seems miles away from Tokyo's relaxed interior.

Key to Price Guide *see p338* **Key to Symbols** *see back cover flap*

CENTRAL LITHUANIA

ALYTUS Dzūkų Svetainė

Rotušės 16 **Tel** *(315) 73 780* **Road Map** *D6*

Fairly nondescript from the outside, this is one of the more reliable spots in this part of Dzūkija for a basic home-cooked meal. Local specialities include pork roast with mushrooms and *koldūnai* (meat dumplings roasted with cheese and sauce). Locally made cheeses are used in snacks that go well with wine or beer.

ANYKŠČIAI Mindaugo Karūna

Liudiškių 18 **Tel** *(381) 58 520* **Road Map** *D5*

This fine-dining restaurant is located in a hotel and sports centre off the Molėtai road, on the town's eastern edge. Well-prepared European dishes are served with a fair selection of European wines as well as locally made wines and brandies. An amiable oak-furnished pub sits in the same complex.

ANYKŠČIAI Romuvos Parkas

20 km (12 miles) E of Anykščia, Žaliosios village, Svedasų region **Tel** *(381) 57 747* **Road Map** *D5*

Part of the Romuva Park Hotel and leisure complex, this small, intimate restaurant rustles up pleasant European and Lithuanian fare that suitably complements the panoramic view of the pine forest. A sunroom can be reserved for small groups and diners can use the equally sunny patio in good weather.

AUKŠTAITIJA NATIONAL PARK Baras Palūšė

Vasario 16-osios g 16 **Tel** *(386) 47 473* **Road Map** *D5*

Standard, though hearty, Lithuanian fare is served at this modest wooden house in the Aukštaitija National Park. However, in addition to the staple beer and fried pork, filling portions of *cepelinai* (stuffed dumplings) and good rye bread are also available .

BIRŠTONAS Birštono Seklytėlė

Prienų 10 **Tel** *(319) 65 800* **Road Map** *D6*

Stunning views are the main attraction at Birštono Seklytėlė, perched on a platform above the densely forested Nemunas Delta region. It may be hard to find a table at the edge, but the seating inside this airy Scandinavian-style lodge is just as pleasant. The food is hearty, with the usual emphasis on chicken, pork and beef.

BIRŠTONAS Sonata

Algirdo 34 **Tel** *(319) 65 825* **Road Map** *D6*

Hidden away by the banks of the Nemunas river in the quiet spa town of Birštonas, the windows of this hotel restaurant peer out onto a lush pine forest. The spectrum of meals on offer is gratifyingly broad, the presentation conscientious and without any of the reliance on mayonnaise common in Lithuania outside the cities.

BIRŽAI 19-tas Kilometras

Raubonių village, Pasvalys, 19 km (11 miles) from the Latvian border **Tel** *(451) 39 676* **Road Map** *D4*

Located on the Via Baltica motorway to Riga, 19-tas Kilometras rustles up canteen-style cutlets, pancakes and salads. This is less a place to dine than a convenient stop to break the journey between capital cities, but the home-made apple pie and *tinginys* chocolate cake available here are very popular.

DRUSKININKAI Kolonada

Kudirkos 22 **Tel** *(313) 51 222* **Road Map** *D6*

Sophisticated jazz, blues and classical music are played at this lovingly restored, 80-year-old colonnade building tucked inside a landscaped park. Lavishly renovated and re-opened in 2004, this modern restaurant and music club now provides delicious meals. Very popular with artists and intellectuals.

DRUSKININKAI Regina

Kosciuškos 3 **Tel** *(313) 59 060* **Road Map** *D6*

The Regina hotel *(see p311)* boasts one of the biggest restaurants in this spa resort. The huge floor-to-ceiling windows add to the sense of space. In summer, the dining area sprawls onto a large patio, providing a sense of Druskininkai's restorative and peaceful environment. The menu contains a broad range of European cuisine.

DRUSKININKAI Europa Royale Druskininkai

Vilniaus 7 **Tel** *(313) 42 221* **Road Map** *D6*

Venison and duck are the staples at this steeply priced restaurant at Europa Royale Druskininkai *(see p312)*. The dishes are carefully prepared and exquisitely presented and the service is as attentive as can be found anywhere outside Vilnius. The glaring white decor makes even a speck of dirt unthinkable.

KAUNAS Bernelių Užeiga

Valančiaus 9 **Tel** *(37) 20 0913* **Road Map** *D5*

Generous helpings of authentic Lithuanian food are served in this restaurant, located within the confines of the Old Town. The interior evokes the feel of a country tavern and the exterior, in gaudy purple peppered with bright red flowers, makes it hard to miss. This 18th-century building is a protected architectural monument.

KAUNAS Metų Laikai

Mickevičiaus 40b **Tel** *(37) 223 253* **Road Map** *D5*

Literally translated as "four seasons", Metų Laikai has a contemporary take on traditional Lithuanian food. This quaint little café is best for beer, snacks or coffee and cake. The prices here are very reasonable, making it a favourite among budget travellers.

KAUNAS Tado Blindos Smuklė

Kęstučio 93 **Tel** *(37) 202 993* **Road Map** *D5*

Named after Lithuania's very own Robin Hood, who roamed the woods and forests of Northern Lithuania in the mid-19th century, the Tado Blindos Smuklė is a lively and unsophisticated eatery that is popular with both the young and old. Meat dishes dominate the menu, along with tasty stews and broths.

KAUNAS Didžioji Siena

Kumelių 7 **Tel** *(37) 220 585* **Road Map** *D5*

Didžioji Siena, with its refined ambience, is the most reasonably priced option for Chinese food in Kaunas. The menu provides some vegetarian choices, but excels in exotic seafood dishes. The set lunch menus make this a convenient option midway through a tour of the Old Town.

KAUNAS Pompėja

Putvinskio 38 **Tel** *(37) 422 055* **Road Map** *D5*

With clay floor tiles and mock-classical Roman frescoes, Pompėja conjures up the spirit of ancient Rome. An unlikely combination of haute cuisine and sizeable portions means that the broadly Mediterranean dishes on offer should satisfy demanding appetites. Weekend evenings see lively entertainment programmes.

KAUNAS Ramzis II

Daukšos 29 **Tel** *(37) 324 301* **Road Map** *D5*

A slice of Egypt tucked down a side street in the Old Town, Ramzis II serves both authentic and Western versions of Egyptian cuisine and provides hookahs and hosts belly-dancing shows during weekends. A restaurant to be enjoyed rather than taken too seriously, as exemplified in the menu, which features "Viagra soup".

KĖDAINIAI Grėjaus Namas

Didžioji 36 **Tel** *(347) 51 500* **Road Map** *D5*

One of the loveliest restaurants in Central Lithuania, Grėjaus Namas is housed in the Old Town hotel of the same name *(see p312)*. Set within the building's subtly decorated cellars, the restaurant offers fish dishes bathed in home-made sauces and the choicest cuts of beef and pork in an optional whiskey sauce.

KERNAVĖ Pušynėlis

Verkšionys, near Dūkštai **Tel** *(699) 48 945* **Road Map** *D5*

Situated above a stunning, thickly forested bend in the Neris river, Pušinėlis commands a stunning view, which is its primary attraction. The food cannot quite match the panorama, but a children's playground makes this an attractive destination for families.

MARIJAMPOLĖ Sudavija

Sodo 1a **Tel** *(343) 52 995* **Road Map** *C6*

In the quiet retreat that is the Sudavija hotel *(see p312)* is a snug dining room with white tablecloths, a warm fireplace, a piano and delicious home-cooked food. A restaurant of the same name once stood on Kęstučio Street in pre-war Marijampolė and this newer incarnation continues its legacy of good food and a homely ambience.

PANEVĖŽYS Forto Dvaras

Savaitiškio 61, Babilonas Shopping Centre **Tel** *(45) 442 887* **Road Map** *D5*

The Panevėžys branch of the reliable Forto Dvaras chain is decorated in Lithuanian-homestead style with wooden clocks and framed old photographs adorning the walls. Calorific traditional local food such as *cepelinai* (stuffed dumplings) and potato pancakes is available here. The service is friendly.

PANEVĖŽYS VIP Martini Club

Respublikos 70 **Tel** *(45) 469 090* **Road Map** *D5*

A great place to combine an evening meal with a night on the town, the VIP Martini Club puts special emphasis on dancing. Dishes available here are generally light, such as hot chicken salad, although the beefsteak with mush-rooms is filling and rather good. Open on Friday and Saturday, from 9pm to late.

PANEVĖŽYS Deja vu

Kranto 24 **Tel** *(45) 584 859* **Road Map** *D5*

The only classy restaurant in Panevėžys is located inside the Romantic hotel *(see p313)*. Its interior of ferns and flowers, rich oil paintings and murals, soft furniture and tableware help maintain the hotel's name. The dishes are refined and stylishly presented. The outdoor terrace looks out onto the Nevėžis river and its former riverbed.

TRAKAI Kybynlar

Karaimų 29 **Tel** *(528) 55 179* **Road Map** *D5*

Traditional Karaim dishes served here include beef, lamb, chicken, vegetables and fresh fish baked in crisp pastry. Karaim decorative patterns and colours pervade the interior, but tastefully and never kitsch. *Kibinai* (savoury pastry) is a favourite, preferably accompanied by strong drink, but the *šišlik* (steak) is fabulous too.

Key to Price Guide *see p338* **Key to Symbols** *see back cover flap*

TRAKAI Senoji Kibininė

Karaimų 65 **Tel** *(528) 55 865* **Road Map** *D5*

The first Karaim eating house in Trakai, this old barn has been in existence for several years. It is informal and hugely popular considering the fact that there are only two items on the menu: *kibinai* pastries and *čenakai* (stewed cabbage hotpot). Guests should try both accompanied with beer in summer and vodka at other times.

TRAKAI Trakų Dvarkiemis

Užukampis village **Tel** *(618) 88 880* **Road Map** *D5*

Nestled amid the forests and fields on the road from Vilnius to Trakai, this newly constructed wooden mansion, though quirky from the outside, offers a unique dining experience. It offers a healthier approach to Lithuanian cuisine with plenty of leafy salads and vegetarian and meat options. A popular stop for families.

TRAKAI Akmeninė Rezidencija

Bražuolės village, 30 km (19 miles) N of Vilnius Airport **Tel** *(614) 8698 30544* **Road Map** *D5*

Hard to find due to the absence of any signposts, this is a delightfully elusive hideaway hotel and restaurant, captivatingly situated on the shores of Lake Akmena. Two of the tables stand on a pier, the others above the grassy banks. Caucasian spices give the dishes an exotic aroma and the wines suit them.

TRAKAI Apvalaus Stalo Klubas

Karaimų 53a **Tel** *(528) 51 790* **Road Map** *D5*

Perched at the water's edge directly facing Trakai's Island Castle, this restaurant benefits from having one of Lithuania's prettiest views. The menu ranges from gourmet French to Lithuanian national flavours with delights ranging from duck to tiger prawns along with some excellent wines that complement the food superbly.

VILNIUS–KLAIPĖDA MOTORWAY Bajorkiemis

Karčiupio village, 15 km (9 miles) from Kaunas **Tel** *(37) 440 770* **Road Map** *D5*

A voluminous roadside inn, Bajorkiemis features a substantial menu of filling Lithuanian dishes. A playground for children lies at the back and numerous pathways stretch into the forest towards Lake Kauno Marios. This is a convenient break for those returning from the coast.

VILNIUS–KLAIPĖDA MOTORWAY Tvirtovė Prie Didžiulio

Dėdeliškių village, 20 km (12 miles) W of Vilnius **Tel** *243 2389* **Road Map** *D5*

Located near the motorway to Kaunas is a modern-day brick-built castle, with three floors of restaurant space. Though massive in size and tastelessly decorated, it serves good, unpretentious food and Lithuanian beer with a fine view of the surrounding lakes and countryside.

VILNIUS–MOLĖTAI ROAD Žaldokynė

Raudondvaris village, 17 km (11 miles) N of Vilnius **Tel** *250 2291* **Road Map** *D5*

An adventure in traditional Lithuanian food can be found on the road to Molėtai. A thatched barn-like mansion conceals a maze of dining rooms with a very complicated floor plan. Much care goes into the varieties of *cepelinai* (stewed dumpling) dishes on offer. Fifty varieties of potato were tested before the right types were found.

VILNIUS–PANEVĖŽYS MOTORWAY Le Paysage

Motorway A2, 17 km (11 miles) N of Vilnius **Tel** *273 9628* **Road Map** *D5*

Set within the upmarket Le Meridien Villon Resort *(see p310)*, Le Paysage is a destination in its own right. Its tall, curved windows overlook the rolling countryside. The French cuisine is exquisite, particularly the seafood and the fabulous array of French cheeses. Combine the trip with a visit to the hotel's Oasis Spa.

VISAGINAS Grilis

Sedulinos 5b **Tel** *(386) 60 237* **Road Map** *E5*

In the extraordinary town of Visaginas, perhaps the best location for a meal or an evening drink is Grilis. The dishes served here are broadly Lithuanian even though, as everywhere else in town, little else except Russian is spoken. In good weather, the rooftop terrace offers fine views.

WESTERN LITHUANIA

CURONIAN SPIT NATIONAL PARK Baras po Vyšniom

Naglių 10, Nida **Tel** *(469) 52 906* **Road Map** *B5*

Edged by a garden of cherry trees and evenly cut grass, Baras po Vyšniom is a pretty wooden chalet on Nida's most enticing street. Home-cooked meals available here go well with local beer or a glass of wine. Especially popular in the summer months, it is advisable to book ahead.

CURONIAN SPIT NATIONAL PARK Lyra

Preilos 15/1, Preila **Tel** *(469) 6124 6447* **Road Map** *B5*

A modest seasonal restaurant, Lyra is located in Preila, one of the Curonian Spit's smaller fishing villages. The back-garden dining area that faces onto the lagoon is a good spot to view the seascape. The dishes here are filling and there is a special menu for children.

CURONIAN SPIT NATIONAL PARK Vella Bianca

Rézos 1a, Juodkranté **Tel** *(469) 50 013*   **Road Map** *B5*

One of the finest restaurants on the Curonian Spit, with panoramic views of the lagoon and Juodkranté harbour, Vella Bianca boasts excellent Italian cuisine and a range of fine wines. Exploiting the location, it presents fabulous seafood creations, although its meat, pasta and home-made pizza dishes are also superb.

KLAIPĖDA Senoji Hansa

Kurpių 1 **Tel** *(46) 400 056*   **Road Map** *B5*

The dominant attraction of Senoji Hansa is its prime location and outdoor seating. This is more a sunny spot for a midday snack, a coffee or a beer than for a romantic evening meal, but the dishes on offer are Lithuanian in style, much of them fried, and the service is as relaxed as most of the holidaymakers.

KLAIPĖDA Anikės Kuršiai

Sukilėlių 8/10 **Tel** *(46) 314 471*   **Road Map** *B5*

This little restaurant makes use of its attractive Old Town location and summertime outdoor seating to serve authentic Curonian cuisine to passing tourists. Curonian coffee and home-made cranberry juice complement set meals, enough for two, based largely on smoked ham, herring, sauerkraut and sour milk.

KLAIPĖDA Ferdinandas

Naujoji Uosto 10 **Tel** *(46) 313 681*   **Road Map** *B5*

One of Klaipėda's two Russian restaurants, Ferdinandas is a short walk along a busy road from the Old Town but is worth the effort, as it presents a quaint and authentic Russian feel. The menu includes soups with pies, stuffed pork and *dičj*, a dish of roasted fowl that was once the mainstay of Tsar-style cuisine.

KLAIPĖDA Petit Marseille

Žvejų 4a **Tel** *(46) 430 472*   **Road Map** *B5*

Reflecting the same winning characteristics as Saint Germain *(see p339)*, its partner restaurant in Vilnius, the Petit Marseille features a wonderful selection of French food and wine, delicious cheeses and satisfying desserts. The Old Town location and outdoor seating by the Danė river add to the charm, making it a relaxing dining spot.

KLAIPĖDA Stora Antis

Tiltų 6 **Tel** *(46) 493 910*   **Road Map** *B5*

A lovely old-fashioned brick cellar in the Old Town, Stora Antis specializes in Russian cuisine and has, in recent years, welcomed many popular Russian cultural figures to its candlelit lair. *Pelmeni* (stewed dumplings) and *borsch* (beetroot soup) feature on the menu, along with seafood and steak and some surprisingly good wines.

KLAIPĖDA Navalis

H Manto 23 **Tel** *(46) 404 200*   **Road Map** *B5*

With wide windows facing onto Klaipėda's bustling shopping street, freshly made coffee and Wi-Fi, this café, housed at the Navalis hotel *(see p314)*, is very popular with visitors. There is also a fine-dining restaurant that prepares divine fish and seafood dishes served with exotic sauces, as well as delicious desserts.

KLAIPĖDA San Marino

Žvejų 21/1 **Tel** *(46) 404 444*   **Road Map** *B5*

One of Klaipėda's most tasteful dining options, San Marino is located in the Europa Royale Klaipėda *(see p314)*. The occasional sculpture and Corinthian column hint at ancient Rome. The fancy Italian dishes served here are perfectly suited for amorous candlelit dinners for two and the choice of wine is among the best in Klaipėda.

KLAIPĖDA Sinbado Oazė

Didžioji Vandens 20 **Tel** *(46) 211 786*   **Road Map** *B5*

Delightful on every level, Sinbado Oazė is one of Old Town Klaipėda's dining surprises. The Middle Eastern food is fabulous yet reasonably priced and the ambience very relaxed. The belly-dancing performances in the dimly lit interior in the evenings are charming. The option of outdoor dining is also available, but the inside is far cosier.

KRETINGA Pas Grafą

Vilniaus 20 **Tel** *(445) 51 366*   **Road Map** *B5*

The elegant café-restaurant Pas Grafą, inside the winter gardens of Count Tiškevičius's 19th-century palace in Kretinga, is perfect for coffee and a light snack. Exotic plants and vines hang from the ceiling, making it a delightful stop, especially in winter. Closed on Mondays.

NEMUNAS DELTA Ventainė

Ventė village, Šilutės region **Tel** *(441) 68 525*   **Road Map** *B5*

A restful, isolated hotel, campsite and aqua park, Ventainė offers everything from Roman baths to tennis. Its restaurant is one of the few places in these parts to serve a cooked meal. The view of the Curonian Lagoon adds to the list of attractions and a well-stocked bar keeps the place humming during summer evenings.

NIDA Sena Sodyba

Naglių 6/2 **Tel** *(469) 52 782*   **Road Map** *B5*

Sena Sodyba is set back slightly from bustling Naglių street, giving the impression of a private dining spot set in a private back garden. The service is pleasantly alert, but it is the freshness of the food, particularly the fish dishes and the fish soup, that is the real highlight of this popular dining venue. Open only from June to August.

Key to Price Guide *see p338* **Key to Symbols** *see back cover flap*

NIDA In Vino

Taikos 32 **Tel** *(655) 77 997*   **Road Map** *B5*

Fabulously positioned, In Vino is a laid-back wine bar that serves a wide choice of alcoholic and soft drinks made from grapes. The views from In Vino are gorgeous, but the menu comes second to the extensive wine list. It is possible to ask the management to keep an unfinished bottle for a return visit a day or two later.

NIDA Prūsų Rūmai

Naglių 29 **Tel** *(469) 52 578*   **Road Map** *B5*

One of Nida's more popular eating venues, the Prūsų Rūmai is popular with both families and tourist groups for serving satisfying portions of broadly European dishes. The ingredients are fresh and the fish is bought straight from local fishermen. The nautical-themed decor inside is predictable but not too cheesy.

NIDA Ešerinė

Naglių 2 **Tel** *(469) 52 757*   **Road Map** *B5*

Strategically placed in the loveliest corner of Nida, this restaurant serves delicious food in a friendly atmosphere. The Hawaiian-style straw parasols juxtaposed with elegant furniture outside is eye-catching. However, the interior is far more brash, giving Ešerinė the feel of a British pub.

PALANGA Elnio Ragas

J Basanavičiaus 25 **Tel** *(460) 53 505*   **Road Map** *B5*

Brazenly decked out with hunters' trophies and a lurid mural dedicated to the joy of the hunt, the Elnio Ragas tempts diners with roe deer and boar meat, served with the predictable potatoes and vegetables. Beer is the beverage of choice here, with fewer wine options.

PALANGA Alanga

S Nėries 14 **Tel** *(460) 49 215*   **Road Map** *B5*

Housed in the Alanga hotel *(see p315)*, this restaurant is a haven of sophisticated calm. The decor of fish tanks, painted seashells and sand-coloured walls are ample reminders of its close proximity to the beach. It offers excellent European cuisine and a range of decent international wines.

PALANGA 1925 Senolių Užeiga

J Basanavičiaus 4 **Tel** *(460) 52 526*   **Road Map** *B5*

A snug wooden chalet located in a bustling corner of town, 1925 Senolių Užeiga rustles up delicious breakfasts of omlettes and porridge, tasty bar snacks and more substantial meals. The sausages and chips served here will surely please kids. A friendly atmosphere, reliable food and sheltered setting beneath trees makes this a favourite.

PALANGA Žuvinė

J Basanavičiaus 37a **Tel** *(460) 48 070*   **Road Map** *B5*

Far more than just another restaurant on Palanga Beach, this wonderful fish restaurant has a menu that features an impressive variety of fish and seafood, from simple herring to a glorified salmon *carpaccio* and the finest black caviar. There is even a scrumptious surf-and-turf tiger-prawn steak.

ŠIAULIAI Juonė Pastogė

Aušros al 31a **Tel** *(41) 540 559*   **Road Map** *C4*

Perhaps Šiauliai's most enjoyable Lithuanian restaurant, Juonė Pastogė serves a wide array of traditional food. Situated in a fairly quiet part of town, it is also a music club featuring a lively programme, and is very popular with families. In summer a spacious, green yard opens up as an extension of the dining area.

ŠIAULIAI Medžiotojų Užeiga

Dubijos 20 **Tel** *(41) 524 526*   **Road Map** *C4*

With a bar made out of cowhide and old photographs of hunters with their trophies, game is undoubtedly the focus of Medžiotojų Užeiga. It is possible to order in advance for an entire roasted boar served on a tray of salad. Much smaller dishes are available too, including fish.

ŠIAULIAI Arkos

Vilniaus 213 **Tel** *(41) 520 205*   **Road Map** *C4*

A high-ceilinged cellar-based café-bar that takes its cuisine seriously, Arkos concentrates on fish in summer and meats ranging from beef to ostrich in winter. The menu also comes with wine recommendations and desserts are worth leaving room for. It also hosts live music on Friday and Saturday.

ŠILUTĖ Rambynas

Lietuvininkų 68a **Tel** *(441) 77 055*   **Road Map** *B5*

One of the biggest restaurants serving Šilutė's needs, Rambynas is centrally located on the town's main street. It is also a morning café, bar and nightclub. Weekend nights even include a programme of adult entertainment. The food, which is also available as home delivery, is standard filling fare.

ŽEMAITIJA NATIONAL PARK Linelis

Paplatelės village, Plungė region **Tel** *(687) 35 058*   **Road Map** *C4*

Part of the lovely Linelis hotel *(see p315)* and aqua park on the shores of Lake Plateliai, this restaurant manages to be delightfully cosy both in summer and in the depths of winter. Candles and romantic music light up the evenings spent amid the ancient forest. The menu includes both national and European dishes, and some good wines.

SHOPPING IN ESTONIA

Traditional handicrafts and souvenirs can be found all over Estonia. The country's retail sector is, in general, quite uniform outside the major towns of Tallinn, Tartu and Pärnu. Shopping malls have had a considerable impact on smaller towns and the same stores and brand names fill out the bulk of these identikit malls. Despite this, towns and villages are good places to find local

Viking, sold in souvenir stalls

specialities, including handicrafts, locally woven textiles such as blankets and rugs, and high-quality organic honey from local farms. Most towns hold small markets where visitors can find food and household items. Antique stores also stock some interesting objects. Prices are usually lower outside Tallinn. Estonian chocolate, alcohol and cigars are readily available in most supermarkets.

Vibrantly painted ceramic bowls, jugs, tumblers and vases for sale

OPENING HOURS

Most shops are generally open from 10am to 6 or 7pm on weekdays, and from 10am to 4pm on Saturdays, and are closed on Sundays. Shopping centres usually open from 10am to 8 or 9pm daily. In small towns and villages, opening hours are more erratic at weekends, with many shops only opening for half a day or staying closed. Grocery stores normally keep longer hours, and in Tallinn there are several 24-hour convenience stores.

HOW TO PAY

All large stores and the majority of small shops throughout Estonia accept most major credit and debit cards. Retail outlets prominently display logos for accepted credit and debit cards. Visitors may be asked for proof of identity when

paying with a credit card. However, most market stalls and out-of-the-way places accept only krooni *(see p385)*.

RIGHTS & REFUNDS

In Estonia, all goods come with a two-year warranty under EU law. However, after a period of six months from the date of purchase, the customer might be asked to prove that the defect existed at the time of buying and was not introduced later. Warranties are only effective on production of a valid receipt.

Refunds remain discretionary on the part of the seller, although most major stores will provide a refund as long as there is no damage to the goods and the receipt is produced. Legal guidance can be sought from the Consumer Centre of Estonia *(see p349)*, which protects consumer rights in the case of cross-border purchases.

VAT EXEMPTION

Nearly all goods and services are subject to the mandatory 18 per cent VAT, which is always included in the display prices. Non-EU citizens can claim a VAT refund of up to 13 per cent on some goods, if they are shown on departure to customs within three months of their purchase, together with a VAT refund application form.

SALES

Throughout Estonia, sales are usually held in the middle and at the end of a season, although the most significant reductions are reserved for the New Year sales. Watch out for a sign in shop windows, which may read as *allahindlus* (discount), *soodusmüük* (sale), *lõpumüük* (final sale), or *tühjendusmüük* (everything must go).

MARKETS

Just about every Estonian town has a market, known as *turg*, although they often only sell fruit, vegetables, household goods and other everyday items. There is little in the way of souvenirs or curios to be found in these markets. Kuressaare market in Saaremaa is a rare exception. It also sells trinkets, such as dolomite-carved objects, in addition to the local produce. For Estonian mementos the best bet is to attend one of the annual folk or town festivals held across the

Trendy clothes displayed in the window of a Kaubamaja store in Tartu

country. Impromptu markets are set up with stalls selling an array of local delicacies, quirky gifts and a fascinating range of handicrafts, including colourful ceramics, stained glass and woodcarvings.

DEPARTMENT STORES & SHOPPING MALLS

The country's best department stores, such as Stockmann and Kaubamaja *(see p349)*, are in Tallinn, although Kaubamaja has recently opened a huge new department store in Tartu. Shopping malls are far more prevalent and are springing up in town centres and suburbs all around the country at a phenomenal rate.

Malls are good for essentials, but they offer little for the discerning shopper.

Supermarkets, such as Selver and Rimi, are extremely common throughout Estonia. These enormous hypermarkets sell just about everything one can think of, from everyday household items to an extensive collection of alcohol, chocolates, cigarettes and music.

REGIONAL SPECIALITIES

Visitors can buy a number of popular local products from all over Estonia. The country has a stunning selection of regional specialities that make ideal souvenirs. In Tallinn,

traditional items, such as hand-knitted mittens and socks, lace, ceramics, amber, leather-bound books, silverware and objects carved out of limestone, are widely available. Kihnu Island *(see p101)* is famed for its colourful and elaborately patterned handmade rugs, as well as thick woollen fishermen's jumpers made by the island's inhabitants.

In southeastern Estonia, home to the Setu people *(see p120)*, one can purchase authentic examples of the embroidered shawls and ornate jewellery that are unique to their culture. The Setu were also the only people in Estonia to commonly use pottery which is sold in several ceramics shops. Today, pottery fairs peddle their wares in the main Setu towns. The use of dolomite is unique to Saaremaa Island *(see pp92–5)*. Dolomite is used to make a wide range of souvenirs, such as carved ashtrays, pestles and mortars. Muhu Island is famous for its embroidered hand-made slippers and bright orange knitwear. Pärnu *(see pp98–9)* is known for its linen and the most popular souvenirs in the coastal resort of Haapsalu *(see pp88–9)* are hand-woven and beautifully patterned white shawls.

Visitors purchasing beautifully crafted cane baskets from a local market

Shopping in Tallinn

Tallinn has witnessed a proliferation of sleek new shopping malls in recent years. Most international brand names can be found alongside a considerable range of popular Scandinavian brands. Tallinn's Old Town, which has some exclusive fashion boutiques and speciality art shops, is also one of the best places in the capital for gift shopping and souvenir hunting. Almost every street has something in the way of traditional handicrafts, such as ceramics, glassware, linen, wooden utensils and toys. There are plenty of stores and market stalls which specialize in art, antiques, jewellery, amber, knitted woollens, patchwork quilts and interesting knick-knacks. The Christmas Market in Town Hall Square is especially popular and brings together virtually every imaginable Estonian product.

Colourful ceramic collection at the stylish Bogapott studio

Russian dolls and amber jewellery for sale on one of Tallinn's souvenir stalls

MARKETS

Tallinn's main market, the open-air Central Market, offers a glimpse into the everyday life of the city's inhabitants. Stalls full of fresh produce may not offer much variety for the average souvenir-hunter, but the Central Market's bustling atmosphere is worth the experience. Those interested in shopping can try and haggle. The market

selling knitwear at the corner of Viru and Müürivahe covers a sizeable stretch of the Old Town wall and is a great place to find a gift. Uus Käsitööturg, a popular stall in the market, has a good selection of traditional handicrafts and souvenirs. The Christmas Market in Town Hall Square *(see pp58–9)*, which runs through December, features everything from knitwear and decorative items to marzipan.

HANDICRAFTS

Much more than just souvenirs aimed at tourists, Estonian handicrafts are synonymous with a traditional way of life that persists even today. Tallinn abounds with a bewildering variety of handicrafts. Wooden toys and utensils are particularly common as are a wide range of ceramics, including candle-holders modelled after the Old Town buildings. Traditionally woven rugs are still made today, some of which are more like works of art with their beautiful and elaborate patterns.

Bogapott, an exclusive ceramics studio, and **Galerii Kaks**, with its wide range of textiles, are worthy of a visit. **Nukupood** stocks handmade toys as well as dolls dressed in traditional folk costumes of Estonia. In **Katariina Gild**, craftsmen can be seen creating handicrafts, jewellery and ceramics. **A-Galerii** has a dazzling selection of local hand-made jewellery.

ART & ANTIQUES

Tallinn's contemporary art scene offers plenty of galleries and small shops that stock all manner of attractive oil paintings, graphic art, textiles, sculpture and off-beat ceramics.

The city has several antique shops selling everything from Soviet-era paraphernalia to exorbitantly priced Russian icons. Emerging only in the 1990s, antique shops have quickly become a fascinating and flourishing retail niche.

Woven baskets, knitting wool and textiles at the Town Hall Square market

Special permission is needed to take some objects out of the country, so check with the shop manager before buying. With a stunning range of bronze items, silverware and crystals, **Reval Antiik**, **Shifara Art & Antiques** and **Navitrolla Galerii** are among Tallinn's best antiques stores.

BOOKS & MUSIC

The best bookstore in Tallinn for English-language books is **Apollo**. This outlet has a range of gift-books relating to Estonian culture and history, as well as a small selection of Estonian novels translated into English. Look out for the English translation of *The Czar's Madman* and *Treading Air* by Jaan Kross (1920–2007), the esteemed Estonian writer.

Estonia's wealth of choral and classical music also makes for a great gift. CDs of the works of renowned composers, such as Heino Eller (1887–1970), Eduard Tubin (1905–82) and Arvo Pärt *(see p23)*, are widely available, as are folk music and choral music compilations. **Lasering**, one of the leading music stores in Tallinn, has an impressive selection of various kinds of music and a separate section on classical music.

Apollo, Tallinn's primary bookstore, stocks a range of gift-books

FOOD & DRINK

Estonian food products are ubiquitous and can usually be found in any supermarket. Rye bread is a local staple, as are sprats, smoked fish and

Kaubamaja store, one of Tallinn's leading shopping venues

cheese, *halvah* and blood sausage, during the Christmas season. Try the gourmet section at **Kaubamaja** for variety. For chocolate-lovers, Kalev, Estonia's largest and oldest chocolate and confectionary producer, offers a wide range of luxury chocolates with picturesque prints of Tallinn on the box. These chocolates can be bought from local food stores. Real chocolate connoisseurs should try the handmade delicacies at **Anneli Viik**. There are also numerous bakeries selling delicious pastries and cakes. **Stockmann**, one of the largest department stores, also stocks cakes, bagels and savouries.

Vana Tallinn *(see p320)*, a very sweet, brown liqueur, is considered to be the national drink of Estonia. Those without a sweet tooth may prefer it mixed with coffee, while some people even drink it with milk. In terms of sheer consumption, beer is by far the most popular drink in Estonia. Saku Originaal is the dominant brand, but Tartu Alexander and A Le Coq beers are popular brews as well. There is an abundance of locally made, as well as quality imported, vodka which is considerably cheaper than in other European countries. Saare Džinn, a gin flavoured with berries from the Estonian islands, is good too. **Liviko**, one of Estonia's leading alcohol producers, has stores all over Tallinn.

Logo of Kalev chocolate

SHOPPING IN LATVIA

Handmade crochet hat

Numerous supermarkets and shopping centres have opened in major towns and cities throughout the country since 1991. However, Rīga undoubtedly has the country's largest range of shopping options. This is particularly true when it comes to items likely to be of interest to visitors, although outside the capital it is usually possible to find typical handicraft items such as amber jewellery and embroidered knitwear. Museum gift shops are normally good places to pick up interesting mementos when a town or village lacks a dedicated souvenir retailer. Several workshops across the country allow visitors to watch artisans at work and even make their own pottery, woodwork and other items to take home. Latvian markets cater mostly to local people, but can still be fascinating places to visit. Local honey, chocolate, beer or a bottle of Black Balsam can make excellent gifts.

OPENING HOURS

Most shops in Latvia open around 10am. Small shops close around 6 or 7pm, while bigger malls and shopping centres usually stay open until 10pm. Many small shops remain closed on Sundays.

HOW TO PAY

In cities and large towns, it is possible to pay with debit cards and major credit cards such as MasterCard or VISA. Some places will also accept American Express and Diners Club. In smaller towns and villages cash payment in the local currency, the lat *(see p386)*, may be the only option.

It is rare for traveller's cheques to be accepted as payment outside Rīga, the capital city, although those issued by major companies can usually be exchanged at most banks.

VAT EXEMPTION

Visitors from non-EU countries are entitled to a VAT refund of up to 12 per cent, provided that the items were purchased in a shop displaying the "Tax Free" logo and the total price of purchases made from the shop was at least 29.50 lats. Identification must be shown at the point of purchase, and a Global Refund receipt completed. Purchased items cannot be used until the receipt is stamped by a customs official when leaving the country. The VAT can be reclaimed at the customs zone in the airport or the land borders with Russia, at Terehova and Grebņeva. For departures from other locations, the receipt should be stamped and sent to Global Refund Latvia *(see p353)* along with the visitor's bank details within six months.

SALES

Although locally made items are fairly cheap compared to other EU countries, prices for imported goods tend to be high in Latvia, a situation which has not been helped by high inflation. One way of picking up a bargain is to go to the end-of-season sales, when shops reduce their prices.

MARKETS

Most Latvian towns have regular or even daily markets, although they are rarely aimed at tourists and are most useful for everyday food purchases. However, some markets, such as the covered market hall in Liepāja *(see pp180–81)*, which is a throwback to the Soviet era, are extremely atmospheric. In the summer months, some markets, like the ones in Jūrmala, sell souvenirs as well as fresh produce.

DEPARTMENT STORES & SHOPPING MALLS

Most sizeable towns have at least one department store or supermarket. Several malls and shopping centres have been built in important cities such as Rīga, Ventspils, Liepāja and Daugavpils. Some of these malls are located in the outskirts of the cities, while others are more central and easy to access. The larger retailers include Rimi, Maxima and Mego.

Collection of fresh produce for sale at the Central Market, Rīga

Handcrafted items displayed at the Ludza Handicrafts Centre, Eastern Latvia

HANDICRAFTS

Traditional Latvian handicrafts include hand-made linen, amber jewellery, woodwork and knitwear embroidered with popular Latvian folk symbols. Motifs from the natural world, such as the sun, stars or trees, are commonly used as part of the repertoire of geometric designs found on many handcrafted goods. A particularly attractive example is the *Lielvārdes josta*, a long red-and-white woven belt which features symbolic patterns, and is a part of Latvian wedding costumes. These belts are available in souvenir shops in Rīga, and can be seen on display at the Pumpurs Museum in Lielvārde, or even made to order.

Visitors can watch artisans at work in several places, such as the House of Craftsmen in Liepāja. The Handicrafts Centre in Ludza has workshops where visitors can try their hand at crafting items themselves. Musical instruments can be purchased from the Musical Instruments Workshop in Gaigalava.

The Smithy of Ancient Jewellery in the New Castle in Cēsis calls itself a workshop of experimental archaeology,

A bar of Laima, Latvia's favourite chocolate

with master craftsman Daumants Kalniņš making replicas of ancient designs. Another place to find handicraft items is the branch of Tornis in the tower of Turaida Castle in Gauja National Park.

FOOD & DRINK

Available in many varieties, Laima *(see p353)* chocolate has been made in Latvia for decades and is among the country's most popular buys. Another common gift is Rīga's Black Balsam *(see p320)*, a herbal liqueur with supposedly medicinal properties, which comes in attractive ceramic bottles. Visitors usually prefer it in cocktails or with blackcurrant juice rather than neat.

Beer also makes a good gift. Latvians are enthusiastic beer-drinkers so there are several brands to choose from. The most popular ones are now internationally owned, but more unusual brews include the yeasty Užavas, which is made near Ventspils.

ART & ANTIQUES

Genuinely valuable Latvian antiques are not easy to find, partly because the 20th century saw many of them destroyed or lost during war

and occupation. In spite of this, antique shops are well worth exploring, especially because they often stock interesting items. The best place to buy art is in commercial art galleries. A licence, which is available at most shops, is usually required before genuine antiques can be exported. The shops are helpful with the paperwork.

AMBER

Amber jewellery is a popular Latvian souvenir, despite the fact that resin is less commonly discovered in Latvia than Lithuania. It is readily available in tourist areas, such as Jūrmala, and in some museum shops.

Buyers should be aware that not all amber is genuine, as various plastics are used to emulate it. Visitors spending a large sum of money on amber objects should ask for a certificate of authenticity, and it is generally safer to buy from an established shop rather than a street-seller.

ROADSIDE STALLS

In the countryside, especially in rural Latgale, it is common to see stalls at the side of the road selling fresh produce. Latvian honey is particularly delicious and also makes a good gift.

Shopping in Rīga

Once a member of the powerful Hanseatic League
(*see p32*), the Latvian capital has had a distinguished
mercantile history. Although its harbour is no longer
one of the most important in the region, commerce has
flourished since the restoration of independence, with
boutiques and department stores springing up throughout the city. Specialist shops can be found all over the
Old Town and in shopping malls, while major high-
street brands are available in Centrs. Souvenir shops,
mostly found in the Old Town, sell handicrafts of
variable quality including linen, amber jewellery and
knitwear. Handmade chocolates and Rīga Black Balsam,
the city's signature drink, are popular gifts.

DEPARTMENT STORES & SHOPPING MALLS

The years since independence
have witnessed the development of many new shopping
centres and department stores
as well as the renovation of
stalwarts such as the 1920s
Galerija Centrs.

Upmarket boutiques and
galleries can be found at
Berga Bazārs, a 19th-century
enclave of shops, offices,
restaurants and apartments.
The **Palazzo Italia** department
store is the hub of designer
fashion, while **mc²** has stores
specializing in gourmet food
and home accessories. For
more basic shopping there
is **Stockmann**, on the edge
of the Old Town.

MARKETS

Housed in five huge zeppelin
hangars, Rīga's Central Market
has most of its indoor space
dedicated to food, while the
stalls and kiosks selling CDs,
clothes and electrical goods
are outside. Also of interest is
the covered outdoor antique
and organic food market on
the second and fourth Sunday
of each month at Berga
Bazārs. Latvians love to give
flowers and the city's main
Flower Market is open 24
hours a day, through the year.

MUSIC

Folk music was a key part
of the National Awakening
Movement (1856), although in
the years since independence
it has become harder to find
a sizeable clientele for folk
recordings. Rīga's best
music outlet is **Upe**,
a chain owned by
the former frontman
of folk-rock band Jauns
Mēness. Upe specializes
in folk music from Latvia
and beyond, and also sells
musical instruments.
Randoms is perhaps
the biggest music shop
in the Baltic States.
Cheap CDs can be bought at
the Central Market, although
bootleg versions are rife.

Decorative wall
lamp

CLOTHING & JEWELLERY

Handwoven garments, lace
items and knitwear are popular souvenirs. Designer clothes
are available at upmarket
stores, while smaller shops sell
traditional woollen garments.
Claiming to be one of the
only amber-free souvenir
shops in the city, **Nordwear**
has sweaters in traditional
designs. **Kleoss** specializes in
trendy knitwear for women.

In addition to countless
places selling amber neck-
laces and bracelets, there are
several shops offering more
unusual jewellery. The stylish
Tornis stocks pieces inspired
by ancient Latvian designs, as
well as more modern styles.

HANDICRAFTS

There are numerous souvenir
shops in the Old Town stock-
ing items such as linen
and wooden toys. In
some cases, however,
these are mass-
produced rather than
handmade. More authentic
and unusual gifts can be
found in **Grieži**, which also
holds craft demonstrations.
Tine boasts a wide
range of souvenirs,
while **Sāmsalas Kalēji**
specializes in metal-
work. Some shops also sell
Russian objects such as
matryoshka, wooden dolls
of various sizes which are
placed one inside the other.

ART & ANTIQUES

There are many commercial
art galleries in Rīga and the
tourist information office can
provide an up-to-date list.
Māksla XO is one of the city's
most highly regarded

A shopper browsing for souvenirs at Art Nouveau Rīga

Amber jewellery displayed in a window at the exclusive A&E store

galleries. **Art Nouveau Rīga**, a leading souvenir shop, offers attractive reproductions, along with scarves, mugs and other objects inspired by early 20th-century designs. The shop is conveniently located at the end of Alberta iela, a street with the city's most impressive Art Nouveau buildings.

Rīga also has a fine selection of antique shops, mostly clustered around Brīvības iela. Upmarket emporiums include **Doma Antikvariāts**, while the chaotic **Retro A** is packed with a bewildering range of Soviet memorabilia. Religious icons and musical instruments are available at **Volmar**.

AMBER

Rīga has dozens of shops selling amber jewellery. A high-end store for an exclusive experience, **A&E** proudly counts Hillary Clinton and Hannelore Kohl among its past customers. Slightly further down the scale are **Dzintara Muzejs** and **Dzintara Galerija**. The former also has a small museum although most visitors will not find it informative enough. There are also several general souvenir shops selling more affordable

Rīga Black Balsam

items. Amber can also be found at street stalls, but it may not be genuine.

FOOD & DRINK

Laima has been one of Latvia's leading chocolate brands since 1870, and it has a dedicated store in Rīga. In recent years, however, its position has been challenged by the more upmarket **Emihls Gustavs Chocolate**, which has stores all over the city, including one in the Valters un Rapa bookshop. For something more traditional, many varieties of honey are available at the **Latvijas Bite** shops owned by the Latvian Association of Beekeepers. The famous Rīga Black Balsam also makes a popular gift, which probably has as much to do with the ceramic bottles it comes in as the drink itself. It is widely available, although **Latvijas Balzams** is among the best places to buy it from. Found across Rīga, Latvijas Balzams stores sell over 50 types of Latvian alcoholic beverages.

DIRECTORY

DEPARTMENT STORES & SHOPPING MALLS

Berga Bazārs
Dzirnavu iela 84.
www.bergabazars.lv

Galerija Centrs
Audēju iela16.
Tel 6701 8018.
www.galerijacentrs.lv

mc²
Krasta iela 68a. *Tel 6700 6868.* www.mc2.lv

Palazzo Italia
K Barona iela 2.
Tel 6707 0930.
www.palazzoitalia.lv

Stockmann
13 Janvāra iela 8.
www.stockmann.lv

MUSIC

Randoms
Kaļķu iela 4.
Tel 6722 5212.

Upe
Vaļņu iela 26. *Tel 6720 5509.* www.upett.lv

CLOTHING & JEWELLERY

Kleoss
Matīsa iela 57/2.
Tel 2962 3353.

Nordwear
www.nord-wear.com

Tornis
Grēcinieku iela 11–2.
Tel 6722 0270.
www.balturotas.lv

HANDICRAFTS

Grieži
Mazā miesnieku iela1.

Sāmsalas Kalēji
Laipu iela 6.
Tel 6722 4496.

Tine
Vaļņu iela2.
Tel 6721 6728.

ART & ANTIQUES

Art Nouveau Rīga
Strēlnieku 9, Laipu 8.
Tel 2836 7112.

Doma Antikvariāts
Doma laukums 1a.
Tel 6781 4401.
www.antikvariats.lv

Māksla XO
Skārņu 8. *Tel 2948 2098.*

Retro A
Tallinas 54.
Tel 6731 5306.

Volmar
Šķūņu 6.
Tel 6721 4278.

AMBER

A&E
Jauniela 17.
Tel 6722 3200.

Dzintara Galerija
Torņa iela 4.
Tel 6732 5157.

Dzintara Muzejs
Kalēju iela 9/11.
Tel 6708 7545.

FOOD & DRINK

Emihls Gustavs Chocolate
Aspazijas bulvāris 24.
Tel 6722 8333.
www.sokolade.lv

Laima
Ģertrūdes iela 6. *Tel 6727 9214.* www.laima.lv

Latvijas Balzams
Audēju iela 8. *Tel 6722 8814.*

Latvijas Bite
Ģertrūdes iela 13.
Tel 6727 9495.

VAT EXEMPTION

Global Refund Latvia
www.globalrefund.com

SHOPPING IN LITHUANIA

Souvenirs and gifts available in Lithuania usually consist of traditional arts and handicrafts made from local materials such as amber, ceramics and wood. Beautiful handmade flax or linen table-cloths and throw blankets, garments and soft toys are often available at reasonable prices. The shops and stalls of the Old Towns in the larger cities as well as the various resorts are flooded with most of these objects.

Mushrooms and berries for sale

Handicrafts of a superior quality and in greater variety can be found at specialist shops, which are commonly located close to the major tourist sights. Food and drink in Lithuania are distinctive in taste. The local cheeses and smoked meats on offer are varied and delicious. The wide choice of Lithuanian alcohol, such as *trauktinės*, often described as a bitter brandy, as well as vodka and beer, are great souvenirs to carry back home.

OPENING HOURS

Shops in Lithuania are usually open from 9am until 6pm on weekdays. Some gift and souvenir shops open at 10am. Food shops and supermarkets belonging to larger chains often open at 8am and close late in the evening.

The Soviet-era practice of closing for an hour for lunch is slowly fading and a handful of supermarkets are open 24 hours a day. Many shops open on Saturdays until 4pm, and some in tourist areas and in large city and town centres are open on Sundays as well. In smaller towns and villages, local stores close early so visitors should avoid leaving shopping until the evening.

HOW TO PAY

As in the other countries of the Baltic region, almost all shops in Lithuania accept major international credit and debit cards. Some smaller retail outlets may accept only the local currency. Bargaining is rarely practised except at some market and souvenir stalls, but visitors are welcome to try.

VAT & TAX-FREE SHOPPING

In Lithuania sales tax, known locally as *pridėtinės vertės mokestis* (PVM), is levied on most goods at a flat rate of 18 per cent. By law, visitors from non-EU nations can claim a refund of sales tax from

customs when they leave the country, provided they have completed a tax-free shopping cheque, available at stores where the "Tax-Free Shopping" sign is displayed. Shoppers should have their passport with them at the time of purchase. VAT can be paid back only if the outward journey is made by air, road or sea; rail is exempt. Visitors need to spend a minimum of 200 litas, including VAT, in a shop in one day to claim the refund of sales tax.

DEPARTMENT STORES & SHOPPING MALLS

To meet the growing demands of local consumers, sprawling modern shopping complexes are being constructed in Vilnius as well as in most of Lithuania's large towns and cities. The malls are replacing the old department stores

dating from the Soviet era, whose interiors were usually adapted in the 1990s to fit the needs of small traders.

Shopping malls have a main anchor tenant, which tends to be one of the leading nationwide supermarket chains. As a result, the range of goods available is practically the same as that found in the rest of Europe. For more authentic shops, visit the Old Towns in the major cities.

AMBER

Lithuanian artisans have applied great imagination to the crafting of amber, an indisputable part of the country's cultural heritage. They fashion it into jewellery, lampshades, writing materials and a great range of other objects.

Amber comes in browns, greens and other colours, besides the more familiar

Europa *(see p356)*, a stylish shopping mall in Vilnius

Souvenir stall on Theatre Square, Old Town, Klaipėda

yellow. It is also available as original polished stones, of which the most valuable and exquisite are those that have insects, plants, leaves and feathers preserved in the fossilized resin.

HANDICRAFTS & REGIONAL SPECIALITIES

Lithuanian craftsmen make all manner of objects out of wood, such as handcarved spatulas and spoons, and grotesque masks of devils and witches, whose distorted, freakish faces are traditionally displayed every Shrovetide. A far more acceptable wooden memento is the *rūpintojėlis*, a constantly worrying Christ-like figure who sits with his chin on one hand. Another religiously themed souvenir commonly made out of wood is the crucifix.

For the musically inclined, handcarved musical instruments, such as the alluring Lithuanian *kanklės*, or zither, make an ideal gift. Russian *matryoshka* dolls are popular souvenirs and can be easily bought from local markets.

Some of the most original items of clothing that can be bought in Lithuania are made of flax. Shirts and blouses, dresses and hand-crocheted hats are all widely available, particularly in the capital's gift and souvenir shops. A hand-woven *juosta*, which is a sash or waistband often used in a wedding attire besides being used as a traditional form of

fortune-telling, is also widely available and makes a good souvenir to take home.

The agricultural nature of Lithuania has helped in preserving many local customs and traditions. Black ceramics, in the form of pots, jugs, cups and figures, are among the specialities of the southern region of Dzūkija. Further north, Aukštaitija is known for its rich tradition of music and instruments, especially its horns and pipes. In the west, the people of Žemaitija value their religious images, miniatures and shrines, which often incorporate traditional pagan symbols.

Cognac bottles on display

FOOD & DRINK

Traditional foods of all kinds are sold in Lithuanian shops, including *blynai* (a thin potato pancake similar to a crêpe with both sweet and savoury fillings), *spurgos* (doughnuts), smoked and steamed cheeses and a range of products made from curd and sour milk.

Smoked meats are usually sold as long, thick sausages or, even more authentically, bound in balls. The best local fish to buy is herring, normally marinated and sold in sealed packets. Some supermarkets also have cafés where a traditional Lithuanian meal of *cepelinai* (potato dumplings), as well as *kugelis* (baked potato pudding) and *vėdarai* (potato sausage) can be sampled. Lithuanian rye bread, such as the widely used black bread or the greyer *palangos*, can be bought from local stores. Traditional *šakotis* (tree cake) and *tinginys* (hand-made cakes) are commonly available. Mushrooms and forest berries can also make unusual gifts, but visitors need a customs clearance to carry them back. Local favourites, such as *starka* (aged, caramel-coloured vodka), or *trejos devynerios* (herbal panacea), should not be missed. The best of the many varieties of *degtinė* include the excellent gold-topped Lithuanian vodkas, while the company Alita makes a popular eponymous brand of brandy. Švyturys Premium Pils and the Švyturys Ekstra Draught are both very fine bottled beers. For more information on food and drinks *see* pages 318–21.

Matryoshka **dolls for sale at one of the many souvenir stalls in Lithuania**

Shopping in Vilnius

The main streets of the Old Town are lined with countless souvenir shops, stalls and galleries that specialize in the national favourites of amber, linen, wood and ceramics. Many of the better-quality craft shops and art galleries are also hidden in the Old Town's labyrinth of narrow lanes and courtyards, so it is worth exploring off the beaten track. Away from the Old Town, Gedimino prospektas (avenue) has a number of clothing stores, bookshops and several shopping centres, while bigger malls with huge spaces for fashionable shopping can be found further afield. With so many choices, Vilnius has evolved into a shopper's paradise.

MARKETS

The most extraordinary market in Lithuania is **Gariūnai**, located next to Vilnius's towering water-heating facility, about 5 km (3 miles) southwest of the city centre. The market sells everything from cheap clothes, shoes, toys, toiletries and cosmetics to food, gadgets and even cars. Traders come from far and wide to sell their wares and, unlike at other markets in the country, bargaining is widely practised in Gariūnai. It is open from sunrise to lunch-time every day of the week except Mondays. The best time to visit the market is during the weekend.

At the southern edge of the Old Town, near the bus and train stations, is **Halės Market**,

One of the paintings for sale on Pilies gatvė

which mostly stocks a variety of fresh fruit and vegetables, cheese, meat and cakes.

FASHION & CLOTHING

The recently spruced-up Gedimino prospektas is the best place to shop for clothes and footwear. **Gedimino 9**, one of the new mini-malls

dotting the avenue, boasts the Baltic region's first Marks & Spencer and Lindex stores. However, most of the outlets for more expensive brands tend to be found in the Old Town along Vokiečių and Didžioji gatvė (street). Vilnius also has its own treasured and highly sought-after designers with their individual boutiques, such as **Ramunė Piekautaitė**. Perhaps Lithuania's most visually impressive shopping mall is **Europa**, which brands itself as a fashion and style centre.

TRADITIONAL ARTS & CRAFTS

Shops and stalls selling traditional Lithuanian arts and crafts are most easily found along Pilies, Didžioji and Aušros vartų streets. Prices vary, so it is best to scan the market stalls before buying anything. Quaint outlets selling hand-made artifacts at cheaper rates are tucked away in the narrow lanes leading off the Old Town artery.

Linen & Amber Studio, an efficiently designed chain of gift shops, are some of the best places to find handicrafts made of amber and flax. These shops stretch up the entire length of Pilies gatvė and beyond; the one on Stiklių gatvė is among the largest.

Market stall displaying traditional amber jewellery in Vilnius's Old Town

For those interested in gifts and accessories made by local textile artists, a good destination is **Aukso Avis**. Funky felt hats, bags and jewellery, screen-printed shirts, garments and silk-printed wall pieces can be purchased here. Visitors can also craft their own souvenirs on the spot. **Sauluva** is one of the best and most reliable options as it stocks an assortment of Lithuanian handicraft items made of wood, ceramics, glass, dried flowers and amber.

ART GALLERIES

Inside the elaborately frescoed Littera bookshop, Vilnius University

Vilnius has an astonishing range of imaginative gift ideas displayed in a number of small art galleries, such as **Rūtos Galerija**. Quirky paintings, colourful plates designed with old photographs, vases and curios for shelves and mantelpieces cover the gallery space. At the **Artists' Union Exhibition Hall**, next to the Contemporary Art Centre *(see p232)*, original artwork, hand-decorated cards and a fine range of Lithuanian and international art books are the main attractions.

Many upmarket galleries in Vilnius mount shows of the work of Lithuania's foremost painters and sculptors. Their works are regularly offered for sale.

Colourful painting at an art gallery

The bohemian district of Užupis is lined with a surfeit of galleries and gift shops. Among them, **Užupio Galerija**, a working gallery selling metal and enamel pieces, is most interesting.

BOOKS & MUSIC

Vilnius has a large number of small, yet very intriguing, bookstores. Most of them sell locally published English-language reference books, coffee-table books, original as well as translated local and international fiction besides maps and postcards. **Vaga** has a whole upper floor which has a good collection of books in English.

Littera *(see p222)*, the bookshop within the Vilnius University complex, is attractive and has a lively atmosphere. It is worth visiting as much for the stunning frescoed walls and ceiling as it is for its books.

There is a lack of a single, all-encompassing record store in Vilnius. However, Muzikos Bomba in the Europa mall has a fair collection of Lithuanian and international music. It also sells music under its own record label. Fans of jazz, blues and rock should not forget to visit **Thelonious**, a quirky basement store in the Old Town stacked with records, CDs and old-fashioned hi-fi equipment. The **Humanitas** bookstore has a fine selection of art books in English as well as a small collection of local music CDs.

DIRECTORY

MARKETS

Gariūnas Market
Vilnius–Kaunas highway.

Halės Market
Pylimo & Bazilijonų street corner.

FASHION & CLOTHING

Europa
Konstitucijos 7a.
Tel 248 7070.
www.europa.lt

Gedimino 9
Gedimino 9. **Tel** 262 9764. **www**.gedimino9.lt

Ramunė Piekautaitė
Didžioji 20. **Tel** 231 2270.

TRADITIONAL ARTS & CRAFTS

Aukso Avis
Savičiaus 10.
Tel 261 0421.

Linen & Amber Studio
Stiklių 3. **Tel** 261 0213.
www.lgstudija.lt
One of several branches.

Sauluva
Literatų 3 &
Šv Mykolo 4.
Tel 212 1227.
www.sauluva.lt

ART GALLERIES

Artists' Union Exhibition Hall
Vokiečių 2.
Tel 261 9516.
www.galerija-lds.lt

Rūtos Galerija
Vokiečių 28.
Tel 231 4537.

Užupio Galerija
Užupio 3–I. **Tel** 231 2318.

BOOKS & MUSIC

Humanitas
Dominininkų 5. **Tel** 249 8392. **www**.vaga.lt

Littera
Vilnius University,
Universiteto 3.
Tel 268 7001.

Thelonious
Stiklių 12. **Tel** 212 1076.

Vaga
Gedimino 50. **Tel** 249 8121. **www**.vaga.lt

ENTERTAINMENT IN ESTONIA

Estonia has a strikingly dynamic and eclectic entertainment scene. The larger towns and cities, especially Tartu and Pärnu, have a crowded cultural calendar as well as a good nightlife scene. Classical music lovers are spoiled for choice all through the year as a range of nationwide and local concerts takes place, given by a fine selection of national and international performers. Saaremaa Island hosts many classical music festivals throughout the summer. Estonians are fond of wining and

Logo of Vanemuine concert hall, Tartu

dining, which plays an integral part in their social lives. A vast array of rustic-style pubs can be found in major towns and cities, offering a hearty meal, a friendly environment and sometimes vibrant, toe-tapping folk music. Smaller towns, such as Haapsalu, Narva and Kuressaare, have numerous bustling nightclubs and bars. A major part of Estonia's cultural life revolves around folk festivals, with almost every town hosting some kind of celebration throughout the year. For entertainment in Tallinn refer to pages 360–61.

A jam session in progress at the Viljandi Early Music Festival

INFORMATION

A good starting point for news about local concerts and events is the nearest tourist information office. *The Baltic Times* also offers information on arts and entertainment. All Estonian towns have their own websites, which usually carry listings of what is happening when. The publication *In Your Pocket* covers Tallinn, Tartu, Pärnu and other major Estonian cities.

BOOKING & PRICES

Bookings for cultural events can be made at the venue or through ticket agencies. **Piletilevi**, the biggest ticketing agency, offers both online booking and ticket purchase. A number of retail outlets throughout Estonia also offer the same service, particularly at the Selver supermarket chain and Statoil petrol stations.

CLASSICAL MUSIC, THEATRE & BALLET

Estonia has an outstanding tradition of classical music and recitals are regularly hosted all over the country. Tartu's main concert venue, the **Vanemuine**, stages theatre, classical music performances, ballet, comedy, musicals and special shows for children. Pärnu Concert Hall *(see p98)* hosts a wide range of concerts and music events.

Logo of Illusioon nightclub, Tartu

MUSIC FESTIVALS

A number of festivals are organized to promote modern and traditional music. Vilandi's annual Suure-Jaani Music Festival is held to commemorate popular composers Mart Saar and Kapp, while

Muhu Island's Future Music Festival, held in June, was established to explore the connections between traditional and world music. Other events that draw large numbers of local and international musicians are the Viljandi Early Music Festival and the Kuressaare Opera Days. For pop music fans, the highlight is the annual Pühajärve Beach Party on the shores of Lake Pühajärve. **Eesti Muusikafestivalid** has a list of nationwide festivals available online.

NIGHTLIFE

Tartu has an impressive range of pubs, clubs and bars to choose from. One of the best-known nightclubs is **Atlantis**,

Brightly lit up exterior of Tartu's favourite nightclub, Atlantis

Performers at one of the many folk festivals held in Estonia

while the most exclusive is **Illusioon**. Another favourite is the **Wilde Pub**, which has consistently attracted a huge clientele. The occasional live performances that take place at the **Illegaard Jazz Club** give it a casual, bohemian feel.

Pärnu also has a lively nightlife. **Lime Lounge** is a stylish place for a drink, while **Postipoiss** is a restaurant-cum-pub with frequent live music. The slickest nightclub in town is **Bravo**, while **Mirage**, another club, is often packed.

In Narva, head for the **German Pub** for a drink in enjoyable surroundings. **Africa** is the biggest and most popular pub in Haapsalu and doubles up as a disco during weekends. Kuressaare has a good choice of quality restaurants, pubs and bars. With an attractive outdoor deck, the **John Bull Pub** is cheerful.

FOLK FESTIVALS

Some of the most important festivals take place in July. Of these, the Folklore Festival in Võru *(see p121)* is the biggest, attracting vast numbers of dancers, musicians and singers each year. Another is the Hiiu Folk Festival in Hiiumaa *(see pp90–91)*, which has a particularly authentic ambience created by its rustic setting.

August is also a busy month. The splendid Narva Historic Festival stages an enactment of the Great Northern War *(see p33)* in Narva. Obinitsa hosts several festivals celebrating Setu culture *(see p120)*. The White Lady Days,

held on the August full moon, is a festival filled with merry-making in the grounds of the castle in Haapsalu *(see p88)*.

CINEMA

Films are shown in their original language with Russian subtitles, though the choice of films outside Tallinn is decidedly poor. Most reasonably large towns have a small cinema which shows the latest blockbusters a few weeks after being shown in the capital. Hollywood films are regularly shown at Pärnu's single-screen **Mai Cinema**. Tartu's trendy **Kino Ekraan**, located in a shopping mall, is part of the same chain as **Forum Cinemas Astri**.

The Black Nights Film Festival *(see p49)*, celebrated in November and December, travels to Tartu, Viljandi, Narva, Jõhvi and Kärdla, while Pärnu has a small film festival of its own in July.

Poster for an Estonian-language film, *Sigade Revolutsioon*

DIRECTORY

BOOKING & PRICES

Piletilevi
www.piletilevi.ee

CLASSICAL MUSIC, THEATRE & BALLET

Vanemuine
Vanemuise 6, Tartu. **Tel** 744 0100.
www.vanemuine.ee

MUSIC FESTIVALS

Eesti Muusikafestivalid
www.festivals.ee

NIGHTLIFE

Africa
Tallinna mnt 1, Haapsalu.
Tel 473 3969. www.africa.ee

Atlantis
Narva mnt 2, Tartu.
Tel 738 5485. www.atlantis.ee

Bravo
Hommiku 3, Pärnu. **Tel** 5344 3887. www.bravoclub.ee

German Pub
Puškina 10, Narva. **Tel** 359 1548.
www.germanpub.ee

Illegaard Jazz Club
Ülikooli 5, Tartu. **Tel** 742 3743.
www.illegaard.ee

Illusioon
Raatuse 97, Tartu. **Tel** 742 4341.
www.illusion.ee

John Bull Pub
Pärgi tänav, Kuressaare. **Tel** 453 9988. www.kohvila.ee

Lime Lounge
Hommiku 17, Pärnu. **Tel** 449 2190. www.wilde.ee

Mirage
Rüütli 40, Pärnu. **Tel** 447 2404.
www.mirage.ee

Postipoiss
Vee 12, Pärnu. **Tel** 446 4864.
www.trahterpostipoiss.ee

Wilde Pub
Vallikraavi 4, Tartu. **Tel** 730 9764.
www.wilde.ee

CINEMA

Forum Cinemas Astri
Tallinna 41, Narva. **Tel** 1182.
www.superkinod.ee

Kino Ekraan
Riia 14, Tartu. **Tel** 740 4020.
www.superkinod.ee

Mai Cinema
Papiniidu 50, Pärnu. **Tel** 443 9451. www.maikino.ee

Entertainment in Tallinn

Entertainment in Tallinn is astonishingly vibrant. Its classical music and opera performances are world renowned and a major tourist draw. In recent years, the city has also started to attract some big international pop artists, although its local live-music scene is far more enjoyable. A plethora of venues in Tallinn regularly host rock, jazz, blues and alternative music performances by local bands. The city's pulsating nightclub scene covers diverse genres, from mainstream pop to underground club music. There is a large choice of places to enjoy a drink. These usually stay open late into the night and range from ultra-chic lounge bars to good old-fashioned, pint-in-hand pubs. Theatre in Tallinn is generally of a very high quality, but is mostly performed in Estonian, except during international festivals.

A scene from *Carlo Gozzi Il Corvo* at the Tallinn Linnateater

INFORMATION

Visitors can check *Tallinn In Your Pocket*, *The Baltic Times* and Piletilevi *(see p359)* for upcoming events in the city.

THEATRE

Tallinn has a proud tradition of theatre and the flagship Estonian Drama Theatre *(see p72)* does a fine job of preserving the national repertoire. The **Tallinn Linnateater** specializes in contemporary work. The best place for serious theatre-lovers is the **Von Krahl Theatre**, the leading avant-garde theatre, though English translations are rare. It often stages various intensely visual multimedia productions. Russian-speakers can visit the **Russian Drama Theatre**, which puts on a range of classic and contemporary Russian theatre.

CLASSICAL MUSIC, OPERA & DANCE

Concerts by the Estonian National Symphony Orchestra, which are often held in the Estonian Concert Hall *(see pp72–3)* and the Estonian National Opera, regularly sell out thanks to their consistently high-quality performances and productions. However, there are also wonderful chamber and choral concerts held in churches and other more intimate Old Town locations every week, such as Niguliste Church *(see pp64–5)*, the House of Blackheads *(see p66)* and the **Estonian Music Academy**. The best of both contemporary Estonian as well as international dance performances are usually hosted at **St Canute's Guild**.

ROCK, POP, JAZZ & BLUES

Live-music lovers are spoiled for choice in Tallinn. **Café Amigo** attracts the biggest local rock, pop and blues bands and holds nightly performances. **Von Krahl Baar** is one of the best places in the city to experience the local alternative music scene, while the industrial setting of the **Rock Café** has a diverse range of live music ranging from blues to funk. Most of the popular international acts that come to Tallinn play at the outdoor Song Festival Grounds *(see p78)*. **No99** hosts cosy jazz concerts on Fridays and Saturdays, as well as some jazz acts during the Jazzkaar festival *(see p48)*.

PUBS & BARS

Tallinn's Old Town is packed with bars and pubs of every imaginable size and description. There are several well-acclaimed Irish and English-style pubs, such as **Molly Malone's** and **Scotland Yard**, which are as much favoured by expats as by foreign visitors. Stylish and classy lounge bars are also extremely popular among the city's well-heeled. Some of the best venues include the chic **Déjà Vu** and the extravagant **Lounge 24**, which affords spectacular views from the 24th floor of the Radisson SAS *(see p294)*. There are

Logo of Molly Malone's pub

Atmospheric interior of the stylish Déjà Vu lounge bar

Parlament, one of Tallinn's most popular nightspots

also several smaller, cosier pubs scattered around the Old Town, which are far less frequented by boisterous visitors. Intimate places, such as **Hell Hunt**, Tallinn's first real tavern, and the **Kolumbus Krisostomus**, which occasionally features live bands, offer an amiable atmosphere for a chat over a relaxing drink.

NIGHTCLUBS

The amazing choice and variety of nightclubs draws people from far and wide to Tallinn. Most of the city's best clubs are situated in the Old Town, or within walking

distance of it. Many, such as Café Amigo, **Bonnie and Clyde** and **Parlament**, are just good, simple, fun places and are equally popular with locals and foreign visitors. For the most exclusive hangouts head to **Club Privé** or **BonBon** and marvel at the preening clientele. Serious clubbers can try the portside **Terrarium**.

Visitors should find out more about a place rather than walking into the first nightclub they come across. It is advisable that visitors choose a nightclub carefully. There are many dubious nightclubs in Tallinn, which should be avoided by travellers.

CINEMA

In Tallinn, films are screened in their original language with Estonian subtitles. The diversity of choice in cinemas has dwindled in recent years due to the arrival of the multi-screen **Coca-Cola Plaza**, which shows the latest Hollywood blockbusters and Estonian films. Art-house and independent house films are screened at the impressive **Sõprus**. The Black Nights Film Festival *(see p49)* is a cinema-lover's treat, when the best in world cinema gets a rare screening in smaller cinemas.

Movie posters displayed at the Coca-Cola Plaza

DIRECTORY

THEATRE

Russian Drama Theatre
Vabaduse väljak 5.
Tel 641 8246.
www.veneteater.ee

Tallinn Linnateater
Lai 23.
Tel 665 0800.
www.linnateater.ee

Von Krahl Theatre
Rataskaevu 10.
Tel 626 9090.
www.vonkrahl.ee

CLASSICAL MUSIC, DANCE & OPERA

Estonian Music Academy
Rävala 16. *Tel 667 5700.*
www.ema.edu.ee

St Canute's Guild
Pikk 20. *Tel 646 4704.*
www.saal.ee

ROCK, POP, JAZZ & BLUES

Café Amigo
Hotel Viru, Viru väljak 4. *Tel 680 9380.*
www.amigo.ee

No99
Sakala 3. *Tel 668 8798.*

Rock Café
Tartu mnt 80d.
Tel 681 0878.
www.rockcafe.ee

Von Krahl Baar
Rataskaevu 10/12.
Tel 626 9090.
www.vonkrahl.ee

PUBS & BARS

Déjà Vu
Sauna 1. *Tel 645 0044.*
www.dejavu.ee

Hell Hunt
Pikk 39. *Tel 681 8333.*
www.hellhunt.ee

Kolumbus Krisostomus
Viru 24. *Tel 615 6924.*
www.kolumbus.ee

Lounge 24
Radisson Hotel, Rävala pst 3. *Tel 682 3000.*
www.madissoni.ee

Molly Malone's
Mündi 2.
Tel 631 3016.
www.baarid.ee

Scotland Yard
Mere pst 6e.
Tel 653 5190.
www.scotlandyard.ee

NIGHTCLUBS

BonBon
Mere pst 6e.
Tel 661 6080.
www.bonbon.ee

Bonnie and Clyde
Olümpia Hotel, Liivalaia 33. *Tel 631 5333.*
www.revalhotels.com

Club Privé
Harju 6. *Tel 631 0545.*
www.clubprive.ee

Parlament
Tartu mnt 17.
Tel 666 2900.
www.clubparlament.com

Terrarium
Sadama 6. *Tel 661 4721.*
www.terrarium.ee

CINEMA

Coca-Cola Plaza
Hobujaama 5.
Tel 680 0684.
www.superkinod.ee

Sõprus
Vana-Posti 8.
Tel 644 1919.
www.kino.ee

ENTERTAINMENT IN LATVIA

Latvia's major cultural events are concentrated in Rīga, although the dynamic festival calendar includes plenty of reasons to explore the country beyond the capital. A few concerts and events are scheduled through the year, but visitors need to consult a website or the tourist board as they are not regular. The major exception is Liepāja, which has a vibrant cultural life and its own symphony orchestra. The city is also considered the home of Latvian rock

Traditional chamber music, Rīga

bands and DJs perform in clubs every evening. There are also some good rock clubs in addition to numerous bars that host live music. The seaside resort of Jūrmala is another hotspot during summer. Here, many bars and clubs open only for the tourist season and the Dzintari Concert Hall hosts concerts ranging from classical to pop. Valmiera, considered to be the cultural capital of the Vidzeme region, is another lively city. For entertainment options in Rīga see pages 364–5.

Hansabank building in Rīga, serving as one of Ticket Service's outlets

INFORMATION

Tourist information offices in Rīga provide details of entertainment in the capital and the rest of the country, while regional tourist offices focus on local areas. The monthly *Baltic Guide*, available in some hotels in Rīga, concentrates on the capital, but includes brief events listings for the rest of Latvia. Online resources include the **Latvian Culture Vortal**, which has a searchable nationwide calendar.

BOOKING & PRICES

Tickets for cultural events are generally very affordable in Latvia, and bookings can be made at the venue or through a ticket agency. **Biļešu Paradīze** has offices in several of Rīga's shopping centres and major venues as well as concert halls and cultural centres

around Latvia. Tickets can be delivered internationally for an extra fee. **Ticket Service** has an even larger network of outlets, including at many post offices, Hansabank branches and Statoil petrol stations. Tickets can be booked online and collected from a sales office, or delivered to an address within Latvia. Both agencies' websites have instructions in English, although most event descriptions are only in Latvian.

THEATRE

Most theatrical performances are in Latvian or Russian. **Liepāja Theatre** produces a mix of intimate drama and expansive theatrical works. The building's restored Art Nouveau and Neo-Classical interior is well worth a look. There are also occasional

travelling performances at **Saulkrasti Open-Air Stage** and at the open-air stage in Reņķa Gardens, Ventspils.

CLASSICAL MUSIC & OPERA

The **Latvian Music Information Centre** is a good resource for details of musical performances across the country. Some of the best classical music concerts take place at annual events, such as the International Early Music Festival, which includes outdoor concerts in Rundāle Palace *(see pp168–9)* and Bauska Castle *(see pp166–7)*.

In Jūrmala, the Dzintari Concert Hall *(see p171)* stages very high-quality events from June to August, on Saturdays. Liepāja's Holy Trinity Church *(see p180)* hosts organ recitals. The **Liepāja Symphony**

Scene from *Uncle Vanya*, by Anton Chekhov, performed at Liepāja Theatre

View of the open-air theatre near Rundāle Palace

Orchestra specializes in romantic music and hosts concerts throughout Latvia in major cities such as Rīga, Valmiera and Cēsis.

With the exception of special events, such as the annual Sigulda Opera Festival, there are few chances to see opera outside Rīga. The Latvian National Opera does leave the capital to perform elsewhere in Latvia, but only occasionally. Venues for these shows include cultural centres in several towns and **Krustpils Open-Air Stage** near Jēkabpils.

ROCK, POP & ALTERNATIVE

The liveliest music scene outside the capital is in Liepāja, which boasts **Latvia's 1st Rock Café**, a four-floor building with pool tables, dining indoors and outdoors and live music every night. Another option is **Fontaine Palace**, which features a mixture of bands and DJs. It has a more relaxed bar downstairs, and a fast food outlet next door. The summer sees performances on Liepāja's open-air stage **Pūt Vējiņi**, as well as the Baltic Beach Festival *(see p133)* in July.

Jūrmala hosts plenty of live music in summer. The programme at the Dzintari Concert Hall features popular Latvian and Russian musicians, and there are occasional concerts at the **Nemo Water Park**. The major Russian-language pop competition, New Wave, held every July, attracts huge crowds. The schedule at the open-air stage in Ogre, on the way to Daugavpils, includes rock and pop acts, while the nightlife

in Jelgava is enlivened by **Jelgavas Baltie Krekli**. Like its sister club, Četri Balti Krekli in Rīga, it has a strictly-Latvian music policy.

JAZZ

Regular jazz nights are scarce outside Rīga, but local tourist offices may provide information. **Saulkrasti Jazz Festival** is an important event in the calendar, as is the more recent **Aile Jazz Festival** in Liepāja.

Latvia's 1st Rock Café in Liepāja, fronted by its signature guitar

BARS & CLUBS

Most places in Latvia have at least a couple of bars, of which some turn into discos on weekend nights. Some of the better ones include Latvia's 1st Rock Café and Fontaine Palace, both in Liepāja. Nemo Water Park hosts club nights.

CINEMA

State funding for Latvian films has almost dried up and many cinemas have closed since independence. Most cinemas tend to screen Hollywood movies with Latvian and Russian subtitles. International short films are shown at **Karaliskais Ķēķis** in Liepāja.

Entertainment in Rīga

Since independence Rīga has been working hard to recapture its reputation as the cultural capital of the Baltic region. Apart from world-class performances of opera, ballet and classical music, the city also has a thriving live-music scene. Local bands play diverse genres from jazz to rock, often alongside international performers. The summer months see a few festivals offering music and more, but in winter there is usually some form of cultural event or other taking place regularly. The city is also renowned for its energetic nightlife. On Friday and Saturday nights, many Old Town bars buzz with foreign visitors, though it is not difficult to find a peaceful place for a drink among local people. Clubs, which range from small and hip to huge and mainstream, stay open throughout the night.

INFORMATION

Most hotels in Rīga stock an assortment of free pocket-sized magazines containing listings and other information, of which the best is *Rīga This Week*. The affordably priced and comprehensive bi-monthly *Rīga In Your Pocket* is available to browse or download as a PDF from the company's website. The larger format *City Paper*, *rigaNOW!* and *Baltic Guide* provide an insider's view of the city. The Latvian Culture Vortal *(see p363)* website is also helpful.

THEATRE

Theatre performances are mainly in Latvian or Russian, making them of limited interest to most visitors. The **Latvian National Theatre**, housed in a Neo-Classical building, has a significant place in Latvian history, as independence was declared

here on 18 November 1918. The **Dailes Theatre**, directed by Eduards Smiļģis (1886–1966) for 40 years, puts on a range of productions, from traditional to experimental. Other options include the **New Rīga Theatre** and the **Russian Drama Theatre**. Rīga's most important theatre festival is Homo Novus, held in September, usually every alternate year. It concentrates on experimental theatre and dance.

OPERA & BALLET

Since the 18th century, Rīga has maintained a strong tradition of opera and ballet. The **Latvian National Opera** has an imposing Neo-Classical building with a Baroque interior. It is the venue for world-class performances that are usually in their original language with surtitles in

Detail, Wagner Hall's façade

Latvian and English. The building that houses the Latvian National Opera is also home to the Rīga Ballet. The strong ballet tradition established during the Soviet period continues today.

Although the National Opera closes in the summer, there are special performances in August. Tours of the building are also available for a minimum of ten people.

CLASSICAL MUSIC

There are a number of concert venues in Rīga, including the Dome Cathedral *(see p142)*, which hosts regular recitals. **Ave Sol** hosts chamber and choral music performances. The Latvian Philharmonic Orchestra performs at the Great Guild *(see p145)*, while chamber music is played at the Small Guild. **Wagner Hall**, named after the composer, who was the music director of the place from 1837 to 1839, is a popular venue for small classical concerts.

ROCK, POP & ALTERNATIVE

Major international artists perform at the **Arēna Rīga**, while local bands play at a host of smaller venues. **Kaļķu Vārti** is noted for booking some of the country's top artistes. **Depo** features alternative music from ska to metal and **Sapņu Fabrika** offers a range of diverse genres from world music to rock. **Četri Balti Krekli** offers strictly Latvian music.

JAZZ & BLUES

The best blues venue in the city is **Bites Blūza Klubs**, which has live music on weekend evenings. It also serves surprisingly good food, while the photographs on the walls are testament to the number of international performers who have visited over the years. The small **Hamlets** club hosts jazz performances, as does the upmarket **Carpe Diem** restaurant.

A lavishly decorated hall of the Latvian National Theatre

BARS & CLUBS

With a wide range of bars and clubs, Rīga has a swinging nightlife. **Rīgas Balzāms** is a popular place to try the eponymous drink in various cocktails. **Skyline Bar** in the Reval Hotel Latvija *(see p302)* is one of the favourite bars in town. **I Love You** attracts a youthful local crowd, while **De Lacy's** Irish pub is a favourite among expats.

The best-known nightclub, **Pulkvedim Neviens Neraksta**, has a young, stylish clientele. Larger venues, such as **Club Essential** and the submarine-themed **Nautilus**, feature DJs on the weekend.

Rīga's gay scene remains low-profile. **XXL**, the only well-advertised gay club, has live shows on Friday and Saturday nights. **Golden**, a gay-friendly bar, plays house music in a warm ambience.

CASINOS

Although there are numerous establishments that describe themselves as casinos, most provide only slot machines. Establishments with gaming tables include the Olympic Voodoo Casinos in the Reval Hotel Latvija and Radisson SAS Daugava *(see p302)*, the **Tobago Casino Club** and **Casino Aladins**. It is compulsory to register at casinos, so carry valid photo ID.

CINEMA

There are several multi-screen cinemas in Rīga, mostly offering Hollywood films. The largest is the **Coca-Cola Forum**, which has 14 halls and several cafés. The **Rīga Cinema**, the city's first cinema house, has been renovated and also shows non-Hollywood films. **K Suns** is the best place for art-house cinema.

Sweeping view of Rīga from Skyline Bar, Reval Hotel Latvija

DIRECTORY

THEATRE

Dailes Theatre
Brīvības iela 75.
Tel 6727 0463.
www.dailesteatris.lv

Latvian National Theatre
Kronvalda bulvāris 2.
Tel 6700 6337.
www.teatris.lv

New Rīga Theatre
Lāčplēša iela 25.
Tel 6728 0765.
www.jrt.lv

Russian Drama Theatre
Kaļķu iela 16.
Tel 6722 4660.
www.trd.lv

OPERA & BALLET

Latvian National Opera
Aspāzijas bulvāris 3.
Tel 6707 3777 *(box office).* **www**.opera.lv

CLASSICAL MUSIC

Ave Sol
Citadeles iela 7.
Tel 6702 7570.

Wagner Hall
Vāgnera 4.
Tel 6720 5492.

ROCK, POP & ALTERNATIVE

Arēna Rīga
Skanstes iela 21.
Tel 6728 1222.
www.arenariga.com

Četri Balti Krekli
Vecpilsētas iela 12.
Tel 6721 3885.
www.krekli.lv

Depo
Vaļņu iela 32.
Tel 6722 0114.
www.klubsdepo.lv

Kaļķu Vārti
Kaļķu iela 11a.
Tel 6722 4576.
www.kalkuvarti.lv

Sapņu Fabrika
Lāčplēša 101.
Tel 6738 8200.
www.sapnufabriks.lv

JAZZ & BLUES

Bites Blūza Klubs
Dzirnavu iela 34a.
Tel 6733 3123.
www.bluesclub.lv

Carpe Diem
Meistaru iela 10–12.
Tel 6722 8488.
www.hamlets.lv

Hamlets
Jāņa sēta 5.
Tel 6722 9938.

BARS & CLUBS

Club Essential
Skolas iela 2.
Tel 6724 2289.
www.essential.lv

De Lacy's
Šķūņu iela 4.
Tel 6722 9045.

Golden
Ģertrūdes iela 33–35.
Tel 2550 5050.
www.goldenbar.lv

I Love You
Aldaru iela 9.
Tel 6722 5304.
www.iloveyou.lv

Nautilus
Kungu iela 8.
Tel 6781 4455.
www.nautilus.lv

Pulkvedim Neviens Neraksta
Peldu iela 26–28.
Tel 6721 3886.
www.pulkvedis.lv

Rīgas Balzāms
Torņa iela 4.
Tel 6721 4494.

Skyline Bar
Reval Hotel Latvija,
Elizabetes iela 55.
Tel 6777 2222.

XXL
Kalniņa iela 4.
Tel 6728 2276.
www.xxl.lv

CASINOS

Casino Aladins
Dzirnavu iela 57.
Tel 2929 6060.

Tobago Casino Club
Aspāzijas bulvāris 22.
Tel 6722 3222.

CINEMA

Coa-Cola Forum
Janvara iela 8.
www.forumcinemas.lv

K Suns
Elizabetes iela 83–85.
Tel 6728 5411.

Rīga Cinema
Elizabetes iela 61.
Tel 6718 1144.
www.cinema-riga.lv

ENTERTAINMENT IN LITHUANIA

Lithuania offers its visitors a wide variety of entertainment, with something for everybody. Most cities have a strong cultural tradition. Panevėžys has a popular drama theatre, while the residents of Klaipėda are more inspired by music, embracing both improvised and traditional jazz, blues and operetta. Trakai and Kernavė provide scenic backdrops to summer events, including medieval festivals of archery and swordfighting

Sign for a nightclub in Palanga

and mystical celebrations of the summer solstice. Lively pop festivals sometimes brighten up summer resorts such as Palanga and Juodkrantė. Outside Vilnius the entertainment options tend to be limited, although Klaipėda provides some atmospheric venues for live music. Baroque and chamber music concerts are regularly performed throughout the year in many of Lithuania's churches. For entertainment options in Vilnius see pages 368–9.

INFORMATION

The English-language *In Your Pocket* guides, found in hotels, at newsstands and online, cover most of Lithuania's livelier towns. Despite its name, *VilniusNOW!*, found in four- and five-star hotels of the capital, occasionally lists events outside Vilnius.

Lithuania has a large number of visitor's information centres with English-speaking staff and English-language leaflets, booklets and up-to-date local information. All of Lithuania's towns and cities have their own dedicated websites, which usually contain schedules and information on culture and events.

BOOKING & PRICES

The booking service **Bilietai** has kiosks in most concert venues and shopping centres in major cities, where tickets can be bought with credit cards or cash. Tickets can also be booked by telephone or through a website and can be collected from a sales office, or delivered to any address in Lithuania. Prices usually vary anywhere between 30 and 100 litas per person.

THEATRE

Lithuanian theatre developed during the period of independence between the World Wars, producing young and talented playwrights such as Balys Sruoga and Kazys Binkis. Vilnius has a

Imposing exterior of the Klaipėda State Drama Theatre in Klaipėda

particularly strong theatre culture, although an equal passion for theatre exists outside the city.

The **Klaipėda State Drama Theatre**, which dates from 1819, is Lithuania's oldest theatre building and the most famous outside Vilnius. In Panevėžys, the **J M Drama Theatre** is named after legendary stage actor and director Juozas Miltinis (1907–94), who taught actors to reject conservatism and to draw on their own life experiences while acting.

CLASSICAL MUSIC

Kaunas has several concert halls that feature music regularly. The **Kaunas State Musical Theatre** and the **Great Hall** of Vytauto Didžiojo University are among the preferred venues, but the Kaunas City Symphony Orchestra and Kaunas State Choir also perform at less formal venues including the Mykolas Žilinskas Art Gallery *(see p260)*. Some churches host classical music recitals that often have no entry charges.

Zapyškis Church *(see p261)*, outside Kaunas, and the famous Church of the Holy Trinity *(see p234)*, near Anykščiai, are some of the more atmospheric venues in the countryside.

On the coast, the **Klaipėda State Music Theatre** holds a wide array of classical music concerts, opera and other performances. The Panevėžys Civic Art Gallery *(see p264)* and the Kėdainiai Multicultural Centre *(see p261)* also hold regular concerts.

Beautiful exterior view of the Kaunas State Musical Theatre

MUSIC FESTIVALS

Several music festivals have grown in popularity over the years. The magnificent Baroque Pažaislis Monastery complex *(see p261)*, near Kaunas, forms the backdrop to the annual **Pažaislis Music Festival**. The **Edvard Grieg and M K Čiurlionis Festival**, hosted in Kaunas each spring, features classical music concerts. The **Muzikinis Pajūris** (Musical Seaside) festival of opera and symphony takes place every summer in Klaipėda.

NIGHTLIFE

Club life is not limited to the capital city. Klaipėda has an increasingly lively and varied nightlife. A popular place is **Pabo Latino**, a branch of the successful club of the same name in Vilnius. Newer venues are gradually taking the place of the duller bars and discos in and around the Old Town. They offer casinos, concerts and restaurants, besides dance floors. Kanto Street also has some spirited bars full of fun and revelry.

Kaunas has a mix of low-key bars such as **BO** in the Old Town and the swinging **Los Patrankos**, a club frequented by the young. The other party-town in Lithuania is the coastal resort of Palanga, where in summer the entire area around Basanavičiaus gatvė (street) turns into a pulsating open-air disco from dusk virtually until dawn.

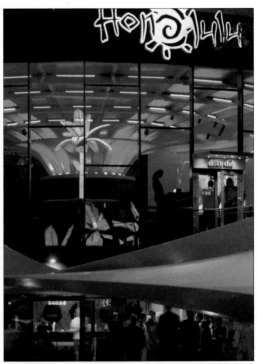

Colourfully lit interior of a nightclub on Basanavičiaus Street in Palanga

JAZZ, BLUES & FOLK MUSIC

Jazz features prominently in the country's cultural scene. Among the best jazz festivals is Kaunas Jazz *(see p208)*. **Kurpiai** in Klaipėda also hosts jazz and blues performances. Folk music features at the Days of Live Archaeology in Kernavė *(see p254)*, in July.

CINEMA

Movies screened in Lithuania are shown in their original language, which means that they can be enjoyed by locals and visitors. Only one modern multiplex, the **Forum Cinemas**, exists in both Vilnius and Kaunas. However, other cities have decent cinemas, such as **Cinamon** in Klaipėda.

DIRECTORY

Entertainment in Vilnius

The range of entertainment on offer in Vilnius has changed rapidly in recent years. Trendy clubs and lounge bars have sprung up, but, at the same time, there has been a resurgence of traditional folk singing and dancing. *Sutartinès*, music with rural roots, helped sustain national identity through the periods of occupation and, today, it has made a comeback in folk-themed restaurants. Classical music was promoted during the Soviet period, but it was also significant in the 20th-century national revivals. Classical music, opera and ballet performances in Vilnius are excellent. Live music is played in several key venues frequented by a small but enthusiastic and faithful crowd. Tourist information points provide news on most cultural events.

On weekdays during term time, students and professors at the Lithuanian Academy of Music often give free-of-charge recitals at different venues in the city.

The standard of opera and ballet is generally high in Vilnius, although the repertoire is fairly conservative. In addition to classical performances, the innovative choreography of the **Anželika Cholina Dance Theatre** attracts big audiences and is very popular among locals and visitors. The famous **National Opera & Ballet Theatre** is funded by Lithuania's Ministry of Culture. Tickets for its performances often sell out quickly and it is advisable to visit the ticket office to check on availability.

A scene from the play *Three Sisters* at the State Small Theatre of Vilnius

INFORMATION

VilniusNOW! is available free of charge in four- and five-star hotels, while *Vilnius In Your Pocket*, which also covers upcoming events, is available in most of the city's hotels. It is also sold in shops and kiosks. Brochures and leaflets of cultural events can be found at the capital's most tourist information centres. Posters are another source of information.

Tickets for concerts, opera, ballet and plays can be purchased at the appropriate venue or booking kiosks. Tickets for all major events in Lithuania can be bought online from **Bilietai LT**.

THEATRE

The residents of Vilnius have a passion for theatre. Productions by two of the country's most outstanding directors, Oskaras Koršunovas and Eimuntas Nekrošius, are highly recommended. The **Lithuanian National Drama Theatre** and the more avant-garde **State Small Theatre of**

Vilnius provide pre-recorded English translation for some performances, which can be heard using headphones.

CLASSICAL MUSIC, OPERA & BALLET

Vilnius has a good classical music scene. Both the opulent **National Philharmonic** and the contemporary **Congress Palace** hold superb concerts. Chamber music concerts are often held at the atmospheric St Catherine's Church *(see p237)* and, occasionally, at St Casimir's Church *(see p232)*.

FOLK MUSIC

Lithuania's folk music can be heard in folk-themed restaurants, which are as popular with locals as they are with visitors. For an authentic experience, enjoy the music with a traditional meal of meat-and-potatoes and Lithuanian beer at venues such as the cavernous Čili Kaimas *(see p338)* or the atmospheric **Marceliukès Klėtis**. Folk festivals are often played out in the courtyards and halls of Vilnius University *(see pp220–21)*, or in more low-key spots such as the **Teachers' House**.

ROCK, BLUES & POP

Several outstanding Lithuanian rock and pop performers play regularly at atmospheric venues such as **Tamsta Club**,

A classical music concert in progress at the Congress Palace

Live band playing at the Tamsta Club in the Old Town

Brodvėjus and the **Forum Palace**. Names to look out for include the punky Biplan, the singer and songwriter Andrius Mamontovas and the more soulful Jurga. International artistes on tour tend to play at the modern **Siemens Arena** or the less pretentious **Utenos Entertainment Centre**, which doubles as an ice rink.

JAZZ

With a small but fanatical following, jazz forms an inextricable part of the Lithuanian lifestyle. During the Soviet era, jazz was associated with freedom. The birth of Lithuania's modern jazz scene was at a recital in 1961, by 17-year-old pianist Vyacheslav Ganelin at the Academy of Music, which mesmerized the audience. Ganelin still makes rare appearances in Vilnius, often with saxophonist Petras Vyšniauskas. Another big name to look out for is singer-flautist Neda Malūnavičiūtė.

The best jazz in town is showcased at the Vilnius Jazz Festival (see p209), but the **Holiday Inn Vilnius** also offers excellent jazz performances.

NIGHTLIFE

Though a little quieter than many other European capitals, Vilnius has an abundance of bars and clubs featuring a variety of music genres and both local and international DJs. Uproarious **Bix** is for heavy metal fans, while **Gravity**, located inside a Soviet-era bomb shelter, attracts the best DJs. A little more central are **Paparazzi**, popular for its friendly atmosphere and wide range of cocktails, and **Pabo Latino**, a nightclub specializing in Latin rhythms. Bands often play live at **Žaltvykslė**.

CINEMA

Vilnius has two modern multiplex cinemas, both operated by Forum Cinemas (see p367). One of them is housed in the Coca-Cola Plaza, while the other is in the Akropolis shopping centre. Films from other countries are usually screened in their original language with Lithuanian subtitles. Lithuanian films do not usually have English subtitles. Art-house cinemas have all but disappeared. A rare survivor, however, is **Skalvija**.

DIRECTORY

OUTDOOR ACTIVITIES AND SPECIALIST HOLIDAYS

Bereft of dramatic peaks and raging rivers, the Baltic States nevertheless abound with subtle charms and this has helped develop rural tourism in the three countries. Exploring the lakes and rivers allows the scenery to unfold at a leisurely pace, while back on land, the forests are perfect for rambling. Fishing, berry- and mushroom-picking and bird-watching are among the most popular activities and can easily be arranged by tour operators. The opportunities for those who wish to discover the region on horseback are endless, with excursions for both novices and experienced riders. Winter changes the landscape, and skiing, ice-skating and snow-boarding take over. For visitors who simply want to relax, the region has a series of stylish spa resorts which draw on decades of tradition. Brewery tours tempt those impressed by local beer. Tourist infrastructure varies between regions and it is best to book activities through a reputable tour operator.

INFORMATION

In the Baltic States, most tourist information centres have lists of both state-run and private tour operators, who organize a variety of outdoor activities depending on the time of the year. Most companies have their own dedicated websites *(see p375)*.

RURAL TOURISM

Development of rural tourism as an organized activity began in the mid-1990s with support from the Ministry of Agriculture along with other organizations. It has now become one of the biggest tourist attractions in the Baltic region, and it is often advisable to arrange for accommodation well in advance. Bookings can be made through the various rural tourism associations

(see p291), such as Estonian Rural Tourism, Country Holidays and Countryside Tourism of Lithuania.

BIRD-WATCHING

Located on major migration routes, with a high proportion of fish-rich wetlands and little intensive farming, the Baltic States are an ideal destination for bird-watchers. Ducks, geese, swans, corncrakes, bitterns, common coots and white storks are easily spotted.

It has been estimated that around 50 million waterfowl, including most of the world's tundra swans and barnacle geese, visit Estonia's coastal wetlands every spring. The peak time for bird-watching is the beginning of May at sites such as Matsalu National Park *(see p89)*. The autumn migration is at its best in October

Bird-watching tower near Lake Lubans, Latvia

at Põõsaspea Cape, close to Haapsalu. Several tour operators, including **Estonian Nature Tours**, arrange bird-watching trips. For further information contact **Estonian Ornithological Society**.

Good bird-watching spots in Latvia include Gauja National Park *(see pp186–9)* and Lake Lubans *(see p198)*. The **Engure Ornithological Centre**, situated in Lake Engure *(see p172)*, has been monitoring and protecting duck populations since 1958. The **Latvian Birding** website keeps up-to-date lists of sightings in the country.

Over 330 species of birds can be spotted in Lithuania, including great snipes, white-tailed eagles, ferruginous ducks, corncrakes and aquatic warblers, among which are endangered species that breed in the country. The main

Latvia's Ķemeri National Park, home to a large number of birds

Cyclists on a winding path in Gauja National Park, Latvia

migration route follows the coast and crosses the Curonian Spit, and a particularly good spot is the Vente Horn on the tip of the Nemunas Delta National Park *(see p283)*. The biggest draws are the migrations in spring and autumn, mainly between September and early October. Early spring is a good time to observe seabirds, owls, woodpeckers and grouse, while the largest number of species can be spotted during the breeding season between late May and early June. The **Lithuanian Society of Ornithologists** also arranges bird-watching tours.

HIKING & TREKKING

Despite their lack of hilly terrain, the Baltic States attract walkers with their extensive forests, attractive rivers, lakes and rural calm. The relatively high chance of spotting wildlife such as roe deer, wild boar, moose and wolves also draws a number of walkers here. Each country has a good selection of well-marked trails with campsites and guest houses along the way, and local tourist offices can suggest routes or arrange guides for visitors.

In Estonia, Lahemaa National Park *(see pp106–107)* has trails of varying lengths covering a diverse terrain. There are also pleasant routes surrounding Tartu *(see pp114–15)* and on the islands of Saaremaa *(see pp92–3)* and Hiiumaa *(see pp90–91)*. A more unusual activity is bog-walking in Soomaa National Park *(see pp100–101)*.

Latvia's Gauja National Park is good for walking, particularly along the well-marked Līgatne Nature Trail *(see p189)*. There are also numerous short trails in the Tērvete Nature Park *(see p167)* and visitors looking for hills might head for the Latgale Uplands *(see p198)*. Tour companies, such as **Eži**, organize walking trips in Valmiera *(see p190)*.

Lithuania has almost 300 hiking trails, of which around 170 are in regional or national parks. Dzūkija National Park *(see p256)* is a favourite and some of its paths and facilities have been especially adapted for disabled visitors. Short, well-signposted walks include the 5-km (3-mile) long Šeirė Nature Trail and the route through the Čepkelių bog from the park's headquarters.

A cycle sign at Vaide, Latvia

Walking trail in the picturesque Tērvete Nature Park, Latvia

Among the Lithuanian companies offering walking trips, the **Nemunas Tour** is one of the most popular.

CYCLING

The relatively flat terrain and breathtaking scenery of the Baltic States makes cycling a pleasant way to get around. However, mountain bikers will find little to challenge their skills. It is not all smooth riding, though, as some roads are in poor condition. A popular international route is the EuroVelo route 10, which runs along the north of Estonia through Tallinn, across to the islands of Hiiumaa and Saaremaa via ferry, on to Rīga and then further south to Klaipėda. Bicycle rental is easy in Estonia and Latvia, while in Lithuania there are hire outlets in the larger towns and cities. A good point of contact for all three countries is **BaltiCCycle**, a non-profit organization which provides details of organized tours, bicycle rental and self-guided cycling. It is also possible to hire a bike in one Baltic country and return it in another.

In Estonia, popular areas for cycling include Lahemaa National Park and the islands of Muhu *(see p91)*, Saaremaa and Hiiumaa. **City Bike** is a notable organization that provides cycling tours and rental services in Estonia.

Easy rides in Latvia include the route from Rīga to Jūrmala *(see pp170–71)*, while the best opportunity for mountain biking is in the Gauja Valley near Sigulda *(see p188)*. There are marked biking routes around Kuldīga *(see p179)* and from Cēsis *(see p188–9)* to Valmiera; Eži arranges trips in the latter area.

The Lithuanian section of the international Baltic Coast route includes an attractive stretch between Palanga *(see p282)* and Klaipėda *(see pp280–81)*. There is also a marked route along the coast of the Curonian Lagoon to the Nemunas Delta National Park.

Riders practising their equestrian skills, Pärnu, Estonia

HORSE-RIDING

Horses are a common sight in the rural areas of the Baltic States, especially in Latvia's Latgale region, where traditional ploughing methods still persist alongside mechanized farming. Horses can be hired at most horse-breeding farms; some farms also offer instruction. It may be possible to hire carriages, traps and even horse-drawn sleighs during winter.

The sandy tracks of Lahemaa National Park are popular for horse-riding in Estonia. One unusual option is the **Tihuse Riding Farm** on the island of Muhu, where guests can also participate in ploughing fields with the help of horses. Visitors to the Tori Stud Farm *(see p101)*, in Estonia, can enjoy a tour of the farm in a

horse-drawn carriage. In Latvia, tourist attractions offering horse-riding include the Līgatne Nature Trail. Disabled visitors may be interested in riding therapy at **Kavalkāde** in Jūrmala. One of Lithuania's most renowned horse-breeding farms, **Žagarė Stud Farm**, about 34 km (21 miles) north of Šiauliai, has stalls built and decorated with materials from England at the end of the 19th century.

FISHING

Fishing is a very popular year-round activity in the Baltic States. In winter, hardy local people trek out onto frozen lakes and cut holes in the ice. Common fish include perch, brown trout, pike, carp, bream, tench and grayling. Fishing permits are

required throughout the region, and additional licences are required for some areas. Major tour operators can provide or assist visitors in obtaining the required permits.

Estonia's long coastline offers numerous angling opportunities. Inland, several companies organize fishing trips to Lake Peipsi *(see p123)* and Lahemaa National Park. A good starting point is the **Tallinn Fishing Club**, which issues permits that can otherwise be difficult to arrange. The club's staff provide assistance, although most of them speak only Estonian.

In Latvia, Lake Engure and Lake Kaņieris in Ķemeri National Park *(see p170)* are particularly good for pike. There are also many other suitable lakes in the Latgale and Vidzeme regions, and fish farms around the country. The **Latvian Fishing Association** can provide information on fishing sites, and permits are usually easy to obtain.

The key spots in Lithuania are in the east of the country, particularly near Ignalina in the Aukštaitija National Park *(see pp266–7)* and Molėtai Lakelands *(see p265)*, and in the south. The Nemunas river is also popular, particularly around the town of Rusnė, as is the Curonian Spit *(see pp284–5)*. Most fishing tackle shops and park offices sell licences; otherwise they are available from the **Department of Water Resources**.

Fishermen angling from the banks of the Lielupe river in Jelgava, Latvia

MUSHROOM- & BERRY-PICKING

Picking berries in spring and mushrooms during autumn are popular activities in the Baltic States. In fact, mushrooms are often a source of income in rural areas.

Often, the best way to arrange mushroom- and berry-picking is to ask your hotel or guest house to organize it. It is advisable to take a local along for guidance on both where to look and which varieties of mushroom are edible and tasty. The Estonian Rural Tourism website has details of farms which can offer mushroom- and berry-picking. The Džukija and Aukštaitija national parks offer some of the best opportunities. Visitors must bear in mind that it is usually illegal to pick the cranberries which grow on peat bogs. Berry-picking with **Vaskna Turismitalu** near Võru also teaches visitors how to make traditional alcoholic Christmas drinks. The website of Countryside Tourism of Lithuania has useful information on mushroom- and berry-picking. The **Žervynos Hostel** can also help with arrangements for the same.

WINTER SPORTS

With long winters usually providing several months of snow coverage, it is not surprising that cross-country skiing is popular. What may be more unexpected is the number of downhill ski runs in a region where the highest point is just about 318 m (1,043 ft) above sea level. Although the Baltic States do not attract hardcore skiers and snowboarders, there are adequate opportunities for those who enjoy the sport.

In Estonia, some of the best skiing, snowboarding, snowmobiling, snowtubing and ski-jumping are found around Otepää *(see p118)*, such as at **Kuutsemäe Resort**. Cross-country skiing is also possible at the Soomaa National Park. Details for winter activities are listed on the Estonian Rural Tourism website *(see p291)*.

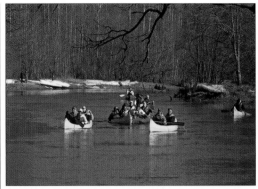
Canoeing in Soomaa National Park, Estonia

A premier spot for downhill skiing in Latvia is **Žagarkalns**, located close to Cēsis, but there are numerous other options listed in the Baltic Country Holidays website *(see p291)*. Visitors seeking adventure should try the bobsleigh run in Sigulda operated by **Taxi Bob**. In Lithuania, Ignalina is a favoured destination for skiers. The **Lithuanian Winter Sports Centre** is one of several options in the area, with four downhill pistes, cross-country skiing and a skating rink. For ice-skating on frozen lakes, including Trakai, visitors may contact **Kempingas Slėnyje**. **Camping Villa Ventainė** regularly organizes snowmobiling and ice-fishing on the Curonian Lagoon.

Enthusiasts enjoying skiing in Kuutsemäe, Otepää, Estonia

WATER ACTIVITIES

With hundreds of rivers and lakes, and an extensive coastline, the Baltic States offer ample opportunities for canoeing, kayaking, windsurfing and rafting. The lack of any serious rapids may deter keen white-water enthusiasts, but it is perfect for leisurely river excursions.

Canoeing is one of the best ways to explore the wilderness of Soomaa National Park in Estonia, where visitors can also try to build *haabjas* (longboats). A number of water activities are provided by **Vesipapp**, **Surf Paradise** and **Reimann Retked**. Of the Baltic countries, Latvia has the most developed water tourism and the Gauja river is a popular spot. Specialist operator **Campo** offers a range of river trips and **Pāvilosta Marina** arranges catamaran sailing lessons. In Lithuania, the Aukštaitija region, with almost 300 lakes linked by waterways, allows tour companies to create multi-day sailing trips. Elsewhere, the **Trakai National Sports and Health Centre** offers kayaking, canoeing, yachting and diving. Similarly, the **Zarasai Water Sports Centre** offers waterskiing and windsurfing. Klaipėda's **Oktopusas** diving centre arranges dives in lakes and the Baltic Sea.

Latvian ice-hockey player in action in an IIHF World Championship match

SPECTATOR SPORTS

The Baltic States are among the few parts of Europe where football is not the dominant spectator sport. The region's most enthusiastic football fans are the Estonians, and their national team has improved in recent years. However, the biggest sport in Estonia is basketball, for which major fixtures can be seen at the **Kalev Stadium**.

In Latvia, the most popular sport is ice hockey, particularly since the national team beat Russia in the 2000 Ice Hockey Championships. Many of the best players are members of overseas teams, making domestic games a little lacklustre, but support is enthusiastic for international games at the **Arena Rīga**. Visitors to Daugavpils will find the city in the thrall of speedway racing. Enthusiasts should not miss a visit to the **Locomotiv Stadium**.

The most popular spectator sport in Lithuania is basketball. The national team has won a bronze medal at the Olympic Games three times and was the European champion in 2003. Žalgiris Kaunas and Lietuvos Rytas Vilnius are the leading domestic teams. To watch players practising, visit the **Siemens Arena**.

GOLF

Soviet Russians were not keen on golf, so the sport is relatively new to the region and there are few good courses.

In Estonia, a number of golf clubs are members of the **Estonian Golf Association**. The **Estonian Golf & Country Club** is seeking to be a part of the PGA Tour. There are 18-hole courses in Otepää, Saaremaa and Tallinn, the last of which is well maintained.

The premier course in Latvia is at the **Ozo Golf Club** on Rīga's outskirts, while the country's other 18-hole course is **Saliena**, located between Rīga and Jūrmala. Golf clubs in Lithuania with 18-hole courses include **Sostinių** and **Europos Centro**. There are also plans to open a golf complex near Klaipėda, featuring an additional spa hotel.

SPA BREAKS

There have been health resorts in the Baltic States since the 19th century, although there is evidence of mud and spring water being used in folk medicine much

earlier. The resorts were hugely popular during the Soviet era, drawing visitors from across the former Soviet Union for relaxation or medical treatment. There was a decline in the spa industry after independence. However, in recent years new spa hotels have opened and older ones have been renovated. Treatments are cheaper than in Western Europe, and there are special deals in winter.

There are several spa hotels on the Estonian islands and also establishments within, and close to, the capital, such as the **Kalev Spa**, a huge facility on the edge of the Old Town, and **Laulasmaa Resort**. The **Estonian Spa Association** represents several of the country's spas.

The main spot for a spa break in Latvia is Jūrmala, a string of seaside towns providing everything from lively bars to secluded beaches. Another good choice is the Spa Hotel Ezeri *(see p307)*.

In Lithuania, the best spas can be found in Druskininkai *(see p255)*, one of which is **Spa Vilnius**. Palanga is also a popular spa destination.

BREWERY TOURS

Beer brewing has a celebrated history in the Baltic States, and there are several brewery tours available in the region. Try **A Le Coq Brewery** in Estonia or the **Užavas** facility in Latvia. Lithuania has the best choice of breweries open to the public, including **Utenos**, **Švyturys**, **Ragutis**, **Kalnapilis** and **Rinkuškiai**.

Entrance to the Spa Vilnius, one of the best spas in Druskininkai, Lithuania

DIRECTORY

BIRD-WATCHING

Engure Ornithological Centre
Tel 742 2195.
www.engure.edu.lv

Estonian Nature Tours
Linnuse tee 1, Läänemaa.
Tel 477 8214.
www.naturetours.ee

Estonian Ornithological Society
Veski 4, Tartu.
Tel 742 2195.
www.eoy.ee

Latvian Birding
www.putni.lv

Lithuanian Society of Ornithologists
Naugarduko 47–33, Vilnius. Tel 8521 30498.
www.birdlife.lt

HIKING & TREKKING

Eži
Valdemāra 1, Valmiera, Latvia. Tel 6420 7263.
www.ezi.lv

Nemunas Tour
Geliu 50, Ringaudai, Lithuania. Tel 3756 3766.
www.nemunastour.com

CYCLING

BaltiCCycle
Tel 6995 6009.
www.bicycle.lt

City Bike
Uus 33, Estonia.
Tel 683 6383.
www.citybike.ee

HORSE-RIDING

Kavalkāde
Asaru prospekts 61, Jūrmala, Latvia.
Tel 2940 6955.

Tihuse Riding Farm
Hellamaa, Muhu, Estonia.
Tel 514 8667.

Žagarė Stud Farm
Žagariškų k, Žagarė, Lithuania. Tel 4266 0860.

FISHING

Department of Water Resources
Juozapavičiaus 9, Vilnius.
Tel 5272 3786.

Latvian Fishing Association
Stabu iela, Rīga.
Tel 6731 6943.

Tallinn Fishing Club
Pärnu mnt 42.
Tel 644 4690.

MUSHROOM- & BERRY-PICKING

Vaskna Turismitalu
Haanja vald, Võrumaa, Estonia. Tel 782 9173.

Žervynos Hostel
Tel 3103 9583.

WINTER SPORTS

Camping Villa Ventainė
Ventės k, Lithuania.
Tel 4416 8525.
www.ventaine.lt

Kempingas Slėnyje
Slėnio 1, Trakai, Lithuania.
Tel 5285 3880.
www.camptrakai.lt

Kuutsemäe Resort
Tel 766 9007.
www.kuutsemae.ee

Lithuanian Winter Sports Centre
Sporto 3.
Tel 3865 4193.
www.lzsc.lt.

Taxi Bob
Šveices 13, Sigulda, Latvia. Tel 2924 4948.
www.taxibob.lv

Žagarkalns
Tel 2626 6266.
www.zagarkalns.lv

WATER ACTIVITIES

Campo
Kronu 23d, Rīga.
Tel 2922 2339.
www.campo.laivas.lv

Oktopusas
Šilutes 79, Klaipėda, Lithuania. Tel 4638 1850.
www.godive.lt

Pāvilosta Marina
Ostmalas 1, Pāvilosta, Latvia. Tel 780 0573.
www.pavilostamarina.lv

Reimann Retked
Tel 511 4099.
www.retked.ee

Surf Paradise
Ristna, Hiiumaa, Estonia.
Tel 639 3288.
www.paap.ee

Trakai National Sports and Health Centre
Karaimų 73, Lithuania.
Tel 5285 5501.

Vesipapp
Tel 529 4614.
www.vesipapp.ee

Zarasai Water Sports Centre
Laukesa, Zaraisi, Lithuania.
Tel 3855 3426.
www.poilsiobaze.lt

SPECTATOR SPORTS

Arena Rīga
Skanstes iela 21.
Tel 6738 8200.
www.arenariga.lv

Kalev Stadium
Juhkentali tänav 12, Tallinn. Tel 644 5171.

Lokomotiv Stadium
Jelgavas 54, Daugavpils, Lithuania. Tel 543 8807.
www.speedwaygp.lv

Siemens Arena
Ozo 14a, Lithuania.
Tel 5247 7576.
www.siemensarena.lt

GOLF

Estonian Golf Association
Tel 630 3080.
www.golf.ee

Estonian Golf & Country Club
Manniva küla, Jõelähtme, Harjumaa.
Tel 602 5290.
www.egcc.ee

Europos Centro
Girijos village, Lithuania.
Tel 6162 6366.
www.golflub.lt

Ozo Golf Club
Milgravja 16, Rīga.
Tel 739 4399.
www.ozogolf.lv

Saliena
Egļuciems, Babītes Pagasts, Latvia. Tel 716 0300.
www.salienagolf.lv

Sostinių
Pipiriškių k, Pastrėvio sen, Lithuania. Tel 6199 9999.

SPA BREAKS

Estonian Spa Association
Sadama 9–11, Haapsalu.
www.estonianspas.com

Kalev Spa
Aia 18, Tallinn. Tel 649 3300. www.kalevspa.ee

Laulasmaa Resort
Puhkekodu 4, Harjumaa, Estonia. Tel 687 0800.
www.laulasmaa.ee

Spa Vilnius
Dineikos k 1, Druskininkai.
Tel 3135 3811.
www.spa-vilnius.lt

BREWERY TOURS

A Le Coq Brewery
Tähtvere 56–62, Tartu, Estonia. Tel 744 9711.
www.alecoq.ee

Kalnapilis
Taikos avenue 1, Panevezys, Lithuania.
Tel 4550 5219.
www.kalnapilis.lt

Ragutis
Kaunakiemio 2, Kaunas, Lithuania. Tel 8007 2427.
www.ragutis.lt

Rinkuškiai
Alyvų 8, Birži, Lithuania.
Tel 4503 5293.
www.rinkuskiai.lt

Švyturys
Kūlių vartų 7, Klaipėda, Lithuania. Tel 4648 4000.
www.svyturys.lt

Utenos
Pramonės 12, Utena, Lithuania.
www.utenosalus.lt

Užavas
Užavas pagasts, Ventspils, Latvia. Tel 369 9484.
www.uzavas-alus.lv

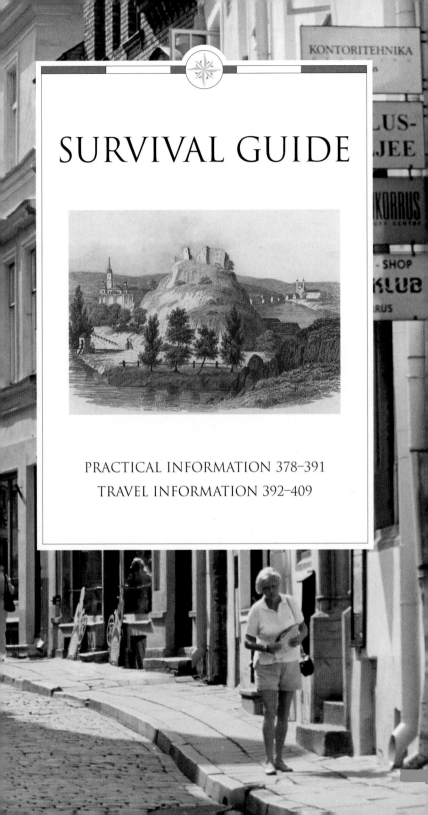

SURVIVAL GUIDE

PRACTICAL INFORMATION 378–391

TRAVEL INFORMATION 392–409

PRACTICAL INFORMATION

After so many years of being excluded from the map of Europe, the Baltic States of Estonia, Latvia and Lithuania are now drawing a great number of eager visitors to discover the region's hidden treasures. These countries are extremely visitor-friendly destinations that offer a wealth of historic sights and cultural activities as well as great natural beauty, good food and fascinating insights into the region's complex past. Each country has a well-developed network of tourist

Logo, Estonian Ministry of Foreign Affairs

information centres that often extends into small towns and offers an abundance of useful literature to help visitors get the best out of their trip. Moreover, with the region's capitals only a relatively short drive away from each other, it is easy to explore the Baltic States either individually or as a whole. Tour operators are growing in number and offer a good variety of packages. The practical information below and on pages 380–81 covers each of the three Baltic States.

WHEN TO VISIT

The best time to visit the Baltic States is from May to October, when the weather is generally pleasantly warm and, quite often, surprisingly hot or cool, but rarely cold. It is an ideal time to explore the region's natural wonders by visiting one of the many national parks or taking long treks in the countryside, camping or going swimming in the sea or one of the numerous lakes. Nearly all the best festivals take place in summer, while some small museums and historic sights are only open between May and September.

The Old Towns of Tallinn and Rīga are especially crowded at the peak of summer due to their compact size. Vilnius's larger Old Town, however, is less cramped. Autumn is often splendid in

Impressive building of the French Embassy in Rīga, Latvia

the Baltic States, but the weather can abruptly turn chilly as early as October.

The capitals are also very atmospheric in winter, when they are blanketed in snow, although winter temperatures can plunge significantly at any time. The worst time to visit is January, the coldest month, and the rainy month of April, when the snow melts into a mass of sludge.

VISAS & PASSPORTS

Citizens of EU-member states, the USA, Canada, Australia and New Zealand only need a valid passport for entry into Estonia, Latvia and Lithuania for a period of up to 90 days in a half-year period. Those wishing to stay beyond the permitted 90 days will need to apply for a national

long-term visa or a residence permit. Visitors from other countries should enquire at the relevant embassy or consulate for visa requirements before travelling. The official websites of the Ministry of Foreign Affairs for each of the three countries offers information on visa regulations.

CUSTOMS REGULATIONS

EU citizens are not subject to customs regulations, provided they adhere to EU guidelines. All visitors should check for any customs duty or special permission required to export a cultural object, before buying it. For detailed information on all these guidelines, entrance regulations and visa cost, it is advisable to visit the official website of the European Commission.

Street café close to Vilnius Cathedral, Vilnius, Lithuania

◁ Shops and cafés lining a cobblestoned street in Tallinn's Old Town, Estonia

Visitors at the tourist information office in Tallinn, Estonia

TOURIST INFORMATION

Estonia, Latvia and Lithuania have a remarkably well-developed network of tourist information centres supported by an equally advanced structure of tourism websites. All cities and most major towns have a tourist information office, which is usually located in or close to the town square. In the case of very small towns, the office is often situated in a museum or within some other historic building. Tourist offices in cities and larger towns are open from 9am to 6pm on weekdays. The offices are open for shorter hours on Saturdays and are usually open on Sundays. In remote places, opening hours are more erratic and it is advisable to check in advance.

Tourist offices are staffed by friendly English-speaking local people, who are always eager to promote their area

Logo, Lithuanian Tourism

and can offer information on accommodation, museums, historic sights, nature trails, entertainment and restaurants. Free brochures covering local and national sights and events are available at these offices, which also sell more detailed maps, postcards and guide-books at nominal rates. For a full list of all tourist infor-mation offices across each country, visit their websites. Latvia and Lithuania also have tourist information centres in London, Finland, Germany, Sweden and Russia.

BUSINESS HOURS

Throughout Estonia, Latvia and Lithuania, banks and state institutions are generally open from 9am to 5 or 6pm. Private businesses are increasingly working longer hours and are open from 9am to any-where between 6 and 8pm. For opening hours of shops see pages 346, 350 and 354.

For opening hours of shops see pages 346, 350 and 354.

DIRECTORY

VISAS & PASSPORTS

Estonia
www.vm.ee

Latvia
www.am.gov.lv

Lithuania
www.urm.lt

CUSTOMS REGULATIONS
www.ec.europa.eu

TOURIST INFORMATION
www.visitestonia.com
www.latviatourism.lv
www.tourism.lt

EMBASSIES & CONSULATES IN TALLINN

Canada
Toomkooli 13. *Tel 627 3311.*
www.canada.ee

United Kingdom
Wismari 6. *Tel 667 4700.*
www.britishembassy.ee

United States
Kentmanni 20. *Tel 668 8100.*
www.usemb.ee

EMBASSIES & CONSULATES IN RĪGA

Australia
Tomsnonia 33-1. *Tel 6722 4251.*

Canada
Baznīcas iela 20/22.
Tel 6781 3945.

France
Raina bulvāris 9. *Tel 6703 6600.*

United Kingdom
J Alunana iela 5. *Tel 6777 4700.*
www.britishembassy.gov.uk

United States
Raiņa bulvāris 7. *Tel 6703 6200.*

EMBASSIES & CONSULATES IN VILNIUS

Australia
Vilniaus 23. *Tel 212 3369.*

Canada
Jogailos 4. *Tel 249 0950.*
www.canada.lt

United Kingdom
Antakalnio 2. *Tel 246 2900.*
www.britain.lt

United States
Akmenų 6. *Tel 266 5500.*
www.usembassy.lt

Imposing exterior of the Hipoteku Bank in Limbaži, Latvia

Exhibition on the Lithuanian partisans, in the KGB Museum *(see p238)* in Vilnius, Lithuania

MUSEUMS, CHURCHES & HISTORIC SIGHTS

Museums in the Baltic States keep rather erratic hours, so it is advisable to check opening times before visiting. Usually, they open from 10am to 5 or 6pm during summer, although in some cases they open at 11am or even mid-day. Monday is the official closing day for most museums, though some are also closed on Tuesdays. Nearly all museums open on Saturdays and many on Sundays. However, tour operators often arrange for museums to open.

Other sights, such as castles and churches, tend to have fairly regular opening hours in summer, between 9 or 10am and 4 or 5pm, Tuesday to Saturday. In winter, however,

St Nicholas's Orthodox Cathedral *(see p181)* in Liepāja, Latvia

many museums open for shorter hours or just remain closed. Some historic sights can only be visited as part of a guided tour. Organizers often try to accommodate single visitors into a group.

DISCOUNT CARD SCHEMES

A cost-effective way of exploring Tallinn and Rīga is to purchase a city card. Unfortunately, Vilnius does not operate a similar scheme. The Tallinn Card offers value for money and costs 130 krooni for 6 hours, 350 krooni for 24 hours, 400 krooni for 48 hours and 450 krooni for 72 hours. The card is also available for children at a 50 per cent discount. It entitles holders to free entrance to 40 major museums and tourist sights, free sightseeing tours, usage of public transport and admission to a range of entertainment venues, including a bowling centre, water park and a major night-club. It can also get visitors a discount in many restaurants and shops. The Tallinn Card is on sale at tourist information centres, hotels, travel agents and at Tallinn Airport and Tallinn Port. The Rīga Card costs 8 lats for 24 hours, 12 lats for 48 hours and 16 lats for 72 hours. It entitles

KONTROLES TALONS

Ticket to St Peter's, Rīga

holders to free admission to many museums, a walking tour of the Old Town and a discount at a range of hotels.

ADMISSION CHARGES

In all three Baltic States, admission charges vary considerably depending on the type of museum and where it is located. Most museums away from the capitals are quite reasonably priced. Ticket prices in Tallinn, Rīga and Vilnius are more expensive, but still reasonable. Students and senior citizens can obtain discounts. State museums in Estonia offer free entrance on the last Saturday of each month. In Latvia, state museums give free admission on the last Wednesday of each month, and in Lithuania many museums do not charge any entrance fee on Wednesdays.

WHAT TO WEAR

The chilly winters in the Baltic countries make thick layers of clothing, as well as gloves, hats and thick-soled water-proof shoes necessary. In summer, lightweight garments are usually adequate, but it is best to carry a jacket for the evenings. In spring, carry an umbrella. Comfortable footwear is recommended for walking on the cobbled streets of Rīga and Tallinn.

TRAVELLING WITH CHILDREN

The Baltic States are extremely child-friendly. Most parks have play areas and some even have a range of distractions, such as bouncy toy castles and trampolines. Many traditional-style taverns and ethnographic museums also provide some wonderfully old-fashioned play apparatus for children. Some hotels offer childcare facilities. For information on eating out with children see page 317.

DISABLED TRAVELLERS

Although there has been a significant improvement in recent years, Estonia, Latvia and Lithuania are not very well equipped in providing facilities for disabled people. Most of the new upmarket hotels and restaurants have taken disabled travellers' needs into consideration, but such places are a distinct minority. Owing to their historic structure, the Old Towns of the three capital cities are extremely difficult for disabled people to negotiate. In Tallinn, there are several steep, winding cobblestoned streets, and Rīga's Old Town is also predominantly cobbled. Although very little of Vilnius's Old Town is cobbled, it is still difficult

Children playing at the Seaside Open-Air Museum *(see p177)*, Ventspils, Latvia

to get around in many places due to the extremely narrow streets and pavements.

Public transport is another major obstacle as trams, trolleybuses and trains do not provide wheelchair access in Tallinn and Rīga, and only a very limited number of buses do. The situation is better in Vilnius, where a large number of new buses and trolleybuses have access for disabled people. For information on access for disabled travellers in hotels, refer to page 291.

Signpost at Limbaži, Latvia

LANGUAGE

Both Latvian and Lithuanian belong to the Baltic family of languages. Estonians speak a Finno-Ugric dialect, which is closer to Finnish. German is quite commonly spoken as a second language in all three Baltic States, while virtually everybody is fluent in Russian. However, communicating in English in the capital cities is seldom a problem – most people speak it to some extent. Knowledge of English is less widespread in rural areas. For common words and phrases used in the three languages, refer to the Phrase Book on pages 427–9.

MEASURES & ELECTRICAL APPLIANCES

The Baltic States all use the metric system. The mains voltage is 230 volts in Estonia and Lithuania and 220 volts in Latvia. Standard Continental European two-pin plugs are used. Although UK plug adapters are available, they are not easy to find, so it is advisable to bring any necessary adapters with you.

LOCAL TIME

The clocks of the Baltic States are set to Eastern European Standard Time and are two hours ahead of Greenwich Mean Time (GMT+2) and seven hours ahead of Eastern Standard Time (EST+7). Clocks go forward one hour on the last Sunday in March and go back one hour on the last Sunday in October.

View of the cobbled Viru Street in Tallinn's Old Town

Personal Security and Health

Estonia, Latvia and Lithuania are generally safe countries, with relatively rare instances of theft and mugging. However, visitors should remain vigilant in the capitals, particularly in and around the Old Towns. Generally, Tallinn, Rīga and Vilnius are far safer than many other Western capitals, although the same precautions should be exercised as in any other major city in the world. The quality of medical care is improving, though at present it may fall short by European standards. Pharmacies in bigger cities are open all day and all three countries provide free emergency care.

Busy western end of Basanavičiaus street in Palanga, Lithuania

POLICE

The Estonian *politsei* (police) usually wear a dark blue jacket and trousers, black boots and a baseball-like cap. They drive white cars with a blue stripe and the word *politsei* written on the side doors and bonnet. In Tallinn, the police have a significant street presence, especially in the Old Town, during summer. The municipal police force wear dark green uniforms and have limited powers. Therefore, the state police should be contacted to report a crime.

In Latvia, the *policija* (police) wear dark blue uniforms consisting of a suit-like jacket with epaulets and a maroon tie, although when on patrol they mostly wear dark blue overalls with a luminous yellow vest and broad cap. The Latvian police drive white cars with a grey stripe along the side. The Rīga municipal police usually wear all-black uniforms and patrol the Old

Town, although they have limited powers of arrest. In an emergency, it is best to call the state police.

In Lithuania, the *policija* (police) uniform consists of a dark green jacket and trousers, black boots and a cap. They drive white cars with a green stripe along the side and "police" written in large letters across the car's bonnet.

GENERAL PRECAUTIONS

Although the vast majority of visitors to the Baltic States do not have any problems with theft, it always helps to take some basic precautions to safeguard valuables. Car theft remains a persistent problem in all three Baltic States, so park in central and well-lit areas, and keep expensive objects hidden from view. Using a guarded parking lot is safer still.

Pickpocketing is a minor problem, but still take care of your wallets and handbags.

In Rīga, avoid using the tunnels around Central Station at night; use the traffic light crossings instead. It is also a good idea to avoid using ATMs in quiet spots at night. Also, never carry large amounts of cash around with you while visiting popular tourist destinations.

PERSONAL SAFETY

As anywhere, using common sense is the best way to ensure your personal safety. Never accept drinks from strangers, no matter how affable they might seem, and never accept invitations from people to go with them to another bar or nightclub. Be vigilant and avoid disreputable-looking clubs, as a number of scams can happen in such places. It is advisable to carry a mobile phone, with a record of all emergency numbers.

Avoid drinking excessively. There are a handful of thugs in each of the Baltic capitals, who make a point of preying on inebriated foreigners as they stumble out of bars in the early hours and head back to their hotels, although they normally target solitary people. Also, refrain from ostentatious behaviour, such as carrying luxury items.

Estonian police car

Latvian police car

HEALTH CARE

Throughout the Baltic States hospitals (*haigla* in Estonian, *slimnīca* in Latvian and *ligoninė* in Lithuanian) are in a rather poor condition after years of chronic under-funding. Emergency treatment is free in each country, but you will need to pay for drugs and any subsequent medical treatment. Most pharmacies stock international drugs.

Private clinics exist in all major cities and are a better option if you require non-emergency treatment. Tallinn, Vilnius and Rīga all have a choice of standard Western European-clinics that offer much better levels of care

Interior of the Town Hall Pharmacy *(see p60)*, in Tallinn's Old Town, Estonia

Exterior of the Medical Diagnostic Centre, Vilnius, Lithuania

than state hospitals and are also significantly cheaper than Western private clinics. Check to see if your existing insurance policy covers all emergencies. If not, it is advisable to take out travel insurance. EU citizens with an EHIC card are entitled to free treatment in Estonia, Latvia and Lithuania.

As there are virtually no significant health risks in the Baltic States, precautionary immunization is not mandatory. However, there is the risk of acquiring tick-borne encephalitis, so if you are planning to spend any length of time in a forest in summer, you should get vaccinated against it. In Tallinn, Rīga and Vilnius, tap water is safe

to drink, but is best avoided as it does not taste very good. Bottled mineral water is a far better option.

PHARMACIES

Minor ailments and accidents can often be treated by staff at a local pharmacy (*apteek* in Estonian, *aptieka* in Latvian and *vaistinė* in Lithuanian), which will usually stock a large selection of international drugs as well as many herbal medicines that are produced locally. Pharmacies generally open from 8am to 7 or 8pm on weekdays and until 3 or 4pm on Saturdays. There are a few 24-hour pharmacies in Tallinn, Rīga and Vilnius.

DIRECTORY

EMERGENCY IN ESTONIA

Ambulance
Tel 112.

Fire
Tel 112.

Police
Tel 112.

Roadside Assistance
Tel 1888.

MEDICAL HELP IN TALLINN

24-Hour Pharmacy
Tõnismägi 5.
Tel 644 2282.

Medicover Swedish-Estonian Medical Centre
Parnu mnt 102c.
Tel 605 1500.
www.medicover.com/ee

Tallinn Central Hospital
Ravi 18.
Tel 620 7040.
www.itk.ee

Tallinn Mustamäe Hospital
J Sütiste 19.
Tel 697 1049.
www.regionaalhaigla.ee

EMERGENCY IN LATVIA

Ambulance
Tel 03, 112.

Fire
Tel 01, 112.

Police
Tel 02, 112.

Roadside Assistance
Tel 1888.

MEDICAL HELP IN RĪGA

24-Hour Pharmacy
Audēju 20.
Tel 6721 3340.

ARS
Skolas 5. *Tel 6720 1007.*

Paul Stradiņš Clinical University Hospital
Pilsoņu 13.
Tel 6706 9600.
www.stradini.lv

Rīga Hospital Number One
Bruņinieku 5.
Tel 6727 0491.
www.1slimnica.lv

EMERGENCY IN LITHUANIA

Ambulance
Tel 03, 112.

Fire
Tel 01, 112.

Police
Tel 02, 112.

Roadside Assistance
Tel 1888.

MEDICAL HELP IN VILNIUS

24-Hour Pharmacy
Gedimino pr 27.
Tel 261 0135.

Baltic-American Medical and Surgical Clinic
Antakalnio 124. *Tel 234 2020.* **www**.bak.lt

Vilnius University Emergency Hospital
Šiltnamių 29.
Tel 216 9140.

Banking and Currency in Estonia, Latvia and Lithuania

The Baltic States have a thriving banking sector and stable currencies which are pegged firmly to the euro. All three countries are in line to adopt the euro but, due to high inflation, the process is taking far longer than initially envisaged, and for the time being, the euro is generally not accepted. The best and most convenient way to obtain local currency is by withdrawing it from debit accounts using the ATMs of major banks. Traveller's cheques are also used. Banks and *bureaux de change* offer money-changing services.

BANKING HOURS

In Estonia and Latvia, banks are usually open from Monday to Friday between 9am and 6pm. Major banks in big cities stay open on Saturdays, from 9am to 2pm in Estonia and from 10am to 3pm in Latvia. In Lithuania, opening hours vary, with bank branches operating from 8am to 5pm on weekdays. Banks in big cities open on Saturdays from 8am to 3pm or 10am to 5pm, and, in rare cases, for a few hours on Sundays.

ATMS

There is an extremely wide network of ATMs in the Baltic States, spread across most major town centres and the capital cities. Some petrol stations have ATMs and most small towns have at least two or three. Most ATMs have English-language options and accept all major international credit and debit cards, such as **MasterCard**, **Visa Electron**, VisaPlus and Cirrus/Maestro, and you can withdraw cash with no additional charges. However, most of the ATM cash machines issue notes of high denominations.

Distinctively signposted *bureau de change* in Latvia

BANKS & BUREAUX DE CHANGE

Estonia, Latvia and Lithuania have a staggering number of banks. The biggest is the Swedish-owned, pan-Baltic **Hansabank**. It has branches in just about every town as well as many branches and ATMs in the cities. Sampo Bank and **SEB** are major banks in Estonia. In Latvia, **Latvijas Banka**, Unibanka, Krājbanka and Parex are well established. In Lithuania, Vilniaus Bankas, **Lietuvos Bankas** and Snoras have the largest network.

DIRECTORY

BANKS & BUREAUX DE CHANGE

Hansabank
www.hansa.ee/eng

SEB (Estonia)
Tornimäe 2, Tallinn. **www**.seb.ee

Latvijas Banka (Latvia)
Jana dalina iela 15, Rīga.
www.lkb.lv

Lietuvos Bankas (Lithuania)
Gedimino pr 6, Vilnius.
www.lb.lt

CREDIT CARDS

MasterCard
www.mastercard.com

Visa Electron
www.visa.com

Banks usually charge between 2 and 3 per cent commission for changing money.

Bureaux de change are extremely widespread in all the three countries. The rates of exchange and commission vary significantly from place to place. The more central ones usually have higher rates. Changing money in hotels should be avoided, as they often have unfavourable exchange rates.

CREDIT CARDS

Major credit cards are widely accepted at high-end restaurants, hotels and shops, and are increasingly being accepted in smaller establishments. Fewer places outside the capital cities and major towns accept credit cards, so it is advisable to carry enough cash when travelling to provincial areas.

TRAVELLER'S CHEQUES

As it is almost impossible to obtain Estonian, Latvian and Lithuanian currency abroad, traveller's cheques are an option, though less popular. They come in various denominations and can be cashed at most banks. A passport has to be shown as proof of identity.

One of the many 24-hour ATMs of Snoras, a bank in Lithuania

ESTONIAN CURRENCY

Estonia's monetary unit is the Estonian kroon, which is divided into 100 sentis. The kroon, translated as crown, is usually abbreviated to EEK. Estonian krooni were introduced in 1992 as a replacement for the Soviet rouble, in order to help stabilize and develop the country's economy. The kroon has officially been a part of the ERM II (European Exchange Rate Mechanism) since 2004.

The country's exchange rate is quite stable since Estonia committed to adopting the euro, which should happen by January 2012 if economic conditions improve. New 1-kroon notes and 5-senti coins are no longer issued.

Banknotes

Banknotes in Estonia are available in denominations of 1, 2, 5, 10, 25, 50, 100 and 500 krooni.

25 krooni

1 kroon

50 krooni

2 krooni

100 krooni

5 krooni

500 krooni

10 krooni

1 kroon   5 krooni

Coins

Estonian coins are available in denominations of 5, 10, 20 and 50 senti and 1 kroon and 5 krooni.

5 senti   10 senti   20 senti   50 senti

LATVIAN CURRENCY

Latvia's monetary unit is the lat, commonly abbreviated as Ls. One lat is divided into 100 santīms. Lats were introduced in the country in 1993, replacing the Latvian rouble, which was used for a short period after Latvia regained its independence. In 2005, the currency entered the Exchange Rate Mechanism II and lat was then fixed to the euro. In small towns and villages, it is sometimes difficult to get change for high-denomination notes. Be aware that visitors have reported a scam in which Lithuanian currency is given as change, as they resemble their Latvian counterpart but are lower in value. There are plans to adopt the euro soon.

Banknotes

Latvian banknotes are available in denominations of 5, 10, 20, 50, 100 and 500 lats. All these notes usually have signature prints of an oak leaf.

5 lats

10 lats

20 lats

50 lats

100 lats

500 lats

1 santīm   2 santīms   5 santīms   10 santīms   20 santīms   50 santīms

Coins

Latvian coins come in denominations of 1, 2, 5, 10, 20 and 50 santīms, and 1, 2 and 100 lats. Commemorative coins are also available, in denominations of 2, 10, 20 and 100 lats.

1 lat   2 lats   100 lats

LITHUANIAN CURRENCY

The national currency of Lithuania is the litas, which is usually abbreviated as Lt. First issued by the Bank of Lithuania in 1922 after World War I, the litas was recalled from circulation after Lithuania was annexed by the Soviets in 1940. The litas was reintroduced in 1993, following a period of transition from the rouble to the litas. One litas consists of 100 centai. The obverse of all coins bears their value and the reverse bears the national coat of arms.

The litas has become a stable currency since it was pegged to the euro in 2002. The euro is to be adopted by Lithuania, but this is unlikely to happen before 2012. Foreign currency can easily be exchanged in banks or in *bureaux de change*.

Banknotes

Lithuanian banknotes currently in circulation are issued in denominations of 10, 20, 50, 100, 200 and 500 litai.

10 litai

20 litai

50 litai

100 litai

200 litai

500 litai

| 1 centas | 2 centai | 5 centai | 10 centai | 20 centai | 50 centai |

Coins

Lithuanian coins come in the following denominations: 1 centas and 2, 5, 10, 20 and 50 centai and 1 litas and 2 and 5 litai. On the reverse side is the national emblem of the vytis, *a sword-wielding knight on horseback.*

1 litas 2 litai 5 litai

Communications in Estonia, Latvia and Lithuania

The three Baltic States have a highly developed communications network, which is almost on a par with that of Western Europe. Mobile phone usage is extremely high, broadband Internet access is widespread and the national postal services are generally dependable. International courier services also operate in all three countries. The absence of high mountains and the flat terrain in the Baltic countries ensure good mobile phone coverage, although there are blind spots in remote areas. International calling cards are easily available. While travelling, one of the best ways of keeping in touch is by email although, in parts of the Latvian and Lithuanian countryside, public Internet access is rare and Wi-Fi access far more limited than in Estonia.

PUBLIC TELEPHONES

The public telephone system in the Baltic States is of a good standard. Payphone booths are plentiful, and most accept pre-paid phonecards, which are readily available from kiosks, post offices and supermarkets. English-language instructions on how to operate the payphone are often posted inside. Discounts on international calling cards are also available from many kiosks. In an effort to win back customers lost to mobile phones, local rates have been kept low but call prices to mobile as well as international numbers are high. In Latvia, some centrally located phone booths offer Wi-Fi access at a range of up to 100 m (109 yards). Hotels charge more than the going rate.

MOBILE PHONES

GSM mobile phone networks have complete coverage in the Baltic States. If you want to use your mobile, however, you should check with your service provider. It is best to inquire about incoming call costs, which can often be exorbitant. The main mobile networks have partnerships with Western European service providers such as Orange and Vodafone. Another option is to buy a pre-paid SIM card from a local provider and insert it into the handset for relatively cheap call and SMS rates.

Estonian postbox outside the Central Post Office, Tallinn

POSTAL SERVICES

Mail services in the Baltic States are efficient and very dependable. Post offices provide a range of services at competitive postal rates. Mail can be sent *poste restante* to any post office in the Baltic region, but a passport is usually essential to collect it.

Postcards should be bought in post offices, as they are cheaper than in most shops.

INTERNET

Internet cafés are abundant and cheap in most major cities and towns in the Baltic States. Nearly all hotels have Internet connections and many cafés and restaurants have Wi-Fi access. In smaller towns they are signposted with an "@" sign. Almost all hotels have fax facilities, and faxes can also be sent through the central post offices.

ENGLISH-LANGUAGE MEDIA

There are several pan-Baltic, English-language publications. *The Baltic Times* newspaper comes out every Thursday and covers news, business, arts and entertainment across the Baltic States. It includes weekly entertainment listings and information on concerts, exhibitions and films.
In Your Pocket provides comprehensive and well-researched write-ups on everything from restaurants and bars to nightclubs and shopping. *City Paper* has a good listings section and some well-written feature stories on local issues. All three are widely available at kiosks and some retail outlets. In addition, the latest editions of *Estonian Weekly*, *Latvian Weekly* and *Lithuanian Weekly* are also available free of charge at airports.

European editions of British and American newspapers, such as *The Financial Times* and the *International Herald Tribune*, are readily available in Tallinn, Rīga and Vilnius.

Customers at a newspaper kiosk in Ventspils, Latvia

Communications in Estonia

Estonia's communications infrastructure is very efficient. All phone lines are digital, ensuring high-quality connections and easy-to-make international calls. Internet and mobile phone usage is particularly high. A staggering range of services can be paid for through mobile phones, including parking charges. The post offices offer a range of express delivery options, including a special pan-Baltic option. There are over 1,000 Wi-Fi areas covering a vast stretch of the country, including the main islands and even some beaches. However, Internet access is limited in the provinces.

One of the many payphone booths in the Old Town, Tallinn

MAKING A PHONE CALL

Estonia has an extremely simple and efficient digital telephone network. In 2004, the country did away with all city codes, as a result of which all landline numbers are now seven digits. The code for Estonia is 372. To call abroad from an Estonian line, dial the international code 00, followed by country code.

To call a number within Estonia, dial the number as it is, as there are no city codes in effect. Landline numbers have seven digits and charges for landline calls are cheaper than those to mobile phones.

Public payphones only accept *telefoniputka* (pre-paid cards), which come in denominations of 30-, 50- and 100-kroon units, and are available at kiosks and post offices. International calls can also be made using pre-paid cards, but the rates are high.

MOBILE PHONES

Estonian mobile numbers all begin with 5 and usually have seven or eight digits. The main mobile phone operators are **EMT**, Elisa and the pan-Baltic **Tele2**. EMT Simpel and Tele2 both offer pre-paid SIM cards, which are useful for visitors planning to stay in Estonia for any significant length of time.

POSTAL SERVICES

The state-owned Estonian *postkontor* (post office) is an efficiently run enterprise. It has 500 outlets around the country opening from 9am to 6 or 7pm on weekdays, and between 9am and 3pm on Saturdays. The **Tallinn Central Post Office** is open till 8pm on weekdays, and 6pm on Saturdays. It is also open till 3pm on Sundays.
Eesti Post (Estonian Post) is the only provider of universal postal services in Estonia. It offers traditional services such as delivering letters, parcels and periodicals, besides express, warehousing and transportation facilities. Postboxes are orange and marked "Eesti Post".

INTERNET & EMAIL

Internet cafés, locally known as *internetikohvik*, are widespread in Tallinn and Tartu. In smaller towns, there may only be one or two and they are often crowded with children playing computer games.

Prices generally range from 15 to 30 krooni for 30 minutes. All public libraries offer free Internet access, although only for 15 minutes at a time, and in smaller towns, this is the only option available. There are over 350 Wi-Fi hotspots in Tallinn, many of which are free, usually in hotel lobbies, cafés, pubs, parks and petrol stations. There are distinctive black-and-orange signs to help spot places offering Wi-Fi access.

Wi-Fi Internet logo, Estonia

Communications in Latvia

The telephone and mail networks in Latvia are both efficient and reliable, although some post office branches need modernization. Nevertheless, post offices are present in most towns and villages of significant size. Public telephones are also common, despite the popularity of mobile handsets. Internet access is excellent in Rīga and other major cities, with Wi-Fi hotspots in many cafés and hotels, and it is improving rapidly throughout the country.

A Plus Punkts kiosk selling SIM-card packages and top-up credit, Rīga

DIRECTORY

USEFUL NUMBERS

Directory Enquiries
Tel 118.

International Information
Tel 115.

PUBLIC TELEPHONES

Lattelekom
www.lattelecom.lv

POSTAL SERVICES

Latvijas Pasts
Stacijas laukums 1. *Tel 6701 8800.* www.pasts.lv

MAKING A PHONE CALL

The partly state-owned **Lattelekom** no longer has a monopoly on landlines, but remains the only operator of public telephones. Most public telephones need either a major credit card or a *telekarte* (phonecard), which can be purchased in denominations of 2, 5 and 10 lats at post offices and newsstands. For international calls, it is better to purchase a pre-paid calling card, which allows connection through a toll-free number and gives automated instructions in many languages.

Since August 2008, all valid telephone numbers now have eight digits. To make a local call on an old seven-digit landline number prefix the existing number with a six. For calls to mobile phones prefix the old number with a two. Latvia has no area dialling codes.

MOBILE PHONES

Latvia's relatively flat terrain helps ensure excellent signal coverage in all the major cities. Today, more Latvians have mobile phones than landlines and Lattelekom is the main service provider.

Visitors who intend using their mobile phones should contact network operators to enable roaming. If there are partnership agreements between the visitor's service provider and the local network, roaming charges are cheaper. If not, both incoming and outgoing international calls are charged at a premium rate.

To avoid roaming charges altogether, purchase a local SIM card issued by a local network operator. This is possible only if the handset is unlocked, as some operators lock phones to specific networks. SIM card packages and top-up credit are available at newspaper kiosks and supermarkets.

Signpost for an Internet café in Rīga

POSTAL SERVICES

Letters and packages weighing up to 10 kg (22 lbs) are handled by the state-owned **Latvijas Pasts** (Latvia Post). Main post offices are usually open between 8am and 7pm on weekdays, and from 8am to 4pm on Saturdays. The largest branches in Rīga, at Brīvības bulvāris (avenue)

19 and Stacijas laukums (square) 1, tend to stay open for longer hours and also open on Sundays, while post offices in villages and smaller branches in towns and cities, often open for shorter hours. Letters and postcards can also be mailed using the bright yellow postboxes.

INTERNET & EMAIL

Most towns have at least one Internet café, variously called a *datorsalon, interneta kafenica* or *interneta clubs*. Prices vary between 0.50 santīm and 1 lat per hour. In villages or very small towns, the library may be the only place with public Internet access. Many hotels offer Wi-Fi access. Internet facility may be available for free or may require a pre-paid Lattelekom card.

DIALLING CODES

- All toll-free numbers in Latvia begin with 8 and all fee-based numbers start with 9.
- To make a call to Latvia from an overseas number, first dial the international access code 00 followed by Latvia's country code (371), and then the landline or mobile phone number.

Communications in Lithuania

The widespread network of telephone and mail services in Lithuania is very efficient. The huge popularity of mobile phones has ensured that public phones are, in fact, rarely used, although they still stand in good working order in many cities, towns and villages. Post offices can be found in all towns and larger villages. Internet usage is fast becoming popular and finding an access point is seldom a problem in most big cities.

Phone card, available with the service provider, Teo LT

MAKING A PHONE CALL

The landline telephone network in Lithuania is run by the private company **Teo LT**. Its payphones are card-operated and easy to use. Cards can be bought at post offices and newsstands, in denominations of 9, 13 and 30 litai. Call tariffs vary according to the time of day, but it is usually about 2 litai per minute for calls made to other countries in Europe or the USA. Telephone rates in hotels vary widely, so it is best to check before making a call.

Lithuania has a complicated system of telephone codes with specific city codes, which can be confusing for most visitors. To make a call from a landline to another landline in the same city or area, dial only the number. If the number is in another city or area add 8 plus the area code before the number. To call a local mobile or landline number from a mobile or landline number overseas, use the international access code followed by the number. To call a local mobile from a local mobile number, prefix the number with 8. For making calls to a landline number from a local mobile number, dial 8, the city code and then the number.

MOBILE PHONES

There are currently three mobile phone operators in Lithuania – **Omnitel**, **Bitė** and **Tele2**. Mobile phone users who wish to avoid roaming costs can buy a SIM card from one of these service providers. Available at newspaper kiosks, these SIM cards help cut local call rates and also reduce international call costs.

POSTAL SERVICES

Lithuania's postal service is very punctual. *Paštas* (post offices) can be found almost everywhere in the country. They open from 8am to 6pm on weekdays and 9am to 2pm on Saturdays. **Vilnius Central Post Office** opens from 7:30am to 7pm on weekdays and 9am to 4pm on Saturdays. A postage stamp for a postcard to any EU country costs 1.70 litai.

It is best to register letters and parcels for a small extra fee. The main post office in every city offers a *poste restante* service for receiving mail. To collect it, you will need to show your passport.

INTERNET & EMAIL

Internet cafés tend to be used mostly by youngsters enjoying computer games. They can be found in many cities and are often located in cellars, rather than standing as recognizable cafés. Hotels offer Internet access to guests, but some provide only a plug-in point for a laptop. Prices for access are reasonable and connections are generally speedy.

DIALLING CODES

- Lithuania's city codes include 5 for Vilnius, 37 for Kaunas, 46 for Klaipėda, 313 for Druskininkai, 460 for Palanga and 469 for Nida.
- To call Lithuania from overseas, dial the international access code 00, followed by Lithuania's country code (370) and the local number.

An everyday scene inside the Vilnius Central Post Office

TRAVELLING TO ESTONIA

It is easy to reach Estonia by air, as several major international carriers from many European cities provide links to Tallinn, the capital of Estonia. The country is also well served by ferries, with regular services to Tallinn and the islands of Saaremaa and Vormsi. In Tallinn, the ferry port and main railway station are conveniently located close to the Old Town and city centre, while

Logo of Estonian Air, the national carrier

the airport and coach station are only a short taxi ride away. The city has good coach connections with the rest of Europe, although travelling by coach can be slow. Reaching Estonia from Western Europe by train is almost impossible, as the only international service is from Russia. However, a pan-Baltic train, Rail Baltica, is being planned and will be operational by 2016.

Gleaming interior of Tallinn International Airport

ARRIVING BY AIR

The sleek-looking **Tallinn International Airport** is the only Estonian airport with regular scheduled flights. In recent years, the airport has become a regional hub with approximately 15 airlines using the airport, including major carriers such as **Finnair**, **airBaltic**, **Lufthansa** and **KLM**.

Founded in 1991, **Estonian Air** is the country's national carrier. Based in Tallinn, it offers a good standard of services in both business and tourist class. The airline has direct links with several major European destinations as well as many Estonian cities and islands. Visitors from outside Europe need to catch a connecting flight from cities such as London, Helsinki, Copenhagen or Stockholm.

As a consequence of the EU "open-skies" policy implemented in 2004, several low-cost carriers, such as

easyJet, now provide daily flights to Tallinn from both Berlin and London.

FROM TALLINN AIRPORT TO THE CITY CENTRE

Tallinn International Airport is about 3 km (2 miles) from the city centre. Taxis wait outside and the ride to the city centre costs 100 krooni. Bus number 2 takes up to 15 minutes to reach the centre and costs 20 krooni. It leaves every 20 minutes Monday to Saturday, and every 30 minutes on Sunday.

Taxi stand near Tallinn International Airport

OTHER ESTONIAN AIRPORTS

Estonia's other airports are situated in Pärnu, Tartu, Kuressaare and Kärdla. Most of these airports are serviced by international flights from Tallinn, besides a few domestic services. There are special summer flight services from Sweden to Saaremaa Island and from Finland to Tartu. A number of smaller private airfields are used for private planes and chartered aircrafts.

ARRIVING BY SEA

Estonia is very well served by ferry, with Tallinn's **Passenger Port** (*reisisadam*) handling about 7 million passengers a year. The main line **Tallink** has routes to Helsinki (Finland), Rostock (Germany) and Stockholm (Sweden), while other carriers, such as **Viking Line** and Eckerö Line are accessible from Helsinki and Stockholm. SuperSeaCat connects Tallinn to Helsinki.

Travellers from Helsinki are spoiled for choice, with a range of catamarans, ferries and even a hydrofoil making the crossing at regular intervals. The Passenger Port is within walking distance of Tallin's Old Town and a taxi ride should cost between 40 and 60 krooni. Tallinn is also included in an increasing choice of Baltic Sea cruises, although these normally only allow for a day's stopover.

Tallink shuttle on its way to Rīga from Helsinki

Pärnu and Saaremaa Island are also included in some cruise ship itineraries.

ARRIVING BY COACH

International coach routes to Estonia are provided by **Eurolines** and **Ecolines**, which operate connections between Tallinn and Berlin, Munich, Kaliningrad, Warsaw and St Petersburg, among others. International coaches arrive at **Tallinn Bus Station** (*bussijaam*), which is a short taxi ride from the city centre. Alternatively, catch the numbers 2 or 4 trams, or numbers 17, 17a or 23 buses from the main bus station into the city centre. Passengers travelling to Tallinn by bus from Rīga or Vilnius can get off at the more central Viru väljak bus stop. There are also limited international coach connections with Pärnu, Narva and Tartu. The coach network is efficiently run and cheap. Services are clearly posted in coach and bus stations.

Luxury coach of Eurolines, Europe's largest coach network

ARRIVING BY TRAIN

Tallinn's main railway station, Balti Jaam, is a short walk away from the Old Town. The only international link is a nightly train to Moscow, and an irregular service to St Petersburg. Tickets should be pre-booked, since Russian visa specifications insist on dates of entry and exit. The Rail Baltica route is due to link Tallinn with Rīga and Vilnius.

ARRIVING BY CAR

Since 2007, when the Baltic States agreed to the Schengen Agreement (under which systematic border controls were abolished), there are no border restrictions for Schengen visa-holders. Crossing the border from Latvia is easy, especially for EU passport-holders. The border crossing with Russia is slower and border guards are likely to scrutinize your documents. To bring along your own car into Estonia, the Vehicle Registration document, an international driving permit and a valid Green Card insurance policy are mandatory.

ARRIVING BY HELICOPTER

Copterline's 12-seater helicopter service between Helsinki and Tallinn takes 18 minutes. There are about 13 hourly services between 7am and 8pm, from Monday to Saturday. Tallinn's heliport is a five-minute drive from the city centre. A minibus service is available.

Getting Around Estonia

The best way of getting around Estonia is by car, as all the main sights are, at most, a few hours' drive away from each other. The country's rail network is cheap but with a limited reach and often frustratingly slow. A far better public transport option is the country's well-developed bus system, which links all the major towns and cities as well as the remote parts of the country. However, rural bus services are sparse, and the buses tend to crawl along at no more than about 30 kmph (19 mph). Alternatively, there is a good range of ferries serving the islands but many of these do not run in winter, when the sea freezes over. No regular domestic flights connect Estonia's mainland cities, although there are regular air connections to several islands.

Local train waiting at Tallinn railway station

TRAVELLING BY TRAIN

Estonia's rail network is the least efficient way to see the country. Services have been so reduced that the choice of destinations is limited. There are rail routes between Tallinn and Narva, Tartu, Pärnu and Viljandi, and an electric train runs between Tallinn and Paldiski ten times a day. It is usually advisable to catch a *kiirrong* (fast train), although these are still relatively slow compared to those in Western Europe. However, there are now express trains, with first-class carriages, between Tallinn and Tartu. **Edelaraudtee** runs inter-city passenger services and **Elektriraudtee**, belonging to the same company, runs local electric trains.

It is best to buy *pilet* (tickets) on board, although some can be bought online or at the ticket offices in Tallinn. There are no passes for rail travel. Timetables are rarely printed or updated and services are usually posted on large display boards at the stations.

TRAVELLING BY BUS

The bus network in Estonia is efficiently run and is good value for money. Inter-city buses run regularly and are generally comfortable. Some companies run express routes, which avoid endless stops in small towns and villages. Express buses are marked with a red "E" on bus time-tables. Tour operators include **SEBE** and **Taisto**. Tickets can be bought from the bus station or the driver on boarding. On busier routes, it is best to buy tickets in advance. Although ticket prices vary according to the operator, they are generally very reasonable, but slightly higher than that for rail travel. The fares of buses bound for the islands are usually higher as they always include the price of the ferry crossing. To check bus schedules visit **Bussireisid**'s website.

Luggage is usually carried onto the bus and passengers may have to pay a small additional fee to stow any large items in the compartment underneath the bus.

TRAVELLING BY FERRY

The Estonian islands are well served by a number of car and passenger ferry connections. There are also regular services between Rohuküla harbour (near Haapsalu), Heltermaa (on Hiiumaa Island) and Vormsi. Virtsu harbour (north of Pärnu) has hourly connections with Muhu Island, which is linked with nearby Saaremaa Island by road. Saaremaa itself is connected with Hiiumaa from Triigi harbour in the north-east. Saaremaa has a special summertime ferry service to Ventspils in Latvia. Check **Saaremaa Shipping Company Limited**'s official website for

Bussireisid's air-conditioned inter-city express bus en route from Tartu

Ferry from Virtsu on its way to Saaremaa Island

route details. **Veeteed** runs a ferry service between Pärnu and the islands of Kihnu and Vormsi, although the service is less regular. In summer, ferries tend to quickly fill up and passengers can be left waiting in long queues if they don't reserve their tickets well in advance. Tickets can be purchased up to 30 days in advance. Passengers travelling by car should reach the harbour about 20 minutes before the scheduled departure time.

In winter, ferry services are often cancelled in the event of the sea freezing over, although officially designated ice roads are established if the ice is thick enough.

TRAVELLING BY AIR

Estonian Air, the country's national carrier *(see p392)*, operates domestic flights that connect the major cities. **Avies** also runs a few daily flights between Tallinn, Kuressaare and Kärdla. It is best to book well in advance because their planes are very small and can only seat up to seven passengers. There are also some flights from Pärnu Airport to Kuressaare and Kihnu which are reasonably priced, and a good option in winter when the sea is frozen. Tartu Airport has no regular domestic flights. Kärdla acts mainly as a stopover point for chartered flights in Europe. The daily domestic service to Tallinn is the only regular service coming from the airport at Kärdla.

TRAVELLING BY CAR

Driving is by far the best way to get around Estonia. Conditions are generally good on main roads and distances are relatively short. However, country roads are severely potholed and dirt roads are also common in many rural parts of the country.

There are no motorways and overtaking is the norm. It is mandatory by law to drive with the headlights on at all times of the day. Wearing a seatbelt is compulsory for drivers as well as passengers. The speed limit is 50 kmph (31 mph) in built-up areas and 90 kmph (56 mph) on the main roads. In Estonia, drinking alcohol and driving is illegal. By law, winter tyres must be fitted between December and March.

Petrol stations are quite rare in remote places so it is advisable to fill up on petrol when leaving a city or town.

CAR HIRE

There are numerous car rental firms in Tallinn, including international chains such as **Avis**, **Budget**, **Europcar**, **Hertz** and **National**. All require a major credit card and a valid international driver's licence. Rental rates are comparable to those in Western Europe. Outside Tallinn, there are few rental options except in major towns. However, some of the Tallinn-based chains can organize car hire in other parts of the country.

Autorent Terminal of Avis, a global car rental chain

Getting Around Tallinn

Most of the main sights in Tallinn are within comfortable walking distance of each other. The Old Town is so compact that it can easily be covered on foot. Public transport in Tallinn is cheap and efficient. It is made up of an integrated network of trolleybuses, buses and trams serving sites away from the city centre. Cycling is another good way of getting around the city. In general, Tallinn's transport options are very good, and there is no need for a car unless you plan to take a day trip or explore the outer parts of the city.

BUSES, TROLLEYBUSES & TRAMS

Tallinn's public transport system operates daily between 6am and midnight. Buses are the best way to reach the airport and other outlying areas. The terminal for many routes is in Viru väljak (gate). The nine trolleybus lines mainly connect to residential areas near the centre. The main stops are on Vabaduse väljak and Balti Jaam. Because of their frequency, trams follow the main arteries in and out of the city centre. The four tram lines running across the city converge at the Hobujaama stop on Narva maanti (road).

The same tickets can be used on all three systems and schedules in English can be found at the **Tallinn Bus Company**'s website. As drivers only sell single tickets at a premium, it is best to buy tickets, either individual or as booklets, at kiosks. Tallinn Card (*see p380*) holders are entitled to unlimited travel on all public transport.

MINIBUSES

Bus sign, Tallinn

Minibuses, or route-taxis as they are often called, are a faster option for travellers. They connect the city centre to outlying residential areas. These white vans, operated by many small private companies, follow set routes, picking up and dropping off passengers at any spot they request along the route. Most minibuses leave from a stop at Estonia puiestee (boulevard) just opposite the Estonian Drama Theatre. Destinations are usually displayed in the window. Tickets cost between 10 and 20 krooni depending on how far the destination is. Tickets can only be purchased from the drivers on boarding.

DRIVING

Driving around Tallinn may be a little disorienting for visitors. There are several confusing one-way systems and traffic jams are common during rush hour. Also, tram tracks are often in the middle of the road. Drivers have to stop and wait for a tram when it pulls in at a station so that passengers can safely alight. Driving conditions are especially difficult at night because of the dangerous habit of overtaking on narrow roads and speeding. The speed limit in Tallinn is 50 kmph (31 mph), except for some larger roads where the limit is 70 kmph (43 mph).

PARKING

There are plenty of parking options in Tallinn, though it can be hard to find a good spot in the heart of the city during weekdays. In the city centre, paid parking is in force between 7am and 7pm on weekdays and 8am and 3pm on Saturdays, although the first 15 minutes are free. Tickets can be bought from street-side machines or kiosks. In some areas, tickets

Tram, a convenient mode of transport for short hops around Tallinn

A taxi waiting in a cobblestoned street in the Old Town, Tallinn

can also be purchased from parking wardens. Rates range from 16 krooni per 15 minutes to 72 krooni per hour. The Old Town has a seven-day, 24-hour paid-parking in effect, which starts at 12 krooni per 15 minutes. A relatively convenient option might be to leave your car at one of several centrally located guarded parking lots. These range in price from about 12 krooni to 30 krooni per hour. In the summer months, paid parking is also in effect in the Pirita district.

TAXIS

There is an abundance of taxis in Tallinn, although it is best to take one from a taxi stand or to book one in advance from reputed companies such as **Linnatakso**, **Klubi Takso** or **Reval Takso**. Taxi stands can be found near large hotels, major inter-sections and also next to the Estonian Drama Theatre. Hailing a taxi on the street is risky, as there are many dishonest taxi drivers who overcharge foreign visitors. Recently, however, a new legislation has helped improve the situation. All taxi drivers are obliged to display their prices in English, on the vehicle's rear right-hand window, and to provide a receipt on request. If the driver fails to give a receipt, the passenger is legally entitled not to pay the fare.

Starting fares normally range from 35 to 70 krooni, with a rate of about 7 krooni per kilometre, although prices can vary considerably from operator to operator. It is advisable to ask the driver for an approximate price before

starting your journey and ensure that the meter is running. All fares must be paid in Estonian krooni.

CYCLING

Getting around Tallinn by bicycle is a good option, although it is not so practical in the cobbled streets of the Old Town. There are plenty of bicycle rental firms in the city, such as **CityBike**, that offer a wide range of organized tours accompanied by a guide. It is also possible to rent a bicycle and take off by yourself. As there are hardly any bicycle lanes in Tallinn, special care should be taken when cycling along congested streets.

WALKING

Walking is the ideal way to experience the busy streets of Tallinn's Old Town and the city centre. In general, Tallinn is a pedestrian-friendly environment, although a good road map is useful to avoid getting lost in its labyrinthine streets. A huge number of

DIRECTORY

BUSES, TROLLEYBUSES & TRAMS

Tallinn Bus Company
www.tak.ee

TAXIS

Klubi Takso
Tel 638 0638.
www.klubitakso.ee

Linnatakso
Tel 644 2442.
www.linnatakso.ee

Reval Takso
Tel 601 4600.
www.reval-takso.ee

CYCLING

CityBike
Tel 683 6383.
www.citybike.ee

VELOTAXI

www.velotaxo.ee

walking tours are available from most hotels and tourist information centres.

VELOTAXI

Velotaxis, or bicycle-taxis, are a novel way of seeing the city. They operate from March to October and cost 35 krooni for an adult and 15 krooni for a child, and can be ordered on the **Velotaxi** website.

Fascinatingly novel velotaxi, available for hire in Tallinn

TRAVELLING TO LATVIA

Most visitors arrive in Latvia by air, at Rīga International Airport. Since independence there has been a rapid growth in the number of European cities directly linked to Rīga, mainly because of the arrival of low-cost carriers that raised the capital's profile as a destination for weekend breaks. In contrast, the country's regional airports are little used

Arrivals sign at Rīga Airport

for international passenger flights. For those who wish to avoid air travel and who have more time, there are sea routes from Germany and Scandinavia, besides comfortable trains and coaches from other parts of the Continent. Arriving by car is also perfectly feasible, provided the driver has the correct documents and is willing to tackle a variable road network.

ARRIVING BY AIR

The majority of passengers arrive at **Rīga International Airport**, which is now connected to most Western European cities as well as to Prague, Moscow, Kiev, Tallinn, Vilnius and Warsaw. Services at the airport include a currency exchange and ATMs, which remain open until the last flight arrives.

The country's national carrier, **airBaltic**, was established in 1995 and now offers some very affordable flights. Rīga is also served by other major airlines including **KLM**, **Aer Lingus**, **Lufthansa** and **Finnair**. Recent years have seen the arrival of several low-cost carriers, such as **easyJet** from Berlin and **RyanAir** from Ireland and the UK.

There are very few direct flights to Latvia from the USA, New Zealand, Canada or Australia. Visitors often transfer at another European airport. It may be more economical to arrange a long-haul flight to a transport hub such as London, along with a separate onward flight with a low-cost carrier.

Exterior view of Rīga International Airport

FROM RĪGA AIRPORT TO THE CITY CENTRE

Rīga Airport is located about 8 km (5 miles) from the city centre. The cheapest way to reach the city is by taking a bus from outside the airport terminal. Bus 22 runs every 10 to 20 minutes from 5:40am to 11pm, taking 30 minutes to reach Abrenes iela (street) with stops including Strēlnieku laukums (square) and the Central Railway Station. Express bus 22A, which runs at half-hour intervals from 7am to 10:30pm, except at 11:30am and 7:30pm, reaches the Orthodox Cathedral in Centrs,

the modern commercial hub, in 25 minutes. Taxis reach the city centre in 15 minutes.

OTHER LATVIAN AIRPORTS

The other international airports are in Ventspils and Liepāja. airBaltic has daily flights to Liepāja from Rīga, as well as regular flights from Copenhagen and Hamburg. Ventspils is rarely used by scheduled passenger services.

ARRIVING BY SEA

Passenger ferries take longer than air travel, though crossing the Baltic Sea has its own appeal. Ferries operated by **Lisco** link the German port of Lübeck to Rīga, while Tallink (*see p393*) connects Rīga to Stockholm (Sweden). **Terrabalt** connects Liepāja to Karlshamn (Sweden) and Rostock (Germany). Ventspils is served by **Scandlines** to Nynashamn (Sweden), Karlshamn and Rostock, and by **SSC Ferries** to Saaremaa Island (Estonia). Rīga's main **Ferry Terminal** can be reached

Express bus 22A waiting outside Rīga International Airport

Passengers queuing up outside the ticket office at a bus station

by trams 5, 7 or 9 from the bus station or outside the National Opera. There are yacht marinas at Rīga, Jūrmala, Liepāja, Pāvilosta, Salacgrīva and Ventspils for those with their own boats. The **Latvian Coast** website offers information.

ARRIVING BY COACH

This is the best way to travel between the three Baltic capitals. International carriers, such as **Ecolines** and **Nordeka**, run services between Rīga and several other European cities. Rīga's main bus terminal, **Autoosta**, is five minutes south of the Old Town.

Travelling by coach costs less than travelling by air. However, the difference in fare is negligible except during the peak season. International coaches are equipped with air conditioning and reclining seats, but can be uncomfortable for long journeys.

ARRIVING BY TRAIN

The main railway station in Rīga, Central Railway Station, is located south of the Old Town. Although there are

no trains from Vilnius to Rīga, there are international rail routes that head east towards Moscow, Vitebsk, Odessa and St Petersburg. The most comfortable way to travel on most routes is a *kupeja* (four-bunk compartment). However, there are more luxurious two-bunk compartments on the trains from Moscow.

ARRIVING BY CAR

Since the Schengen Agreement *(see p393)*, there are no border controls between Estonia, Latvia and Lithuania. Busy border crossings can take up to 20 minutes to negotiate, though cars queue separately from the long lines of lorries. Entering from Russia or Belarus may take longer.

It is essential to bring along the vehicle's registration document, a valid third-party insurance policy and either a European driving licence or an International Driving Permit. Vehicles must be in roadworthy condition and it is compulsory to have a first-aid kit, fire extinguisher and hazard-warning triangle. From December to March, winter tyres must be used, and between September and April, drivers should fit spiked tyres.

ARRIVING BY BICYCLE

Since Latvia acceded to the Schengen Agreement, cycling into Latvia has been simple from Estonia or Lithuania. The flat landscape makes it an attractive option during summer. It is sensible to carry appropriate spares and a waterproof jacket.

DIRECTORY

AIRPORTS

Liepāja Airport
www.liepaja-airport.lv

Rīga International Airport
10/1 Mārupes civil parish.
Tel 9000 6006.
www.riga-airport.com

Ventspils Airport
www.airport.ventspils.lv

AIRLINES

Aer Lingus
www.aerlingus.com

airBaltic
See p393.

easyJet
See p393.

Finnair
See p393.

KLM
See p393.

Lufthansa
See p393.

RyanAir
www.ryanair.com

FERRY COMPANIES

Lisco
www.lisco.lt

Scandlines
www.scandlines.lt

SSC Ferries
www.slkferries.ee

Terrabalt
www.terrabalt.lv

FERRY PORT

Ferry Terminal
Eksporta iela 3A, Rīga. *Tel* 6732
6200. www.freeportofriga.lv

Latvian Coast
www.latviancoast.lv

COACH COMPANIES

Autoosta
See p401.

Ecolines
See p393.

Nordeka
www.nordeka.lv

Passenger train passing through lush pine forests of the Latvian countryside

Getting Around Latvia

The public transport network in Latvia is extensive and affordable. Travelling by coach tends to be quicker than by train, although the buses are often old and can be uncomfortable. Major urban areas and places of interest to visitors usually benefit from frequent coach services. However, in the countryside, there may be only one bus or train per day in each direction. This means that visitors who wish to get off the beaten path will find it difficult to rely on public transport. Car hire is a popular choice, despite the variable state of the roads in the country. The combination of a flat landscape and relatively short distances makes cycling pleasant, especially in good weather.

Commuters entering the Central Railway Station, Rīga

TRAVELLING BY TRAIN

Trains tend to take a little longer than buses to reach their destinations, but the journey is slightly more comfortable, especially if travellers bring along cushions for the hard benches. However, the windows rarely open, making the carriages stuffy in summer. The heating can be erratic.

The most useful routes are from Rīga to Jūrmala, Jelgava and destinations in Gauja National Park. There are also train services to places further afield such as Liepāja, Valmiera, Daugavpils and Rēzekne. Rail enthusiasts may wish to try the narrow-gauge railway line between Alūksne and Gulbene.

TRAVELLING BY COACH

Regular coach services run between most large towns and cities. Other places are less frequently served, therefore careful planning is important to visit several towns in a single day. Although more expensive than travelling by train, travelling by bus is still good value. For overnight journeys, it is advisable to carry a blanket or sleeping bag.

Autoosta (Rīga's Central Bus Station) runs services to Bauska, Cēsis, Sigulda, Daugavpils, Liepāja, Valmiera and Ventspils. If the journey starts at a major station, it is best to buy a ticket before boarding. Otherwise tickets can be purchased from the driver. If your luggage is very large, you may have to pay to stow it in the luggage compartment, but otherwise it is normal to take it on board.

UNDERSTANDING TIMETABLES

Outside of Rīga, it can be difficult to find station staff who speak English. Time-tables are written on boards at the railway station and are also available by telephone and on the Internet. Details of several common routes are also available in the publication *Rīga in Your Pocket (see p403)*. For further enquiries visit the **Latvian Railways** website.

Timetables at train or bus stations rarely include timings of return journeys from various destinations. Express buses are generally indicated by the letter "E", while the equivalent for trains is indicated by three-digit route numbers. *Pietur* indicates that a train or bus stops at a particular destination, while *nepietur* means that it does not. Buses and trains listed as *darbdienās* run on weekdays, and the days of the week are often listed by their initial. Latvian stations number their *perons* (platform) and *ceļš* (track) separately.

TRAVELLING BY AIR

Having revived its domestic flights, airBaltic *(see p393)* runs twice every day between

One of the many extra-long public buses typical of Daugavpils

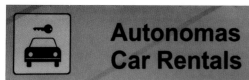

Typical car rental sign at the Domestic Airport, Rīga

DIRECTORY

TRAVELLING BY TRAIN

Latvian Railways
Gogoļa iela 3. *Tel 6723 1181.*
www.ldz.lv

TRAVELLING BY COACH

Autoosta
Prāgas iela 1. *Tel 9000 0009.*
www.autoosta.lv

TRAVELLING BY CAR

SOS Motor Club
Tel 6733 3333. **www**.motor.lv

CAR HIRE

Budget Rent A Car
Tel 6720 7327. **www**.budget.lv

Rīga and Liepāja. If booked well in advance, flights to Liepāja cost little more than those for train or bus, and are very reasonable by European standards. Rīga International Airport is 8 km (5 miles) from the city centre.

TRAVELLING BY CAR & MOTORCYCLE

Bringing or renting a vehicle is an excellent way to see Latvia for those who come for short trips, or wish to visit out-of-the-way corners of the country. However, neither car rental nor petrol is cheap, and road conditions vary dramatically. Most major routes are in an acceptable state, but minor roads can be in poor condition. Many are surfaced with gravel or dirt. In winter, gritting is not widespread and some minor roads become impassable without a sturdy 4WD.

Latvians tend to drive aggressively and overtaking on blind corners is common. Congestion is rare outside the capital. The legal blood alcohol limit is 0.05 per cent, with a ten-day prison sentence for exceeding it. Seat belt use is mandatory in the front seats, as well as in the rear if fitted, and crash helmets must be used on motorcycles. It is compulsory to drive with the headlights switched on at all times. The speed limit is 50 kmph (31 mph) in built-up areas and 90 kmph (56 mph) elsewhere. Traffic police cannot always be spotted outside towns and cities, but they are strict about speeding and collect fines on the spot. Remember to ask for a receipt if you are fined.

In the countryside, changes in speed limit are not always signposted and it is up to the driver to notice signs

Bumpy road sign at Krāslava

indicating built-up areas. These are white rectangles usually bearing the name of the town or village.

Signposting is poor across the country, making it essential to buy a good roadmap. For vehicle breakdown and towing, it is advisable to contact **SOS Motor Club**. On major roads, *degvielas stacija* (service stations), are often open 24 hours, but in rural areas it can be hard to find a place to refuel.

Parking is usually easy outside Rīga, although some cities, notably Daugavpils and Liepāja, have parking meters in certain areas. There is also a fee of 1 lat to enter Jūrmala, collected at a roadside booth.

CAR HIRE

Vehicle hire is most easily arranged in Rīga, although other towns and cities have hire offices. Most international car rental companies are represented in the capital, and many of them have offices at the airport. They are many smaller companies as well. Check the condition of the vehicle and the insurance cover provided. Car hire services are operated by companies such as **Budget**

Rent A Car. Most companies stipulate a minimum age for the person hiring the car. Requirements state that the driver should have held a licence for at least a year. The driver may also need to leave his credit card details or a large deposit.

TRAVELLING BY BICYCLE

Cycling is a good way to get around the relatively flat terrain of Latvia. Bicycles can be hired in many towns and cities. The tourist information board can provide details of cycle routes, such as the popular and easy trail from Rīga to Jūrmala and routes in Gauja National Park and its surrounding valley.

Cyclists riding through a field of dandelions in Gauja National Park

Getting Around Rīga

Rīga's compact Old Town is a pleasure to wander around and is best explored on foot. The cobbled streets, however, can prove difficult for those with mobility problems. Several hotels are located within the Old Town, while many others are within easy walking distance. It is also a short walk to the unmissable Art Nouveau district from the city centre. Attractions further afield, such as the Open-Air Ethnographic Museum, can be reached via the city's extensive network of buses, minibuses, trolleybuses and trams. Tickets are available on board, while passes valid for various lengths of time can be purchased from newspaper kiosks. Taxis are readily available outside the Old Town.

Passengers boarding a bus at Rīga Bus Station

BUSES, TROLLEYBUSES & TRAMS

With several bus, trolleybus and tram routes, Rīga's public transport system is a cheap and efficient way of getting around the Old Town. There are timetables at the various bus stops, but usually no route maps are available, therefore it is advisable to carry one when travelling. Public transport on most routes runs between 5:30am and 11:30pm, with some services operating hourly throughout the night. Autoosta *(see p401)* is close to both the Central Railway Station and Central Market. Other transport hubs include the stretch in front of the Orthodox Cathedral.

Various organizations merged in 2005 to form a single body responsible for public transport, **SIA Rīgas Satiksme**. The system is not yet fully integrated and a separate type of ticket is needed for each mode of transport. A flat fee of 0.40 lats is charged,

irrespective of the length of the journey. Tickets can be purchased on boarding in both buses and trolleybuses from the ticket inspector, while tram tickets can either be purchased from a kiosk or from the driver and then validated in one of the on-board machines. Kiosks sell passes covering various lengths of time, but they are not valid on the whole range of transport options. They may, for example, only apply to trams and trolleybuses.

MINIBUSES

Rīga's *mikroautobuss* (minibus) network runs along the major boulevards and out into the suburbs, and usually offers a little more comfort and speed. The main stops are outside the Central Railway Station, the Orthodox Cathedral and the Central Post Office. Tickets cost marginally more than those for other public transport.

DRIVING

Driving in Rīga is seldom a pleasant experience, marred by heavy traffic and aggressive drivers. Entering the Old Town is also very expensive, as it requires a permit that costs 5 lats per hour. Permits can be obtained from various outlets including branches of Parex bank at Smilšu 3 and Kaļķu 28, and the 24-hour Statoil service station at Eksport 1 C.

PARKING

Parking can be difficult to find in the city centre. It is also expensive. Rates are 1.40 lats for the first hour and 2 lats per hour on the streets of the Old Town. For those who really need a car, it is best to choose a hotel with parking space.

TAXIS

Taxis are abundant in Rīga and are a comfortable, though relatively expensive, way of getting around. They do not come in a standard colour, although all official cabs have

Taxis for hire outside Rīga International Airport

yellow licence plates. From 6am until midnight, the meter starts at 0.4 lats and rises by 0.35 lats per kilometre. After midnight, the meter starts at 0.6 lats, increasing by 0.4 lats per kilometre. A better price can be obtained by calling a reputed company such as **Rīga Taxi** or **Rīgas Taxometru Parks**. It is also better to book a taxi in advance, rather than hire one in the street. Taxis waiting outside the upmarket hotels tend to be more expensive.

Passengers must note that drivers often refuse to accept a fare of less than 3 lats, and try to charge at least that much to take passengers from the bus or railway station to a nearby hotel. Visitors must ensure that the meter is used, or at least negotiate a fare in advance. It is rarely difficult to find a taxi during the day, while at night taxis congregate at each end of Kaļķu iela.

Pedestrians at a zebra crossing, Aspazijas bulvāris

Cycling in Rīga, a quick and easy way of getting around the city

CYCLING

Getting around Rīga by bicycle is a good option, despite the Old Town's cobbled streets and the heavy traffic in other parts of the city. One of the more pleasant places for a ride is the pristine suburb of Mežaparks *(see p156)*. The **Active Holiday Centre** on the left bank of Daugava river offers help with bicycle rental.

WALKING

The Old Town is relatively small, with plenty of recognizable landmarks, making the walk manageable as well as enjoyable in spite of the cobblestoned streets. It is particularly pleasant to wander around in summer, when many streets and squares are lined with terrace seating outside bars and cafés, and the weather is more suitable for walking. The area immediately north of the Old Town is home to some impressive Art Nouveau buildings and several smart shops and restaurants. The main street in Rīga's Art Nouveau district is Elizabetes iela, which intersects with Brīvības bulvāris (avenue). In addition, Alberta and Strēlnieku iela also feature examples of this style.

The **Rīga Card** *(see p380)* offers free entry to many museums, a free walking tour of the Old Town, and free public transport within Rīga and Jūrmala. Since public transport is already so cheap in the country, investing in the card is worthwhile only if visitors are interested in the walking tour or in visiting several museums in a single day. The card is available in hotels, Rīga Airport and the tourist information offices.

MAPS

The most widely available map of the city is published by Jāņa Sēta, at a scale of 1:20,000 with the centre shown at a detailed 1:7000. A much smaller version of the map is included in the popular *Rīga In Your Pocket* guide, but it is only detailed enough if you do not plan to stray far from the centre. However, the guide also indicates public transport routes.

DIRECTORY

BUSES, TROLLEYBUSES & TRAMS

SIA Rīgas Satiksme
Tel 8000 1919.
www.rigassatiksme.lv

TAXIS

Rīga Taxi
Tel 8000 1010. **www**.taxi.lv

Rīgas Taksometru Parks
Tel 8000 1313. **www**.rtp.lv

CYCLING

Active Holiday Centre
Bauskas iela 2. *Tel* 6762 3122.
www.aac.lv

CITY CARD

Rīga Card
Tel 6721 7217. **www**.rigacard.lv

MAPS

Rīga In Your Pocket
Elizabetes iela 75. *Tel* 6722 0580.
www.inyourpocket.com

TRAVELLING TO LITHUANIA

The quickest and easiest way to reach Lithuania is by air. Most airlines fly to Vilnius, which has direct connections with many European cities. Some international flights arrive at Kaunas and Palanga airports. Lithuania has only one sea port, at Klaipėda, which offers a limited number of passenger ferry services across the Baltic Sea to Germany and Scandinavia. By land, it is best to travel to Lithuania by coach. There are regular departures from London, Paris and other European capitals. However, getting to Lithuania by car is long and hazardous given the bad roads in Poland. A daily train service links Warsaw with Kaunas and Vilnius, with a change at Sestokai, on the Polish-Lithuanian frontier. Lithuania is not covered by Eurail or InterRail, making travelling by train from Western Europe expensive.

Klaipėda port logo

ARRIVING BY AIR

Lithuania is well connected with Europe and, via major European transport hubs such as London, Copenhagen and Amsterdam, to the rest of the world. Connectivity has been improving rapidly in recent years, with flights to and from Vilnius timing in well with intercontinental flights. Since March 2008, the control of internal borders among the Schengen states, which also include Estonia, Latvia and Lithuania, was abolished.

Opened in 1944, **Vilnius Airport** is the arrival point for most flights. It is the only airport among the Baltic capitals to have maintained its original appearance of a formulaic erstwhile Soviet-era terminal. A large extension of Vilnius Airport terminal building that opened recently has raised its capacity to 3 million passengers a year. Services at the airport include car rental offices, currency exchange, cafés and newspaper kiosks that also sell bus tickets.

FlyLAL, or Lithuanian Airlines, is the country's national carrier. Vilnius Airport is also used by about 17 other airlines, including **Lufthansa**, **Finnair**, **Czech Airlines** and **Austrian Airlines**. British Airways pulled out of Vilnius as a result of stiff low-cost competition on UK-Lithuania routes offered by FlyLAL, **airBaltic** and **RyanAir**,

International check-in hall at Vilnius Airport

which fly to **Kaunas Airport**. As a result, major international flights and low-cost carriers from around 40 cities arrive in Lithuanian airports. These include almost all the capitals of Western Europe, as well as Prague, Moscow, Minsk, Gomel, Kiev, St Petersburg, Tbilisi, Kaliningrad, Baku, Tel Aviv and other cities further east. Additional frequencies laid on by airlines serving Lithuania also mean a greater choice of arrival and departure times. This is good news for the fast-growing number of business travellers in the country.

Since airBaltic started to challenge the existing price structure in Vilnius in 2004, airline ticket prices have undergone a revolution. By implementing a one-way ticket system, the airline has ensured that the prices of tickets depend directly on demand. The traditional

Official logo of FlyLAL

"Sunday rule", with prices being higher on weekdays than on the weekends, does not hold true. The majority of tickets are purchased on the Internet. In accordance with international agreements, most airlines operate a system of reduced rates for children, students and pensioners as well as pre-arranged groups.

FROM VILNIUS AIRPORT TO THE CITY CENTRE

Vilnius Airport is located 5 km (3 miles) south of city centre. From Vilnius Airport, bus route 1 runs to the railway station and route 2 goes to Lukiškių aikštė (square). Tickets are cheaper if bought at airport kiosks. However, tickets can also be purchased while boarding the bus. The bus stop and taxi rank are both outside the arrivals area. Taxis at the airport are reliable. They charge a fare of 30 litai and take 20 minutes to reach the city centre.

OTHER LITHUANIAN AIRPORTS

The airports at Kaunas and Palanga have scheduled international flights, although they are fairly limited compared to those at Vilnius Airport. New terminals are being built at both the airports in an effort to make them better equipped. From Kaunas Airport, shuttle bus number 120 goes to Savanorių prospektas (avenue) and the Old Town, while bus number 29 goes to the bus station. A minibus shuttle travels twice daily between Kaunas Airport and Vilnius connecting all Ryanair flights, as that is the only carrier operating in Kaunas at the moment. For information on airport bus services, log on to **Aurakom**. There are hourly buses from **Palanga Airport** to Palanga and many buses operate between Palanga and Klaipėda. FlyLAL offers its passengers free mini-bus services from Palanga Airport to Klaipėda. Buses head north from the airport to Liepāja in Latvia.

ARRIVING BY CAR

As Lithuania is part of the Schengen zone, there are no restrictions to entering it from Schengen countries. Drivers entering the country by car do not need an international driver's licence, but it is essential to carry the vehicle's registration documents, insurance papers, a passport and a licence from their country. All cars must carry a first-aid kit and fire extinguisher.

International cargo and passenger carrier sailing out of Klaipėda

ARRIVING BY SEA

Lithuania's only commercial maritime harbour, **Klaipėda State Sea Port**, is linked by ferry to ports in Germany, Sweden and Denmark. There are connections between Klaipėda and Kiel and Mukran in Germany, Copenhagen-Fredericia, Aabenraa-Aarhus in Denmark and Karlshamn in Sweden.

ARRIVING BY COACH

Lithuania has an extensive network of roads connecting the country to neighbouring states. It is fairly simple to reach Lithuania by bus or coach from Estonia or Latvia as there are numerous crossing points. There are express passenger coaches from Vilnius to Rīga and Tallinn, as well as other cities including Warsaw, Berlin, Prague, Vienna, Kaliningrad and Moscow. On the other hand, the journey from countries such as Germany or the UK is very long and the inconvenience is best avoided.

DIRECTORY

AIRLINES

airBaltic
See p393.

Austrian Airlines
www.austrian.lt

Czech Airlines
www.czechairlines.com

Finnair
See p393.

FlyLAL
www.flylal.lt

Lufthansa
See p393.

RyanAir
See p399.

AIRPORTS

Kaunas Airport
Karmėlava. **Tel** (37) 399 396.
www.kaunasair.lt

Palanga Airport
Liepojos pl 1. **Tel** (460) 52 020.
www.palanga-airport.lt

Vilnius Airport
Raudūnios kelias. **Tel** 273 9305.
www.vilnius-airport.lt

AIRPORT BUS SERVICES

Aurakom
www.airport-bus.lt

FERRY INFORMATION

Klaipėda State Sea Port
www.portofklaipeda.lt

Airport terminal building, Palanga Airport in Western Lithuania

Getting Around Lithuania

Lithuania's excellent road network makes it very easy to get around. Buses are the fastest and most convenient mode of public transport in the country. Express buses link virtually every town in Lithuania and are also a great way to see the countryside. Trains are cheaper, but also less frequent and with far fewer routes. The roads in Lithuania are some of the best-maintained in Central and Eastern Europe, which often makes hiring a car the most comfortable way to travel. The country's relatively flat landscape, punctuated by low hills, makes it ideal for cycling as well.

International luxury coach at the bus station in Panevėžys

TRAVELLING BY BUS

Buses form the main mode of Lithuania's public transport network. The privately owned bus company **Toks** operates comfortable buses on more than 50 routes countrywide as well as 11 international routes for **Eurolines**. Although travelling by bus is usually a little more expensive than by train, buses are quicker and connect more places.

Schedules are written on signs at the head of each stand, as well as inside the bus station building. Express buses, marked by an "E" in the schedules, sometimes operate on intercity routes, bypassing smaller towns and villages along the way. Many of the bus services to the coast, for instance to Palanga or Nida, are seasonal and operate in summer only. For more information on frequency of services check the official website for Toks.

Vilnius Bus Station is the country's biggest bus transport hub, although **Kaunas Bus Station** also has links with various European cities.

Tickets can be bought at ticket desks in bus stations in larger towns, although you can also buy them from the driver on boarding, especially on minor routes. In summer, or during weekends when services are more regularly used, it is worth buying tickets in advance. Tickets have to be paid for in cash and there are no facilities for reserving them by telephone or on the Internet. Disabled passengers, senior citizens over the age of 70 and children below the age of ten, are entitled to a 50 per cent discount. Pre-school children travel free. Groups of ten passengers or more get price reductions if travel is arranged in advance.

TRAVELLING BY TRAIN

The national rail network is run by **Lietuvos Geležinkeliai** (Lithuanian Railways). The main routes are from Vilnius to Šiauliai and Klaipėda, Vilnius to Visaginas, which passes by Ignalina and Aukštaitija National Park, Šiauliai to Panevėžys and Rokiškis, and the comparatively speedy and regular Vilnius to Kaunas route. The Vilnius to Varėna line continues to Dzūkija National Park before heading into Belarus. One of the most enjoyable and scenic train journeys in Lithuania is on the Narrow-Gauge Railway, which runs from Panevėžys to Lake Rubikiai.

All train tickets must be purchased at the ticket desks at railway stations. Reductions are available for young children, pensioners and also disabled passengers.

Lithuania's *autobusų stotis* (bus stations) and *traukinių stotis* (railway stations) are generally located close to one another and are within easy walking distance of the town centre. Theft is rare, although it is best to keep an eye on your belongings. Risk to personal safety is seldom an issue when travelling in Lithuania, but security guards are often deployed at Vilnius Bus Station.

However, bus and train stations place little emphasis on cleanliness and hygiene, although the stations at Vilnius and Kaunas have now been modernized. At

Narrow-Gauge Railway, one of the most scenic and enjoyable train journeys

Well-maintained ticket office in the railway station, Vilnius

the larger railway stations it is also possible to leave your baggage at the left luggage room for a small fee, or deposit the luggage in a self-service locker.

TRAVELLING BY CAR

Roads in Lithuania are excellent by post-Soviet standards, and present no special problems to drivers. There are different categories of roads, with different speed restrictions. The highest category of roads in Lithuania is the motorway, but there are only two of these, Kaunas to Klaipėda (A1), and Vilnius to Panevėžys (A2). Although the Vilnius–Kaunas and Kaunas–Klaipėda roads look the same, the former stretch is not the "motorway" class because of its hilly terrain. There are no toll roads in Lithuania except through the Curonian Spit National Park.

Lithuanian regulations state that every car must carry a small fire extinguisher, a first-aid kit, a reflective warning triangle and reflective safety vest. It is mandatory for passengers to wear seat belts. Motorists must use headlights at all times, both during the day and night. The traffic police may not be able to speak fluent English but are stringent about rules and can collect fines on the spot.

The maximum permissible speed limit on motorways is 130 kmph (81 mph) from May to October and 110 kmph (68 mph) for the rest of the year, the exception being the Vilnius–Kaunas motorway

where the speed limit remains 110 kmph (68 mph). The speed limit in built-up areas is 50 kmph (31 mph), but drivers are rarely stopped for speeding unless they exceed a speed of 60 kmph (37 mph).

Drunken driving is a punishable offence and local authorities sometimes use roadblocks and breathalyzer tests as enforcement tools.

CAR HIRE

A large number of local and well-known international car hire companies offer a wide range of vehicles for rental in Lithuania. Some have desks at Vilnius Airport and upmarket hotels. Many others can be found in Vilnius city centre. Local firms, such as **Aunela**, have a range of newer and older Western makes of cars. The minimum rental period is usually 24 hours. Payments for car hire can be made both with cash or through any major credit card.

DIRECTORY

TRAVELLING BY BUS

Eurolines
See p393.

Kaunas Bus Station
Vytauto 24. **Tel** (37) 409 060.

Toks
www.toks.lt

Vilnius Bus Station
Sodų 22. **Tel** 8900 01661.
www.toks.lt/en/schedule

TRAVELLING BY TRAIN

Lietuvos Geležinkeliai
www.litrail.lt

CAR HIRE

Aunela
www.aunela.lt

ROAD SIGNS

Signposting on motorways, country roads and minor roads is comprehensible. When entering a town or village, the settlement's name appears on a sign with black lettering on a white background. This indicates that drivers must slow down to the speed limit for built-up areas. Small blue signs near road junctions in Vilnius city centre point the way to streets, sights and landmarks. Key road signs to look out for are those regulating speed, controlling roadside parking and preventing right or left turns. These are often monitored by traffic police.

Part of Klaipėda's recently modernized road network

Getting Around Vilnius

The best way to explore Vilnius is on foot as most sights such as churches, museums, restaurants and cafés are within easy walking distance of each other. It is only a short walk to the main sights from the city's main thoroughfare, Gedimino Avenue. Vilnius's Old Town is among the biggest in Europe and much of the city's inner traffic is kept to roads that circle its boundary. To reach the sights and restaurants that lie outside the city centre, a reliable network of trolleybuses and buses exists. Taxi services are usually trustworthy. However, getting around by road is best avoided at rush hour.

Modern trolleybus, part of Vilnius's public transport network

BUSES & TROLLEYBUSES

Vilnius has a very dependable network of trolleybuses and buses with frequent services that span the city. Some of the older vehicles are now being replaced with modern ones. However, public transport is best avoided during rush hour, when trolleybuses and buses are crowded.

A detailed map of the city's bus routes is available on the **Vilnius Transport** website. The timetables for every *stotelė* (stop) can be viewed by clicking "*autobusų*" for buses and "*troleibusų*" for trolleybuses. Few services run between 11pm and 5am.

A standard *bilietas* (ticket) is valid on both buses and trolleybuses. This must be bought in advance at a kiosk or from the driver on boarding, and then validated by punching it in one of the machines on board. Passes for one, three and ten days are available. Penalties for travelling without a valid ticket are high.

DRIVING IN VILNIUS

Traffic density has increased rapidly in Vilnius in recent years, resulting in traffic congestion during peak hours, especially early mornings and late evenings. The problem is further compounded by the erstwhile Soviet city planning. The lack of roads is a serious issue that Vilnius's city council is struggling to solve with the help of EU funds. However, road construction causes further blockades, adding to drivers' woes in the short term. With the rise in the number of vehicles, tailgating and overtaking have become standard practice. Central Vilnius has an extensive one-way system, which can be quite tricky to negotiate without a road map.

PARKING

Multi-storey car parks in Vilnius are few. Most often drivers use roadside parking. In the city centre, drivers can use controlled parking between 8am and 6pm, using a pay-and-display machine. Parking is more expensive in the Old Town. Failing to pay results in a wheel-clamp, a lengthy wait and then a very heavy fine.

In parked cars, all objects including bags and clothing should be locked out of sight.

TAXIS

Taxis are easily available in Vilnius, although during rush hour and late on weekend evenings it may be necessary to call several companies before finding a free cab. Ordering a taxi by telephone is cheaper than hailing one on the street. The average charge is 2 litas per kilometre, but companies, such as the

View of a busy road in Vilnius during peak traffic hour

Martono Taksi, an expensive but reliable option

more expensive **Martono Taksi**, charge 3 litas, although they are generally more reliable. **Ekipažas** charges 2 litas per kilometre. Charges are higher at night. All taxis must have a working meter so check the initial reading as you get in.

CYCLING

Conditions for cyclists vary considerably around the city. Bicycle routes are clearly marked on many of the pavements in the Old Town, along roads such as Gedimino and Konstitucijos avenues and into districts such as Žvėrynas and Vingis Park. EuroVelo route 11 is an Eastern European cycle route that runs through the eastern Baltic region, taking in Vilnius and Tartu. It has now been extended to Vilnius from the southwest to the northeast, towards Verkiai. However, cycling along roads that do not have bicycle lanes is not recommended. Bicycles can be rented at **Baltic Cycle**.

WALKING

Each sight is just a few steps from the next one, allowing visitors to experience the Old Town's magnificent architecture from close quarters. There are many pedestrianized streets and, despite the occasional reckless driver, traffic is rarely a hindrance.

Crossing roads in Vilnius can sometimes be hazardous. At many crossings a "red man" and "green man" guide pedestrians on when to cross. However, at road junctions, there are traffic lights just for cars. When at a pedestrian crossing without lights, cars must give way to pedestrians, but they do not always do so.

Gedimino Avenue is the city's main street for shopping, festivals and parades, besides being an attraction in itself. Stretching from Cathedral Square in the east to Žvėrynas in the west, it becomes pedestrianized in the evenings and night. The lush districts of Žvėrynas and Užupis are on either sides of the Old Town. The former leads to the splendid views of the Neris river and Vingis Park, reachable by a pedestrian bridge. A walk to Užupis may culminate in a breathtaking panorama at the Tores restaurant (*see p339*), the peaceful Bernadinų Cemetery or as far as even Belmontas and the Church of Sts Peter and Paul.

Visitors walking down Pilies Street towards Upper Castle, Old Town

SIGHTSEEING TOURS

Tour guides in Vilnius are professional and speak fluent English. A typical sightseeing tour arranged by **Senamiesčio Gidas** or **Mano Gidas** includes a trip to the Old Town, Užupis and the Church of Sts Peter and Paul. Customized tours can also be arranged.

Travel agencies such as **Visit Lithuania** also arrange guided tours as well as accommodation and transport. **West Express** organizes specialized tours, such as Jewish Vilnius.

CAR HIRE

A convenient alternative for getting around the city and taking day trips to nearby attractions such as Trakai is to hire a car. International car rental companies, such as **Europcar**, **Avis** and **Hertz**, and local companies, such as Aunela, offer insured vehicles.

DIRECTORY

BUSES & TROLLEYBUSES

Vilnius Transport
Sodų 22. **Tel** 216 0054.
www.vilniustransport.lt

TAXIS

Ekipažas
Justiniškių 14. **Tel** 240 0064.
www.ekipazas.lt

Martono Taksi
Kalvarijų gatvė 53. **Tel** (85) 246
1487. **www**.martonas.lt

CYCLING

Baltic Cycle
Vytenio 6–110. **Tel** 6995 6009.
www.bicycle.lt

SIGHTSEEING TOURS

Mano Gidas
Krokuvos 59-1a. **Tel** 6123 4000.

Senamiesčio Gidas
Aušros vartų 7. **Tel** 6995 4064.
www.vilniuscitytour.com

Visit Lithuania
Odminių 5. **Tel** 262 5241.
www.visitlithuania.net

West Express
A Stulginskio 5. **Tel** 255 3255.
www.westexpress.lt

CAR HIRE

Avis
See p395.

Europcar
See p395.

Hertz
See p395.

General Index

Page numbers in **bold** refer to
main entries

Acknowledgments

Dorling Kindersley would like to thank the many people whose help and assistance contributed to the preparation of this book.

Contributors
Howard Jarvis has been editor-in-chief for several publications including *The Baltic Times*, *VilniusNOW!* and *Baltic Stand By*. He has been a regular contributor for the Jane's Information Group since 2000.

John Oates, winner of the Guardian newspaper's Young Travel Writer of the Year award, has contributed to numerous newspapers, magazines and guidebooks.

Tim Ochser has been living in Rīga since 2001 where he works as a freelance journalist. He also contributes to Latvian media and has written several Latvian plays.

Neil Taylor is a writer, a tour operator and a consultant. He writes for British news-papers on the Baltics and has published several guidebooks on the region.

Fact Checkers
Nicholas Archdeacon, Joel Dullroy, Brigita Pantelejeva

Proofreader
Deepthi Talwar

Indexer
Ajay Lal Das

Design and Editorial
Publisher Douglas Amrine
Managing Art Editor Jane Ewart
Project Editor Michelle Crane
Production Controller Lousie Daly
Picture Research Ellen Root
DTP Designer Natasha Lu

Additional Photography
Peter Dennis, Rose Horridge, Rajnish Kashyap, Ian O'Leary.

Additional Illustrations
Chapel Design & Marketing Ltd

Cartography
Casper Morris, Stuart James

Cartographic Research
Netmaps

Special Assistance
Dorling Kindersley would like to thank the following for their assistance:
Sonata Šiaučiulytė at Vilnius Tourist Information Centre

Photography Permissions
Dorling Kindersley would like to thank the following for their assistance and kind permission to photograph at their establishments:

Ainaži Naval College Museum, Andrejs Pumpurs Museum, Anton Hansen Tammsaare Museum, Aqua Park, Arsenal Museum of Art, Art Nouveau in Rīga, Aviation Museum, Beekeeping Museum, Bicycle Museum, Calvary Church of the Holy Cross, Cathedral of Christ the King, Cathedral of St Anthony of Padua, Cathedral of St Mary the Virgin (Toomkirik), Cathedral of Sts Boris and Glebe, Cat's House, Church of St Casimir's, Church of St Theresa, Church of Sts Peter and Paul, Coca Cola Plaza, Tallinn, Contemporary Art Centre, Dauderi, Déjà Vu Lounge Bar, Tallinn, Dome Cathedral, Dominican Church, Dominican Monastery, Old town, Dundaga, Europa Mall, Vilnius, Folk House of the Livs, Franciscan Church, Friary of the Virgin Mary, Tytuvenai, House of Blackheads, KGB Cells Museum, KGB Museum, Vilnius, Kohtla Underground Mining Museum, Kiek in de Kök, Tallinn, Kumu Art Museum, Latgale Culture and History Museum, The Latvian Ethnographic Open-Air Museum, Latvian Museum of Photography, Rēzekne, Liepāja Museum, Lithuanian National Museum, Littera Bookshop, Vilnius University, Mentzendorff House, The Mihkli Farm Museum, Mikalojus Konstantinas Čiurlionis National Museum of Art, Motor Museum, Museum of the Barricades of 1991, Museum of Decorative Arts and Design, Museum of History and Applied Arts, Preiļi, Museum of Horns, Museum of Rīga's History and Navigation, Niguliste Church, Tallinn, Palmse Manor House, Pedvāle Open-Air Museum, Peter The Great House Museum, The Palanga Amber Museum, Photo Museum, Tallinn, Porcelain Museum, Powder Tower/Latvian War Museum, Railway Museum, Vilnius, Rundāle Palace, Latvia, Sea Museum-Aquarium and Dolphinarium in Smiltynė, Setu Village Museum (Lake Peipsi), Shakespeare Boutique Hotel, Skaistkalne Roman Catholic Church, Skyline Bar (Reval Hotel, Latvija), St Anne's Basilica, St John's Church, Tallinn International Airport, Tamsta Club, Tērvete Nature Park, Theatre, Music and Film Museum, Town Hall Pharmacy in Tallinn, Trakai Island Castle, Tukums, Vilnius Cathedral, Vilnius Picture Gallery, Vilnius University, Vincents Restaurant, Rīga, Vytautas The Great War Museum, Žemaitija National Park

Picture Credits
Placement Key- t=top; tc=top centre; tr=top right; cla=centre left above; ca=centre above; cra=centre right above; cl=centre left; c=centre; cr=centre right; clb=centre left below; cb=centre below; crb=centre right below; bl=bottom left; bc=bottom centre; br=bottom right; ftl=far top left; ftr=far top right; fcla=far centre left above; fcra=far centre right above; fcl=far centre left; fcr=far centre right;

fclb=far centre left below; fcrb=far centre right below; fbl=far bottom left; fbr=far bottom right.

Every effort has been made to trace the copyright holders, and we apologize in advance for any unintentional omissions. We would be pleased to insert the appropriate acknowledgments in any subsequent edition of this publication.

The publisher would like to thank the following individuals, companies, and picture libraries for their kind permission to reproduce their photographs:

Works of art have been reproduced with the kind permission of the following copyright holders:

The Offering 1909 by M. K. Ciurlionis, Tempera on canvas, 71 x 78.5. Inv. No Ct- 172 © Mikalojus Konstantinas Čiurlionis National Museum of Art; *Funeral Symphony II* from the cycle of 7 paintings by M. K. Ciurlionis, 1903 Pastel on paper, 62.3 x 73. Inv. No Ct-107 © Mikalojus Konstantinas Čiurlionis National Museum of Art Tarvas 2002 by Tauno Kangro, 9 x 4 x 2m, bronze, Rakvere on the Castle Hill, Estonia 112bc

4CORNERS IMAGES: Cozzi Guido 249b

AKG-IMAGES: 32cl, 34br, 36tr, 36-37c, 50crb, 51tl, 135bc, 136tc, 215tl; Erich Lessing 30, 212-213c; RIA Nowosti 39t, 39c, 212cl

ALAMY: A.P. 84, 163b, 181br; Urmas Ääro 45b, 102; Stuart Abraham 42br; Ace Stock Limited 17br, 93crb, 291bc; AllOver photography 206b; Arco Images 233cb; Andrew Barnes 26bc; Caro 202bl, 206tr; China Span/Keren Su 183b; Content Mine International 129b, 131tr; Gary Cook 187tl; Kitt Cooper-Smith 27ca; Dennis Cox 2-3; Danita Delimont 12bc, 24br, 131br, 174-175, 371tl, 401br; Ilja Dubovskis 284cl; Cody Duncan 19c; Sindre Ellingsen 253tl; Maciej Figiel 27tl, 27cla; Peter Erik Forsberg 45c; FotoIJ 54; Johan Furusjö 133bl; Christopher Griffin 69cr; Andrew Harrington 85b; Simon Hathaway 318cl; Pete Hill 390cla; Ula Holigrad 18cr; Peter Horree 3c; !hotimagery! 248; Imagebroker 19cl, 93tl, 80tr, 138; Images&Stories 129c; INSADCO Photography 388c; InterFoto Pressebildagentur 201c; Jevgenija 187br; Michael Juno 288c; Stanislovas Kairys 239bl; Christian Klein 363tl; Stan Kujawa 319c; Yadid Levy 37cr, 243tl; Robin Mckelvie 110crb, 172bl; The Natural History Museum 27tc; Natural Visions 26br; Kari Niemeläinen 397bc; Indrek Parli 48bl; PCL 133tl; Pictorial Press Ltd 22cl; Les Polders 58br; The Print Collector 125c; Robert Harding Picture Library Ltd 130t,/Yadid Levy 376-7; Jonathan Smith 24cla; David Soulsby 394cl; Sylvia Cordaiy Photo Library Ltd 362tc; Vario images GmbH & Co.KG/Stefan Kiefer 53c, 395br; Tiit Veermae 17tr, 18tr, 47t, 57cr, 96-7, 106clb, 110cra, 117br; Martyn Vickery 20br, 68clb, 243tr, 356b; Visual&Written SL 70tl; World Pictures 47br; Sven Zacek 92cla, 103b
APOLLO RAAMATUD : 349bl

AUKSTAITIJOS SIAURASIS GELEZINKELIS: 406br
BANK OF ESTONIA: 385tl, 385tr, 385cla, 385cra, 385cl, 385cr, 385clb, 385cb, 385cb(1), 385crb, 385bl, 385bc, 385br, 385fbr.
BANK OF LATVIA: 386cla, 386cra, 386cl, 386cr, 386clb, 386crb, 386br, 386fbr
BANK OF LITHUANIA: 31c, 39bl
BOGAPOTT: 348tr
THE BRIDGEMAN ART LIBRARY: King Charles XII (1682-1718) of Sweden, on horseback, 1702 (engraving) (b/w photo), Picart, Bernard (1673-1733)/Bibliotheque Nationale, Paris, France, Archives Charmet 33br, Catherine the Great, 1793, Lampi, Johann Baptist I (1751-1830)/ Hermitage, St. Petersburg, Russia, 34bl, Arms of the Hanseatic League (stone), German School/© Museum of London, UK, 134bc, Shipping off a Baltic Port (oil on canvas), Larsen, Carl E. (1823-59) & Neumann, Carl Johan (1833-91)/Private Collection, Bourne Gallery, Reigate, Surrey Art Library 135crb
Bussi Reisid: 394br
CLUB ILLUSION: 358c
CORBIS: Niall Benvie 370bl; Christophe Boisvieux 57br; Epa/Toms Kalnins 207br,/Kay Nietfeld 119bc,/Ljubo Vukelic 39bc; Franz-Marc Frei 202cl; Jon Hicks 40-1, 232t; Robert Harding World Imagery/Yadid Levy 21tr; Hans Georg Roth 364bl; Sygma/ Gérard Rancinan 22bl; Peter Turnley 215crb; Zefa/Goebel 16cl, 203br
DANITA DELIMONT STOCK PHOTOGRAPHY: Janis Miglavs 11br, 182; Keren Su 216, 217b
VYDAS DOLINSKAS: 213tl, 213tc
ESTONIAN AIR: 392tc
FOCUS: Kaido Haagen 24clb; Tiit Hunt 90tl; Jarek Jõepera 10cl, 19cra, 46tl, 119cra, 119clb, 119crb, 123tr; Didzis Kadaks 26crb, 171br, 186bc; Mati Kose 49cr; Arnold Kristjuhan 19ca; Heinrich Lukk 29br; Kalju Suur 23tc, 23cra, 25tl, 53tl; Tiina Tammet 75tl; Andres Teiss 44, 359tl, 361tl, 373tr; Toomas Tuul 10br, 11t, 15tr, 46br, 48tc, 48cr, 74cl, 89b, 92bl, 93bl, 94cl, 101br, 105cr, 106cla, 107cra, 113br, 321tr, 358br, 372tl, 373bc, 395tl; Tips International/ Didier Givois/Vandystadt 119tc
GETTY IMAGES: AFP/Tim Sloan 137bc,/Ilmars Znotins 130br,/Stringer 37br; AFP/Petras Malukas/ Stringer 207tl; De Agostini 204; Hulton Archive/ Austrian Archives/Imagno 212br; Hulton Archive/ Stringer 36br, 136clb, 214c; Jeff Gross 374tl; Robert Harding World Imagery/Gary Cook 12tl; Stu Forster 23bl; Time & Life Pictures/Ben Martin 196bl,/David Rubinger 137tl
THE GRANGER COLLECTION, NEW YORK: Ullstein Bild 137crb
ILGI BAND: 25tr
HOWARD JARVIS: 220cl
JONATHAN SMITH PHOTOGRAPHY: 24-5c, 208bc, 209tl, 268, 269b, 319tl, 366cr
KALEV CHOCOLATES: 349c
LINAS KARDASEVICIUS: 262-263
KAUBAMAJA STORE: 349tc
KGB CELLS MUSEUM: 115cb
KLAIPEDA CLOCK MUSEUM: 280crb
THE LATVIAN ETHNOGRAPHIC OPEN AIR MUSEUM: Uldis Veisbuks 159cla, 159clb
ARCHIVE OF THE LATVIAN TOURISM DEVELOPMENT AGENCY: 198cl, 198bc
LIEPAJA THEATRE: 362br

LILIJA PLUS LTD.: 289cb
LITHUANIAN NATIONAL TOURISM OFFICE: 379c
LITHUANIA STATE DEPARTMENT OF TOURISM: 212tl
DAOYONG LIU: 16ca
LONELY PLANET IMAGES: Jonathan Smith 208cl
MARY EVANS PICTURE LIBRARY: 9c, 34tl, 52c, 134bl, 287c; Mary Evans Iln Pictures 41c; Rue Des Archives 377c
MIKALOJUS KONSTANTINAS ČIURLIONIS NATIONAL MUSEUM OF ART: 22cra
MOLLY MALONE'S: 360c
MONIKA CENTRUM: 288tc
NATIONAL AERONAUTICS AND SPACE ADMINISTRATION: 14cl
NATIONAL GEOGRAPHIC IMAGE COLLECTION: Klaus Nigge 18bl
NATUREPL.COM: Niall Benvie 19crb; William Osborn 19clb; Igor Shpilenok 19bc; Artur Tabor 18br.
NORTH WIND PICTURE ARCHIVES: 26cl
PALANGOS TOURISM INFORMATION CENTRE: Tomas Smilingis 27br
JOAN PARENTI: 275br
PHOTOGRAPHERS DIRECT: Andrew Bain Photography 200-201, Peter Erik Forsberg 346cl, Didzis Kadaks 153; James A. Krug 8-9, Stefan Sollfors Photography 132tc, Wandering Spirit Travel Images/Louise Batalla Duran 55b.
PHOTOLIBRARY: Niall Benvie 124-125; Jon Arnold Travel/Peter Adams 13tl; JTB Photo 128, 347b; Roland Marske/Voller Ernst 205b
PHOTOSHOT: NHPA/Lee Dalton 18cb
PRIVATE COLLECTION: 22tr, 24tr, 33tl, 33crb, 34cb, 35c, 35cb, 35bc, 36cl, 36bl, 38tl, 50ca, 51cr, 52tl, 77tr, 79cl, 79cr, 79bl, 99cr, 135tc, 198cra, 210c, 210crb, 210bc, 211tc, 211crb, 212bl, 213tr, 213bl, 213br, 214br, 239cl, 239cr.
PROMENADE HOTEL: 291tl
JON REKSTEN: 132bl
ERIKS REMESS: 13br
REUTERS: Alexander Demianchuk 119br
AIVAR RUUKEL: 100cl, 100cla, 100br, 101cl
SALACGRVAS NOVADA TIC: 190cr
SCANPIX BALTICS: 133cr; F64 23crb, 132cr; LT 25cr; Postimees/Lauri Kulpsoo 19tc,/Henn Soodla 19cla
SIGADE REVOLUTSIOON LLC: 359bc
STAROVER.EE: Piirissaare 122bc

STATE SMALL THEATRE OF VILNIUS: Dmitrij Matvejev 368cl
SUPERSTOCK: Age Fotostock148tl,/Wojtek Buss 257cl; Yoshio Tomii 49bl
COURTESY OF THE TALLIN CITY MUSEUM: 73c
TALLIN CITY THEATRE: Siim Vahur 360cl

TEATER VANEMUINE: 358tc

TOPFOTO.CO.UK: The British Library/HIP 214tl

TRAVEL-IMAGES.COM: A. Dnieprowsky 43br, 165tr, 184bl; G. Frysinger 243br

VILNIUS CONGRESS CONCERT HALL: 368br

VILNIUS JAZZ FESTIVAL: Vytautas Suslavicius 209bl

JONATHAN WASSERSTEIN: 72crb

WIKIMEDIA COMMONS: 23cl, 118br

WIKIPEDIA, THE FREE ENCYCLOPEDIA: 20cl, 22crb, 38cb, 38bc, 51bc, 378tc; GNU Free Documentation License 26bl, 37tl, 51crb, 52br, 53bl, 211bc [http://en.wikipedia.org/wiki/Wikipedia:Text_of_the_GNU_Free_Documentation_License]; U.S. Department of Defense 53bc

Front Endpaper: ALAMY: A.P. ftl, Urmas Ääro tl, FotoIJ fcl, !hotimagery! bl, Imagebroker ftr; DANITA DELIMONT STOCK PHOTOGRAPHY: Janis Miglavs fbr, Keren Su br; JONATHAN SMITH PHOTOGRAPHY fbl.

Cover Picture Credits
FRONT COVER: DK IMAGES: Linda Whitwam clb; PHOTOLIBRARY: Gary Cook main.
BACK COVER: ALAMY IMAGES: China Span/Keren Su bl; Inga Sõelsepp cla; DK IMAGES: Linda Whitwam tl; FOCUS: Andres Teiss cl.
SPINE : DK IMAGES: Linda Whitwam b; PHOTOLIBRARY: Gary Cook t
All other images © Dorling Kindersley
For further information see: www.dkimages.com

Phrase Book: Estonian

In Emergency

Help!	Appi!	*Awpy!*
Stop!	Peatuge!	***Beb****-atu-gay!*
Call a doctor!	Kutsuge arst!	***Coot****-soo-gay arst!*
Call an ambulance!	Kutsuge kiirabi!	***Coot****-soo-gay keer-awbi!*
Call the police!	Kutsuge politsei!	***Coot****-soo-gay po-leet-say!*
Call the fire department!	Kutsuge tuletõrje!	***Coot****-soo-gay too-lei-****tur****-ye!*
Where is the nearest telephone?	Kus on lähim telefon?	*Coos onn la-him telefon?*
Where is the nearest hospital?	Kus on lähim haigla?	*Coos onn la-him bigh-glaa?*

Communication Essentials

Yes	Jah	*Yab*
No	Ei	*Ey*
Please	Palun	*Pa-loon*
Thank you	Aitäh	*Ai-****tab***
Excuse me	Vabandage	*Va-ban-da-gay*
Hello	Tere	*Te-re*
Goodbye	Head aega	*Heyad ayga*
Good night	Head õhtut	*Heyad ewh-toot*
morning	hommik	***bom****-mik*
afternoon	pärastlõuna	***pa****-rawst-lew-na*
evening	õhtu	*ewh-tu*
yesterday	eile	*eilay*
today	täna	*ta-naw*
tomorrow	homme	***bom****-may*
What?	Mida?	*Meeda?*
When?	Millal?	*Meelal?*
Why?	Miks?	*Meeks?*
Where?	Kus?	*Coos?*

Guidelines for Prounciation

The Estonian alphabet consists of the following letters: a, b, d, e, f, g, h, i , j, k, l, m, n, o, p, r, s, š, z, ž, t, u, v, õ, ä, ö, ü. The letters c, q, x, y, z are used only in proper names (of places and people) and in words borrowed from foreign languages. Unlike English, all letters in Estonian are pronounced (for example: the silent k in "knee").

Some letter sounds:

a	as in the "u" in cut
b	similar to "p" in English
g	similar to "k" in English
j	as in the "y" in yes
r	like in English, but rolled
š	"sh"
ž	as in the "s" in pleasure
õ	like the "o" in own
ä	as in the "a" in bat
ö	similar to the "u" in fur
ü	as in the "u" in cube

Some letter combination sounds:

ai	as in the "ai" in aisle
ei	as in the "ei" in vein
oo	as in the "a" in water
uu	as in the "oo" in boot
öö	as in the "u" in fur

Some points to remember:
• Usually the first syllable of a word is stressed. However, quite a few words with foreign origins and some native Estonian words, such as *aitäh*, don't follow this pattern.
• Vowels and consonants can be short (written with one letter), long or extra long (written with two letters).

Useful Phrases

How are you?	Kuidas läheb?	*Cooi-das la-beb?*
Very well, thank you.	Aitäh, väga hästi.	*Ai-****tab****, va-ga ****bas****-ti.*
Pleased to meet you.	Meeldiv tuttavaks saada.	*Mayl-div too-taw-vawks saa-daw.*
See you soon!	Varsti näeme!	*Vaarsti nay-me!*
Is there … here?	Kas siin on …?	*Cos scene onn …?*
Where can I get …?	Kust ma saaksin …?	*Coost ma ****sawk****-sin …?*
How do you get to?	Kuidas minna …?	*Cooi-dass ****min****-na …?*
How far is …?	Kui kaugel on …?	*Cooi cow-kel onn …?*
Do you speak English?	Kas te räägite inglise keelt?	*Cos tay ****ra****-gi-tay ing-li-say keylt?*
I can't speak Estonian.	Ma ei oska eesti keelt.	*Maw ey oska ****eys****ti kaylt.*
I don't understand.	Ma ei saa aru.	*Maw ey saw aru.*
Can you help me?	Kas saate mind aidata?	*Cos ****saw****-tay meend eye-data?*
Please speak slowly.	Palun rääkige aeglaselt.	*Pa-loon ra-ki-gay ayg-la-selt.*
Sorry!	Vabandust!	*Va-ban-doost!*

Useful Words

big	suur	*suur*
small	väike	*vayke*
hot	kuum	*coom*
cold	külm	*kewlm*
good	hea	*be-ya*
bad	halb	*balb*
enough	küllalt	*cool-alt*
well	hästi	*basti*
open	avatud	*aw-va-tud*
closed	suletud	*soo-laytud*
left	vasak	*vaw-sawk*
right	parem	*paw-rem*
straight	otse	*ot-say*
near	lähedal	*la-bay-dawl*
far	kaugel	*kaw-gbell*
up	ülal	*oolal*
down	all	*all*
early	vara	*va-raw*
late	hilja	*bill-yaw*
entrance	sissepääs	*see-say-pa-es*
exit	väljapääs	*val-yaw-pa-es*
toilet	tualett	*too-a-****lett***
free/unoccupied	vaba	*vaw-baw*
free/no charge	tasuta	*taw-soo-taw*

Making a Telephone Call

Can I call abroad from here?	Kas ma saan siit välismaale helistada?	*Cos maw sawn seet va-lees-****maw****-lay bay-lees-taw-da?*
I would like to call collect.	Tahaksin helistada vastaja kulul.	*Taw-baw-ksin bay-lees-taw-da vaws-taya koo-lool.*
local call	kohalik kõne	*kobaw-lik kew-ne*
I'll ring back later.	Helistan hiljem tagasi.	*Hay-lees-tawn beel-yem taw-gau-si.*
Could I leave a message?	Kas ma saaksin teate jätta?	*Cos maw ****sawk****-seen tyate ya-taw?*
Could you speak up a little, please?	Kas saate natuke valjemini rääkida?	*Cos saw-tay naw-too-kay vawl-ye-meenee ra-ki-daw?*

Shopping

How much is this?	Kui palju see maksab?	*Cooi pawl-yu say mawk-sab?*
I would like …	Tahaksin …	*Taw-bawk-sin …*
Do you have …?	Kas teil on …?	*Cos tayl onn …?*
I'm just looking.	Vaatan lihtsalt.	*Vaw-tan libt-sawlt.*
Do you take credit cards?	Kas krediitkaardiga saab maksta?	*Cos kre-****diit****-kawrd-eega sawb mawk-sta?*
What time do you open?	Mis kell teil avatakse?	*Mees kell tayl a-vaw-tawk-say?*
What time do you close?	Mis kell teil suletakse?	*Mees kell tayl su-lay-tawk-say?*
this one	see	*cee*
that one	too	*toe*
expensive	kallis	*kaw-lees*

cheap	**odav**	*oh-dav*
size	**suurus**	*soo-rus*
antique dealer	**antiigipood**	*an-**tiiki**-pode*
souvenir shop	**suveniiripood**	*sou-ve-**niiri**-pode*
bookshop	**raamatupood**	***raw**-maw-too-pode*
café	**kohvik**	*koh-fik*
chemist	**apteek**	*ap-tayk*
newspaper kiosk	**ajalehekiosk**	*a-ya-le-he-**kii**-osk*
department store	**kaubamaja**	*cow-ba-mawya*
market	**turg**	*toorg*

Staying in a Hotel

Have you any	**Kas teil on vaba**	*Cos tayl onn*
vacancies?	**tuba?**	*vawba too ba?*
double room	**kahene tuba**	*ka-hay-ne tooba*
with double bed	**laia voodiga**	*la-ya **vo**-diga*
twin room	**kahe voodiga tuba**	*ka-hay **vo**-diga too*
single room	**ühene tuba**	*ew-bene too-ba*
non-smoking	**mittesuitsetajatele**	*meetay-sooitse-ta-ya-lay*
room with a	**tuba**	*too-ba*
bath/shower	**vanniga/dušiga**	*vaw-niga/doosh-iga*
porter	**portjee**	*port-ye*
key	**võti**	*vew-ti*
I have a	**Mul on**	*Mool onn re-se-**veri**-*
reservation.	**reserveeritud.**	*tood.*

Sightseeing

bus	**buss**	*boos*
tram	**tramm**	*trawm*
trolley bus	**troll**	*trol*
train	**rong**	*row-ng*
bus stop	**bussipeatus**	*boo-si-peya-toos*
tram stop	**trammipeatus**	*tra-mi-peya-toos*
art gallery	**kunstigalerii**	*koonsti-gale-**ree***
palace	**palee**	*pa-lay*
castle	**loss**	*lowss*
cathedral	**katedraal**	*caw-tay-dral*
church	**kirik**	*kee-reek*
garden	**aed**	*eye-ed*
library	**raamatukogu**	*raw-maw-too-kogu*
museum	**muuseum**	*mu-seum*
tourist information	**turismiinfo**	*too-ris-me-info*
closed for public	**külastajatele suletud**	*koo-las-taya-tayle soo-le-tood*
holiday	**puhkepäev**	*pooh-ke-payev*
travel agent	**reisibüroo**	*ray-see-bu-roh*

Eating Out

A table for ...	**Palun üks laud ...**	*Pa-loon ooks*
please	**inimesele**	*la-ood ...eenee-me-selay*
I want to reserve	**Tahaksin reserveerida**	*Taw-hawk-sin re-*
a table.	**lauda.**	*ser-**veri**-da la-ooda.*
The bill, please	**Palun arve**	*Pa-loon arvay*
I am a vegetarian.	**Olen taimetoitlane.**	*Olayn tai-may-toyt-lanay.*
I'd like ...	**Tahaksin ...**	*Ta-hawk-sin...*
waiter/waitress	**kelner/ettekandja**	***kel**-ner/etay-kandya*
menu	**menüü**	*men-**oo***
wine list	**veinimenüü**	*veini-men-**oo***
chef's special	**firmaroog**	*feer-ma-rogue*
tip	**jootraha**	***yot**-rawha*
glass	**klaas**	*klas*
bottle	**pudel**	*poo-del*
knife	**nuga**	*noo-ga*
fork	**kahvel**	*kauf-fel*
spoon	**lusikas**	*loo-si-kaws*
breakfast	**hommikusöök**	***bom**-miku-sook*
lunch	**lõuna**	*lewna*
dinner	**õhtusöök**	*euh-tu-sook*
main courses	**praed**	*prayed*
starters	**eelroad**	*el-rowad*
vegetables	**köögiviljad**	*koo-gi-vilyad*
desserts	**magustoidud**	*maw-gus-toy-dud*
rare	**pooltoores**	*pole-**toe**-res*
well done	**küps**	*cewps*

Menu Decoder

äädikas	*a-di-kaws*	vinegar
aurutatud	*ow-ru-tawtud*	steamed
friikartul	***free**-kartool*	chips
grillitud	*grilly-tud*	grilled
jäätis	*ya-tis*	ice cream
juust	*youst*	cheese
kala	*kaw-la*	fish
kana	*kawna*	chicken
kartul	***kar**-tool*	potatoes

kaste	*kaws-tey*	sauce
keedetud	*kay-day-tud*	boiled
klimbid	*klim-bid*	dumplings
kohv	*k-oh-v*	coffee
kook, saiad	*coke, sigh-ad*	cake, pastry
koor	*core*	cream
küüslauk	*koos-lauk*	garlic
lambaliha	*lawm-ba-leeha*	lamb
leib/sai	*layb/sei*	bread
liha	*lee-ba*	meat
loomaliha	***lo**-ma-leeba*	beef
mereannid	*mayrey-awnid*	seafood
mineraalvesi	*min-e-**rawl**-vaysi*	mineral water
muna	*moona*	egg
õli	*ewli*	oil
õlu	*ewlu*	beer
pannkook	*pawn-coke*	pancake
peekon	*paykon*	bacon
piim	*peem*	milk
pipar	*peepar*	pepper
pirukas	*piru-kaws*	pie
praeliha	*praey-leeba*	steak
praetud	*praeytud*	fried
punane vein	*poo-naw-nay vein*	red wine
puuvili	***puu**-veelee*	fruit
puuviljamahl	***puu**-vil-ya-mawbl*	fruit juice
riis	*rees*	rice
rull	*rule*	roll
salat	*sawlat*	salad
sealiha	*seya-leeba*	pork
seened	*say-ned*	mushrooms
sink	*sink*	ham
šokolaad	*shok-o-lawd*	chocolate
sool	*sole*	salt
suhkur	*suhkoor*	sugar
suitsukala	*suit-soo-kawla*	smoked fish
supp	*soup*	soup
tee	*te*	tea
täidetud	*tayde-tood*	stuffed
valge vein	*val-gay vein*	white wine
vorst	*vorst*	sausage
võileib	*voi-layb*	sandwich

Numbers

0	**null**	*nul*
1	**üks**	*ewks*
2	**kaks**	*kawks*
3	**kolm**	*colm*
4	**neli**	*ne-li*
5	**viis**	*viis*
6	**kuus**	*kuus*
7	**seitse**	*say-tsey*
8	**kaheksa**	*kaw-hex-a*
9	**üheksa**	*ew-hex-a*
10	**kümme**	*kewmme*
11	**üksteist**	*ewx-taste*
12	**kaksteist**	*kawks-taste*
13	**kolmteist**	*colm-taste*
14	**neliteist**	*nayli-taste*
15	**viisteist**	*viis-taste*
16	**kuusteist**	*kuus-taste*
17	**seitseteist**	*saytse-taste*
18	**kaheksateist**	*kawheksaw-taste*
19	**üheksateist**	*ewheksaw-taste*
20	**kakskümmend**	*kawks-kew-mend*
30	**kolmkümmend**	*colm-kew-mend*
40	**nelikümmend**	*nayli-kew-mend*
50	**viiskümmend**	*viis-kew-mend*
60	**kuuskümmend**	*kuus-kew-mend*
70	**seitsekümmend**	*say-tse-kew-mend*
80	**kaheksakümmend**	*kaw-beksa-kew-mend*
90	**üheksakümmend**	*ew-beksa-kew-mend*
100	**sada**	*sa-da*
1000	**tuhat**	*too-bawt*

Time

one minute	**üks minut**	*ewks minut*
hour	**tund**	*toond*
half an hour	**pool tundi**	*pole toondi*
Sunday	**pühapäev**	*pew-ba-payev*
Monday	**esmaspäev**	*esmas-payev*
Tuesday	**teisipäev**	*taysi-payev*
Wednesday	**kolmapäev**	*kolma-payev*
Thursday	**neljapäev**	*nelya-payev*
Friday	**reede**	*re-de*
Saturday	**laupäev**	*lauw-payev*

Phrase Book: Latvian

In Emergency

Help!	Palīgā!	*Pu-lee-gaa!*
Stop!	Apstāties!	*Up-staat-eas!*
Call a doctor!	Izsauciet ārstu	*Iz-sowts-eat abr-stoo!*
Call an ambulance!	Izsauciet ātro palīdzību!	*Iz-sowts-eat aa-troa pu-leedz-ee-boo!*
Call the police!	Izsauciet policiju!	*Iz-sowts-eat po-lits-ee-yoo!*
Call the fire department!	Izsauciet ugunsdzēsējus!	*Iz-sowts-eat oo-goons-dseb-say-oos!*
Where is the nearest telephone?	Kur ir tuvākais telefons?	*Koor ir too-vaak-ais tel-e-fons?*
Where is the nearest hospital?	Kur ir tuvākā slimnīca?	*Koor ir too-vaak-aa slim-neets-u?*

Communication Essentials

Yes	Jā	*Yaa*
No	Nē	*Neb*
Please	Lūdzu	*Loodz-oo*
Thank you	Paldies	*Pul-deas*
Excuse me	Atvainojiet	*Ut-vy-noa-yeat*
Hello	Sveiki / Labdien	*Svay-key / lub-dean*
Goodbye	Uz redzēšanos	*Ooz redz-ee-sbun-oas*
Good night	Ar labu nakti	*Ur lub-oo nukt-i*
morning	rīts	*reets*
afternoon	pēcpusdiena	*pebts-poos-dea-nu*
evening	vakars	*vu-kars*
yesterday	vakar	*vu-kar*
today	šodien	*sboa-dean*
tomorrow	rīt	*reet*
What?	Ko?	*Kuab?*

Guidelines for Prouunciation

Latvian is, for the most part, a phonetic language and the stress is almost always on the first syllable. Each letter and vowel combination (dipthong) has a particular sound, as indicated below:

Vowels

Either short or long (with a macron):

a	like "u" in "under"
ā	like "a" in "star"
e	like "e" in "bed", or "a" in "cat"
ē	like "ai" in "hair", or "a" in "glad"
i	like "i" in "sit"
ī	like "ee" in "feet"
o	like "o" in "corn", or "oa" in "oar"
u	like "oo" in "book"
ū	like "oo" in "school"

Dipthongs

ai	like "i" in "line"
au	like "ow" in "cow"
ei	like "ay" in "clay"
ie	like "ea" in "clear"
oi	like "oy" in "boy"
ui	like "ui" in "ruin"

Consonants

Same as English, except for:

c	like "ts" in "hats"
č	like "ch" in "church"
dz	like "ds" in "hands"
dž	like "j" in "joke"
ģ	like "d" in "duty"
j	like "y" in "yellow"
ķ	like "c" in "cute"
ļ	like "li" in "million"
ņ	like "n" in "new"
r	like "r" in "run"
š	like "sh" in "shut"
ž	like "s" in "treasure"

When?	Kad?	*Kud?*
Why?	Kāpēc?	*Kaa-pebts?*
Where?	Kur?	*Koor?*

Useful Phrases

How are you?	Kā jums klājas?	*Kaa yooms klaa-yus?*
Very well	Ļoti labi	*Lyot-ee lu-bi*
Pleased to meet you.	Prieks iepazīties.	*Preaks ea-pu-zeet-eas.*
See you soon!	Uz drīz redzēšanos!	*Ooz dreez redz-e-sbun-oas!*
Is there ... here?	Vai šeit ir ....?	*Vi sbayt eer ...?*
Where can I get ...?	Kur es varu dabūt ...?	*Koor es vu-roo du-boot ...?*
How do you get to?	Kā es varu tikt līdz?	*Kaa es vu-roo tikt leedz?*
How far is ...?	Cik tālu atrodas ...?	*Tsik taa-loo ut-roa-dus ...?*
Do you speak English?	Vai jūs runājat angliski?	*Vy yoos roon-aa-yut ung-lees-kee?*
I can't speak Latvian.	Es nerunāju latviski.	*Es ne-roon-aa-yoo lut-vees-kee.*
I don't understand.	Es nesaprotu.	*es ne-sup-roat-oo.*
Can you help me?	Vai varat man palīdzēt?	*Vy vu-rut mun pu-leedz-ebt?*
Please speak slowly.	Lūdzu, runājiet lēnām.	*Loodz-oo roon-aa-yeat lebn-aam.*
Sorry!	Atvainojiet!	*ut-vy-noa-yeat!*

Useful Words

big	liels	*leals*
small	mazs	*muzs*
hot	karsts	*kabrsts*
cold	auksts	*owksts*
good	labs	*lubs*
bad	slikts	*slikts*
enough	pietiekami	*pea-teak-um-ee*
well	vesels	*vas-als*
open	atvērts	*ut-vebrts*
closed	slēgts	*slebgts*
left	kreisi	*pu krays-i*
right	labi	*pu lu-bi*
straight	taisni	*tai-sni*
near	tuvu	*toov-oo*
far	tālu	*taal-oo*
up	augšā	*owg-sbaa*
down	lejā	*lay-aa*
here	šeit	*sbayt*
there	tur	*toor*
early	agri	*ug-ri*
late	vēlu	*vebl-oo*
entrance	ieeja	*ea-ey-u*
exit	izeja	*iz-ey-u*
toilet	tualete	*toou-le-te*
free/unoccupied	brīvs	*breevs*
free/no charge	bezmaksas	*bez-muk-sus*

Making a Telephone Call

Can I call abroad from here?	Vai no šejienes var zvanīt uz ārzemēm?	*Vy noa sbay-ean-ess vur zvun-eet ooz aar-zem-ebm?*
I would like to call collect.	Es gribu, lai zvana saņēmējs.	*Es grib-oo, lai muks-aa zvu-nu suny-eb-mebs.*
local call	vietējā saruna	*veat-ay-aa su-roo-nu*
I'll ring back later.	Es atzvanīšu vēlāk.	*Es ut-zvun-ee-shoo vebl-aak.*
Could I leave a message?	Vai es varu atstāt ziņu?	*Vy es vuroo ut-staat ziny-oo?*
Could you speak up a little, please?	Lūdzu, runājiet mazliet skaļāk?	*Loodz-oo, roon-aa yeat muz-leat skuly-aak?*

Shopping

How much is this?	Cik tas maksā?	*Tsik tus muk-saa?*
I would like ...	Es vēlētos ...	*Es veb-leb-toas ...*
Do you have ...?	Vai Jums ir ...?	*Vy yooms ir ..?*
I'm just looking.	Es tikai skatos.	*Es tik-ai skut-oas.*
Do you take credit cards?	Vai es varu maksāt ar kredītkarti?	*Vy es vu-roo muk-saat ur kred-eet-kurti?*
What time do you open?	Cikos tiek atvērts veikals?	*Tsik-oas teak ut-vebrts vay-kuls?*

What time do you close?	Cikos tiek slēgts veikals?	*Tsik-oas teak slebgts vay-kuls?*
this one	šo	*sboa*
that one	to	*toa*
expensive	dārgs	*daargs*
cheap	lēts	*lebts*
size	izmērs	*iz-mebrs*
antique dealer	antikvariāts	*un-teek-vur-i-aats*
souvenir shop	suvenīru veikals	*soo-ve-near-oo vay-kuls*
bookshop	grāmatu veikals	*graa-mut-oo vay-kuls*
café	kafējnīca	*ku-fay-neets-u*
chemist	aptieka	*up-teak-u*
newspaper kiosk	avīžu kiosks	*u-veezb-oo kee-osks*
department store	universālveikals	*oo-ni-ver-saal-vay-kuls*
market	tirgus	*tir-gus*

Staying in a Hotel

Have you any vacancies?	Vai jums ir brīvas istabas?	*Vy yooms ir breev-us is-tu?*
double room with double bed	istaba ar divvietīgu gultu	*is-tu-bu ur div-veat-ee-goo gool-too*
twin room	divvietīga istaba	*div-veat-ee-gu is-tu-bu*
single room	vienvietīga istaba	*vean-veat-ee gu is-tu-bu*
non-smoking	nesmēķētāju	*ne-smee-kyeb-taay-oo*
room with a ...	istaba ar vannu/dušu ...	*is-tu-bu ur vun-oo/doosb-oo ...*
porter	portjē	*port-yay*
key	atslēga	*ut-sleb-gu*
I have a reservation	Man ir pasūtīts	*mun ir pus-oo-teets*

Sightseeing

bus	autobuss	*ow-to-boos*
tram	tramvajs	*trum-vuys*
trolley bus	trolejbuss	*trol-ay-boos*
train	vilciens	*vilts-eans*
bus stop	autobusa pietura	*ow-to-boos-u pea-too-ru*
tram stop	tramvaja pietura	*trum-vuy-u pea-too-ru*
art gallery	mākslas galerija	*maak-slus gul-e-ree-yu*
palace/castle	pils	*pils*
cathedral	katedrāle	*kut-e-draa-le*
church	baznīca	*buz-neets-u*
garden	dārzs	*daarzs*
library	bibliotēka	*bib-li-oa-te-ku*
museum	muzejs	*mooz-ays*
tourist information	tūristu informācija	*toor-is-too in-for-maats-i-ya*
closed	slēgts	*slebgts*
holiday	brīvdiena	*breev-dea-nu*
travel agent	ceļojumu aģentūra	*tsely-oy-oo-moo udy-en-toor-u*

Eating Out

A table for ... please.	Galdiņu .... personām, lūdzu.	*Guld iny oo ...pebr soa naam, loodz oo.*
The bill ...	Rēķinu ...	*Rebky-i-noo ...*
I am a vegetarian.	Es esmu veģetārietis.	*Es as-moo vedy-e-taar-ea-tis.*
I'd like ...	Es vēlos ...	*Es veb-loas ...*
waiter/waitress	oficiants / oficiante	*of-its-i-unts/of-its-i-unte*
menu	ēdienkarte	*eb-dean-kurt-e*
wine list	vīnu karte	*veen-oo kurt-e*
chef's special	īpašais šefpavāra ieteikums	*ee-push-ais sbef-pu-vaa-ru eat-ay-kums*
tip	dzeramnauda	*dzer-um-now-du*
bottle	pudele	*poo-de-le*
knife	nazis	*nu-zis*
fork	dakša	*duk-sbu*
spoon	karote	*kur-oa-te*
breakfast	brokastis	*broa-kus-tis*
lunch	pusdienas	*poos-dea-nus*
dinner	vakariņas	*vuk-ur-iny-us*
main courses	galvenie ēdieni	*gul-ven-ea eb-dea-ni*
starters	uzkodas	*ooz-koa-dus*
vegetables	dārzeņi	*daarz-eny-i*
desserts	saldie ēdieni/deserti	*sul-dea ee-dea-ni/dess-er-ti*
rare	asiņains	*us-iny-ains*
well done	labi sacepts	*lu-bi suts-apts*

Menu Decoder

alus	*ul-oos*	beer
augļu sula	*ow-gly-oo soo-la*	fruit juice
baltvīns	*bult-veens*	white wine
bekons	*bek-ons*	bacon
cepts	*tsepts*	fried
cūkgaļa	*tsook-guly-u*	pork
cukurs	*tsoo-koors*	sugar
desa	*des-u*	sausage
etiķis	*et-iky-is*	vinegar
frī kartupeļi	*free kur-too-pely-i*	chips
grilēts	*gril-ebts*	grilled
jēra gaļa	*yebr-u guly-u*	lamb
jūras veltes	*yoor-us vel-tes*	seafood
kafija	*kuf-i-yu*	coffee
kartupeļi	*kur-too-pely-i*	potatoes
kūpinātas zivis	*koop-in-aat-us ziv-is*	smoked fish
krējums	*kray-ooms*	cream
liellopa gaļa	*leal-loap-u guly-u*	beef
maize	*maiz-e*	bread
mērce	*mebr-tse*	sauce
minerālūdens	*min-er-aal-oo-dens*	mineral water
ola	*oal-u*	egg
pankūka	*pun-koo-ku*	pancake
piens	*peans*	milk
pildīts	*pild-eets*	stuffed
pipars	*pi-purs*	pepper
rīsi	*rees-i*	rice
saldējums	*sul-day-ums*	ice cream
sāls	*saals*	salt
salāti	*sul-aa-ti*	salad
sarkanvīns	*sur-kun-veens*	red wine
siers	*sears*	cheese
šķiņķis	*sbkyinky-is*	ham
smalkmaizīte	*smulk-maiz-ee-te*	pastry
šokolāde	*sbok-o-laa-de*	chocolate
steiks	*stayks*	steak
tēja	*tbey-a*	tea
tvaicēts	*tvai-tsebts*	steamed
vārīts	*vaar-eets*	boiled
vista	*vis-tu*	chicken
zivis	*ziv-is*	fish
zupa	*zoop-u*	soup

Numbers

0	nulle	*nooll-e*
1	viens	*veans*
2	divi	*di-vi*
3	trīs	*trees*
4	četri	*cbet-ri*
5	pieci	*peat-si*
6	seši	*se-sbi*
7	septiņi	*sept-iny-i*
8	astoņi	*us-toany-i*
9	deviņi	*dev-iny-i*
10	desmit	*des-mit*
11	vienpadsmit	*vean-puds-mit*
12	divpadsmit	*div-puds-mit*
13	trīspadsmit	*trees-puds-mit*
14	četrpadsmit	*cbet-r-puds-mit*
15	piecpadsmit	*peats-puds-mit*
16	sešpadsmit	*sesb-puds-mit*
17	septiņpadsmit	*sept-iny-puds-mit*
18	astoņpadsmit	*us-toany-puds-mit*
19	deviņpadsmit	*dev-iny-puds-mit*
20	divdesmit	*div-des-mit*
30	trīsdesmit	*trees-des-mit*
40	četrdesmit	*cbet-r-des-mit*
50	piecdesmit	*peats-des-mit*
60	sešdesmit	*sesb-des-mit*
70	septiņdesmit	*sept-iny-des-mit*
80	astoņdesmit	*us-toany-des-mit*
90	deviņdesmit	*de-viny-des-mit*
100	simts	*simts*
1000	tūkstotis	*took-stoa-tis*

Time

one minute	viena minūte	*vean-u min-oo-te*
hour	stunda	*stoon-du*
half an hour	pus stunda	*poos stoon-du*
Sunday	svētdiena	*sveet-dea-nu*
Monday	pirmdiena	*pirm-dea-nu*
Tuesday	otrdiena	*oa-tr-dea-nu*
Wednesday	trešdiena	*tresb-dea-nu*
Thursday	ceturtdiena	*tset-oort-dea-nu*
Friday	piektdiena	*peakt-dea-nu*
Saturday	sestdiena	*sest-dea-nu*